Maryland Voices

of the Civil War

For the Reynolds-Yellott Family

All the best

Chazz

Maryland Voices
of the Civil War

Edited by CHARLES W. MITCHELL

THE JOHNS HOPKINS UNIVERSITY PRESS   Baltimore

© 2007 The Johns Hopkins University Press
All rights reserved. Published 2007
Printed in the United States of America on acid-free paper
9 8 7 6 5 4 3 2 1

The Johns Hopkins University Press
2715 North Charles Street
Baltimore, Maryland 21218-4363
www.press.jhu.edu

Library of Congress Cataloging-in-Publication Data

Mitchell, Charles W., 1954–
Maryland voices of the Civil War / Charles W. Mitchell.
    p.   cm.
Includes bibliographical references and index.
ISBN-13: 978-0-8018-8621-8 (hardcover : alk. paper)
ISBN-10: 0-8018-8621-x (hardcover : alk. paper)
1. Maryland—History—Civil War, 1861–1865—Personal narratives.
2. Maryland—History—Civil War, 1861–1865—Social aspects.
3. United States—History—Civil War, 1861–1865—Personal
narratives. 4. United States—History—Civil War, 1861–1865—
Social aspects. I. Title.
E512.M58 2007
975.2′03—dc22   2006036776

A catalog record for this book is available from the British Library.

For my parents…

Braxton Mitchell, who gave me the push

and

Polly Mitchell, who gave me the paint

Contents

April 21st 1861
Baltimore Md.

Preface

Maryland Voices of the Civil War has its origins in the proverbial "box of Civil War stuff" that my wife, Betsy, inherited after it had sat, long neglected, in her parents' attic. The stuff, gathered by her great-grandfather, Alexander P. Watson, a private in the Sixty-seventh Pennsylvania Infantry from the small town of Indiana, Pennsylvania, arrived at our house in 1985 to take up residence with fourth-generation family.

Watson's box contained many personal effects from the war: a leather cap case taken from a dead rebel was filled with acorns from a tree under which he had buried a comrade, his Bible with notes jotted in the margins during his time in a rebel prison on Belle Isle in Richmond, and a jagged cannonball fragment and a piece of stone from a wall behind which he'd fought during the Battle of Cedar Creek in October 1864. Notes and writings described the circumstances in which he had obtained many of these artifacts.

We began learning the story of young Private Watson. We relished the tale of this uneducated and patriotic young man, who enlisted at age eighteen, was captured at the second battle of Winchester, and survived imprisonment and war. The story grew richer as we learned more about him from articles he wrote for his hometown newspaper, his military and pension records in the National Archives, and battle accounts of the Union army's Sixth Corps, which included his regiment.

Then, one of my ancestors, heretofore unknown, ambled into the picture. While researching a travel article on the Battle of Cedar Creek, I discovered that Col. Carter Braxton, a Confederate artillerist from Norfolk, Virginia, had been on the field against Watson's regiment there. I read (and, from the Sons of Confederate Veterans, heard) about Braxton and learned more from a history of his artillery unit and his military records from the National Archives. (Confederates received no federal pensions, so he had no pension records.) One winter day, I stumbled upon Braxton's tunic and pistol on display in the Visitor Center museum at the Fredericksburg Battlefield.

Ken Burns's 1990 PBS documentary on the Civil War, which led millions of us to cancel appointments and neglect our children, drew on letters and diaries to relate the compelling personal dimension of the war. I began wondering what had been written about my home state of Maryland during that time. I confronted my ignorance: I didn't *think* Maryland had seceded, and I *thought* it sanctioned slavery. As I write, some years later, I've forgotten what I didn't know, except that it was embarrassingly much.

I discovered a good deal written about the subject. I found books on politics, the best of which effectively argue that Maryland tilted strongly toward Unionism, a sentiment that annoyed many Southern sympathizers who believed in a right of secession. Some books advocate—with transparent bias—a secession impulse, while poorly researched polemics express fist-pounding, dogmatic convictions. Books by Mayor George W. Brown of Baltimore and about Gov. Thomas H. Hicks of Maryland reveal how hard they labored to keep war from Maryland's door. A half dozen books about the Battle of Antietam, still the nation's single bloodiest day, chronicle the fate of Lee's first incursion onto Maryland soil.

Watson and Braxton had stoked my interest in stories. I tapped into a rich Maryland vein of letters, diaries, newspapers, slave stories, legislative resolutions, business records, military directives, muster rolls, proclamations, slaveholder affidavits regarding slave "property," telegrams, and reports from recruiters of black soldiers and documents of the postwar Freedmen's Bureau. Though previously published works drew on some of these documents, the broad social narrative built on the voices within was missing from Maryland's Civil War story.

Three themes make up the architecture for this tale. Part 1, "Indecision," explores how Lincoln's election and the crisis in Charleston Harbor, leading to the federal capitulation of Fort Sumter on April 12, 1861, resonated in Maryland and recounts the passion and uncertainty of the autumn of 1860 through the summer of 1861, when Marylanders grappled with the threat of secession and danger of war. Part 2, "Occupation," delves into the presence of both Union and Confederate troops in Maryland, the arrests and imprisonment of dissidents, how troops were recruited, and the timeless topic of suppression of civil liberties in wartime. Part 3, "Liberation," recounts the demise of slavery in Maryland, recruitment of black troops for the Union army, and postwar efforts by frustrated owners to retain the antebellum social order. Throughout are stories of merchants, women, shopkeepers, slaves, children, farmers, slave owners, soldiers, clergymen, students, lawyers, and public officials from a state pivotal to Lincoln's struggle to protect the capital and ensure the loyalty of a Maryland essential to Union war aims. A brief essay introducing each theme provides background and context.

The faces of soldiers and civilians in Civil War–era photographs captivate me. I stare at eyes and mouths and wonder what they thought as they posed for the lengthy periods required by the cameras of that time. My imagination teases forth the sound of voices, especially accent and pitch.

An epilogue discusses the ways in which Marylanders of all stripes memorialized their versions of the Civil War. They wrote memoirs, delivered and listened to speeches, created memorials, and established social organizations so the nobility of their cause might endure.

A series of letters exchanged in April 1861 between two brothers, John C. Pratt of Boston and Jabez D. Pratt of Baltimore, drills to the heart of this book. These Baltimore-born brothers had starkly different views of the events then cascading into conflict, and their words to each other that fearful spring grew increasingly bitter. The appeal of Maryland's stories from those terrible years has its roots in the odyssey of Alexander Watson, forever a brave, frightened lad of eighteen years.

Acknowledgments

Historians of Maryland's Civil War cannot navigate the massive quantity of material on the subject without assistance. My years at the Maryland Historical Society in Baltimore bore much fruit because of the dedicated archivists and librarians who oversee its rich collection of Civil War–era materials. In the Manuscripts Department, Mary Herbert, associate director of Special Collections, and Elisabeth Proffen, Special Collections Librarian, repeatedly went above and beyond the call to be sure I saw all relevant documents, always anticipating what might strike a chord in a researcher. Jennifer Bryan, Mary Markey, Emily Hubbard, and David Angerhofer helped me during their tenures in the Manuscripts Department. In the Maryland Historical Society Library, I benefited from the skills of Robert Bartrum and, especially, Francis O'Neill, senior reference librarian, whose knowledge of sources about Maryland history is probably unsurpassed.

Robert "Ric" Cottom Jr., former editor of the *Maryland Historical Magazine* and director of the Maryland Historical Society Press, has irrepressible enthusiasm for Maryland's Civil War, reflected in his own writing on the topic. His editorial guidance on three articles drawn from my research material, on early topics in Maryland's Civil War story published between 1997 and 2002 in the *Maryland Historical Magazine*, sharpened both my writing and understanding of key themes.

Robert W. Schoeberlein directed me to obscure collections at the Maryland Historical Society in his role as curator of Prints and Photographs and, following his move to the Maryland State Archives in Annapolis as director of Special Collections, supplied images for Part 3 of this book. Catherine Baty, curator of Collections at the Carroll County Historical Society, and the staff of the Library of the Historical Society of Frederick County cheerfully guided me through their collections, as did the staff at the Baltimore City Archives.

I especially thank Jean H. Baker of Goucher College, who helped me in countless ways throughout this twelve-year endeavor. She critiqued proposals and drafts and encouraged me to weigh competing perspectives and explore approaches that could cast fresh light on matters such as secession, Unionism, slavery, and emancipation in Maryland. William Freehling of the University of Kentucky also commented on early drafts and helped shape the project's direction, for which I express my gratitude.

Leslie S. Rowland at the Freedmen and Southern Society Project (FSSP) at the University of Maryland–College Park gave me generous amounts of her time and expertise, along with free rein in the FSSP's collection of documents from the National Archives that capture the complex transition from slavery to freedom in Maryland during and following the Civil War. I am most grateful to her and her colleagues for their efforts, which did much to broaden the scope of Part 3 of the book.

ACKNOWLEDGMENTS

I thank Jennie A. Levine, curator of Historical Manuscripts; and Anne Turkos, university archivist, of the Archives and Manuscripts Department of the University of Maryland's Special Collections Library at College Park, for introducing me to the diary of Leonidas Dodson and other documents in their jurisdiction; and Elizabeth Schaaf, archivist and curator of the Archives of the Peabody Institute of the Johns Hopkins University, for guiding me through the papers of John Pendleton Kennedy. James F. Reaves, director of Archives and History, and Rev. Edwin A. Schell at the Lovely Lane Museum and Archives in Baltimore kindly shared the diary of Rev. Henry Slicer and lent me his photograph. I am grateful for the assistance of Rev. Garner Ranney and, especially, Mary Klein at the Episcopal Diocese of Maryland's archives in Baltimore, who provided vital research assistance as deadlines loomed. I also thank the staff of Emmanuel Episcopal Church in Baltimore for allowing me to peruse the church's vestry records.

Braxton D. Mitchell rendered invaluable research assistance by relentlessly cranking microfilm versions of Baltimore newspapers and the correspondence of two Maryland governors of the early 1860s, Thomas H. Hicks and Augustus W. Bradford. His skillful persistence at identifying and capturing material he knew I would want to read was indispensable to much of my work. I admire his talents and am most grateful for them.

David Hein of Hood College offered numerous insights and was particularly helpful with my questions about the Allen Bowie Davis family of Montgomery County, while Laurie Taylor Mitchell's incisive comments on early drafts helped keep me from straying too far afield. Charles Wagandt helped me grasp the subtleties of slavery and emancipation in Maryland. I thank them all.

I am indebted to many individuals for providing images. Mary Ellen Hayward generously lent a number of slides from her extensive collection of Civil War–era Maryland. Jeff Korman, manager of the Maryland Department of the Enoch Pratt Free Library, shared several dozen photographs, while Dee Dee Thompson and Cameron Caswell of the Maryland Historical Society expeditiously supplied nine late in the game. Sharon Snow at the Z. Smith Reynolds Library at Wake Forest University provided three images from the library's collection of Confederate Broadsides that satirized Maryland on behalf of the Confederacy, while Ana Luhrs of the Gilder-Lehrman Collection at the New York Historical Society and Jennifer Boston of the Historical Society of Frederick County, respectively, supplied a Frederick Douglass recruiting broadside and (to my knowledge) an unpublished Confederate receipt documenting payment of a ransom by the City of Frederick. Daniel Toomey kindly lent a rare photograph of U.S. Colored Troops Chaplain William Hunter.

Martha E. Marshall, Lucy Neale Duke, and Arthur B. Steuart, all of Baltimore; Sidney Wanzer of Connecticut; and Achsah Henderson of Virginia went out of their way to share with me their unpublished family letters, papers, and photographs pertaining to their ancestors from the Civil War era.

I also thank the public-spirited librarians at Goucher College, Towson University, the University of Maryland–College Park, Rice University, the University of Florida, Yale University, Duke University, the University of North Carolina–Chapel Hill, Bowdoin College, Northwestern University, and Brown University, all of whom helped me find at times obscure information without asking if I was a dues-paying member of their university community.

I am especially grateful for the talents of Robert J. Brugger, my editor at Johns Hopkins University Press. His knowledge of the subject and vision for this project are reflected in these pages, as is his relentless encouragement that nursed it through a transition from a chronological narrative to the structured documentary approach that follows. Brendan Coyne at the Press ably oversaw the manuscript's journey from editorial to production, while the vigilant pen of manuscript editor Andre Barnett caught numerous small errors and averted a few howlers.

At last I have the opportunity to thank publicly Thomas N. Longstreth, an extraordinary teacher who helped me get traction as a young writer at St. Paul's School in Brooklandville, Maryland, so many years ago.

I thank my family for their willingness to tolerate my obsession to finish this story that truly has no end. My children, Abbie and Alec, came to look bemusedly upon this book as their youngest sibling, while my wife, Betsy, brought to it keen insights into the military dimensions of the Civil War and the social mores of that era. Her sharp editorial eye and ability to rework passages of prose and headnotes made this book better.

Editorial Method

Each original document in this book is part of Maryland's Civil War story. Each is given as written to preserve the flavor of its message in the prose, style, and spirit of its time. There is little editorial interference, tempting as that was. Words are as they were spelled. Poor or missing punctuation and incorrect grammar are presented not as I thought the writer may have intended, but as he or she actually wrote—with my occasional editorial intervention to supply the rare missing word only when clarity demanded. Many nineteenth-century writers concluded sentences not with periods, but with dashes, which I have captured faithfully.

The occasional word or letter stumped me and, ever so rarely, even the able Maryland Historical Society archivists who were so generous with their skills. In those instances I used brackets around either the word I thought was meant or a question mark when the document speaks clearly despite the missing word. Virtually every letter, diary entry, or newspaper excerpt is complete—a handful contain ellipses to indicate the absence of large portions of text irrelevant to the point or to present the document as quoted in a secondary source. Emphases are captured as the writers intended. A few documents are transcribed versions of unavailable originals.

Maryland Voices

of the Civil War

Mid-nineteenth-century America was a literate land, unburdened by the techno-logical distractions that pervade twenty-first-century life. Men and women wrote to one another often, about their families, affairs of the heart, political and business matters, sickness, and social events. Politics engaged them. Men petitioned their elected officials and wrote to their many newspapers; the affluent expressed their views in public letters and privately published pamphlets. Adults and children kept diaries and journals.

In 1848, Americans were relishing victory in the Mexican War and war booty that included territories annexed from Mexico. These vast new lands stoked fresh debates over slavery, and they raged through Congress, state capitals, and parlors alike. Which would be free and which slave? This uneasy equilibrium came under increasing pressure from the unyielding abolitionists and Southern fire-eating na-tionalists who occupied the extremes. The latter vehemently opposed any federal interference with slavery—a prerogative historically reserved for the states, they claimed. The 1850s, however, sprouted an amalgam of Northern abolitionists, free-soilers, and former Whigs and Know-Nothings who organized a new Republican Party that by 1860 was pledging to thwart the expansion of human bondage.

When the election of Abraham Lincoln in 1860 led to the secession of South Carolina, war between North and South became increasingly likely. The cries of the righteous doomed efforts at compromise. The storm broke over Fort Sumter in Charleston Harbor in April 1861, and Americans found themselves caught in a conflict over slavery, the "peculiar institution," which, like a persistent mist, had soddened so much of our history.

Maryland, with proclivities North and South, found itself trapped—culturally, economically, and geographically. Lincoln's stance on slavery was clear and firm: He had pledged to prevent its taking root in new lands but not to interfere with it where it existed. Other states of the Deep South prepared to secede in early 1861. The adamant Republican position and militant Southern rhetoric alarmed many in the Upper South. Unnerved especially were citizens in Maryland's southern and Eastern Shore counties, which for more than two hundred years had prospered from the cultivation of tobacco and other crops—all made possible by the labor of slaves. Proslavery Democratic legislators from these agrarian areas remained a potent political force, and they had long worked diligently both to insulate slavery from government meddling and to keep even Maryland's free black citizens in posi-tions of near servitude. It was small wonder, then, that Lincoln received only 2,249 Maryland votes (of 86,290 cast), finishing last of four candidates, and that, in seven Maryland counties, he received not one vote.

Maryland's economy in 1860 was a blend of Northern mercantilism and South-ern agrarianism. Baltimore City reflected this dichotomy. The business climate in the nation's fourth-largest city was unmistakably Northern, the character of her citizenry more traditionally Southern. One historian portrayed the contrast by noting how the city's "Northern characteristics of finance and commerce . . . greatly resembled Philadelphia, New York or Boston, but culturally and socially Baltimore had Southern ties which were most evident."[1] The city's unskilled and lowly paid laborers included free blacks and recent European immigrants, many from Ireland and Germany. Western Marylanders, including a large number of pro-Union, anti-slavery Germans, worked small farms and mined coal.

The state, founded on principles of religious toleration, seemed poised for great things. The nearly completed Baltimore and Ohio Railroad linked Baltimore with western Maryland and the Ohio Valley, making the city a major center of trade. The Chesapeake and Ohio Canal reached its western terminus in Cumberland in 1850, connecting the Maryland coal region to the District of Columbia, while the Susquehanna and Tidewater Canal between Wrightsville, Pennsylvania, and Havre de Grace enabled Maryland to tap the rich harvests of the Susquehanna River valley. Since 1850, ship tonnage had grown almost 30 percent, to more than $11.7 million, and the value of improved Maryland farmland had almost doubled, to $146 million.[2] Police reform had finally curtailed the decades of election violence inflicted on Baltimore by political gangs that had given the city the moniker "Mob-town."

A clash in Baltimore on April 19, 1861, between the Sixth Massachusetts Infantry Regiment en route to Washington, D.C., and a mob of Southern sympathizers, secessionists, and street thugs left fourteen people dead and scores injured. Three days of lawlessness and civil unrest ensued. Mobs seeking arms sacked gun shops and warehouses, while Unionists were terrorized and looters grabbed what they could. An outbreak of civic pride mobilized Baltimoreans of all persuasions to collaborate to prevent more federal troops from passing through their city. Both Unionist and Southern militia companies rushed to their armories. Squads of men galloped to the city's perimeter to erect barricades against the Northern hordes; some rode farther to burn railroad bridges that spanned the rivers north and east of the city. A viable secession movement in the state might have exploited this episode, but an absence of leaders and organization and a hastily enacted solution to move troops to the nation's capital by water, avoiding Baltimore, precluded further strife. The door to secession slammed shut.

Maryland would not come close to leaving the Union to which, in June 1788, she had bound herself in perpetuity. To be sure, Gov. Thomas H. Hicks had for months resisted intense pressures to summon the state assembly into special session so that the state's "course of action" might be determined, but when he relented late in April 1861, lawmakers promptly refused to consider secession and buried the concept for good. Proposals for Maryland neutrality went nowhere. Winter and spring brought widespread indigenous opposition to a Maryland secession from diverse interests that encompassed Unionist slaveholders and even Southern sympathizers, well before the national government began imposing suppressive measures. Nonetheless, the unconsummated notion of a Confederate Maryland, while having lost the vitality of youth, lingers on the shores of the Chesapeake.

In mid-May 1861, Gen. Benjamin Butler's Massachusetts men marched into Baltimore and occupied Federal Hill, a site overlooking the city from which Butler promised to answer any hint of disloyalty with his heavy guns. Lincoln and General-in-Chief Winfield Scott were furious at Butler's unauthorized move and relieved him of command. The Massachusetts troops remained. Marylanders reacted variously to their presence: Unionists, Southern sympathizers, and secessionists found creative ways to express their sentiments. Views changed as Lincoln suspended the writ of habeas corpus (initially along rail lines only, to ensure that troops could travel to Washington), and in the autumn, he sanctioned arrests of suspected disloyalists, including state legislators, the mayor of Baltimore, newspaper editors, and other prominent citizens. Letters from those incarcerated describe frustration at indefinite detainment without charges, anxiety at being deprived of liberty, and principled refusals to take loyalty oaths in exchange for release. The complexities of the June 1861 election—a triumph of pro-Union conservatives who opposed both secession and growing antislavery sentiment—must have puzzled and confused many observers. Marylanders began to confront both the seemingly abstract and irreconcilable concepts of federalism and states' rights and the practical need to choose sides in a rapidly escalating conflict.

The term "occupation" in Part 2 appears inside quotation marks for two reasons. Disagreement persists over the extent to which the presence of Union troops in parts of Maryland constituted a state of affairs normally associated with military rule. Second, "occupation" also encompasses the presence of Confederate forces on Maryland soil. Major rebel incursions occurred in the early days of the war and in 1862 and 1863, as Lee tried in vain to add Marylanders to his ranks en route to Antietam and Gettysburg, and in 1864, when rebel troops terrorized Frederick and Baltimore at the Battle of Monocacy prior to their desperate, abortive assault on Washington.

The story of slavery in nineteenth-century Maryland is one of economics and redemption, as the slaves themselves played a central role in the eradication of the rotting institution. Slave-cultivated tobacco had long been the economic bedrock of the southern and Eastern Shore counties; however, depleted soil unable to sustain consistent production had for decades been allowed to undermine the crop. By the middle of the century, cereals and corn were flourishing in eastern and southern Maryland, and the seasonal labor needed to harvest them made hiring free laborers a better economic deal than slave ownership. The consequent rise in manumissions had helped make Maryland, at the outbreak of the Civil War, home to 74,723 free blacks, the largest number in any state in America.[3]

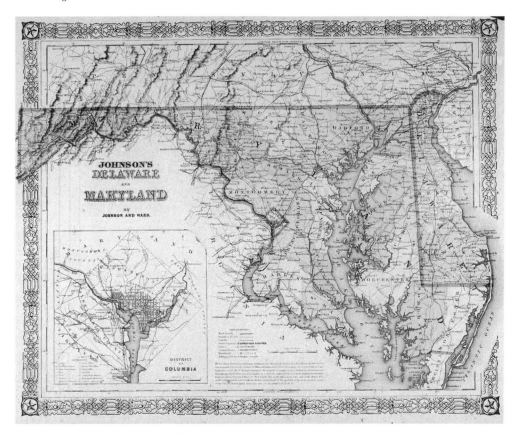

Map of Maryland and Delaware at the outbreak of the Civil War (Johnson and Ward). MdHS.

Though in Maryland Unionism quickly trumped secession—the latter seemed, even to Southern sympathizers, like economic suicide—such was not the case in the fight over slavery. Indignant slave owners and their allies demanded protection for their constitutionally sanctioned property and enforcement of the Fugitive Slave Law in return for their loyalty. Gov. Augustus W. Bradford, a Unionist elected in November 1861, labored indefatigably for his slaveholding constituents. In March 1862, he conveyed a set of Maryland legislative resolutions to Lincoln that rejected the right of secession but made clear that Marylanders would look askance at any effort allowing the war to interfere "with the domestic institutions of the States; and they solemnly protest against all schemes, the object or tendency of which is, to excite insurrection among the slaves."[4] The president responded craftily. His emancipation policies toward Maryland exploited both recruitment of black troops and divisions between conservative and radical Unionists to trigger the death rattle of slavery before the war was over. Consistent with his objective of keeping Maryland in the Union, Lincoln dealt aggressively with disloyalty while simultaneously courting and splitting slaveholders with offers of compensated emancipation.

While white men complained, black slaves ran. Some fled to the District of Columbia, where the abolition of slavery in April 1862 further weakened it in Maryland. Other enterprising escapees found refuge in the camps of the Union army, working as laborers and, in 1863, taking up arms as the United States Colored Troops. Union recruiters scouring the Maryland countryside for black men enlisted freemen and defied government policy with creative ways of absorbing slaves into the ranks of the black troops (in whose six Maryland regiments more than eight thousand seven hundred blacks would fight). These circumstances enabled Lincoln and his Maryland allies to transform the slavery debate from slaveholder compensation to constitutional abolition. Poignant letters of escaped Maryland slaves to loved ones still in bondage and the unctuous complaints of slaveholders to military and elected officials projected their own brand of emotional power.

When Maryland's new constitution banning slavery took effect on November 1, 1864, many slaveholders refused to accept the new social order. Compliant judges of county orphans' courts readily invoked a provision of the state's black code that allowed them to bind black children as apprentices to white masters if the judges determined that parents were unable to provide adequate care. Although some indentures were legitimate, abuse was widespread. Many whites, military authorities, and the Freedmen's Bureau vigorously opposed these indentures, whose pervasiveness in parts of Maryland for several years after emancipation perpetuated de facto slavery.

Maryland Voices of the Civil War helps puncture the enduring myth that Maryland ever stood at the abyss of secession. It illuminates how dramatically the issues of secession and Civil War affected men and women from all walks of life and sheds direct light on the poignancy of the African American experience of becoming free. Marylanders felt the effects of events between 1860 and 1865 as did few other Americans. Here are their stories.

part one

Indecision

The presidential election of 1860 split the electorate in Maryland. Results revealed allegiance to both the Union and states' rights—proponents of the latter especially aroused by the threat of Abraham Lincoln and his "Black Republicans." The enmity of Southern Democrats toward presumptive nominee Senator Stephen Douglas of Illinois had driven them to run their own man, Vice President John Breckinridge of Tennessee, splitting the Democratic vote and making a Republican victory more likely. In Maryland, Lincoln received less than 3 percent of votes cast, earning a distant last-place finish behind Breckinridge, Tennessean John Bell of the Constitutional Union Party, and Douglas.

Lincoln's triumph was poorly received in southern Maryland and Eastern Shore counties, where slaves still worked soil depleted of nutrients from two centuries of tobacco cultivation. Men in the Charles County town of Beantown passed a resolution requesting that anyone who had voted for Lincoln leave the county by January 1. The reticence of the *Baltimore Sun*, which withheld its endorsement, spoke volumes: "As we cannot offer to the readers of *The Sun* one word of congratulation on so inauspicious a result, we are disposed to do no more than announce the fact this morning."[1]

Nevertheless, 54.2 percent of Maryland ballots were cast for Unionist candidates. Breckinridge's plurality—just under 46 percent—endorsed neither disunion nor secession. Most Marylanders saw no contradiction in simultaneously embracing Unionism and slavery. Many were enraged by Northern states' refusal to enforce the federal Fugitive Slave Law of 1793 (and strengthened in the Compromise of 1850), which allowed slave owners to recover slaves who had escaped to free states. Faithful they were to Union and Constitution, however, and more than half of their ballots were cast for the three men who believed as they did.

Lincoln's victory galvanized the South, where legislative bodies began appropriating money to purchase weapons; by the end of November, Northern ships laden with munitions were headed for Southern ports. "Great quantities of arms continue to be ordered in the North by parties in the South," reported the *Sun* in early December. "In all of the armories there is enough work for a year. So great is the demand beyond the capacity of labor that southern agents report it impossible to have all their orders filled." When Maj. Robert Anderson, commanding the federal garrison in Charleston Harbor, consolidated his forces in late December inside Fort Sumter in the harbor's mouth, tensions grew between lame-duck President James Buchanan and South Carolina. Confederate recruits from Maryland began departing via steamship for Charleston, eager to bear arms for South Carolina's Palmetto flag.[2]

The South Carolina legislature convened, its long-simmering desire to leave the

Union at the boiling point. Georgia, Florida, Mississippi, Texas, and Louisiana began laying plans for secession. "Secessionists stressed the vital need to cut all ties to the Union before Lincoln's inauguration," wrote Daniel Crofts. "They insisted that governors call legislatures into session, that legislatures immediately schedule dates for voters to select convention delegates, and that conventions meet promptly. Across the lower South the secessionist strategy worked. The process unfolded in an atmosphere of crisis and haste."[3] South Carolina's secession on December 20 sparked statewide celebrations, and the fever spread as far as New York City, which threatened to leave the Union to become a free city.

In the weeks following the election, congressional committees worked feverishly to avert further secessions. As members futilely debated legislative and constitutional compromise, Southern nationalists labored to lure the upper South border states of Kentucky, Missouri, and Maryland into the Confederate fold. Lincoln was adamant about keeping them in the Union, and appeasing their slaveholding legislators and citizens became, under the circumstances, a small price to pay. His secretaries recognized that "of more immediate and vital importance, however, than that of any other border slave State, was the course of Maryland in this crisis. Between that State and Virginia lay the District of Columbia, originally ten miles square of Federal territory, containing the capital, the Government, and the public archives," they wrote years later in their biography of Lincoln. "In Baltimore, the chief city of Maryland, centered three of the great railroad routes by which loyal troops must approach Washington." Getting these troops to Washington was imperative, for the U.S. Army had been in a shambles since the end of the Mexican War, and rebels across the Potomac appeared ready to strike a vulnerable capital.[4]

Thomas Holliday Hicks, a slave-owning Eastern Shoreman, had become Maryland's governor in 1859. The 1860 state legislative session had ended in the spring, not to meet again until 1862.[5] Hicks came under great pressure to summon the lawmakers into special session. In the winter of 1861, he entertained entreaties of seceded-state emissaries who promised much for a Confederate Maryland. The governor would prove a steadfast Unionist, resisting the legislative call until the fourth week of April 1861 and then finding ways to neutralize dangers from Southern sympathizers.

Early in 1861 rumors circulated of a plot to assassinate President-elect Lincoln in Baltimore as he changed trains en route to Washington to be inaugurated on March 4. Although a railroad detective preposterously claimed that he thwarted the conspiracy by infiltrating the plot, no arrests were made, and the tale became consigned to the memoirs of the sleuth and a handful of Lincoln advisers and railroad officials. When Fort Sumter surrendered on April 13, the president two days later called on the Northern states to supply seventy-five thousand troops to put down the rebellion and protect the capital. The passage of some through Baltimore would quickly force Marylanders to examine their loyalties as their nation edged toward war.

"April is the cruelest month," wrote T. S. Eliot, and so it was for Marylanders in 1861. They confronted a bewildering array of choices. Abolitionists, slaveholding Unionists, antislavery Southern sympathizers, non-slaveholding secessionists, and proponents of neutrality all made their views known. The intentions of neighboring Virginia and the recalcitrance of Governor Hicks to call the legislature into special session exacerbated tensions.

Northern governors responded with alacrity to the call for troops. Militia companies in Pennsylvania, New York, Massachusetts, and others began journeying south by rail. They passed through Baltimore, where their cars were unhooked from arriving locomotives and pulled by horses through city streets to Camden Station for the final leg to Washington. Baltimoreans of many persuasions saw the arrival of these troops as the vanguard of an assault on the Southern states. City streets were teeming with politically passionate citizens and a rabble of agitators and onlookers. News that the Confederacy had issued its own call for troops unleashed passions that led to fisticuffs.

Though Governor Hicks and Mayor George Brown each issued proclamations on April 18 appealing for calm, events were moving beyond politicians. That day, several fresh-faced regiments of Pennsylvania troops pulled into the Bolton Street Station, where they began their transfer to Camden Station. Baltimoreans taunted them mercilessly. In the only documented act of violence that day, Nickoles Biddle, a black man with the Pennsylvanians, was hit by a rock.[6]

In Baltimore, Confederate recruiters were working and Palmetto flags of South Carolina were flying. Word of more Northern troops headed for Mobtown had the city in a fever pitch. The next morning—Friday, April 19—thirty-five cars carrying men from Massachusetts and Pennsylvania steamed into the President Street Station. The cars were quickly hitched to horses for the mile trek to Camden Station. The men from Massachusetts went first. As word spread of a large number of armed, uniformed men on Baltimore streets, the throng on the sidewalks grew. It spilled into Pratt Street, the major thoroughfare between stations.

The crowd dragged anchors from nearby wharves onto the street, blocking the tracks embedded in the road and stopping the cars. Insults were hurled at the Bay State men, and then pieces of cobblestone smashed into the sides and windows of the cars. Screaming soldiers covered their heads amid the missiles and flying glass. Cars containing four Massachusetts companies, consisting roughly of 220 men and their regimental band and a number of the Pennsylvanians, could no longer move. Officers ordered their men to disembark into a crowd growing larger and angrier by the minute. The men in blue were ordered to move at double-quick through the mob. Two muskets discharged. Stones flew, then fists. Weapons were wrested from their owners and turned against them.

This episode, known as the "Pratt Street Riot," or "Baltimore's Civil War Riot," left twelve Baltimoreans and two Massachusetts men dead and scores wounded and forever marked Baltimore as the site of the Civil War's first fatalities. For the next three days, lawlessness driven by smoldering anger against the federal government lit the fuse to propel Maryland into the Confederacy. Although the immediate mission of these soldiers was to protect Washington from what Lincoln feared was an imminent attack by rebels massed across the Potomac River, the day was lost in the volcanic emotions that flowed from the deaths of Baltimoreans at the hands of Bay State militiamen.[7]

Mayor Brown, with the support of Governor Hicks, quickly convinced Lincoln that the outrage stemming from another trainload of troops arriving in Baltimore would lead to more violence. The three devised a water route, via the Susquehanna River, Chesapeake Bay, and Annapolis, for getting Northern men to Washington. In late April, Lincoln, mindful of the city's sensitivities, ordered Army General-in-Chief Winfield Scott not to interfere with the special session of the state legislature that Hicks had finally called.

For months, many Baltimore businessmen had publicly opposed secession, fearing the consequences for business of further civil unrest, a federal blockade of their port, and Maryland's long, indefensible border with Pennsylvania. News of the Baltimore bypass spread, and Union spirit began appearing in Baltimore. Brown and Hicks, along with Lincoln, had crafted a masterstroke that deprived leaderless and poorly organized Maryland secessionists of their best chance to mobilize.

In mid-May, the state legislature adjourned; its refusal to consider secession a powerful harbinger of Maryland's Union fealty. During the night of May 13, Gen. Benjamin Butler of Massachusetts marched into Baltimore, where from atop Federal Hill, he threatened to level the city at the first sign of disloyalty. Lincoln and Scott were incensed at Butler's unauthorized action, which risked sparking further civil unrest and undermined the president's intent to respect Maryland's sovereignty. Butler was relieved of command, having sired the enduring myth that Lincoln sent troops into Baltimore in spring 1861—though the troops, once in place, remained.

On April 27, Lincoln suspended the writ of habeas corpus in Maryland—the first such suspension in U.S. history, and one still misunderstood today. The president's action allowed arrest and indefinite detention without charges and was to be applied *only* along the railway lines to ensure they remained unimpeded for the movement of troop trains. Lincoln adopted this measure quietly; he alerted only his senior military commander and issued no public proclamation. His announcement on the same day of a federal blockade against Southern ports excluded Maryland. Later in the year, by the time Lincoln had broadened the suspension of habeas corpus throughout the state, the dim light of secession had been long extinguished.

Lincoln remained true to his reason for suspending the writ; it was an action taken for military, not political, purposes. No arrests were made in April, and only two in May: The detention of Baltimore industrialist Ross Winans, briefly held on suspicion of manufacturing and distributing arms for resisting the movement of troops through the state, was insignificant. The arrest of Baltimore County farmer John Merryman, for destroying railroad bridges in the wake of the riot, ignited a constitutional furor.

Military authorities ignored a petition for a writ of habeas corpus signed by Supreme Court Chief Justice Roger Taney, then serving on a circuit court, to produce Merryman from his cell at Fort McHenry for charge and trial in a civilian court. Taney challenged Lincoln's authority to suspend the writ and prepared for his own arrest. Military detention of Marylanders would accelerate under Secretary of State William Seward and later Secretary of War Edwin Stanton, infuriating many and supplying administration opponents a potent issue during elections later that year.[8]

As spring slid into summer, Maryland men were slipping into Virginia and points south to join the Confederate army, and many who remained were seething at the ubiquitous presence of federal troops in Baltimore. Family fissures widened between siblings, sons and parents, and friends as attitudes hardened and positions were staked. When Maryland slave owners began demanding protection under existing law for their investment in black labor, their politicians would give them false reason for optimism.

Baltimore in 1860 boasted a number of daily newspapers. Some were partisan organs of political parties, such as the *Exchange* and the *South*, which advocated the
Southern cause and right of secession, and the *Clipper*, the official paper of the
American, or Know-Nothing, Party. Widely read were the *Baltimore Sun*, which
was critical of Lincoln and sympathetic toward Southern goals, and the *Baltimore
American and Commercial Advertiser*, which supported Lincoln, the Union, and
the Constitution. County and city papers throughout the state also expressed the
views of their citizens. Two papers in Centreville, in Queen Anne's County on
Maryland's Eastern Shore, expressed contrasting views on the political issue of the
day. One advised that differences be resolved inside the Union; the other endorsed
South Carolina's right to secede—a harbinger of divisions to come.

> There appears to be a fixed determination, upon the part of some of our sister
> States, to sever the political bonds of the Union which was formed by the wis-
> dom of our ancestors. Such action threatens to involve our country in that worst
> of evils, civil war; therefore it is resolved: we do not recognize the success of the
> Republican party as a cause for dissolution . . . We believe any existing griev-
> ance that is or has been inflicted upon the South can be more fully redressed in
> the Union than out of it. We look upon the action of South Carolina as uncon-
> stitutional and unworthy of the support or sympathy of Maryland. We hereby
> pledge ourselves to maintain our position as citizens of the United States. We
> furthermore are determined to maintain inviolate the present Constitution and
> the Union.[1]
>
> Lincoln is elected, and it becomes us, as law-abiding and Union-loving citi-
> zens to submit quietly and await the result. We trust that the same Providence
> which guided our infant bark amid the surging tide of the revolution will still
> overrule all things for our good and direct our noble ship of State safely through
> the dark and troublous waters of the present. Should the North attempt to sub-
> vert our rights it will be ample time to speak of redress, and even then dissolution
> will be madness. Redress in the Union is possible, and, if rightly sought, certain;
> out of it, impossible.[2]

The *Exchange*, while sympathetic to the South, agreed:

> though we in common with the South have just reason to feel aggrieved at the
> treatment we have received from the North, we do unhesitatingly assert that we
> have not yet been driven to the point at which revolution alone can remedy the
> wrongs of a people. We do aver, therefore, that Baltimore has not by her vote yes-
> terday sanctioned any disunion scheme or sentiment whatsoever, and it is our

earnest hope that she may never feel herself impelled to seek for justice through secession.[3]

The *Kent Conservator*, in Kent County on Maryland's Eastern Shore, was more outspoken against the Southern nationalists, noting that "this section of the country is almost unanimous against secession":

> Yet, while our sympathies are with our Southern brethren, we cannot but deplore their precipitation in the movements which threaten evil consequences to us all.

The newspaper then considered its home state:

> The State of Maryland, we think, is opposed to secession, and does not consider the mere fact of Lincoln's election as sufficient to justify a revolution. The Union has given us, for seventy years, peace among ourselves. This, in itself, is a blessing of inestimable value. We say peace, not meaning to contradict what we have said of Northern aggression. But we have had no wars among ourselves, no mutual ravaging of our fields, no sacking of cities, no desolation of homes and hearts.[4]

In late October, Leonidas Dodson, a prominent Unionist in Easton, attended a Constitutional Union Party event, in anticipation of the presidential election:

> As the general election approaches political excitement rises higher. Yesterday the Grand Mass meeting of the Union party was held. We had a barbecue and a plentiful supply of provisions, at an early hour the people from our own, and the adjacent counties poured in. A very large platform had been erected in front of the court house, the meeting organized at 11 oclock, and was addressed by several gentlemen at about two, the "Minute Men of '60" from Balto nearly 600 strong entered our town, when every thing was wild with excitement, the long line of procession caps, & capes, and lamps, glittering in the sunlight the strains of martial music, all tended to beget a perfect furor. After dinner the meeting was again called to order, and addressed by Hon A. Kennedy, U.S. Senate, and Hon. J. Morrison Harris,—after supper the minute men gave us a grand torch light procession, one of the most beautiful scenes I ever witnessed, along the whole line torches gleamed and rockets flew and the streets were as if in a blaze.[5]

Though many newspapers in Maryland's counties and smaller cities would change their views in 1861, in the autumn of 1860 a number shared the pro-Union views of the *Frederick Herald*, the largest city in western Maryland, fifty miles west of Baltimore:

> For ourselves, looking at the question in all its mighty relations, and connections, we say yes—hold on a little longer. Though we have been taunted and insulted, until every nerve of every limb seemed to cry out for shame or further

Leonidas Dodson, a Unionist in the town of Easton, in Talbot County, kept a detailed diary throughout the war. UMdLib.

forbearance—though they have spit upon the dust of our fathers—though they have vilified the bond of our association—though day by day they are distilling the venom of their slanderous and corrupting treachery into the whole body politic, we say hold on to the Union! They are our brothers still by the ties of common memories, a common glory, and common hopes for the future.[6]

The weekly *Catholic Mirror* in Baltimore wondered in early November, before the presidential election, "what true American could be insane and vicious enough to arrest this country's march to greatness by destroying her unity?" A month later the paper changed its tune, suggesting the Union should be broken apart rather than allowing the Republicans to "destroy what we believe to be southern State Rights." The *Mirror*'s editors would later be arrested for their "treasonous" views.[7]

Leonidas Dodson, undoubtedly disappointed at the loss of his candidate John Bell, revealed little reaction to Lincoln's victory:

> The agony is past, and the tremendous fact known that Abraham Lincoln, the Republican candidate is our President elect. This is the first time in the history of the nation that a purely sectional man has been elected on sectional issues to the presidency. We look now with intense solicitude upon the reception of the news of the South.[8]

Secession fervor in South Carolina politics accelerated rapidly after Lincoln's election. South Carolinians exploited the situation; sympathetic Marylanders rushed to their aid. Washington Yellott, the brother of state senator Coleman Yellott, pledged a thousand National Volunteers to the Southern cause:

> We desire to have some Palmetto flags made here. Please send us immediately a copy of one drawn in colors, or a small flag. We appreciate the pluck of the gallant little South Carolina. Send us her flag—we are ready to defend it![9]

Young Marylanders such as Philip Harry Lee (who claimed descent from "Light Horse" Harry Lee, George Washington's cavalry commander and father of Robert E. Lee) promised South Carolina one thousand three hundred Light Horse National Volunteers:

> We promise to show, like the old and famous *Maryland Line,* that our soil can produce a few more men whose metal will prove too hard for the digestion of a certain class of people.[10]

James Hicks of Montgomery County, a lieutenant in a volunteer company, had a similar view:

> if it should become necessary, we would go with the South; that if a war should break out between the two portions of our nation, the north and the south, we should certainly side with the south.[11]

Other Marylanders had little patience for Southern vitriol. Pro-Union meetings were held in December and January in Baltimore, Frederick, and Cumberland, and a pro-Union resolution was issued from Howard County. A petition from Unionist leaders in Anne Arundel County, just south of Baltimore, endorsed Governor Thomas H. Hicks's refusal to summon the state legislature to consider secession.[12]

> To His Excellency Governor Hicks: The undersigned, citizens of Anne Arundel county, beg leave to express to your Excellency their full approval of the course you have pursued on the subject of calling an Extra Session of the Legislature. And they assure your Excellency that they confide in your patriotism and discretion to preserve for us and our children, to the extent of your ability, the integrity of our glorious and happy Union.[13]

In December, a Baltimore newspaper recounted the behavior of a man emboldened by Lincoln's election:

> Several evenings since a colored man entered car No. 43 of the Madison avenue line, and sat down among the lady and gentlemen passengers who were in the car at the time. The conductor accosted him, and demanded on what authority he violated one of the well known rules of the railroad company. The man replied that Lincoln was elected, and he would ride like "any other man." The conductor, not having the fear of Lincoln before his eyes, jerked the intruder from the car, which proceeded without him.[14]

Governor Hicks explained his reason for refusing to convene the state legislature, replying to a petition from former Governor Thomas Pratt, whose passionate support for the Confederacy would earn him brief arrest in 1861. Hicks stated that a special session would tax the state financially, tempt winter weather, and send a poor signal:

> I cannot but believe that the convening of the Legislature in extra session at this time would only have the effect of increasing and reviving the excitement now pervading the country, and now apparently on the decline. It would at once be heralded by the sensitive newspapers and alarmists throughout the country as evidence that Maryland had abandoned all hope of the Union and was preparing to join the traitors to destroy it.
>
> Is such the true position or wish of Maryland? I think I have had very full opportunities of learning the wishes of the people upon this question, and I have no hesitation in declaring it as my opinion that an immense majority, of all parties, are decidedly opposed to the assembling of the Legislature at this time.[15]

Hicks revealed his convictions in a letter to his friend William L. Wilcox, who had asked the governor for arms for his "Minute Men," a Union militia:

> I have felt it necessary to hold the Executive rein with a firm hand, and none but myself can tell how gratifying it has been, to see the bone and sinew of Baltimore City and of the counties standing firmly by the Union ready to face the disecessionists, if they dare to lay violent hands upon that sacred legacy of our Patriot Fathers—I still trust all may be right, but think we should not lull into ease + quiet, but look to movements of secessionists.[16]

Both sides had Minute Men. One writer described "a parade of the Minute Men, a volunteer militia outfit dedicated to the support of the Unionist candidates, who marched by torch-light past the illuminated stores of pro-Union merchants." But Baltimorean William Platt, in a 1909 letter to Richard D. Fisher, described the Southern version:

> Baltimore, being a Southern city, in March 1861, a large secret society was formed to give material aid, and help to the South, embracing the leading men of the city. It was called the "Minute Men," and consisted so far as I recollect of about 4,000 men. The badge of this Society was a pin, with the head turned down, and stuck in the left lapel of the coat. Of the career of many of these men later on they went South; and their bones are found on every battle field from the Potomac to the Mississippi.
>
> We held meetings in small numbers. Col Kimball had an office on Calvert St. near Lexington St, and the leaders met in the 3rd story of this office building; and from thence reports were made, and orders sent out accordingly, to the different subordinate companies or groups.

As regards the arms to be used in case of necessity, there was collected a large number of muskets and cartridges and stored in a warehouse on Gay St opposite the old Post Office (the warehouse belonged to the late Johns Hopkins).[17]

Baltimorean George Steuart commanded militia in defense of his city in April 1861 before joining the Confederate army to fight at Gettysburg and other battles. Shortly after Lincoln's election he implored the *National Intelligencer*, a Washington newspaper, to investigate voting by blacks, even in free states, suggesting that this "unconstitutional" action invalidated Lincoln's election and insisting that the paper "ascertain and publish without delay whether such negro votes were so cast and counted in the States I have named":

> I am aware that the nature of the case (voting by ballot) does not admit of exact and specific data as to the color of the votes deposited in the ballot boxes (however strong the odor,) but as a Marylander, knowing my rights as a voter to the exclusion of all negro voters, here or elsewhere in all Federal Elections; and knowing also that the deliberate and intentional extension of the elective franchise to a single negro in any one State, at any election of Federal officers is a gross violation of the Federal Constitution, and if practically carried out will vitiate the election (unless the votes of the offending state or states are rejected).

Steuart proclaimed that if any state authority had sanctioned such violations he would not acknowledge the election of Lincoln and Hannibal Hamlin:

> I believe the only remedy left for the case is the rejection of the votes of the offending State or States, or for our good old state to stand erect and firm on her reserved rights.

He closed with a reminder of his status as a Maryland aristocrat:

> I am as your worthy Senior Editor knows a native born and now very old citizen of Maryland known as a tobacco planter & to possess some landed Estate and some appurtenant slave property, all fairly and rightfully acquired by my ancestors and I believe so held and administered by me as a slave proprietor under our laws. I acknowledge with gratitude this and with it many other blessings which I consider of a higher order than any amount of any kind of property; but at the same time I declare on the honor of a gentleman, that in my estimate all of these blessings weigh but little in comparison with my rights as a Citizen of Maryland and of the United States guaranteed by our State and Federal Constitutions, and that I will risk life and all I possess in support of my own rights or those of any one of my fellow citizens when assailed and violated as they have been and now are, and until the injury is addressed.[18]

1861

As the new year dawned, Leonidas Dodson recorded in his diary the political atmosphere in Easton:

> The truth is the people are divided, and this division of sentiment on the exciting questions of the day takes in great part its character from the party sentiment of each class. The Democrats hold to the Union and a tacit justification of the course of S. Carolina, the opposition hold to the Union, and maintain that the action of the Palmetto State has involved us in almost ruin, and greatly retarded the progress of an amicable adjustment of our difficulties.[19]

As secession gained momentum in the Deep South, on January 10, Illinois Congressman Elihu Washburne shared with President-elect Lincoln his worry over matters in Maryland:

> To my observation things look more threatening to-day than ever. I believe Va. and Maryland are both rotten to the core. We have had one of our friends from New York (the kind I wrote about) in Baltimore, sounding matters there, and he gives most unfavorable reports. *Great danger is to be apprehended from that quarter.* The very worst secessionists and traitors at heart, are *pretended* Union men.[20]

A woman wrote to warn Lincoln of trouble in Baltimore, namely:

> a league of ten persons who have sworn that you should never pass through that city alive,

while William Snethen, a leading Republican in Baltimore, urged caution:

> it has been deemed unadvisable, in the present state of things, to attempt any organized public display on our part, as Republicans.[21]

The day after Christmas, Lincoln friend Joseph Medill, editor of the *Chicago Tribune*, who was in Washington, described Baltimore as a Southern hotbed:

> The evidences of my eyes and ears are forcing me to believe that the secessionists are seriously contemplating resistance to your inauguration in this Capitol. There is certainly a secret organization in this city numbering several hundred members having that purpose in view—sworn armed men, and bunches or lodges affiliated with them in design, extend south to Richmond, Raleigh & Charleston. The malakoff in their way, is Baltimore and that fortress they have laid seige to. The Union & loyal sentiment of her citizens is gradually giving way, and the vicious rabble are getting control. If things go on there for the next 60 days as they have for the last 30, the city will be under the complete control of Disunion Vigilance Committees and a reign of terror will domineer over that

As Southern states seceded and the nation moved toward war, Jefferson Davis became celebrated as the personification of Confederate aspirations. In February, he was inaugurated as the first, and only, president of the Confederate States of America, which would consist of eleven states with almost 9 million people, including 3.5 million slaves. MdHS.

city. When this key point is stormed by the enemy and in their hands, Maryland will go the same way. The city rules the State—the southern and central counties especially. It is the intention of the dis-unionists, if they get Baltimore on their side to prevent you reaching this city by force, and with the aid of the lodges here and in Virginia and south to "clear out" the Republicans here, take possession of the Capitol and proclaim the Southern Confederacy.

Medill believed the "dis-unionist" strategy to prevent Lincoln's inauguration and the counting of electoral votes hinged on their success at flipping Maryland to the South:

> The secession epidemic is spreading with fearful rapidity and violence thro' the Slave States, and if Maryland gives way your friends will have to fight their way with the sword from the Pa. line to the Capitol. And rather than let the rebels hold possession of Washington and exclude the rightful Administration, it were better to lay wast Maryland to reach here.[22]

A New Year's Day message to Hicks from an anonymous correspondent urged him to stand firm and referred to Lincoln's inauguration on March 4:

> I take the liberty of apprising you that from intelligence which has previously come into my possession that the Disunion leaders in this city intend to make

Maryland the basis of their operations during the next two months. Apparently satisfied that the "Cotton States" are sufficiently pledged to the overthrow of the Federal Government, they hope to bring Maryland into the line of the "seceding States" *before the 4th of March next.* To this end they will stimulate your people by every variety of appeal calculated to undermine their loyalty to the Constitution; will, if necessary, resort to threats of violence in case the allurements of ambition should be powerless to move you from your steadfastness, and will, by industriously manufacturing public sentiment in Baltimore and all other points in the State, seek to give it factious strength to their ill-omened cause.

The motive of their labors is this: If they can succeed in bringing Maryland out of the Union, they will inaugurate the new "Southern Confederacy" in the present Capitol of the United States. If this can be accomplished before the 4th of March next, they will succeed in divesting the North of the seat of Government, and by retaining in their possession the public buildings and the public archives they hope at once to extort from foreign governments a recognition not only of their *de facto* but of their *de jure* pretensions.[23]

George B. Cole, a proslavery Unionist, Baltimore insurance executive, and early Maryland photographer, expressed optimism to his brother, even though "I am heart sick of hearing men talk of the demolition of our nation, the grandest earth has ever seen":

I send you by the mail a pamphlet by Jno P Kennedy—an admirable thing. I had a half- hour's talk with him last night that made me feel that there was some hope that *every body* was not yet made. He is hopeful of a settlement shortly. The Border States certainly do at this moment show the early signs of hope. Our Governor, Hicks, has shown himself a true and staunch man, and has kept the state out of the hands of a faction of scoundrels who are striving to make Maryland a cat's paw for the seizure of the seat of Government, and of course the battle ground of the civil war that must ensue. We will have a Union meeting on Thursday night that will be a strong one.[24]

Samuel A. Harrison, a Talbot County physician in St. Michael's, kept a detailed diary of political and military events during the Civil War. Many of his entries were verbatim editorials from his local newspaper, the *Easton Gazette,* while others commented on the editorials and recorded his impressions of a county in conflict. One in late January suggested that Unionism and slavery were fundamentally incompatible.

The Union party of the slave-holding border states were very much embarrassed by its position. Those who constitute it were ardent advocates of the maintenance of the Union, yet they were also advocates of the maintenance of the institution of slavery. They wished that no rupture should be made of the integrity of the nation, yet they revolted at the thought of "coercing" any State to remain in connection with the federation.

While acknowledging that "disunionists" also lacked a coherent message:

> On the other hand the disunionists were equally troubled. A series of queries were put to the candidates of both parties and answered. It will be seen that while the replies of the Unionists were direct and unequivocal, those of the disunionists were evasive, and equivocal. The latter saw that the people of the county, the majority at least were not favorable to secession and did not approve of the action of the Southern states. While therefore the Unionists were troubled by the political fallacy of coercion and the fact of slavery, the Disunionists, were troubled by apprehension of popular disapprobation of their proceedings. The Unionists wished to preserve the integrity of the nation unimpaired but saw not how it could be done, the disunionists wished to disrupt the confederacy knew how it might be accomplished, but were fearful they had not the power.[25]

Leonidas Dodson celebrated the Unionist triumph on February 4, when Talbot County voted against convening a convention to discuss matters that may well have included a Maryland secession:

> Old Talbot has spoken trumpet tongued for the Union! After all the efforts of the extremists, their candidates are defeated by the glorious majority of 261 votes, and the Convention movement put down by a majority of 181! This result in a county belonging to the Democrats by over two hundred maj. has astonished every body.—and shows that the people are right.[26]

On February 8, amid investigations by two congressional committees into rumors of plots, Lucius Chittenden of Vermont arrived to interview Gen. Winfield Scott about security measures for the tally of the electoral vote, scheduled for February 13:

> The grand old man lay upon a sofa. He raised his gigantic frame to a sitting posture. There was infirmity in the movements of his body, but it was forgotten the moment he spoke, for there was no suspicion of weakness in his mind.

When Chittenden told the general of widespread concern that the "vote will not be counted nor the result declared," Scott replied, "Pray tell me why it will not be counted?":

> I have said that any man who attempted by force or unparliamentary disorder to obstruct or interfere with the lawful count of the electoral vote for President and Vice-President of the United States should be lashed to the muzzle of a twelve-pounder and fired out of a window of the Capitol. I would manure the hills of Arlington with fragments of his body, were he a senator or chief magistrate of my native state! It is my duty to suppress insurrection—*my duty!*

Scott then spoke more reassuringly:

> I will say further that I do not believe there is any immediate danger of revolu-
> tion. That there has been, I know. But the leaders of secession are doubtful about
> the result. They are satisfied that somebody would get hurt. I have the assurance
> of the Vice-President of the United States that he will announce the election of
> the President and Vice-President, and that no appeal to force will be attempted.
> His word is reliable. A few drunken rowdies may risk and lose their lives; there
> will be nothing which deserves the name of a revolution. But no promises relieve
> me from my duty. While I command the army there will be no revolution in the
> city of Washington![27]

Chicago detective Allan Pinkerton had worked for the Illinois Central Railroad,
where he became acquainted with George McClellan, vice president of the rail
line. Samuel Felton, the president of the Philadelphia, Wilmington, and Baltimore
Railroad, hired Pinkerton to watch the company's tracks for sabotage. Pinkerton,
using the alias E. J. Allan, claimed to infiltrate what he described—in increasingly
dramatic terms as time passed—as a cell of Baltimore secessionists planning to assassinate President-elect Lincoln as he changed trains in the city en route to Washington to be inaugurated:

> Upon arriving at Baltimore I distributed my Operatives around the City for the
> purpose of acquiring the confidence of the Secessionists. One of these Detec-
> tives, named Timothy Webster, accompanied by a Lady, was stationed by me at
> Perrymansville, a Station about 9 miles South of Havre-de-Grace, on the P.W.
> and B.R.R. [Philadelphia, Wilmington & Baltimore Railroad], where a Rebel
> Company of Cavalry were organizing. Webster, as you will find from his reports
> under the heading of T.W., and those of the lady who accompanied him, un-
> der the heading of H.H.L., succeeded admirably well in cultivating an acquain-
> tance with the Secessionists. You will find much of interest in Webster's Reports,
> showing the manner in which the first Military organization of Maryland Seces-
> sionists was formed, and the promises repeatedly made by Governor Hicks of
> arms being furnished to them; and, if my recollection serves me aright, of arms
> finally being furnished to that Company; their drilling at Belle Air, etc. Webster
> was afterwards executed at Richmond, Va., as a Union spy, and was the first who
> paid the penalty of his life for such Service.[28]

Lincoln dispatched Thomas Mather, the adjutant general of Illinois, to Washington
to confer with General Scott about rumors of plots to murder Lincoln as he passed
through Baltimore. After several attempts to see the general, who was "confined to
his room by illness," Mather got in to see him:

> I found the old warrior, grizzly and wrinkled, propped up in the bed by an em-
> bankment of pillows behind his back. His hair and beard were considerably

disordered, the flesh seemed to lay in rolls across his warty face and neck, and his breathing was not without great labor.

Mather related Scott's message:

"General Mather," he said to me, in great agitation, "Present my compliments to Mr. Lincoln when you return to Springfield, and tell him I expect him to come on to Washington as soon as he is ready. Say to him that I'll look after those Maryland and Virginia rangers myself; I'll plant cannon at both ends of Pennsylvania Avenue, and if any of them show their heads or raise a finger I'll blow them to hell."[29]

The Reverend Henry Slicer, a Baltimore Unionist who objected to Lincoln's suppression of civil liberties, drew the attention of federal authorities during the war, when he served as pastor of Seaman's Union Bethel Church on Aliceanna Street in Fells Point. Slicer's wartime diary in February noted the tension in the nation's capital:

Dr. Cockrill and I went to Washington Returned Home in the evening—saw plenty of soldiers there—under the idea of Genl Scott that that Capitol is to be seized, and Mr. Lincolns Inauguration prevented—.[30]

John Kennedy, superintendent of the New York City Metropolitan Police, visited Baltimore in January to investigate the plot. Two of his men who stayed behind and infiltrated the "Southern Volunteers" would flee after learning they had been exposed:

alarmed at the state of public feeling in Maryland, especially in Baltimore . . . Riots were feared, and there were sinister rumors of threatened attempts to assassinate the President-elect . . . Upon reaching Washington we were instantly admitted to consultation with a Government officer, high in position, whose nervousness was proof of the gravity of the crisis. With secret instructions from this gentleman we went to Baltimore.[31]

Pinkerton's three versions of his work on the "Baltimore plot" became increasingly grandiose. His 1866 account mentioned a barber, Cypriano Ferrandina, a leader of the National Volunteers who plied his trade at Barnum's, Baltimore's fanciest hotel. Pinkerton offered a colorful description of the hotel swarming with boorish Southerners:

The visitors from all portions of the South located at this house, and in the evenings the corridors and parlors would be thronged by the tall, lank forms of the long-haired gentlemen who represented the aristocracy of the slaveholding interests. Their conversations were loud and unrestrained, and any one bold enough or sufficiently indiscreet to venture an opinion contrary to the righteousness of their cause, would soon find himself in an unenviable position and frequently the subject of violence.[32]

Pinkerton took offices in Baltimore as John H. Hutchinson, a "Stock Broker." He cultivated one John Luckett, whose office was on the same floor, describing him as a secessionist furious at Hicks's inaction. Pinkerton gave Luckett twenty-five dollars, to be "employed in the best manner possible for Southern rights, and that when more was required I hoped he would call on me." Luckett divulged that Ferrandina had a plan to keep Lincoln from getting through Baltimore, and he introduced Pinkerton to Ferrandina and "Captain Turner" at Barr's Saloon on South Street:

> Ferrandina said that never, never shall Lincoln be President—His life (Ferrandina) was of no consequence—he was willing to give it for Lincoln's—he would sell it for that Abolitionists, and as Orissini had given his life for Italy, so was he (Ferrandina) ready to die for his country, and the rights of the South, and, said Ferrandina, turning to Captain Turner, "we shall all die together, we shall show the North that we fear them not—every Captain, said he, will on that day prove himself a hero. The first shot fired, the main Traitor (Lincoln) dead, and all Maryland will be with us, and the South shall be free, and the North must then be ours." "Mr. Huchins," said Ferrandina, using Pinkerton's alias, *"If I alone must do it, I shall—Lincoln shall die in this city."*[33]

Pinkerton agent Joseph Howard infiltrated the plotters, "many of whom he had met in the polite circles of society." He reported that they gathered one night in a darkened room, where Howard was inducted into the group. Ballots were placed in a box, with a red ballot "conferring the honor." As conspirators blocked the streets surrounding the Calvert Street rail depot, a diversionary fight would break out as Lincoln made his way to the street. "Mr. Lincoln would find himself surrounded by a dense, excited and hostile crowd, all hustling and jamming against him, and then the fatal blow was to be struck." A Chesapeake Bay steamer would spirit the assassin safely to a Southern port.[34]

Senator (and Secretary of State–designate) William Seward handed a note from General Scott to his assistant Frederick Seward, who was also his son, about danger awaiting in Baltimore:

> Whether this story is well founded or not, Mr. Lincoln ought to know of it at once. But I know of no reason to doubt it. General Scott is impressed with the belief that the danger is real. Colonel Stone has facilities for knowing, and is not apt to exaggerate. I want you to go by the first train. Find Mr. Lincoln wherever he is.
>
> Let no one else know your errand. I have written him that I think he should change his arrangements, and pass through Baltimore at a different hour. I know it may occasion some embarrassment, and perhaps some ill-natured talk. Nevertheless, I strongly advise him to do it.[35]

On the evening of February 21, Frederick Seward found Lincoln at the Continental Hotel in Philadelphia, where he joined others urging the president-elect to pass through Baltimore furtively, late at night. Though Lincoln refused to cancel his engagements the following day—a morning ceremony in Philadelphia to raise the flag at Independence Hall and an afternoon address to the Pennsylvania legislature in Harrisburg—"under any and all circumstances, even if he met with death in doing so," he agreed to pass through Baltimore secretly. Pinkerton discredited the story that Lincoln traveled disguised in a Scotch kilt and cap:

> He wore an overcoat thrown loosely over his shoulders without his arms being in the sleeves, and a black Kossuth hat, which he told me somebody had presented to him. The story of the Scotch cap I may as well at this time pronounce a falsehood made up out of the whole cloth.[36]

In 1918, George C. Latham of Springfield, Illinois, a member of Lincoln's party, stated that reporter Joseph Howard Jr. was the source of the Scotch kilt story:

> I think there was, among many other correspondents, one by the name of Howard, who represented the *New York Times*. In the morning at Harrisburg, after Mr. Lincoln had left the night before, he said he must get up some sort of a story for this paper, and he is the one who fabricated the Scotch cap story. Mr. Lincoln wore a slouch hat and not a Scotch cap, as I learned while staying in the family during the week I was in Washington. He wore a cloak, but it was the same one that he had worn from Springfield and was fastened in front near the neck like many that were worn at the time.[37]

Cartoonists nonetheless satirized Lincoln mercilessly over this incident. Newspapers then were as nasty as today's tabloids; one headline described Lincoln's journey as "More Ass-ass-in-nation."[38]

Baltimore Mayor George Brown discounted any serious threat against Lincoln, describing the episode in his 1887 memoir as

> an unfortunate incident occurred which had a sinister influence on the State of Maryland, and especially on the city of Baltimore. Some superserviceable persons, carried away, honestly no doubt, by their own frightened imaginations, and perhaps in part stimulated by the temptation of getting up a sensation of the first class, succeeded in persuading Mr. Lincoln that a formidable conspiracy existed to assassinate him on his way through Maryland.[39]

Brown had been ready to receive the president-elect:

> An open carriage was in waiting, in which I was to have the honor of escorting Mr. Lincoln through the city to the Washington Station (Camden Station), and of sharing in any danger which he might encounter. It is hardly necessary to say

A lively crowd awaited President Lincoln's arrival in Baltimore, where he would change train stations en route to Washington. Southern-leaning conspirators intent on assassination may have been ready to strike, but Lincoln thwarted them by passing through the city the night before. Pratt Lib.

that I apprehended none. When the train came it appeared, to my great astonishment, that Mrs. Lincoln and her three sons had arrived safely and without hindrance or molestation of any kind, but that Mr. Lincoln could not be found.[40]

Baltimore Unionist William Schley wrote to Lincoln on February 23 that an assault on him was imminent, police protection notwithstanding:

A vast crowd was present at the Depot to see you arrive this morning, but at "Ten" you may judge the disappointment at the "announcement" of your "passage" through *unseen, unnoticed* and *unknown*—it fell like a thunder clap upon the Community—was denied as a "hoax"—&c until the truth was made [known] beyond a doubt—A large "police force" was present to preserve the peace, besides your many friends to resist *attack*—which I now declare *was meditated* and *determined.* By your course you have saved *bloodshed and a mob.*[41]

Lucius Chittenden described in his 1891 memoir a plot by "a mob of twenty thousand roughs and plug-uglies" in which the train taking the president-elect to

Washington would be boarded in Baltimore by five men who would stab him to death.[42]

Lincoln's journey had begun on February 11, 1861, when he left Springfield for Washington. His route took him more than one thousand nine hundred miles, on eighteen railroads, to Indianapolis, Cincinnati, Columbus, Pittsburgh, Cleveland, Buffalo, Albany, and New York City, stopping in small towns along the way. Lincoln later told his friend Isaac Arnold why he acted in a way that lent credibility to a plot:

> I did not then, nor do I now, believe I should have been assassinated, had I gone through Baltimore, as first contemplated; but I thought it wise to run no risk, where no risk was necessary.[43]

Governor Hicks made pronouncements his opponents could use to portray him as less than a staunch Unionist. In early December 1861, he replied to John Contee, a delegate from Prince George's County who had urged him to convene the legislature, that the South had never objected to personal liberty laws before Lincoln's election. (These were state laws enacted in the North to counteract the Fugitive Slave Law, which had given force of law to slave owners seeking to recover escaped slaves.)

> These laws should be repealed at once, and the rights of the South, guaranteed by the constitution, should be respected and enforced. If they are not, *then* in my judgment, we shall be fully warranted in demanding a division of the country.[44]

Unionist Henry Winter Davis, a prominent Baltimore lawyer and Know-Nothing member of Congress, disliked Hicks but, agreeing that Maryland should remain in the Union, urged friends to support him—telling a friend that "I have been writing letters all day instead of going to church on this matter":

> There is a very determined effort to compel the Governor to convoke the Legislature. Under various pretexts the real purpose is to entrap Maryland into revolutionary opposition to the United States: & I have reason to believe that hope is entertained here by persons anxious to destroy the Government & create a Southern Republic, that they will be able, if they can get the Legislature of Md. convened, to secure some act placing Md. in opposition to the Government before or on the 4th March. They are especially anxious to have the Legislature called both because without it they cannot affect the position of Maryland & the refusal of the Governor and the consequent quiet opposition of Md. is a severe rebuke to the noisy agitation elsewhere & a serious obstacle in the way of uniting the middle slave states in their contemplated rebellion. They say too that Md. is between the Seat of Government & other free states & if she joins them, they can use her as a shield against them in any effort to get possession of

the Capital & archives. All this means armed opposition to Lincoln's inauguration if it can be accomplished. How Maryland would fare between Penn. & her
3,000,000 men & the capital you can judge. If we can hold the Governor where
he is we are safe till the government is in the hands of men who will protect it.
It is now in the hands of its enemies. There will be trouble elsewhere; I wish
to avert it from Maryland. It is my deliberate judgment that the calling of the
Legislature is the first step towards civil war: & Maryland has not a single interest that could survive a struggle carried on over her own soil & resulting in the
overthrow of the Government of the United States. That must be averted at all
hazards. Everything else is subordinate to that great necessity. Whether we join
Va. or Pa. we are ruined: we must prevent their being divided. I therefore beg
you to exert yourself actively in securing a petition signed by the most influential
of your mercantile & business friends, remonstrating against the calling of the
Legislature & sustaining the Governor's refusal. It is necessary to sustain him
against the inordinate pressure to which he is being subjected by bad men for
revolutionary purposes.[45]

Maj. Robert Anderson commanded the federal troops in the fortifications surrounding Charleston Harbor. On December 26—taking advantage of darkness and
the holiday cheer in which the South Carolina militia indulged—he spiked the guns
of Fort Moultrie on the northern shore and moved his men to Fort Sumter, a more
defensible fort in the middle of the harbor. One Baltimorean saw Anderson's move
as ominous:

> The exciting news by telegraph has just reached here of the burning of Fort
> Moultrie by the U.S. troops & their occupation of Fort Sumpter.
> The telegram seems to be believed. What this will lead to God only knows.
> Whether done by order of the government or not it precipitates events.
> We have a wretched Know nothing Govr. in this state, who refuses all solicita-
> tions to call our legislature together.

And speculated about the prospects for a "Middle Confederacy":

> I am decidedly in favor of a united South. If the free border states will not give us
> our rights in the present confederacy what faith can we have in them in a middle
> Confederacy?[46]

The *Frederick Herald* advocated neutrality for Maryland, but inside the Union:

> As far as we have been able to gather the sentiment of the people of Maryland,
> we think one thing is menifest, that while they do not think that the election of
> Lincoln to the Presidency is sufficient cause for any Southern State to secede,
> they will oppose the use of measures to coerce a State into the Union, whose
> people may think differently from them upon the subject. They believe that such

a course, upon the part of the general government, would only make the breach wider and more irreconcilable, and destroy the little change there may be left of ultimately putting things to rights again.

> Though Maryland should assume a position of neutrality, it should be one of *armed neutrality*. We should be fully prepared for any emergency that may arise. In these uncertain times no one can tell what a day may bring forth.[47]

The November 13 inaugural address of Democrat George W. Brown as Baltimore's mayor struck a delicate balance between Unionism and acknowledgment of the right of states to sanction slavery:

> While the citizens of this State are sensitive in regard to their constitutional rights, and are justly indignant at the enforcement of laws by some of the States which practically nullify one of those rights, and while they have suffered at least as much from unwarrantable interference with the institution of slavery as the people of any other part of the United States, they have always been steadfast in their devotion to the Union; and will doubtless so remain, unless acts of aggression should be perpetuated or sanctioned by the general government—a contingency which I hope and believe there is no reason to apprehend. I am confident that I express the unanimous sentiment of the people of Baltimore—the largest of the Southern cities—when I say that the true policy of Maryland is to adhere to the Union, so long as she can do so with honor and safety.[48]

Hicks disapproved of secession in principle and opposed South Carolina's on December 20:

> Should I be compelled to witness the downfall of that Government inherited from our fathers, established, as it were, by the special favor of God? I will at least have the consolation, in my dying hour, that I neither by word or deed assisted in hastening its disruption.[49]

A January 7 editorial in the *Baltimore American and Commercial Advertiser* expressed incredulity at a civil war:

> It is computed that at least one million citizens of the South are natives of the Northern States, who have settled in the South, and in many instances intermarried with Southern families.

After providing examples of Southern cities with larger Northern populations, it looked at the reverse:

> The number of citizens in the North of Southern birth is also very large. They may be found everywhere—in the most remote portions of New England, and are scattered all over the Northwestern States. There are more natives of Virginia now resident in New York than of New Yorkers resident in Virginia. In many

instances they too have intermarried into families in the land of their adoption. Thus linked together by the most sacred ties, what new and unspeakable horrors are involved in the idea of civil war! Does it not become all good men, all men who have humanity, all men who are not given over to hardness of heart and demonical malice and cruelty, to labor with their whole souls, and to besiege the throne of Heaven with their supplications, that this hitherto the happiest of all nations may be saved from such an unnatural collision and fearful catastrophe?[50]

Early in January Henry Winter Davis forecast calamitous consequences from a Maryland secession:

Ambitious and restless men, availing themselves of facetious fear which they have inspired, and sectional passion which they have inflamed, are conspiring the overthrow of the government. They hope to found a Southern confederacy on the fragments of the United States of *America.*

Maryland has been formally asked to join a Southern confederacy. The advocates of ruin speciously deny their treasonable plans under the form of Southern prejudice, and ask if Maryland will desert the South and join the North. But that is not the question which Maryland is called to answer.

Maryland is now joined to both the free and the slave States, under the wisest Constitution, and by the best government the world ever saw.

That government has never wronged her, or failed to protect her. The formation of a Southern Confederacy must be preceded by the destruction of that government. Till it is broken up and its armies defeated, there can be no Southern Confederacy.

He asked whether Marylanders really wanted to "break up and destroy the Constitution which Washington founded":

That is the true question you have to consider, for peaceful secession is a delusion, and if you yield to the arts now employed to delude you, the soil of Maryland will be trampled by armies struggling for the national capitol. The only question is, Will you fight to maintain or to destroy the existing government?

Davis noted that slaveholders stood to suffer as much as anyone:

If the present government be destroyed, Maryland slaveholders lose the only guarantee for return of their slaves. Every commercial line of communication is severed. Custom-house barriers arrest her merchants at every frontier. Her commerce on the ocean is the prey of every pirate, or the sport of every maritime power. Her great railroad loses every connection which makes it valuable. If two republics divide the territory of the United States, Maryland is ruined, whichever she join. If the South, her slaves will walk over the Pennsylvania line unmolested. The African slave-trade will reduce their market value below the cost of raising or supporting them.[51]

With Maryland's position on the sectional crisis a subject of growing national speculation, newspapers in Philadelphia, New Orleans, and New York noted the deleterious effects of civil strife on the state's business climate:

> Business here continues terribly oppressed. Merchants are doing scarcely anything. The banks are obliged to restrict, and unable to accommodate customers, except limitedly. Stocks are much depressed, large hypothecations being forced to sale at heavy reductions. Confidence is generally weakening . . . The value of property, rents, everything, is tending downward. Produce of all kinds has declined . . . Many laborers and mechanics in Baltimore are being discharged, and manufactories are curtailing operations.[52]

> Stocks have gone down to almost nothing and many dealers therein are ruined. The banks have great difficulty in accommodating their customers. Money is abundant but capitalists will not let it out.[53]

> The leading hotel was reported to have closed more than half of its house and discharged two thirds of its servants. Other public houses in Baltimore were said to have suffered in proportion.[54]

Maryland businessmen grew frustrated at the silence of their state officials. In December, John Roberts, of the Baltimore hardware firm Magruder, Taylor & Roberts, was traveling in the South seeking customers. In three letters from Georgia, he described the poor business climate and the perception of Maryland in the South:

> Things grow more gloomy daily business seems to be at an end the Towns generally look like mid summer
> I have no hope of selling goods to this country this season nearly every man is for winding up business. Guns will not even sell.
> I will continue to do my best, but you must not expect much from me.

Roberts closed his December 23 letter with another observation about his home state:

> I regret the position of Maryland—the people here complain bitterly of her position

Five days later he wrote again:

> You can give up all hope of selling goods out here next spring, for I am satisfied that good men will not want them.

The greatest expectations prevail from an act [account] of the late news from Charleston. The Minute men are forming and all seem anxious for a fight.

I am sorry to see Maryland so backward for I think it is time she had taken a position.

I hope to be able to send you some more money in a few days.

And closed on December 30 with more pessimism:

I would not think of ordering one dollars worth of goods of any kind for spring sales

In your last letters you still speak of the trouble blowing over of this have not the shadow of a hope for the Union is gone and the Southern people will have more use for muskets than hardware. What will Maryland do? Where will she be found when our rights are trampled upon? Your Union meetings answer with the Black Republicans. Would to God it were otherwise, for to day I am in Georgia & for the first time in my life am ashamed to say I am a Marylander.[55]

Several Confederate states sent emissaries to inveigle Maryland leaders to join their cause. Ambrose Wright, Alabama's commissioner to Maryland, reported on his visit with Governor Hicks:

I can only give to your honorable body the result of the personal interview I had with the Governor, and I regret to say that I found him not only opposed to the secession of Maryland from the Federal Union, but that if she should withdraw from the Union he advised and would urge her to confederate with the Middle States in the formation of a central confederacy. He also informed me that he had already, in his official character, entered into a correspondence with the Governors of those States, including New York, Pennsylvania, New Jersey, Delaware, Virginia, Missouri, and Ohio, with a view, in the event of an ultimate disruption of the Federal Union, to the establishment of such central confederacy. He thought our action hasty, ill-advised, and not justified by the action of which we complain, and that we were attempting to coerce Maryland to follow our example; that he had great confidence in the Peace Conference then in session in Washington, and had assurances that body would agree upon a plan of adjustment that would be entirely acceptable to Maryland.[56]

Baltimore lawyer and Southern-rights' supporter William Wilkins Glenn purchased the pro-Southern *Exchange* newspaper shortly after the war began. He noted in his diary the reluctance of many Marylanders to leave the Union:

Subsequent events convinced me that the majority of the people of the State were by no means ready for separation. They were opposed to coercion and clung to the Union.[57]

In a letter to Maryland's Episcopal bishop, Reverend William Whittingham, Governor Hicks described his interest in mediating the conflict between North and South:

> It is my purpose, so far as I am able to do so, to keep Maryland out of strife that now seems to be inevitable; not only, that she may be free from the horrors of civil war; but also that she may continue to be, in a position to mediate between the hostile sections.
>
> I have almost lost all faith in the disposition of Congress to settle our troubles. Mans wisdom having failed us, I am still trusting that Providence will so overrule the madness of the people, that what now seems to threaten our national destruction, may ultimately be for our national advantage.
>
> I thank you most sincerely for your kind sustaining letter, and if agreeable to you, shall be glad to publish it, believing that it will greatly assist in quieting the clamor for immediate state action.[58]

Daniel Thomas, a native of West River in Anne Arundel County, practiced law in Baltimore and belonged to the pro-Southern National Volunteers. In February 1861, he declared his views in a letter to his sister:

> Matters are frightening here—at one time I thought we were sold to the North, but the feeling which has manifested itself here recently makes me hope everything is not lost yet. We are going on now to stir the matter in the wards by ward meetings & speeches and so forth. Nearly Everybody here has given up all hope of compromise, and the only question is, whose cause shall Maryland embrace, that of the North or that of the south. I am satisfied that not only our sympathies and honor but also our material interests require us to side with the south. If Maryland does go North I for one go south.[59]

Elizabeth Blair Lee, daughter of Lincoln confidante Francis Preston Blair, sister of Lincoln's Postmaster General Montgomery Blair, and wife of U.S. naval officer Samuel Phillips Lee, recounted fisticuffs between U.S. Senator Robert Toombs of Georgia and Gen. Winfield Scott, who tipped the scales at close to three hundred pounds. The fracas occurred at the home of Democratic Senator John R. Thomson of New Jersey:

> Mr. Tombs & Genl Scott had a *bout* at No. 4 (John R's). The first called the Old Hero a liar—whereupon the Genl rushed into him—but they were promptly parted—it was at a dinner party—Civil War seems inevitable—even at friendly dinner parties.[60]

Signs of Maryland Unionism were abundant in early 1861. A January meeting in Frederick resolved to prevent any effort "to commit 'noble old Maryland' to any sectional issue" that would disengage the state from "the Constitution and the laws." Baltimorean John Fulton quoted a resolution passed by several Maryland counties that urged support for a compromise:

> *Resolved,* as the opinion of this Conference, Maryland is this day, as she ever has been, true to the American Union; that she will exert all her influence for its peaceful preservation, and that in her efforts to that end, she will rely upon the wisdom and patriotism of her tried and faithful sons, and upon an all-wise and overruling Providence.

The second resolution noted:

> That the people of Maryland will accept the proposed constitutional and legislative guarantees known as the Crittenden compromise, as a fair and proper settlement of the fatal controversy which is now distracting the republic.[61]

When Maryland Congressman J. Morrison Harris, in a speech on the House floor, referred to his state as a Southern state and himself as a "southern man," the retort of his fellow Rep. George W. Hughes elicited applause from the galleries:

> I have no objection to my colleague speaking for his own district; but I must dissent, when he undertakes to speak for the State of Maryland, and especially the district I represent. I repeat my declaration; and say now, that at this moment, according to my honest, and I believe well-informed judgment upon the subject, the doctrine of secession cannot, in the State of Maryland, to-day raise more friends than would make up a corporal's guard.[62]

Some Marylanders felt an affinity with Virginia and wished to await events there before determining Maryland's course. The *Richmond Enquirer* approved:

> Can there not be found men bold and brave enough in Maryland to unite with Virginians in seizing the Capital at Washington?[63]

A speaker at a celebration of Washington's birthday in St. Mary's County expressed a similar sentiment:

> The States of Virginia and Maryland having grown together in prosperity, they should cling together in adversity. Like the Siamese Twins to divide them, would be to kill them both.[64]

While a Bladensburg physician urged bold, collective action:

> Noble South Carolina has done her duty bravely. Now Virginia and Maryland must immediately raise an armed force sufficient to control the district, and never allow Abe Lincoln to set foot on its soil.[65]

The new Congress scrambled to control the secession conflagration. The House quickly assembled the Committee of Thirty Three and the Senate the Committee of Thirteen. Their first order of business—to keep the entire upper South and all the border slave states from seceding—failed. The Washington Peace Conference began on February 4 in Washington—"the last, sad effort to avert war," wrote Allan Nevins. Hicks appointed seven distinguished men to represent Maryland— Reverdy Johnson, Augustus Bradford, William Goldsborough, John Crisfield, J. Dixon Roman, John Dent, and Benjamin Howard. This group gave the Maryland delegation a Unionist mien, leaving Eastern Shore Congressman Roman to voice the Southern position:

> I have not hitherto addressed the Conference, but I should do myself injustice if I remained silent any longer. I came here in good faith, encouraged with the hope that this conference would do something which would indicate a purpose to protect and acknowledge the rights of the slave-holding States. I have patiently attended your sittings, and little by little that hope has faded, until to-night it has almost passed away. What good can come of these deliberations when upon every question which is presented the lines of sectionalism are tightly drawn, and with one or two exceptions every northern State is arrayed against us?

Roman complained that compensated emancipation would be nothing "but an inducement to mobs and riots":

> If the peace of this country is to be hereafter established on a permanent basis, and the Union is to be preserved, you, gentlemen of the North, must recognize our rights, and cease to interfere with them. You have nothing to do with this question of slavery. It is an institution of our own. If it is a crime, we are responsible for it, and will bear the responsibility. We have never interfered with your institutions. You must now let us alone.[66]

In February, Captain John C. Robinson took command at Fort McHenry, which protected the Patapsco River approach into Baltimore. He quickly found what he was up against:

> The officers at the post were on friendly and visiting terms with some of the leading families of Baltimore, but when secession became the harbinger of war, they found many of these acquaintances were intensely Southern in their feelings, and ready to unite with the seceding States in their efforts to destroy the Union.[67]

In the winter of 1861, U.S. soldiers and civilian laborers (including some Baltimoreans) working feverishly to fortify Fort Sumter received little support from Washington, and Major Anderson rationed their dwindling supplies. With the Congress unable to craft a compromise, the possibility that conflict would erupt in the waters of Charleston Harbor grew. Hester Davis, wife of Allen Bowie Davis, a prominent planter in Montgomery County, anticipated the failure of the Washington Peace Conference:

The Commissioners from 13 states yesterday met in Washington. It is hoped they will agree on something which will be submitted to Congress and meet its approval. As to war—that is a question no one at this time can answer. If this matter is not settled before the 4th of March—I much fear the policy of the incoming administration will be the enforcement of certain government laws in the southern states. This will induce resistance and of course Civil War must follow.[68]

Members of the Shriver family, of Union Mills in Carroll County, would populate both sides of the conflict. A letter in February from Christopher Columbus Shriver to his cousin, Frederick, was a harbinger of the political differences between them throughout the war:

We Southerners are settled in the belief that the North will do nothing and it is time for us to help ourselves. Self preservation is the first law of nature. The Stars and Stripes ain't doing their duty and we must disown them.[69]

In February, Josephine Tilton heard a shot from the upper floor of her home. Mrs. Tilton, mother of five, hurried upstairs to discover her husband, Navy Capt. Edward G. Tilton, dead of a bullet in the brain. Elizabeth Blair Lee recorded the incident:

I was grieved to the heart to learn by the city papers that Capt Tilton had committed suicide yesterday. I have not met him this winter & think I saw across the Senate one day—The paper says it was owing to the Countrys troubles—forgetting that there is a "better county" for which we ought to work on bravely & honestly in this one. Oh the bitter pang to his wife to feel that there was no love of God or any of his creatures not of himself even to protect them from such wretchedness. The amount of unhappiness to result in such a deed is fearful to think of [.] May God be more merciful to him than he has been to himself—He looked ill when I saw him here in the summer & perhaps his mind was clouded with illness—His State was still in the Union & all prospect of Md. seceding is given up by the frantic fire eaters.[70]

Early in February W. W. Glenn complained about the lack of leadership in the crisis:

Every one saw that matters were getting worse daily and still nobody in Maryland at least dreamed of the terrible revolution into which we were drifting. What astonished me most was that there were no leaders in Maryland who were willing to take a prominent part or act independently. There was but one opinion. Everyone said "Wait for Virginia. See what she does."[71]

A Pinkerton operative in Baltimore, using the alias "A.F.C.," promised $500 to any man who would kill Lincoln. The pledge was made to a National Volunteer named O. K. Hillard, who agreed to commit the deed "between here and Havre-de-Grace" if the money were given to his mother. Over supper at Mann's Restaurant, Hillard—who two weeks before had testified to Congress that he knew nothing of any organization opposed to the government or Lincoln—further enlightened A.F.C.:

> "Five Hundred dollars would help my Mother, but it would do me no good, because I would expect to die—and I would say so soon as it was done—here gentlemen take me—I am the man who done the deed." Hillard also remarked "If our Company would draw lots to see who would kill Lincoln, and the lot should fall on me, I would do it willingly, even if my Captain should tell me to do it I would do it."[72]

Hillard explained to Pinkerton the conspiracy's extreme secrecy:

> We have taken a solemn oath, which is to obey the orders of our Captain, without asking any questions, and in no case, or under any circumstances reveal any orders received by us, or entrusted to us, or anything that is confidential, for instance I was called to Washington City before the Committee—I must not divulge the object nor the nature of our organization, but evade and if necessary decline to answer their questions.[73]

Edward Spencer lived at the Martin's Nest, a farm near Randallstown in Baltimore County. In 1851, he struck up a friendship with Anne Catherine Bradford Harrison ("Braddie") of Mount Pleasant in Talbot County. Ten years later, Spencer was courting her, principally by letter, many of which describe both his anger at coercion against the South and embrace of Confederate views:

> Honey, the times are awful, and I am fearful that very many persons do not appreciate them properly. We are on the brink of civil war, and I see no possible means of averting it. The Peace Congress has failed, Congress does nothing, & before May, Maryland & Virginia will certainly be out of the Union. This means war, for the Republicans are determined to hold Washington, at all hazards. I had the opportunity, while in Washington, of conversing with & learning the views of very many prominent men of that party, and it is their universal resolve to coerce Maryland. Until now, I have thought it possible to save the Union, but now, I am a positive, unconditional Secessionist. Md will go out, and, if there is war, I must and shall take part in it—not for the sake of distinction, but for the South. We will have a terrible time, much blood will be shed, but the South will conquer—unless the negroes are roused against us.[74]

Luther Bruen was in Washington on March 3, when he wrote to his wife in Dayton, Ohio:

> I arrived this morning, ready to take part in the "wild hunt for office," which has now fairly begun.

I saw a man to-day who went to Baltimore to ferret out the conspiracy to assassinate Mr. Lincoln. He thinks an attempt will be made to take his life to-morrow. If it is there will be a lively time you may well believe. I shall not be surprised myself if his life is attempted.

I would not write thus to you, if there was any possibility of this letter getting to you before the Inauguration Day was passed. If there is any trouble you will learn by telegraph whatever has happened. I hope everything will pass off smoothly & that our country may not be disgraced by a scene of violence which is seriously apprehended.[75]

Bruen gave his wife an eyewitness account of Lincoln's swearing-in:

The inauguration passed off very quietly & without the least disturbance. There was a large display of military & a tremendous crowd of people. Upon the plat form there was the whole body of Foreign Ministers. I had never seen them in their court costume & I regarded them with a very curious eye.

Everybody was armed, nearly, & the southerners were very mad, so that you can easily believe it would not have taken very much to have started a bloody fight. I am very glad that nothing occurred to commence it, for I am afraid I should have been obliged to take a hand in it.[76]

John Pendleton Kennedy, a lawyer, novelist, and member of the Maryland House of Delegates, was a Whig member of Congress from 1838 to 1846 representing Maryland, who in 1852 and 1853 served as Millard Fillmore's secretary of the navy. March and April diary entries contained observations about the new president:

In the evening we get Lincoln's inaugural. It is conciliatory and firm—promising peace, but brooking no purpose to visit aggression against the Government (March 4).

I read the Inaugural again and like it better. I thinks its tone is dignified and truthful, and its spirit for promotion of concord (March 5).

Magraw calls to see me and sits a great part of the morning. Tells me anecdotes of Lincoln in the White House. From these representations he must be pretty rough, and uneducated. The pressure for office they say is awful.

We have a rumor today that Lincoln has determined to abandon Fort Sumpter. This is a great stride towards a peaceful solution of difficulties (March 11).

(Mayor Thomas) Swann calls to see me to tell me of his visit to Washington and interview with Mr. Lincoln. The cabinet seems to be very unsteady and vacillating. One would think they were bewildered by the complications of the crisis.[77]

TO THE PEOPLE OF FRED'K. COUNTY.

FELLOW-CITIZENS,

The wide-spread prevalence of the political heresy of Secession which has resulted in the withdrawal of seven States from that Union which for nearly a century has been our pride and boast, demands our instant action, so that our silence may not be misconstrued and that our example may afford moral aid and encouragement to the loyal & patriotic men who still cling to their Country with unabated love and fidelity.

Notwithstanding the many grievances of which the South justly complains, and against which none has juster cause for remonstrance than the State of Maryland, we hold that *Secession is no remedy* for ... but on the contrary, is an intolerable aggravation of and an addition to th...

We hold that in a government of laws, the first duty of every citizen is obedience. That whatever injustice or wrong may be perpetrated, in a free government where the largest exercise of liberty compatible with the stability of government and the security of the people is guaranteed to every individual, no such wrong or injustice can be permanent, but that a fair and candid appeal to the honesty and intelligence of the people of the whole country, will inevitably result in a full and cordial recognition of all our constitutional rights and the removal of all our existing grounds of complaint.

We hold that the temporary and accidental triumph of the Republican Party in the election of a President, while the real and substantial power of the government remained in the hands of their opponents, was no such overwhelming calamity as to compel or justify the dissolution of this Confederacy; the total abandonment of our rights and privileges in the Union and the renunciation of the glorious heritage bequeathed to us by our Revolutionary ancestors.

We hold that the remedy for all these things is to be found, not in Secession, but at the ballot-box; and we feel justified in believing that there is already a returning sense of justice on the part of our Northern brethren.

Therefore, the undersigned earnestly invite their fellow-citizens of Frederick County, who stand by the Union of these States and oppose Secession for any past or present cause, to unite with them in

MASS CONVENTION

AT THE COURT HOUSE, IN THE CITY OF FREDERICK AT 10 O'CLOCK, A. M.,
ON TUESDAY, THE 26TH DAY OF MARCH 1861,

to form a Union Organization in this County and to take steps for holding a Union State Convention at an early day thereafter.

Jacob Bear	Otho Norris	Jacob Sahm	Ephraim Creager	Lewis H. Bennet	Daniel S. Loy,
R. Potts	J D Getzendanner	Jacob Reifsnider	Spencer C Jones	P. Jefferson Hawman	William Dean,
L. J. Brengle	Ulysses Hobbs	Charles E Mealey	Grafton W Elliott	Lloyd Dorsey,	W. H. C. Dean,
John Loats	Charles Cole	Charles W Haller	John Poole	Robert Shafer,	Josiah Harrison,
Chas E Trail	J A Simmons	Frederick Main	Frederick Kehler	George W. Summers,	Harrison Conley,
Wm P Maulsby	Frederick Keefer	Geo C Johnson	Jacob Detre	Henry C. Steiner,	Nicholas T. Haller,
James Cooper	Christian Steiner	Charles Mantz	Wilson R Boyd	John J. Kantner,	L M. Englebrecht,
Frederick Schley	Charles Lease	E Y Goldsborough	Erasmus West	Lawrence Bentz,	James W. Phebus,
Grayson Eichelberger	James T Smith	Samuel R Hogg	L V Scholl	Daniel A. Staley,	C Getzendanner,
James Whitehill	D C Winebrenner	Jacob Fox	G R Kephart	Anthony Kimmel,	John T. Martin,
Edward Shriver	James Hopwood	David Weaver	Daniel H Rohr	Francis T. Rhodes,	Henry Lorentz,
Adam Wolfe	Barney Fisher	Wm Johnston	George K Birely	George W. Derr,	William Lorentz,
Nicholas Whitmore	James Hergesheimer	Edward Trail	D W Brooks	Isaac P. Suman,	John Routzahn,
Wm D Reese	Zephaniah Harrison	W G Moran	John Lyeth	George W. L. Bartgis	Mathias Abalt,
J W L Carty	A Gault	Daniel Haller	I W Suman	John Wilson	John Sifford,
Basil Norris	Edward Buckey	George Engelbrecht	C T Albaugh	George Gittinger	Geo T. Williard,
W Tyler, Sr	Thos M Holbrunner	Thomas M Markell	John T Schley	James Bruner	Thomas Hooper,
Jacob Markell	John Mackechney	William T Haller	Isaiah Mealey	H. K. Hilton	John Cramer,
R Y Stokes	Edward Sinn	John E Sifford	John Sanner	Michael Englebrecht	James W. Hood,
John Schreiner	Val S Brunner	John Goldsborough	George S Groshon	William Glessner,	J George Sinn,
R H Macgill	Wm G Cole	George F Webster	John H Mumford	George Kantner,	J. R. Marken,
P L Storm	Tobias Haller	G W Delaplane	Robert Boone,	A. H. Hunt,	John Hooper,
W B Tyler	Jacob Hammell	Daniel Sweaner	... Boyd,	W. R. Sanderson,	James Hooper,
Francis Markell	John J Woodward	E Albaugh	Levi Vanfossen,	W. J. Lynn Smith,	W. H. R. Kelty,
P M Englebrecht	L M Schaeffer	George W. Ulrich	Dennis Scholl,	Simon Parsons,	O. F. Butler,
George Markell	Wm G Schneffer	Abraham Haff	Isacher Himbury,	Frederick Shipley,	Gideon Bantz,
Lewis Markell	M Keefer	Charles E Albaugh	William Higgins,	Abraham Kemp,	David Kenega,
Emanuel Mantz	T J McGill	D T Runner	Richard T. Dixon	George M. Tyler,	Upton Buhrman,
John Ramsburgh,	George Salmon,	Andrew Boyd,	Lewis H. Dill,	Maurice Albaugh,	W. L. Hays,
Jacob Knauff,	Jonathan T. Wilson,	Hiram H. Mullen	John J. Suman,	William T. Duvall,	A. E. Smith,
George A. Abbott,	William H. James,	John H. Abbott,			

John McPherson, Wm. B. Tabler, W. Loehner, Fairfax Schley, Grafton Fout, Charles W. Eader, Jacob Ramsburg, Clark Eldridge, Saml. B. Preston, Wm. T. Gittings, R. G. McPherson, Hiram M. Nusz, George Metzger, Jacob Leilich, George Buhrman, M. G. Arnold, Dewalt Williard, Isaac Keller, William Stokes, John T. Martin, Adam Custard, Michael H. Haller, Henry C. Frazier, Hanson T. C. Green, Samuel Carmack, Wm. T. Preston, B. A Cunningham, N. D. Hauer, G. W. Dertzbaugh, John Stimmel, William Mahony, J. J. Moran, J. McPherson, of W James Williamson, John H. Keller, John S. Burucker, T. E. Getzendanner, Charles W. Miller, John H. Young, George R. Dennis, Sebast'n Ramsburg, Wm. H. Derr, James M. Harding, John Fauble, Benjamin Ebert, Benjamin Roatzsho, B. G. Fitzhugh, Dr. J. Bonne, Jacob Grove, John M. Ebert, Henry M. Nixdorff, G. P. Ramsburg, of Jdl. F. Schindler, George D. Miller, Henry Schley, L. A. Brengle, Jr, Jacob Kiehl, William H. Grove, Henry B. Fessler, John T. Moore, Samuel Haller, A. P. Kessler, A. H. Reinhart, G. J. Doll, John T. Green, David K. Schaeffer, Samuel B. Ebert, Mason R. Marsh, George W. Custard, William H. Rice, Christian Woerner, Isaac Wisong, Hiram Schessler, Charles H Keefer, Chas E. Campbell, Lewis Medtart, N. H. Pitts, Henry A. Cole, George Hoskins, T. M. Morgan, jr. Philip Cramer, George W Cramer, Philip H Sinn, Edward Young.

Printed at the Office of "The Maryland Union" Frederick, Md. [March 19, 1861.

In March, dozens of Unionists in Frederick summoned citizens to a "Mass Convention" at the courthouse, "to form a Union Organization in this county" and to plan a Union state convention. Their broadside stated that remedies to problems lay "not in Secession, but at the ballot-box." MdHS.

In March, Baltimorean Elizabeth Patterson Bonaparte, wife of Napoleon Bonaparte's younger brother Jerome, received a letter from her property manager in Baltimore expressing frustration at economic conditions thwarting his efforts to collect her rents:

> I have collected a great deal of money but never experienced such difficulty as at present. Our Country is in such a state that it is almost impossible to get money, owing to the fact that no business is doing. I have been compelled to take dribs on account running daily after them, and in some instances to take Virginia money which is at 6 per cent discount, for fear I should get none if I refused, the discount being more than my commission.[78]

Edward Spencer lashed out about economic conditions and the newly inaugurated Lincoln:

> No one has any idea of the distress in Baltimore. There are 8000 persons unemployed, and as many more working on half-time. If there should occur any disturbance it will be awful, for men become fiends when bread is lacking. Yet, "nobody's hurt" says that infamous clown of the White House, anchored in Washington like a black & white buoy to warn people off from hope & reasonable expectation. It makes me savage when I think we have fallen so low as to have such a man for President.[79]

Confederate Gen. Pierre Beauregard dispatched two aides to Fort Sumter to demand that Major Anderson (his artillery instructor at West Point) vacate it immediately. The major, under orders to hold the Fort, refused. At 3:20 on the morning of April 12, Beauregard's men announced the start of the Civil War:

> By authority of Brigadier General Beauregard, commanding the Provisional Forces of the Confederate States, we have the honor to notify you that he will open the fire of his batteries on Fort Sumter in one hour from this time.[80]

Leonidas Dodson told his diary of his feelings about April 12, a day that

> Will be ever memorable in our annals as a nation as the day the revolutionary forts attacked Sumter,—the firing was continued all day.[81]

One of Beauregard's aides later described Anderson's mood as he refused to surrender:

> He seemed to realize the full import of the consequences, and the great responsibility of his position. Escorting us to the boat at the wharf, he cordially pressed our hands in farewell, remarking "If we never meet in this world again, God grant that we may meet in the next."[82]

South Carolina forces shelled Sumter for thirty-three hours, reducing parts of the massive structure to rubble. Sumter's barracks caught fire and threatened the magazine; the hail of burning debris allowed the men to evacuate only a portion of the powder. When Anderson, supplies depleted, surrendered on the afternoon of April 13, miraculously no casualties had occurred. Major Abner Doubleday, Anderson's second in command, wrote how one group of men erased doubts about their loyalty:

> To my great astonishment the battery I had left recommenced firing. I could not imagine who could have taken our places. It seems that a group of the Baltimore workmen had been watching our motions, and had thus learned the duties of a cannoneer. They could not resist the fun of trying their hand at one of the guns. It was already accurately pointed, and the ball struck the mark in the center. The men attributed it to their own skill and when I entered they were fairly in convulsions of laughter. One of them, in answer to my question, gasped out, "I hit it square in the middle." After this first attempt, each of them was desirous of trying his skill at aiming. The result was, that we soon had them organized into a firing party.[83]

W. W. Glenn noted the home-front reaction:

> Fort Sumter fell, after nearly two days bombardment. There was great excitement in Baltimore. The general feeling however was against the action of South Carolina.[84]

An ardent Unionist once the Civil War began, J. P. Kennedy wrote about the dangers of secession—"out of this Union, there is nothing but ruin for [Maryland]":

> We may not shelter ourselves under the plea of revolution. No man in Maryland can lay his hand upon his heart and say that this Government of ours has ever done him wrong.

Kennedy also warned of the dangers of the Maryland secession:

> But if Maryland should be a member of that Confederacy, then the North, in time of war, may also shut up the Chesapeake against us; and not only that, but may also shut up our Western and Northern railroads. It may deny us the Ohio River; it may deny us access to Philadelphia, to New York & utterly obliterate not only our trade, but cut off our provisions. In the other case, Virginia could not do that, nor even impede our transit on the Baltimore and Ohio Rail Road, as long as Western Virginia shall stand our friend, as assuredly it will if we are true to ourselves.[85]

The *Sun*, while advocating a peaceful solution to the national crisis, equated South Carolina with the American colonies at the outbreak of the Revolutionary War:

*John Pendleton Kennedy—
congressman, novelist,
lawyer—became an articulate
defender of the Union. MdSA.*

Now is the time for every good citizen to use all his influence to stay the onset, push back the advancing and furious contestants, and insist upon a peaceful adjustment of the cause of the strife. Failing in this, no man can conceive the terrible consequences that may ensue. The war spirit of the North, that war spirit which it is so difficult to arouse against a foreign foe, is instantly inflamed versus the members of our national household—against our own people, the common brotherhood of the States. And for what? Not for an aggressive deed of war, not because of invasion, not because of design or even declaration against rights of the North, but simply because they have captured a fortress within their own territory.

In the attack upon Sumter they have done just what the United States would have done with respect to England at the opening of the revolutionary war, just what any nation would do under the same circumstances.[86]

The *Baltimore American and Commercial Advertiser* noted on Monday, April 15, "the excitement consequent upon the stirring news from Charleston Harbor" that "was indicated by an unprecedented demand for the *American*—the heavy morning edition of which was exhausted before ten o'clock":

> The groups increased rapidly in number, taxing the constant attention of the squads of policemen judiciously distributed throughout the excited throngs to keep the sidewalks in the vicinity of North and Baltimore streets sufficiently clear for the passage even of individual pedestrians, and the manifestations of popular excitement were occasionally marked with alarming exhibitions of personal feeling or of partisan rancor. The predominant sentiment was, however, unmistakably one of devotion to the Union.

When a man expressed Southern views the crowd reacted quickly:

> Shortly before the excitement had reached the inflammatory stage of fever a large, knotty looking individual, dressed in an orange colored jumpsuit, and hailing, it was said from North Carolina, appeared among the crowd at South street and Baltimore, with a secession cockade conspicuously displayed in his hat. It is probable that a discreet bearing would have secured the stranger from any manifestation of popular indignation more expressive than good-natured ridicule or satire, but the North Carolinian—who, by the way, had about him an air of resolution and self-poised coolness indicating an ability to "hoe his own row"—was bent on proselytism, and, running counter to the excited sympathies of the Unionists, soon provoked an ebullition of dislike and of practical opposition which, but for the prompt interference of the police, who escorted the stranger to his hotel, followed by a shouting a throng, might have led to a serious collision.

The evening ended with rumors of Anderson's surrender:

> Men hurried about in all directions—to the hotels, the newspaper offices (then closed for the night), and other popular resorts, in the eager desire to gain some confirmation of the rumor. In this particular endeavor crowds were engaged until nearly midnight, when thousands of earnest Union loving men returned to the [h]omes, many of whom doubtless vainly sought to "—Draw around an aching breast the curtain of repose."[87]

Allen Bowie Davis wrote to his son William, a student at St. James Academy in Hagerstown, to tell him that Sumter had fallen and with it Maryland's chances of avoiding an inevitable war:

> I write with a heavy heart, our beloved Country is now involved in Civil War, the most horrible of all national contests, and God only knows where it will end. We here in Maryland I fear are to be the innocent victims of the wicked and insane Slavery agitation between the North & the South. We have not provoked the

contest and cannot rightfully be made parties to it—but I fear we cannot escape its consequences. Since Sumpter has fallen, in the [inaugural] contest hoped against her the next point of attack I fear will be Washington. A Nepolian at the head of the Southern army would be there in forty eight hours after the fall of Sumpter to anticipate the reinforcements Lincoln will call around him from the North. A Southern army will meet no resistance in Virginia as they have too many Sympathizers in Maryland—Washington would therefore be an easy pray to their usurpations. I was sorry the other day to hear Mr. Hutton avow himself a thorough Secessionist—this he did to me. I hope he will have direction enough not to repeat it or to propagate such political heresy.

Davis had harsh words for Lincoln:

It is a great misfortune that we have at such a time a President for whom we cannot entertain political sympathy & hardly personal respect—it greatly weakens the chances of sustaining the Government. I think as Marylanders we should if possible keep out of the contest—but this may not be practicable.

And fatherly advice for his son:

Do not suffer yourself to become too much excited upon the subject so as to lett it interfere with your studies and the advantage you *now* have for the opportunity may never return to you again—not even the opportunity of completing your collegiate course.[88]

In April, a Baltimorean warned Lincoln of a plot against the government:

I take this method of informing you that you better prepair yourself for an assailing mob that is organizing in Baltimore as far as i can inform myself is about 12000 m. strong they intend to seize the Capitol and yourself and as they say that they will tar & put cotton on your head and ride you and Gen Scot on a rail this secret organization is about 70000 m members in Maryland and Virginia.[89]

Leonidas Dodson was one of many Unionists who favored neutrality for Maryland. On April 19, he appeared optimistic about such a prospect, unaware of events transpiring across the Chesapeake Bay in Baltimore:

We have news of no further conflict between the unhappy beligerents in our civil difficulties, Gov Hicks is understood to say to the President, that he will only obey the demand, to call out troops in our State, upon conviction that it is imperative upon him so to do, and then not without the written guarantee of the Government that these troops shall be held only to preserve the peace of Md, and protect the District of Columbia.

This is in my view the course of prudence, and will have the effect to make Md a sort of armed neutrality.[90]

chapter two

April 1861

Two days after Lincoln's call for Northern troops, William Wilkins Glenn attended a meeting of Southern extremists at the home of William Norris, a lawyer who lived at 92 West Monument Street:

> The Southern men in Maryland assumed a more determined attitude and expressed great indignation at the idea of troops being raised in one state to subjugate another. Still nothing was done. There was no concerted action. The Clubs met more frequently and Mr. Norris addressed them repeatedly urging them to arm and drill.
>
> This evening there was a meeting at Norris'. Wallis and Frank Howard both advised me not to go, saying that I only compromised myself by associating myself with so extreme a party. But I decided to go, because, as I told them, I thought one of us ought to know what was going on and because too I thought I had some influence which I had at least exercised for good, in the case of the Maryland Institute meeting. When I got to the house, I found there were just thirteen of us present. I could not help smiling at the ill omen although I little thought that before the summer was over half of us would be in Fort (McHenry) or skulking in the woods. The meeting was in secret. Its object was evidently to organize an armed resistance to the passage of troops through Maryland.[1]

An advertisement in the *Baltimore Sun* saw opportunity amid the uncertainty gripping Maryland:

> Many inquiries have been made by parties interested as to the effect of service in the army or navy upon life insurance. The New England Life Insurance Company, of Boston, has established a war rate, at two per cent, above the ordinary rates, and has commenced the issuing of policies.[2]

An April 18 letter from "X" of Trappe, on Maryland's Eastern Shore, in the April 20 edition of the *Easton Gazette* expressed the view that slavery and Unionism were compatible ideals and the South was the aggressor:

> It cannot but grieve a true union man to see the state of affairs in the country at present. If we acknowledge that there is such a thing as a Southern Confederacy, we see the strange sight of a nation making an attack upon us, while perhaps a third of our citizens—*American Citizens*—openly saying that we must not raise an arm in our defense, even when our Federal Capitol is threatened with an attack.

"X" rhetorically asked who could support the South:

> And whence comes all this sympathy for the cotton growers? Is it because they have injured our trade, ruined our credit, and "taken from us our good name?" Is

it because they have tried to break up this Union, the foundation of which is laid upon the graves of thousands of the heroes of '76, who gave up their lives that they might transmit the blessings of liberty to their posterity? Is it because they basely deserted us at the time of our greatest need, when assailed by the North, and when their voters might have protected us? Or is it because of the common institution of slavery? May the border States, while firmly breasting the waves of abolition North, never be driven upon the breakers of secession South.

The secessionists are improving the opportunity (but let no true union men be deceived), who cry out "coercion" while their guns are aimed at Fort Sumter. Who cry out "coercion" if the government calls for troops when the Federal Capitol is openly threatened by the southern, would be, president. We have no more cause now for secession than we had three months ago. Let the union men only continue to be true and submit to be called "abolitionists" even if they hold fifty slaves, and all may yet be well.[3]

Samuel A. Harrison took note of that letter and presciently noted in his journal that slavery lay at the root of the crisis:

The first public enunciation by the *Gazette* of the right and duty of the Government to defend itself against the rebellions of the South is in a Communication signed "X" of Trappe. Even now, the plain right of self protection, even by force, is timidly uttered and with a kind of qualification. This which was written about the time of the attack upon Fort Sumpter. I here insert it as indicating the gradual steps taken by the loyal men of the county towards the light a proper position ultimately assumed. It will be seen too from this article, that the Union men of the County began to awaken to the true issues of the contest—the perpetuation or destruction of slavery.[4]

Northern governors moved quickly to meet their troop quotas requested by the president. With soldiers preparing to move through Maryland toward Washington, federal and Confederate recruiters in Baltimore enlisting Maryland men, and South Carolina's Palmetto flag flying in the city, a newspaper described passions in the city:

In the forenoon a politician at the corner of Baltimore and South streets used some harsh language towards the Confederate States which for the time excited the mirth of those who stood around him, but offense was finally taken by some who heard his expressions, and his friends deemed it prudent, during the excitement to persuade him to leave.[5]

On April 18, two companies of U.S. artillery and four of militia left Harrisburg on the Northern Central Railroad for Baltimore. Recruits gazing through their windows at the Maryland town of Havre de Grace might have seen a large American flag bearing the message, "By the Eternal, the Union must and shall be preserved." Though taunted by crowds as they changed stations in Baltimore, the Pennsylvanians passed through Baltimore without incident. Mayor George Brown, however, wrote to Lincoln that day of his misgivings about further troop passage through his city:

> The people are exasperated to the highest degree by the passage of troops, and the citizens are universally decided in the opinion that no man should be ordered to come.
>
> The authorities of the City did their best to day to protect both strangers and citizens and to prevent a collision, but in vain and but for their great efforts a fearful slaughter would have occurred. Under these circumstances it is my solemn duty to inform you that it is not possible for more soldiers to pass through Baltimore unless they fight their way at every step.
>
> I therefore hope and trust and most earnestly request that no more troops be permitted or ordered by the Government to pass through the City. If they should attempt it the responsibility for the bloodshed will not rest upon me[6]

Confederate Attorney General Judah P. Benjamin advised Capt. J. Lyle Clarke of Baltimore that the services of men from the Union slave states were not yet needed, but when they were, men such as Clark could count on transportation costs, subsistence, and "40 cents per day for the use and risk of their horses":

> The Government of the Confederate States regards your patriotic effort as among the most agreeable and important evidences of true Southern feeling in the State of Maryland. Such friends of this Confederacy as yourself in Maryland will continue to hold yourselves in readiness for the promptest movement.[7]

A New Yorker who wrote to the president recognized both the vulnerability of the nation's capital to rebel attack and the significance of the border slave states for the Union cause:

> I am able to inform you that it was the intention of the conspirators to march on Washington, rendezvousing at Richmond Va., immediately after Fort Sumpter was evacuated, of which by the way they consider a certainty. The rapidity of movement on the one side, and expected demoralization on the other side of the North from loss of Sumpter, (which they are signally mistaken) contain according to the plans of conspirators, the element of success so as to secure Washington city and perhaps force Border Slave States into Secession. They inform me also that there are 5000 men in Virginia, 3000 in Maryland, and 1000 in Washington city, (several hundred in employ of government) who are ready to assist in movement contemplated by the conspirators.[8]

Robert E. Lee, who had spent thirty-six of his fifty-four years in the U.S. Army, declined the offer to command the Union forces. He gave fuller vent to his feelings in a letter to his sister Anne Marshall, a Unionist who lived in Baltimore:

I am grieved at my inability to see you. I have been waiting for a more convenient season, which has brought to many before me deep and lasting regret. Now we are in a state of war which will yield to nothing. The whole South is in a state of revolution, into which Virginia, after a long struggle, has been drawn; I had to meet the question whether I should take part against my native State.

With all my devotion to the Union, and the feeling of loyalty and duty of an American citizen, I have not been able to make up my mind to raise my hand against my relatives, my children, my home. I have, therefore, resigned my commission in the Army, and save in defense of my native State (with the sincere hope that my poor services may never be needed) I hope I may never be called upon to draw my sword.[9]

On Friday, April 19, Pennsylvania and Massachusetts troops left Philadelphia for Baltimore's President Street Station, where horses would pull their uncoupled cars along tracks embedded in the street to the Camden Station, just a mile west, for trains to Washington. This common connecting maneuver allowed the various railroads serving Baltimore to move passengers easily between their own stations around the city. As the locomotive rumbled south, the young men saw through the windows the rolling hills of central Maryland and the broad expanse of the Susquehanna River, thoughts undoubtedly on families behind and adventures ahead. Their officers warned of trouble on the passage through Baltimore. Col. Edward Jones of the Sixth Massachusetts Regiment warned his men they might have to vacate the cars to march

in columns of sections, arms at will. You will undoubtedly be insulted, abused, and perhaps assaulted, to which you must pay no attention whatever, but march with your faces square to the front, and pay no attention to the mob, even if they throw stones, bricks, or other missiles; but if you are fired upon, and any of you are hit, your officers will order you to fire. Do not fire into any promiscuous crowds, but select any man whom you may see aiming at you, and be sure you drop him.[10]

Thirty-five rail cars, carrying almost two thousand men, arrived at 11 a.m. and were hitched to horses for the transfer to Camden Station. Sidewalks quickly filled with Southern sympathizers, Unionists, and onlookers, who began spilling onto Pratt Street and the embedded rails. Epithets gave way to stones and shots, igniting the battle that left fourteen dead and many wounded. Mayor Brown recalled four companies,

in all about 220 men, formed on President street, in the midst of a dense and angry crowd, which threatened and pressed upon the troops, uttering cheers for Jefferson Davis and the Southern Confederacy, and groans for Lincoln and the North, with much abusive language. As the soldiers advanced along President street, the commotion increased; one of the band of rioters appeared bearing a

Confederate flag, and it was carried a considerable distance before it was torn from its staff by citizens. Stones were thrown in great numbers, and at the corner of Fawn street two of the soldiers were knocked down by stones and seriously injured. In crossing Pratt-street bridge, the troops had to pick their way over joists and scantling, which by this time had been placed on the bridge to obstruct their passage.[11]

Many witnesses described their recollections of the April 19 clash in the mists of old age. William Bowley Wilson, a member of the Southern-leaning Maryland Guards, did so forty-nine years later:

> Believing firmly that the Government had no right to coerce the Southern States, and that it was outraging the State of Maryland by bringing Northern militia through it for that purpose, I ran down to the depot to assist in preventing their passage. I found a large and angry crowd gathered outside, some thousands. The Sixth Massachusetts were drawn up in two ranks on the north of the station, just outside. They had unwisely allowed the crowd to surround them so closely that the men of the regiment would have been unable to use their arms in case of an attack. There were people of all sorts in the crowd and it was no common mob; most of them with my feelings, I imaging.
>
> A big man came forward with a Palmetto flag and planting it in front of the Colonel with an oath, dared him to touch it. The Colonel was prudent and did not. The men of the regiment were very pale and quiet; the Corporal on the left was especially exposed. I saw a man spit in his face, and another kick him. Tears ran down his cheeks, and he was as pale as death. It was he who a little later was killed on the Pratt Street bridge. The crowd did their best to provoke them to action. Had they made any move I think they would have fared very badly, as they could not use their arms to any effect.
>
> I did not see any arms displayed by anyone in the crowd.[12]

Henry Wagner was carrying checks from his place of business on Bowley's Wharf, near the foot of South Street, to Baltimore Street for deposit when, at the southeast corner of South and Pratt, he came upon

> several car loads of Soldiers, passing westward on Pratt Street, with an excited and angry crowd of men and boys at the side of and following the cars, throwing sticks stones etc., and hurling opprobrious epithets at the Soldiers, declaring vehemently that no Yankees should be allowed to pass through the City of Baltimore to war upon the South. No shots were heard, but missles were thrown into the car windows which were open, and several negro draymen cracked their whips at the faces of the occupants, who seemed calm and unmoved, scarcely noticing the taunts and curses of the mob. It was difficult to tell whether this conduct of the Military was caused by fear, or strict disciplinary orders. Cheers

were given for Jeff Davis, South Carolina, the Confederacy etc. A single cheer for the Union was heard. The writer found it came from an old schoolmate and valued friend, James A. Gary of the "Alberton Cotton Mills." The writer ran up to him and begged him to desist, or trouble would ensue. "No," said he. "I'll hurrah for the Union forever." Soon thereafter, as the writer had feared, he was felled by a treacherous blow.[13]

Augustus J. Albert was walking to the home of his grandfather, Mr. Taylor, on Lombard Street, when he heard that Northern troops were marching along Pratt Street. His description is consistent with other accounts of lawlessness on April 19 and the days immediately following:

> I ran down to Camden Station, where I found that part of the 6th Mass. Regiment which got through to Washington later, on a train of cars in the depot. The other part of the regiment was stopped on Pratt St. and driven back by volleys of stones to President St. depot and returned to Philadelphia. A party of about 20 of us got on the train that was about to start for Washington with the troops and tried to jerk their muskets from them, but the police came to their aid and put us off the train. We then started out beyond the limits of the City, tore up the R.R. track, and prepared to attack them with large rocks which we collected on a bridge running over the R.R. track but realizing how foolish it was, when we did not have even have a pistol among the whole of our party, we decided to start back to the City. Just then the train arrived and I had my first opportunity of looking into the Muzzles of a lot of guns. The train stopped as they saw the track was torn up, and the officer in command gave the order "Ready! Aim!" The guns came crashing through all the windows of the cars which were closed, breaking the glass and shutters. I folded my arms and held my breath, but fortunately for me the order to "fire" did not come.[14]

William Platt, a resident of South Stricker Street, in 1909 recorded his recollection of the Southern-leaning "Minute Men":

> We marched down to capture Ft. McHenry and marched back again. When we arrived we were told by the commanding officer that the guns of the Fortress were loaded, and at any attempt made he would open fire, so we concluded not to make an assault.[15]

Daniel M. Thomas, a member of the Maryland Guards, described the events leading to April 19:

> I suppose you will like to hear some of the details as gained from personal observation. All last week we were apprehending trouble here from the *Masses* without knowing from which *side* it would come. Consequently, we were keeping strong guard at our armory.

After digressing about preparations and saying of his friend Bill Murray "that a truer man in time of danger I have never seen," Thomas continued:

About 9 o'clock Friday morning news was brought to us (for we could not go out) that 2000 men from New York were at the Philadelphia depot and were going to pass through the city—and that the citizens were pulling up the railroad track on Pratt Street and were going to stop them. At half past 11 our captain was notified that before 12 we would be called out as the Police had notified the Commissioners that they could not keep the mob down. This you may imagine gave us no little trouble as we were on the side of the mob, and we were sorely exercised in mind as to how far our duty required us to go in the matter. I will say for our credit, however, that we resolved that if called out we would do our best to put down the mob short of firing on them. In a few minutes our men came running in fearfully excited and crying, "They are firing on our people in the streets and shooting them down like Dogs." Then came the news. "Frank Ward, one of our men, is shot dead." And then followed such a scene as pen could not describe. Men insisting that if the battalion would not turn out they would take the guns and go on their own hook. This of course would have been madness.[16]

Thomas was incorrect about the death of Frank Ward, who survived to become a lieutenant in the First Maryland Infantry Regiment, C.S.A.

Among the contemporary accounts of that day was a call to Mayor Brown for assistance from the "Office of the Baltimore Clipper," a Know-Nothing newspaper, bracing for an assault on the paper's office:

There is reason to apprehend an exhibition of mob violence directed against the building and the occupants of the office of the Baltimore Clipper, numerous threats of violence have been publicly uttered and there is ground for apprehension that their execution may be attempted. In accordance with legal requirements we give you notice of this fact in order that the city may be held responsible for any damage that may be done, and that you may take such action in the premises as you may be necessary and proper.[17]

The mayor's courage amid the violence endeared him to many. While assessing the situation at Camden Station, he heard of the chaos along Pratt Street and hastened toward the President Street Station. Witnesses substantiated his account of the incident, which he recounted in his memoirs:

When I was about to leave the Camden-street station, supposing all danger to be over, news was brought to Police Commissioner Davis and myself, who were standing together, that some troops had been left behind, and that the mob was tearing up the track on Pratt street, so as to obstruct the progress of the cars, which were coming to the Camden-street station.[18]

Baltimoreans and Massachusetts troops clash in the "Pratt Street Riot," as the Bay State men pass through the city en route to Washington. The first fatalities of the Civil War occurred during this incident on Friday, April 19, 1861. MdHS.

Brown raced to "the point of danger" and ordered that anchors placed on the tracks be removed. As he approached the bridge on Pratt Street:

> I saw a battalion, which proved to be four companies of the Massachusetts regiment which had crossed the bridge, coming towards me in double-quick time.
>
> They were firing wildly, sometimes backward, over their shoulders, so rapid was the march that they could not stop to take aim. The mob, which was not very large, as it seemed to me, was pursuing with shouts and stones, and, I think, an occasional pistol-shot. The uproar was furious. I ran at once to the head of the column, some persons in the crowd shouting, "Here comes the mayor." I shook hands with the officer in command, Captain Follansbee, saying as I did so, "I am the mayor of Baltimore." The captain greeted me cordially. I at once objected to the double-quick, which was immediately stopped. I placed myself by his side, and marched with him.[19]

As he marched, Brown observed "neither concert of action nor organization among the rioters"—an important comment in view of claims that Baltimore political gangs, albeit weakened by recent political and police reforms, helped mobilize resistance to the passing troops. Brown wrote that the rioters were armed only with such stones or missiles as they could pick up, and a few pistols. My presence for a short time had some effect, but very soon the attack was renewed with greater violence. The mob grew bolder. Stones flew thick and fast. Rioters rushed at the soldiers and attempted to snatch their muskets, and at least on two occasions succeeded. With one of these muskets a soldier was killed. Men fell on both sides . . . the soldiers fired at will. There was no firing by platoons, and I heard no order given to fire.[20]

Sixteen-year-old George W. Booth, a member of the "Independent Grays" militia, was returning home from evening guard duty at an armory, when, from the corner of Pratt and Commerce streets, he saw the clash in full furor. Booth, who joined the Confederate army early in the war, recalled the incident many years later:

A soldier, struck by a stone, fell almost at my feet, and as he fell, dropped his musket, which was immediately seized by a citizen, who raised it to his shoulder and fired into the column. The rear files faced about and delivered a volley into the crowd, who responded with pistol shots, stones, clubs and other missiles. A perfect fusillade was kept up between the troops and the enraged mob, the troops taking the double quick and the crowd closely following. As the Maltby House was reached, the police, under the Mayor and Marshal (Kane), intervened between the flying soldiers and their pursuers.[21]

Brown described rapidly escalating violence:

At the corner of South street several citizens standing in a group fell, either killed or wounded. It was impossible for the troops to discriminate between the rioters and the by-standers, but the latter seemed to suffer most, because, as the main attack was from the mob pursuing the soldiers from the rear, they, in their march, could not easily face backward to fire, but could shoot at those whom they passed on the street. Near the corner of Light street a soldier was severely wounded, who afterward died, and a boy on a vessel lying in the dock was killed, and about the same place three soldiers at the head of the column leveled their muskets and fired into a group standing on the sidewalk, who, as far as I could see, were taking no active part. The shots took effect, but I cannot say how many fell. I cried out, waving my umbrella to emphasize my words, "For God's sake don't shoot!" but it was too late.

Following an aside to rebuke a rumor that he had "seized a musket and killed one of the rioters," the mayor resumed his narrative:

Marshal Kane, with about fifty policemen (as I then supposed, but I have since ascertained that in fact there were not so many), came at a run from the direction of the Camden-street station, and throwing themselves in the rear of the troops, they formed a line in front of the mob, and with drawn revolvers kept it back.[22]

Businessman Richard D. Fisher watched from the second-floor window of his "counting-house" at 54 West Gay Street. Years later, as president of the Maryland Historical Society, he asked eyewitnesses for their written recollections of April 19, and offered his own, of a racially and ethnically diverse mob:

I was an eye-witness of the "moving picture" at the junction of Gay and Pratt Streets. I saw the scene from the window of my counting-house on the second floor of No. 54 South Gay Street, about 150 feet off. Car after car, each filled with troops, was drawn along Pratt Street by horses, amid the hoots of the crowd, the incitement steadily increasing until the last car was saluted with stones and brickbats, and I can still hear the crashing of the glass windows; altho' in this car no troops were visible, and I have since heard they were "lying low." Immediately afterward, I saw an acquaintance of mine seize the bridle of a horse attached to a sand-cart, and dump the sand on the R.R. track. This set the example. Gentlemen merchants, Irish draymen and Negro laborers tumultuously joined in dragging across the track anchors, chains and other obstructions, rendering the further transit of cars impracticable. After an interval, came the four last companies on foot, marching from the direction of President Street Depot, and following the Pratt Street track, amid volleys of yells and missles; and just after the corner of Gay Street was passed, the heavy firing began.

I well remember that, standing beside me, was a Spanish Sea-captain, whose vessel was then in port to my consignment, and who said to me in Spanish "You seem much agitated; this is nothing; we frequently have these things in Spain."—and I replied "In Spain, this may mean nothing; in America, it means Civil War."[23]

L. A. Whiteley was one of the first to advise the federal government of the troubles in Baltimore, in an April 19 message to Secretary of War Simon Cameron:

Mob violence begun. Attempts made to obstruct railroad in streets. Governor and mayor in consultation. Will skeleton companies be received to be subsequently filled, and the pay of the men begin from date of their reception? If so, a large number ready at once. Answer.[24]

A rare reference to a Maryland secession movement appears in a brother's letter to his sister on what was surely the day of the clash:

The passage of the northern troops through here has caused an immense revolution of feeling and men who a day or two ago would have done anything for the "Union" are now (as is usual with those who change) the most ranting secessionists.

There was a very large crowd last night in front of Barnums and I was very much surprised when Willie Thomas came out on the steps and addressed them. He made a very nice little speech which was enthusiastically applauded. A half cracked individual next appeared who announced his name as Tom Jones the first Know "Nothing" of Baltimore and said he was for the Youth all over and then proposed three cheers for Jeff Davis which were given with a will. The meeting last night of the secessionists was a secret one and no one seems to know anything about it.[25]

His sister replied days later:

I am delighted to hear that your Southern prospects are so good, for I am afraid poor old Maryland is union forever. I feel really ashamed of her.[26]

Secretary Cameron replied unequivocally to railroad officials in Philadelphia who asked how troops might best be sent to Washington:

Governor Hicks has neither right nor authority to stop troops coming to Washington. Send them on prepared to fight their way through, if necessary.[27]

On the day after the riot, Catherine Smith referred to terrified soldiers seeking refuge in a house:

We are amid fearful excitement. You will I dare say have seen an account of the Massachusetts soldiers passing through. Our citizens became frantic and attacked them in the street and altho the Hon. Mayor and police accompanied them the enraged Mob prevailed urged on no doubt by those who should have acted differently and a good deal of blood was spilled on both sides some 15 or 20 besides many wounded. It was one battle from the President Street Depo—to the Camden Street depot—I can say no more. We are all well. I will send the newspapers. There is great excitement—the rabble are now attacking a house in Pratt Street occupied by some company going to Washington.[28]

The Reverend Henry Slicer also recorded the chaos the day after:

Found my family in a great state of excitement—apprehending Civil War—
A force of Penna troops some 3,000, were reported to be at Cockeysville on sabth morning, on the way to Washington via of Baltimore—The whole city was thrown into alarm and the church is closed &c—and the military order'd out—The troops were order'd back by the govmt—on Friday last (19th) a collision took place in our streets between an unorganized body of our people, and the Massichusets troops, who were on the way to Washington—In which several were Kill'd on each side, and a considerable number wounded—They should have been warn'd by the authorities not to come this way, or to come this way, or to have been let pass unmolested—several innocent persons not in the fight were killed by the *balls* of the soldiers, our people attacked them with stones and bricks.

We have fallen upon evil times—God only knows what will be the issue, and when we shall see the end—

The danger now is, that the border slave states will secede—[29]

Jabez David Pratt told his brother John C. Pratt in Boston of Baltimore's resolve to keep troops out of the city:

We, both Lucy and myself, are not disposed to run—much less into the arms of infernal abolitionism. We know there is danger. We have expected for thirty-six hours war to the knife. Possibly all may be slaughtered; but by the God in heaven, we are determined to die in the work, and not a man or woman I have seen or heard of but are so determined.

Let any more Northern troops attempt passage of this city and not one will live to tell the story. It is a yawning gulf as long as a man is left to do the death.

Thirty-six hours ago a majority of our people were for peaceable separation, and I may say for peace at all hazards, but now the man does not exist in these parts who is not for the defense of our city against the inroads or passage of troops from the North. We are not to be subjugated by Lincoln and his hordes.[30]

Daniel Thomas believed April 19 a watershed that would lead to a Maryland secession. He had rushed that day with William Bowley Wilson and McHenry Howard to Carroll Hall to protect Maryland Guard weapons stored in the armory there. There they found a dozen Guard members with bayonets keeping looters at bay:

Against the real enemy we were crazy to march. But the Colonel steadily refused until he should receive orders from the Mayor. In a short time we heard him sing out below. "Now then—Throw out the flag." And such a shout as went up would have done your hearts good. I'll undertake to say that never a flag was flung to the breeze with such a will as ours was on that occasion. Their thinking it was of course for the purpose of going to fight the northern soldiers. The next hour after that was one of the most exciting ever passed. I was on guard at the street door, and to see our fellows rushing in from all sides, with their firm resolved faces and eagerness to avenge the murder of our citizens was something for patriotism to feed on. All our West River men were there looking as cool as cucumbers and ready for the fight. At the same time applicants for enlistment crowded on us, and men were so anxious to get in that it was as much as we could do to keep them off. Old men would come and with tears in their eyes beg us to take them along. Others would come and ask for their sons or brothers to bid them goodbye and some of the parting scenes were really affecting. By this time the fighting spirit of Baltimore was fully aroused, as the papers will show you, but before anything could be done, the enemy had escaped, part by way of Washington and the other part back to Philadelphia. The rest of the incidents of the day you will get from the papers. But be assured it was a thing to live for, to see a large town like this that up to this time had been on the eve of civil war in its own midst, uniting almost to a man, in one common cause, and that cause the one I have had at heart so long. The first blood shed in our streets settled the vexed question and the union cause is dead in Maryland. How singular it is that this affair, so similar an incident to the battle of Lexington, should have happened on the anniversary of that battle.[31]

Civil unrest escalated. Throughout the night of April 19, raiders from Baltimore, including sixty policemen, destroyed railroad bridges that spanned the Gunpowder and Bush rivers north and east of the city. The City Guards burned Northern Central Railroad bridges connecting Harrisburg and Baltimore, including one at Cockeysville; the Melvale Bridge in Mt. Washington was doused with camphor and burned; and the Canton Bridge was destroyed.[32] By April 20, federal authorities were moving decisively to keep Maryland's rail lines open—and hinted at occupying Baltimore:

There has been no arrival from the North. Some one or more bridges have been destroyed; where it is not known; telegraph interrupted. Warford has sent by horses along the road to find where the trouble is; will send me and General Keim with his staff through by an express train, if locomotives are on the north side of the break.

This road must be under military control at once, and in charge of the Government. So must the road between here and Washington. This is absolutely indispensable. Our rapid communication with the North is otherwise cut off. Troops coming on your road could leave it about three miles from Baltimore, and by a march of five miles reach the Washington road some two and a half miles from the city on the Washington road. This would avoid the city. But the city must be under the Government control. You should not rely upon any sending dispatches. Trusty agents should keep you informed, and carry your directions. Depend upon it, a vigorous and efficient plan of action must be decided on and carried out, or we will have to give up the capital.

The communication with the South is perfect both by railroad and telegraph, and we must have the same, or we are gone. No arrivals from Philadelphia or New York, and no information. Rumor says the bridge across the Gunpowder is destroyed, and also a bridge some six or eight miles out of the city. The Northern Central should be the base of operations, and the communications by water be kept open. Havre de Grace, it seems to me, is a point at which our Pennsylvania troops might concentrate with advantage, as from there they could reach here by water or Annapolis by rail. We could keep the railroad open easy from the east bank of the Susquehanna.

Let there be prompt action. Let the Government as soon as possible take possession of the railroad necessary to keep open communication with Washington.

THE CIVIL WAR.

BURNING OF BRIDGES.

CORRESPONDENCE WITH THE PRESIDENT.

TROOPS TO PASS AROUND THE CITY.

Five Hundred Thousand Dollars Appropriated for the Defence of the City.

MILITARY MOVEMENTS.

Seizure of Government Munitions of War.

DOINGS OF FRIDAY NIGHT.

The city during Friday night was a scene of wild excitement, equal almost to that which prevailed during the day previous. Shortly after 1 o'clock information was conveyed to the military headquarters that a

Headlines in the Baltimore American and Commercial Advertiser *trumpeted the chaos of the aftermath of April 19, 1861, and actions by state and city officials to prevent further civil unrest. MdHS.*

Take, if necessary, two steamers here for transporting troops by water. A few thousand men with artillery on the high grounds about this city would secure it to us.[33]

Lincoln, worried about the precarious state of the capital's defense, received callers at the White House, as recorded in the diary of his secretary, John Hay:

After tea came Partridge and Petherbridge from Baltimore. They came to announce that they had taken possession of the Pikesville Arsenal in the name of the Government—to represent the feeling of the Baltimore Conservatives in regard to the present embroglio there and to assure the President of the entire fidelity of the Governor and the State authorities. The President showed them Hick's and Brown's despatch. Which "Send no troops here. The authorities here are loyal to the Constitution. Our police force and local militia will be sufficient." Meaning, as they all seem to think, that they wanted no Washington troops to preserve order, but as Seward insists, that no more troops must be sent through the city. Scott seemed to agree with Seward & his answer to a despatch of inquiry was "Gov. Hicks has no authority to prevent troops from passing through Baltimore." Seward interpolated, "no right." Partridge and Petherbridge seemed both loyal and hopeful. They spoke of the danger of the North being roused to fury by the bloodshed of today and pouring in an avalanche over the border. The President most solemnly assured them tht there was no danger. "Our people are easily influenced by reason. They have determined to prosecute this matter with energy but with the most temperate spirit. You are entirely safe from lawless invasion."[34]

Mayor Brown and former Baltimore Mayor Enoch Lowe claimed that Governor Hicks authorized destruction of railroad bridges north of Baltimore, and Brown always denied authorizing such action himself. However, Col. Isaac Ridgeway Trimble, a Baltimore engineer who would later command the militia companies in Baltimore, claimed that Brown instructed him to destroy the bridges. Trimble wrote:

> The Mayor, I am convinced, had but one object in view, viz. the peace of the City and preservation of life, which he knew alone could be accomplished by keeping troops out of the City.

Summoned to Brown's office at midnight on April 19, Trimble claimed that the mayor had stated that "it had been decided to destroy the bridges on the two roads." Brown "wanted me to break down those on the Philadelphia Road," but Trimble replied that he "preferred that someone else would be selected for the service." But after being assured that Governor Hicks had approved, Trimble consented upon receiving a written order from the mayor:

> He wrote the order at once (see copy) and in a few hours two of the bridges on the Philadelphia had been rendered impassable for a week by burning the draw bridges, 18 & 20 miles from the City. I refrained from doing other damage to these costly structures, than burning the draws in the channel. Marshall Kain, the same night burned two bridges on the Northern Central Road about 16 miles from the City.

Trimble reproduced the order in his statement:

> By the authority of the Governor of Maryland and for the protection of the City of Baltimore, I hereby direct Col. Isaac Trimble to proceed up the Philadelphia

R.R. and break down the bridges thereof up to the Susquehanna River, and also require all persons to refrain from opposition thereto. I require the agents of the road to furnish all necessary facilities.[35]

William Seabrook, commissioner of the Maryland Land Office, defended Hicks:

It is charged that at a conference of city officials and prominent private citizens with him he either gave orders to have the bridges on the P.W. and B. Railroad burned, or gave his assent to that act, which was one of the incidents connected with the effort to obstruct the passage of Northern troops through Maryland to the national Capital. This he always strenuously denied. He was under duress at the time and his life was endangered. A lawless mob had followed him on the street threatening violence and crying "Hang him, Hang him."[36]

In a letter to a Baltimore newspaper, Hicks promised to

lay before the public a full refutation of this nefarious attempt to involve an innocent person in an unwarranted proceeding. Until that time, I request a suspension of public opinion.[37]

Orville Browning, a Lincoln friend and adviser from Illinois, told the president what he must do:

The fall of Washington would be most disasterous. Communication ought to, and must be kept open to Washington. Baltimore must not stand in the way. It should be seized and garrisoned, or, if necessary to the success of our glorious cause, laid in ruin. No city or state can be allowed to interpose between the government, and the final and triumphant termination of this quarrel, and if they get in the way give them up to their doom.[38]

Governor Hicks explained to Secretary Cameron his refusal to supply Maryland regiments to the federal government, as the president had requested on April 15:

Since I saw you in Washington last I have been in Baltimore City laboring, in conjunction with the mayor of that city, to preserve peace and order, but I regret to say with little success. Up to yesterday there appeared promise, but the outbreak came; the turbulent passions of the riotous element prevailed; fear for safety became reality, what they had endeavored to Conceal, but what was known to us, was no longer concealed, but made manifest; the rebellious element had the control of things. We were arranging and organizing forces to protect the city and preserve order, but want of organization and of arms prevented success. They had arms; they had the principal part of the organized military forces with them, and for us to have made the effort, under the circumstances, would have had the effect to aid the disorderly element. They took possession of the armories, have the arms and ammunition, and I therefore think it prudent to decline (for the present) responding affirmatively to the requisition made by President Lincoln for four regiments of infantry.[39]

A newspaper reported on Hicks's address to an afternoon rally in Baltimore's Monument Square on April 19, where the governor sought to mollify slaveholding Marylanders:

> Mayor Brown introduced the Governor with a few prefatory remarks, which were not distinctly heard by our reporter, who was just then assiduously engaged in relieving himself of an outside pressure so strong and dense as to effectually pinion his limbs.

In his address, Hicks uttered a line that opponents would long use to challenge his Unionist feelings:

> If separate we must, in God's name let us separate in peace; for I would rather this right arm should be separated from my body than raise it against a brother.[40]

Men raced about seeking arms, and volunteer militias assembled amid reports of thousands of Pennsylvania troops at Cockeysville, headed for Baltimore:

> The scene of excitement that followed was one of those events that are placed among the marked memories of a life time. The tocsin of war was sounded, not metaphorically but literally; the population of the city poured into the streets, and thousands upon thousands gathered towards the points where the news could be learned, and the preparations for resistance witnessed or participated in.

The *American* urged Maryland lawmakers to act:

> The feeling is general, finding expression, we believe, from all classes of sentiment, that the Legislature of the State should be assembled in extra session by the Governor, as soon as possible. The events of the last few days have precipitated us into the midst of difficulties and responsibilities of a character so momentous that there must needs be a concentration of all the authority and power of the State to meet them. In the fullest sense, the State is in a condition of revolution.[41]

In the confusion of April 19 and the ensuing days, as men thought about their loyalties, Christopher Columbus Shriver—soon to enlist in the rebel army—described to his cousin the uncertainty in Baltimore:

> I have just passed through a day of the most intense excitement, I ever experienced. You have heard not doubt of the little war we had on Friday—so I will not say anything about it, but will continue the story only from this morning.

The cry at 11½ O'clock was, that there were at Cockeysville some 4000 armed troops ready to make an attack upon the City, and as many more down on the Philadelphia road. The union said they were to act in concert, and lay the city in ashes. John and I were on our way to church at the time, and not having arms of any kind thought perhaps it was as good a place as one could get. The Clergy had been officially informed of the attack, and in consequence of which we had *low Mass* instead of High Mass, which is usual. When we got into the Church and saw how deathlike the silence was, and how much affected all the ladies were—I tell you I felt might badly We had no music—and as the service was very short we were soon through

The whole congregation was almost in tears ever one had heard the news, and of course was interested, when we got on the street every man we met had a gun, pistol, or sword, and all running as hard as they could toward the mayor's office. Officers on horses were riding through the street as hard as their horses could leg it, and each man you met had a more horrible tale to tell. Some said that the President had ordered the troops from Fort McHenry to fire upon the town—and that of course considerably raised the [?]—ladies along the street were begging their friends not to go, and when we got here at the house found our folks worse scared than any others, Mr. Myer Johnson & myself went down to Barnum's Hotel and found the streets so crowded with soldiers, volunteers and cavalry that one could hardly get through the crowd. A long row of wagons were extended out Calvert St. with *beds upon them intended for* the *wounded,* and a lot of young [Doctrs] tearing linen into to pieces for bandages. Oh God! It was a sickening sight, I hope I may never see another like it. The "*Maryland Guards*", were all in their uniforms—ready to march. The "Grays" City Guards and all just ready to go to work Every one of them seemed anxious to commence, The whole town was wild.[42]

On Saturday, April 20, Lincoln sent a message to Governor Hicks, which Mayor Brown also received:

I desire to consult with you and the Mayor of Baltimore relative to preserving the peace of Maryland. Please come immediately by special train, which you can take at Baltimore, or if necessary one can be sent from hence. Answer forthwith.[43]

Hicks and Brown feared the catastrophic consequences of more Northern troops arriving in Baltimore. The mayor sought the governor's approval of his response to the president:

Letter from President and Gen. Scott. No troops to pass through Baltimore, if as a military force, they can march around. I will answer every effort will be made to prevent parties leaving the city to molest them, but cannot guarantee against acts of individuals not organized. Do you approve?[44]

Hicks answered that he "hoped they would send no more troops through Maryland, but as we have no right to demand that, I am glad no more are to be sent through Baltimore. I know you will do all in your power to preserve the peace." Brown assured Lincoln that, were troops to avoid Baltimore, city authorities would endeavor to keep citizens from harassing them—but with the caveat that city officials

> have no authority to speak for the people of Maryland, and no means of keeping any promise they might make. They do sincerely & earnestly trust that the government will be warned by the melancholy occurrences of yesterday, & avoid precipitating further disastrous results. Baltimore seeks only to protect herself.[45]

Brown departed for Washington at 7:30 Sunday morning, accompanied by George Dobbin, John Brune, and Baltimore lawyer Severn Teackle Wallis. At the White House, the Baltimoreans pled their case, but the mayor had to explain why Baltimore militiamen were destroying railroad bridges above the city:

> It was a measure of protection on a sudden emergency, designed to prevent bloodshed in the city of Baltimore, and not an act of hostility towards the General Government; that the people of Maryland had always been deeply attached to the Union, which had been shown on all occasions, but that they, including the citizens of Baltimore, regarded the proclamation calling for 75,000 troops as an act of war on the South, and a violation of its constitutional rights, and that it was not surprising that a high-spirited people, holding such opinions, should resent the passage of Northern troops through their city for such a purpose.[46]

The president, recalled Brown, said he had been misunderstood:

> Mr. Lincoln was greatly moved, and, springing up from his chair, walked backward and forward through the apartment. He said, with great feeling, "Mr. Brown, I am not a learned man! I am not a learned man!" that his proclamation had not been correctly understood; that he had no intention of bringing on war, but that his purpose was to defend the capital, which was in danger of being bombarded from the heights across the Potomac.[47]

Shortly after Brown left the White House, he received a telegram from Baltimore & Ohio Railroad President John Garrett:

> Three thousand (3,000) Northern troops are reported to be at Cockeysville. Intense excitement prevails. Churches have been dismissed and the people are arming *en masse*. To prevent terrific bloodshed, the results of your interview and arrangements are awaited.[48]

At 1:25 p.m. Brown replied: "Be calm, and do nothing until you hear from me again." He returned to the White House; at 3:15 p.m., he telegraphed Garrett: "We have again seen the President. The troops are ordered to return forthwith to Harrisburg." Lincoln remained true to his word, and Brown for the moment had accomplished his mission.[49]

On Sunday, George Whitmarsh, a Baltimore shoemaker, recorded his observations:

> Just as I started for church this morning early at 10 o'clock, the alarm spread that 3,000 volunteers from the North were coming in city. All up in arms and with arms—people frightened from church. I went, but many of terrified congregation stood outside. Consternation all day.[50]

Reverend Charles Coffin Adams, rector of St. John's Huntington, asked Bishop Whittingham to use less incendiary language in the prayers the bishop had instructed the clergy to recite:

> I write now to beg of you, if it seems agreeable & proper, to permit me to use, in my congregation, the word *peace* instead of "victory" in the last prayer.
>
> It seems to me, that what we most need now is Peace—"the Peace of God"— the Peace which the Blessed Savior left behind as His last, best legacy to the church & the world.
>
> This request I make in all lowliness, not as wishing to dictate to your greater wisdom & knowledge, or to interfere with your authority, which I always acknowledge & cheerfully *submit* to: but to satisfy a desire I feel for my people, & the Church of God.[51]

A man told his sister how he was ready for action:

> I suppose you have long since heard that we are again threatened with an invasion of northern troops. The whole town is in arms. We boys that is the Thomas Winans Hambleton have formed a sharpshooting company and I have not been to bed before 2 o clock for 3 days. I never leave the house but with the but of a revolver projecting from my bosom a 10 in bowie knive at my side and a carbine slung across my shoulders. This day Sunday we have been under arms all day as there are 3000 Penn volunteers who are within 17 or 18 miles of us. Armed men are to be seen in every direction galloping too and fro.[52]

Police Chief George P. Kane sent an emissary to General Wikoff, commanding the two thousand four hundred Pennsylvania troops at Cockeysville, to plead with him to avoid Baltimore. Wikoff offered a reassuring response:

> I have no intention of going to Baltimore, and have been endeavoring to get a map of the county, so as to pick out some other route to Washington. I am a Marylander, born in Montgomery county, and nothing would give me more pain than to be compelled to shed the blood of Maryland citizens.[53]

The *American* learned that the Baltimore men "were cordially received and entertained" by the Pennsylvanians, encamped at "Cockey's Fields":

> Far from entertaining any idea of forcing a passage through Baltimore, they held our citizens in peculiar and friendly regard. One of the companies composing the force—a corps from Lancaster—were earnest in their inquiries after the Baltimore City Guard, with whom they have heretofore enjoyed relations of friendship and of pleasant social intercourse.[54]

The *Sun* described the Sunday atmosphere:

> Such a Sabbath as yesterday, perhaps, never dawned upon Baltimore. The weather was fine and the sky clear, and citizens eagerly sought the streets with anxious faces. Even the ladies became accustomed to the sight of a volunteer rushing along with his musket, and the sight of a firearm caused no more remark than had it been an umbrella. As early as 9 o'clock thousands of persons were upon the streets approaching the City Hall, the headquarters of all the defensive operations, and the clamor for arms increased when it was reported that the Northern troops were at Cockeysville on the line of the Northern Central Railroad. Mounted cavalry were dashing in every direction; the artillery, with horses to the guns, stood in position, and citizens with arms in their hands stood at the various street corners loading them or run in double quick time to the rendezvous. Squads of volunteers, armed with muskets and weapons of every description, started out the Hookstown and York roads on horseback and in vehicles, for the purpose of waging a guerilla warfare on the troops.[55]

However, not all was tranquil on that Baltimore sabbath:

> The unarmed clamored for weapons and rushed to the gun shops on Baltimore Street, which were quickly broken open, and what arms they contained passed out indiscriminately to any who were alert enough to get within reach of the supply. The bells of the church on Second Street rang out a startling alarm, communicating the excitement in every part of the city. In the churches in which services were at the time in progress, of course the wildest apprehensions were at the time in progress. A general attack upon the city, a bombardment from Fort McHenry, with all the addenda of horrors that the fertile imagination could depict, presented themselves. Services were interrupted, ladies shrieked and fainted, congregations dismissed themselves, and terrified women hurried to their homes.[56]

U.S. Senator Anthony Kennedy of Maryland and former Congressman J. Morrison Harris also called upon Lincoln, who reassured them that troops would be on Maryland soil as little as possible. Boarding steamers at Perryville on the Susquehanna River, they would sail down the Chesapeake Bay, south to Annapolis, then

Officers of the Sixth Massachusetts Regiment demanded that Marshal Kane return arms seized on April 19, 1861, by Baltimoreans. Pratt Lib.

go by rail to Washington. The Marylanders informed the president that the B&O would move the men on this last leg, despite the railroad's April 20 decree that it would cease transporting soldiers into Maryland. Lincoln responded gratefully to Brown and Hicks:

> I tender you both my sincere thanks for your efforts to keep the peace in the try-ing situation in which you are placed. Troops *must* be brought here, but I make no point of bringing them *through* Baltimore. Without any military knowledge myself, of course I must leave the details to Gen. Scott. He hastily said, this morning, in presence of these gentlemen, "March them *around* Baltimore, and not through it." By this, a collision of the people of Baltimore with the troops will be avoided, unless they go out of their way to seek it. I hope you will exert your influence to prevent this.
>
> Now, and ever, I shall do all in my power for peace, consistently with the maintainance of government.[57]

B&O officials were not enthused about transporting more men through Baltimore, amid threats to burn the company's office at Camden Station if its trains moved more troops, and the police seizure of four of its cars loaded with arms and provi-sions. A B&O official later recounted to a congressional committee damage to its track along the thirty-one miles between Relay House and Washington.[58] Garrett himself received an anonymous threat:

> One Hundred of us, Firm, Respectable, Resolute men—have determined & Sworn to each other, to destroy "every" Bridge & tear up your Track on both lines of your Road—(the Main & the Branch) between this City & their head points—If you carry another Soldier over either line of your Road after Saturday April 20th. We trust Dear Sir that you will hearken unto the request of your Southern Fellow Citizens & save us this labour which we will very much regret to undertake. This organization of ours extends from here to Grafton & Washington & your trains will be watched. Spare us Dear Sir this to us unpleasant duty. Many of our Committee know you personally, some intimately, but the nature of our Oaths prevent us from seeing you in person. I am requested Sir to thus notify you. We have a large force ready to answer our calls.[59]

Jabez David Pratt sent brother John in Boston an account of the shooting of Robert W. Davis, a merchant whose death further inflamed Baltimore passions—notwithstanding the claim by the Massachusetts commander that Davis had hurled a stone at the train:

> (My last) letter was written under the most intense excitement in this city, and the most of it, so far as it affected me and my friends and the business community, was caused by the deliberate murder (outside of the city after the cars had left for Washington) of my dear friend, Robt. W. Davis, a merchant and one of nature's noblemen. I saw and conversed with him at his store and in the best of humor and spirits. We were starting together to go and see the soldiers pass, without the least idea of any obstruction being offered. I had to go to the office first and we parted, or I should have been with him. He was standing quietly laughing and talking with two of his and my friends, totally ignorant of any riot or difficulties in the city, and not in any crowd for they had gone away from the city crowd, when a soldier from the platform of the car in very slow motion deliberately aimed and shot him down.[60]

On April 22, Governor Hicks finally announced that the legislature would meet in special session, not in Annapolis but in the western city of Frederick, a Unionist stronghold. Hicks's biographer noted that this change of venue "strengthened the impression that Hicks was in heart and soul with the friends of the South"—a view some would never disavow. Hicks may have had good reason for the change, for Gen. Ben Butler, commanding the state militia troops moving to Washington via Annapolis, had warned him about legislative consideration of secession:

> I also told him that if the legislature undertook with or without his recommendation to discuss an ordinance of secession, I should hold that to be an act of hostil-

ity to the United States, and should disperse that legislature, or, more properly speaking, would shut them up together where they might discuss it all the time, but without any correspondence or reporting to the outer world.[61]

W. W. Glenn noted the pressure that Richard Steuart, a Baltimore physician and ardent Southern partisan who would go into hiding, placed on Hicks:

> While everything was in this state of confusion, Maryland was in no condition to act. Hicks had withstood every effort made to call a convention and even steadfastly refused to call together the Legislature. Doctor Rd. S. Steuart was in Baltimore. He followed Hicks to Annapolis & forced him to convene the Legislature. I am satisfied he would have shot him if he had refused.[62]

Steuart's own account, written shortly after the war, describes his visit to Annapolis, accompanied by Unionist Alexander Randall. Steuart implies that his readiness to shoot Hicks was not so far-fetched:

> I had passed all Friday, nearly all of the night, Saturday, and part of that night among the soldiers of the city and new levies being organized, and I can confidently aver that I scarcely heard a man dissent fro the opinion that Maryland must be cut off from the North. And that the sooner a Convention could be assembled to do this the better for all parties. Hundreds who had belonged to the Hicks' party so declared and expressed a wish that some one would appeal to Gov. Hicks again to call the Legislature. Influenced by this generally expressed opinion, I determined to ask a few prominent gentlemen to meet and take this point into consideration. Accordingly at an early hour on Sunday morning, I went out to call of such gentlemen as I thought most likely to embrace this idea.
>
> On the way (just at sun-rise) I met a party of friends all armed just from Talbot Co., who had taken the steam boat the night before. I had brought quite a considerable company to offer their services in defence of the City. These volunteers I soon put in connection with the Commander in chief, and proceeded to call together the friends I desired to consult on the question of calling upon the Governor, as a committee of the citizens, to insist on his issuing his proclamation for the Legislature to convene believing that this body (and not himself and his party) should decide the fate of our State. The gentlemen thus invited, met at a friend's house at 8 o'clock A.M. thirteen were invited, and 8 or 10 came. The object of the call was stated, several were name as proper persons to go to Annapolis to call on the Governor, who had left Baltimore on Saturday fearing the excitement of the people. I believe I may state that every one concur'd in the opinion that some rush action was necessary, and that if the Gov'r and his party continued to refuse this demand that it would be necessary to depose him, revoluntionize the State.[63]

On April 21, Daniel Thomas reveled in the achievement of keeping more troops from Baltimore:

> By one of the most astonishing performances recorded in history, Maryland has fully redeemed her tarnished character, and old Baltimore may now hold up her head again. That which the united efforts of our statesmen were unable to do has been triumphantly accomplished by the *people* by a sort of spontaneous combustion.[64]

Hicks's April 22 message to Lincoln reveals he still clung to the chimera that troops might avoid Maryland altogether:

> I feel it my duty most respectfully to advise that no more troops be ordered or allowed to pass through Maryland and that the troops now off Annapolis be sent elsewhere, and I most respectfully urge that a truce be offered by you, so that the effusion of blood may be prevented.[65]

General Butler, commanding the troop movement from Perryville to Annapolis and thence to Washington, informed General Scott about a threat in Baltimore:

> I have received what I believe to be authentic intelligence from the information of Mr. [Purnell], of Baltimore, who had the honor to receive the nomination of postmaster of that city, and who is comptroller of the State of Maryland, and whom I believe to be a loyal and true man. He states, in a personal conversation with me, that he has positive information that scaling ladders are being prepared, and that a force is being organized for the purpose of throwing up batteries on the heights, with the intention of making an assault upon Fort McHenry. This information, if true, as I believe it to be, is important.[66]

J. P. Kennedy exonerated the Baltimore officials and its police department for the April troubles:

> No man laments more sincerely and truly than I do the deplorable occurrence of the 19th of April; but it is due to truth to say here, that the police and the city government of Baltimore resisted and put down that mob . . . no body of men were ever more zealous to perform their duty, and did it more daringly and openly, than the mayor, city authorities, and police of Baltimore, on that day. It is true, a mob did suddenly spring up. No one knew anything of it. It was unorganized, not led, whatever may have been the impressions regarding its organization throughout the country . . . It was one of those sudden outbreaks that have been of frequent occurrence, not only in Baltimore, but in all the large cities of this country.[67]

John H. Dike, a Massachusetts officer wounded in Baltimore, agreed with Kennedy, telling the *Boston Courier* on April 25 that

The Mayor and city authorities should be exonerated from blame or censure, as they did all in their power, as far my knowledge extends, to quell the riot, and Mayor Brown attested the sincerity of his desire to preserve the peace, and pass our regiment safely through the city, by marching at the head of its column, and remaining there at the risk of his life.[68]

George Whitmarsh was confident that Northerners seeking vengeance would understand the forces behind April 19:

But I hope now their savage natures are cooling off when they read authentically that the proceedings were only the fruits of a lawless mob. Balto will yet (tho it may take some time) redeem her good standing amongst the Cities of the world.[69]

The *Sun* sympathized with the South and for much of the war was anti-Lincoln, as this April 22 dispatch suggested:

A number of spies are prowling about Howard county and Ellicott's Mills procuring information for the Lincoln government, and stiffening the backbone of its sympathizers, and using their pernicious and abolition influence among the working classes especially. One seen near Roxbury Mills on Sunday last was suddenly pounced upon whilst busily engaged with paper and pencil platting the Westminster Road, which extends in almost a line from Washington to Harrisburg—a distance of 100 miles. The spy hastily put his sketching implements into his pocket, and then, Yankee like, began to ask questions of his discoverers as to how much flour was stored in Roxbury Mills, etc.[70]

Charles Howard, president of the Board of Police, on Sunday, April 21, asked Col. Isaac R. Trimble to take command of the various militias forming to protect the city:

A large number of our fellow Citizens, have apprized this Board that they are organizing themselves into associations for the defense of the City; various rumours having led them to believe that it's safety is seriously endangered.—

The Board of Police will be glad to avail themselves of the aid of all such Associations as desire to act in a regular and combined matter. They respectfully request that you will place yourself at the head of this movement, and take command of all organized Bodies who may choose to place themselves under your Orders.—[71]

When Trimble accepted the offer that day, Howard issued further instructions:

To avoid however all causeless excitement, you will please direct the Associations under your command, to refrain at the present-juncture from using martial music in the streets.—The sound of a drum at once collects crowds, and gives

Col. Isaac Trimble, a railroad engineer, organized the Baltimore militia companies to protect the city from further Northern incursions. He would become a Confederate general, losing a leg and his freedom at Gettysburg. MdHS.

rise to the circulation of all sorts of rumours, calculated to produce unnecessary, and mischievous excitement.

For the same reason we desire that all unnecessary parading of bodies of Men, not at the time in execution of your Orders, may be dispensed with.[72]

The same day Lincoln was visited by a group from the Young Men's Christian Associations of Baltimore, whose members pleaded that no more troops be sent through their city. John Hay, the president's secretary, recorded the encounter:

This morning came a penitent and suppliant crowd of conditional Secessionists, who having sowed the wind seem to have no particular desire to reap the whirlwind. They begged that no more Federal troops should be sent through Baltimore at present; that their mob was thoroughly unmanageable and that they would give the Government all possible assistance in transporting its troops safely across the State by any other route. The President, always inclined to give all men credit for fairness and sincerity, consented to this arrangement contrary to the advice of some of his most prominent counsellors.[73]

Though no formal record of this meeting with Lincoln is known to exist, Rev. Richard Fuller, a nationally prominent Baptist minister, pastor of the Seventh Baptist Church in Baltimore, and a slave owner, recounted his impression of the president in a letter to Treasury Secretary Salmon Chase:

From President Lincoln nothing is to be hoped—except as *you* can influence him. Five associations—representing thousands of our best your men—sent a delegation of thirty to Washington yesterday. I was not at their meeting, but they called & asked me to go with them as their chairman.

We were at once & cordially received. I marked the President closely. Constitutionally genial & jovial, he is wholly inaccessible to Christian appeals—& his egotism will forever prevent him comprehending what patriotism means.[74]

Another member of the delegation offered a blunter assessment of the president:

God have mercy on us, when the government is placed in the hands of a man like this![75]

Lincoln's reply to this "Baltimore Committee" made clear that the Northern troops were to protect Washington, and not to invade the South:

You, gentlemen, come here to me and ask for peace on any terms, and yet have no word of condemnation for those who are making war on us. You express great horror of bloodshed, and yet would not lay a straw in the way of those who are organizing in Virginia and elsewhere to capture this city. The rebels attack Fort Sumter, and your citizens attack troops sent to the defense of the Government, and the lives and property in Washington, and yet you would have me break my oath and surrender the Government without a blow. There is no Washington in that—no manhood nor honor in that. I have no desire to invade the South; but I must have troops to defend this Capital. Geographically it lies surrounded by the soil of Maryland; and mathematically the necessity exists that they should come over her territory. Our men are not moles, and can't dig under the earth; they are not birds, and can't fly through the air. There is no way but to march across, and that they must do. But in doing this there is no need of collision. Keep your rowdies in Baltimore, and there will be no bloodshed. Go home and tell your people that if they will not attack us, we will not attack them; but if they do attack us, we will return it, and that severely.[76]

John Hay recorded a Saturday visit to Lincoln from a visitor from Baltimore:

A young lady called today from Baltimore, sent by her father, H. Pollock, Esq., to convey to the Gvt information as to the state of affairs in the plug-ugly city. She was very pretty and Southern in features and voice and wonderfully plucky and earnest in the enunciation of her devotion to the Stars and Stripes. She stated that the mails had been stopped at the Balto. P.O.—arms expected from Va.—Ft. McHenry to be attacked tonight.[77]

After Jabez Pratt sent brother John a news clipping describing his visit to the White House with the Baltimore YMCA delegation, John's sarcastic reply revealed the growing hostility between the brothers:

We shall now have the song of the six wise men of Baltimore who went all the way to Washington to ask the President to make an infernal fool of himself, and if his boorishness was equal to your consummate folly and impudence, he would deserve a place in Barnum's museum.

What an astonishing piece of information it must have been to the President to be told by Dr. Fuller and then to be endorsed by yourself that peace would at once be restored if he would recognize the Independence of the Confederate States, give them up all the property they had stolen, and evacuate Washington.

I wonder he had not called his Cabinet together to consult upon the proposition, seize upon it before it "grew cold". I wonder that instead of smiling with ill concealed contempt he had not grasped your hands and said, "Gentlemen, you have saved the country," and you should each of you have a monument of brass erected to your memory, that being the only material to perpetuate this great event.

Pardon me, my dear brother, if I treat this matter with levity, but I am surprised that you should be a party to this consummate folly.[78]

Daniel Thomas provided an eyewitness account of the weekend bridge burning:

About half past two that night (April 19) I was aroused by a violent pulling at the street bell, and going to the window was hailed by one of our men with,

"OUR UNION FOR EVER"

*Union symbols began
reappearing in Baltimore
early in the week of Monday,
April 22, in response, some
said, to the presence of
Northern troops in Annapolis,
their point of departure for
Washington. MdHS.*

"All our men are wanted at once at the armory—some more soldiers are coming through." This sounded like battle indeed, and by the time I got into the street I found our men were about, hurrying in from all sides. The scene at the armory was splendid—every man at his post and evidently resolved to do some desperate deed. A body of thirty men, of which I was fortunate enough to be one, was immediately detailed to do work which ought to make us famous. In face of the momentary expectation of the arrival of 1700 men from Philadelphia we were sent with about 30 of the police, out to Harris Creek to burn the bridge if possible before the cars got there, and to keep the enemy in play till the bridge was destroyed. After a slapping march of over two miles we reached the bridge, and in less than no time it was making night day with blaze. Before the destruction of it was complete we heard the whistle of the cars and in a moment up they came and halted. I doubt much if any men in our company counted on more than five minutes of life from that time, and yet granite rock could not have stood firmer than they did. Officers and men had come there to kill time while the bridge burned, and but for an unforeseen event, I truly believe Thermopylae would have had a rival.

That event was, the *non arrival* of the expected troops but being told they were coming on in a special train, we took possession of the train which had just arrived and started off to burn the bridges on the road, *provided* we did not meet the enemy in the meantime. We went on very slowly, till we had passed the farthest bridge (at Bush River) and then we went to work and burnt that down, taking care to place ourselves on the side towards town, then we came down to the Gunpowder Bridge and burnt that and then we started for town thinking we had done a very smart thing. And I can tell you, would think the soldiers and citizens thought so too if you had heard them cheer us as we returned to the armory.[79]

Jabez Pratt's reply to John countered the impression that Baltimore was a city aflame. He closed with an assurance of brotherly affection that had been sorely tested:

I see the Northern papers filled with inflammable matter and dispatches as to Baltimore which are false. There is no city more peacable and quiet and not the first particle of "reign of terror." We have in our city Black Republicans and Union men, the latter in large numbers, and who are not fearful in expressing their sentiments, and the B.R. are as safe as in Boston.

There is no muzzling as in the North. The excitement of our citizens caused by the shooting of our friends has entirely abated. The mob of Friday is deprecated now that reason has its sway. I think the same would have happened in New York or Boston if places and circumstances had been changed to those cities.

Maryland is not going to be hasty and the feeling which before the trouble was prevalent is again shown, that of a peaceable solution of the dispute between North and South.

The whole irritation has been caused by the foolish acts of the administration in declaring war and making enemies of those who were for peace and union for and with the Border States. We hope for peace and will do all we can for peace.

Accept my kind regards and best wishes for yourself and be assured that I hold nothing in my heart of bitterness towards you.[80]

Just after sending that letter, Jabez received John's letter criticizing his visit to the White House. He answered at once:

Dear Brother:
You are fast driving me to consider that term inappropriate.

I have received your letter of the 27th, and if you consider me a "fool and a boor" why so be it.

The only answer I have to make is that you are crazy. I will only say further that you entirely misinterpret and misunderstand the mission to Washington and what was asked of Mr. Lincoln. We asked nothing of what you so glibly ridicule.

If such is to be your correspondence it had better be stopped till you get your senses.[81]

The president of the Baltimore Police Board offered Capt. John C. Robinson the services of local militia to foil incursions against Fort McHenry:

> From rumors that have reached us, the Board are apprehensive that you may be annoyed by lawless and disorderly characters approaching the walls of the Fort to night. We propose to send a guard of perhaps 200 men to station themselves on Whet-stone Point, of course entirely beyond the outer limits of the Fort, and within those of the City. Their orders will be to arrest and hand over to the Civil authorities any evil disposed and disorderly persons who may approach the Fort. We should have confided this duty to our regular Police Force, but their services are so imperatively required elsewhere, that it is impossible to detail a sufficient number of them to your vicinity.[82]

Robinson declined the offer upon learning that the Maryland Guard had been chosen to protect the Fort, "having made the acquaintance of some of the officers of that organization and heard them freely express their opinions."[83] Testimony of Maryland Guard member Augustus J. Albert suggested that Robinson's decision had been wise:

> The next excitement after April 19, was the determination of the citizens to capture Fort McHenry. Gen. Huge who had resigned from the U.S. Army, had been elected to command the Maryland Guard. Early one night my regiment was called in line, and a request made for about 200 volunteers. I was selected as one of them. We were marched down towards the Fort, thinking we were to have the honor of capturing it. We were placed in picket line across the neck of land leading to the Fort, where we were kept until sunrise, when we discovered we were there to prevent the mob of the city from doing what we wanted to do ourselves; the authorities wishing to prevent useless bloodshed.[84]

Ten days later Robinson claimed that "the reign of terror was over, and Baltimore became a quiet city." He then received a visitor:

> One day word came in that there was a stranger at the picket who wanted to see the commanding officer. When I met him he wished to see me privately, and when out of view of the guard he informed me that he was the bearer of a letter from the Secretary of the Navy, that as he did not know what might happen to him in Baltimore he had concealed it in a queer place. He then removed his hat, and lifting his wig, drew out the letter from between it and his bald crown. It was rather oily, but, nevertheless, a document I was glad to receive.[85]

By Sunday, thousands of Northern troops were steaming down the Chesapeake for Annapolis, headed for Washington. Hicks, despite the arrangement avoiding Baltimore, was not reassured by the prospect of these men flooding into Maryland's capital, and protested to General Butler:

> I would most earnestly advise you do not land your men at Annapolis. The excitement here is very great, and I think that you should take your men elsewhere. I have telegraphed to the Secretary of War, advising against your landing your men here.[86]

Butler refused to take his men elsewhere, short of an order from the secretary of war:

> I am sorry that your excellency should advise against my landing here. I am not provisioned for a long voyage. Finding the ordinary means of communication cut off by the burning of railroad bridges by a mob, I have been obliged to make this detour, and hope that your excellency will see, from the very necessity of the case, that there is no cause of excitement in the mind of any good citizen because of our being driven here by an extraordinary casualty.[87]

Sunday services at the First Lutheran Church were disrupted:

> Several members of the congregation ascended the pulpit, and informed (Rev. Dr. McCron) that an immense army was about entering the city, and war had commenced. Service was then suspended, after a few remarks were made by the pastor, and the congregation, especially the ladies, hurried out of the edifice with all imaginable haste, and proceeded to their homes.[88]

Hester Davis, wife of Montgomery County planter Allen Bowie Davis, was not so quick to abandon the hands of Providence:

> The state of affairs is truly alarming. The City Council have appropriated $500,000 for the defence of City. And our only hope now is in Almighty God, who holds in His hands the destinies of the children of men.[89]

Late in April a Southern visitor to Baltimore wrote to Lincoln:

> Some three weeks ago I wrote an old friend and classmate, who now resides in Mobile, Ala On my arrival here last evening I found a letter from him. I learn from it that it is the settled policy to attack the capital by the Southern Confederacy. It is to be done by foes within as well as without. He says there is not a department at Washington that is not well filled with friends of Jeff Davis. And they are ready to strike at any moment. He further states that a large number of the citizens of Washington will be prominent in the move, and that desperate men dressed in citizens garb will infest your city to take their part in the contest

"Raising the Stars and Stripes over the Custom-House at Baltimore." Harper's Pictorial History of the Civil War *(New York, 1866), 102.*

against you. This information comes from a high source. It is imparted in that manner that I cannot betray the name, or expose the letter. I give it to you only at its market value.[90]

John Hay described a colorful evening meal April 23 at the White House evening:

At dinner we sat opposite Old Gen. Spinner who was fierce and jubilant. No frenzied poet ever predicted the ruin of a hostile house with more energy and fervor than he, issuing the rescript of destiny against Baltimore. "We've got 'em," he said. "It is *our* turn now."[91]

Hay's account noted the appearance of Jim Lane of Kansas, "the ally of Montgomery, the King of the Jayhawkers, and the friend of John Brown of Ossawatomie":

A gaunt, tattered, uncombed and unshorn figure appeared at the door and marched solemnly up to the table. He wore a rough rusty overcoat, a torn shirt, and suspenderless breeches. His neck was innocent of collar, guiltless of necktie. His thin hair stood fretful—porcupine-quill-wise upon his crown. He sat down and gloomily charged upon his dinner. A couple of young exquisites were eating and chatting opposite him. They were guessing when the road would be open through Baltimore. "Thursday," growled the grim apparition, "or Baltimore will be laid in ashes."[92]

From Boston, John Pratt wrote of his joy at learning that Baltimore was calm:

We are rejoiced to hear as we do this morning that there is a reaction in sentiment in Baltimore and that there is a prospect that our troops will be allowed to pass without a fight. I hope so, for it would be a terrible alternative to be obliged to apply the torch to your city and widen the streets with artillery, for there is no question that if Maryland is obstinate in this matter, she will have to be subjugated. Her secession will amount to nothing: she will not be permitted to go: we like your people too well to part company so easy. The North is just waking up like the "lion from his lair" as there is a force coming down through the South that will crush out, annihilate and sweep away all before it. Let the South look out for its cherished institution, let this war continue a few months, and the whirlwind now gathering will sweep within its vortex the South and slavery, and all will perish together.[93]

Years later Captain Robinson recalled the morning of Sunday, April 28, 1861, on the Patapsco River, as seen from Fort McHenry:

A sailing vessel came down the river crowded with men, and covered from stem to stern with national flags. She sailed past the fort, cheered and saluted our flag, which was dipped in return, after which she returned to the city. The tide had turned. Union men avowed themselves, the stars and stripes were again unfurled, and order was restored. Although after this time arrests were made of persons conspicuous for disloyalty, the return to reason was almost as sudden as the outbreak of rebellion. The railroads were repaired, trains ran regularly, and troops poured into Washington without hindrance or opposition of any sort.[94]

Newspapers reported the fate of A. H. or S. H. Needham, a Massachusetts trooper badly injured during the April 19 clash who was cared for in the Lombard Street infirmary and was

injured by a brick thrown from the assailing crowd. It fractured the skull just above the left eye, and caused a terrible wound. He was received into the Institution on Friday afternoon, and is now lying in a hopeless condition. He is insensible at times.

Needham died of his wounds and was buried at the Greenmount Cemetery in Baltimore.[95]

Baltimore businessmen displayed the American flag on April 21. MdHS.

Lincoln was turning his attention to a Maryland legislature he feared poised to consider secession, by legislative fiat or state convention and referendum. On April 25, he instructed General Scott not to interfere with the lawmakers—contradicting enduring and erroneous claims that Maryland remained in the Union only because troops were then arresting legislators suspected of Southern sympathies:

> The Maryland Legislature assembles to-morrow at Anapolis; and, not improbably, will take action to arm the people of that State against the United States. The question has been submitted to, and considered by me, whether it would not be justifiable, upon the ground of necessary defence, for you, as commander

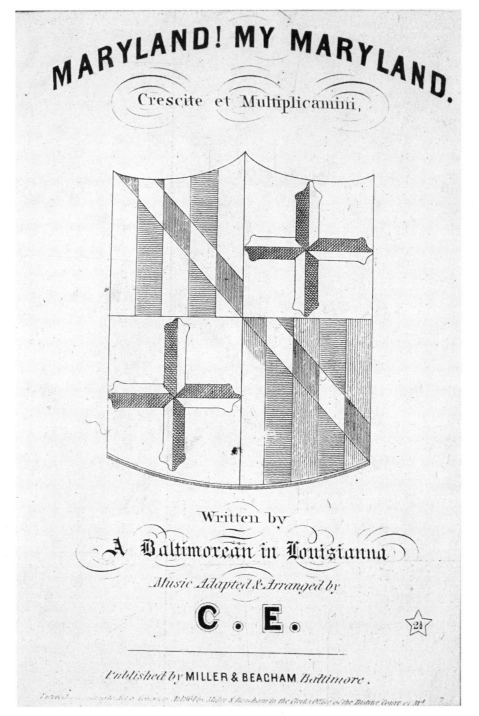

Reacting to the presence of Northern troops in Baltimore, James Ryder Randall, a Marylander living in New Orleans, wrote "Maryland, My Maryland," a song harshly critical of President Lincoln and the federal government. Music and lyrics were published by Miller and Beacham. MdHS.

in Chief of the United States Army, to arrest, or disperse the members of that body. I think it would *not* be justifiable; nor, efficient for the desired object.[96]

The president explained that he would not sanction arrest or dispersal of Maryland's legislators, for reasons both legal and practical:

> First, they have a clearly legal right to assemble; and, we can not know in advance, that their action will not be lawful, and peaceful. And if we wait until they shall *have* acted, their arrest, or dispersion, will not lessen the effect of their action. Secondly, we *can* not permanently prevent their action. If we arrest them, we can not long hold them as prisoners; and when liberated, they will immediately re-assemble, and take their action. And, precisely the same if we simply disperse them. They will immediately re-assemble in some other place.[97]

Lincoln then ordered Scott to respond forcefully to Maryland's actions to bear arms against the government. The president's willingness to suspend habeas corpus triggered a debate over the right of the executive branch to do so when the Constitution seems to reserve such action for the Congress:

> I therefore conclude that it is only left to the commanding General to watch, and await their action, which, if it shall be to arm their people against the United States, he is to adopt the most prompt, and efficient means to counteract, even, if necessary, to the bombardment of their cities—and in the extremest necessity, the suspension of the writ of habeas corpus.[98]

On April 26, the opening day of the special session, the *Baltimore Sun* suggested that Baltimore's interest lay with a Confederate Virginia, noting that Maryland voters, not legislators, should decide the state's course—"for the Legislature to pass an ordinance of secession would be, in our opinion, to arrogate powers not vested in it":

> We find in certain quarters a disposition to urge the immediate passage of a secession ordinance by the Legislature; in others the expectation of such a measure. These propositions take us by surprise, and we cannot, of course, maintain the consistency of The Sun and assent to them. Some of our citizens who have been willing to believe what others have said of us, rather than what we have said ourselves, will now perhaps accept the fact that The Sun is *not a secession paper.*
>
> In one word, it is not and never has been *for or against secession;* and it has never contained a line to justify the imputation one way or the other. It has been slandered in this as it is with regard to almost every other thing in which it is supposed that misrepresentation can impair its influence. We have insisted, that, with the secession of the Confederate States an accomplished fact, and Virginia in alliance with them, the interests of Baltimore, commercial and manufactur-

ing, would also identify her with them. This is our opinion; but this, with the actual question of secession, is for the people themselves to pass upon. The Sun has been through all the early stages of our present troubles a staunch Southern Rights paper, earnest and zealous for the salvation of the Union.[99]

The same day Mayor Brown suspended some rights:

> For the purpose of preserving the peace of the city, I hereby direct and proclaim that for the period of their days from this date no Banners nor Flags of any description shall be publicly displayed in the City of Baltimore, except on buildings or vessels, occupied or employed by the United States Government, and I call on all good citizens to aid the enforcement of this regulation.[100]

When Governor Hicks told legislators that the events of April 19 impelled him to summon them into special session, he intimated that a loyal Maryland might remain neutral:

> I honestly and most earnestly entertain the conviction that the only safety of Maryland lies in preserving a neutral position between our brethren of the North and of the South. We have violated no rights of either section. We have been loyal to the Union. The unhappy contest between the two sections has not been fermented or encouraged by us, although we have suffered from it in the past. The impending war has not come by any act or by any wish of ours.—We have done all we could to avert it. We have hoped that Maryland and the other border slave States by their conservative position and love for the Union, might have acted as mediators between the extremes of both sections and thus have prevented the terrible evils of a prolonged civil war. Entertaining these views, I cannot counsel Maryland to take sides against the general government, until it shall commit outrages upon us which would justify us in resisting its authority. As a consequence, I can give no other counsel than that we shall array ourselves for Union and peace, and thus preserve our soil from being polluted with the blood of brethren.—Thus, if war must be between the North and the South, we may force the contending parties to transfer the field of battle from our soil, so that our lives and property may be secure. It seems to me that, independently of all other considerations, our geographical position forces us to this, unless we are willing to see our State the theatre of a long and bloody civil war, and the consequent utter destruction of every material interest of our people, to say nothing of the blood of brave men and innocent women and children.[101]

George Whitmarsh speculated on April 30 about the legislature's actions:

> Business—city improvements and all mercantile and mechanical pursuits paralyzed! War civil war that worst of wars is now stalking round this once favoured Union! The fire of secession like a baleful spark rose last Novemb in South Caro-

lina, and since that time has steadily overspread the great south until the 19 of this month it spread its [?] in Baltimore. Since that time arms & munitions of war is seen daily in the Streets, especially in the hands of half-grown men and boys without seeming consideration. The good old Stars & Stripes sunk in the abyss of confusion for a time—but its uprising these few days past is restoring wanted peace and tranquility. From the accounts of the Legislature, I don't think our State will secede at least for the present the temporary vote yesterday was 13 for secession & 53 against.

And recorded concerns about Baltimore's business environment:

Business has been nearly broken up. Merchants are failing every day. Stores that continue business are scarcely making expenses. But the torn up railroads broken and burnt bridges will give employment to some who live in different portions of our state. Hope all these things may yet be settled amicably without shedding of fraternal blood for the South has been entirely too hasty the north too sectional & stubborn & I think old Maryland in her Union ticket truly proved herself so to be. I see nothing before us now but a divided nation resolving itself in two republics for the future Union almost seems idle talk but we will hope for the best & put our common trust in that high & holy Providence that ruleth all things well for his own beloved Church & his own Glory—amen. went down town today in the shower and saw many small flags offered by boys instead of the wild secession ones offered last week—very dull day only took one dollar day & night. I hope I may write better times in a new journal.[102]

A newspaper listed suggestions for men heading into the field:

1. Remember that in a campaign more men die from sickness than by the bullet.
2. Line your blanket with one thickness of brown drilling this adds but four ounces in weight, and doubles the warmth.
3. Buy a small India rubber blanket (only $1.50) to lay on the ground or to throw over your shoulders when on guard duty during a rain storm. Most of the eastern troops are provided with these. Straw to lie on is not always to be had.
4. The best military hat in use is the light-colored soft felt; the crown being sufficiently high to allow space for air over the brain. You can fasten it up as a continental in fair weather, or turn it down when it is wet or very sunny.
5. Let your beard grow, so as to protect the throat and lungs.
6. Keep your entire person clean; this prevents fevers and bowel complaints in warm climates. Wash your body each day, if possible. Avoid strong coffee and oily meat. Gen. Scott said that the too free use of these (together with neglect in keeping the skin clean) cost many a soldier his life in Mexico.
7. A sudden check of perspiration by chilly or night air often causes fever and death.—When thus exposed do not forget your blanket.[103]

Edward Spencer, a resident of Baltimore County, risked arrest for disloyalty because of his vocal criticisms of the federal government. Courtesy of Sidney H. Wanzer.

William Chauvenet, a professor of mathematics at the U.S. Naval Academy in Annapolis, sought news from Baltimorean George B. Cole, a proslavery Unionist, late in April:

> We are quite anxious about you and yours. We can tell nothing by the papers; they are so contradictory. What is the true state of public sentiment in Baltimore and Maryland? Will you escape a reign of terror? Here we have been quite, but expecting every day a mine to explode under our feet. The union men here are confounded with black republicans, and if the state secedes there will be waged an indiscriminate war on both. All that we can hope for here of course is that the state will remain neutral.[104]

Edward Spencer told "Braddie," on the Eastern Shore, about the deteriorating conditions in Baltimore—from the Southern perspective:

> There is no telling what tomorrow may bring. You can have no idea, darling, of the terrible threats breathed out against Balto. by Northern people. The pa-

Edward Spencer's courtship of Anna Bradford Harrison, member of an Eastern Shore Unionist family, was an example of family ties and personal relationships prevailing over political sentiments. Courtesy of Sidney H. Wanzer.

pers here, especially the American, dare not publish them. I have seen many private letters & they all advise our citizens to flee, pretty much as Lot was urged to leave Sodom. The treatment promised us is worse than any Chinese or Sepoy vengeance, and is enough to make one incredulous of the influences of civilization. John Brown jr is drilling negroes near the Penna. Line. Lieut. Morris defies Judge Giles from Ft. McHenry & U.S. vessels run down innocent trading steamers in our waters. So it goes.[105]

On April 27, alarmed at reports of bridge destruction and insurrectionary behavior in Baltimore, Lincoln quietly authorized General Scott to broaden the suspension of habeas corpus:

You are engaged in repressing an insurrection against the laws of the United States. If at any point on or in the vicinity of the [any] military line, which is now [or which shall be] used between the City of Philadelphia and the City of Washington, via Perryville, Annapolis City, and Annapolis Junction, you find resistance which renders it necessary to suspend the writ of Habeas Corpus for

"Occupation of the Post Office, Corner of Gay and Lombard Streets, Baltimore, MD, by a Detachment of the Twentieth Pennsylvanian Troops, to Protect It, in a Case of a Riot. By Order of Major-Gen. Banks." Pratt Lib.

the public safety, you, personally or through the officer in command at the point where the [at which] resistance occurs, are authorized to suspend that writ.[106]

Lincoln's instruction to Scott was not made public, nor was it circulated to military commands, courts, or other civil authorities. The president would soon issue his first public suspension of the writ of habeas corpus, via a proclamation, in Florida—the first in American history.

William Seabrook described Governor Hicks as a pragmatic Unionist:

There was never a moment when Maryland's governor was willing that she should follow Virginia into secession, notwithstanding there were times when his words and his deeds seemed to justify a different opinion, or to indicate that he was, at least, opposed to the employment of force to prevent the success of the secession movement. And it is but truth to say that the employment of the military power of the government for the preservation of the Union was regarded by Governor Hicks as the last resort and only justified when all efforts at conciliation had failed. And that was the general sentiment of the unionists of Maryland as well as of many friends of the Union in the Northern States. When all other reasonable means to prevent the disruption of the nation had been tried and failed, the governor was as decidedly in favor of prosecuting the war as was Lincoln himself.[107]

Though the Maryland General Assembly would pass a number of resolutions hostile to Lincoln and the Union, its members determined it had no right even to debate a secession ordinance, or to call a convention to discuss the issue. The legislature adjourned sine die on May 14.

chapter three

May 1861

On May 1, Governor Hicks complained to Virginia Gov. John Letcher about depredations by Virginia troops on Marylanders along their common border, around Harpers Ferry:

> Cattle, grain etc. have been seized; canal boats laden with produce have been detained; private houses have been forcibly entered; and unoffending citizens have been insulted and threatened. I am confident that these outrages have been committed without orders from you. But your Excellency will readily perceive that they are liable to provoke hostilities.[1]

Commodore Isaac Mayo, a twenty-five-year veteran of the United States Navy who lived on the South River in Anne Arundel County, resigned in protest:

> I hereby most respectfully tender to you my resignation of the office of Captain in the United States Navy.
>
> For more than half a century it has been the pride of my life to hold office under the government of the United States. For *twenty-five* years I have been engaged in active service, and have *never* seen my flag dishonored or the American arms disgraced by defeat. It was the hope of my old age that I might die, as I had lived, an officer in the Navy of a free government. This hope has been taken from me.
>
> In adopting the policy of *coercion,* you have denied to millions of freemen the rights of the Constitution. In its stead you have replaced the will of a sectional party, and now demand submission in the name of an armed force. As one of the oldest soldiers in America, I protest—in the name of humanity—against this "war against brethren." I cannot fight against the Constitution, while *pretending* to fight *for it.*[2]

In 1861, Franklin Buchanan, the first superintendent of the U.S. Naval Academy, commanded the main arsenal at Washington. After resigning from the navy in the wake of the Pratt Street riot, he asked Navy Capt. F. Engle to support the rescission of his resignation:

> You no doubt are aware that I *very* hastily, to use *no other expression,* resigned during the great excitement in Baltimore a few weeks since. I now regret it, as there was no occasion for it, and as my resignation "is still under consideration," I have this day written to the Secretary and asked to withdraw it. The Secretary no doubt will consult with you on the subject.
>
> I wish to say to you that I never was a *Secessionist,* and all my friends have heard me express my views on that subject, and strongly denouncing the extremists of both sections who have ruined our glorious country. My attachments

Admiral Franklin Buchanan resigned from the U.S. Navy and took the same rank in the Confederate Navy. MdHS.

to the service are too strong to wish to leave it. I shall be miserable out of it; therefore if I am retained in it, my duty shall be performed faithfully, as it always has been. When we meet, I will tell you how peculiarly I was situated at the time I tendered my resignation; and, as I remarked to Mr. Welles at the time, "the most painful and disagreeable duty I ever performed was to hand him my resignation." I will not trouble you now with a long letter. As an old friend, I have written to you with a hope that you may serve me.[3]

Several weeks later, in a letter to George B. Cole, Buchanan explained his decision:

I made a mistake in resigning *when I did,* I will admit to you, but I did so in *good faith to my state;* at the time, the belief was general throughout the state that she was virtually out of the Union.[4]

Buchanan's midsummer appeal to U.S. Senator James A. Pearce of Maryland noted that "I have not sought a situation in the Southern Confederacy, but I have recd. letters informing me that I could get a high position. I have never made a reply; I cannot think this unholy, fratricidal war can continue much longer."[5] Buchanan would join the Confederacy, command the CSS *Virginia* as an admiral, and suffer as a prisoner of war, held by the military he once served.

Early in the month, with Maryland firmly in the union, Edward Spencer expressed frustration and resignation:

> Baltimore is ruined forever—the grass will grow in her streets. Lincoln himself said he only wanted three weeks to conquer Maryland, and, alas for human nature, he has done it in less time even. I don't care what comes, now. I shall go forth whenever I can sell out to advantage, & meantime, I shall stay at home how I can. You and I will live as quiet as Yankee insolence and intrusion will permit & you'll teach me to forget that the State I love & yearned to fight for has refused the honorable and glorious gaze of battle.[6]

Elizabeth Patterson Bonaparte's property manager wrote to her in Paris with more bad news about her Baltimore affairs:

> We are so fully engaged in war here now that all business is well nigh suspended, indeed since April 19th the general fear has been that our City would be burned up.

After recounting the events of April 19, he presented the bad news:

> We are now surrounded with U.S. troops to keep Maryland in the Union and what things will come to, I cannot imagine. A great number of persons has fled from the City—I am sorry to say also that on that same day 2 of your houses came near being in ruins—the arch over the alley between Reuter and Coates (upon which a heavy dividing wall rests) fell in carrying with it the whole of Reuters stone wall smashing up his cases filled with hardware. his stock however did not damage.[7]

The *Protestant*, a pro-Union Baltimore newspaper, suggested that on April 19 Baltimoreans were guilty only of defending home and hearth:

> We do not pretend to say that the riot of the mob on the 19th ult. was not calculated to inflame the North. It certainly was. It struck with terror everybody here. It was difficult to find out what was the matter. All was consternation—dread. Nobody seemed to be himself. It was as though all social, domestic and national foundations were sinking beneath our feet. Most of our people were as much terrified as if an earthquake had suddenly rocked the city to its foundations. Home instincts prompted to home defense. There was no time for reflection. Men thought only of their own lives and the lives of their women and children. It was a moment of popular frenzy—a delirium of municipal terror.—But some of our Christian editors of New York—away from the scene and its excitement—did

A paean to the "Maryland Line," the name given to the first state troops organized during the Revolutionary War—and who, in late 1863, reconstituted themselves to fight for the Confederacy—was superimposed over the state seal as war broke out. MdHS.

not pause for a moment to philosophize upon such a condition of things. They assumed all Baltimore to be guilty of throwing stones and firing pistols.[8]

Early in May Governor Hicks dispatched former U.S. Senator and Attorney General Reverdy Johnson to call upon Lincoln or other high officials:

in regard to the difficulties now agitating our government and people, and having full confidence in the integrity and ability of Mr. Johnson, this will authorize him to act for me, and will oblige more to endorse whatever he may do with reference to staying the march of troops through Baltimore City, for a few days, until the furor originated by the secessionists shall subside. Mr. Johnson can also inform the President and Cabinet how far the innocent will suffer with the guilty if a second disgraceful outbreak shall occur in the streets of Baltimore.[9]

From the armory of the Maryland Guards, where he reported each morning, C. C. Shriver described the humdrum nature of guard duty:

> Since my last letter to you times have considerably quieted and now, if it were not for the newspapers reports, and the seeing of a good many soldiers on the streets you would imagine any thing else but, war. In consequence of the complete prostration of business, it is even more quiet than usual—There is not half the bustle and excitement on the streets, as there was before the war. Every person keeps quiet.
>
> My life now is a rather monotonous one. I come down to the armory at 9 in the morning. We are all then placed in our places, and have to answer to our names, as they are called out to us, after that some person preaches or reads, or prays for a half hour or so—It seems to make no difference, about whom they get, anything so he professes answers the purpose—after prayers, we are either drilled in squads or in full companys—for an hour—then if we are not placed on duty we can run around town until six in the evening.

Shriver described his feelings about conflict:

> I do not know how I would feel about being marched out to fight—but I think perhaps I would be able to stand it. The third night after I had joined I had a trial of my courage. The signal for us was given in this way—just before we left for our homes at night, the Captain said that when all the bells in town were rung we should all come prepared for action as quickly as we could. At three O'clock that night I heard "all" (or what I imagined to be all) the bells ringing, and saw a great fire down in the direction of the fort. I thought my time had come but was bound in honor to respond to the call. I jumped out of bed & put on my clothes, strapped on my cartridge box and ran down towards the armory as hard as I could leg it, when I got as far as Howard st. I met one of our company and he told me it was not our alarm, but only a fire. As you may imagine I was considerably relieved—I came home as willingly as I ever did in my life—Since then we have had no occasion for courage.[10]

One Baltimorean was apprehensive about the mood in Baltimore:

> Our beloved City is very quiet but gloom hangs over us and Death & destruction seems to await us.[11]

On May 5, Col. Isaac Trimble received a report from Francis J. Thomas, adjutant general of the Volunteer Forces, whom he had sent south to procure weapons for the protection of Baltimore:

> I have the honor to report my return from the confidential mission on which I was sent, and to render the following history of my proceedings.

From the nature of my duties, and the importance of secrecy, my instructions were purely verbal, and I was left entirely to my own discretion.

Following visits to Norfolk and the "Navy Yard," Thomas reported the procurement of twenty 20-pound guns, twenty-four 24-pound guns, and five 8-inch/60-pound Columbiads, "together with a small quantity of shot, some cannon locks, as models, and a few such articles":

I at first intended to send these arms by water, as I previously informed you, and had a portion of them loaded when the Blockade by the U.S. Government of the Virginia waters and Cruisers in the Chesapeake Bay rendered that proceeding, in my opinion, too hazardous. I therefore at once shipped them overland by Rail.

Thomas continued:

The Guns will be held at Winchester, where they will await my orders, between now and Wednesday next, and, in all probability from 10.000 to 15.000 stand of small arms furnished by the authorities of North and South Carolina.[12]

By May 6, Baltimore officials were sufficiently confident about the restoration of order that they instructed Trimble to disband the local militias:

The Board of Police, believing that the immediate and pressing danger to the safety of the city, has in a great measure, if not altogether, passed away, deem it proper to disband the Volunteer forces of the city—*organized to preserve order.*

They desire to express to the officers and men, their sincere acknowledgments and thanks for the readiness with which they came forward for the preservation of order, and for the protection of our beautiful and beloved city.

In taking leave, I beg to return my own thanks to the officers and men, for their good conduct, and for the respect shown their superior officers. Should any further difficulties call us together, I hope our future intercourse may be as pleasant as the past. I request you all, in returning to your homes, that you will set a good example of peaceable and orderly behavior to your fellow-citizens.[13]

One Marylander referred to B&O Railroad officials when recounting the flight of Baltimoreans to safety in the North:

I think they were afraid the Baltimore mob would burn them (the cars) and on Sunday only one train passed down and that was loaded with stock. On Monday nothing went either way. It began to be very lonesome for three or four days after the riot in Baltimore. The passenger trains were crowded with people going north from Baltimore to get out of the way of battle. They went by Frederick and Hagerstown to Chambersburg and then Harrisburg to Philadelphia, New York and Boston.[14]

An Annapolis resident, "R.J.," described the atmosphere in Maryland's capital, which—along with the nearby Annapolis and Elk Ridge Railroad—remained under Union control to ensure a continuous flow of Northern soldiers to Washington:

> Now, my dear Hester, I have told you the state of affairs here in such a way that, should this prove a case of "intercepted correspondence," I may not be hung as a spy via the army here, nor you for holding communications with an alien enemy. In sober seriousness, everything is quiet here—more so than usual, because there is no drunkenness, nor meetings of Rowdies in the streets. You meet soldiers with, and without arms, at every store & almost at every street in the town—but they are orderly and respectful. The General in command, Butler of Massachusetts, a first rate Breckinridge democrat, who with Cushing, Yancey &c. seceded from the Charleston convention because they nominated Douglas, has possession of the Rail Road, which has been put in complete order and now runs 2 or 3 times a day with troops and passengers. They are now laying a track from the depot to the Navy yard wharf to facilitate transportation. All the Professors and other occupants of the houses in the Yard have moved out to make room for the troops.

R.J. was ready to flee at the first sign of trouble:

> The valuables &c, however, to which Cousin Hester refers, in her letter rec'd last evening, have been packed, ready "for a start," when it becomes necessary to flee. For the present, they decline Cousin Hester's kind invitation to visit the Parsonage near Scottsville, even by way of Winchester—thinking that were they to attempt it, they would not be much wiser than the fish inn the frying pan. Altho' some of our "coloured fellow citizens," encouraged by the presence of their friends of the North, attempted to play the secession game, Aunt Hester has no fear that her body-guard aforesaid, will secede—since, if they were not restrained by motives of gratitude or self interest, the ill success which attended the efforts of others, having been sent back to their masters, would restrain them. Matilda says the street has never been so quiet as now, and they all sleep as soundly as they ever did. So Cousin H. may be quite easy about her dear ones in the big house, until Jeff Davis drives the Yankees from Washington, and they run pell mell to the water & set fire to the old town and murder its inhabitants, from revenge at this defeat—for which contingency some of our present ones have provided, and accordingly emigrated to distant parts. Marriage is still perpetrated in our beleagured city, and women will, in spite of war's alarms, have babies.[15]

A Baltimore newspaper described the behavior of Union soldiers, who were probably marching from Annapolis to Relay House for trains to Washington. These men included Germans who were "very agreeable":

while others of them, especially the German companies from Washington, are overbearing and disgusting in their behavior towards our citizens, and not even our *ladies* are exempted from their insults. "We can't talk much English, but we can talk with this," as they brandish their muskets.[16]

A Maryland soldier told his sister about an incident that befell troops traveling via steamboat from Perryville to Annapolis:

> The troops under Gen Butlar's command from Massachusetts suffered terrably from hunger and thirst. The pilot on board the boat which took them from Havred (e) grace to Annapolis ran them a ground on a sandbar where they had to stay forty hours without any provisions they all most died with thirst for they had not even their cantenes filled so some were so thirty that they drank salt water which (s) caused some to be crazy two of them hopelessly so.[17]

The *True Union* styled itself a "religious and family newspaper" and used the motto, "One Lord, one faith, one baptism." It advocated a constitutional convention, peaceful separation, and either recognition of the Confederacy or compensated emancipation in lieu of war; its editorials drew denunciations from all sides. William Crane, a friend of its editor Franklin Wilson, objected to the paper's recent political tone:

> Among the wide circle of my particular friends there is scarcely one for whom I feel a more sincere Christian regard, or with whom I more deeply regret a variance of opinion than with you. But I have for months past regretted that your management of the True Union, seemed to me, decidedly favorable to the ultra doctrines and actions of the Secessionists—and in this I have differed from you in toto. I have had no taste for reading any of your Editorials or selections of this character, fully believing that you only need time and experience to convince you, that the whole work of Secessionism is *evil* and *only evil.*

Crane further chastised Wilson for glorifying April 19 and implying that the mob was motivated by anything other than destructive impulses (at the end of his letter, Crane stated, "you force on me an willingness to see no more of the True Union"):

> I had overlooked in your issue of the 25th ult. your notice of our diplorably diabolical mob on the 19th untill I saw it so sharply noticed in the N York Examiner, and I don't think anything the paper has ever contained, has caused me a tenth part of the surprise and chagrin—that I felt in recuring to it. I hardly know which is the most seriously objectionable—the superlative arogance, assumed by you for the city and state authorities—that the nineteen millions of the free states *should not be allowed* the simple, long established, direct, right of way, to their own capital, or, the palpably false statement, that this scandalous event, "was

The Boston Light Artillery (the "Bouquet Battery") occupied the railroad junction at Relay in May to ensure the unimpeded movement of troops from Annapolis to Washington. Harper's Weekly, *June 1, 1861, 346/Pratt Lib.*

sanctioned by the united voice of the people." The mass of the tear stricken people, know then, as well as now, that it was a most wicked, murderous mob—no one of the reckless instigations or actions in it, dares to acknowledge himself as such—But you have glorified it, as "the momentuous Lexington battle" of this most unnatural secession war!! I fear that history will truthfully record this affair, as the *foulest, most injurious* blot, on the *character* and *interests* of our city—in the entire annals of our country, but it has fired up to boiling heat, the war spirit of the entire population, of the free states—far more effectually than anything else has done it.[18]

Even Southern sympathizers such as Richard Sprigg Steuart thought April 19 more an effort to keep troops out of Baltimore than a harbinger of Maryland secession:

> I happened to be in Baltimore on the 19th of April, 1861, and witnessed the outburst of feeling on the part of the people. Generally, when the Massachusetts troops were passing thru the city of Baltimore, it was evident to me that 75 p.c. of the population was in favor of repelling these troops. Instinctively the people seemed to look on them as intruders, or as invadors of the South, not as defenders of the City of Baltimore. How or by whom the first blow was given can not be now ascertained, but the feeling of resistance was contagious and powerful. The Mayor of the City, nevertheless, thought it his duty to keep the peace and to protect these troops in their passage thru Baltimore.[19]

On May 7, the "Brengle Home Guard" was organized at the Frederick Court House, where it received the flag from ladies of the town (any member found "under the influence of intoxicating liquor, asleep, or off of his beat" was subject to dismissal). The *Minute Book* described the reaction of Frederick citizens to young Marylanders heading south to join the Confederate army:

> About 120 of the most wretched specimens of humanity passed through this city from Baltimore, en route for Virginia, to join the rebel forces concentrating along the line of that State bordering on Maryland. When the announcement of the proximity to this city was first made, the Union men felt much like driving them off, but when their miserable condition become known they excited no other feelings than pity and contempt, and they were allowed to remain a few hours on the outskirts of the city to rest themselves, whilst those whose sympathies were excited in their behalf took up subscriptions to provide them something to eat, and after satisfying the cravings of hunger were made to leave.[20]

Early in May Maj. William W. Morris, the commander at Fort McHenry, was served with a writ of habeas corpus ordering him to relinquish John George Mullan, a soldier at the fort. In his May 7 reply to U.S. District Court Judge William Fell Giles, Morris recited a litany of complaints:

> At the date of issuing your writ, and for two previous, the city in which you live, and where your court has been held, was entirely under the control of revolutionary authorities. Within that period United States soldiers, while committing no offense, had been perfidiously attacked and inhumanly murdered in your streets; no punishment had been awarded, and I believe no arrests had been made for these atrocious crimes.

Morris conceded the suspension of the writ but defended his refusal to comply with the order:

> If all this be not rebellion, I know not what to call it. I certainly regard it as a sufficient legal cause for suspending the writ of *habeas corpus*. Besides, there were certain grounds of expediency on which I declined boeying your mandate. 1st. The writ of *habeas corpus* in the hands of an unfriendly power might depopulate this fortification and place it at the mercy of 'a Baltimore mob,' in much less time than it could be done by all the appliances of modern warfare. 2d. The ferocious spirit exhibited by your community to the United States army would render me very averse from appearing publicly and unprotected in the city of Baltimore to defend the interests of the body to which I belong. And now, sir, permit me to say, in conclusion, that no one can regret more than I, this conflict between the civil and military authorities. If, in an experience of thirty-three years, you have never before known the writ of *habeas corpus* to be disobeyed, it is only because such a contingency in the political affairs as the present has never before arisen. I claim to be a loyal citizen, and I hope my former conduct, both official and private, will justify this pretension. In any condition of affairs, except that of civil war, I would cheerfully obey your order, and as soon as the present excitement shall pass away, I will hold myself ready, not only to produce the soldier, but also to appear in person to answer for my conduct; but in the existing state of sentiment in the city of Baltimore I think it your duty to sustain the Federal military and to strengthen their laws, instead of endeavoring to strike them down.[21]

When Mullan was discharged for being underage, the crisis over the fate of the writ was but briefly postponed.

Baltimorean George H. Steuart, a West Point graduate, commanded one of the city militias in April. Unionist sentiment and actions of the state legislature soon drove him to an illustrious career in the Confederate army, where he rose to the rank of general:

> I found nothing but disgust in my observations along the route and in the place I came to—a large majority of the population are insane on the one idea of loyalty to the Union and the legislature is so diminished [?] and unreliable that I was rejoiced [?] to hear they intended to adjourn on today or tomorrow. It seems that we are doomed to be trodden on by these troops who have taken military possession of our State, and seem determined to commit all the outrages of an invading army.[22]

Ross Winans was a wealthy industrialist and state legislator whose manufacture of pikes for resisting passage of Northern troops through Baltimore attracted the attention of General Butler. Winans also perfected and tested the centrifugal "steam gun" invented by Charles Dickinson, reputed to fire numerous rounds per minute.

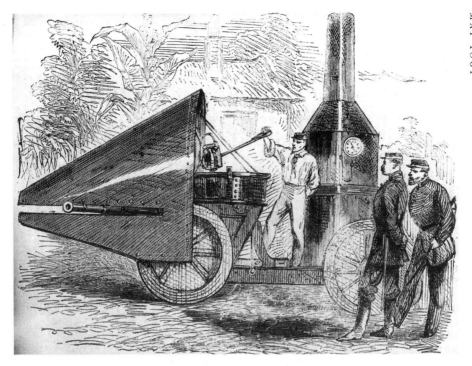

Winans's steam gun, tested on Baltimore streets as a weapon against Northern troops, led to the arrest of legislator Ross Winans—and to some mystified soldiers instructed to disassemble it. Pratt Lib.

A newspaper described it as "the subject of much curious inspection" in camp and "as harmless as an old barn fan."[23] A soldier recounted the effort to find this weapon:

> An order came for two companies to march out capture a baggage train they reported that there were three hundred men with it but it turned out to be a steam gun four miles and three men it is a strange looking thing about the sise of a steam fire engine.[24]

Another observer described the contraption:

> The guard captured the man that invented the steam gun that Gen Butler captured last week that gun is the damdest thing I ever saw it looks like a shovel more sharp at one end and at the other it looks a spike [driver].[25]

On May 14 Massachusetts troops dragged Winans from a train at Relay House as he returned home from the legislative session in Frederick. Not even the pleas of Governor Hicks and other legislators riding with Winans could save the bearded Southern sympathizer from twenty-four hours behind bars at Fort McHenry. A Union soldier described the arrest:

I had just got asleep when we were all turned out by the firing of the guards for they thought there was an attack on depot but it that they had arested the richest man in Maryland for we set a trap for him the night before he was coming home with the rest of the legislature when he was taken out of the cars the whole of the legislature got out and began to bluster and say they would take him away.[26]

Winans, one of only two Marylanders detained in the spring of 1861, was released the following day after taking a loyalty oath.

Governor Hicks complained to Butler about the presence of free black men in the Union camps at Annapolis—a harbinger of difficulties Maryland slaveholders would soon face:

Several free negroes have gone to Annapolis with our troops, either as servants or camp followers; that they are armed and insolent; that they seek the company of, and are corrupting our slaves. Also, that on the 7th instant two of the negroes grossly insulted a storekeeper in Annapolis, and drew their pistols with threats to shoot him.

I respectfully suggest to you that the mere presence of these negroes in our state is a violation of our statutes, and even if they should comport themselves in an orderly manner, the General government ought not tolerate a violation of our laws by permitting them to accompany its troops.

You can readily see that their presence here will be provocative of disorder and ill feeling. I am sure you desire nothing of the kind. I must urge you to send them back, and to permit no more to come here.[27]

The *Baltimore Sun*, objecting to Northern papers accusing Maryland of secession inclinations, captured the often misunderstood difference between Southern sentiment and secession:

A natural and irrepressible sympathy with the cause of Southern rights is constantly and willfully misinterpreted as a spirit of secession. In this thing very great injustice is done to our citizens.[28]

A Baltimore newspaper recommended to readers, "The Sentiments of a Southern Wife and Mother," written by a Maryland woman to female relative in the North, noting "We bespeak it for a careful perusal":

The South has never asked anything of the North but the quiet and peaceable enjoyment of their constitutional rights, and when that has been denied they have determined, to the last of life and property, to resist the aggressive spirit which seeks to strike down their liberties and to rob them of their property. Were the South to make a donation of her slaves to the North and permit them to sell them in the West Indies and then occupy our territory by Yankee labor, we would hear no more of war, but as that cannot be, she has determined, while she has a gallant man within her borders, a gun and an ounce of powder, to appeal to just Providence and fight for her rights.[29]

Catherine Smith described soldiers passing near Baltimore and at the rail junction south of the city:

There were a good many Troops landed last night at Locust Point—they passed along unmolested to Washington. Our Citizens go out to the Relay to see the Troops—there yesterday [T h S] took Nat and Eddy and Nathan Pusy and young Nate—they said they conversed very pleasantly with some of the Military there, they are polite.

She noted that Northern civility did not prevent Maryland boys from heading south:

A good many young men here, have joined the Southern Army I suppose George Smith Lucys Brother with others about 100 left here either yesterday morning or the day previous so I was told none of our family have been seized with the military fever but Roberts Matt.

Eddy and Matt are great Secessionists and Richards Family very much that way inclined all the rest of our folks good Union men—Nate Pusy great for the Union.[30]

One pacifist was prepared to head the opposite direction:

I do not feel like taking any part in the fight as I cannot bear the Idea of hurting any of my fellow beings from time to eternity unprepaired if they get to fighting here I will leave and go somewhere North I have kept my boys out of it up to this time and if I can I will continue to keep them from fighting.[31]

Allen B. Davis cited reasons why many Maryland businessmen opposed a Maryland secession:

Ma was quite excited in passing through the troops at the Relay House the other day—the sight of the muskets, bayonets, swords and cannon quite unnerved her. I am glad that Maryland is still in the Union—it would be utter ruin and devastation for her to attempt to secede. The South could not protect her and she would be a prey to the northern border. The Legislature has adjourned because they found they could not take her out.[32]

George N. Moale described the views of his friends to his uncle—on the reverse side of his letter, dated the next day, appeared, "Neutrality becomes Maryland":

I have heard the opinion of all my Northern friends—or rather most of them—in relation to the troubles between the North & South and they all agree in thinking the North entirely right—with the exception of Mr. Page.[33]

An encampment high on the bluff gave the troops a panoramic view of the rail lines in and out of Relay. Pratt Lib.

The Reverend John Milton Peck, a Connecticut native and rector of Deer Creek Parish in Harford County, felt the acute divisions in his congregation:

> Prejudice out of the Parish was never so great as now about Darlington, and to me personally has been shown some of the vilest meanness ever tolerated, short of bodily assault or mob law. The little band of communicants is lessened by scandal. The sworn soldiers of Christ are examples of sinfulness and world-liness.
>
> Our National troubles have come, and my Eastern birth is now held up (the only *political* wrong I am guilty of) though by silence and care I do not fear from that much. Yet there is a feeling here I do not like.
>
> Just after the Baltimore riot, partially for that reason as well as for another, I took my family to Mass., and have just returned. A month ago my father was taken dangerously ill with hemorrhage—it is painful to me to be far away from him. Though now on his feet, yet his condition is somewhat critical.

Three weeks ago I made a kind but formal request of the vestry for my salary overdue—I doubt very much that any real effort is made to obtain it. The Church and I have some of the noblest and truest friends here, but they are almost powerless, if not negligent or discouraged—rather incongruous situation for "*friends*" you think?[34]

Catherine Smith attributed difficulties in procuring life's essentials to a labor shortage rather than scarcity of goods:

All kinds of business that I know any thing about is prostrate I really do not know where very many get bread. This is no scarcity but all kinds of labour is suspended—a great many persons that keep their servants only pay just half wages that they did. Indeed there are many that would work for a home and food—so many families left and went out of town during the Panic. Mary and Sallie have had Emily Brooks this last week.

I have not had heart to have my garden done up yet. Did thee hear that Douglass lawn had failed I feel very sorry but hope when things if they ever do come round he may be able to resume. Alexandria is occupied pretty much by the Military I was too sorry when Virginia went out of the Union.

She took note of consequences of the federal presence:

A great many Jews left the city. William Talbott's house and grounds are occupied by General Butler's brigade—the tents are spread around the house.[35]

Baltimorean Frederick W. Brune, law partner and brother-in-law of Mayor George W. Brown, wrote in May to his wife Emily Barton Brune about "the horrors of this threatened Civil War":

Though the prospect is gloomy enough, I cannot believe but they will stop & think, before they bring so much misery here, what good they are to gain, for they will meet with opposition, even if they murder thousands, they can never restore a Union which is broken up for ever—& if they wished, could settle it peacefully and seperately.[36]

One publication noted the innocence of children in a tense time:

It is a happy thing for childhood that it anticipates no evil. Childhood takes no thought for the morrow. It lives in the present. It is happy when actual suffering is absent, and playful whenever its immediate wants are supplied.

As we pass through the streets of Baltimore, towards nightfall, and look into the faces of the men and women, we meet, sober, serious, full of anxious, desponding care, it is a pleasant relief to notice the groups of happy little girls, in the more retired neighborhoods, full of life and merriment, singing their "Here we go, two by two, Dressed in yellow, pink and blue." Or to notice the boys, in their mimic soldiering, happy as princes, albeit the pastime, is suggestive of some unpleasant reflection. The poor man's child shares this happiness alike with the rich . . . that boy yonder who is picking up the coal that has fallen about the *depot* from the locomotives, to take to his widowed mother, will, when he has laid down his basket at the hearthstone of poverty, bound out to play with as light a heart and as merry a laugh as though he were the son of a millionaire.[37]

John Pendleton Kennedy told Congress that, since April 19, he had seen little in Baltimore suggesting Southern sympathies:

Before I take my seat, let me say a word in regard to the secretion of arms in the city of Baltimore, about which we have heard so much . . . the whole aggregate of the arms discovered has been three hundred and twenty-one. Sixty-five of these were pistols that were taken from a mob in former days in a contest between the Governor of Maryland and Mayor Swann of the city of Baltimore . . . The whole story of eight thousand arms is a fabrication . . . I do not believe to-day the armed secession fighting force of Maryland is 5,000 men.[38]

Mayor Brown sent physician Charles H. Bradford to General Butler's camp near Relay House to investigate reports that a soldier had been poisoned by an itinerant vendor who laced his wares with strychnine. Bradford ruled out poisoning, citing instead tetanus induced by cold rain in a camp with no tents, fatigue, and exposure as responsible for the victim's cramps and spasms:

on the day of his attack he had from his own admission eaten freely of pies, cakes, and pickles, and that in a short time thereafter he was seized with violent pain in the stomach which was quickly followed by spasms of all the voluntary muscles . . . I was also informed that he is in the habit of occasionally indulging in intoxicating drinks to excess, and at such times will lay down in any position however much exposed.[39]

Two weeks following the riot, Daniel Thomas attributed the quiet in Baltimore to an absence of secession fervor and the army's conclusion that its citizens posed no threat to the Union. Thomas revealed his opposition to secession, which, having missed its opportunity, must now wait for more propitious circumstances:

I suppose you are sharing the general state of quiet that has succeeded the storm. We are as quiet here as mice. The military has been disbanded and everything has been going on as usual except business. That is entirely suspended, and what we are to live on if things go on thus much longer I am at a loss to know. Our town was in a great state of excitement Sunday in consequence of the arrival of the Massachusetts troops at the Relay House, it being supposed by the foolish ones that they must necessarily come here the next day and take possession. I don't think they design coming any nearer than where they are, and that if we

Union soldiers fill Monument Square, presumably awaiting assignment to federal camps around Baltimore. In the nineteenth century, the square was frequently the site of speeches and revelry—notably in June 1860 during the Democratic National Convention that nominated Stephen Douglas and in May 1870 celebrating passage of the Fifteenth Amendment that gave black citizens the vote. MdHS.

keep our own city quiet they will let us alone. The spirit put forth here two weeks ago, notwithstanding our relapse has inclined the Government to let us alone as long as possible, as they have now learnt that we can shout hurrah and talk on *one* side and fight *on the other.*

Charlie Steele says I am represented on West River as being even now for secession. Such is not the case and I don't know what I have ever said that would warrant such an opinion. I am and always was a secessionist on principle, but I never advised or desired the attempting impossibilities. The very substance of my arguments last winter was that unless we took proper steps in advance of the inauguration of Mr. Lincoln, our hands after that event would be completely tied, so that if every man in the state should desire to secede we would not be able to do it. And such now every body admits to be the case. If Virginia and the south could have backed us up at the time of our outbreak on the 19th we might have gone out with a rush, but they were not ready and as a matter of common sense we had to fall back to our old condition. Our position is fully understood at the south, and they do not desire Maryland to do anything at present, and neither do I. by our own culpable blindness & folly we have allowed this emergency to take us wholly unprepared, and we must now abide the consequences. Cut off from all help as we are, and wholly without arms it would be madness for us to attempt to do anything. We must remain on the defensive and "bide out time."[40]

A Georgetown man described the effects of civil strife on the mills along the Potomac River, referring to sabotage on the Chesapeake & Ohio Canal, a principal method of shipping goods—mainly coal—between Washington and Cumberland:

We are in a bad way business of all kind is stoped the government has taken all the flour we had in town or nearly so but paid us well for it gave us a good price but we cannot get wheat to make any more as our Canal is broke and if it was in operation the Va. People would not let it come we will have to get our supply of flour from Baltimore. I do not know how we will get along the people of this district I believe are worse of than any other part of the United States we are hemed in by the Southern States as Mereland will be out of the union if she is not already out . . . most of our young men who belong to the Church have joined the Military company in this place which I have grait fear of [them?] looseing what little religion they had for this soldering it is very demoralizing.[41]

Charles C. Grafton, the assistant rector at Baltimore's Old St. Paul's Church, described the spring as:

a most trying political time. I had felt it my duty . . . to read the pastorals which Bishop Whittingham, who was a most decided Unionist, put forth. They were couched in very trenchant language, and with quotations from the homilies on

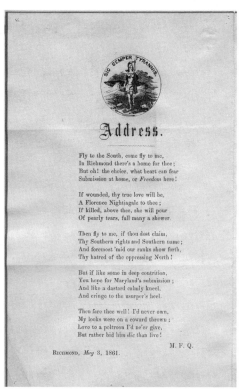

Left, *"Address to Her Maryland Lover, By A Virginia Girl, And His Reply."* Right, *This broadside poem, which began "Fly to the South, come fly to me," was typical of Confederate portrayals of Union repression in Maryland as the alternative to "Submission at home, or* Freedom *here!" Rare Books and Manuscripts Department, Z. Smith Reynolds Library, Wake Forest University, Winston-Salem, North Carolina.*

the sin and wickedness of rebellion. During the illness of the rector, when I was forced to read them, I can well remember the way the pew doors were slammed and the people left during their delivery. A number of Confederate church people loved me for my ministrations, but when a vacancy occurred in the rectorship the people naturally chose a southerner to succeed Dr. Wyatt.[42]

The Reverend William R. Whittingham, bishop of Maryland, reminded his clergy of their duty toward parishioners:

I have learned with extreme regret, that in several instances, the "Prayer for the Presdt of U.S. & all in Civil Authority" has been omitted of late in the performance of divine service in this Diocese.

Such omission, in every case makes the clergyman liable to presentment for the violation of his ordination vow, by the mutilation of the worship of the

Church, & I shall hold myself bound to act on any evidence of such offense laid before me after the issue of this circular.

I beseech my brethren to remember that current events have settled any question that might have been started concerning Citizenship & Allegiance. Maryland is admitted & declared by the Legislature & Governor of the State to be at this time one of the United States of A. As residents in Maryland, the clergy of this Diocese are bound to the recognition & discharge of all duties appertaining to that condition.

To my keep distress & disgust I have too much reason to fear that in at least one instance a minister of Christ may have so far forgot himself his place & his duty, as actually to commit the canonical offense known as "brawling in church," while venturing to do what an Archangel I wish not do, & to defend transgression of the Word of God.

We of the clergy have no right to intrude our private views of the questions which are so terribly dividing those among whom we minister into the place assigned us that we may speak for God & minister in His Worship.[43]

By mid-May, Edward Spencer described himself as "the rebel, conspirator and traitor":

I left town Tuesday night, *on foot*, having missed the omnibus, & being *forced* to go, to keep out of jail. I saw enough of the outrageous occupation of B. & of the infamous disregard of property & person on the part of our masters to provoke me beyond reason. I was nearly crazy, was four times arrested, & at last told by Marshall Kane to leave town forth-with under penalty of being committed for Court. I bade the folks goodbye and started on foot, walking three miles & spending the night at a country tavern. Thence I traveled home, starting next morning early, in company with three volunteers for Harper's Ferry who had lost their comrades, and were without money, but had nevertheless resolved to walk to Liberty, 45 miles. I took them to McHenry, my neighbor, & made him provide them with money & breakfast. I was very tired when I got home & am pretty sore and stiff yet, but more sick in soul than body.[44]

Spencer took issue with "submissionists" whose "masterly inactivity" made them a "conquered people":

We are to be subject to arrest, confiscation & every indignity. Every provocation is to be hurled upon us, and, if we dare revolt, because there is a limit to human endurance, we are to be swept from the face of the earth, by murders, ravishings and fire. The troops quartered in B. are the merest rabble, insolent blackguards, the veriest offscourings of cities, jails, and almshouses, amenable to no laws, no decency. I do not exaggerate. There is *no* protection for us. It is not safe for women to be in Balto. I know of outrages committed by these scoundrels in Washington already, which I cannot repeat to you, & which so fill my soul with bloodthirst that I scarcely know myself. I am *so* glad you are not coming to B. you must not, darling, indeed. These villains may provoke an outbreak at *any* moment, & then B. will be utterly destroyed.[45]

General Butler's presence in Baltimore notwithstanding, rumors of insurrection continued to circulate:

It was reported last night that an attempt would be made from about Perryman-ville to burn Bush or Gunpowder bridges again, and the utmost vigilance was used by the road guards and the military, but nothing of an incendiary character made its appearance. Edward Bayne, of company H, who had the fore finger of his left hand shot off by the premature discharge of his Allen revolver, is doing well, and will soon be able to go out.[46]

Union camps were popular with Baltimoreans, especially ladies. At the Locust Point camp milk, ice cream, beer, and cakes were sold outside the picket lines, and officers gently dislodged intruders, apologizing to the ladies and citing their orders. Though "spirituous liquors" were permitted only with rations, most soldiers carried a "'pocket companion' in the shape of a canteen, to which they refer pretty often." One early May day the camp at Relay saw a record number of visitors, who observed battery practice—"the target, distant half a mile, was struck at nearly every discharge"—and soldiers fishing and sleeping.[47]

One Unionist newspaper described the subtle shades of secession:

The more conservative Secessionists counsel patience and moderation. While they neither fight nor plead for the maintenance of the American Union, they steadfastly oppose the madness of the violent portion of their own party, and while they look to the ultimate union of Maryland with the Confederation that claims Virginia, they still demand that this union shall be perfected under legal forms, and without the precipitate haste that has marked the passage of Secession Ordinances in other localities.[48]

On a day when more men departed from Camden Station to join the rebels—with about six hundred Baltimoreans already in Confederate service—a newspaper headline entitled "An Outrage" related a situation that usually ended badly for black men:

Henry Stokely, a negro, has been committed to jail at Towsontown, charged with attempting to commit an outrage upon a Mrs. Carback, a white woman. He was positively identified by another woman who was riding with Mrs. C. at the time in a wagon.[49]

A simple depiction of the Confederate flag showed fifteen stars—reflecting, perhaps, Southern hopes that the four border slave states, including Maryland, would join the Confederate 11. MdHS.

The Kirkwood family farmed at White Hall, Baltimore County, near Calverton Mills. Three of the four Kirkwood sons fought for the Union. Robert Kirkwood's many letters to his parents and siblings describe the political atmosphere in the Baltimore region and trace the movements of his First Maryland Infantry Regiment throughout the war. In May, he described recruiting in Baltimore:

> They are recruiting very fast here. There is five or six will be ready for the field in a week or two slades kenery is going along with us for a waiter I hardly knew him he has got so fleshy we will get to fort Mc Henry to get out clothing and equipments well as I expect to be called to duty I must bring my letter to a close it is not worth while to rite untill wesar stationed and then I will let you know where to direct I hope we will be so fortunate as to see each other again if not on earth I hope it will be heaven where wars and troubles can never reach.[50]

Ross Winans's sons, William and Thomas, were also railroad engineers and inventors, and they often collaborated on projects such as the "Cigar Boat," a sleek passenger vessel powered by high-pressure steam engines designed to cross the Atlantic in four days. In May, William wrote to Thomas from Paris to express concern at reports from Maryland:

> Besides the general news I get from America showing our loved & great country divided & in a state of civil war and its worst horrors staring us in the face, by many of the New York papers I see mention of Father and yourself as counted with secession in Maryland, that you have subscribed enormous amounts to aid the southern Confederacy & Baltimore in that course, that Father's establishment is engaged with 400 men in making Pikes, and in making cannon to take

Black citizens, presumably Marylanders, helped the Eighteenth Massachusetts Regiment repair railroad bridges between Annapolis and Washington. Harper's Pictorial History of the Civil War *(New York, 1866), 93.*

to Fort McHenry & sweep the streets of Baltimore if Northerners enter to pass through, that Father is elected as a secession delegate . . . of course I do not believe the rascally reports which are sent from Baltimore to the New York & Republican papers about you.[51]

The *Sun* continued to advocate Unionism and Southern rights or a "peaceable separation" if that would avoid war:

There are very few people in Baltimore who desire to see the two sections of our country engaged in war. There is not a man, we believe, in any of the seceded States who desires war. It may be safely assumed and asserted therefore, that the 'war party' is alone to be found in force in the Northern States. It is a fact, *we know*, that there is also in the Northern States a large number of the people who are for peace, and who would prefer a peaceable separation from the seceded States, if separation there must be, to a war with them.[52]

Daniel Thomas described the effects of General Butler's departure from Baltimore after General Scott relieved him of command:

Since "Dearest Butler" has taken his lamented departure we have had a pretty quiet time of it. An Eel is said to like being skinned alive, *after he gets used to it,* which only means I suppose that people can get used to anything, and so with the people of Baltimore. The fact having been clearly established that we are a conquered people and are under a military despotism equal to any that ever prevailed in Europe. The people, after the first burst of indignation had sub- sided—finding there was nothing better to be done—have made up their minds like sensible people to "*grin and bear it.*" Since General Cadwalader has taken command here, our chains have not been drawn quite so tight. They are none the less around us. He seems disposed to act decently but how long he is to be permitted to do so is the question. People are leaving here very fast & I am afraid there will be no voters left here by the time of the election.[53]

With Northern troops occupying Relay House and Maryland militia disbanding, Maryland exile George W. Booth in later years described the creation of Company D of the Confederate First Maryland Infantry, whose officers included George H. Steuart and Bradley T. Johnson:

Being invited by James R. Herbert to unite with him in raising a company for service in the southern army, and all prospect or opportunity for action on the part of the State having passed, this work for some time received my attention. About the middle of May, 1861, a sufficient number of men to establish a nucleus for a company having been enlisted, Captain Herbert took his departure for Harper's Ferry, marching across the country and taking the train at Sykesville, on the B. &O.R.R., while I remained in Baltimore, forwarding daily additional men, until it became unsafe to linger longer, as arrests were being freely made by the federal authorities.[54]

Late in May Walter F. Southgate, a Baltimore Unionist visiting Christiana, Dela- ware, praised Maryland's governor:

We are all pretty well. I am visiting out in this monotonous region. I supposed tho in these times one & all are in the same state. Some rabid bloodthirsty Re- publicans in this region stigmatize Gov Hicks as a traitor, I give him every credit for wisdom, sagacity & prudence. To him Maryland, no matter what the issues of the present struggle, owes her salvation, I do not know what your sentiments are, here I am called a secessionist because I cry out for peace and the rights of the South in the Union. You can't make a man your friend by beating out his brains, nor can the Pulpit make Christians by hounding on their congregations to cut the throats of their fathers & brothers, I close abruptly. Love to all.[55]

David Creamer's newspaper collection included a May 20 account of a raid to iden- tify disloyal Northerners:

At precisely three o'clock in the day, the telegraph offices in all the principal cities and towns north of Washington, and throughout the free States were seized. The movement, prepared with the utmost secrecy, was simultaneously executed, so that no chance of apprising other offices, and destroying their contents could be had. All the telegrams of a year previous, kept recorded as they were in the offices, were seized, at the same instant, and in this manner the Government came into possession of an immense amount of information, as the telegraph had been freely used by many persons at the North in sympathy with the secession leaders of the South.[56]

The Protestant chastised other papers for their coverage of Baltimore:

The secular papers have all run into the sensation school. They are making the most of the present war fever. "Extra" follows "Extra," and the newsboys on Baltimore street have increased a hundred fold. Experts in the paragraph line are busy as bees. If they hear no news they event "items." The public ear is athirst. "*They say*" has become oracular. It may be truthfully affirmed, that non one-half of the marvelous things stated in the newspapers have any reality in them. They are manufactured to keep up the excitement. Men live by them.

The religious press ought to be wiser than to suffer itself to be imposed upon by those who trade in falsehood for the purpose of pandering to the morbid curiosity of the multitude. But alas, they too have drifted from stable moorings. They too are adrift on the mad whirl of political excitement. They copy and endorse the exciting paragraphs of the day, without the slightest apparent suspicion of imposture. In one of our religious exchanges the other day, we saw a picture of Baltimore which was really amusing, and yet it was very provoking. According to that statement, in addition to other marvels, there were loop-holes in the window of our private residences, from which guns were to be fired upon government troops passing through the city! To read it, one would have supposed the whole community here, were a set of desperate ruffians, blood-thirsty and unfit to live. To destroy Baltimore, the tone of even our religious journals of the North, inclined to speedy and swift action. Poor Baltimore! She has, like every other city, her noisy and turbulent rowdy element. They are often hard to manage. But they certainly do not form the majority of her citizens.[57]

As spring stretched toward summer the government continued to clamp down on dissent. Daniel Thomas told his sister that a friend, Billy Murray, had gone south, with the promise of a position as "Master of Drill":

He had to leave secretly and a little more hurriedly than he intended in consequence of notice recd of his intended arrest. Arrests are very prevalent now, & the general fancy on the part of suspected parties seems to be to prefer the open air in Virginia to a dungeon here.[58]

Capt. William Murray commanded the Maryland Guard City Militia in Baltimore in the spring of 1861, when he went to Virginia and organized Company H of the First Maryland Confederate Infantry Regiment. He was killed on Culp's Hill on the second day of the Battle of Gettysburg. MdHS.

Rebecca Davis, daughter of Allan B. Davis, discovered that her parents and brother all had different views on the crisis in Maryland. From her father, the Unionist:

> I am glad that Maryland is still in the Union—it would be utter ruin and devastation for her to attempt to seceed. The South could not protect her and she would be a prey to the northern hordes. The Legislature has adjourned because they found they could not take her out.[59]

And from brother William Wilkins Davis, student and newly proclaimed Southern radical:

> For your benefit I hereby announce myself, henceforth, a straight out "Southern Rights" man, and want nothing to do with Lincoln, his party, or anything connected with him, or it, unless it is to help thrash him. I remained by the Union as long as I could, but when I saw it was the intention of Lincoln & his crew, to convert into a despotism, the fairest, & best government ever instituted by mortal man I can no longer support a man whose avowed intention is to subjugate the South. The very act of trampling upon, and treading in the dust the most sacred rights guaranteed to all the states, alike, in the Constitution, converts the government into a despotism, justifies revolution, and renders the duty of defending their rights & vindicating their honor an imperative on the Southern end. And so I am henceforth for the *"Southern Confederacy," & the right."*
>
> If you could only see the tyrannical way in which "Abe" wields his despotic sceptre over Maryland, and the insults he offers, & continues to offer to her, I think your Union, or rather *ExUnion* proclivities would be a little weakened. And our contemptible, cowardly, lying governor winks at every thing (he) does without the least compunction.[60]

And from a neutrality-favoring mother:

> To my mind we are living in the World's Saturday night, that you and perhaps I will witness most extraordinary and unlooked for changes in the aspect of things, perhaps the entire abolition of slavery, the Northern press seem sanguine that this will be the result of the war, and seem anxious to impress on the minds of the soldiers that it is some of their business to stop runaway negros or suppress insurrections with all their horrors, but rather to take advantage of this weakness of the Enemy. This seems very wicked, but I fear it will prove true and we shall hear of awful massacres by the negros as it was in St. Domingo—and yet many in our state helpless, unarmed, and entirely surrounded by the U States troops at the risk of having Baltimore sacked and burned (which I think she narrowly escaped) the whole country devastated, even the wealthy utterly impoverished, the poor made poorer, thousands abused and massacred in cold blood, would rush our state into secession. Now what benefit can it ever be to the poor creatures who should survive—to solace themselves Maryland proved to the whole

William Wilkins Davis, a student in Hagerstown, became a vocal Southern sympathizer during the spring of 1861. His parents were strong Unionists. MdHS.

world that her people were so reckless as to play the part of a set of daredevils. At the cannons mouth—on the point of bristling bayonets, bidding defiance to Fort McHenry's shells, which in a few hours could lay her principal city in ruins. I hope your brother will escape this *strange delusion.* we may not like the present administration, nor endorse its acts, but we had better bear the ills we have than fly to others that we know not of. Let Maryland remain neutral and she may ride out safely this awful storm. Oh if I only could feel sure she would—but I fear this secession element. It would be certain ruin to all *our hopes as a family* in this world.[61]

St. Mary's County was a center of tobacco cultivation. Lotty Leigh Gardiner expressed her views in a letter from St. Mary's Seminary to John Bowie:

Have you heard recently from Johnny. I suppose he & you & all my friends are now interested in nothing but the war question "to be or not to be," what say you? Are you belted and spurred, ready for the contest! I was made most happy to hear of your resignations. I must tell you that I am heart & soul with the south, & had I ten thousand brothers I would be glad to see them go forth. Every man should have a strong arm.[62]

On May 25, Baltimore County farmer John Merryman was arrested and held in Fort McHenry, charged with burning railroad bridges spanning the rivers above Baltimore:

> This is to certify that Mr. John Merryman was arrested by orders of Colonel Yohe as first lieutenant of a secession company who have in their possession arms belonging to the United States Government for the purpose of using the same against the Government. The prisoner acknowledged being lieutenant of said company in the presence of Adjutant Miltimore, of First Regiment of Pennsylvania Volunteers, and Lieutenant Abel, Company D, First Regiment. It can also be proven that the prisoner has been drilling with his company and has uttered and advanced secession doctrines. The prisoner was arrested on the morning of May 25 at his residence about two miles from Cockeysville.[63]

Gen. George Cadwalader received a writ of habeas corpus for Merryman:

> You are hereby commanded to be and appear before the Hon. Roger B. Taney, Chief Justice of the Supreme Court of the United States, at the U.S. court room in the Masonic Hall in the city of Baltimore on Monday, the 27th day of May, 1861, at 11 o'clock in the morning, and that you have with you the body of John Merryman, of Baltimore County, and now in your custody, and that you certify and make known the day and cause of the capture and detention of the said John Merryman, and that you then and there do submit to and receive whatsoever the said court shall determine upon concerning you in this behalf according to law, and have you then and there this writ.[64]

Cadwalader sought guidance from the War Department:

> I was yesterday evening served with a writ of habeas corpus issued by the Hon. Roger B. Taney, Chief Justice of the Supreme Court of the United States, commanding me to be and appear at the U.S. court-room in the city of Baltimore on Monday (this day), the 27th day of May, 1861, at 11 o'clock in the morning, and that I have with me the body of John Merryman of Baltimore County now in my custody, and that I certify and make known the day and cause of the capture and detention of the said John Merryman and that I do submit to and receive whatsoever the said court shall determine upon concerning me in this behalf. I have the honor to inclose herewith a copy of said writ together with a copy of my reply thereto which will be handed to the court at 11 o'clock this day, the hour named in said writ. Requesting to be furnished with further instructions as to the course I am to pursue in this case.[65]

Daniel Thomas described the constitutional issues at stake in the Merryman case (though he erred in saying that the Supreme Court had ruled that the writ of habeas corpus could be suspended only by the Congress):

> This morning a new act in the Great Drama was performed. Mr. John Merryman who was arrested on Saturday appealed to Judge Taney for a writ of Habeas Corpus which was served on Gen. Cadwalader & made returnable this morning. The Judge came over himself to sit upon the case. At the appointed hour this morning the Court Room was crowded & a Col. Lee appeared & Read his answer to the writ, by which he respectfully but decidedly declined to produce the prisoner & announced amid the most profound sensation that he had been instructed by the President to *suspend the operation of the writ of Habeas Corpus!* This was what cost Charles 1st his head, & would at this day shake Queen Victoria from her throne. No right has ever been held so dear to Englishmen as the right to the writ of Habeas Corpus. And our Supreme Court has repeatedly decided that it can only be suspended by *Act of Congress.* Judge Taney very cooly & quietly ordered an attachment against the General returnable tomorrow morning. If resistance is made we will have the *Judicial* arm of the Government arrayed against the *Executive,* the result of which of course will be the downfall of the former under the military power of the latter, & then what becomes of the star spangled Banner, when one of the three arms of Government of which the three colors is the Emblem is trodden out of Existence by the armed heel of one of the other two. The right of arbitrary imprisonment of all *suspected* persons is the necessary consequence, & you may look for numerous arrests in the future.[66]

William Chauvenet acknowledged reports from George Cole that Maryland appeared safe for the Union:

> You put the Union men of Maryland where I had already asserted they were in my conversations with people here. The state I knew was loyal and by a very large majority, and could not be dragged into revolution by a few secessionists.[67]

Edward Spencer reassured his fiancée on the Eastern Shore that he was safe as the Union army expanded its presence in Baltimore County:

> I have been extremely busy the last few days, darling. I cannot say more than that it is in the cause that has my best wishes—it will not do for one to commit himself further on paper at these times. I am pretty well fatigued, riding at night, but I take extreme good care of myself, and run no risk whatever. So don't you worry, pet. The Lincolnites are drawing the lines closer and closer upon us every day. On Wednesday they were at Towsontown, entering the private houses

of gentlemen, in search of arms. Think of it! They searched Grason's, Bedford's, Acy's, Wheeler's etc—all men of name, and as orderly citizens as can be found anywhere.[68]

At the end of May, the *True Union* framed war in a religious context:

One thing, however, seems certain. *A War upon the seceded States is about the worst thing that can be done.* The Capital must be defended, and the officers and archives of the government protected, of course, but we speak of an *aggressive war*. It will raise new questions for division even more fatal to Union than the Slavery question. It cannot bring them back into love and Union. It might *conquer* them, but the conquest would be worse than worthless. It will inflict incalculable distress on the whole country—on the *North* perhaps more than on the *South*, for they are mutually dependent on each other. It will destroy everything lovely, virtuous, philanthropic and Christian among us. It will result in the everlasting *Disunion* of States which might otherwise have been *allied*, if not *united*, and it will turn this beautiful land of ours into a Gehenna, a vale of slaughter, from which men will flee with horror as the very vestibule of hell.

And all this *for what?* To end only where it might have been settled in the beginning, without slaughter, without increased hatred, without letting loose the fiendish passions of men. Christian Patriotism then demands *Peace*—a settlement of the controversy without further bloodshed, whatever form that settlement may take. We see no alternatives except compromise, exterminating war or immediate separation. There may be others, but we cannot perceive them. May God in infinite mercy include the hearts of the *five millions* of Christians on this continent to demand of our leaders on both sides such a settlement.[69]

chapter four

Summer 1861

Following Roger Taney's ruling in the Merryman case that Lincoln's suspension of the writ of habeas corpus was unconstitutional, W. W. Glenn described the reaction when the authorities refused to produce Merryman to face charges in a civilian court:

> The court was crowded. Great indignation was expressed against the Administration. Andrew Ridgely was very decided in his views and was willing to form one of a posse comitatus to proceed to the Fort, demand the prisoner and sustain the majesty of the law. The Administration had however determined to support its authority by the sword.[1]

In June, J. P. Kennedy sent a copy of his pamphlet *The Border States* to a man in St. Louis who had requested it. Kennedy's cover letter stressed the importance of those states to the Union cause:

> I trust you will be able to secure your state against the persistent and wily tactics of the Disunionists. With Missouri, Kentucky, Western Virginia and Maryland sustaining their loyalty through this tremendous trial, I think it impossible that secession can make any permanent government in the South.[2]

Correspondence in the early months of the war between the Shriver cousins, Christopher Columbus Shriver (C.C.) and Frederick Austin Shriver (Aust), remained friendly despite their political differences. In June, C.C. wrote about having left Shriver Brothers, his new job at James R. Herbert & Bros., and that:

> Almost all my friends have gone to Richmond & Harper's Ferry, and I was just spoiling to be with them, I have heard from them frequently and all of them write in the best of spirits. They say they are treated most hospitably by the Virginians and the ladies almost worship them.[3]

Later in June C. C. Shriver explained his support for Southern rights:

> Tis a strange thing, this difference of feeling in politics. I am sure I cannot understand how any one, who justifies the "Old Revolution", could help supporting the South. It is a thing I cannot comprehend how any honest man, who believes in a just God, and has read Jefferson Davis's proclamation, is not with the South. Not for an instance do I doubt your sincerity, in your choice of opinion; but what surprises me, is your saying the South "has lost nothing;" "that her grievances are only imaginary." This is preposterous. If in a monetary point of view she had not lost a cent, 'tis for her constitutional rights she has been asking, and they being refused, she, I think, is perfectly justified in doing what she has already done. When pleadings are of no avail, when truly patriotic addresses are

scorned in derision; and every honorable means of redress, is disregarded, how can you expect patriots under such circumstances to act? I will first point to the Old Revolutionists, and next to the southern men of the country. The latter in my humble opinion are more worthy of praise than the former They asked to be allowed to govern themselves; all they wanted was peaceful separation, but those who denied them their *constitutional rights,* laughed at such an idea, and commenced by trying to reinforce Fort Sumpter.

This is no one-sided account. 'Tis what I consider a fair and impartial view of the whole case. You must know and admit that it is.

After noting that "your President whom you endorse; usurps his power," that Southerners were the only patriots, and that he "would sooner live under the Queen of England than our present ruler," C.C. closed with cousinly affection:

I will stop tis useless to extenuate. I suppose you will hardly read what I have already written, and I might in my warmth of feeling say something which would provoke you to anger. Though, dear Aust, we can not agree upon the political subject now before us, you will now, and ever after and under all circumstances have in me, I am sure, as good a friend and as affectionate a cousin as "ever jumped" "or any other man." Let not political differences intrude upon our friendship.[4]

Frederick's reply recounted mundane activities at Union Mills:

I guess it is about time for me to say something in reply to your last letter. I have been busy during the last week at the *healthy* employment of mowing and making hay. So you may be sure I did not at that time feel much like writing a letter. I was helping your brothers, yesterday, to get in their *'tea'* (as John calls the hay, from its resemblance to that article) and was as hard at it as I knew how, the whole day, and felt so stiff this morning that I could hardly roll out of bed. I have not a great deal to say as regards our "Political differences." My feelings on the subject are unchanged.

And politics, including an account of an article by Clement Vallandigham supporting the South:

If I understand Vallandigham, all the South asked, was *guarantees* for their Rights. They were not deprived of them but they wanted guarantees. The Supreme Court has decided that they can take slaves to the territories, and at this very time they can take them (slaves) to any territory they please and nobody can stop them.

And besides this have not the opposition (including the Seceded states) at this time, a majority in Congress. What more guarantees could the south want. As for the growing of the Republican party, and what they would have done—any party that is founded on a *wrong principle* or one *of injustice* must go down—and 4 years hence, had they attempted during the Lincoln administration, to do any injustice, they would not have elected another president—because the real sentiment of the people North are not those of a few senseless fanatics, which are so much spoken of—I admit that the Crittenden Compromise would have been a wise measure on the part of the North, but the South ought not to complain, because not long ago there *was* such a Compromise, and it was repealed mainly by the South. The constitution has not been broken as regards the "Fugitive Slave Law." It has not been *executed* as well as it should have been, but as well as could be under the circumstances. *Under Lincoln's administration it has been executed better than ever before*—Does that show a desire to impose upon the South. If they ever thought of abolishing slavery, it is singular that they *themselves* made an *irrepealable* amendment to the constitution which prevents Congress from ever interfering with Slavery where it now is. When Lincoln said that these states had to be either all free or all slave, he meant that in the Natural course of events they would ultimately be so. He did not mean that the Republican Party intended doing it. This is the true meaning of that speech—Lum, I have told you all this, because I want you to know there are reasons for my course, and not only the ones I have given, but numerous others—How anyone can compare the revolution down South, with the glorious one in which our forefathers rebelled against a government whose *very "oppressions planted them"* in America, I am unable to conceive. This tyrannical Lincoln, as you think, is only trying to save us and our *nation* from eternal ruin.[5]

The Reverend Henry Slicer had a pessimistic, if practical, outlook:

I am for the Union, and have resisted for a quarter of a century the sectional agitation which has brought about the unhappy state of things—*but I do not believe that war waged agt the south will reconstruct the Union—but will bankrupt the country, and make thousands of homes desolate*—

Civil war is now upon us—my judgment is, that this is not the way, to win back our erring brethren of the seceded states.[6]

Two weeks later, C. C. Shriver, on duty in a Baltimore militia camp, told Frederick about an Independence Day celebration that included a ride on what was likely a merry-go-round:

You will no doubt be interested in my telling you how I spent the 4th. Well, in the morning early I was awakened from a delightful night's rest by the discharge of cannon in almost every part of the city. As they kept it up for some time I did not get to sleep again, so, dressed and amused myself until breakfast by reading. After breakfast I went with a couple of my friends, Eugene Diders & Will Neale, out beyond the Park to shoot at marks with pistols. I had one of my "Al-

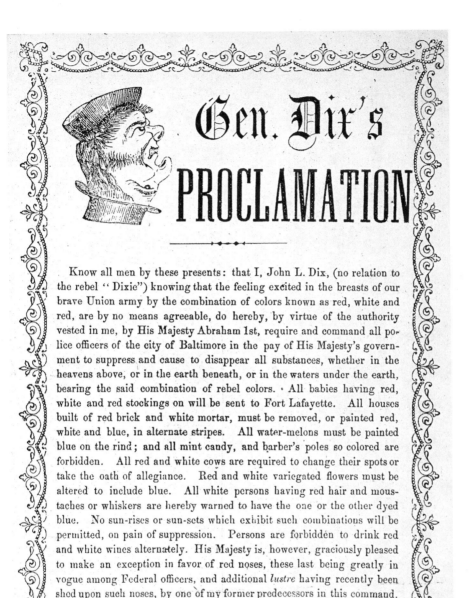

Gen. Dix's
PROCLAMATION

Know all men by these presents: that I, John L. Dix, (no relation to the rebel "Dixie") knowing that the feeling excited in the breasts of our brave Union army by the combination of colors known as red, white and red, are by no means agreeable, do hereby, by virtue of the authority vested in me, by His Majesty Abraham 1st, require and command all police officers of the city of Baltimore in the pay of His Majesty's government to suppress and cause to disappear all substances, whether in the heavens above, or in the earth beneath, or in the waters under the earth, bearing the said combination of rebel colors. · All babies having red, white and red stockings on will be sent to Fort Lafayette. All houses built of red brick and white mortar, must be removed, or painted red, white and blue, in alternate stripes. All water-melons must be painted blue on the rind; and all mint candy, and barber's poles so colored are forbidden. All red and white cows are required to change their spots or take the oath of allegiance. Red and white variegated flowers must be altered to include blue. All white persons having red hair and moustaches or whiskers are hereby warned to have the one or the other dyed blue. No sun-rises or sun-sets which exhibit such combinations will be permitted, on pain of suppression. Persons are forbidden to drink red and white wines alternately. His Majesty is, however, graciously pleased to make an exception in favor of red noses, these last being greatly in vogue among Federal officers, and additional *lustre* having recently been shed upon such noses, by one of my former predecessors in this command.

Done at the Baltimore Bastile, this 4th day of September, the 1st year of Abraham's glorious and peaceful reign.

(Signed),   JOHN L. DIX, Maj. Gen.

Even Unionists objected to Gen. John Dix's proclamation suppressing displays of support for the Confederacy. In September 1861, Marylanders parodied the Dix directive with one that referred to "His Majesty Abraham 1st"; threatened prison for babies wearing "red and white stockings"; and ordered removed or painted red, white, and blue "all houses built of red brick and white mortar." MdHS.

len Revolvers" and Neale had some "three shooters" I don't know whose make. We shot about seventy times and made some pretty good shots, a good many though were not so good. We staid out in the woods until 1½ when we turned to come in town—Just before cousin Alex on Madison Ave—some fellow has such a Machine as you will remember to have seen at Old Myers called the "Flying Horses" Well, when we got there I met a lot of fellows who I knew and all of them were riding—I was invited to get in the Coach, by three fellows who had charted one of them. I accepted the invitation, and was soon flying around at a 2.40 rate. After making three or four rounds, I forgot where the starting point was and just felt as though all creation was flying away. I laughed until I thought I would choke, the air flew down my throat so, I never in my life had such a ride. When the machine was stopped I could not see, and had as much as I could do to get out, and when I was on the ground could hardly walk.

But he could not avoid politics:

Why did you not send your political letter, I would like to know your reasons for still supporting the "Republican Party" as it can be not called justly any thing else, for the constitution is a thing they lay aside when ever it suits them.

I agree with you though—that is if our political feelings are not exactly alike do not let them interfere with our other feelings so I will leave you to the *fates* and *times* and hope soon to hear of your being on the side of "*Justice and Truth.*"[7]

A month earlier C.C. had complained about Lincoln:

Old Lincoln ought to have better sense, than to try to coerce the South. We can never do it, and if after ten years fighting he wishes to compromise, it will be harder to do than it is now. He might as well try to subjugate England, as the south. The Old Tyrant I wish he had never been born, or since he is, I wish that he were now in Heaven—instead of where he is. But I fear for his ever getting in the latter place.[8]

In June, Leonidas Dodson described the presence of Union troops in Easton:

The quiet of our town was broken on Sabbath last 9th inst, by the sudden apparition of a detachment of U.S. troops 400 strong entering our town about 4 o clock P.M. It proved to be a detachment of the 13 Regt. N.Y. Volunteers part of the force at Annapolis, under command of Col. Smith. The object of the visit was to take possession of the Armory, and remove all arms to Fortress McHenry.

The Col commanded the expedition in person, and treated the people here very civilly. One of two persons were arrested for a short time because of unguarded remarks. The troops remained at the Ferry until Monday morning, when they started landed at St Michael's, and exhibited the drill, of the army to the people there.[9]

Some Maryland slaveholders believed the Union would best protect their invest-ment in black brawn. Typical of this conservative view was R. L. Merced, who wrote from his estate, Parkhurst, to Rep. J. Morrison Harris:

I have been intending for some time to write, & congratulate you upon failing to get the nomination for Congress in your District, because you refused to sell your birthright—like you I am a Union man, do not wish my state to secede ei-ther now, or hereafter; because it would entail upon us, domestic confusion and strife without limit, besides probably making us at once a free state, by the forc-ible abduction of our slaves.

I regret to see, as evinced by the platform submitted to you & other public men, that the tendency of the Union party is merging it rapidly into the ranks of unmitigated black Republicanism. They fail to understand & appreciate the fact, that we have now to deal with a great Revolution instead of a contemptible rebellion!—& that preserving the integrity of the Union by force, meant the in-auguration of an interminable & bloody civil war, the result of which, can only plunge the whole country in poverty & wretchedness—and although victory may crown the policy of Mr Lincoln & his invading army, battle after battle may be won, but every drop of blood shed in the unnatural war, will only tend to widen, & make eternal the existing breach.

Merced expressed his hope for his home state:

Here in Maryland, as in the other border States, union men should be the great nucleus around which conservative men in all sections may hereafter rally.[10]

Baltimore businessmen demanded protection from the mayor:

Agreeable to the provisions of Article 82 Section 2 of the new Code, I hereby notify you that I am apprehensive of an attack being made on my dwelling situated on the corner of Broadway and Gough Streets, and respectfully request that you will take such measures as in your judgment will tend to prevent any such occurrence.[11]

On May 30, Governor Hicks ordered all arms owned by the state collected and stored. Shortly thereafter he expanded the order to include all state arms in the possession of individuals—an order many saw aimed at militia companies sympa-thetic to the South. The state senate, calling Hicks a "military despot," demanded he be reined in:

It is the imperative duty of the Legislature to make a direct issue with the Gover-nor of the powers thus claimed, and to confine him to the exercise of the powers and duties confided to him by the constitution and the laws.[12]

Young William Wilkins Davis bitterly criticized the governor's denial of culpability in the destruction of railroad bridges:

Federal troops occupied Locust Point, near Fort McHenry, in the summer of 1861. Pratt Lib.

We have been laughing, for the last twenty four hours, over the milk and water attempt of that time serving old tody, Gov. Hicks, to get himself out of the scrape, into which he got himself, by letting such an egregious falsehood about the bridges.[13]

Edward Spencer pledged to stick to his principles in the face of arrest, and the occupation of the federal arsenal at Pikesville by Union troops:

The U.S. Arsenal was occupied last night by three hundred troops (only 6 miles from here) and, among the arrests certainly to be made in a day or two, are those of I. Howard McHenry, Dr. J.Z. Offutt, Atwood Blunt, Sam'l Mettam, Robert Spencer, and one "little fellow" who is I think tolerably well known to Miss A.C.B.H. [Braddie]. I don't know what charge is to be trumped up, but the source whence I got the information is such that I cannot fail to give it credence. Now, they can't *hurt* us, honey, of course, and I'll get into no trouble unless they insult the women folks—but, I *vow I will not take the oath of allegiance,* and so, if I am arrested, I may expect to be imprisoned indefinitely. I write to you about this now, so that you need not to be alarmed if you see the matter in the papers. *No harm can come to me*—I will be well cared for, and have friends who will spare no pains to effect my release as speedily as possible, so, if it *does* come, I forbid you to feel the slightest uneasiness or apprehension. I shall be guarded, will stand on my dignity, and will *permit nothing to provoke me,* except insolence to my mother. In that event, of course, I shall be apt to fare badly.[14]

The Brengle Home Guards passed one resolution disapproving of Hicks's order and a second mandating expulsion for any member complying:

> Whereas the Legislature of Maryland now in session in this city, have passed a resolution requesting the Governor to return to the armories of the State the arms which have been "placed, in the hands of ununiformed companies" and Whereas
>
> The Home Guard of Frederick City—an ununiformed company—having been regularly organized and mustered into the 16th Regiment, Maryland Militia, in accordance with law, would naturally come under the purview of the resolution, having probably excited the ire of this body by their honest zeal and careful efforts in protecting the town from the villainous designs of incendiaries and imprincipled scoundrels who have been found prowling our streets at night; and
>
> Whereas, the present Legislature, by it's high handed legislation, unparalelled in the history of any civilized nation, have legalized riot, robbery & bloodshed in the city of Baltimore, one T. Parkin Scott, now unjustly and shamefully holding a seat in the legislature of this state, and thereby taught us a lesson which must be looked upon with indignation and horror by all good citizens, and
>
> whereas, we, the members of the Home Guard of Frederick, have organized the Company for the purpose of protecting life and property from mobs and rioters, and have obtained our arms legally from the *proper* military authorities of the State, *Therefore be it unanimously Resolved,* by the Home Guard of Frederick, that we will resist the enforcement of said order or requisition if made on us, *at all hazards and to the death.*[15]

Elizabeth Blair Lee hoped for a victory in June elections by Charles Benedict Calvert, a Union Whig from Prince George's County:

> It has been our first real summer's day—Blair is chirping Becky is well again—Our people here are in a fever about the election—All are keen to elect Calvert It will be a great Union triumph I hope—The fight down the Bay will insure a quiet election in Baltimore.[16]

Two days later Lee attributed Calvert's victory to her father's political skills:

> Prince George's went for Mr. Calvert—& Maryland for the Union almost without dissent—Mr. Calvert's vote is a great tribute to his character He was Father's & Bonifant's nominee & so managed that our Prince Georges friends feel as if he was theirs—but dont *ever* tell this.[17]

With staples low and business suffering, Baltimore's mayor and city council petitioned the state legislature to repair the railroad bridges, so trade might be reopened. But the House of Delegates disagreed:

> (As) facilities for invasion were offered to the fanatical and excited multitudes of the northern cities . . . whose animosity to Baltimore and Maryland is measured

by no standard known to Christian civilization, and who publicly threaten our destruction, without subordination even to the Federal authority . . . it would hardly be consistent with the commonest prudence to reopen the avenues which would bring them to our very doors.[18]

A woman in Wilmington, Delaware, commented on Baltimore's dire straits:

As you intimate: *Balt.* is in a *dangerous* condition, and the reports *now pending* assume a darker colour. I shall not be surprised to hear of the city's destruction at any moment, as also our whole Country.[19]

Elizabeth Patterson Bonaparte spent much of the war in France. William Mentzel, who managed her properties in Baltimore, sent her unwelcome news in May:

My object in writing you at present is to inform you that most of your tenants are going to leave their premises and have given me notice to that effect; unless the rents are reduced until they can be able to resume business—all kinds of trade and labor is at a perfect stand still. War and bloodshed has taken the place of peace and prosperity and we have nothing to hope for but a bloody, horrible civil war for sometime.[20]

Three weeks later he delivered more bad news:

If this is civil war I hope forever to be delivered from it in the future. Our city; although at present exempt from war, is feeling its sad and bitter effects, we are surrounded by military encampments, there is no business doing, mechanics and laborers are nearly in a state of starvation. Property stocks are reduced very much in value. The Balto & Ohio RRroad has stopped for several weeks by reason of the Bridges having been burned and we are perfectly prostrate. There is some thousands of houses idle and rents have been reduced to a mere nominal price, some even living rent free to take care of the premises until times shall change, for if a house is vacated there is no earthly chance of renting it.

Many of Bonaparte's tenants

Gave me notice that they would be compelled to move at the expiration of their quarter as they must reduce their expenses or have nothing for support. I am convinced from daily observation among them that such is the fact. Mears has not sold a piece of furniture since April 20th a few coffins being the extent of his business—some stores on Balto st engaged at $1500. per annum have been reduced to $600—some have taken off one half and others one third, your tenants on Balto st claimed one half off or they would move, this I could not comply with, unless I had your consent. I asked them to wait until I hard from you.[21]

Individuals and businesses demanded economic relief from Baltimore City:

On account of the entire stagnation of businesses in our Line—since January 1, 1861. (Having Rec'd but three cargoes of trunks since that date) We respectfully request that you will bring the subject before the Comit. of Finance with a view of reducing our Rent.[22]

In mid-June pro-Southern verse, "Rebel Poetry," appeared in a Baltimore newspaper:

Maryland! Maryland!
Stainless in story!
True in heart—true in hand—
Cling to thy glory!
Land of the Virgin name!
Land of Untarnished fame!
Oh, be thou still the same,—
Now, and forever!

Baltimore! Baltimore!
City of beauty!
Daring, as heretofore,
Spring to thy duty!
Spurn the invader forth!
Tell the despotic North—
That, when two hearts are wroth,
Union must sever![23]

In July, Armstrong Berry described the tense atmosphere in the city:

Business activities *strangely dull*—our sales for cash yesterday and day before was about 2 to 3 per day. We are not alone multitudes are in like prostration of Business. We can not give you any assurances that our City will remain quiet—there are a great many secessionists here and some are violent and may by foolish acts produce difficulty with the Military. If the Union Army should meet with reversals there is reason to fear that the secessionists would quickly ride up in our midst, and might bring the war to our doors. A few days will no doubt find the two armies engaged in fierce conflict. The Almighty only can foresee the terrible consequences.[24]

The War Department complained of interference with Northern troops arriving in Baltimore:

The general-in-chief has heard that on several occasions when troops have arrived in Baltimore from the North the police and others have interfered to prevent friendly persons from furnishing them with water at the depot. Two worthy

An Appeal for Peace

SENT TO LIEUT. GEN. SCOTT,

JULY 4, 1861.

THE mission of woman, has ever been a holy work, consecrated by that patient suffering, which calls forth a world's sympathy for her gentle fortitude. Has her claim ceased, that her agonizing cries are no longer heard, and is that care vouchsafed from the beginning, forever closed to her sorrows?

To you, our once great Nation's Chieftain, we call aloud in bitter anguish, to stay the strife which now desolates, our homes, and gives to America a bereaved sisterhood. To you we appeal, as the guardian of our once unstained and spotless Banner, to still those waves of passion, which surge over our unhappy land, sundering our dearest ties. As Man, endowed by the GIVER OF GOOD with all that station values, as Husband, whose—heart beats responsive to woman's love, as Father, the gentle whisperings of whose children cannot be forgotten in times going; by the memory of our holy dead, whose hushed voices speak again through our tears, we appeal, with all the earnestness of a grief more sore than any enlightened woman has ever borne. The unclosed graves now open for their victims, you can deny their tenants!

We claim, to know no distinction in party broils, as the pure element of the nation's greatness; we demand, in appealing, that protection GOD has entrusted to man in our behalf. Are only sorrows to be meted us? Has party strife, for gold's gain, obliterated all sense of right? Can the wail of our anguish for all ties rent, by the ruthless violence of men, forgetful that they are formed in GOD's image be unheard? Have we no natural rights? Husband, Son, and Brother, torn from their our homes, and incarcerated in the decaying atmosphere of a military prison, each day taking from us all that supports life! We call upon you to arise in the majesty of Freedom's chieftain, and restore our fettered nation to its primal greatness.

The halo of woman's prayers will encircle with its radiance the closing years of a life now far waning to its end, and will bear up on high the record of love to plead for that blessed eternity promised by the cross.

The children perfected in *your* art have gone sorrowfully to the stern duty of its use, (necessitated upon them), but would gladly lay aside the bloody weapons of defense, and turn in grateful happiness to your outstretched arms. The good and noble Lee upon the tropic plains of Mexico placed the fairest leaflet in the laurel which adorns your brow; the great Johnston gave the victorious Cerro Gordo to the glorious galaxy of your battles; Beauregard, whose mighty intellect is impressed by the Divine Essence with the mysterious knowledge of "numbered science;" Davis, the loved Davis, whose name is a talisman of virtue, to whom a suffering people cling. These are the sons of your training! These the comrades of your battles. Let the clustering years of your age be wreathed with the hallelujahs of an enfranchised people! We plead as those perishing, for that Peace, which your might alone can give; rising above the wicked machinations of the recreant to high Heaven's mandates, cast off the petty spirit of party jealousy, and give to us that blessed Peace whose rays illumine the inner sanctuary of the Most Holy. Can our unhappy land give you back for the labor of your earning, a greater boon, than the brightened page of History, whose inscription transmits the cessation of that carnage so unnatural and so fearful the world looks on in horror?

Can the emblazoned record of any victory confer a greater glory than this legacy of Peace? Can the angelic host who watch, lay upon the altar of your GOD an offering more pure?

As the Daughters of that State whose men in solemn legislative council fearlessly protested that her soil should not be profaned by the tread of martial feet, led on to devastate the domestic sanctuaries of the "Old Dominion." We implore you by all you value in Time's great Past, or hope for in unwritten Future, to stay the sorrows of our souls!

To you we appeal as Hope's last beacon, looking for the light which can alone point to a brighter day; and we thus place upon the register of our archives, this our cry of woe, whose piteous tones will be known as the appeal of the

WOMEN OF MARYLAND.

"An Appeal for Peace" from Maryland women to Gen. Winfield Scott may have been Confederate propaganda, designed to neutralize the federal presence in the state. Rare Books and Manuscripts Department, Z. Smith Reynolds Library, Wake Forest University, Winston-Salem, North Carolina.

Quakers named William Robinson and James D. Graham have it seems been threatened with violence for no other cause than this. The general asks your attention to this matter and suggests that by having a detachment of your troops at the depot at the proper time the regiments arriving might be duly supplied with water.[25]

On June 28, Baltimorean Richard Thomas, his disguise in women's clothing giving rise to the moniker "French Lady," hijacked the steamer St. Nicholas off Point Lookout at the southernmost point of St. Mary's County, where the Potomac River meets the Chesapeake Bay. Thomas delivered the steamer to the Confederacy at Fredericksburg, Virginia, and was promptly captured. W. W. Glenn recounted a conversation with Thomas:

> News came this morning of Dick Thomas' famous exploit of capturing the steamer St. Nicholas. A few days before he had walked into (Severn Teackle) Wallis' office took a seat & began to converse . . . "Well, if neither of you know me I think I am safe"—& he moved back his wig from his forehead, when they recognized him. He told them they should shortly hear from him. He went on board the St. Nicholas disguised as a French lady. He jabbered French most profusely and made great confusion. He took supper with the ladies & made quite a scene at the supper table. Afterwards he took possession of the Steamer with his accomplices made several prizes and carried them all up the Rappahanock.[26]

Leonidas Dodson approved of the first arrests of suspected Maryland disloyalists:

> Marshal Kane chief of Police in Balto has been arrested and sent to Fort McHenry by order of the War Department on a charge of treason. I am not surprised at this for if any individual in the State is susceptible of an implication of this crime it must be Kane, who officially telegraphed to Brad Johnson on the fearful 19th April to raise the war cry in the Mountains of Western Maryland, and hasten down to Balto to resist the "Northern Hordes."
>
> It is also foreshadowed by the Proclamation of Gen Banks that there is a conspiracy in Md, having its head in Kane, for the purpose of aiding & abetting the rebellion, and that his arrest is only the beginning of an effort to bring all the parties to justice.[27]

By July, one Marylander had abandoned hope that Congress would acknowledge Southern rights. Explaining that the south was well armed and amply provisioned, the anonymous writer asked "Lou" to "burn this letter as soon as read":

> There were many in the south who opposed (secession) on the ground that their rights could be obtained from Congress, but such hopes were not long entertained and the people have long since become a unit. There is not the slightest foundation for the assertion that a strong union party exists anywhere in the south and I really believe that if the North were to give the South a blank sheet

of paper and tell them to write the terms of reunion and promise by all the oaths we know to abide by it the south would refuse."[28]

A few days later, Rev. William Augustus White, rector of Spring Hill Parish in Salisbury, on the Eastern Shore, informed Bishop Whittingham that he was resigning his position:

> Should it be in your power to aid me in obtaining another care, or my people here in securing the services of a Pastor, it will be a great kindness to us all.
>
> The sad political struggle, now going on in the land, is the immediate cause of my leaving here. My thoughts have been directed to the Diocese of Tenn. as my future home, but I shall await intelligence which you may possibly be able, from a knowledge of my past career as a Priest, to furnish me of work still in your own Diocese. All that I desire is to preach "Christ and Him crucified," & to have no part or lot in the awful troubles wh. make our country tremble to its foundations.[29]

White remained in Maryland, serving as rector at My Lady's Manor in Baltimore County from 1862–1865.

The "Monument Street Girls" of Baltimore began meeting in 1861 to sew garments for boys headed for the Southern army. In 1904, one of the members, Rebecca Lloyd Shippen, recounted a July morning when H. Rozier Dulany arrived at the home of James Carroll with a tale about "Maryland, My Maryland," the song by James Ryder Randall memorializing the view of Lincoln's tyranny in Maryland:

> He came in very much pleased with some printed verses—that he had been handed on Baltimore St. and he proceeded at once to read them. My pen is inadequate to describe the enthusiastic reception, those verses met with, and when Mr. Dulany himself suggested they surely should be published as a song—it was seconded by all present. These verses were the lines written by Mr. James Randall.—and now known as "Maryland! My Maryland"—with one accord—Mr. Delany & these young girls present, proceeded to the piano—picking up—a "Yale Book of Callege Songs"—to see if any time there in could be found to sing these verses to. One—after another—was tried—without success—finally Mr. H. Rozier Dulany—exclaimed this one [?]—if we add "My Maryland" (for each verse of Mr. Randalls ended only with the word "Maryland".)—selecting the tune called—in this Book of Callege Songs—"Lauriger Horations" but it is the German—"Tannenbaum—O Tannenbaum"—This tune was found to [?] exactly with the added word—and forthwith—the Song—peeled forth from every voice—as "Maryland! My Maryland." It was then suggested by Mrs. William Henry Norris that it should be published as a *Song*—and asked Mr. Dulany if he could not have this done—but to this, Mr. Dulany gave a refusal saying—oh— thank you, no—Fort McHenry is too near.

The Monument Street Girls surreptitiously made clothes for their young male friends from Baltimore who had gone south. MdHS.

The group, having chosen a tune, walked to what was probably Monument Square and, near the statue of George Washington:

> And these enthusiastic young people, proceeded to sing it with a will—led by Mr. Delany and—General Washington on his Monument two squares away, might have heard the singing of this now well known song—had his ears been aught but marble.

One of the women offered to explore having the song published, explaining that her father, a Union man, could get her out of prison were she arrested. She took the verses and the Yale songbook to the Miller & Beacham music store on the west side of North Charles Street, just below Fayette. At the end of her letter, Shippen—"daughter of Mr. James M. Nicholson, who while a true Southerner, was opposed to secession—and was known as a 'Union Man'"—identifies herself as the woman in question.[30]

In August a police officer asked to be paid:

> Learning that the force of permanent Police of Balto. have rec'd their pay with some few exceptions, and being one of the number who has been overlooked, I would most respectfully ask of your Honor, the reason why I have not received my pay for the last month; by returning an answer to the above, you will confer a favor on your humble Servant.[31]

Benjamin Kirkwood, of the Seventh Maryland Infantry Regiment, told his brother that he was ready for action:

> I say if there can be no union by compromise there must be one by the force of arms, and I would like to go to have a hand in it for I begin to feel bloodthirsty just now.[32]

In the summer of 1861, the U.S. government authorized Francis Thomas to organize four regiments on the Maryland and Virginia sides of the Potomac River to protect commerce on the Chesapeake & Ohio Canal from the Monocacy (River) to the west boundary of Maryland; for the protection of the Canal and property and persons of loyal citizens of the neighbourhood.[33]

In late July, Edward Spencer still clung to secession hopes:

> Maryland is like a volcano, shivering already with the eruption about to take place—while old Scott stuffs himself upon pate's de Perigood, and Abe Lincoln cracks ribald jokes at the White House. Hurrah for the C.S.A.!
>
> The troops in our neighborhood make their presence continually felt. They beat some fellows very severely a week since—on Monday last they searched Ridgely's premises very strictly for arms, though the old man is a great Unionist. Clay gave them a wild goose chase about his barns, in the hay and straw, and they left in high dudgeon, finding nothing, although one of the famous Md. Guard muskets was standing in a corner of his bedroom. They took it to be a shot gun. This has made the young man more of a Secessionist than he ever was before.[34]

Mary Jane Kirkwood described to brother Robert war's divisive effect on their acquaintances:

> The secessionists at dogtown are very high they are allmost fit to bite themselves. Two of Sally Wright's Brothers has joined the Northern army and she does not like it, she is a great secessionist, one of them said he would not be home for three years or until every Rebel was killed. Henry Baker started this morning—he is bound for the union.[35]

On the same day, another sister, Hannah Kirkwood, sent Robert a letter that could bolster a soldier's morale:

> Well Robert you say you have had a little brush with the enemy I suppose you let them see that one Northern man was as good as two Southern you said I ought to been there to see them blow after the Battle I expect it would have been worth seeing, if you all stand your ground as well every time you will whip the south in a little time.

Hannah expressed delight at a young Unionist who muzzled some secessionists of the fairer sex:

> at a party at Mr. William Wileys he says he got in company with Miss Joanna Sterrett. She is a great secessionist she began to talk very smart about the Northern Army being such a set of cowards he says he just set to and shut her up so she could not say a word but got most awful mad. There is some very smart ladies in this neighbourhood any how some is almost to sharp for their own good.[36]

Spencer revealed the fissures in his relationship with Braddie's family over their conflicting views of the war:

What must I do about visiting you? Can I, *ought* I to come, consistently with my own pride, my own independence, my sensitiveness, my self-respect—and moreover, without danger of the visit contributing still more to my darling's discomfort and to our mutual embarrassments? You say "You would even now be received cordially, I am sure"—but what an "even now" that is—how significant—how pregnant with unpleasant suggestions.[37]

Recriminations and explanations related to April 19 circulated in Baltimore through the summer. In July, Mayor Brown told the City Council that

the facts, which I witnessed myself, and all that I have since heard, satisfy me that the attack was the result of a sudden impulse, and not of a premeditated scheme.[38]

Judge Richard Carmichael expressed his outrage to U.S. Senator James Pearce at Northern action toward the South:

For God's sake do, without a moment's delay, make your speech denouncing this unholy war, and the unconstitutional proceedings with which it has been gotten up, and conducted.

Do it for your friends, for your state, for your country and for your self.

As for myself I do not want a word. But for yourself and the body of your friends many are wanted; pouring upon the usurpers the piercing *fire* of truth.[39]

One business threatened to sue Baltimore City if not reimbursed for cannon seized by the police in the aftermath of April 19:

We have made several efforts to get our bill against the City collected but without success so far. Our Bill of $225 is for cannon taken by the Police on the 22nd of last April—from Mohler & Graff's yard, where we had them stored. Now we can prove by Mr. Mohler that the Police broke open his yard & took out the cannon—afterwards gave him a receipt for the guns. We can further prove that the City took and held possession of them and sent the same cannon to Messrs. Denmeads to have them mounted on carriages.[40]

In August, the *True Union* chided those who expected either quick Union victory or negotiated peace:

Some of our friends are pleasing themselves with the hope of a speedy peace, and even go so far as to say that in sixty or ninety days the war will be over. Would that we could cherish such a hope. From a careful survey of the whole subject, by the best lights at our command, we have been forced to the conclusion that, unless Providence shall interpose, this war will be one of great length, of unparalleled expense and awful suffering.[41]

On June 27, Marshal George P. Kane was arrested:

The arrest was made with suddenness and secrecy, no intimation of any such purpose having transpired. About two hours past midnight a company of soldiers composed of a portion of the Maryland Union volunteers from Camp Carroll, and some of the Pennsylvania regiment stationed on Federal Hill, were marched as quickly and quietly as possible to Colonel Kane's resident, No. 136 St. Paul street, where the Marshal was summoned to appear. He obeyed the summons, coming down to the door partially dressed, when he was at once seized and placed in a carriage, which guarded by soldiers, conveyed him shortly to Fort McHenry. On nearing the house, every avenue of approach to the dwelling was guarded, and as a measure of precaution, the military, as they marched through the city, seized all the police they met, and obliged them to accompany them.[42]

Elizabeth Blair Lee told her husband about the arrest and the consolidation of Union feeling in Baltimore:

Spent most of yesterday at John's—the arrest of Marshal Kane made him a little bitter but when he sees by to days papers—the Cannon Caps—guns & all sorts of warlike provisions found secreted in his cellars & etc I think he will feel that Genl Banks was right. As you supposed—it is evident that there was arrangements made by the Secessionists in Baltimore to rise & act if there was a reverse met by the federal troops—they are now disarmed & the City police will soon be reorganized & then it will be a safe city—The people by 2 thirds are unconditionally for the Union as the late vote shows—& the whole state is of the same way of thinking except St Mary Charles & Prince Georges This last County only gave 28 majority for Calvert The Secessionists expected to beat him by hundred but they dont know the people.[43]

A newspaper described two blockade runners in Baltimore. One was en route with approximately $2,500 worth of goods to North Point to rendezvous with rebels, while a second sought subterfuge in a funeral:

Mr. N. Williams, a coachmaker, No. 56 German street, was arrested about five o'clock on Sunday morning, September 8th, just as he about leaving his shop with his little daughter and driving a wagon and pair of horses. The police had learned several days before that the wagon had been ordered for certain parties, to be constructed with a false top and bottom, with a view of smuggling articles contraband of war for the Confederate forces. A strict watch was kept and the arrest made at the hour named, when it was supposed that Mr. Williams was about driving down to North Point to communicate with the party before mentioned, and to furnish them with arms for the expedition. On examination of the wagon, by first removing the oil cloth flooring, a recess was discovered about six inches deep, and in this were eighteen large navy revolvers, some gold lace and bullion, and a package of over one hundred letters addressed to various prominent business men who had formerly belonged to Baltimore and had gone south.

A hearse containing a coffin was driven across Light street bridge, and either from the irreverent manner of the driver of some other cause of suspicion, the funeral party was challenged by a sentinel, when the attendants, two or three in number, took to their heels and escaped arrest. On examination the coffin was found to contain a quantity of guns, pistols, percussion caps and other contraband articles.[44]

As state legislators gathered in Frederick during the second week of September for another special session, W. W. Glenn's diary recorded a wave of arrests by a federal government still anxious about Maryland's proclivities:

> I arose, breakfasted & went to my office. I soon heard the rumor of arrests. The Legislature was to meet in a day or two. All the Baltimore members had been dragged from their beds late in the night. Tom Hall, Editor of the South and Frank Howard as Chief Editor of Exchange were also arrested. The Members of a Legislature which had refused to arm the State and had advised non resistance were imprisoned on the Charge of planning the secession of the State. So much for the middle course. What folly in a revolution! These men were all taken to Fort McHenry. I found John Thomas, took my carriage and drove down. Many of my friends opposed my going and declared I would be arrested. They were very sadly frightened. My reply was "that if they wanted me, they would take me anyhow." In the fort we saw Col. Morris—in comman—but were allowed no communication with the prisoners, except a few words at a distance. We conveyed them some money through Morris.[45]

In August, Gen. John Dix, now the Union commander in Baltimore, outlined to Postmaster General Montgomery Blair the difficulties of shutting down Baltimore newspapers. Dix's letter included Blair's recommendation that "the Exchange, Republican and South should be suppressed. They are open disunionists. The *Sun* is in sympathy but less diabolical":

> I have received the letter of the postmaster of Baltimore with your indorsement in regard to the Exchange and other secessionist presses in that city. I presume you are not aware that an order for the suppression of these presses was made out in one of the Departments at Washington and in consequence of strong remonstrances from Union men in Baltimore was not issued. Under these circumstances it would not be proper for me to act without the authority of the Government. Any action by me without such authority would be improper for another reason that probably does not occur to you. The command of General McClellan has been extended over the State of Maryland. I am his subordinate

*This Unionist cartoon
parodied the leadership of
Jefferson Davis. MdHS.*

JEFF DAVIS.
TAKEN FROM LIFE.

and have corresponded with him on the subject. I cannot therefore act without
his direction. But independently of this consideration I think a measure of so
much gravity as the suppression of a newspaper by military force should carry
with it the whole weight of the influence and authority of the Government especially when the publication is made almost under its eye.

There is no doubt that a majority of the Union men in Baltimore desire the
suppression of all the opposition presses in the city but there are many—and
among them some of the most discreet—who think differently. The city is now
very quiet and under control though my force is smaller than I asked. There is
a good deal of impatience among some of the Union men. They wish to have
something done.[46]

As the number of arrests grew, John Fulton became incensed at the actions of federal authorities in Maryland:

Brutal outrages such as had never disgraced the soil of Maryland, and acts of
petty tyranny which any would, a twelvemonth before, have been ashamed to order or execute, were perpetrated without eliciting a word of public remonstrance

or denunciation from the "Union" party. Persons were dragged from the homes upon the mere order of some contemptible underling of the Government. The houses of citizens were invaded and ransacked in the search for arms, papers and flags; and oftentimes without even the pretext of an excuse for the outrage being vouchsafed to the occupants. Newspapers were denied the privilege of passing through the mails, and were finally suppressed by the arrest of their editors. Men and women were stopped on the streets and ordered to strip from their persons ribbons or scarfs, of which the colors were obnoxious. Nurses were borne off to the Station House for carrying in their arms babies wearing red and white socks. Free speech became an act of treason.[47]

Others also despaired:

> Every week we hear of some new encroachment on our liberties, they are now trying to control the Press—oh, what next?![48]

A Baltimorean beseeched Mayor Brown for employment—sending his son to City Hall after several letters from his wife had failed to bear fruit:

> I send my dear little boy to see you, this morning, with regret, to ask you, if you can not give me something to *do,* yet, my only hope is *upon you.* If you could see my dear dear little family, I am sure you would make some arrangement for me . . . I find I shall have to make application to the [?] association for aid . . . I can not see them starve, and, bare of clothing.[49]

In August, Edward Spencer told Braddie of disappointments—refraining from visiting her because of discomfort from her family's Unionist sentiments, "the miserable uncertainty of my own domestic affairs" and "the political condition of things, and especially of Maryland":

> I have never urged this hitherto—but anything—riot, civil war, burnings, murder, all desolation and misery, rather than the infamous servile misery of submitting like a whipt cur to the Lincoln dynasty. I love Maryland well, but I cannot and will not stay here with that shame resting upon us. I cannot and will not be the fellow citizen of men who so persistently lick the foot that spurns them. Our party is about to be reorganized under the august banner of Peace, and, as it is entirely essential for us to carry the fall election, I will submit to the disguise— but I am for war, ruthless war, if need be, till our rights are fully recognized.[50]

He proclaimed "I shall fling myself into the campaign with ardor"—and found another matter worthy of complaint:

> It is probably that Baltimore will be made a central military depot—large bodies of troops concentrated there, and the influence of large sums of money unscrupulously profited by.[51]

A few days later Spencer speculated on the repercussions of a Confederate advance for a Unionist Maryland:

> The indications now are of a speedy advance on the part of the Confederates towards Washington—and this promises us of Maryland a succession of untold horrors. If the Federal forces are driven back through our state they will ravage and lay waste with the ruthless fury of the Cossacks. There is no calculating, no imagining the horrors that will be heaped upon us. Baltimore I fear will be the signal victim of their revengeful hatred—indeed I am sure that our city will experience the utmost limits of their impotent and fury. Missouri has been rescued—Virginia is safe—*through war*—but poor old Maryland, which Hicks has been so anxious to *save*, is to be plunged into the profoundest depths of intolerable misery through him and his party—or else, to remain a conquered Yankee province. I begin to think of merciless revenge towards these authors of our ruin when I contemplate the position of affairs—and there are many, very many like me.[52]

The following week Spencer complained about the nomination of "Gus Bradford" for governor. Spencer believed himself "in imminent peril of arrest" and that "the Confederates intend an almost immediate advance into Maryland":

> The Federal army is terribly disorganized—they are not recruiting any new men scarcely—and many regiments are in such a state of insubordination that they dare not lead them into the field. This will bring about consequences in Maryland of such a character that no one can foresee what will happen to him individually. There is more to be dreaded from a *retreat* of the Federals through our State than from anything else—they will burn, ravage & destroy everything within their reach. Baltimore will suffer terribly—the hatred against it is malignant.[53]

He closed his letter with his feelings for his soon-to-be wife:

> Now, my love, about that visit. If nothing prevents, I will go to Baltimore on Friday next, and be in St. Michael's, and see my darling, on Saturday, Aug 24th. I shall make a *very* short visit, honey, for I must return by the boat on Wednesday. It is imperative that I shall be in our famous village on Thursday 29th. So make up your mind to have as much as possible of me and to give me every moment of your time. It is precious . . . and oh, in these terrible times a thousand fold more so, because I cannot say certainly when I shall see you again. The war may come among us and snatch me off in its whirlwind—or I may be in Fort Lafayette. There is no telling, so sweetest, let us resolve to make the most of our brief meeting. Love, pure joyous holy love shall crown us and fill and all the hours.[54]

Despite disapproval from the Harrison family, Edward and Braddie married in Philadelphia on November 25, 1861. In 1882, Braddie would die of tuberculosis, and

Edward would die two years later "of grief, overwork, heart failure—or all three, as the newspapers said."[55]

S. E. Horgewerff, a member of Grace Church in Elkridge Landing, Howard County, asked Bishop Whittingham for help in keeping the parish free of politics—including those of the rector, William G. Jackson:

> We are not to have the benefit of services in our church on Thursday a day of fasting & prayer appointed by the President, owing to the Political predgudices of our pastor. Could you not appoint some one to officiate for the congregation on the occasion? Apart from being deprived of the services it may have the effect of giving a political character to the congregation which would be unpleasant to the majority of its members. As I do not desire to have any unpleasant personal relations with my pastor & neighbor, while I consider it right that you should be informed of Mr. Jacksons intention, I desire that you will not mention my name, but consider this communication as confidential.[56]

The bishop replied the following day that "it is not in my power to appoint some one to officiate in Grace Church, as you suggest" and that he had written to Rector Jackson asking him to observe the day appropriately.[57]

Just before the 1861 gubernatorial election, the *Baltimore American and Commercial Advertiser* championed Unionist candidate Augustus Bradford:

> To-morrow is the election, the most important, beyond all comparison, that has ever occurred in the State. That any citizen can be indifferent to its tremendous issues seems impossible; for on one side or the other every one must have determined by this time to take his stand. That any in Maryland could hesitate in determining to stand by the Union seems the most marvelous condition of things possible, when we remember that eighteen months ago there was no more affiliation here with Nullification and Secession than there is now with the views of government held in the Celestial Empire. Presuming, however, amidst the marvels of the times, that there are some yet wavering in their allegiance amongst us, let us make to them another appeal to stand by the Government so long the pride of our people, so long the admiration of the nations of the earth.[58]

Another editorial, "The Hypocrisy of Secession," reminded readers of the government's repeated pledges not to interfere with slavery:

> But Maryland *will* be true to the traditions of her noble past. She will maintain her position; she will proclaim her persistent attachment to the Union. And there will come a day—mark it—when every citizen within her borders will blush for any proclivities he may have entertained for a heresy so destructive to peace, so

A Baltimore City election poster urged support for the proslavery Unionist Augustus Bradford for governor and Criminal Court Judge Hugh Lennox Bond. Bond would be a strong advocate for the rights of freed Maryland slaves. MdHS.

fraught with all that is evil. There will come a day, once more, when patriotism will again be in the ascendant, and men will recur with horror to the thought that they could have been untrue to the splendid system of free government already theirs, that it could be presumed to give place to a pitiful and imbecile Oligarchy.[59]

"A Few Practical Suggestions with Reference to the Election" exhorted voters to get themselves, and others, to the polls for election day on November 6:

To those who are anxious for a Union triumph in Maryland in the election at hand, let us urge a few practical suggestions as means to that end. That we have the strength there can be no shadow of doubt; but it must be *brought out.* Let no one, then, who is a recipient of the blessings of free government as dependent on the Union, fail to give *one day's work* in order to prove that he appreciates what the Union has done for him. The election will not carry itself. It demands true hearts and willing hands, and it is not sufficient to vote oneself; each ought to see that his neighbor votes also, if possible. There are always more of less of the lukewarm, or the careless, who would go to the polls and cast their votes with a little persuasion; and let all who can think of such within the bounds of their acquaintance be on the alert to urge them to the line of their duty. Then, too, there are the infirm, or those who may need a vehicle in order to vote. Let all such be provided for in this election, the most important ever known to us; let it not be said after it is over that any failed to exercise a privilege so vital to the preservation of free government. Let each also resolve *to vote early,* so as to have ample time afterwards to hunt up those who are derelict. Unless the day is freely given to the country, unless men rise in the morning determined to abate nothing of their exhortations until the last vote is secured, it will avail little or nothing to regret the result, should we come short of an overwhelming triumph.[60]

The newspaper portrayed the November 6 election in populist terms, with Maryland's salvation from secession coming from "the people":

> To-day, if every Union man, every patriot, in the State does his duty, will witness the political regeneration of Maryland, so successfully begun at the last election, confirmed by this. She will be finally saved from those deadly toils thrown around her by a treasonable conclave of legislators who sought to hand her over, despite her protests, bound hand and foot, to Jefferson Davis. All was ready for the horrible sacrifice; but a strong hand interposed, the people came to the rescue, and now, by their vote this day to be deliberately recorded, they must reaffirm their own decision, and they must endorse the action of the General Government. The argument is at last exhausted. Let to-day witness action. And let the sun as it goes down to-night shine upon countenances illumined and bright from within with that gladness which comes of a glorious victory achieved over the enemies of one's county.[61]

The paper took satisfaction at Bradford's overwhelming victory. While conceding that some opposition voters were prevented from voting and, in some cases, arrested, the editors claimed that suppression of Unionism on April 19 created a backlash that explained the outcome:

> The election for Governor and State offices yesterday passed off quietly and peaceably, though there was quite a number of arrests made on the charge of disloyalty, which prevented a full vote being cast by the opponents of the Union candidates. The intimidation caused by these arrests is to be regretted, as there has been no doubt at any time since the 19th of April that a large majority of the legal voters of the city are devoted to the preservation of the Union. The intimidation at the April election for the Legislature, which, sustained by the authorities of the city, effectively silenced the Union sentiment, lead yesterday to a desire for retaliation, which was, to a considerable extent, practiced in all the wards.
>
> The Judges, however, were all men of standing and character, and in most of the precincts Opposition judges were in attendance. In all other respects the election was a fair one, the greatest care being taken everywhere to prevent illegal voting.[62]

The Reverend Leonard J. Mills, rector of Zion Church in Beltsville, Prince George's County, reported to Bishop Whittingham shortly after taking his post that

> Having arrived so recently I am not able to say much of the Parish & its profile. Things look more encouraging than at first; & I trust that God will soon restore amity to a congregation that has been very much divided by the political troubles of the times.[63]

The tumultuous middle years of Maryland's Civil War brought systematic efforts to suppress dissent through arrests and imprisonment, consolidation of Unionism that further minimized likelihood of secession, federal and Confederate troops occupying parts of Maryland, and two battles on the state's soil (one still the single bloodiest day in American history). Troops—white and black, free and slave—were raised for the Union army through voluntary enlistments, national conscription passed by Congress in March 1863, and the establishment of the U.S. Bureau of Colored Troops later that year. The emergence of a radical, antislavery Union Party generated mounting pressure to end slavery in the state, and the state's slaveholders deprived themselves of a chance for government compensation by failing to devise a collective response to this new political dynamic.

In the wake of Lincoln's limited suspension of the writ of habeas corpus on April 27, 1861, along Maryland's railroad lines, the U.S. State Department that year assumed broad powers to arrest and imprison suspected dissidents in the state without charges or trial. (The president suspended the writ throughout the nation on September 24, 1862, two days after issuing his Emancipation Proclamation.) Marylanders were detained on the slightest suspicion of Southern sympathies—some were offered release in exchange for a loyalty oath, while others faced indefinite imprisonment with no charges. These circumstances underscored the strategic importance of Maryland for North and South. Southern leaders were quick to exploit Lincoln's extreme measures to hold the state in the Union, which provided fodder for Confederate propaganda that portrayed events in Maryland—beginning with the Northern "invasion" of April 19 and consequent presence of federal troops, arrests, military oversight of elections, and general suppression of civil liberties—as rationale for rebellion against a central government that would impede the right of a state to set its own course. The notion of Maryland as an occupied state, though, is misleading, as Union soldiers were permanently encamped only during the war's first year (along the Potomac River and outside Washington), and permanent military installations were in Baltimore and Annapolis only.

Though public officials and private citizens were detained throughout the North, the border states were replete with putatively Southern sympathizers who made their views known by their own public expressions, professions, prewar southern travel, or relatives and friends who had fled into the Confederacy. These individuals bore the wrath of federal officials determined to seize every advantage in suppressing the rebellion. Mark Neely found of the 509 military arrests of civilians in 1861 (where the home state of the detainee was known), 166, or 32.6 percent, were Marylanders.[1] This heavy federal hand on Maryland reflected both the importance of ensuring the state's loyalty and the imperative to thwart communications and smuggling through the state's many avenues south via the Potomac River, Chesapeake Bay, and Eastern Shore routes. When the Maryland legislature again met in Frederick in September 1861, the Secretary of War ordered the arrests of lawmakers, editors, and prominent citizens throughout the state suspected of disloyalty, including Henry May, a member of Congress. Though Lincoln may not have been aware of the arrest order when issued, he subsequently endorsed it and refused to provide Congress any details about the rationale for the arrests. Many Marylanders, including Baltimore's mayor, George W. Brown, and top police official George P. Kane—who, though jeopardizing their own safety to tamp down the violence against the Massachusetts troops on April 19, 1861, nonetheless had given federal authorities legitimate reason to suspect their allegiance—recorded their experiences at the hands of arresting officers and prison commanders. The diary entries of William Wilkins Glenn, a Baltimore lawyer and founding newspaper editor, vividly recount both his detentions and narrow escape from a police party sent to arrest him.

During this middle period, Marylanders as far east as Baltimore thrice confronted the fearful uncertainties introduced by large Confederate forces moving through the western part of the state. In September 1862, the northward advance of Lee's army—looking for fresh forage on Maryland and Pennsylvania soil—prompted Hagerstown bankers to send their reserves north to New York and city officials to move the post office to Chambersburg, Pennsylvania, while civilians jammed into railroad cars to escape what would become the carnage of Antietam. Nine months later Lee again passed through the state and into Pennsylvania, from which the Confederates retreated after their defeat at Gettysburg that sealed their fate. Both Maryland campaigns were grave disappointments to the Confederates, who fell short of military objectives and saw even hospitable western Marylanders refuse to embrace the Southern cause.

The Confederates on both occasions passed through Frederick, followed hours later by the Union army in pursuit. Diaries, letters, and newspaper dispatches recount the fortitude of the citizenry in dealing with enemy soldiers, followed immediately by the boisterous welcome showered on McClellan's forces. The Gettysburg campaign incited western Maryland and turned out alarmed Baltimore militiamen and citizens to dig entrenchments, erect barricades, and man fortifications to counter the movements of an enemy force that with a quick change of direction could have marched into the state's largest city. In the third Confederate invasion, a force under Gen. Jubal Early in July 1864 moved north from the Shenandoah Valley into Maryland. Following a Pyrrhic victory over a hastily assembled Union force along the Monocacy River south of Frederick, Early's troops executed an eastward turn to threaten the nation's capital that terrified nearby Baltimoreans, who set about fortifying the city with more than five hundred laborers who worked for twenty days for a wage of $1.50 per day.[2]

Unionist sentiment solidified in Maryland as the war ground on. Recruiting grew to include black men. A Union Club in Baltimore was organized in spring 1863 and quickly formed a militia, and a variety of municipal and statewide elections—increasingly presided over by pro-Union election judges as soldiers became less ubiquitous at polling places—produced Unionist victories. The state legislature in March 1862 passed a wide-ranging "Treason Bill," which threatened death or imprisonment for lending aid and comfort to the enemy, engaging in acts of rebellion, belonging to organizations advocating secession, displaying "to public view what is commonly designated the Secession Flag, with a view and intent to excite seditious feelings," and inducing others to engage in any of these activities.[3]

Abraham Lincoln would capture 54 percent of the Maryland vote in his November 1864 reelection—a vast improvement from his 1860 showing in the state, when only a small percentage of the state's 54 percent Unionist vote had gone to him. Contrary to some claims, the soldier vote did not carry the state for Lincoln in 1864—subtracting his 2,800 soldier votes (to George McClellan's 321) from his total would have left him a margin of just over 51 percent.

Emancipation in the District of Columbia in April 1862 had made the nation's capital a magnet for runaway Maryland and Virginia slaves, while Union army camps in and near Maryland attracted increasing numbers of escaped, or "contraband," slaves. The risks taken by these men and women, and the recruitment of blacks into the Union army beginning in 1863, further undermined the state's crumbling artifice of bondage. Slavery throughout this middle period edged closer toward the abyss, pushed by black and white citizens alike who, by exploiting the cracks in the old Maryland slaveholder alliance, ensured its collapse.

chapter five

1861

Early in the year federal troops apparently tried to stop "Mrs. T." from smuggling Southern-bound contraband aboard a Chesapeake Bay steamer:

> Being a good friend to the South, she carried, to be smuggled across the river, a lot of gray flannel for soldiers' shirts, quilted in her skirts, a quantity of letters in an india-rubber bag, and some packages of quinine, morphine and strychnine, which last she had made into a "bishop" and hid around her waist under her dress. When the boat had gone a few miles, the stewardess requested the attendance of all the ladies in the private cabin. They assembled there, but Mrs. T., suspecting something, took the precaution to drop her bag of letters overboard. Sure enough, when the ladies were all in the private cabin, the doors were fastened, and some females attached to the boat announced that the ladies were all to be searched for contraband goods. In the confusion that followed Mrs. T. found opportunity to break the string of her packet of medicines, and not knowing what to do with it, took the lid off the water-cooler and dropped it in. Hardly had she done this, when she remembered that there was strychnine and morphine enough in it to kill five regiments. Half desperate she turned the spiggot and drew off all the water into the pan for the drippings. In the mean time the search proceeded, so rigorously that even the ladies' stockings were pulled off. Luckily the gray flannel was not detected. In the midst of it all, somebody grew thirsty, and finding the cooler empty, calls for water. When a pitcher was brought, the thirsty individual presented a tumbler and received what she wanted directly from the pitcher, and the stewardess poured the remainder into the cooler without looking in. Mrs. T. found another chance, and drew off all the water again.
>
> The search being ended and nothing discovered, the ladies were free to go where they pleased; and Mrs. T. when unobserved, withdrew the perilous packet from its hiding place and as it was saturated with water, threw it overboard. The rest of her journey she accomplished without molestation.
>
> But the bag of letters was brought up by the tide and drifted ashore at Canton, and a boy found it and carried it to his Employer. The latter was, happily, a good Southerner and finding a letter addressed to a name which was also the family name of a gentleman that he knew in the city, took him the whole package and left them with him.[1]

C. C. Shriver described the sight of troops from Maine on Baltimore's streets:

The weather has been very unpleasant all of this week, These soldiers on Federal Hill are having a mighty unpleasant time, A great many of them are now, on the street and almost always look as though they were never clean; but I suppose it is almost impossible for them to keep clean as they have no water over there, I have been over to see them drill, and must say they get through with all their evolutions, very well—

I just now saw up on Lombard st, a company from Maine, they were passing thro, at double quick time, as though they were needed down in Va. You ought to see what a big Company like 1000 men make. They fill the streets for about four squares, and the clatter of their feet and the noise of the crowd following is quite exciting. This company had a pretty good Band with them, and played as they marched. Poor fellows a good many of them will never return I am sure, Tis by George an awful sight to see so many men with muskets, marching down to kill a fellow's best friends. I wish I were 100,000 men with myself—if I could not clean Maryland of the *blackguards* there is no hereafter—Aust I can't even write about this war without getting provoked, it seems to me.[2]

In June, a Northern soldier encamped at Elkridge Landing, southwest of Baltimore, supplied a taste of his duties on election day in Baltimore:

The whole regiment went to Baltimore the 13th it was election there and they expected truble there so we went down and stayed all night. We marched round the city a little in the afternoon and frightened the women half to death.[3]

Van gave more details the next day to "Friend Charley":

Our regiment went down to Baltimore on the thirteenth, it was election day and they expected some disturbance but every thing passed of quitly. We went down in the morning and stayed untill the next morning and bivouac on the ground in an open field in the form of a square with the flying artiliary in the center with us out side as a guard some of the horses broke loose and run over the men. I brought the whole regiment onto their feet in a moment they all sprung for their guns thinking they were attack.

Charley I wish that you could see about a hundred soldiers in a crowd sleeping in a cold night like that. They all crowd up to each other for the closer they lay the warmer. they look like a pack of hogs than any thing else with their blankets around them. On the afternoon the day we got there we left the ground where we had stopped and went into the city of Baltimore and commenced to drill. we went on the double quick down the streets with the artiliary between the wright and left wing we went sofast that the horses went upon a gallop to keep up to us. Just before we reached one of the cross streets in the midst of the City the order came for the infantry to halt and the artiliary to forward and the guns were sent down the three streets right, left, and in front then one company was datatched to each gun to protect it and some thrown out as scurmishers and the rest were held as a reserve It sounded splendid And it was a good sight to see this rush along over the pavements with sabers clashing and to hear the rattle and roar of the artiliary. As they galloped along the linch pin of one of the gun carriages came and went the wheels and away on to side walk parting the people right and left.[4]

Edward Spencer was unimpressed by federal troops in Baltimore:

The Yankees are terribly afraid of Baltimore—witness that valorous N.Y. regiment, pigeon-shooting at the Camden depot the other day. They have Fort McHenry with 1700 regulars—Fort Carrol with a garrison—and 8000 men and 24 cannon in the city—half our arms and all our powder seized—yet they are afraid of us—make continual arrests—find out innumerable bogus conspiracies—& close all the bar-rooms for fear of excitement.[5]

In July, Daniel Thomas wrote to his sister Julia about his premonition of what may have been the Battle of Manassas and his view of troops exercising adjacent to Mrs. Foy's boardinghouse, where Thomas had recently moved:

I feel very confident that there must be a big fight in a few days at farthest, and when it does take place look out for scampering on the part of the Northerners.

I celebrated *the* 4th most delightfully in Harford County at the house of Mrs. McHenry where the Miss Robinsons are passing the summer. I went up Wednesday; Miss Margie McKim & Carvel Hall had gone up the day before, so that we had quite a large party. Leaving here a little before 10 in the morning I got there by Railway & stage at 2½ and returned on Friday. The contract between that place & this was very marked & agreeable.

Yesterday & today have been the two hot days of the season; today particularly it is fearfully warm.

I have soldiers all about me now. They eat & sleep in the Court House & go through their exercises every morning in the Court House yard just under my window.[6]

The *Leonardtown Beacon* reported the presence of federal troops in towns in St. Mary's and Charles counties:

On yesterday morning, about sunrise, our town was favored with another Federal visitation. About 200 marines and sailors, under the command of Major Reynolds and Captain Budd, were landed from the steamers Freeborn, Baltimore and Resolute, and entered the town and made a thorough search of the dwellings and adjacent premises. They told the old tale, about having received

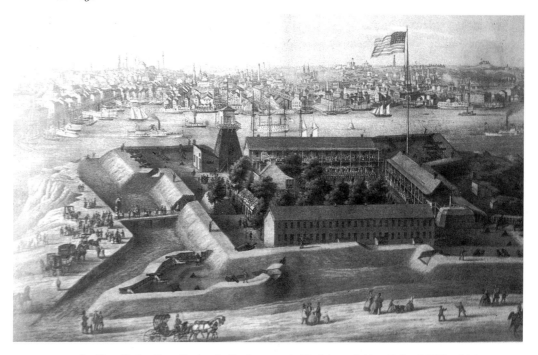

In May, Union Gen. Benjamin Butler occupied Baltimore's Fort Federal Hill, which overlooked the city from the south. Pratt Lib.

direct information that cannon, rifles and other contraband articles were concealed here, and stated that information to that effect had been received on yesterday. The search, as heretofore, resulted in disclosing nothing. The officers and men behaved well, and, after remaining about an hour with us, returned to the steamer and took their departure.[7]

Robert Kirkwood wrote to his brother about his duty near Sharpsburg:

I don't feel very well at present. I have a slight touch of the diariea it is the first attack that I have had since I inlisted but it has been a general complaint among the troops all summer but I am able to do duty but I hope when these few lines reach you they will find you all enjoying good health four Companies of us have moved about 16 miles down the river within 3 miles of Sharps Burg it is about 2 miles long and about as nice a little town as I ever was in. We are encamped close to the river and have a full view of Shepardstown it is on a high piece of ground.

Kirkwood described an encounter with the enemy:

A company of rebel cavalry quartered (across the river) it is full of Secesionists about 20 of them came down to the side of the river and fired us as we was washing in the canal. We did not leave. Captain Willson and about a dozen more came down with their muskets. Captain fired the first at them they started and run like white heads we fired about a dozen shots and wounded one of them by shooting him through the thie & they are actualy too cowardly to live they say themselves that they would sooner fight any other rigiment than ours these Baltimoreans are too bloodthirsty they say.[8]

Late in August George Carpenter, confined to his home with "the bilious fever," speculated on the motives of federal troops who, he claimed, destroyed his boats that ferried cargo on the C&O Canal. He urged his friend Robert Spear to confer with friends in Lincoln's cabinet:

I wrote you in reply to your cash, (long enough ago to have heard from you in reply-) Saying that I sawn no difficulty in you shipping your timber. I now think the only difficulty will be with the Federal Government, They have become very exacting—indeed oppressive on the river—day before yesterday they distroyed all my boats whither serviceable or otherwise. They assigned no reasons—other than general orders. What was the reason—or what the purpose I cannot conjecture—unless it be to drive the people of Md. into open revolt in order that they May have an untrameled excuse for our entire subjugation.[9]

Franklin Wilson described the scene in the city shortly after the events of April 19:

Our streets for a few days swarmed with men in uniform, and with guns & cannon. For a time I thought Baltimore was doomed, and the threats of the infuriated North were fearful. After a time however a calm succeeded, and thousands of soldiers have not only passed through, but have encamped here. Some of the camps are in full view of my house, and the sounds of the drums & brass band are daily, almost hourly heard.

Wilson was angry at the government's suppression of civil liberties in Maryland and worried that rumored atrocities in Virginia and Missouri might occur in Kentucky and Maryland:

The President on his own notion has increased the army and Navy, suspended the *habeas corpus,* overthrown our city police-system, and imprisoned the Police Commissioners without warrants or indictment. People are arrested and imprisoned everywhere without law, papers interdicted and suppressed, and the display of white and red badges or emblems of any kind in this city summarily stopped. Even ladies' ribbons, children's dresses and baby's socks have been seized by the police under this ridiculous and despotic order![10]

The Maryland Club, founded in 1857, was a hub for socially prominent Baltimore businessmen. In September, Gen. John A. Dix ordered a raid of the club:

General Butler threatened the city with the Fort Federal Hill's heavy guns. MdHS.

The Maryland Club House, the social resort of an association of gentlemen, situated on the northeast corner of Franklin and Cathedral streets, was searched yesterday morning by the Provost Marshal's police. The search was for arms, it is supposed, but none were found. The reconnoissance of every department was most complete, and was acquiesced in by the occupants very willingly, as they knew the result would vindicate the house.[11]

William Russell of the *London Times* recounted in his memoirs how the troops

searched every room, took up the flooring, even turned up the coals in the kitchen and the wine in the cellar. Such indignities fired the blood of the members, who are, with one exception, opposed to the attempt to coerce the South by the sword. Not one of them but could tell of some outrage perpetrated on himself or on some members of his family by the police and Federal authority.[12]

Samuel W. Smith, the president of the Maryland Club who had two sons in the rebel army, protested:

I cannot permit this occasion to pass without expressing my sense of the insult which has been put upon each member of the club—and of the outrage upon legal rights that it involves.[13]

Under the heading "Contraband in a Coffin," a Baltimore newspaper reported a discovery by troops at a checkpoint:

> On Monday afternoon (9 Sept) the sentinels of the Second Maryland Regiment, on guard at the Long Bridge, on the Anne Arundel shore of the Patapsco, had their attention attracted to the approach of a funeral procession, consisting of a somber hearse and attendants. The first sentinel allowed the hearse to pass, but the second stopped it, and an examination revealed a lot of muskets and ammunition concealed in the coffin. The attendants escaped, but the hearse and horse were captured.[14]

Dix's worries over disloyal elements extended to Carroll County and slaveholding Eastern Shore counties, as recounted in a September report to McClellan, who approved Dix's plan to act:

> There are several companies in Caroline, Queen Anne, and Carroll Counties under arms once or twice a week drilling. They are composed exclusively of secessionists, and are armed with rifled muskets. I have not been able to ascertain whether they are organized in every instance under the laws of this State, but it makes no difference. If they are, they are acting in violation of the order of the governor, who called on them some months ago to give up their arms. If they are unauthorized organizations, they ought to be broken up. If you approve of the suggestion, I will send a few policemen, with a competent military force, from 50 to 100 men in each case, and take their arms from them. I know the governor approves the measure, and I propose to consult him in each case before I act. We can get a few hundred arms of the best quality, and take them out of the hands of men of the worst character.[15]

Baltimorean Virginia Warner apologized to Elizabeth Patterson Bonaparte for her lack of correspondence, complaining that she was the only loyal member of her family, "compelled, as I am, to dwell in so large an insane asylum as Baltimore is at present":

> we who are loyal suffer most & each day to me is so sad and sorrow-laden that I have often to seek my bed from utter frustration of my nervous system. I sometimes think that I could bear up more bravely if my husband was loyal, but himself & children having been carried away with the "fashionable heresy" my daily meals are seasoned alternately by the bitterest denunciations of our government & by the most alarming reports of the near approach of their grand leader Beauregard with his legions, who are coming as they say to free downtrodden Balt.[16]

Both armies used manned "war" balloons to monitor enemy troop movements. General Dix offered Gen. Henry Lockwood in Cambridge, on the Eastern Shore, a "Steamer Balloon" for use in disrupting southward commerce and hostile militia:

The cover of the September 7, 1861, Harper's Weekly *showed a stylish Baltimore woman confidently striding past Union soldiers around Monument Square. The legend read, "A Female Rebel in Baltimore—An Everyday Scene."* Harper's Weekly/MdHS.

I send you the Steamer Balloon, Capt. Kirwan, which is placed at your disposal for the purpose of aiding you in breaking the commercial intercourse, with the confederate States of which the Eastern Shore of Maryland furnishes the material. You have, as I suppose, ere this taken measures to seize all merchandize brought from Delaware & Salisbury by rail and destined to Virginia—With aid of the Balloon you may intercept much of that which finds its way down the Chesapeake by water. I trust be able to confine this illicit traffic to very narrow limits.—

It is believed that the Balloon will also be of essential use in sending to different points the forces necessary to disarm such companies of Militia or such unauthorized military bodies as are training with intentions notoriously hostile to the government. The duty is one of the greatest delicacy, and requires the utmost prudence and discretion. It is not doubted that numbers of individuals on the Eastern Shore of Maryland have been led into the support of disloyal measures by gross misrepresentations of the views and intentions of the Government. While the purpose you have in view should be steadily maintained and carried out with inflexible firmness, those who have been deceived and misled, instead of being confirmed in their prejudices and driven hopelessly off by harshness on our part, should, if possible, be reclaimed by kind treatment, and convinced of their error by correcting the misapprehensions under which they labor. If, in spite of all efforts to induce them to discontinue their acts of hostility to the Government, they persist in carrying on correspondence with the enemy and in giving him aid and comfort, they should be arrested and sent to Fort McHenry; but unless a case of extraordinary urgency should occur, I trust it may not be necessary to make an arrest without first consulting me. I have full authority from General McClellan to act in all cases.

You will bear in mind that we are on the eye of an election in Maryland of vital importance. The preservation of this State is indispensable to the safety of the capital. It is not doubted that all your measures will be so tempered with discretion as to give strength to the cause of the Union; but while all the just rights even of those who are disloyal should be respected, they should be made to feel that no act of open hostility to the Government will be tolerated for a moment.[17]

Leonidas Dodson recorded his son's interactions with Union soldiers in Easton:

We have been so long accustomed to the presence of U.S. Soldiers in our midst that they cease to attract any considerable attention I was amused yesterday to see my little Son, running to school, and working his way on the pavement through a file of soldiers passing the side arms of soldiers in his dodging between them, dear little boy he is not, (and it is well it is so) aware of the fearful crisis that is upon us, which is now threatening the peace of our State as well as the permanency of our national government.[18]

In November, as the federal authorities monitored polling stations in Baltimore City, Maryland voters went to the polls to fill offices that included election of Unionist Augustus W. Bradford as governor:

Throughout the city, as soon as the polls were opened, the Federal police began to make arrests, and continued until all the police stations were filled to repletion. The charges upon which they were arrested were disorderly conduct, holding treasonable tickets near polls, using treasonable language, and attempting to pollute the ballot box by offering to vote treasonable (democratic) tickets, while a few were charged with having been concerned in the affray of the 19th of April last, and others with having subsequent to that time taken up arms to prevent the passage of Federal troops through the city. Several of those arrested were charged with having been in the army of the Confederate States, and re[t]urned to the city for the purpose of participating in the election. In several instances candidates for magistrates and constables were arrested and sent to the police station, and some others were arrested because they declined to take the oath of allegiance to the Federal Government.[19]

Also that month a delegation of prominent Baltimoreans complained to President Lincoln about the poor state of business induced by the war. In his reply, Lincoln commended their election of Bradford and promised that the "wishes for a fair participation by the mechanics and laboring men of Baltimore in the benefits of supplying the Government with materials and provisions" would "be referred to the proper Departments":

> I thank you for the address you have presented to me in behalf of the people of Baltimore. I have deplored the calamities which the sympathies of some misguided citizens of Maryland had brought down upon that patriotic and heretofore flourishing State. The prosperity of Baltimore up to the 19th of April last, was one of the wonders produced by the American Union. He who strangles himself, for whatever motive, is not more unreasonable than were those citizens of Baltimore who, in a single night, destroyed the Baltimore and Ohio Railroad, the Northern Pennsylvania Railroad, and the railroad from Baltimore to Philadelphia. From the day when that mad transaction occurred, the Government of the United States has been diligently engaged in endeavoring to restore those great avenues to their former usefulness, and, at the same time, to save Baltimore and Maryland from the danger of complete ruin through an unnecessary and unnatural rebellion.
>
> I congratulate you upon the declaration which the people of Baltimore and Maryland have made in the recent election, of their recent approbation of the federal government, and of their enduring loyalty to the Union. I regard the results of these elections as auspicious of returning loyalty throughout all the insurrectionary States.[20]

In December, "An old Correspondent" in Baltimore, suspecting widespread disloyalty in Maryland, advised Secretary Seward of same, suggesting he watch espe-

Federal troops searched for rebels in November 1861. This scene may be near Annapolis, with the state capitol on the hill in the background (not shown). Harper's Weekly/Pratt Lib.

cially Congressman Henry May, who "with other rebels were loitering about the city, and took a private boat and went down the river and around Fort McHenry taking observations":

> I fear too much confidence is placed in the loyalty of Baltimoreans. I am sure that the rebel spirit here if not closely watched is as dangerous as ever; that many persons professing loyalty are base traitors to their country, and unfortunately some few such are kept in office under the Government. I have been a close observer and have had some opportunities to know. I have been engaged since April last in attending to the wants of soldiers, carrying water and such like and nothing else. About the 19th April last I with others were threatened with violence, but I told them publicly on that day and at the risk of violence that the Stars and Stripes would be perpetuated, and that the time would come when many of them would be hung, and that I was a candidate for hangman general, and as I was one of the number who voted for Abraham Lincoln I found there was no chance for anything else in Baltimore, consequently I urge my claims on the Government.[21]

1862

John Donnell Smith left Baltimore on a vessel steaming south to Richmond. Once there he smuggled a letter via an imprisoned captain about to be exchanged, describing to his sister how his boat, carrying "contraband cargo," was grounded as it evaded federal gunboats, forcing the crew to make its way through southern Maryland on foot before being rescued by a Confederate vessel:

> We walked half a mile, and came across a negro cabin. The negro guided us to his Master's house, whose name was Langley. We had on the way a good deal of conversation with the Boy about all sorts of matters; for instance, how far it might be to the nearest Camp, who was in command; whether his Master was a good Southern man, whether he could hire us a wagon etc. At length something, I forget exactly what, started our suspicious; and we discovered that we were *not in Virginia but in St. Marys Co. Maryland.* I could not believe it at first, and it was not until we had roused up & questioned Langley, that I permitted myself to believe I was the victim of such a stupid and fatal blunder. Langley refused to open his house to us, or even to take in the lady, or give any assistance. The Capt had got into the Potomac, supposing he was still in the Bay, & mistook the Land mark on his right hand for the Virginia shore. We had landed I suppose about four miles from Point Lookout. The negro conducted us to a house nearer to the place of our landing, where lived a Mr. Jones. We found him in no wise more civil than his neighbor. I appealed to him to suffer the Lady at least to pass the night in the Cabin of one of his negro's. he said he would not turn her out. The whole county was occupied by the troops & the people were in a state of abject terror. We returned to our comrads on the beach, and you can imagine their consternation at the dismal report.[22]

In January, Baltimorean Unionist Dr. Harvey Colburn congratulated his son, Rev. Edward Colburn, pastor at Trap Church in Harford County, on the birth of his son, offering to "not trouble you with advice about a name for the child beyond saying that if you should contemplate calling him Jeff., that you omit not to add Beelzebub." Dr. Colburn expressed his lack of enthusiasm for John Bell, the Constitutional Union candidate in 1860, and believed secession inevitable regardless of the outcome of the presidential election:

> I was sorry to hear from your mother that you entertain so bad an opinion of Mr. Lincoln. You know very well that he was not my choice, and that I worked for the Union nominees; but think for one moment what a predicament we should be in if we had elected Mr. Bell. The same difficulties would have occurred, & he could not have resisted them as is evident from his backing down so soon. The Breckenridge party denounced him as an abolitionist, (as the Democrats

did Mr. Clay,) and the leaders were determined on secession no matter who was elected. They had been concocting the movement for ten years, and Jeff. Davis, as Secretary of War under Pearce, commenced sending the largest quantities of arms & ammunition South.

Colburn's view of Lincoln was typical of many Maryland Unionists:

> Mr. Lincoln said some things on his way to Washington that I regretted; but every man has his weaknesses, his foibles, & his faults.
>
> Look at the circumstances under which he came into office, and if he were not possessed of much talent, & great decision of character, we should have been completely broken down months ago.
>
> By the 1st of March we shall probably find the rebel army is nearly or quite broken up, and when that difficulty is settled I think that neither England or France will be over anxious to pick a quarrel with us.

He implied that the president had won him over:

> I have come to think of Mr. Lincoln as a conservative man, good old Whig, and of undoubted honesty, combined with excellent practical talents. He is somewhat singular; but faithful.
>
> So much to endeavor to induce you to open your eyes wide enough to see the good points of our President—the President of the U. States.[23]

Farmer John M. Buchanon wrote to his son Horace from Ellerslie, near Cumberland, in western Maryland, about Union hospitals and troops—and the dramatically increased prices of hay, wheat, oats, gathering beef, flour, and corn:

> Cumberland is crambed full of soldiers, and by far the best dressed men, and the finest looking men I have seen since they War commenced, is the Illinois 39th Regt. I was in town last Saturday. A call was made for troops to go to New Creek, in Virginia—and in one hour, the Illinois soldiers, mustering more than one thousand strong, with a full band of musick, with their Rifles on their shoulders and their knapsacks on their backs, were on their march to meet the Southern thieves and Cutthroats.
>
> The Belvedeir Hall, the Barnum Hotel, the National Hotel, on the corner of Baltimore and Mechanic streets—Doct. James M. Smith's Dwelling house, Knost's tavern house opposite the Catholic church, and many other houses, are all turned into Hospitals, for the Poor sick Union soldiers—and not less than 30 or 40 other houses are used as Barracks for the soldiers. Notwithstanding so many men are quartered in Cumberland, and so many Teams and Cavalry horses are kept there, times are very bad, money is extremely scarce

In the letter, he apologized to Horace for not sending money and revealed his fealty to country:

> Mr. Gordon is still confined at Fort Warren. I very much pity his little family. He could no doubt, get released, if he would take the oath required. Cousin Kate is very spunky and says a great many very hard things of Mr. Lincoln and his friends. But I would rather be called anything before any one should call me a Rebel and a traitor to my Government.[24]

Horace received a letter from his thirteen-year-old sister revealing the divisions in the Buchanon family:

> I am now going to school to Mr. Kriebaum's. I like him very much as a teacher and then he a good secesh. Sissy N is an awful secesh. She is abusing the Yankees awful, she calls them thieves, murderes and every thing else that is bad. I am a secessionist myself. I think his *satanic majesty* will have a good time with Yankees, for I know when they die they will go there. They carry on high here steal every thing they can lay there fowl hands on.[25]

Second Lt. George F. Young, stationed at a camp near Sandy Point in Charles County, Maryland, was a member of Company G, Second Regiment, known as the "Excelsior Brigade." Young, whose real name was revealed to be Joseph Hill, was charged with "Conduct unbecoming an Officer and a Gentleman" for allowing his wife

> to keep near the encampment of the 2nd Regt. in the house of George H. Waters on Sandy Point, a kind of Sutlers Store for the sale of whiskey etc. etc. in gross violation of General Order No 12 Head Quarters, Hookers Division dated December 26 1861; and this Said "Mrs. Young" has sold her whiskey to both Officers and Privates, causing great rioting and disorder in the encampment.[26]

After George Steuart joined the Confederate army, Union troops seized his estate at Union Square, in West Baltimore, and named it "Camp Andrew" for Massachusetts Gov. John Andrew. In February, a Massachusetts soldier described the duty to a cousin in Salem:

> We are nicely quartered on a high hill situated on the west of Baltimore formerly owned by Gen. Stewart now of the Rebel Army and the property is now confiscated. There are about 36 acres in the field and a house and out buildings and it must have been a very nice place before the troops went in there. It is the same place that the Eighth were and the Fourth Penn—so it is an old stand. The weather is very mild and there has been no snow hardly this winter and it is very muddy & raing most all the time. We have got Barracks now which we built and I tell you we have nice times in them dancing and playing Checkers most of the

time as we do not have much drilling this winter. We are on the left of the Regt and drill as Skirmishers.

We have had the misfortune to lose 6 of our Co since its formation one in Lynnfield and 5 in Baltimore all of the Typhoid Fever but we have only one dangerously sick he has the Lung Fever. The Vollunteers that go for three years do not have the privelidges that the State Militia had the Officerrs are too overbearing and think themselves more that human beings about all of them have been under arrest and all of them had ought to be.

I have been sick twice but am well now and enjoying the best of health better than I did shoemaking. We have not had any fighting nor do not expect to here but we did expect it when we went down to the Eastern Shore but the rebels scattered all ways when the Union troops made their appearance.[27]

W. W. Glenn noted the reaction to news that Fort Donelson, a Confederate stronghold in Tennessee, had fallen:

Of course there was great excitement among the loyal citizens of the North and in Baltimore, where loyalty was at a much higher premium, than in the Northern cities, on account of its scarity, there was a great display of flags. A party of roughs went into the News Sheet office and ordered the flag to be put out.[28]

Samuel Streeter, the "Military Relief Agent" for Maryland, reported that he

attended a session of the City Council, went to a military ball, and attended a meeting of the Executive Committee of our Union Relief Association. To night, Mrs. [S] and I are enjoying a quiet cosy *séance,* at home, and you are getting the benefit, if it can be so called, of the unusual circumstances.

But war was not far out of mind:

We are looking anxiously now, towards the line of the Potomac. An advance is to be made, and if the confederates stand their ground, there will be a tremendous battle. The plan is, to crowd in upon them on every side, and by vigorous and concentrated blows to crush out the rebellion. I believe it can and trust in God, it will be done.[29]

In February, a woman in Hancock, a town in western Maryland, described to her cousin the devastation in her town, from the troops of both armies:

All is sad around us, war, sickness, and death in the last four weeks; there has been sixteen corps passed our house, besides a number of persons in the country and soldiers. The hand of affliction hath laid heavily upon Jimmie D—death entered his household and bereft him of his dear *Jennie;* she was an interesting child—it was a sad sad affliction, yet she is now a little angel taken from the evil

Jarvis U.S. General Hospital, on the west side of Baltimore, one of many hospitals in the city. Pratt Lib.

to come: it is our duty when death comes, to bow in humble submission to him who entireth the annels of Heaven and among the children of men.

Our town is very muddy; we have had almost perpetual snow and rain for the last month—the streets are impassible for ladies—just go to the doors. The streets are lined with Northern Soldiers, and those who are southerners are in great danger. I suppose you read an account of the condition Hancock is in: some families are not able to get their houses—there is great complaint among persons—Mr. Henderson's house is all torn every way, not any fence around the yard and soldiers still in,—not a cent of rent do they pay: it is the house where your Pa and Ma lived. The church has everything burnt around it but that in front; windows out, doors open: a great many persons say they would be afraid to go in it, as the wall is cracked. No one in town preaches, as all the churches are occupied. You would hardly believe your eyes if you would visit here again. Genl. Williams promises us that he will see us paid for what we have lost; if we get the money all well and good, but I am afraid we may look for it when we see it; as I received a letter from Washington stating there was not one cent of silver or gold in the Treasury: nothing but paper money: if we get that I will be glad as Mr. B. has lost a great deal. The confederates burned his store across the river. Captn. Russell broke his store open on this side the night the Northern troops had to run to Maryland.[30]

In Poolesville, on the Maryland side of the Potomac River, J. V. Van Ingen described the federal presence in the area:

Poolesville & its neighborhood has been for a year a region of Camps. Galloping up and down the river by country road or on canal bank, striking up into the hills & traversing the plantations & farms. Every where the deserted log hut, and the tattered remnants of tents in clustered villages or scattered hamlets meet the eye—& surprize by the strangeness, please by the picturesque transformations & then shock & sadden by the desolation which fratricidal ambition has wrought. The overlooking eminences near the river are crowned by blockhouses, of no mean proportion, into which the [?] oak forests have been transformed.

Van Ingen described war's impact on the landscape:

The log-hutted encampments are very fine—and so well built that a little finishing would readily convert them into villages for rural population, or into an apparatus for education. They are now most of them deserted & abandoned—and the process of dismantling & demolition transforming these sites into rail stacks for the enclosure of the open & defenseless farms.

Here at Poolesville the broken fragments of many regiments, and a few companies of our 8th N.Y., either fill the hospitals or are guarding the public property accumulated from the occupation & departure of so many successive regiments.

And his "circuit," probably as a minister or medical aide:

My own circuit is from Poolesville camp & hospital to 7th Michigan (3 miles below, toward river) to Edward's Ferry—then 12 miles up—& 12 miles down—and back again. You may be sure I enjoy it—and bless God for the privilege.

Socially—our officers—and every commissioned officer whom I have conversed with, are conservative men—and hence have formed very pleasant & healing bonds of friendship with the principal inhabitants. The result is matter of congratulation and thanksgiving to God. I have embraced every opportunity for visiting both gentry & plain people, over my district dining with them by invitation with our officers, and discussing all topics with the utmost freedom, not excepting religion in the Church.[31]

B. Adelman lived at Mrs. Parkinson's boarding house, at Green and Saratoga Streets in Baltimore, where his $3 weekly rent included meals and washing. His

Northern troops posed at Relay House, the rail junction nine miles west of Baltimore that they occupied in May 1861, giving commanders control over east, west, and southbound rail traffic. MdHS.

1862 diary recorded taking girls "on the horse-cars" to Druid Hill Park and Washington Gardens. His May 12 entry blended national events and the minutiae of daily life:

> Union people quite elated. Southerners little dejected but still firm. On 10th & 11th great numbers of wounded reached the city some few confeds but great majority Federals from Williamsburg Federals within 27 miles of Richmond Fix up Garrett. Fix muff boxes get dubbin and grease shoes Dr. Rich send box to Cole's send after Miss Duvals' Furs Make deposit in P S Bnk leave hat to be scoured at Fishers.[32]

Chaos in Baltimore thwarted Adelman's plan to go south:

> News arrived of Kents' defeat and Banks retreat into Maryland. Rows and Riots in Balt. Got Bag & Baggage with intention of joining C's but found R.R. communication cut off—consequently had to return home Alex got a hell of a drunk last weeks.[33]

In May Southern-leaning Marylanders despaired. The Confederate ironclad vessel *Merrimac* had been destroyed, and McClellan appeared ready to take Richmond. W. W. Glenn described the reaction in Baltimore when Union Gen. Nathaniel Banks retreated from the vicinity of Harpers Ferry, across the Potomac:

> An extra demonstration of loyalty was made. Flags were hung out in all directions, throngs crowded the streets, the roughs moved around in squads and it was dangerous for a known Southerner to walk along the thoroughfares. I had not gone far up town before I heard that they had taken possession of the Maryland Club. I immediately changed my programme and endeavored to assemble a party of gentlemen to resist Mob Violence. This I found very difficult to effect.

After the "roughs" vacated the Maryland Club, Glenn expected further trouble and organized a defense:

> I knew that the Military authorities were not at all inclined to protect "disloyal" men and I anticipated further trouble. I represented to the men in the Club, that later in the day the roughs would probably return in force and that as this Club was particularly obnoxious to them, they would commence by an attack upon it; that in the heat of excitement they would then probably go to Hanson Thomas, then to our house, then to Robt. McLane's, then to Howard's & so on, making no particular distinction of persons at all obnoxious to them. I begged them to arm themselves, come to the Club & make their defense there and I assured them that if resistance was made, the military authorities would then certainly interfere and prevent further strife. But one man present, Jas. H. Barney, was willing to adopt this course. Fortunately for us, later in the day Genl. Wool thought that the excitement had had sufficient sway, that the Southerners had been sufficiently insulted & took steps to prevent any outbreak.[34]

A resident of Plum Point, on Mattawoman Creek in Charles County, later petitioned the U.S. government for

> damages done by the United States troops to the same while occupied by the aides of General Joseph Hooker, as place for landing & deposit for army stores for the benefit of Hooker' division from November the 17th 1861 to June the 15th 1862 & for which no compensation has been received in no manner, shape or form $3000 All we ask is justice. Evr'y panel of fence was destroyed as well as evr'y f'lr & shrub on the premises. Houses were rendered untenable the fishing outfit was destroyed & a Wharf—300 feet—the remnant of which still stands in the center of the Fishing Birth.[35]

John Hay replied to Bishop Whittingham's complaint to Lincoln about Baltimore churches being used as hospitals. Whittingham had likely referred to the wounded

"Women of Maryland Entertaining the Federal Recruits While en Route through Baltimore, MD," in September, 1862, prior to the Antietam campaign. The Soldier in Our Civil War.

from the battle of Second Manassas, on August 29 and 30—in the days following, the *Sun* referred to 1,300 wounded and sick troops arriving throughout the week, with 50 surgeons and 80 nurses from Pennsylvania and 127 surgeons from Delaware traveling to Baltimore to help:

> The President directs me to acknowledge the receipt of your communication protesting against the occupation of the Episcopal Church edifices in Baltimore for Hospital purposes.
>
> He directs me to state that he has referred the matter to the consideration of the Surgeon General, recommending that your wishes should be treated with that respect which is due not only to your high and venerable offices, but also to your unwavering loyalty and patriotism.[36]

In September, Anne Schaeffer of Frederick recorded the arrival of large numbers of soldiers wounded at Antietam:

"Maryland and Pennsylvania Farmers Visiting the Battlefield of Antietam, while the Federal Troops Were Burying the Dead, Friday, September 19th, 1862.—From a Sketch by Our Special Artist, F. H. Schell." Famous Leaders and Battles in the Civil War.

I with my neighbors determined to confine our attention for the present, to these poor fellows in the ambulances and found them sadly in need of refreshment.[37]

The next day, Saturday, was spent "All day in the kitchen preparing broth, porridge and jelly for the wounded."[38]

Then came Sunday:

A lovely Sabbath day—but it does not appear like the Sabbath. Churches filled with the wounded and dying, streets thronged with lades and servants carrying baskets and buckets . . . strangers going the rounds to find friends.[39]

Glenn described the fate of a young woman accused of smuggling:

Sometimes the travel was very dangerous and the the treatment to those caught very rough. I recollect on one occasion, a young lady, who was a governess in a private family in St. Mary's County, crossed over from Virginia to return to her home. She was seen, by the Commander of the Gunboat who overhauled the boat, putting something in her bosom. The boat was hailed and hauled alongside. The officer ordered her on deck. She replied that he might have the civility to hang over a companion way. This was done and she came on deck. The officer immediately seized her and thrust his hands in her bosom for the papers he said were concealed there. He did not ask for them. He then said that he did not believe she was a woman at all. She replied that "she thought his own indecent act had already convinced him of that". His answer was "that he had known many a man with as large breasts as she had" and in spite of her entreaties took her down into the cabin for further examination. The brute was afterwards Killed.[40]

William Preston, an attorney who lived at "Pleasant Plains" in Baltimore County, apologized to his daughter for not writing sooner, explaining that he had been distressed over the war. He encouraged her to get a "good substantial education" so she might "be found among the distinguished women of your Country discharging duties such as have characterized the noble women of every land that has had to struggle with heartless or ambitious tyrants":

> I have lived to see good men like T. Parkin Scott and others at the dead hours of the night torn from their homes and the bosoms of their families—and unjustly and cruelly consigned to the privations and horrors of distant and unwholesome dungeons. I am fast becoming an old man and can scarcely hope to live to see my country free again.[41]

1863

In January Gov. Augustus Bradford welcomed Gen. Robert Schenck as the new commander of the Middle Department in Baltimore, with a speech extolling Unionism as the principal objective of the war. The phrase scrawled across one page of the speech—"PRESERVE SLAVERY ALONG WITH UNION!"—reflected a powerful view held by many Marylanders, including Bradford himself:

> Such my friends I would have our guest and others believe is the loyalty of Maryland's loyal men. Such I believe it to be. Such I know it should be—and I have confidence it will continue to be. It will repudiate all local all sectional, all subordinate, all selfish considerations, every consideration in fact that has the power or possibility of [?] its hand from the great work that occupies its heart—the loyal men of Md. have but one purpose and one hope, but one ambition and one thought and that is the Union, its restoration, its preservation, its perpetu-

ity. We would save it at all hazards, and if not with all the improvements that
some of us might suggest then with all the interests and institutions that have
ever found shelter beneath it. We would then at least be saving it in the identical shape in which our fathers themselves received it from their own patriotic
ancestors.[42]

Baltimore physician Alexander C. Robinson received permission to travel into the
Confederacy to minister to his ill son:

> The Secretary of War has given a pass to Dr. Alexander C. Robinson, of Balti-
> more, to go through our lines, via Fort Monroe, and City Point, to visit his sick
> son, and to return by the same route.
>
> The Secretary accordingly directs that you facilitate his passage by the first
> flag of truce boat which goes up James River after his arrival at Fort Monroe.
>
> Dr. Robinson has given his parole of honor to afford no information, aid, or
> comfort to those in arms against the United States Government.
>
> He is permitted to take with him a bottle of chloroform and any reasonable
> supply of medicines or restoratives for the use of his son, but for no other use,
> furnishing to this Department, in advance, a list of what he proposes to take, and
> to be approved by you.[43]

Joshua Webster Hering, a Frederick native who practiced medicine in Westminster, was a proslavery Southern sympathizer whose 1890s memoir characterized
that town during the winter of 1862–1863 as "practically, under military rule." The
provost guard had

> head-quarters in the front room of the first floor of the Odd Fellows Hall, was
> here all the time. Deep and intense feeling pervaded the community, social con-
> ditions continued to be greatly broken up, and those who were of Southeren
> proclivities had to walk with the utmost circumspection, lest for no cause what-
> ever, they would be the victim of the arrogant upstart, who commanded this
> Provost Guard, led on and aided by a coterie of town associates who could be
> found at almost any time lounging about his place, men whose character would,
> in ordinary times, have been a bar to entrance into any respectable home in
> Westminster or elsewhere, where they were known.[44]

Glenn complained in February about the social vacuum in Baltimore:

> There were few general entertainments this winter. Society was almost entirely
> Southern—and every annoyance was given to those who attempted to encour-
> age gaiety. The Union Shriekers who knew they would not be allowed to share
> in the amusements of the Southerners gave information that the parties, which
> were apparently given for social amusement, were in fact treasonable gather-

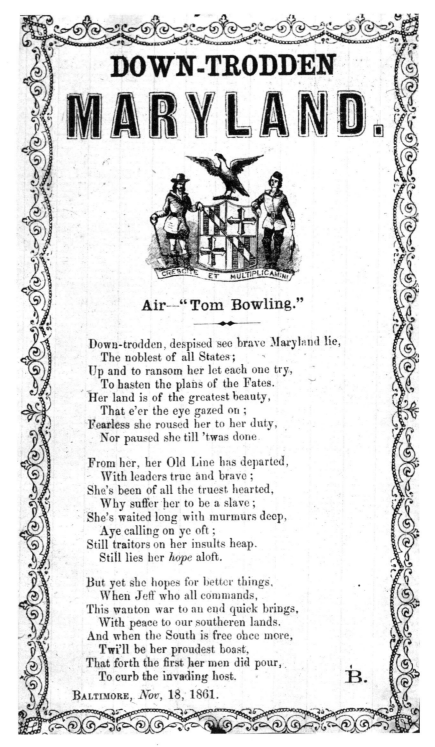

DOWN-TRODDEN
MARYLAND.

CRESCITE ET MULTIPLICAMINI

Air—"Tom Bowling."

Down-trodden, despised see brave Maryland lie,
   The noblest of all States;
Up and to ransom her let each one try,
   To hasten the plans of the Fates.
Her land is of the greatest beauty,
   That e'er the eye gazed on ;
Fearless she roused her to her duty,
   Nor paused she till 'twas done.

From her, her Old Line has departed,
   With leaders true and brave ;
She's been of all the truest hearted,
   Why suffer her to be a slave ;
She's waited long with murmurs deep,
   Aye calling on ye oft ;
Still traitors on her insults heap.
   Still lies her *hope* aloft.

But yet she hopes for better things,
   When Jeff who all commands,
This wanton war to an end quick brings,
   With peace to our southeren lands.
And when the South is free once more,
   Twi'll be her proudest boast,
That forth the first her men did pour,
   To curb the invading host.

                             B.

BALTIMORE, *Nov*, 18, 1861.

The poem "Down-Trodden Maryland" yearned for the state to follow "her Old Line" south to the Confederacy. MdHS.

ings. The Assembly Room was decorated with flags and the Assemblies were consequently broken up, as this kept away the Southerners. A few young people quietly met once a week to dance the German Cotillion. General Schenk determined to stop this because his daughters, who were here, were not invited. He sent his aide one evening and a small guard to inspect the premises. They entered the room uninvited took a look & were speedily asked out.[45]

Seaman's Bethel Church was ordered to hoist the American Flag, to the chagrin of Rev. Henry Slicer:

> They have evidently been imposed upon by some mischief making person—and have been induced to believe that the U.S. flag was formerly, but not latterly, raised upon the Church—whereas the church has never had any other than the Bethel flag, which is still run up, on every Sabbath, as formerly—[46]

Slicer objected to the order as government interference with religion, noting that "it was not in my line of business to put up flags of any kind":

> The govmt is being weakened every day, by the blunders of weak or wicked men, who attempt to represent the govmt—
>
> Genls Dix & Wool never belittled themselves, by interfering with ministers or churches. I trust in God, that the liberties of the American people, will not be totally overthrown before the end of this horrid Civil War—[47]

An anonymous letter Governor Bradford received in April criticized his Unionism but ignored his staunch support for Maryland slave owners:

> Do you truly think, as you remember what has taken place and reflect upon the present position of affairs, that the Union and the Constitution can ever again exist as they existed two years ago? You cannot really believe this. The issue you affect to make is an utterly false one. There is so much Southern blood on your hand that this generation of Southern men will never again grasp it in amity. The blackened walls of too many Southern homes stand now an eternal barrier between you and those with whom you wish to live. The memory of the rapine, the arsons and the murders, which this Government has suffered its officers to commit without rebuke, will keep the blood of a million men at too near fever heat for life, to render it possible that you and men like you should approach them, except sword in hand. If, too, there is any lesson which history should, by this time, have taught rulers, it is the difficulty of subjugating a united people.[48]

Because Maryland's proximity to the nation's capital facilitated gathering information about federal forces, Glenn believed his home state aided the Southern cause by remaining in the Union:

It was astonishing to me that more harm did not result from the perfectly loose manner in which Marylanders behaved. Matters of the greatest importance and often very compromising were talked of with the greatest publicity. Still they never seemed to get to the ears of the Federals, so unanimous was the feeling of the native born Marylanders and so distinct was the devision between them and the Yankees. Genl. Dix had a proper appreciation of this. When some one asked him how he could send a letter South, he replied, "Go, ask any little girl you see in the street in Baltimore" and he was right.[49]

At the end of May, a Baltimorean wrote to Reverdy Johnson suggesting he try to have revoked an army order to oversee statewide elections in June, on grounds that the order would harm the cause it was designed to aid:

I have just learned from Rev. as coming from Dr. Cox of the Army here, that an order has been prepared in view of Wednesday's election, to the effect that any secessionist seen lingering about the polls will be arrested; and that all persons whose loyalty is suspected, before being allowed to vote, will be required to take the oath of allegiance. As all candidates are Union men, differing only in the case of Moffit and Goldsborough, as to the *political* support they are inclined to render to the present administration, there can be but one object in the issuing of any such order as that alluded to, and that object is certainly not one in which the military officers should by the administration be allowed to interfere.[50]

In June, Robert Kirkwood was encamped at Camp Maryland Heights at Harpers Ferry, where he wrote to his father about the Unionist cause in Baltimore County in upcoming elections:

The emigration from the city has been so great to Harpers fery that it is almost impossible to walk the streets of Bolliver and the Ferry for hoop skirts these last few days the cars are loaded with cittizens every day all the houses unocupied is now filled with boarders if old Lee was to make his appearence i ll bet there would be an uproar and a sciddadel I am glad to learn of our making a move in Balt County to do something in behalf of our cause at the coming election. I hope you will select an unconditional and firm union man and one that will please all good and Loyal voters. I also hope that we will be permitted to aid you some way or other at the Ballot box if we are spared next fall if we are successfull this fall in making a clear sweep I think Copperheadism will be pretty well swampt in Maryland my Maryland.[51]

Joshua Hering explained why the women of Westminster were busy during the occupation of their town:

The soldiers, as a rule, had money and were on the lookout for something better than the ordinary army rations. The ladies with a keen eye to the main chance, and with a desire to gratify this very natural instinct of the American soldier, and with a desire also of replenishing their exchequer, concluded to furnish the "boys" with "Mother's Bread" and especially with "Mother's Pies". And so there were Bakerys established in almost every kitchen in the town. And such baking and eating of pies Westminster had never heard of or witnessed before. The quality of the pies did not cut as much of a figure in the business as the quantity.

Tables were placed on the pavements in front of doors, or else the front windows would indicate by having some apetizing pies on exhibition, that the good Matron of the household was in the pie business. Pies were made of about everything that the human mind could think of as going into such an article, and with a suspicion of sugar in them, were sold with great readiness for 25 cents a piece. But a good green currant pie, such as the soldier's Grand-Mother used to make, went off like "hot cakes" at double that amount. And especially was this the case when the servant of some officer was sent out on a forageing expedition. And so the pie business went on, and it was a great time, to be sure, the ladies piling in the money and the soldiers piling in the pies. Just how many of them died from indigestion, as a result of their visit to Westminster on this occasion, the army records have never disclosed, but I think any good judge would have considered some of pies about as indigestible as a confederate bullet, and nearly, if not quite as dangerous.[52]

Two letters from "Lou," a Union soldier in Baltimore, give a flavor of the city in June. The first refers to Fort Federal Hill, above Baltimore Harbor; a creative use of an old tree; and secession sentiment among Baltimore ladies. The second, on June 22, likely refers to the city's response to news that the rebel army was moving into Maryland, in the prelude to Gettysburg:

The boys found this place in the most filthy condition, the barracks were like pig stys, and it was first necessary to hoe and shovel out the dirt, and then go to work and clean house. The place is now pretty clean, and had it been clear today we should have had it looking as bright as a pin. As usual the N.C. Staff are very comfortable. We have a room in the Officers quarters on the 2nd. story and are very comfortably situated. The rest of the staff all laugh at me because I will bunk on the floor with nothing but my blanket. However I like it now. I thought it might be just as well to get used to it before they send us where we could not get mattresses.

This fort is on a high hill, overlooking, and commanding the whole of Baltimore, so if the Sesesh should happen to kick up a row, this fort would soon burn the City.

We find the people on this end of the town more of the Union Stripe than when we were on Federal Hill. We had a great many visitors on Sunday, which was a charming day, but they did not "move into our circle". We are working very hard, drilling & trying to keep up our reputation.

One of the greatest institutions in the place is the 7th Co. pipe. On the center of the parade is a tree which has had a branch cut off, about four feet above the ground; the end has rotted in a little ways in the center, which the 7th Co. cleaned out, and they bored through the side of the butt, and inserted seven flexible pipe stems. The "pipe" is filled with tobacco, and seven men squat around and all smoke the same pipe. It excited a great deal of interest. I have tried it and pronounced it good.

I understand Kate & Uncle Lathrop have gone to Fort Monroe. I wonder whether they will visit Fort Federal Hill. Probably not, as it is the fashion here to be secesh—I was walking thru Hanover St. last evening about dusk and some ladies and gentlemen were sitting on the stoop as is the custom here. As I passed one lady remarked "she was going to have it trimmed red as she wanted to wear white and red." I am sure I didn't care what colors she wore. The same evening I stopped into a "Darkie meeting." The officiating "passon" wore a white "surplus." I did not stay long.[53]

On June 22, now a quartermaster lieutenant, Lou again wrote to the "Girls," from Coleman's Eutaw House, a hotel, referring to anxiety over the entry of Lee's army into Maryland:

I have been very busy since I arrived, but have now about got through my hurry, and I am glad of it. We are trying hard to get the fort clean enough to exist in, but it is hard work, scrub, scrub, and plenty of whitewash, but the place is full of L——, B. Bgs, and all other sorts of horrid things. The men are very hard at work on the big guns, and could already show a pretty good account of themselves. The place here is still in a very much excited condition. Some 2 & 3000 Darks are at work, throwing up entrenchments, mounting cannon etc. They are also barricading the street with H.hds. tobacco etc.[54]

A soldier, probably Robert Kirkwood, wrote to his mother from Harpers Ferry about matters serious:

There is another shot man in the hospital Frank Temple. When they were striking tents Temple wanted to tear it down. Lisenring (both of Co. C) did not want him to do it for a while. Lisenring got to jawing him. Temple was going to fight him their 1st Lieut caught Temple and run him back. Lisenring said he would shoot him. Lieut told him to shoot—he shot him with a pistol through the right

An interior view of Fort Federal Hill. The Fort quickly became a popular weekend destination for Baltimoreans. Pratt Lib.

breast the first time he jumped behind the Lieut and shot him again through the right arm above the elbow

And mundane:

> You said you wanted us to send you some of our old pant to mend our over-coats with. We generaly patch them up and wear them until they are pretty well gone. I get William to do my patching and mending, he makes a splendid old woman.[55]

Reverdy Johnson opposed ending hostilities short of victory. When invited to a June 23 convention he replied, "you will readily see that I should be out of place at a meeting called only of 'those in favor of a cessation of hostilities'":

> Before the rebellion disclosed itself, I was most solicitous, & did all I could to avert it (as it might, I believe, at one time have been) "by conciliation & compro-mise." Most happy therefore, should I now be, if it could now be so terminated. An assurance that will hold out a promise to secure to all, every right, State & personal, would, I believe, materially contribute to such a blissful result. But, in the existing temper, and with the present power of the leaders of the rebel-lion over their deluded and comparatively helpless masses, I am satisfied that an offer of the kind, at the present time, would not only not be accepted, but be rejected, with their usual rude & insolent arrogance. Every indication given by them personally, & by the people under their control, conclusively, I think

evidences this. No "cessation of hostilities" therefore, is in my judgment, advisable. The military power of the rebels must first be destroyed. And for this, the government is abundantly competent, if they will properly employ the means in money & men, which a patriotic people have so liberally & confidingly placed in their hands.[56]

In June, the authorities ordered a raid on the Maryland Club, which they believed a viper's nest of secessionism and weapons caches. Federal soldiers burst in, expelled six members, and posted a proclamation from General Schenck:

> There is an association existing in the city of Baltimore known as the "Maryland Club." The meetings of this body, and of those who frequent its rooms or are entertained by its members, take place at a building on the corner of Franklin and Charles streets. Departing from the original character and purpose of its institution, this club has, for a long time past, degenerated into a resort for those who are disaffected towards the government, hostile to its legally constituted authorities, and who give countenance, encouragement and aid to the unnatural and causeless rebellion by which our institutions and national integrity are sought to be overthrown. So dangerous and mischievous an association cannot be permitted longer to maintain this attitude in a loyal community. The "Maryland Club" is therefore suspended, and its house of meeting taken possession of and closed.
>
> In the execution of the order the names of all persons found in the building, and of all who belong to the association, and of all who habitually frequent it, will be taken, and an inventory will be made of the property and records or papers of the association.[57]

As preparations continued for the defense of Baltimore, Henry Shriver, in the Twenty-sixth Pennsylvania Regiment, described a Pennsylvania evening in pursuit of the rebel army:

> We are camped in the woods about four miles from Oxford, along the RR. We slept last night in the open air & very soundly too—we spread our tents on the ground, laid on them, rolled ourselves in our woolen blankets & covered our gum covers over the top—this keeps out the damp some of the men put their gum blankets below—the dew saturated the wool blankets so as to make them quite wet before morning—a great many complained of cold but Dave & I were very comfortable—The woods looked so pretty by the light of the camp fires—all around you could see the sleeping soldiers in all sorts of positions. You cannot imagine how quiet they become. I was awakened a short time about 1 o'clock & had it not been for the extensive *snoring* going on, I could have imagined myself alone in the woods.[58]

A drawing by Baltimore dentist Adalbert Johann Volck, a Southern sympathizer who used the pseudonym V. Blada (part of his first name reversed), depicted a thuggish Union officer, bottle protruding from his jacket, finding only a small Confederate flag in a woman's bedchamber as other soldiers restrain her protesting father. MdHS.

Just before Gettysburg, Lt. Col. A. Steiner of the First Maryland Potomac Home Brigade of Frederick happily noted Union Gen. Joseph Hooker's dismissal (to be succeeded by Gen. George Meade):

> heard this afternoon that Genl Hooker has been relieved by Genl Mead, temporarily & that Genl McClellan will very soon be at the head of the army cheering news.[59]

W. W. Glenn left his home in Baltimore City and evaded a dragnet by the authorities:

> I awoke to find Martial law declared. It had in fact prevailed for a long time. I was satisfied it was time to be off. I did not know it until after I left the house and then had no time to go back. I went to my office, found my clerk Mr. Hardy and told him that I had some important payments to arrange for, which I would do in the street. I made an appointment to meet him at 12 o'c. I chose the most public corner in the City knowing that that would be the last place the detec-

tives would expect to find me. I had hardly gone off, before a detective came & asked for John. He saw John who promised to go to the Marshall's office. Soon after they sent to my office, but I was not to be found. I sent word by Hardy to my people that I was gone, and at noon started to leave town. All the railroads were guarded. Pickets were on all the carriage roads. You could not possibly get out without a pass. Strict orders had been issued forbidding anyone to leave. I quietly took the Passenger Cars out Baltimore street and rode as far as the toll gate. There I saw the first line of pickets just ahead and I got out.

Glenn arrived at "Hill Top," the home of lawyer William F. Frick on Frederick Road, "reeking with perspiration and fagged out." After dining he arrived at Hilton, his estate in Catonsville:

I knew perfectly well from the British Legation that Seward and Stanton were both very annoyed at my supposed communications with the South.

He moved north through Baltimore County, going via New York to Canada. Glenn returned to Baltimore in April 1864.[60]

George J. Cornwell, at Fort Federal Hill in Baltimore, wrote to his mother as the rebel army retreated through Maryland following the Battle of Gettysburg:

Last night we were all called out at 12 o'clock armed and equipped as there were rumors of an attack by the rebels. The bells in Baltimore were all ringing for two hours to arouse the union citizens. We waited some time expecting to get definite orders, but I soon lay down in my bunk and went to sleep and I believe all the rest did the same soon after, so you see it did not amount to anything serious. Some of our boys broke up a secession club house Saturday night. It was the hot bed of secession in the city. We have about 40 of our boys down in the city acting as a provost guard to arrest all deserters and also to suppress any demonstration that the secessionists may make. Today the orders are to allow no man to go out of the fort, not that they feel any of our men will desert us, for none would leave the regiment at the present time, but that they may all be here in case we are needed.

He closed with words of reassurance:

It looks as if we were to have some warm work very soon, although I do not think the rebels will attack the city as they have more friends than enemys here. Their game is to cut the railroad communication between here and New York and also between here and Washington which will probably be done before you get this letter, but you need not be alarmed. I do not fear, if it should come to fighting you will not have cause to be ashamed of your son. Do not worry about me, Mother. I am willing to place my life in God's care. He will do whatsoever is for the best.

Again I ask you not worry about me. I know you cannot help thinking of me, but I shall feel relieved to know that my mother is willing to trust all to God and that she will not be over anxious. Our fort is strong—it is well protected by breast-works—we would not be exposed scarcely at all in case of an attack, but this will all blow over in a few days and you will be glad I came.[61]

On July 3, General Schenck suggested that Baltimore homes and businesses show the American flag from 10 a.m. to 6 p.m. on Independence Day and that "if there be any spot where it does not appear, its absence there will only prove that patriot hearts do not beat beneath that roof":

Although there was much anxiety manifested yesterday in the city, in regard to the fight in progress in the vicinity of Gettysburg, there was no undue excite-ment.

The order for the display of the national flag will, doubtless, be generally ob-served today, if we may judge from the number already displayed last evening, and the quantity said to have been sold by the storekeepers. A special order was issued yesterday morning by Major Gen. Schenk, allowing certain kinds of busi-ness, and also the city markets, to remain open until 11 o'clock last night, and the citizens availed themselves of the opportunity to lay in a supply of the necessar-ies until Monday morning.[62]

By July 4, Frederick Shriver was at the Shriver family homestead at Union Mills, where he recounted his relief at Henry's well-being after Gettysburg and the scene after the Union army had marched through:

You have no doubt received, ere this, mine & Sis's letters telling you how things have been going on here before & since the battle of Gettysburg—We were all very glad to find you had been at Harrisburg during all the fighting, as it had been so long since we heard from you we did not know whether *you* had been ordered on to take part in the fight, or not—I think we all have occasion to be thankful that we escaped so well thus far, but as we heard tremendous cannon-ading yesterday in the direction of Frederick, we cannot be certain that you are out of the mess yet—

Things about here have returned pretty much to their usual channel. Were it not for the few fences they have destroyed & the remains of their camp fires a stranger would not know we had had army here at all. There is not a soldier to be seen any more, not even a straggler. That part of the Army of the Potomac which went by here left the most favorable imppression on the citizens, imagin-able—For my part I never expected to find any army as well behaved and who were as gentlemanly *throughout* as that one was—I do not think I conversed with *one soldier* who did not talk like a gentleman & behave like one. The only trouble we had was with the stragglers who kept about for a few days after the army had

This collection of pro-Union images reflected events such as a "Union Concert" and "Union Soiree" and satirical thrusts at the Confederacy, using devices such as depicting George Washington as "One of the Rebels" and as "The Southern Gentleman, and Slaveholder." MdHS.

left—some of them were extremely saucy & every saucy one was an *Irishman*. Even they did not do us any material damage.

Shriver recounted the experience with Union Gen. John Sedgwick, who, with his staff, took breakfast at the Shriver home:

> They left a very unfavorable imppression on the family. They seemed to think a great deal of themselves & their position & were inclined to have the best of everything & then did not seem to be the least thankful for it. I hated those fellows.[63]

Franklin Wilson described the post-Gettysburg atmosphere in Baltimore and the effects of Schenck's proclamation to show the U.S. flag:

> This awful battle was fought within 40 miles of Baltimore. About 4000 prisoners have been sent through this city, and many dead and wounded. Fears of invasion here seem to have subsided, though the barricades are still kept up. On Monday night June 29th the alarm bells were rung at midnight, and the cry "to arms" resonated through the streets, causing intense excitement and alarm. We heard the bells, but kept quiet. On Saturday July 4th Gen. Schenck issued an order denouncing every man as a traitor who did not hang out the U.S. flag and the consequence was an almost universal display, though some flags were ludicrously small.[64]

Margaret "Maggie" Mehring, a thirteen-year-old in New Windsor, Carroll County, recorded the movements of the rebel army north through Maryland, and what she heard about the clash at Gettysburg. By July 14, life's routines were resuming:

> The heat has been very oppressive to day. It is again clouding u[p] for rain. I expected to get a letter from Sister at noon but did not. I have known all of my lessons very well as far as I went to day. We did not say our Physiology yesterday evening and will say it this afternoon. Clay has toothake very badly. She was not at school to day. My piece in the instructor is the scale of C magor, and Mr. Dielman brought me a new piece called the Elfin Waltz. I think it is very easy to run the scales but at firs though I could never do it with both hands at the same time. It takes but a little perseverance to overcome apparently great difficulties *some times.*[65]

The military authorities announced conditions under which Confederate "sick and wounded prisoners of war" from Gettysburg would receive medical care in Baltimore:

> No rebel officer or soldier can be received or entertained in any private house, or in any place other than the hospital to which he is regularly assigned by proper medical authority.

Separate hospitals for prisoners of war will be established.

No person not thoroughly loyal will be permitted under any circumstances to visit or have access to any military hospital.

If any person or persons, within this Department, be found harboring, entertaining or concealing any rebel officer or soldier, in his or her house, or on his or her premises, or in any place, after twenty-four hours from the publication of this order, the person so offending will be at once sent beyond the Union lines into the rebel states, or otherwise punished, at the discretion of the military authority.[66]

By summer, Rebecca Davis shared brother William's political views:

Ester & I were taking a moonlight ramble, as we approached the gate singing in loudest key Maryland! My Maryland! up rode three Federals. We retreated to the house knowing such treacherous refrain would not be agreeable to their ears. They brought a summons for Pa to appear in Mr. Cashell's case to be tried before Court Martial; before leaving they came in to take refreshment. Sister & I do not make our appearance when Yanks are in the house, entertaining no sympathy for them.[67]

In September, W. W. Glenn, aboard a ship leaving Quebec for England, described the aftermath of the government's seizure of the Maryland Club:

After suffering every possible annoyance, the club was finally closed by Military order and taken possession of in June last. A guard of the 7" New York Regiment was placed there. The men took entire possession, played billiards, drank all the wine and segars they could find—and which they broke open cupboards to find—and even stole the clothes of the servant men, which were left in their sleeping rooms upstairs. The Club was closed because the members did not choose to issue invitations to Officers of the Federal army. That was of course high treason.[68]

In October, George Vickers, the proprietor of McKim Mansion—used by the Sixth Michigan Volunteer Regiment beginning in August 1861—warned Governor Bradford that "Radicals" planned to impose oath requirements at the polls to help their candidates in fall elections. Bradford agreed "that their policy is to prevent if possible a full Conservative vote by creating an apprehension" of military interference, but given Lincoln's lack of concern, the Governor urged caution and reliance on election judges:

The President apparently hooted the idea, said that no such purpose was entertained, nor had he received any intimation of any desire to that effect. With this assurance from the President, it would hardly be necessary or proper for me to interpose any remonstrance against the use of force, as I certainly shall not hesitate to do did such reasonable ground exist for such an apprehension.[69]

Bradford complained to Lincoln that federal troops were being dispatched to monitor elections:

> These troops are not residents of the State, and consequently are not sent for the purpose of voting, and as there is no reason, in my opinion, to apprehend any riotous or violent proceedings at this election, the inference is unavoidable that these military detachments, if sent, are expected to exert some control or influence in that election.
>
> I am also informed that orders are to be issued from this military department on Monday presenting certain restrictions or qualifications on the right of suffrage—of what precise character I am not apprised—which the judges of election will be expected to observe.
>
> From my knowledge of your sentiments on these subjects, as expressed to Hon. R. Johnson in my presence, on 22nd Inst., and also disclosed in your letter of instructions to Genl. Schofield, since published, in reference to the Missouri election, I cannot but think that the orders above referred to are without your personal knowledge, and I take the liberty of calling the subject to your attention, and invoking your interposition to countermand them.
>
> I cannot but feel that to suffer any military interference in the matter of our election, or to prescribe any test of oath to voters when all the candidates in the State—with the exception perhaps of two or three in one Congressional District—are all loyal men, would be justly obnoxious to the public sentiment of the State.[70]

Lincoln responded on November 2. He defended the requirement for loyalty oaths and the need for troops at some polls, noting "nor do I think that to keep the peace at the polls, and to prevent the persistently disloyal from voting, constitutes just cause of offence to Maryland":

> Yours of the 31st. ult. was received yesterday about noon, and since then I have been giving most earnest attention to the subject matter of it. At my call Gen. Schenck has attended; and he assures me it is almost certain that violence will be used at some of the voting places on election day, unless prevented by his provost-guards. He says that at some of those places Union voters will not attend at all, or run a ticket unless they have some assurance of protection. This makes the Missouri case, of my action in regard to which, you express your approval. The remaining point of your letter is a protest against any person offering to vote being put to any test not found in the laws of Maryland. With the same reason in both States, Missouri has, by law, provided a test for the voter, with reference to the present rebellion, while Maryland has not. For example, Gen. Tremble, captured fighting us at Gettysburg, is, without recanting his treason, a legal voter by the laws of Maryland. Even Gen. Schenck's order, admits him to vote, if he re-

cants upon oath. I think that is cheap enough. My order in Missouri, which you approve, and Gen. Schenck's order here, reach precisely the same end. Each assures the right of voting to all loyal men; and whether a man is loyal, each allows that man to fix by his own oath. Your suggestion that nearly all the candidates are loyal, I do not think quite meets the case. In this struggle for the nation's life, I can not so confidently rely on those whose elections may have depended upon disloyal votes. Such men, when elected, may prove true; but such votes are given them in the expectation that they will prove false.[71]

Bradford's reply took issue with many of Lincoln's points. He also told the president that, because he had read his letter in the Baltimore papers the day before, "Your Excellency has in this respect the advantage of me, for though, following your example, I shall send a duplicate of this to the press":

If the sending out of one or more Regiments of soldiers, distributing them among several of the Counties to attend their places of election, in defiance of the known laws of the State prohibiting their presence; ordering military officers and provost marshals to arrest voters guilty, in the opinion of such officers, of certain offenses; and menacing judges of election with the power of the military arm in case this military order was not respected, is not an "undue interference" with the freedom of elections, I confess myself unable to imagine what is.[72]

In early November, Fayette Thrall, a soldier at Fort Federal Hill in Baltimore, sent a lady friend a pen-and-ink image of the fort along with a depiction of daily life there:

I shall have to stay here until I here from the colonel commanding my regiment and I am in hopes that will be soon. I will give you a little detail of our fair here our living consisting of a cup of coffee and a piece of meat with one third of a loaf of bread in the morning for dinner a cup of bean soup and a third of a loaf of bread the supper the same as breakfast our sleeping is fare worse than you could expect not being where we could expect worse it is the soft side of a pine board which is rather harder than the virginia mud we as soldiers should not complain at this for there is many in the field who would rejoice for the place we are in.

When Thrall's hands grew too cold to write, he warmed them, ate dinner, and continued:

There is all kinds of enjoyment here among the boys from whistling down to dancing while others are singing spiritual hymns and others reading there bible while the others are gambling and cursing some are siting with their fingers in there mouth lamenting of there enlistment and wishing themselves home again very sorry they took the bounty after it is to late such men in my oppinion came for money not for there country.[73]

In November, Gen. Fitz-John Porter—who had been cashiered from the army by Congress following the second Battle of Bull Run—expressed his disapproval of the federal role in Maryland elections to Reverdy Johnson:

> The outrages upon the rights of citizens and upon those of states committed under the shadow of authority in the late Maryland election, are attracting much deserved attention. The Journal of Commerce of yesterday had an article on the subject and there will be another to day. Although Republicans are pleased at the result—they fear the means by which it was effected, and the evils of a large standing army.

Porter enclosed an excerpt from a *Journal of Commerce* article that complained of military interference in the election:

> In the accompanying extract you will see but a shadow of what is hoped for i.e.—that Gov. Bradford will refuse to give certificates of election to the parties claiming election where the soldiers appeared—and this on the ground that the election was interfered with in the state in violation of state law.[74]

A correspondent of Jerome Bonaparte complained about repressive actions at the polls during Maryland's 1863 elections:

> The Mechanics & other labourers are flying from a service odious to them as Marylanders. All such of these as may be arrested will be shot as deserters. The recent election here shows conclusively that over two thirds of our voters did not attend the Polls. Schenck's order was that the Judges should receive no votes except from those who would take the oath. This order was protested against by Gov. Bradford but Maryland as a state is wiped out.[75]

An officer in the Union army's Second Corps thanked a Westminster woman for her kindness during the Gettysburg campaign:

> As my duties took me with the baggage trains that were parked around Westminster, I found myself on the morning of the 4th of July, 1863, in the streets of your pretty town searching for a place where I might be able to purchase a loaf of bread.
>
> After searching sometime I passed your residence, and as I passed I asked a young lady who was seated upon your door step—and whom I judged to be your daughter—"If she would be kind enough to sell me a loaf of bread", She looked up and raising her glasses said with a pleasant emphasis "No Sir, I can't sell any bread to soldiers" but at the same time invited me to the kitchen, where I met Mrs. Gehr and was very kindly pressed to seat my self at the breakfast table and between visiting and eating I passed a very pleasant half-hour.
>
> Since that day when I have thought of the Glorious 4th of July—Birthday of

Weapons searches by Union soldiers sometimes bore fruit.
Harper's Weekly, *November 16, 1861, Pratt Lib.*

our Nation's Freedom—I have thought of the 4th as spent in Westminster, Maryland, and asked God of the Good and True to bless Mrs. Gehr and family, and all patriotic mothers and daughters of our Common Country.[76]

Rebecca Davis was angered at the treatment of her relatives by Union troops:

> Pa went to Balto. Tuesday & returned Thursday. Says Cousin Etta Harwood's correspondence with her husband in the Confederacy has been discovered and she is ordered to go South the 12th inst. Is also falsely accused of having previously been there. Aunt Glenn's house was subjected to the most minute & disgusting search, all private papers perused & some seized.[77]

A diary entry shortly before Christmas suggested that Rebecca did not share her parents' view of Union soldiers:

> Raining fast all day. A Yankee officer & boy came in this evening for a night's lodging. Pa & Ma have the pleasure of entertaining him.[78]

1864

Governor Bradford's speech to the state legislature on the first day of its 1864 session included charges of military interference with autumn elections, wherein disloyal citizens faced arrest and voters asked to take a loyalty oath had to comply to vote. In Kent County on the day before the election, Bradford claimed the military arrested "some ten or more" citizens, and voters were urged to support "the whole Government ticket":

> a yellow ticket, and armed with that, a voter could safely run the gauntlet of the sabres and carbines that guarded the entrance to the polls, and known sympathizers with the Rebellion were, as certified to me, allowed to vote unquestioned, if they would vote that ticket.[79]

In February, Almon D. Jones was on duty at Point Lookout, at the junction of the Potomac River and Chesapeake Bay and site of a large Union prison. He told his sister Carrie that rebel prisoners were enlisting in the Union army:

> It is warm out here and I have a nice time. The rebs are interesting in to our army Four hundred has inlisted already and more will inlist as soon as these states come back in to the union. Three states has com back allready more is coming back soon old Jeff has sent a word to Lincoln that he will give up there slaves and lay down there armes if Lincoln will do two or three things I don't now whether he will or not I was on gard the other day in side of the rebs camp and they all say that Jeff is bout plade out Jeff is moving out of richmond as fast as he can for he is feared of his head and I don't blaim him much.

Jones related his culinary regimen at Point Lookout:

> I don't finde any trouble in eating . I had a pie to nite . . . we have beans twice a week and fresh meat and hastey [fruches?] and molaces once in a while we made some malaces candy the other night we have soft bread to eat all the time and coffee three times a day and sugar in it.[80]

Baltimore businessmen began a Union Club to support the war effort. Early in 1864 Joseph Cushing described its status in a letter to Jerome Bonaparte:

> I am about to call in the second subscription to the Union Club & by request of Mrs. Bonaparte I write to request you to send me an order for the amount ($500.00) five hundred dollars of the second half of your subscription. The Club is progressing well, and the membership constantly increasing. All seem satisfied with the house, and desirous to make the concern a permanence. We had a memento of you on the occasion of Genl. Schenck's visit to the Club, in the form of your tremendous punch bowl, kindly loaned to us by your wife. Its

John T. Ridgely of Howard County, shown here in 1868 at age 26, was the colorbearer in Company A of the First Maryland Cavalry. Courtesy of Achsah Henderson.

size was a subject of general comment and admiration, and our barkeeper filled it with a potation worthy of the receptacle.[81]

In March came a comment on the social scene in Baltimore:

> In my last letter I wrote you of a masquerade fancy ball to be given (by) a very wealthy merchant of this city. I attended dressed in a black velvet suit hung with bugles with a fancy cap, the character I assumed was Hamlet.[82]

Jacob Grove, a Westminster native serving in the Sixth Maryland Infantry Regiment, wrote from his camp near Alexandria about a straw poll for the autumn's presidential election:

> There was an election held here in the Regiment in order to find out how many is in favor of Abraham Lincoln. He got the majority.[83]

In April, William McKim ascribed the effects of Gen. Ulysses S. Grant's campaign in Virginia—where he was pursuing Gen. Robert E. Lee and moving toward Richmond—on the economy:

> Gold and Exchange continue to advance, notwithstanding the efforts of the Govt. to keep them down, and I see no probability of a decline until the movements of Genl. Grant begin to have some effect on the future prospects of the rebellion—which I hope may be ere long. Troops are going to the front in large numbers, and a considerable army is being concentrated at Annapolis, under command of Genl. Burnside, for some useful purpose, I hope.[84]

Not all were happy about the state of Baltimore social life. Styling his Charles Street home the "Den of the Attic Philosopher," a man complained in April about the closure of social clubs:

> In these "troublous times" of awful strife and bloodshed, it is seldom that one can forget the horrors that are around us and find time to indulge in cheerful thoughts.
>
> I am glad to know that you sometimes think of Baltimore and that you retain pleasant recollections of your short stay here—although you saw it under the most unfavourable circumstances in which any place could be viewed—that is as a sullen, conquered city—a Venice in America—and its people undergoing much heart suffering. Alas! It is still so—and will be until the "end of the chapter." (I hope no "detective"—so ubiquitous—has been looking over my shoulder while I have been writing down these rather "treasonable" thoughts—but I can't help myself, & feel very bitter at times) Only think of us poor bachelors deprived of the solace of our clubs ever since Genl. Robert E. Lee came into "My Maryland" last summer. We scarcely know what to do with ourselves during our leisure hours, and as I pass by the "Allston" (I hope you have not forgotten it) and look

at its closed doors and windows, "now a days," denying me admittance, I almost "drop a tear" to think that such an institution should have been considered so dangerous as to call forth the "ukase" which closed it because in the imagination of the powers it threatened the existence of the "best government that the world ever" &c.&c!!!

Thus, you see, even our much cherished and time honoured social enjoyments are abolished; but why pursue the "harrowing topic"—woe, woe is me! If you have any sympathy give me a tear![85]

In April, Baltimore women sponsored a Maryland State Fair to benefit U.S. Sanitary and Christian Commission efforts to aid Union troops. President Lincoln arrived in the city on April 18 and, after staying at the home of Unionist attorney William J. Albert on Monument Street, visited the fair, where the president

made his appearance, with Mrs. Governor Bradford on his arm. His towering figure was plainly visible above the throng, and from the floor and the galleries there was a waving of handkerchiefs and continuous cheers until he reached the platform immediately in front of the Floral Temple, which had been erected for the occasion.

At twenty minutes past nine o'clock the President arose to leave the platform, when the ladies rushed upon him, and he was occupied for some time in shaking hands with all who could get near him.

The President then went through the fair, and expressed himself highly pleased with the whole arrangements.[86]

The *Baltimore American and Commercial Advertiser* described the scene:

The traducers of Baltimore, and those who represent its population as Secessionists or disloyalists, should have taken a stroll through its streets yesterday afternoon. It was a bright and beautiful evening, business was temporarily suspended by many of our tradesmen, and everything was favorable for a turnout of the people in their strength. The "Old Flag" was displayed from many a house-top and window of rich and poor alike. The streets, we venture to say, never presented a more pleasant aspect, or were more crowded, old and young availing themselves of the opportunity to see the parade of the troops and enjoy the holiday. Battle Monument Square, from whence the military parade started, was jammed and crowded so that had it not been for the exertions of the police force accidents would have happened during the evolutions of the troops. Broadway, the point where the column was reviewed by Gen. Wallace, presented a magnificent appearance. We think it no exaggeration to say that two-thirds of the dwellings between Baltimore street and the Point Market were decorated with the National flag.[87]

The federal Camp Small, in Mount Washington, helped protect the Northern Central Railway passage through Baltimore to its stations at Bolton Street and Calvert Street. Pratt Lib.

At Camp Cole near Frederick, Union soldier Thomas Sutton missed his family:

> If it was not for having my wife and child I wold like soldiering first rate but I cannot help thinking of them but as I have got into it I hope that I may come out safe and also see the Southern men lay down their arms within the next six months.[88]

On April 27, W. W. Glenn "reached Baltimore in the Morning, after an absence of 10 months" in Canada and England, beyond the reach of the federal authorities. On May 1, he "showed publicly & went to church":

> My friends all tell me that I am mad to come home. There is no law—no protection. Arbitrary force rules. The negro population is in a state of ferment. Few servants can be trusted any longer and it is scarcely possible to get along with decent comfort. Genl. Schenck who was bitter and violent has been removed. Lew Wallace, who is worse, is in his place.[89]

Robert Kirkwood told his father that John Merryman suffered a beating at Unionist hands:

Hay Field John Meryman was Knocked down and badly beaten at Cockeysvill this evening by some of the boys belonging to Co. G after they done it they sung rally around the bridge burners.[90]

Capt. F. W. Alexander's May report of the Baltimore Battery of Light Artillery at Camp no. 20 described the loss of one of its men, Pvt. Jeremiah E. S. Ried:

> While on guard on the 17th of May his pistol slipped from his holster and falling on the ground exploded the ball entering his body from the effects of which he died on the 18th of May 1864.[91]

In June, Governor Bradford sent General Wallace, commanding the Middle Department in Baltimore, a petition from Queen Anne's County, whose citizens protested excessive levies assessed them as compensation for damages committed against property belonging to U.S. Army recruiters. Bradford, who conceded that such outrages did occur, took the opportunity to complain about the president:

> Already as you are doubtless aware General, even some of the political friends of the President are making an outcry against what they term his arbitrary exercise of Authority and assumption of unconstitutional power, and I feel sure that every true friend of the Administration will take pleasure in removing as far as possible all just cause for such complaints, as well as in upholding the acknowledged rights of the Citizen in all cases unless the most unequivocal necessity requires that they should for the time be suspended.[92]

In a series of July diary entries, C. T. Simpers, a Union surgeon, described a bout with diarrhea and the effort to see his wife:

> July 13: Returned to my Regt. at Druid Hill Park, a pleasant place, but am sick. Suffering a great deal of pain. Wrote to my wife and mailed the letter last night. Heard through [Sogby] Harvy that I had been captured by the Rebels on Saturday last near Frederick town Md.

> July 14: was respectfully referred to Dr. Hasson by Medical Director Simpson for medical treatment, after having obtained permission to go to Gen. Hospital for treatment.
>
> Dr. Hasson prescribed chlorodine/cholordim 15 drops every 2 hours and Elixs of Calisaya Bark 3 times daily.

> July 18: Had prescribed for me Oak Bark as an astringent. Went to the cars to meet my wife and was disappointed on her not being on the train.[93]

In June the rebel army entered Maryland for the third time in less than two years. The Monocacy campaign included cavalry strikes into Baltimore County and the burning of Governor Bradford's home on Charles Street. Baltimore quickly raised "an Independent Company of Military," which on July 12 quickly ordered sixteen men

> to start at 4 AM next day and march to the residence of W.P. Preston, near Towsontown to search for arms alleged to have been there concealed, and if they were found on the property to arrest the owner (W.P. Preston) and bring him to the Fort.

No arms were found, and on July 15, the company was relieved of further duty.[94]

A reminder that the Civil War was an "uncensored" war came from Robert Moore, a soldier assigned to Fort McHenry. His description of the fort to his mother included a detailed drawing and noted that the fort was never intended to threaten Baltimore:

> I suppose you have been under the impression that we have been quartered in the fort but such is not the case, as you will see by my drawing we are inside of the fortifications but not in the fort. This is what is called a birds eye view or in other words you are supposed to be looking down from above. now you will see that this fort was never built to fire the city its sole strength is pointing out in the bay and it can do considerable damage in that direction. its largest guns and mortars are turned on the cit since this war as you will remember Genl Dix at one time threatened to shell the city and he turned his large guns on that side of the fort for that purpose. when this fort was built it was never expected that this country would be at war with itself. Now the water battery is a good deal lower than the fort: if the enemy should take the lower or water battery they would have to scale a wall about 25 ft high to get to the fort. the upper tiers of guns in forts are always considered the best and they would have to do some tall fighting before they could take it too the water battery has no guns in it: but in case the enemy should take it the guns would not do them any good as they cannot be turned on the fort. The round ring in the center of the fort is the reservoir that supplies the ground with water. It is pumped full twice a day by the prisoners. The buildings on each side of the sally port are prisons. The far one on the left is the one that that spy was confined in. the far one on the right is the one that the ex Mayor of Washington is confined in he is sencensed to stay there for the remainder of the war he has already served two years he is a political prisoner.

Moore's apology for his poor pen might have included one for his literacy:

> Mother I am ashamed of this letter and I hate to send it but I have got the drawing of the fort (and it is a good one too) and don't like to tear it up. My pen is a miserable one as you will see by the writing I have been all over the barracks to get a good one but cannot so I hope that you will excuse me and remember the

inconveniences I am in I am well and doing first rate. Tell Anna I will answer her letter tomorrow or next day. I am on guard at the prison tomorrow so you know where I am 1 month from to day our time is up.[95]

Interactions between Baltimore's citizens and occupying troops were not always smooth, as related in a newspaper dispatch entitled "Assaulting the Provost Guard":

Alexander Joseph Cutino, keeper of a barber shop on Conway street, near Eutaw, was arrested yesterday, charged with employing boys to sell liquor to soldiers. Upon the guard attempting to arrest him, he turned upon them and assaulted one of them with a razor. He was locked up for trial.[96]

George Washington Kimball, a carpenter and soldier in the Fifth Massachusetts Volunteer Militia, wrote to his wife and children from Fort McHenry that Union troops were not embraced by Baltimoreans even late in the war:

We came through the prettiest part of the city of Baltimore we past the Washington monument whitch is a splendid thing. They received us in silence & no doubt they would like to throw Brick Bats at us if they dared to. They druged a soldier yesterday. He was a well & hearty man he lived just long enough to get into the fort & died. He was buried at 10 this morning. It seamed rather a solum introduction to camp. The first thing I saw this morning was the Gallos close by where we slept. They say there is to be a Rebil spy hung tomorrow on it. But I shall endeavor to ceap clear from it.[97]

Kimball's letter a week later helped explain the attitude of Baltimoreans toward the Union troops:

There is 4 men to be hung here the 29. as you will see by a slip of paper I will put in this. The Gallos that we have is only large enough for one. These men are to be hung all at once. So I have received orders to build a new one & am to work on it now have got to get it don this weak, it is not a verry pleasant job for me. I sort of emajin I am framing a Barn so I get along verry well.[98]

In October, Jacob Grove's Sixth Maryland Regiment was in Baltimore:

Early this morning I went to the (Federal) Hill again and found out we would not leave. Went up street again. They do not know my pass is not good. Had me before the colonel. I took a young lady to the theatre had a pleasant time. Went to the parks to sleep. Weather cool.[99]

George Buchanan Cole recorded his voting experience in Baltimore on election day, November 9. He wrote that election judges also asked if he had sent letters south or assisted any communications with the South:

Abt 9 A.m. I called at the Polls of my precinct 2nd, 10th w and finding no McClellan tickets on the grounds, I went down to St. Paul St. to procure one among the lawyers of that neighborhood. I obtained one and erasing the word "Democratic," and the names of all men known to me as secessionists, I returned to the polls. On presenting myself the constitutional oath was administered to me, and the judges, to whom I was well known, proceeded to ask me numerous questions. Among them, one of the earliest was "If the armies meet in battle which do you deem shall succeed?" This was amended before I could reply by one of the judges adding—"If the Northern and the Southern armies meet—" I replied "I know no Northern army—I desire always the success of the Federal army—of the Army of the United States—is that satisfactory?"[100]

The following day he described his election judge:

I called this morning on Isiah Cobb, the judge of election who put the questions to me. I asked him to let me see them. He consented to read them to me, saying they were devised by himself. The last one was "Have you in your church associations changed from listening to a loyal preacher to one of disloyal character?" He told me, [?], after reading this question that he would not have allowed any man to vote who did not answer it in the negative. He also said "I put the question to some men "Do you sustain the Administration in all its measures and I added, the measures of emancipation, confiscation and subjugation"—I asked "had you put that to me and I had answered in the negative, would I have been allowed to vote?" He replied No.[101]

In December, Eudocia Stansbury, owner of Eudowood on Hillen Road, southeast of Towsontown, described to May Preston, daughter of William and Madge Preston of the adjacent "Pleasant Plains" farm, the travails of the time:

The Government has placed on my farm 1,500 head of cattle and taken the old cottage for there quarters so the place is alive with men and cattle; and I am affraid your dear mamma is affraid to come and see us as she has not been hear since the dinner company, and aunt Christy and Johnney have just gone over to sea why it is that they have not bean over. I must ask you how you spent thanksgiving day and as it will be some time before you will tell me I shall have to tell how we spent ours, I expect you know that I never pay any attention to the day whatever not have any particular regard for the Commader but on this particular day I was doomed to make merry; I had forgot that it was thanksgiven day until two gentleman came from the citty and reminded me of the fact by saying they had come to dinner; so I commenced in my yousual way to make ready by sackrifising the lives of the geese and turkeys, in about two hours after I received intiligence that there was three Carriges more on there way so you can immgin the bussel the news created at our quiet Eudowood.

She closed with an apology:

> now my dear May you must excuse all imperfections and remember that I am not a young lady any longer, but am growing old so you must right whenever you can as nothing can give me more pleasure than to hear from you and now must say farewell once more to my dear little girl hoping that you are in the injoyment of the best of gods Blessings good health and a contented mind.[102]

Writing from his headquarters at the Eutaw House, Gen. Lew Wallace, now commanding the Middle Department, sought to introduce historian Benton Lossing to Jerome Bonaparte:

> Mr. Lossing, the historian, with a couple of gentlemen friends from Philadelphia, are with me this morning. They are very desirous of an introduction to you and Mrs. Bonaparte. If agreeable, I would like to present them this evening. In making this request, I hope you will be frank eno' to prevent us from intruding upon you or Mrs. B.[103]

chapter six

1861

In May, Robert Kirkwood described to his father his first duties, and his commitment to the cause:

> I am now at the National Hotel in camden St near the station—our recruiting office and drilling place. I was on duty until 2 oclock this evening, engaged in drilling and guarding the outside doors there is two guards placed at each door. We will not stay here no longer than we can get our Company filled up which will take 10 or 12 more men. I am not certain where we will be sent—it will be either at frederick or to guard the Baltimore and Central rail road we have not got our uniforms and weapons yet. it might be that we will part of next week try and come to the National hotel in camden street near Howard and [in]quire for Captain Willson you will find two guards at the door well Father I am in good spirits so far we get very good fare such as fresh and corned beef baken and good beding but I don't think it will last long but I feel determined and willing to endure all the hard ships and dangers to save that flag which has so long protected us and if I should be so unfortunate as to fall in battle I feel it will (be) in a good cause.[1]

In August, General Dix told Postmaster General Montgomery Blair that he could secure Baltimore with a sufficient number of trained troops—but that the serious danger to Maryland lay on the Eastern Shore:

> There is no doubt that a majority of the Union men in Baltimore desire the sppression of all the opposition presses in the city but there are many—and among them some of the most discreet—who think differently. The city is now very quiet and under control though my force is smaller than I asked. There is a good deal of impatience among some of the Union men. They wish to have something done. The feeling is very much like that which prevailed in Washington before the movement against Manassas. It would not be difficult to get up a political Bull Run disaster in this State. If the Government will give me the number of regiments I ask and leave them with me when I have trained them to the special service they may have to perform I will respond for the quietude of this city. Should the time for action come I shall be ready. In the meantime preparation is going on. I am fortifying Federal Hill under a general plan of defense suggested by me and approved by General Scott. Two other works will be commenced the moment I can get an engineer from Washington. On the Eastern Shore there should be prompt and decisive action. I have urged it repeatedly and earnestly during the last three weeks. Two well-disciplined regiments should march from Salisbury, the southern terminus of the Wilmington and Delaware Railroad,

Union Capt. Richard Wills lured recruits for the Second Maryland Infantry Regiment with the promise of a $300 bounty and offers of "a $15 premium for a Veteran and $10 for a New Recruit." MdHS.

through Accomack and Northampton Counties and break up the rebel camps before they ripen into formidable organizations as they assuredly will if they are much longer undisturbed. No man is more strongly in favor of action than I am but I want it in the right place. We are in more danger on the Eastern Shore than in any other part of the State.[2]

One missing Baltimorean may have been dragooned into the Confederate army:

Robins went down in Virginia in May to collect some money—but I have not heard from him since the 28th of May. I expect they have forced him to join the army—if they have it is contrary to his wishes—as he is not a fighting man. He can swear a great deal, but not fight.[3]

In October, Eliza Marsh of Palmyra complained to Charles Ridgely about the inability of civilians to provide assistance to young Confederate soldiers:

I see day by day so much in the Federal papers, respecting the rebel traitors, murderers, robbers, with every other epithet that can disgrace a civilized community. I feel disposed to vindicate the reputation of my neighbors sons who have left their comfortable homes, and many who were accustomed to the ease and elegancies of life, are now enduring all the hardships of a soldiers life. Their cloths in tatters and no parent or friend dare give them aid or comfort, that is treason. The attempt was made, and some have been betrayed and dearly have they suffered for it, their carriages and horses taken and property destroyed. If the rebels were allowed a single newspaper, the curtain would be lifted, and you would say that the dark ages of the world had returned. Believe me as one Regt after another comes here that they help themselves in town and country, the grocers have nothing left, the livery stables, have all the feed taken by force, there is nothing now but the growing crop of corn, a Regt. of Cavalry is to be quartered here and one of infantry for the winter the fear now is, that houses will be ransacked for beds and beding. They occupy the court house, and order any citizen to give up his house as they require it, without compensation, sometimes give government script. all this under a certain species of pretence to protect the law and to keep order.[4]

Thomas M. Cathcart of Jarrettsville, Baltimore County, noted the anxiety surrounding the draft of friends in a letter to John Hershey:

The friends are all well as far as I know, though well, Bro Hersey some are in great trouble on account of having been drafted. Your old friend, Sister Hall, near Ebenezer, and her daughters are almost beside themselves on account of Bro. James Hall's having been drafted, and old Bro. Walter Watters and family on account Howard's having been drafted and George Watters, was drafted also. Many more I might name who were drafted but it is unnecessary. These are days of sorrow, from being one of the most prosperous and healthy nations on earth, our sins have made us in a few short months a nation of mourners. Oh, that our sighs and tears were for our sins, then might we hope for peace.[5]

1862

On New Year's Day parishioners of Emmanuel Church in Baltimore found cards entitled "Objects of Benevolence for the Year 1862" on their pews. The list of offerings presented included "Union Societies," which encompassed the American Bible Society, American Tract Society, and the "Am. S.S. Union." Notice of the difficult times was made:

The Rector is well aware that the charitable ability of many of our number is much reduced by the evil times upon which we have fallen, but he ventures to express the trust that the Ransomed of the Lord will be so jealous of their Master's honor as to see to it that His cause is the last to suffer.[6]

Washington Hands, a Marylander in the Confederate army's First Maryland Regiment, was furious when, in spring 1862, his men resisted orders to go to the front near Front Royal during the Virginia campaign:

> Before this day I was proud to call myself a Marylander, but now, God knows, I would rather be known as anything else. Shame on you to bring this stain upon the fair face of your native state—to cause the finger of harm pointed at those who confided to your keeping their most sacred trust—their honor and that of the glorious old state. Marylanders you call yourselves. Profane not that hallowed name again. What Marylander ever before them threw down his arms and deserted his colors in the presence of the enemy, and those arms, placed in your hands by a woman? Never before has one single blot defaced her honored history.[7]

John G. Noyes, a Marylander in the Union army, wrote to his aunt from camp at Budds Ferry, on the Potomac River, about his homesickness and reasons for fighting:

> I take great pleasure in answering your kind letter which I received last evening when when I read your kind letter it makes me think of the happy times I used to have at your house what a change has taken place since then. I would like to have those days come back again. I can hardly express my happiness in words them times were the happest of any in my life. I am happy to see that I am not forgot and am sorry that I did not get your letter that you sent to Boston but never mind that now now we have found each other we will keep run of each other I am very glad to hear that you take so much interest in the poor soldiers especially me you talk of promotion there ain't much of a chance for that besides I didn't come here for that I came here to fight for the union and liberty not for money or promotion. I am a soldier only when soldiers are needed to defend our country. I am happy to know that I have the honor in representing the family in this wicked rebellion.[8]

The Fire Inspector's Office advised advised the mayor's office of hazardous items in Baltimore, suggesting that "some restriction be placed upon their sale and use":

> I respectfully call your attention to the fact that there is now sold in our city an exceedingly dangerous article, called the "Parlor Match." It is of an explosive character, and well calculated to frighten horses and increase the number of accidental fires. This article of match are mostly purchased by small children, and are used by them in various mischevious ways. There is no telling what amount of loss of life and property may be the result of the continued use of these matches unless some restrictions are placed upon their manufacture and sale, or use. One building has already been destroyed by fire, caused by children playing with these dangerous things.[9]

In July, Governor Bradford convened a meeting of fifty men (including Enoch Pratt, former Mayor Thomas Swann, Johns Hopkins, and John P. Kennedy) in the office of the mayor of Baltimore to discuss incentives for raising volunteers to meet Maryland's quota of four regiments. They discussed bounties, drafting with paid substitutes and taxes, and passed resolutions to press their case upon the Governor.[10]

With Mayor George Brown in a federal prison in July, acting mayor John Lee Chapman called upon the city council to

> borrow on the credit of the city $300,000 for volunteers in the regiments authorized to be raised in the State of Maryland. This bill doubtless needs perfecting in some of its parts, and I would respectfully suggest that the loan should take the form of city stock, redeemable in 1882 or 1892, and that sinking fund be established for its redemption. Public sentiment imperatively demands the passage of this ordinance, or one having the same object in view, and I beg your honorable body to give the subject an immediate and favorable consideration. The Government and the people of the loyal States are engaged in a mighty struggle for the existence and perpetuation of the Republic. Free institutions and all that we hold dear are at stake, and when the rebellion is crushed, and peace and Union once more prevail, it must not be said that our city failed to do its whole duty.

A crowd gathered outside the council chamber disapproved:

> In the Second Branch chamber, outside of the railing, and in the passage leading thereto, there was a crowd of fifteen or twenty persons, who evidenced their disapproval of the course pursued by the Branch by their language, but made no manifestations of any design to act violently.[11]

By early 1862, "The Maryland Society" had formed to seek information about fallen soldiers in both armies from Maryland and the District of Columbia.[12] John Donnell Smith wrote his sister Ellen from Richmond about his attendance at two meetings in late 1861–early 1862, finding it

> a highly useful Organization. It serves as a medium of communication with Maryland in the Army throughout the South, forward letters & packages and receives donations. The generosity of Baltimore to Southern prisoners has had a remarkable effect throughout all the South. 15 thousand dollars worth of articles have been donated to the Society.

He mentioned an item from his home state:

> *Maryland buttons* are greatly sought after here. I should have a set myself.

And told Ellen that

> There are many young men here from Baltimore who in the hope of *something turning up here* become mere loafers. They talk of expecting commissions—of

raising companies and of waiting until Spring. I saw a very good letter from young Lyon, a private in the 1st Maryland. He says he has never regretted the step he has taken—that he is satisfied to do the work before him, because others as deserving as himself are in the same position & because he came here not to advance any personal ends. He advises all who are in earnest, & who feel confident of their health & strength, to come down to Camps *at once* & join.[13]

On July 4, 1862, Governor Bradford responded to Lincoln's call for an additional three hundred thousand men, combining pleas for Union with language suggesting the serious threat to Maryland:

Men of Maryland I look to you with confidence to be among the foremost in responding to this call. There are reasons why you should be. You are, as it were, the natural bodyguard of the Capital of the Nation. If this diabolical rebellion ever makes another forward movement, its first step will be upon your soil. In your very midst there lurks a comparatively small, but still influential, plotting, determined, treasonable element, watching the first opportunity to pilot the rebellion's host into your midst and to give up to the desolation of war your present peaceful firesides.[14]

Jacob Eugene Duryee resigned from the Second Maryland Volunteer Regiment following the Battle of Antietam:

Shortly after the Battle of Antietam I decided to resign as I had heard that Governor Bradford had been on the field, and had ignored us, not even visiting the regiment or our cowshed hospital where so many brave Maryland soldiers lay wounded and dying. We needed the Governor's sympathy, besides our wants were many, especially for medical supplies, etc.

General Ambrose Burnside initially refused to accept the resignation, but when Duryee spoke up the next day, Burnside accepted it:

General, at reveille this morning less than 100 men answered the roll call, out of 953 men who had reported to you in North Carolina for duty in April, not five months ago.[15]

John G. Noyes described his bucolic camp near the James River in Virginia, following McClellan's retreat from the Peninsula campaign, writing that "we had a pretty hard time of it I assure you the enemy were on our heels all the way and we had some very hard battles with them we had a fight every day." Noyes reported that "We are encamped in the woods near a mill Pond":

a splendid place to bathe as I was batheing yesterday General McClellan passed by and seemed very much pleased to see us enjoy ourselves and well we might enjoy ourselves it is the first oppitunity we have had for many a month we have not had time to even wash our clothes for the last few months but now we can make up for lost time as we are to camp here 2 or three weeks.

I spent the fourth in picking Blackberries which are plenty here it didn't seem much like the fourth of July I assure you.

I would like Ellens likeness very much I can remember as well as though it was yesterday when I used to hold herr in my lap and amuse her.

At the end Noyes wrote, "hopeing to live through the rest of this Campaign."[16]

A Harford County woman expressed to her aunt in Howard County her worry about the effects of the draft on the local voting population:

mother is very much troubled, about the present prospects of our once happy county. they are already, about, enrolling the names in preparation for the draft, which has caused quite a number to volunteer. brother still remains at home, but how long he will be, permitted, to stay I do not know, as it is, thought that it will take one man out of every four men, which will thin out the number very much in our district, as there, is only about 750 voters in the district, dear aunt thee must excuse me for writing so gloomy, but there appears, to be, a general gloom on every face although in the midst of gloom, we must have faith and look to *him,* who rules, the universe for *aid* and *comfort,* for he only can aid us.[17]

In a letter to Father John Hershey, Robert Wilson prepared to seek redemption from the misfortune of the draft:

I have not as yet been drafted, and I hope I will be blessed with the luck of drawing a prize, but should the chances be against me, I will have to bear my portion of the work and trust in the Lord for the results.

I feel very unworthy and think sometimes, that I have lost that good desire; I feel cold and careless as regards to my future, then again I feel as if I am resigned to the will of God; I know that I have been to careless, and have sinned with a high hand, and have fail to walk in that straight and narrow way as I SHOULD, BUT BY THE HELP of God I will try and live from this time forward in his favor, and I wish you to bear me before the throne daily, that I may be made the creature that God would have me be.[18]

When the Second Branch of the Baltimore City Council on July 23 rejected an ordinance that would have appropriated money to prevent the passage of Northern troops through the city, council members felt the wrath of an angry crowd estimated at four hundred people:

The members of the Second Branch voting against the ordinance, the disloyalty of all of whom is well known, were protected by the police from the excited multitude who followed them to their homes, and two of them were slightly assaulted.

Marshal Van Nostrand announced that he would "preserve the peace and that they must be quiet," whereupon "an elderly man, with a broad Scotch dialect, cried out that Decatur H. Miller was a traitor, and should be hung."

As the crowd grew larger and more agitated, Van Nostrand offered Miller and three other members sanctuary in his office. Councilman Baker (one of two members who voted against) left via carriage and was followed by a crowd of fifty screaming, "traitor" and "hang him," and 150 policemen arrived to escort home the council members:

> The last member who left was Mr. Miller, whose appearance excited the hostility of the crowd, who surrounded the officers with the intention of rescuing and perhaps hanging him from the nearest lamppost, as they swore they would, but the entire police force at the building rallied, and after a hard struggle at the corner of Holliday and Saratoga streets succeeded in repulsing the assailants and in conducting Mr. Miller to his residence, on the corner of Monument and Cathedral streets, the distance being a full half mile. The crowd, however, followed, crying out "come and look at a live rebel," "a d—d traitor to the best Government upon the earth." The Marshal, Capt. Mitchell and Commissioner Hindes walked along side of Miller as far as his house, where he thanked them for their protection. A guard of about thirty officers was left in front of the house for the purpose of protecting it.[19]

"Immense Union Meeting in Monument Square," trumpeted a newspaper on July 29, at which "the appearance of the veteran General Wool and his staff was greeted with warm and enthusiastic cheers" and Governor Bradford took the speaker's stand:

> I thank you from my heart, my fellow-citizens for the warmth and cordiality of your greeting. It was nine months since he last occupied that stand. It was when your State and your city were in a state of jeopardy and alarm, from which nothing but your ballots could have rescued them. It was then that reckless demagogues had combined with faithless officers to give a death-blow to your continuance in the Union.
>
> But nobly did you come to the rescue, and show conclusively to the world that Maryland, in her central position, was in her heart as true and loyal to the Union as any State at the utmost verge of its circumference.
>
> Your country is now assailed by wanton hands, and I know that you will not shrink from its defense. You have not only a common but a particular interest in the perpetuity of the Union. Maryland is offended at any doubtful reputation of her loyalty. The rebels and traitors, pressing into its ranks old and young, the rebel and the true man, are endeavoring to march hither, and to place their foot first upon your soil.

But Maryland will not hesitate a moment to march to the front; she will send her four regiments to oppose them.

Bradford explained that he had not called the legislature into special session because it had just met a few months before, and so doing

would afford an opportunity to the horde of traitors in our midst to foment the inordinate agitation of sectional questions for the purpose of aiding the rebels.

Marylanders will have, proclaimed Bradford,

in a week at furthest a municipal legislature, both branches of which will be unquestionably loyal. One branch has already made a most liberal appropriation in connection with the bounty to be paid to your volunteers—a bounty which will cheer him on his forward march, so that he will cast no lingering look behind.[20]

From his James River camp, John Noyes related details of army medical care:

I am not wounded or hurt in any way and am thankful for it for the way Doctors treat sick and wounded soldiers on the Battlefield is a shame they are not fit to fill the positions they do. On the late retreat I saw a Doctor take a wounded soldier out of an ambulance and lay him beside the road saying he wouldn't live to lay there and die and then the doctor took and helped a sick nigger into the same ambulance he had taken the poor soldier out of a moment before. If this is humanity it is time this war was ended. It is actually murder to see how the poor wounded soldiers are treated by brutes professing to be Doctors but this is times of war now and so soldiers are supposed to be dogs and are treated as such but the time is comeing when we will be on an even footing with those who profess to be our superiors. We have a butiful young lady with us now acting as nurse in the hospital. She is from Chelsea Mass. I had the honor of being detailed to guard her tent last night to see that no one disturbed her peaceful slumber and pleasent Dreams. I am afraid there will be a great many more sick on her acount. I've a great mind to be sick myself would you blame me I don't believe ou would.[21]

In September, Bradford asked the secretary of war for "Infantry arms and equipments for say four or five thousand men" for Marylanders wishing to organize militia companies:

The people of our State excited by current events are manifesting a strong desire for immediate Militia organization, and their great anxiety is to be able to procure arms—unfortunately we have but very few at command—Although the purpose of those proposing thus to organize looks chiefly to domestic emergencies, yet those emergencies are just now so intimately connected with the National cause, that it would seem important in every aspect that we should avail ourselves of the spirit now aroused and arm as many as possible of our loyal people.[22]

As in any major military campaign, the logistics of supporting troops are significant. These dined al fresco *outside the U.S. Naval Academy in Annapolis before departing for Washington. Pratt Lib.*

Stanton replied positively the next day:

> We shall supply your organized force with arms as fast as they can be needed. Two thousand stand were sent yesterday to Genl Wool for that purpose.
>
> In distributing arms to other persons too much care cannot be exercised. I have ordered One thousand stand to be sent to you at Baltimore and will endeavor to keep you supplied.[23]

Eager to capitalize on Stanton's willingness to oblige, the governor requested assistance in implementing the Maryland draft:

> I would take this occasion again to call your attention to the absolute necessity of providing a small Military force to be stationed in some six or eight of our Counties to ensure the peaceable execution of the Draft—it would require some 500 men.—The Enrolling books in two of the Counties having been captured by the Rebels, and other causes of delay existing, we have been compelled again to postpone the Draft until 15th October.[24]

In the Eastern Shore counties of Worcester and Somerset, men were selected randomly in the draft:

> A detachment of Company K, Capt. L. Long, was present to preserve order but there was no need of their services, as everything went off quietly. Tickets were drawn by Mr. John R. Rowland, who was blindfolded.[25]

1863

James Farnandis, who lived at "The Homestead" near Bel Air in Harford County, complained to Governor Bradford of "an outrage inflicted on my Mother and myself by a detachment of the Purnell Cavalry, commanded by Captain Theodore Clayton."[26] Bradford's reply explained the cavalry unit's assignment and that he had both expressed his disapproval to Clayton, who was to ensure that his men are "promptly and properly punished," and contacted the quartermaster "urging the necessity of a prompt and liberal payment for it":

> It is unnecessary for me, I hope, to express my unqualified condemnation of the proceedings of which you complain on the part of a detachment of Capt. Clayton's Cavalry Company in taking violently and against your remonstrance 15 Bushels of Oats from your Granary.
>
> I am surprised however that Capt. Clayton should have so entirely mistaken the character of the State's connection with his Command, as to represent it as "entirely a State affair the expenses of which were to be paid by funds provided by the State"—His Company, it is true was detailed by the War Department to aid in enforcing the draft in this State, that being a Government and not a State affair—and for that purpose were ordered to report to me. This however was only that I should indicate where they could be most serviceably employed in accomplishing the object for which they were detailed; And although I assigned them to the Rendezvous of drafted men near Baltimore, where they have been for the last two months employed in guarding that Camp and hunting up deserters from it, yet their Military government and especially their Supplies of Subsistence and forage have been exclusively under the control of the usual Military Authorities, entirely unconnected with the State which has not paid nor is expected by the Government to pay for their supplies.[27]

In March, Bradford appointed Samuel Streeter head of a new agency, "Superintending the Ward of the Sick and wounded officers and men, who have volunteered into Maryland Regiments." In his appointment letter, Bradford told Streeter that because no appropriation existed for compensation, "I will take it upon myself to pay out of the Executive Contingent fund all reasonable personal expenses connected with your agency as you shall from time to time present accounts for the same." The governor also noted several problems requiring Streeter's attention:

1. A sick or wounded soldier being absent from his Regiment when the Paymaster visits it, is frequently overlooked, and his pay is not only considerably in arrear but is frequently several months behind that of all others in the Corps.
2. He is often desirous, when he has received his pay, to transmit a part of it to his family at home, and unable to do so from the want of some trusty friend at hand to whom he can confide it.

3. Circumstances may frequently exist which would authorize the transfer of an inmate in some particular Hospital to some other nearer to friends and home, and where the transfer could work no possible detriment to the Government and would be allowed, if some one was at hand competent to make the proper representation.[28]

As Lee began preparing his army in early summer to move north, rumors swirled westward from Baltimore. Frederick Shriver wrote to cousin Henry, recently departed to meet his unit in the Army of the Potomac:

The day after you left was rather a gloomy one here. All sorts of rumors were going and of course all of the worst kind, that, with your & Daves leaving tended to make every body feel blue. One story was that the Confeds were before Hanover & requested the women & children to leave as they were going to burn the town. That report did not disturb anybody much though, for it was contradicted immediately after by a man straight from H[eadquarters]. It was really funny to read of 8000 Rebels being at Westminster & as many more at Littlestown. As the truth comes to be known there seems to have been a great cry and *very* little wool I think.

The girls seemed to take your departure pretty much to heart that evening after you left, they all had a pretty good cry in the parlor, & didn't want to do anything else until they went to bed. I was sitting on the porch at the time and as the sobs came through the open doors I felt *almost* like doing the same thing myself—(When I said *you*, above there I meant you & Dave)—Though they were low spirited for a day or so after you left, as the danger from the Rebs decreased their spirits rose & I think fully made up for what they had lost. I took them boat riding yesterday evening & I don't think I ever saw a noisier, jollier set in my life.[29]

John Noyes wrote again in July of the young woman nursing injured soldiers:

We have got one of those Angels in this regiment a young Lady from Chelsea Mass named Miss Gibson she is doing a great deal of good. She devotes her whole attention to the sick. She even sings to them and in the evening she sings with the glee club which we have in the regiment.[30]

Thomas Sewell Ball, known as "Sewell," was a Corporal in Company B of the Tenth Maryland Volunteers stationed in September at Harpers Ferry, where he received a letter from a cousin:

Your father is quite as uncompromising a union man as ever; and perhaps both of us are a little more so than formerly—if possible. We are in daily expectation of the ultimatum from Charleston—and that is that treason may be utterly eradicated and exterminated, in its original cradle: that one stone may not be left upon another, if need be, as a resting place for its fiendish presence! Charleston is a great and lovely city, and other circumstances its destruction would be heartily deplored: but in the choice between our beloved country & our glorious old Star-spangled Banner, and *that* city of *all* cities, of the South, let them perish—let them be as Lyre & Babylon, sooner than yield an inch to the demon of Secession![31]

From Camp Porter, Ball wrote to his sister Lou in Baltimore:

I was sorry I could not be with you on the pic-nic. I know they could not help but miss me and my straw-hat. I was exceedingly glad the Maggie had entirely recovered and hope she will continue well. As she & Miss Lou send their love I suppose there would be no harm in returning the compliment. You can give my best love and confections. I hope they will enjoy themselves, during their visit to Phila. I am glad Mag. likes the album. Ask Mag. if she promised me her picture if she did to enclose it in an envelope directed to you and I will possibly get it. It is very seldom we see a lady's face here. We see now and then a country-woman but they are generally as ugly as sin. I would like to see somebody.

How are all my friends Sunday school and day school friends. I will hardly get back some say before my six month's are out, but nobody but the General commanding knows. We were reviewed by Gen. Lockwood on Friday. He thinks much of the regiment.

After writing "I guess we'll all go to Butcher's when I am discharged if I should live," he described the weather, camp routine, and that "John's cheese was full of skippers from one side to another" before closing:

The candle is going out. Write soon and send the picture if she will give it to you. I am very well. P.S. Tell Ma not to send any more pitchers or crockery of any kind. They can sell it, and send me what they want to, in a bottle which I can throw away when useless.[32]

Lou wished her brother to write more:

Enclosed you will find some *stamps*. If you will only write often I will supply you with *all the necessary articles*. Ma will write in a few days and send you some money. They expect Charlie [Henry] son on soon, and perhaps that would be a safer way of sending it. Write soon a *long, long* letter. Do you want some more *live cheese*. Ha! Ha! Ha! Or, do you prefer *ice-cream and strawberries at Butchers. Olden times, we often talk of them. Good Bye.*[33]

Several weeks later Ball's cousin wrote again:

We enjoyed ourselves in Baltimore as well as could be expected. You were on the lips of some one every hour in the day. Sewall, no one in the army, I judge,

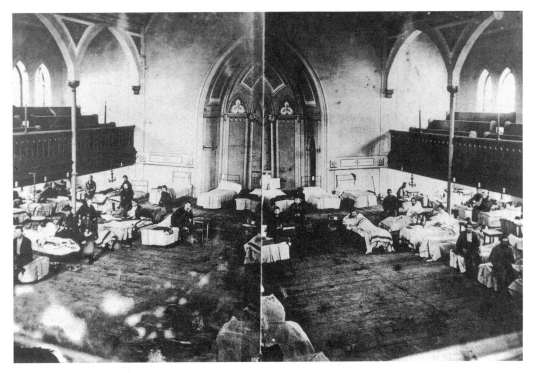

Wounded soldiers from Antietam were tended to in the makeshift hospital at the Evangelical Lutheran Church in Frederick. Wooden planks were laid atop the pews to make a floor for cots. MdHS.

is more sincerely beloved, and has more fervent prayers offered for him, than, yourself. But all this will avail you but little, if you be not yourself vigilant, guarding against sin.[34]

In October, Governor Bradford complained that Maryland volunteers were not being properly credited to the state's draft quota and that Maryland's quota for the 1863 draft was disproportionately higher compared with 1862. Bradford cited a letter from the provost marshal general:

That orders had been sent to Boards of Enrollment—directing a draft to be made in the 1st, 2nd & 3rd Congressional Districts of our state.

I have since had a conference with Major Jeffries the Dep. Pro. Marshal for Maryland, who, I was in hopes would be able to furnish me with some of the data or calculations by which the number of the draft from these three Districts has been ascertained. It does not appear from any information possessed by Major Jeffries or myself that any credit whatever for the three years or six months volunteers, white or colored, has been made either to these Congressional Districts or to the Counties composing them, and the number ordered from these

Districts would seem to confirm that view of the case. Indeed the number as compared with the previous draft is calculated to startle us.

The number of drafted men called for by the President's order of 1863 is I believe the same ordered in the draft of 1862, viz 300.000—and yet the quota of the whole state under the 1862 draft was but six thousand, or less by upwards of two thousand, (and exclusive of the 50 per cent margin) than is now claimed from three only of the five Congressional Districts in which the state is divided. And this too in the face of the fact that is indisputable, that the number now in the state subject to military duty is far less than at the time of the former draft.[35]

Bradford sought military and financial support from Washington to enforce the draft in Prince George's County:

Mr. Clark the Commissioner whilst in the Court House engaged in hearing applications for exemption was openly assaulted and grossly insulted by an armed Rebel, who has been it is said for a year past in the Rebel service, and who though the room was crowded with people where the Commissioner was engaged, was permitted to enter and commit this outrage and to depart without even an attempt to arrest him—Mr. Clark who will bear you this will detail more particularly the circumstances of the outrage.[36]

Bradford reminded an officer of a cavalry company attached to Purnell's Legion of his responsibility to enforce the draft:

I would take this occasion to impress upon you the delicacy and importance of the duties required of you and that you take care that your Command act with all possible discretion. Whilst they will avoid all unnecessary force and abstain as far as possible from all actions calculated to offend or irritate the citizens of the County, they will at the same time exhibit such a firm & determined course as to manifest to all inclined to resist the enrollment the folly and necessary failure of such an attempt, and the determination of the authorities to enforce the enrollment and draft in said County as thoroughly as in all the others of the State.[37]

In November, two citizens of Worcester County asked that Pvt. James Snead be released from military service because he had been "violently and attacked and prostrated by rheumatism":

Being entire strangers to you we must ask pardon for the liberty we have taken, and we are only induced to do so from the fact that our people are disposed to relieve men with large depending and helpless families like Snead here from military Service and to Substitute in their place. *"Colored Volunteers"* who are now entering the Service in large numbers from our County as by this management the Government looses nothing, and the poor white man is relieved.

Another reason is because all of poor Sneads family are among our most loyal men, and aided in our late polit-struggle to carry forward that banner of "Union & Emancipation."[38]

The Reverend John Rose, a native of Bavaria, in February 1861, became Missionary of the South Eastern District of Baltimore. In November 1863, he sought counsel from Bishop Whittingham:

> I have this day been drafted for military service, & most respectfully ask your advise as to the proper course for me to pursue—I am neither physically fit for service, nor able pecuniarly to pay the commutation money. My severe illness for the last four weeks prevents my seeing you personally.[39]

Late in November came a reaction to the exemption policy for conscription in Maryland:

> (William) Pennington has saved $300 by leaving the Country, as I see he has been drafted for the army. This expedient for managing the war has been in progress all the week in this City. It is believed that all those who have been drafted who favor the war will obey their Country's call by paying the $300. Those who desire to see this struggle ended will be compelled also to pay if they can afford it while those who are too poor, will be very reluctant soldiers. The poor negroes who have been drafted, are in a state of abject horror.[40]

James L. Baylies presented to his boss, Jerome Bonaparte, a strategy for confronting the draft:

> The draft in this City is now progressing rapidly and this week will finish it as the draft of my ward the 19th will not take place until Saturday next I am unable to say whether I will have to enter Uncle Sam's service [is no]—the quota being about two in every thirteen. I guess my chances are about as good as any for a prize, but should I fail in this one, I will have another and perhaps better chance in the Draft of January 5th '64. It looks very much like that I will have to shoulder a musket some time with in the next three months, but I hope not, as I am sure it would not agree with me, at all.[41]

The draft ended earlier than Baylies predicted and made him a member of the army—so he asked Bonaparte for an increase in salary so he might procure a substitute:

> The draft in this City was completed Saturday last, and according to my usual luck, I drew a prize, and consequently am now considered as belonging to Uncle *Sam*.
>
> As I am very certain that the hardships of a soldier's life will not agree with my delicate Constitution I have no desire whatever to become one, and will endeavor to commute by paying the three hundred dollars, which will exempt me

"Ministering to the Wounded"—women waited outside a Hagerstown hospital bearing packages for men in October 1862. Harper's Weekly/Pratt Lib.

from serving as a soldier for three years, before which I hope this war may be at an end.

In thus relieving myself, it will take all the [mon]ey that I can raise and [?] together, and reduce [me] very small compass indeed.

All the necessaries of life are enormously [?], and are advancing every day, and with my present Salery [I] find it a very hard matter indeed to make both ends meete.

I am fully aware that you would have no difficulty in getting some one to take my place at the same salary, or perhaps less, but my unConscience tells me that you can get no one to be more attentive to your affairs nor study your interest more than I do, however you are the best judge of this.[42]

After apologizing for taking five months to reply—explaining that Baylies's letter had arrived when he was ill—Bonaparte declined to help:

I should feel it impossible to increase my expenses on the collections of my income, when it is so very materially reduced, that I have been obliged to diminish my own expenses much lower than they have ever been before. In times of great national calamity every one must suffer & reduce their living, both employed and employees. Should things return to their normal state, I do not suppose you would expect an increase of salary, should they get worse (they cannot remain as they are), I may not have the means of employing anyone but may be reluctantly obliged to perform myself what you are now doing for me. From the above I hope you will not infer that I do not fully appreciate the value of your services, or that I am insensitive to the hardships of your case, particularly in having been obliged to pay for a substitute for the war, which must have been very onerous to you last year.[43]

1864

Governor Bradford's speech to the state legislature on the first day of its 1864 session included a nod to Marylanders fighting in the Union army:

> We who remain at home, surrounded by its comforts, and with our ordinary avocations in most cases scarcely interrupted by the casualties of the war, are hardly prepared to estimate, as we ought, the value of the service which these soldiers render, or to realize the extent of the privations they endure.[44]

Provost Marshal James B. Fry wrote to Bradford in May defending the army's method for crediting Maryland for troops raised in the state:

> Due credit has been given for all the men both white and colored, who are in any way known to this Department to have been mustered into the U.S. Service. Yesterday an additional credit of 2250 colored men was given upon a certificate of Col. Jeffries that they were creditable—,this was done without waiting as customary, for more certain & formal Rolls & Returns. The total number of colored recruits now credited to the state is 6404. I know of no data upon which to base further credits, nor of any reason to postpone the draft. If however, any further musters are reported they will be credited up to the latest possible moment. I am unable to discover wherein this Bureau has disregarded the "circumstances which have justly entitled" the loyal citizens of Maryland to "liberal considerations," as set forth in your Excellency's letter, or that you have been dealt with "ever so strictly." The facts are these as they appear to me.
>
> 1st—The quotas assigned to you since March 3rd 1863 have all been based upon an enrollment of the white persons found to be still in that state after the disloyal persons have gone south. The quotas being in proportion to the number of men left,—the fact that some men had gone south previous to the enrollment worked no hardship.
>
> 2nd—after having assigned quotas *in proportion to the enrollment of white men* as above, the slaves were enrolled and are used for filling the quotas of volunteers and drafts but have not been counted to increase the quota. That is surely not dealing "strictly" with you.[45]

Two weeks later Fry sent the governor an opinion from the solicitor of the War Department describing the government's policy regarding Marylanders who either had joined the Confederate army or taken up residence "between the Rebel lines" and their eligibility for enrollment:

> The statement of His Excellency the Governor of Maryland, shows that persons, formerly citizens of that State, who have gone into the rebellious States, and have not within two or three years last past, been residents within any town or district of Maryland, have nevertheless been enrolled in some instances as part of our Military forces, and have been credited in estimating quotas. The requests that the names of such non-residents may be removed from the enrollment, whenever it shall be again revised and corrected.
>
> This request is reasonable and is according to law. The Statutes require the enrollment only of persons residing in the respective districts &c of the loyal States, and do not include in the forces of the United States, persons who have some years since joined the forces of the enemy, or who have permanently taken up their residence in territory at present under their military control.
>
> It would be a hardship not imposed by Congress upon the people of any loyal State, and not in accordance with your intention, to assign their quota on a basis of enrollment which should include non-residents. While it will be the duty of the Board of enrollment to see that no name shall be improperly removed from the lists on the plea of non residence, the reenrollment lists should be corrected as requested, and the quotas should be assigned accordingly.[46]

Rev. John Kerfoot, president of the College of St. James, asked J. P. Kennedy for help for a colleague:

> One of the officers of our College, the Rev. Mr. Coster, has been drafted as a soldier. He cannot out of his very moderate salary, pay the commutation money #300; & he has no means besides. I have undertaken the effort in his behalf to procure the money from those who as Churchmen & Union-men, will be most likely to regard the request favorably. Mr. Coster is a Marylander by birth, of Charles Co., & a decidedly loyal man—the plan requested to me was to ask twelve gentlemen to share my effort by procuring a giving equal shares of the sum.[47]

William R. Wilmer of Port Deposit sought Bishop Whittingham's aid in securing a surgeon's position in the Union army, asking for "a certificate that I am a loyal man":

> I am drafted, and I do not wish to be exempted. I want to obey my country's call. Being lame I am physically disabled from performing the duties usually required of drafted men, but I do think I am able to perform a surgeon's duties, particularly if not required to ride much on horseback. I graduated the year before your son in Baltimore and attended lectures the following year in Philadelphia. I have been engaged in quite an active country practice whenever my health would permit it, which has been, except the time I have been sick, about ten years.

Attention
MARYLANDERS!

The undersigned is raising a Company for the Maryland Line, now rapidly organizing in Richmond. He will be in Charlottesville, at the Farish House, on Saturday morning; at Staunton, at the Virginia Hotel, on Saturday evening and Sunday morning, and after that in Richmond, 12th Street, three doors from Main. Persons wishing to join can be mustered in on application, and transportation furnished to Richmond.

McHENRY HOWARD.
Late A. D. C. to Gen'l. C. S. Winder.

Baltimorean McHenry Howard recruited Marylanders in Virginia for the Maryland Line, "now rapidly organizing in Richmond." Howard, from a prominent Maryland family, served as aide-de-camp to Gen. Charles Winder until Winder was killed in August 1862. MdHS.

During the war I have generally attended the soldiers stationed in this county when they have been without their regular officers (medical) making about fifteen hundred altogether that I have had under my medical care. I have an earnest and peculiar desire not to be exempted, principally because I love my country and wish to do all in my power to preserve the Union; and because I wish to be, and to show my secessionist friends that I am, a consistent Union man. While all around me are seeking exemption I wish to set them an example of genuine loyalty.[48]

Samuel B. Lawrence, the assistant adjutant general on Gen. Lew Wallace's staff, reported on efforts in Baltimore to raise additional troops during Confederate Gen. Jubal Early's assault at Monocacy Junction, to the west:

I have the honor to report that matters are progressing favorably here. The Union Leagues are forming companies, and as fast as the companies are reported I send the captain a copy of the circular herewith inclosed, so as to prepare them for a call. They seem pleased with it. I think they will raise twelve or fifteen companies. They prefer battalion organizations, of four companies, to select their own field officers, and say there will be no great objection to your appointing the field officers. I have issued a special order to-night to arrest all officers in this city without authority. Copy of the special order is inclosed for your information. It is said there are a great many such officers in town.[49]

Lawrence explained plans for a new cavalry company:

> The current business of the office is about as usual, all finished up to to-night. I am at the office almost constantly, and can keep up I think. The Union League asked permission this a.m. to organize a cavalry company. I told them to go ahead and report when they were ready. Then if you approve I will seize horses from the rebels here and mount them—that is, if necessary. The list of persons who own horses has been furnished by the police. The cavalry company prepared by the Union League will be mainly composed by those who have had experience in the cavalry service. I think it a good idea. Captain Leib with his cavalry marched this afternoon.[50]

The Baltimore Union Club formed a militia company in July, following the Confederate army's eastward march toward Washington:

> The excitement caused by the third invasion of the state by the Rebel forces, the Cavalry raid around the City, and threatened attack upon the City, drew a large number of members together, early in the morning. Among them it was at once determined to raise an Independent Company of Military and tender its services to the defence of the City.[51]

Horace Shipley of Westminster learned that he had been drafted:

> It was mid day the eleventh of July eighteen hundred and sixty four that I while in the discharge of my merchantile duties was informed by a much esteemed lady friend Miss Susanna Gilliss that my name had been drawn from the State enrollment list to serve or to do military duty in defense of the government of the United States for the period of one hundred days I replide to Miss Gilliss by saying that I was a going to answer the call myself and I should not get any substitute upon making further inquiery I assertained that all the drafted men that failed to report on or before the fifteenth of July were to be considered dissirters
>
> As I had no dissire to be classed with that unfortinate class of men I resolved to make immediate preperations for entering the military service I according in gaged my sister Ann R. Shipley and my Brother John B. Shipley to endeaver to cary on my Store under the immediate controal and advice of my Father
>
> But here let me remark that the presence of Henry Gilmore and his band of rebble gurillas had caused me to stow some of my goods in to places not likely to meet his view

"At sunrise," Shipley met his friend Thomas B. Gosnell "for the purpose of traveling to gether in his carriage to the city of Baltimore the place named for us to report ourselves for military duty."

Avoiding capture by rebels said to be prowling the roads between Westminster and Baltimore, Shipley arrived at Lambert's Hotel on July 14:

> I stayed at the tavern that night and the next morning I went to the Adgentant Generals office and was examined by Doctor C.C. Cox and by him I was pronounce fisically able to do military duty But General Shriver granted me six days longer time to close my buisiness and arrainge my affairs preparatory to entering the Service of the United States.[52]

Rebecca Davis's father Allen led an effort to raise funds to exempt all males in the area from the draft:

> Pa having been appointed to receive contributions for buying off our district from the draft, Wednesday evening received between $4 & $5000, it being known to the whole neighborhood made us feel a little uneasy that night. Mr. T. Riggs came in to tea and was pressed into service for the night. We discussed all the robberies & murders imaginable & Priscilla became too alarmed to sleep way over in the front room, so she & Mary came to keep us company. We had much fun arming ourselves in defence. Pa had a carbine, revolver & sabre, Mr. R. a revolver, me a big cane & neglected till too late our intention to bring up the *Indian war club.* Under the watchful eye of an ever gracious Providence, all slept in peace & safety, though Priscilla & Mary declared they heard queer noises which did not justify alarming the gents, but kept them in a nervous *tremor.*[53]

A cavalry company in Westminster requested a commission and arms from Governor Bradford:

> They have adopted the name of the "Carroll County Union Cavalry," and are comprised of excellent material at their request I write to ask you to commission the officers, and furnish them arms & equipments as early as possible. I think they will be serviceable in the community.[54]

Lieutenant Col. Gregory Barrett Jr., Fourth Maryland Volunteers, recounted a raid in Virginia on the Weldon Railroad, in which his men moved on Jerusalem Plank Road, crossed the Nottoway River, and passed through Sussex Court House toward Jarrett's Station. Rebel cavalry captured many stragglers:

> On nearing Sussex C.H., three of our men were found by the roadside having been shot through the head and stripped of all their clothing; this act was evidently the work of guerrillas and so exasperated our men that they fired every house, barn, stable and pen on the route from that point to our old lines in front; the destruction was terrible and I felt sorry for the women and children who were thus rendered homeless, but the innocent must suffer with the guilty in such cases, for such is war.

Barrett complained that storming rebel fortifications does not succeed, for the federals lose men as enlistments expire—a problem the Confederates did not have because they did not discharge their veterans. The government, he claimed, needed more men:

> If our Government does not awake from the lethargic doze under which they have been laboring for so long, you will find that not even all the time of the incoming administration will suffice to put down the Rebellion; we should at once put into the field three hundred thousand men, not substitutes and Bounty jumpers, and then we would hurt somebody.
>
> Mr. Lincoln now has his seat firmly for four more years and he should go to work and get every man we want; if we are not strong enough to stand it, let us test the strength of republicanism; but I am afraid he will not do it unless our representatives force him to it, which I sincerely hope they will if they seen any signs of flinching on his part.

He praised his foes:

> The people of the south deserve credit for the manner in which they have submitted to the privations and devastations which this war has subjected them to, and their leaders for the manner in which they have conducted the war; more than one half of Virginia, part of Tennessee, Georgia, Louisiana, Arkansas, N and S Carolina have been devastated by our arms, and the inhabitants thereof reduced to extreme poverty.
>
> I have seen ladies who have moved in the highest walks of society dressed in tatters that they would not have at one time allowed their slaves to wear, yet they are as determined and defiant as ever; how great the contrast between them and the women of the North, whose whole ambition seems to be that they shall be more extravagant than ever.

And expressed gratitude to Baltimoreans for remembering Marylanders in the Union army at Christmas:

> I see by the papers that the folks in Baltimore are getting up a Christmas dinner for the soldiers of our state; of this I am glad, as all other troops were supplied by their states on Thanksgiving day, and it would be a source of comfort to think that our people had not forgotten us, while they were enjoying the blessings of peace.[55]

Following the Battle of Monocacy, Walter Shriver wrote cousin Henry:

> Your letter of 8th May last has laid on my desk nearly ever since it came to hand. I have kept it there as a reminder, & faithfully it has done its duty—for every time I have "set things to rights," on the desk I have seen the letter, & just so often have

I been impelled to answer it—having nothing very pressing on hand this after-noon, I will do myself the pleasure of paying you a *onesided* visit, on paper—and do all the talking myself

He criticized Lincoln and his advisers:

I don't know what to think of our administration, from the President, with his ill-timed jokes, to Stanton the incompetent head of the War Dept. and old Gideon Welles, surely the man least fitted for his place that the Prest. would dare to nominate. Let it go—will talk of something else—before dismissing the subject, I must congratulate you on yr. share of the glory of "Gettysburg"—& tender you a vote of thanks for the patriotism evinced in your going to meet the invader. Deeds are *real*—words not always so—and I appreciate & admire the man who under similar circumstances takes up his arms & goes forth to meet the foe:—I am glad you did not feel the reality of war, in the shape of a ball through any por-tion of yr. frame corporeal.[56]

The conscription law passed by Congress in March 1863 allowed draft-eligible men to procure substitutes for $300. Brokers surfaced to facilitate such arrangements, as described by Joshua Hering, who engaged such a firm when drafted in August 1864 (the gruesome incident he recounts probably occurred that summer):

John L. Reifsnider and I were selected by the contributors and the drafted men, to go to Baltimore and procure the substitutes and obtain the releases for the drafted men. A camp was established near Baltimore, known as "Camp Brad-ford" to which drafted men or their substitutes were taken. We spent a week, or perhaps more, in arranging the matter, and finally through the agency of the firm of Blick & Stevens, who were engaged in the business of furnishing substitutes, we got all our substitutes in and our drafted men furnished with certificates of release. It was a novel experience to us and we were delighted, as were the men for whom we were acting, when we got the matter concluded. It was really a responsible and somewhat dangerous position to be placed in, as we were com-pelled to carry the cash with us to the Camp, for the payment of the substitutes, and the Camp and its surroundings were about as tough and uninviting as you can well imagine. I remember one morning when Mr Reifsnider and I went into the camp, we found a dead soldier lying right inside the enclosure, in a very pub-lic place, and uncovered, except for the uniform he had on. We inquired what it meant, and were told that the fellow was put in as a substitute the day before, and was attempting to get over the fence at night and desert, when under orders, the guard shot and killed him, and that they had him laid in the conspicuous place as a warning to others.[57]

*Mark Owings Shriver joined
the Confederate First Virginia
Calvary in 1863. He was
arrested by federal authorities
in May 1865 and subsequently
acquitted of charges. MdHS.*

1865

Men went to great extremes to find the money for substitutes.

> The bearer of this, Henry Michard, having been drafted and not being in circumstances to procure a Substitute would most respectfully beg of you what you can conveniently give to aid him to procure one.

Michael found sixteen people to donate to his cause—one gave $25, eight gave $5, one gave $3, and the remainder $1 each.[58]

Even in late 1865, men were still avoiding the draft; businesses sprung up to handle the details:

> We have this day furnished a substitute for Samuel Bowley enrolled in the 3rd district of Washington County State of Maryland, and should he prove to be

a Deserter, or liable to draft, we hereby obligate ourselves to furnish another, free of any charge whatever, and this obligation shall be binding upon us on the above conditions for the term of three years.[59]

Henry W. Shriver eventually procured a substitute:

We have this day furnished a Substitute for Mr. Henry W. Shriver, enrolled in the 3rd E. Dist. Of Carrol Co., State of Maryland, and should he prove to be a deserter, or liable to draft, hereby obligate ourselves to furnish another, free of any charge whatever, and this obligation shall be binding upon me as the above conditions for the term of three years.[60]

One business enterprise found substitutes for seven Shrivers, who as of March 9, 1865, were mustered into the Union army for three years. William Colton wrote to A. K. Shriver to conclude the deal, "which fills the Contract you made with us for the seven men" closing with "if other opportunities of Business should offer give us a call."[61]

chapter seven

1861

Augustus J. Albert narrowly avoided arrest shortly after General Butler's men occupied Baltimore:

> The night before they took possession of the City the Maryland Guard was disbanded and my brother Taylor and I got a wagon and went to the Armory where we loaded it with muskets and took them to my father's residence, then 81 Monument Street and carried them up to the top of the house and stowed them away in a space between the roof and the ceiling. Afterwards when the U.S. troop commenced searching the City for arms, my brother brought a wagon in form the farm near Cockeysville and carried them out and buried them in a large hole had had prepared for them in the garden, and where the rusty remains possibly even now are resting undisturbed.[1]

Edward Spencer told his fiancée about his options for avoiding arrest:

> The arrest of Mr. Winans is but the beginning. Col. Kane, Wallis, Parkin Scott, Norris, Dallam, John Merryman, &c, are all to be taken & tried for treason. There is no saying where it will end. I dont suppose they will take me (so very fortunate is my insignificance) but, I am not safe. I can, however, always get to Harper's Ferry from here, so long as Frederick is not seized. They will be within 5 miles of our place, this week, at the U.S. Arsenal—but the Liberty road is still open, and about 200 volunteers are passing up every day, en route for Virginia. Dont be alarmed about me, honey—unless there is a collision in Md. I shall keep very quiet, at home, henceforth—and I am as safe here as any man can be where there is no law.[2]

Civilians held without charges were sometimes offered freedom in exchange for their "parole," wherein they promised to refrain from hostile acts against the U.S. government. Some refused, believing that doing so implied they had been disloyal. Ross Winans accepted parole the day after his arrest:

> The Lieutenant-General desires me to add that he has just been instructed by highest authority to cause Mr. Ross Winans, of Baltimore, now a military prisoner at Fort McHenry, to be liberated on condition of his written parole, to this effect: "I solemnly give my parole of honor that I will not openly or covertly commit any act of hostility against the Government of the United States pending existing troubles or hostilities between the said Government and the Southern seceded States or any one of them."[3]

Winans was quickly released:

> On receipt of your letter which gave me the first official [information] I had that Mr. Ross Winans was a military prisoner at Fort McHenry I sent an officer to read to him the condition of the written parole upon acceptance of which I was instructed to liberate him. The result was that Mr. Winans signed the parole and was immediately liberated.[4]

Early in the war Secretary of State Seward oversaw arrests for disloyalty, such as the arrest of Baltimore's police chief in June:

> George P. Kane, marshal of police, was arrested at 3 o'clock this morning by a detachment of troops. The marshal was in bed at his residence. The arrest was effected without excitement. The policemen on the route were taken into custody to prevent an alarm. Kane was taken to Fort McHenry where he is now confined. On arriving at the fort the police officers were released. The arrest is not generally known. No excitement manifested.[5]

In an effort to defuse tensions during June elections in Baltimore, Gen. Nathaniel P. Banks, commander of the Department of Annapolis, reassured Mayor Brown that "no soldier will be permitted to leave his post or enter the city during this day without positive orders from the general in command except those who are voters." Banks also issued a proclamation explaining Kane's arrest:

> It is not my purpose neither is it in consonance with my instructions to interfere in any manner whatever with the legitimate government of the people of Baltimore or Maryland. I desire to support the public authorities in all appropriate duties—in preserving peace, protecting property and the rights of persons, in obeying and upholding every municipal regulation and public statute consistent with the Constitution and laws of the United States and of Maryland. But unlawful combinations of men organized for resistance to such laws, that provide hidden deposits of arms and ammunition, encourage contraband traffic with men at war with the Government and while enjoying its protection and privileges stealthily wait opportunity to combine their means and forces with those in rebellion against its authority, are not among the recognized or legal rights of any class of men and cannot be permitted under any form of government whatever. Such combinations are well known to exist in this department. The mass of citizens of Baltimore and of Maryland loyal to the Constitution and the Union are neither parties to nor responsible for them. The chief of police, however, is not only believed to be cognizant of these facts but in contravention of his duty and in violation of law.[6]

Gen. Winfield Scott suggested to Banks that a dangerous secessionist movement in Baltimore warranted detention of the Baltimore Police Board:

Mr. Snethen, of Baltimore, a gentleman of standing, will deliver to you this communication. He has just given to the Secretary of War and myself many important facts touching the subject of [the] Union in that city. It is confirmed by him that, among the citizens, the secessionists, if not the most numerous, are by far more active and effective than the supporters of the Federal Government.

It is the opinion of the Secretary of War, and I need not add my own, that the blow should be early struck, to carry consternation into the ranks of our numerous enemies about you. Accordingly, it seems desirable that you should take measures quietly to seize at once and securely hold the four members of the Baltimore police board, viz: Charles Howard, Wm. H. Gatchell, J. W. Davis, and C. D. Hinks, esqrs., together with the chief of the police, G. P. Kane.[7]

Six days later the military authorities in Annapolis ordered Col. Edward Jones, commander of the Sixth Massachusetts Regiment, to make the arrests:

Major-General Banks directs that you will proceed with a detachment of nine companies of your regiment immediately upon receipt of this order to the residence of Mr. Charles Howard, late a member of the board of police commissioners, or wherever else he may be found and him the said Howard arrest and securely hold and bring him to Fort McHenry in this department without fail.[8]

Banks reported the mission's success:

The board of police was arrested this morning at 4 o'clock. Troops have been stationed at the principal squares of the city. All is perfectly quiet. We greatly need cavalry for patrol duty.[9]

J. P. Kennedy defended Baltimore's police chief following his arrest:

No one did more to suppress that mob, and to protect the troops from Massachusetts marching through, than one of the persons now suffering under this very suspension of the writ of *habeas corpus*—I allude to Marshal Kane.[10]

Secretary of War Cameron ordered more discretion on Maryland arrests:

Complaints are received at this department of arrests and searches in Maryland by troops from this District. You will please give directions to prevent such proceedings except for good cause and by your order and to have your own necessary orders for such arrests and searches executed by discreet officers from the native troops.[11]

Col. John R. Kenly, provost-marshal in Baltimore, deputized four hundred Baltimore men as police officers to replace the regular force, who had quit to protest Kane's arrest. Banks reported on progress:

Baltimore lawyer John R. Kenly was appointed by Governor Hicks in May to organize Maryland regiments in response to Lincoln's call for troops from the loyal states. Kenly, commanding the First Maryland Infantry Regiment, was badly wounded in May 1862 in the Battle of Front Royal. He oversaw many arrests as provost-marshal in Baltimore. MdHS.

The city has remained in perfect order and quiet since the organization of the new police. The headquarters of the police when vacated by the officers appointed by the board resembled a concealed arsenal. Large quantities of arms and ammunition were found secreted in such places and with such skill as to forbid the thought of their being held for just or lawful purposes. An inventory of the arms and ammunition will be forwarded.[12]

And Banks pledged that federal troops would vacate Baltimore when the police force stabilized:

In view of possible occurrences and the better to meet contingent action of disloyal persons rumors of which have reached me from quarters entitled to respect I have placed a large part of the force under my command within the city and in possession of the principal public squares. No building of importance will be occupied and no obstruction to the business of the city will occur unless it be upon the strongest public necessity. The troops will be withdrawn from the city as soon as the question of the conflicting forces of police can be arranged. This I believe will be done at once.[13]

In July, Banks complained that Fort McHenry was too small to accommodate the rising number of Maryland detainees:

Its limited dimensions make it insufficient for the secure possession of persons whose arrests and detention is indispensable to the public peace. I have discouraged arrests for the expression of political opinions or upon unimportant charges, and when they have been made I have promptly ordered a discharge unless important or positive testimony could be found against them; nevertheless arrests multiply to such extent as to endanger the safe-keeping of prisoners.[14]

Edward Spencer referred to the arrest of "Captain Tilghman," probably of the Eastern Shore (other Tilghmans would face similar fates: one in October and "General Tilghman" in 1863):

Mrs. Agle Tilghman did not *shoot* at the Yankees who arrested her husband. One of the *gentlemen* pointed a pistol at her child who was looking out the window, whereupon she presented her revolver and threatened to shoot if he did not instantly withdraw it. She prepared breakfast for the whole crew of them—in return, Capt. Tilghman was not allowed a mouthful for 24 hours, and was kept at the fort, out in the rain, with no shelter, for two days more.[15]

In August, Gen. John Dix—having been promised relief from crowding at Fort McHenry—was encouraged to continue an aggressive detention policy:

Before many days some place will be designated where prisoners of this description can be sent for safe-keeping until everything is settled. When there is good reason to suppose that persons are giving aid and comfort to the enemy they should be arrested even when there is a want of positive proof of their guilt.[16]

A Baltimore newspaper carried a dispatch from the *Washington Star* about the attempted arrest of a prominent hotel owner:

> We learn that the baggage of Mr. Gilmor, of Baltimore, (the owner of the building known as the Gilmor House,) was followed and overtaken near Port Tobacco, it being understood by the authorities that he was sending it secretly into secession, proposing to follow it in person. In it was found his full secession uniform, a magnificent affair. Last night an effort was made to capture him in Baltimore, but the bird had flown.[17]

In an August report on his work in Baltimore, Dix asked General Scott "not to change my regiments":

> The deputy marshal told me this morning the city had not been so tranquil since April 19. I have adopted stringent measures to secure quiet but they are so ordered as to attract no notice. The regiments are well drilled to street-firing and in half an hour I can have 1,000 men in any part of the city; in forty minutes five times that number.[18]

That September Lincoln remained worried about the intent of the Maryland legislature when it met in Frederick again in special session. Frederick Seward's memoir fifty-five years later recounted the rationale for detentions and an incident in which the president and the two Sewards—later joined by Gen. George McClellan, commander of the Army of the Potomac—rode to meet General Banks at his headquarters in Rockville:

> On a bright summer day in 1861, callers at the White House in Washington were informed that the President had gone out for a drive, and that he was accompanied by the Secretary and Assistant Secretary of State. When the more curious observers noted the course of the carriage, they saw that it stopped at the door of the headquarters of the Army of the Potomac. Presently, General McClellan came out and joined the party, taking the vacant seat. The carriage was then rapidly driven over toward Georgetown Heights. It was a natural and reasonable conclusion, that the official party had gone up to inspect the camps and fortifications now beginning to cover the hills in the direction of Tennallytown. So the event was duly chronicled in the press, and the statement was deemed satisfactory by the public.[19]

Seward recalled that "only cursory glances were bestowed on camps and troops," after which "the carriage whirled on, as fast as the rather rutty and broken roads would permit, until, some hours later, it drew up at the door of a tavern in the little village of Rockville," the headquarters of General Banks, who escorted his visitors to a small grove where they could speak privately:

> The Secessionists had by no means given up the hope of dragging Maryland into the Confederacy. The Legislature was to meet at Frederick City on the 17th of September. There was believed to be a disunion majority, and they expected and intended to pass an ordinance of secession. This would be regarded as a call to active revolt by many who were now submitting to Federal rule. In Baltimore and throughout Maryland the bloody experiences of Virginia and Missouri would probably be repeated. Governor Hicks was a loyal Union man, but would be unable to control the Legislature. The Union members were understood to be divided in opinion as to the expediency of going to Frederick to fight the proposed ordinance, or staying away, in the hope of blocking a quorum.
>
> The Administration, therefore, had decided to take a bold step that would assuredly prevent the adoption of any such ordinance. To forcibly prevent a legislative body from exercising its functions, of course, savors of despotism, and is generally so regarded. But when, departing from its legitimate functions, it invites the public enemy to plunge the State into anarchy, its dissolution becomes commendable. So the Administration reasoned and decided.[20]

En route Lincoln reported that William Seward had been to Baltimore to brief General Dix, who would monitor events there. Dix and Banks were to watch the legislators as they traveled to Frederick. The men discussed the covert operation against the Maryland lawmakers:

> Loyal Union members would not be interfered with. They would be free to come and go, perform their legislative duties, or stay away, just as they pleased. But disunion members starting to go there would be quietly turned back toward their homes, and would not reach Frederick City at all. The views of each disunion member were pretty well known, and generally rather loudly proclaimed. So there would be little difference, as Mr. Lincoln remarked, in "separating the sheep from the goats."[21]

The party returned to Washington late that night:

> The public anxiously awaited the coming of the eventful day which was to determine whether Maryland would sever her connection with the Union. When the time arrived which had been appointed for the assembling of the Legislature, it was found that not only was no secession ordinance likely to be adopted, but that there seemed to be no Secessionists to present one. The two generals had carried out their instructions faithfully, with tact and discretion. The Union members returned to their homes rejoicing. No ordinance was adopted, Baltimore remained quiet, and Maryland stayed in the Union.[22]

Seward declared the operation a success, without mentioning that arrests had in fact occurred:

> Of course the Administration were prepared for the storm of invective that was hurled at them through the press. Their "high-handed usurpation" was said to be paralleled only by "the acts of Cromwell and Napoleon." But even the denouncers were somewhat mystified as to the way in which things had happened. Cromwell and Napoleon were more spectacular, but Dix and Banks were equally effective.
>
> There are still some who unconsciously lament these events in the history of "My Maryland" to the melodious strains of *Lauriger Horatius.* But Union men and disunion men alike had good reason, during the next three years, to thank God that Maryland had been spared the misery and desolation that overtook her sister Virginia.[23]

On September 4, Dix briefed McClellan on his actions in Baltimore, which included mobilization of a revamped police force and plans for extensive arrests of disloyal citizens:

> No secession flag has to the knowledge of the police been exhibited in Baltimore for many weeks, except a small paper flag displayed by a child from an upper window. It was immediately removed by them. They have been instructed to arrest any person who makes a public demonstration by word or deed in favor of the Confederate Government and I have prohibited the exhibition in shop windows of rebel envelopes and music. The informant of the Secretary of the Treasury does not appear to have mentioned special cases and you know how unreliable general statements are.
>
> The old police when disbanded consisted of 416 persons. Twenty-seven are in our service. Several have been discharged. There are now about 350 left. The great part of them are obscure and inoffensive persons. Some of them are Union men. There are I am confident not over forty or fifty who would not take the oath of allegiance. There are some very mischievous, worthless fellows, but they are quiet. We only want a pretext for arresting them. They have up to this time been paid by the city. Yesterday I addressed a letter to the mayor ordering the payment to be discontinued. I think he will obey it. If he does not I shall arrest him and make a like order on the city comptroller who will obey.[24]

Dix sought to reassure McClellan that his areas of responsibility were stable:

> As I perceive by Colonel Marcy's letter that the condition of things has been represented to you by zealous persons as less favorable than it really is I have thought it best to mention now what I am doing. The city is perfectly quiet and perfectly under control by the police force alone. If there is an uprising on the Eastern Shore under the influence of the rebel organizations in Accomack

"Monument Square, Baltimore, MD—Section of Cook's Boston Light Infantry with Artillery in Position, by Order of Major Gen. Banks to Quell an Anticipated Riot on Account of the Arrest of Marshall Kane and the Police Commissioners [in June 1861]." Pratt Lib.

and Northampton, or if the Confederate forces cross the Potomac we may have trouble. I shall endeavor to be ready for it whenever it comes.[25]

Secretary Cameron a few days later reversed the plan to have suspected Southern sympathizers "quietly turned back toward their homes," instead authorizing their arrest:

> The passage of any act of secession by the legislature of Maryland must be prevented. If necessary, all or any part of the members must be arrested. Exercise your own judgment as to the time and manner, but do the work effectively.[26]

Cameron ordered the arrest of a group of Baltimore lawmakers, editors, prominent citizens, and Henry May, a member of Congress:

> You are directed to arrest forthwith the following-named persons, viz: T. Parkin Scott, S. Teackle Wallis, Henry M. Warfield, F. Key Howard, Thomas W. Hall, jr., and Henry May, and to keep them in close custody, suffering no one to communicate with them, and to convey them at once to Fortress Monroe there to remain in close custody until they shall be forwarded to their ultimate destination. You will also seize their papers and cause them to be closely examined.[27]

Prison assignments revealed the wide range of arrests:

Thirty political prisoners left Fort McHenry this day for Forts Columbus and Lafayette via the Delaware and Chesapeake Canal and Camden and Amboy Railroad under a guard of eighteen enlisted men from the Twenty-first Regiment Indiana Volunteers, commanded by Capt. James Grimsley. Four prisoners are ordered to Fort Lafayette, viz: George P. Kane, late marshal of police of Baltimore City; Robert Drane, citizen of Fairfax County, Va.; Arthur Dawson, citizen of Fairfax County, Va.; Benjamin Eggleston, citizen of Washington, D.C. The other twenty-six have been sent to Fort Columbus. The only person of note among them is Col. John Pegram.[28]

One detainee explained his disappearance to his landlady, the proprietress of a Baltimore boardinghouse, at 26 Cathedral Street:

I dare say you were quite as much surprised as I was at not finding me at your breakfast table at the usual hour on the morning following the night when I was "spirited away," but indeed it was not my fault.[29]

At his headquarters near Darnestown, on September 16, General Banks ordered the Third Wisconsin Regiment, "on special service at Frederick," to move against Maryland legislators:

The Legislature of Maryland is appointed to meet in special session to-morrow, Tuesday, September 16. It is not impossible that the members or a portion of them be deterred from meeting there on account of certain arrests recently made in Baltimore. It is also quite possible that on the first day of meeting the attendance may be small. Of the facts as to this matter I shall see that you are well informed as they transpire. It becomes necessary that any meeting of this Legislature at any place or time shall be prevented.

You will hold yourself and your command in readiness to arrest the members of both houses. A list of such as you are to detain will be inclosed to you herewith, among whom are to be specially included the presiding officers of the two houses, secretaries, clerks and all subordinate officials. Let the arrest be certain and allow no chance of failure. The arrests should be made while they are in session I think.

You will upon the receipt of this quietly examine the premises. I am informed that escape will be impossible if the entrance to the building be held by you; of that you will judge upon examination. If no session is to be held you will arrest such members as can be found in Frederick. The process of arrest should be to enter both houses at the same time announcing that they were arrested by orders of the Government. Command them to remain as they are subject to your orders.

Any resistance will be forcibly suppressed whatever the consequences. Upon these arrests being effected the members that are to be detained will be placed on board a special train for Annapolis where a steamer will await them.

Everything in the execution of these orders is confided to your secrecy, discretion and promptness.[30]

A Banks aide-de-camp reported on the operation:

> We have seized seven members of the house of a very bitter character, and four officers, clerks, &c, who are intensely bitter and are said to have been very forward and to have kept some of the weaker men up to the work. Several arrests were made of violent or resisting persons whom I shall let go after the others are gone. I shall send four men at least to General Dix, at Baltimore, who are very bad men.[31]

During the night of September 17, the dragnet netted nineteen state legislators. Most were taken to Fort McHenry before being sent to various federal prisons (as would most Marylanders arrested throughout the war). Many were never charged.

General Banks reported a successful campaign, implying that better coordination might have "bagged" even more prisoners:

> I have the honor to report, in obedience to the order of the Secretary of War, and the general commanding the Army of the Potomac, transmitted to me by letter of the 12th instant, that all the members of the Maryland Legislature assembled at Frederick City on the 17th instant known or suspected to be disloyal in their relations to the Government have been arrested.
>
> The opening of the session was attended chiefly by Union men, and after rigid examination but nine secession members were found in the city. These were arrested, with the clerk of the senate, and sent to Annapolis, according to my orders, on the 18th instant, under guard, and safely lodged on board a Government steamer in waiting for them. Of their destination thence I had no direction. The names of the parties thus arrested and disposed of were as follows, viz: B. H. Salmon, Frederick; R. C. McCubbin, Annapolis; William R. Miller, Cecil County; Thomas Claggett, Frederick; Josiah H. Gordon, Alleghany County; Clark J. Durant, Saint Mary's County; J. Lawrence Jones, Talbot County; Andrew Kessler, Jr., Frederick; Bernard Mills, Carroll County; J. W. Brecolt, chief clerk of the senate.
>
> No meeting of the senate occurred; but three senators were in town, and those were Union men. Three subordinate officers of the senate, the chief clerk and printer of the house, and one or two others were also arrested, but released after the departure of the members for Annapolis upon taking the oath of allegiance.
>
> Milton Kidd, clerk of the house, is in the last stages of consumption, beyond the power of doing harm, and was released upon taking the oath and making a solemn declaration to act no further with the legislature under any circumstances whatever. This course was adopted upon the urgent solicitation of the

Union members present. The same parties desired the release of R. C. McCubbin, of Annapolis, upon the same condition. I telegraphed to the commander of the steamer that he might be left at Annapolis under sufficient guard until the orders of the Government could be ascertained.

Colonel Ruger Third Wisconsin Regiment; Lieutenant Copeland, my aide-de-camp, and a detachment of police rendered efficient aid. Sufficient information was obtained as to preparations for board, &c., to lead to the belief that the attendance of members would have been large had not the arrest of some of the leaders been made at Baltimore on Saturday and Monday before the day of meeting.

I regret the attempt at Frederick was not more successful.[32]

Lincoln told Marylanders that these arrests of their legislators and other public officials, including Baltimore's mayor, were essential and legitimate—the reasons for which would be explained to them "at the proper time":

> The public safety renders it necessary that the ground of these arrests should at present be withheld, but at the proper time they will be made public. Of one thing the people of Maryland may rest assured: that no arrest has been made, or will be made, not based on substantial and unmistakable complicity with those in armed rebellion against the Government of the United States. In no case has an arrest been made on mere suspicion, or through personal or partisan animosities, but in all cases the Government is in possession of tangible and unmistakable evidence, which will, when made public, be satisfactory to every loyal citizen.[33]

The day following this journal entry, W. W. Glenn was arrested and his paper, the Baltimore Daily Exchange, shut down:

> I arose, breakfasted & went to my office. I soon heard the rumor of arrests. The Legislature was to meet in a day or two. All the Baltimore members had been dragged from their beds late in the night. Tom Hall, Editor of the *South* and Frank Howard as Chief Editor of *Exchange* were also arrested. The Members of a Legislature which had refused to arm the State and had advised non resistance were imprisoned on the Charge of planning the secession of the State. So much for the middle course. What folly in a revolution! These men were all taken to Fort McHenry. I found John Thomas, took my carriage and drove down. Many of my friends opposed my going and declared I would be arrested. They were sadly frightened. My reply was "that is they wanted me, they would take me anyhow." In the fort we saw Col. Morris—in comman—but were allowed no communication with the prisoners, except a few words at a distance.[34]

Glenn took a principled stand:

I was privately informed that I was to be arrested. I could easily have gotten away, but it was a point with me. The Administration evidently wanted to stop the paper, without having the odium of directly suppressing it. It thought by the arrest of Frank Howard to frighten me. Now after I had committed myself I was allowed the chance of escape. Even my brother urged me to go; but stir I would not I determined to force the Government to have recourse to military power if they wished to muzzle free speech in Maryland.[35]

And arrived at Fort McHenry:

After dinner, McPhail came to the house with a small force and took me off. I was allowed time to get my trunk. It was very hard parting with my wife and sisters. This kind of thing was new to us then and they had no idea what was in store for me.

I was driven to Fort McHenry and locked up in a room furnished with one table, a chair, a blanket & some straw. It had evidently been used by other prisoners and had not been cleaned out. All the other prisoners had been sent off during the day, to make room for others, for the wholesale arrests which were afterwards so common, were just being inaugurated. Late in the evening I received some bedding from home.[36]

One man expressed his appreciation for the government's program of arrests:

I thank you in the name of every truly loyal man in Baltimore and in my own poor name too for your arrest of the traitors whom you have sent to Fortress Monroe. A great and a good work has been done. Rebellion has received a staggering blow. I hope General Banks will take care that the Legislature shall not sit at all.

And offered suggestions for improvement:

The arrest of W. Wilkins Glenn, the proprietor of the *Exchange*, has given intense satisfaction. Beale Richardson and his writing editor Joice, of the *Republican*, are very violent and would grace the Tortugas. If the *Exchange* should go on a Doctor Palmer and a William H. Carpenter are the ostensible editors, and both write with bitterness. They too would do well at Tortugas.

After fulminating about the *Exchange*, he proposed a mechanism to prevent rebel sympathizers from voting:

The effect of these arrests must determine very rapidly the status of the floating population who are ever on the watch for the stronger side. I have already heard of cases in our favor. We are determined to prevent any rebel voting if he will not take the oath of allegiance. It is to be done by a system of challenging. The new mayor has already surrendered the pistols retained by the old police and evinces a readiness to co operate with the Federal authorities. His name is Blackburn. It is intimated that General Howard has taken the hint and will not accept the rebel nomination for Governor. If he does he should be sent at once to Fortress Monroe, and so too of Jarrett, the rebel nominee for comptroller. I hope the Government will not release a single one of these prisoners let the circumstances be what they may. The effect upon the public mind depends largely upon firmness at this juncture.[37]

Governor Hicks congratulated General Banks on the success of the operation:

We have some of the product of your order here in the persons of some eight or ten members of the State Legislature soon I learn to depart for healthy quarters. We see the good fruit already produced by the arrests. We can no longer mince matters with these desperate people. I concur in all you have done.[38]

Detained also were Frank Key Howard, editor of the *Daily Exchange*:

arrested at midnight Sepr. 13th 1861 at my own house, by armed men & by order; they said, of Wm H. Seward. Conveyed to Fort McHenry, & thence to Fortress Monroe. Transferred Sep. 26th to Fort La Fayette, N.Y. & thence Nov. 1st to Fort Warren, Mass. Arrested for expressing political opinions distasteful to the Administration.

And Lawrence Sangston, a member of the House of Delegates from Baltimore City:

taken from his bed at midnight on the 12th September by a body of armed men, without warrant or process of Law—conveyed to Fort McHenry, thence to Fort Lafayette, thence to Fort Warren, where he now remains without having been able to ascertain the cause of his arrest, or the existence of any charge against him.[39]

In September Gen. John Wool, commanding the Department of Virginia at Fortress Monroe and now in charge of political prisoners, sought clarification on the treatment of newly arrived Baltimoreans, including Mayor Brown:

The prisoners Brown, May, Winans and others were landed at this post yesterday afternoon and have been placed in the casemates where they are strongly guarded. I have no other instructions or communications from the Government in regard to these prisoners than those contained in the above extract from a letter addressed to General Dix. Those instructions so far as the treatment of the prisoners while here is concerned may be susceptible of two constructions. Is it the intention of the Government that the prisoners shall neither receive nor send letters to their families and friends of a purely domestic and private character to be ascertained by inspection?[40]

Dix clarified procedures for military searches:

> I do not wish any searches made in private dwellings by the military. I prefer it
> should be done by the police. You have very properly reported to me the case
> of Doctor Henkle and I shall put it in the hands of the provost-marshal in Bal-
> timore. I do not wish any persons to be stopped who have shotguns and who
> are evidently going on sporting excursions. They should not be detained or
> interfered with in any way. Your duty is to examine vehicles passing out of the
> city of Baltimore and suspected of having concealed arms or goods destined to
> the disloyal States.[41]

Samuel B. Rogers expressed to brother Nathan his anger over the Maryland arrests:

> Four or five days ago they arrested nearly all the Legislature and other promi-
> nent men. Henry Warfield your ex-partner was one of them. T. Parkin Scott
> was another, he has two sons in the Southern Army, his family are left without
> hardly any thing to live on. Is not that hard! What is the sentiment of California
> is it North or South! The Confederates have beaten the Unionists in every battle
> of any size they have had yet and I trust will continue to do so and thereby put
> an end to the war. In Baltimore there are said to be spies paid eighty dollars per
> month by the Government to find out who are the prominent Secessionists.
> These spies are women.[42]

This September petition to Lincoln from Johns Hopkins, Enoch Pratt, Reverdy
Johnson, John P. Kennedy, and other prominent Baltimoreans protesting Mayor
Brown's arrest fell on deaf ears:

> We, the undersigned, citizens of Baltimore, declaring our absolute and uncom-
> promising loyalty, fidelity and attachment to the Government of the United
> States, respectfully represent to your Excellency;
> That we have heard, with the deepest pain and regret, of the arrest by the Fed-
> eral Authority of our esteemed fellow citizen, George William Brown, Mayor of
> the City of Baltimore;
> That from our knowledge of his private and official character and conduct,
> we unhesitatingly declare our conviction that he is a man incapable of treason or
> conspiracy;
> That we most earnestly believe that, in all his intercourse with the officers of
> the Federal Government, he has been guided and governed by a most conscien-
> tious regard for the obligations of his official oath, and never by treasonable or
> hostile design against the Government.[43]

Anna Maria Tilghman of the Eastern Shore lamented the arrest of her father in
September:

The calamity we have so dreaded has befallen us—last Friday night the house was surrounded, just after midnight, by soldiers in number about a dozen & arrested Father. The officers behaved in the most considerate manner allowing Father to take a cup of coffee before leaving. Ma & Tench accompanied him to Easton, where he only remained a few hours before going to Cambridge.[44]

Samuel A. Harrison's description of Gen. Tench Tilghman may have explained the latter's arrest:

He was the main instigator in putting our county on a war footing, in opposition to the Government, by repairing & putting in complete order the arms in the Easton Arsenal, and refused to give out arms to the Citizens of St. Michael's District, the most loyal district of the county. He was wrested from power by a proclamation from Governor Hicks—was arrested—took the oath of allegiance, and is now an ardent sympathizer of the rebel cause. [of Genl. Tilghman much is said in these annals. Indeed he has been one of the most conspicuous characters in this county for many years. A sketch of his life will be found among the Biographical Annals no I. p. 70—and it is my purpose to give a more complete sketch hereafter. His opinions during the war were of the most ultra southern character, and his conduct most ill-advised, imprudent and culpable. He is essentially aristocratic, and I am disposed to think his advocacy of the cause of the South had its origin in this feeling. Genl. Tilghman is my personal friend, whose many fine traits of character do not prevent me from seeing those effects which so sadly mar that character. After his arrest I called upon him, while in duress, and offered to him my services to secure his release. I regarded his arrest, in this case, as wrong & as calculated to harm the cause which I espoused. However, my services were not required, for he was soon paroled, and at liberty].[45]

By early October, General Dix had become wary of informers who denounced the disloyal:

I have become somewhat suspicious of charges against individuals unless they are well supported by statements from reliable sources. I arrested in an interior county and brought to this city two men charged with open acts of hostility to the Government on testimony vouched by the U.S. marshal, and yet they turned out to be two of the most consistent and active Union men in the neighborhood.[46]

October brought allegations that the U.S. mail system was a conduit for smuggled correspondence in and out of Virginia from a post office in St. Mary's County, six miles from the Potomac River that separated Maryland and Virginia:

On examination I find a large number of letters addressed to parties in Virginia and other parts of the South, also letters coming from Virginia to parties in Baltimore, Washington, Philadelphia, &c., the most important of which accompany the report.

The postmaster at Great Mills seems to have made his office a repository or depot for this contraband correspondence although he professes to be a very strong Union man. We arrested one John S. Travis, a resident of the above-named locality, and brought him a prisoner to this city. Travis is charged with carrying the mails to and from the Great Mills Post-Office into Virginia. This morning I received a telegram from Major-General Dix, at Fort McHenry, stating that the provost-marshal of Baltimore would furnish me with an abundance of proof against Travis. I shall detain him until such proof arrives. The post-offices at Leonardtown and Ridge Road I think should be immediately seized. I have positive information that an extensive Southern correspondence is now being carried on through these offices.[47]

Concern over secessionists in western Maryland, disguised as "peace candidates," led to the arrest of four:

The result of the election in Baltimore proves the wisdom of the action of the Government in having the prominent traitors arrested. Even the secessionists in Western Maryland are reconciled and even approve it for they dread civil war within the State.

At the same time, however, I learn from a very reliable source in Allegany County that a secret movement is on foot by the peace party, i.e., secessionists in disguise to nominate an opposition ticket; and for the purpose of defeating the Union ticket the commissioners, nearly all secessionists, have lately had a meeting and appointed the rankest secessionists as judges of election. I mention the name of one so appointed for Cumberland, W. O. Sprigg, well known as a rabid secessionist, having a son in the rebel army. Amongst the opponents of the Government the foremost in Allegany County are Judge Perry and Doctor Fitzpatrick. The former appointed young Brien, now an officer in the rebel ranks, foreman of the grand jury and permitted him to come into court with a large secession badge on his breast. I mention this fact as a glaring instance of his proclivities. He and his confederates Doctor Fitzpatrick, W. O. Sprigg (who I believe has also a son in the rebel ranks) and if I mistake not Deveemon, the lawyer, are the head and front of the secret movement now going on. They are in constant communication with the rebels in Virginia and are doing all the mischief they can. Now it seems to me these people should for a while be placed where they can do no harm. If the Government could be made aware of the state of things, I think they should give these gentlemen free quarters at Fort McHenry or Fort Lafayette from now until after the election. The quiet and safety of the State of Maryland would be promoted by such a proceeding and an election result obtained which could not but have a most beneficial effect upon the whole country.[48]

When Rev. John Kerfoot sought John P. Kennedy's intervention in the arrest of William G. Harrison, the uncle of W. Hall Harrison, a teacher at the school, Kerfoot implied that arbitrary arrests would undermine loyalty:

> The prevalence among us in Maryland of a bold, unyielding devotion to the Union, must be hindered by the belief that any needless & injurious restraints are laid upon our friends. Such rumors uncontradicted, or such facts commonly believed, must impair the good cause. Without referring to particular cases, I understandingly recognize the necessity & therefore the justice of prompt arrests in such revolutionary times. Delay or indecision will destroy the government.[49]

Late in October an official in Montreal wrote to Frederick Seward about Frederick Brune, a state delegate:

> Mr. Brune, a member of the Maryland Legislature, was in my office yesterday. He admits that he fled from Maryland under a feigned name, is a secessionist, &c., but is anxious to obtain his trunk which is detained at Rouse's Point. He asserts there was nothing in the trunk that can afford any evidence for or against him and is only anxious to obtain [it] on account of his wardrobe. He has friends here who are excellent Union men, and at their request I address this note asking that the trunk may be given up unless there are reasons for detaining it.[50]

W. W. Glenn remained busy in Fort McHenry, arranging for his paper to reappear under a different name:

> Everyone would see and understand from the type, & advertisements, that it was the old thing in another shape. The only thing I did was to control the name. I insisted on calling it the "News-Sheet", as a sort of token to the people of Maryland, to keep fresh in their memory the fact that their press was muzzled and that the publication of anything more than a simple News Sheet was not permitted.[51]

> Today the first copy of the paper was issued under the name of the Times. Neilson, our foreman in the composing room, now that he appeared as principal instead of sub, began to assume magnificent proportions. He did not wish to run a paper with no name, a mere offshoot of a former publication. So he must needs issue the new paper as The Times. I sent him word very shortly to obey my instructions or to shut up shop.[52]

General Dix again complained about the excessive number of prisoners at Fort McHenry:

Fort McHenry is very small and is filled up by the garrison. We have not room for the accommodation of prisoners or the means of pro-riding for their comfort. Seven prisoners of war from General Banks' column and four State prisoners engaged in secreting a balloon in Delaware came in last night. We have now over twenty confined in one room and cell.[53]

Military officials in Maryland authorized stern measures to prevent interference from "disunionists" in elections. The final line of an October 29 order—"For the purpose of carrying out these instructions you are authorized to suspend the habeas corpus"—revealed the depth of their concern:

> There is an apprehension among Union citizens in many parts of Maryland of an attempt at interference with their rights of suffrage by disunion citizens on the occasion of the election to take place on the 6th of November next.
>
> In order to prevent this the major-general commanding directs that you send detachments of a sufficient number of men to the different points in your vicinity where the elections are to be held to protect the Union voters and to see that no disunionists are allowed to intimidate them or in any way to interfere with their rights.
>
> He also desires you to arrest and hold in confinement till after the election all disunionists who are known to have returned from Virginia recently and who show themselves at the polls, and to guard effectually against any invasion of the peace and order of the election. For the purpose of carrying out these instructions you are authorized to suspend the habeas corpus. General Stone has received similar instructions to these.[54]

On October 29, Dix received a letter from two "election inspectors" in New Windsor, Carroll County, seeking authority "to administer to all persons of doubtful loyalty who offer their votes at the approaching election an oath to support the Constitution of the United States." Dix replied that, while sympathetic, he was committed to minimal interference and a fair election:

> The constitution and laws of Maryland provide for the exercise of the elective franchise by regulations with which I have no right to interfere. I have this day issued an order of which I inclose a copy to the U.S. marshal and the provost-marshal at Baltimore to arrest any persons who have been in arms in Virginia if they appear at the polls and attempt to vote as we are told some such persons intend, and to take into custody all who aid and abet them in their treasonable designs; and I have requested the judges of election in case any such person presents himself at the polls and attempts to vote to commit him until he can be taken into custody by the authority of the United States. I consider it of the utmost importance that the election should be a fair one and that there should be no obstruction to the free and full expression of the voice of the people of the

State believing as I do that it will be decidedly in favor of the Union. But it is in the power of the judges of election under the authority given them to satisfy themselves as to the qualifications of the voters—to put to those who offer to poll such searching questions in regard to residence and citizenship as to detect traitors and without any violation of the constitution or laws of Maryland to prevent the pollution of the ballot boxes by their votes.[55]

Baltimore attorney and Unionist William Schley was friendly with many arrested Marylanders. In November, he wrote to Secretary Seward about the arrest of Baltimore attorney S. Teackle Wallis, explaining that he had tried several times to see Seward, both in his office and at his residence—though he did meet Frederick Seward, "by whom I was assured that all the cases would be examined without unnecessary delay":

> Shortly after the arrest of Mr. Wallis and others I went several times to Washington for the purpose of having with you if the opportunity should occur a full and frank conversation in relation to all the citizens of Maryland who were detained as prisoners of state. Your numerous engagements prevented me from seeing you although besides calling at the Department I called repeatedly at your private residence.
>
> I have always said and have said truly I am sure that the various arrests made in Maryland by the orders of the heads of the department were made on the basis of representations which the officers of Government were not at liberty to disregard and for the full investigation of which before taking action thereon there was neither time nor opportunity. But I wished to say in the desired interview that I was myself satisfied from my personal knowledge of many of the gentlemen who had been arrested that they were unjustly accused, and that I had the fullest confidence that you would come to that conclusion if the cases were fully investigated and I meant to ask on behalf of all that the case of each of them should be examined as early as possible; that is without any delay not actually unavoidable. I desired also to state to you so far as I could do so from personal knowledge some of the reasons which induced me so earnestly to desire the liberation of gentlemen from unnecessary detention at the earliest practicable moment, Failing to find you disengaged I had on the occasion of my last visit a brief interview with the Assistant Secretary of State, by whom I was assured that all the cases would be examined without unnecessary delay. I should be wanting in candor if I did not say that there are undoubtedly in Maryland a great number of persons who sympathize strongly with the South. I deeply lament that such is the fact. At the same time I have always believed that the great body of our people are loyal in their feelings, and that there never was a moment when Maryland could have been forced into secession, even if the General Government had not interfered. But it is right that I should further add that I am not aware nor do I

MARYLANDERS KNOW THEIR RIGHTS,
AND KNOWING, DARE MAINTAIN THEM.

Patriotic images adorning stationery enabled Unionists to show their pride—and Southern sympathizers to avoid trouble. MdHS.

believe that either the mayor, the police commissioners, the marshal or any one of the arrested members of the Legislature have done anything whatever beyond speaking or writing in favor of secession.[56]

The election was a triumph for Unionists, and some in southern Maryland did not react well:

> Throughout Calvert County I found very warm receptions from Union men and others. At Prince Frederick alone was there any open attempt of violence directed toward Union men. The following persons were arrested: Hon. Augustus R. Sollers, ex-M. C. He used the most violent and treasonable language, drew a large knife and cut to the right and left. He was secured and brought in by Colonel Welch to Lower Marlborough where he was taken so ill with gout that I could not bring him but left him on his parole to report at Washington as soon as he is able to move. Mervin B. Hance, Walter Hellen, William D. Williams and John Broome were arrested charged with treasonable language and with carrying weapons. They also were brought to Lower Marlborough. I released them under oath of fealty and that they had not borne arms against our forces.
>
> At Lower Marlborough Colonel Rodman made several arrests but subsequently released the individuals. They had been disorderly while under the influence of strong drink. At Saint Leonard's all went off very quietly without any arrest.[57]

General Dix's response to a complaint about the arrest of Snow Hill lawyer E. K. Wilson (for allegedly speaking disrespectfully of Lincoln) articulated the government's rationale for its military presence in Maryland:

> to show the people of Maryland of all classes that their rights of person and property are not only to be scrupulously respected but protected instead of being invaded by the military forces we have sent among them. No arrest is to be made without your special order in each case and then only for overt acts and giving aid and comfort to the enemy. I am well aware that such an order has not had your approval and I should direct the officer who issued it to be arrested if I were not sure that it originated in mistaken zeal. You will please have it rescinded and do all in your power to repair the wrong done under it. And I request your especial and prompt attention to Mr. Wilson's case, leaving it to your discretion and good judgment to do what is right. If his alleged offense is no more than the alleged memoranda above stated specifies he should be instantly discharged. Our mission is not to annoy or invade any personal rights but to correct misapprehension in regard to the intentions of the Government. And while all open acts of hostility are to be punished we should labor to win back those who have separated themselves from us through a misunderstanding in regard to our motives, and objects by kindness and conciliation, and above all by rigid abstinence from all invasion of their constitutional and legal rights.[58]

Samuel Harrison's diary recorded the arrest of a smuggler:

> A detachment of U.S. soldiers was sent down to the Bayside on Tuesday last, and captured a man by the name of Gibson, who has been conveying passengers across the Potomac, to join the Rebel army. He is said to be a very expert hand with a boat, and had a canoe large enough to carry a number of persons, fitted up with black sails to keep from being detected at night. His last exploit . . . was to carry 15 or 20 young men from this different parts of this county, to the land of Dixie.[59]

In December, Charles County delegate Augustus R. Sollers, in custody a month, detailed government persecution against him, denied the charges, and proclaimed fealty to the United States:

> My arrest was a simple outrage only to be excused upon the ground of over zeal in the officer who ordered it. He declared here he had no orders from Washington to arrest me, but that since he had arrived he had been informed that I and others had formed a plan to take the polls on the day of the election and prevent the Union men from voting Now this may have been told Colonel Welch, but it was as pure a fabrication as ever was invented by wit and malice combined, and I have certificates and affidavits from nearly all the leading Union men in the district and county to that effect. The truth is I took no part in the election; never

attended a public meeting and never publicly or even privately expressed any opinion about it or the questions upon which the canvass was.

Colonel Welch says he was also informed that I had forced my son to go to Virginia and join the Confederate Army. This is equally false, and I produced to General Dix abundant proof of this. My son and my only son did join the Confederate Army, but against my earnest entreaties and the tears of his mother and sisters. I commanded him not to go. I held out every inducement for him to remain that I was able to hold out. In truth when he did go I denounced him for doing so and ordered him to hold no further intercourse with me or any of the family But he was twenty-four years old and beyond my authority.

These are the charges against me. "The very head and front of my offending hath this extent, no more." I have before heard of this last charge and that it had been brought against me in Washington, and when the First Massachusetts Regiment under Colonel Cowdin visited this county some two months ago they sought to arrest me. I was driven from my home, family and business and lived in the woods for weeks. They visited my house the night of their arrival and searched for me; they placed a guard of 150 men around it; they killed my hogs, sheep, poultry and wantonly shot the best horse on the farm, for all of which I was never offered a cent nor have I since received a cent. Now, all this has been endured by as loyal a citizen as any in this State; so help me Heaven I have never perpetrated or dreamt of perpetrating an act that malice could construe into treason, for I hold that allegiance and protection are reciprocal obligations and that it is both treasonable and dishonorable for a citizen living under the protection of the Government to assist or aid in any way the enemies of that Government. God knows I have not received much of its protection lately; but notwithstanding all my persecutions I have sternly refused (although importuned very often to do so) to aid those in arms against the Government. Many persons have passed through this county on their way to Virginia, and contraband of many kinds have also been sent by the same route and I have been called upon to assist in the work. I have always refused to have anything to do with such matters, and have even refused to let strangers enter my house when I suspected where they were going.

For all this I have incurred the displeasure of some of my best friends and looked upon with suspicion and distrust by many others. But for my loyalty I have received nothing but persecution; I have been driven from home, my property destroyed, my family harassed and insulted, and finally arrested. True, I have been discharged but the next regiment that visits the county will be told the same tales by some poor timid wretches who in that way seek the favor and protection of the officers and I shall be again arrested.[60]

A draft of a Lincoln proclamation in late 1861 revealed plans to ease up on Maryland following the election of Unionist Augustus Bradford as governor:

In view of the recent declaration of the people of Maryland of their adhesion to the Union so distinctly made in their recent election, the President directs that all the political prisoners who having heretofore been arrested in that State are now detained in military custody by the President's authority be released from their imprisonment on the following conditions, namely: That if they were holding any civil or military offices when arrested the terms of which have not expired they shall not resume or reclaim such offices; and secondly, all persons availing themselves of this proclamation shall engage by oath or parole of honor to maintain the Union and the Constitution of the United States, and in no way to aid or abet by arms, counsel, conversation or information of any kind the existing insurrection against the Government of the United States.[61]

1862

A January letter from John M. Buchanon to his son underscored the economic difficulties of wartime:

> You wrote to me, to try and send you one hundred dollars—you know, my dear Horace, that I would share with you my last dollar, but it was entirely out of my power to give you any aid whatever.

And war's divisions in his family:

> Mr. Gordon is still confined at Fort Warren. I very much pity his little family. He could not doubt, get released, if he would take the oath required. Cousin Kate is very spunky and says a great many very hard things of Mr. Lincoln and his friends. She calls me a Black Republican and an Abolitionist. I am very far from being either. But I would rather be called anything before any one should call me a Rebel and a traitor to my Government.[62]

Prominent Jewish families in Baltimore included the Cohens, bankers and industrialists with at least one member in the Confederate army, and the Friedenwalds, Democrats and strong secessionists (though Dr. Aaron Friedenwald, an eye doctor studying in Europe from 1860 to 1862, later became a staunch Unionist who served in the Union army). In 1863, Friedenwald was arrested for blockade running. His wife claimed that he was falsely implicated by informers, who extorted money by promising to procure his release:

> He was put in a nasty place in what used to be a Negro jail . . . the real reason for his arrest was that one of his brothers was in the Southern army . . . The people to whom papa owed his arrest were some friends who made a lot of money that way, by informing on innocent people and then going to them and telling them: "If you can pay $50 or more we know someone who can help you out of this."

Papa often related how he answered the Provost Marshall, who tried his utmost to get papa to say something which would be brought up against brother Ike, but he answered him without fear; "Do you want me to testify against my brother? Such things are not done."[63]

In February, Attorney General Edward Bates wrote to the U.S. Attorney for Maryland about the case of a man detained for carrying out orders allegedly issued by Isaac Trimble, by then a Confederate officer:

I have every disposition to deal as leniently as possible with John Henderson, jr. In that spirit I have had some conversation about him with others connected with the Government here on view of the documents you sent me not long ago. The main difficulty seems to be this: How a man of Mr. Henderson's reputed intelligence could in a moment of high popular excitement and threatened insurrection proceed to destroy the buoys (the Government guides into and out of the port) on no better warrant than an order of one Major Trimble, who pretends to act by authority of the mayor. It is assumed by some and I find it hard to convert the idea that a man of Mr. Henderson's intelligence must have known that it was a crime in Major Trimble and in the mayor of Baltimore to do the thing, and therefore that the order itself was insurrectionary and hostile to the Government.[64]

Henry M. Warfield, a Maryland legislator held in Fort Warren, refused parole. In a letter to the War Department, he related the details of his arrest:

About midnight of the 12th Septem 1861, a body of armed men, by practicing deception, obtained entrance into my House, and without warrant, or any other mode known to the Law arrested me, as I then understood, upon a Telegraphic Despatch from Wm. H. Seward Secy of State. I submitted to that arrest, only on account of the force which was brought against me. Immediately upon my surrendering myself, my House, from cellar to Roof, was taken possession of, by armed men, and I was forced to deliver up, all my papers and keys, then upon my person. Amongst the papers, then given up, was a Letter containing money, and which I have never heard as having reached its destination. The sanctity of my Bedchamber, was invaded by the armed servants, who were doing the bidding of the Secy. of State. My private papers, were taken possession of: doors and drawers of my furniture, were broken open: every indignity heaped upon my Home and its decencies. During the period of the outrageous proceedings thus enacted in my House, my Brother and relatives, were denied admission, whilst I was on my way to Fort McHenry, and my wife alone in the House, without even being allowed the company of one of her servants. After my arrival at Fort McHenry, a prisoner, and after midnight, I was ushered into a room, without even a chair to sit upon, the luxury of a Bed, being entirely out of the question.[65]

In March, General Dix informed the Baltimore Police that he was relinquishing control of their department—but the "government's man" remained in charge:

> I give notice that the police force established under its authority will be placed under your control on the 20th instant. In making this communication to you I respectfully request the retention of Mr. McPhail, whose great executive ability has been of incalculable service to the Government. There is still as you are well aware a suppressed feeling of disloyalty in a portion of the population of this city, and I deem it of the utmost importance to the Government that Mr. McPhail should be retained on account of his familiar acquaintance with the transactions of the last eight months and the public necessities which have grown out of those transactions and which still continue to exist.[66]

A. Chaplain, a Maryland state legislator from Trappe in Talbot County, demonstrated solidarity with his fellow lawmakers:

> I have been awaiting for some time with no little degree of concern the release of the members of the late General Assembly of Maryland from Fort Warren. I was one of the members of that body and whatever may have been their real or imagined nature of their offense against the Government I feel myself bound in honor that my guilt was the same as theirs both in degree and kind. Neither can I reconcile it with my own ideas of the duty which I owe both to myself and them to witness their confinement without sharing their sufferings with them.
>
> Being engaged at Annapolis in performance of the duties of a legislative committee at the time of the reassembling of the Legislature in September last accounts for my absence from the city of Frederick then and perhaps for my enjoyment of my liberty now.
>
> Please communicate with me at your earliest convenience and I will surrender myself to Colonel Dimick at Fort Warren at any time you name unless my case be otherwise disposed of.[67]

A public debate erupted over the arrest of Charles C. Fulton, editor of the *Baltimore American and Commercial Advertiser*. From Fort McHenry, Fulton published an appeal to Lincoln:

> I find myself under arrest and on my way to Fort McHenry. I appeal to you for a hearing and prompt release in behalf of my family, who will be in great distress at the execution of this inexplicable order. The Secretary of War authorized me to publish my statement.[68]

Franklin Wilson recorded the calamities befalling his congregants as a result of the war:

> Bro. Adams was imprisoned for a month at Fortress Monroe but was released on taking the oath of allegiance, and is now in this city. Bro. Stevenson, deacon of

our church, was arrested last week on the charge of going South as a mail agent & c. Saml. Sindall a member of our church, joined the Confed. army about 14 months ago, and was killed by a wound in the face at Harrisonburg on the 10th of June. Our church has suffered much. There is a division of sentiment among the members, the prayermeetings are very small and cold, and the finances greatly straitened. I feel deeply the effect of the times on my own religious condition. I feel cut off from both sides in a great measure and have seen so many exhibitions of unchristian and anti christian conduct on both sides as greviously to wound my regard for those whom I have esteemed as Christian brethren.[69]

Franklin Wilson noted the divisions in his church:

Our pastor, Rev. T.H. Pritchard, has left us, and gone to the South. We had, ever since the commencement of the war, betrayed a warm sympathy for the Confederates, laboring much for their wounded and prisoners, but doing nothing openly against the regulations of the Government, except corresponding with the South. However, the so-called *Union* men of the Church have been greatly disaffected, have absented themselves from our meetings, and have apparently lost all interest in the church. He had abstained from any allusions to politics in the pulpit, has prayed for those in authority, and for peace, but he has long felt out of place. His heart was with the South, and not with his work here.

Two days later Wilson wrote that Reverend Pritchard was "arrested on the charge of trying to go South."[70]

W. W. Glenn recounted the seizure of two passenger steamers, the Mary Washington and the George Weems:

About six o'clock as we neared North Point, the Mary Washington hove in sight. An officer hailed us from the deck, the boat bore down upon us, the two ran alongside of one another and a company of soldiers preceded by half a dozen detectives came quickly aboard. The Mary Washington then proceeded on her way. All the gang ways of the George Weems were immediately taken possession of & guarded. The men passengers were orderd back to the upper cabin, the women to the lower one.[71]

He was again taken to Fort McHenry to appear before William Morris, the commander:

I was asked if I would take the oath. "Of course not" was my reply. I was ordered to stand aside & placed under guard. Most of the passengers stood firm and joined me. Some few, who half an hour before had been most ardent Southerners became suddenly quite loyal, some wanted to know what the oath was, some man wanted to consult his wife first who was in the cabin below. The boat was finally taken to Fort McHenry where those of [us] under guard were marched on shore, through a crowd of soldiers, who jeered and hooted as we passed, into the garrison.[72]

In May, authorities at Easton arrested Judge Richard Carmichael, of the Queen Anne's County Circuit Court. Friends leapt into action—one wrote to U.S. Senator James Pearce:

> We are all greatly concerned about the arrest of our Friend Judge Carmichael. We could wish earnestly to have yr. counsel as to the best course to be pursued. It is not only important to put in motion all the machinery which can be employed to effect his complete release, but it would seem to be necessary to his comfort to have some immediate change in his accommodation. I propose to see Genl. Dix, but with very little hope of producing on his mind any favorable impression, as he probably regards me as quite as much an offender as the Judge. However in defence of a friend I feel bound to peril the consequences.[73]

W. W. Glenn gave his opinion of Carmichael's arrest, widely reported to have involved excessive force:

> The whole details were most shocking. He was perfectly upright & manly and determined to do his duty as an officer of the law and not of the Government. Some soldiers and police officers were sent over to arrest him. They entered the Court while it was in session. They knocked him over the head with the butt of a pistol and dragged him bleeding and senseless out of the room.[74]

A Baltimore newspaper recorded the fate of William H. Cowan, who was arrested and taken to Fort McHenry

> on a general charge of treason; but the particular cause for his arrest, it is supposed, was on account of the expressions made use of by him in the Criminal Court on Wednesday morning, during the trial of Frank Fitzpatrick, "that a person had a perfect right to drink a toast to the health of Jeff. Davis or any other man, and to express any sentiments, even if it was considered treasonable, if he chose to do so." In addition to the above, it is stated that he was among the first to raise the Palmetto flag at the Liberty Engine House during the times preceeding the eventful 19th of April, and that he participated in the transactions of that day.[75]

Late in November Glenn commented on the rebirth of the *Exchange* and described the return from Fort Warren of a group of Maryland political prisoners who "were very much feted and entertained for some time":

> They were in excellent spirits and had high hopes of being able to restore a better tone to the State. They could not understand that the Administration had

released them simply because it was indifferent to the little influence they could exercise. They imagined that they had triumphed over the Government. One of the first things proposed was the reissue of the Exchange. Both Frank Howard & Wallis desired to start it on the first of January. I objected to this. I was satisfied it was too soon, but thought that the time was fast approaching and that we might safely count upon the freedom of the press being sufficiently restored by April.[76]

1863

In March, Daniel Thomas, amid recounting his busy law practice, complained about the heavy hand of the authorities and expressed optimism about the outlook for the Confederacy:

> Arrests are still the order of the day. Many ladies were arrested last week, some of whom were discharged—others are to be *banished.* Among others Mrs. Frederick Steuart was arrested on the charge of giving aid & comfort to a *Deserter.* She was at once released, but the question of her banishment is still held under advisement. We are in the hands of a nice set here at present; they are capable of doing anything bad; and no one knows when his turn will come. The prospect in other respects, I think is remarkably encouraging. In every quarter the aspect of things is just the reverse of what it was this time last year. The southern armies are said to be in splendid condition, and when military operations do commence "somebody will be hurt" to a certainty. The war steamers from Europe, that have been so long looked for, will be heard from soon, I think. I think the next four weeks will bring stirring events of several kinds. The conscription act for one thing, is big with events.[77]

A week later Thomas told his sister of another arrest:

> A very large number of troops have been passed though here today, and it is supposed they are going to Kentucky under Burnside. If they don't hurry, they will be too late. I saw Miss Mary Hall at church today and having supposed she had gone home weeks ago, I asked her when she had come to town, and got a proper scolding I tell you. Miss Nannie McCaleb was there too and heard her friend Mr. Gibson preach. He was arrested yesterday on the charge of harboring Confederate soldiers. It seems his nephew came up from Virginia, and brought with him a supposed friend, whose expenses he paid, and took him out to his uncles to stay, and the miserable sneak went and informed on them. His case (Mr. Gibbons) has not been decided on yet, but they threaten to send him south. Mrs. Steuarts case also is still undecided.[78]

James S. Downs and J. Leeds Barroll were, respectively, editors of the *St. Mary's Beacon* in Leonardtown and the *Kent Conservator* in Chestertown. In a letter to the *Richmond Enquirer,* they told of their arrest and confinement in Fort McHenry and Harpers Ferry, where they "were confined in the guard-house at that place for two days, amidst filth and a disorganized and demoralized soldiery." After an overnight stay in the jail in Berryville, Virginia, they were released to the Confederacy at Newton, "never again to return, under the penalty of being treated as spies":

> Since Mr. Lincoln first declared his intention to wage a war of subjugation against the South, we have been decided in our opposition to him. We have been careful, however, to violate no law, either State, national, civil or military, and have confined this position to simple expression of opinion adverse to his policy. For this, we suppose, we have been sent into exile. The Baltimore "American" so states, and we presume it has reliable information on the subject. Our offices have been closed,—ere this, perhaps robbed of their contents,—our business broken up, and our families left to care for themselves as best they may. And all this has been done without even official notification that there was a charge, against us. An this, too, within a few leagues of the capital of the Great American Republic!!![79]

Leonidas Dodson recorded the arrest of an Eastern Shore newsman:

> Thomas K. Robson, Editor of the "Star" was arrested this afternoon by order of Gen Schenck and, carried on board the Gvt Steamer Baloon en route for Balto. How strange it is that he has not foreseen this as the inevitable result of his abuse of the government and its agents.
>
> It is very likely that he will be sent South.[80]

In July, Rev. Henry Slicer attended the Baltimore funeral of Capt. William Brown, a Confederate who had been killed at Gettysburg—apparently not all mourners were acquaintances of the dead man:

> The military authorities, after the funeral, arrested a number of the males attending the funeral in the Greenmount Cemetary, among whom was the father, and Rev Mr. Parrish the Brother-inlaw each of whom were taken from the sides of their wives—I had left before the arrests in order to Baptize a dying child on Lancaster St.
>
> I had not the most remote idea of any difficulty, until informed of it at my house subsequently—The parties arrested were all released—and all declined (under the circumstances) to take the oath, although loyal men.[81]

In August, a number of Westminster citizens were arrested on charges of disloyalty, "in one day, perhaps forty or more of our best citizens, both men and women, were arrested by the soldiers," including Joshua Hering, who with his wife and a friend was escorted to headquarters:

In July 1863, Rev. Henry Slicer's house was searched by federal troops, who seized his rifle but did not detain him. Lovely Lane Museum and Archives.

But the iron heel of the military was upon us and what could we do? When we arrived at the Provost Headquarters, and the soldier had delivered his prisoners, we found a number of others there, all under arrest. The Lieutenant was a good deal abashed in our presence, and to some extent, I thought realized that he was doing a very disreputable piece of work, in which I felt assured he was led on by some of the very worst elements of our town; people who were in every way equal to such a job.[82]

Hering was informed that the charge against him was "general disloyalty" and that he would be freed upon taking the oath of allegiance:

I said "all right, let us have it." And so our party stepped up to the bar and went through the humiliating farce of swearing an allegiance that neither of us had ever violated. He then issued to each of us a certificate attesting our renewed loyalty and let us go.[83]

A group of Anne Arundel County citizens, including former Gov. Thomas G. Pratt, complained to Governor Bradford that they were arrested and ordered to report to military authorities in Baltimore to explain why they had refused to take a loyalty oath at the polls—and that failure to report would cause their "arrest and confinement":

> It was in the exercise of the right thus secured to us that we attempted to vote at the late Election. We declined to take the oath tendered to us because we had, without it, the qualifications prescribed by the Constitution and laws of our State entitling us to vote.[84]

Bradford met with the group and concluded that they must have committed some other offense, noting that many who had refused the oath were not arrested:

> You however protest that you have been guilty of no such acts of hostility to the Government or aid or encouragement to the Rebels, and seem to feel assured that the sole cause of Complaint against you is the fact that you declined to take the oath referred to, declining to do so you did not, as I understand, vote at said Election—I think as I stated to you this morning that there must be other causes for your arrest than the one you assume, for I cannot believe that it is the intention either of the President or the Commander of this Military Department to arrest or punish any one for simply declining to take the oath as prescribed in, and for the purpose contemplated by, the aforesaid order.[85]

Rebecca D. Davis described her father's efforts in August on behalf of a relative, who refused a loyalty oath that could have earned release:

> Pa returned from Baltimore where he has been, at Cousin Culp's request, for several days past endeavoring in vain to procure her brother, John Dorsey's release; charge against him disloyalty. No alternative would be given but the oath of allegiance or Fort McHenry, though Pa plead the urgency of his case, the only male member of his family, now left with a widowed mother & sister looking to him for protection, whose business affairs now require his presence at home. The Gen was inexorable & Mr. D. prefered the Fort to swearing allegiance to a government for which he felt no sympathy.[86]

1864

Arrests of Marylanders suspected of disloyalty continued throughout the war. One longtime resident implied that he might have been but a step ahead of the authorities:

> It was with deep regret that I was compelled to leave my native city without bidding my long-cherished companion of many years "goodbye" but in a moment

least expected I had to leave. I was detainted two thirds of the day, and did not arrive in Washington until after 10 P.M. I landed about two miles from the city, and had to walk the whole distance through a marsh piloted by negroes through a drenching rain with the mud over my shoe tops—I had cause however to congratulate myself upon my *safe* arrival. I remained in Washington until the 4th Jany, saw Miss Scott who enquired after you and desired to be remembered when I wrote.

He returned to Baltimore in January 1864 to discover that the renaissance of the city's vibrant social life had not precluded searches for the disloyal:

Immediately upon my arrival in Baltimore I proceeded to my boarding house, a more desirable location could not be found in the city being central churches of all denominations surround us, our rooms being in the second story were furnished in a style exceeding our anticipations, soon I hung some of my little pictures upon the wall, a home like appearance. We are *all* delighted with the move, and have no regrets at leaving Alex[andria] with the exception of parting from esteemed friends

Our table is not only supplied with the substantials, but the luxuries of the season. Ma's card basket is beginning to tell of the number of calls we have received, the night after my arrival I was invited to a party on Eutaw Street where I spent a most agreeable evening—to-morrow night I attend one of the largest parties that will be given here this season at Mr. Geo Small's on Franklin Street. I understand a full band of Music has been engaged, my tailor has just sent me my suit which I ordered, it being a party suit.

Night before last I called on Miss Mary Wilson & Miss Sanford had a pleasant evening, and promised to join them in a skating party next week on a private pond.

Last Wednesday [-muk] a little circumstance occurred which quite alarmed us—while sitting in our room, several detectives entered our room and informed us we were under arrest and the house was to be searched You can well imagine our feeling—they examined our trunks but finding nothing they informed us we were released, they arrested Miss Mclery an account of which you no doubt read in the paper but as powerful union influence was exerted in her behalf she was released.[87]

In April, a Baltimore newspaper issued two reports of disloyal activity:

Mrs. Otey, arrested under the name of Leroy, who was arrested several days since by government officers at Princess Anne, Somerset county, and brought to this city, charged with having returned from the South, and obtained a quantity of goods, with which she intended to have run the blockade, is still in custody of Provost Marshal, Col. Woolley. Mrs. Otey was arrested by Col. Fish, and sent

South, for engaging in the blockage running business, about one year ago, but managed to get back again into Maryland. Her case will be disposed of by Gen. Wallace in a few days.[88]

Frank A. Price and John Ferguson, arrested in February last, charged with disloyalty, were yesterday sentenced to six months' imprisonment in Fort McHenry. Price, it will be recollected, a short time since attempted to escape from the military prison in this city and was shot by one of the guards.[89]

On June 4, W. W. Glenn, just returned from England, was again arrested, on charges of carrying messages from Mason and Slidell between England and Richmond (he was released two days later):

> The front door bell rang. I went to it myself and found a detective there. They had evidently been on the watch for me since my last presence in Baltimore. I was in my slippers. The fellow would not even let me go upstairs alone to put on shoes. He signalled to another man & in a moment half a dozen more appeared on the scene. They entered the house, keeping me in strict custody, and commenced a search. The first thing picked up was Lucy's photograph album of Southern Generals. The names were written under each. On the front page was a picture of Genl. Lee not yet published in the North. Under it was written "Commander in Chief". The fellow looked at it, turned it round, said "Commander in Chief—Commander in Chief" and then suddenly, as if a bright idea had struck him, cried out "God bless my soul, I believe it is meant for General Lee". The book was confiscated.[90]

The Reverend Edward A. Colburn wrote to his father about a report describing the November 18 arrest of a friend, Jacob Enfield, who had been sentenced to six months at "hard labor" at Fort Dix on charges of disloyalty and displaying a rebel flag. Colburn believed the circumstances of Enfield's case, and the strong Union position so late in the war, made his fate unduly harsh:

> Jacob Enfield's wife is a member of my congregation, and a communicant—a most estimable, though uneducated person. Mr. Enfield himself is a Presbyterian—but a very excellent man. I can express the same opinion of all his family.
> You see he is charged with displaying a rebel flag. There is some mistake here. He had an old flag—with the names of Buchanan & Breckenridge on it. He had written on a piece of paper, McClellan and Pendleton—and pasted that paper over the other names. He hung the flag, thus fixed, upon the side of his barn—but a rain coming, washed off the paper, leaving the old names. This will tell what kind of a flag it was. He was arrested, and taken to Balt—where he was confined in the city jail—till the day when sentenced to work on Fort Dix. He has always been a strong southern man—but still I have always found him not

unreasonable. About the time of the election, he took this flag to various meetings—and was very imprudent in his display of it. He is an uneducated man—yet, hard working.

Can anything be done for him. His family are in a great deal of trouble about his arrest—but do not yet know of his sentence. Cannot some of you, who are in the interest of the government, present this statement to some one, who has power to move in his behalf? I feel anxious, on his wife's account—and on account of his farm—all will suffer from his absence.[91]

1865

Union Gen. Philip Sheridan banished eight women south into the Confederacy just six weeks before Lee's surrender at Appomattox (the details of their offenses may be best left to the imagination):

The following named persons are hereby ordered out of the lines of the Army. Mrs. Hugh H. Lee, Miss Lee, The Misses Burnell (two), Mrs. W.A. Shenard and three daughters. These ladies, placed with in the lines of this Army by the fortune of War, have so far forgotten themselves as to provoke an exercise of Military power by giving constant annoyance, either for the sake of notoriety or from want of reflection or a want of being true to themselves, and they are now sent beyond the limits of the command that they may be freed from the slight restraint Military necessity requires here.[92]

Marylanders continued to draw the attention of the authorities after Lee's surrender, as demonstrated by a note dispatched in late April to Charles Vocke, Esq., the consul of the Netherlands for Maryland and Washington at Charles Street near Camden:

You will please report at this office without fail at 9 oclock tomorrow morning on particular business. By command of William Wiegel, Major and Asst. Provost Marshal.[93]

chapter eight

Prison

1861

Two of the three Winder brothers of Maryland ran afoul of the military authorities. William was the Philadelphia correspondent of the *New York Daily News*, while brother John was a Confederate general. Charles was imprisoned in Washington and, though confident of a brief detention, nonetheless asked for experienced legal counsel:

> I am in custody of the military authorities & unless I am detained merely for my opinions, I will be released tomorrow I presume.
>
> I shall therefore only require a shirt & my tooth brush. I have a pocket comb which will answer my purpose tomorrow.
>
> If you want anything send for Walter Davidge.

And a postscript: "Send me a towel. Let Mollie call on Mr. Reverdy Johnson & inform him of my arrest if I can see him I would like it."[1]

In early July, Gen. Nathaniel Banks was pleased "to report that Baltimore is perfectly orderly and quiet night and day," but when he learned that one of the imprisoned police commissioners was seriously ill, he foresaw a public relations disaster should the prisoner die in custody:

> Charles D. Hinks, one of the commissioners of police arrested on the 1st instant and now a prisoner in the fort, is in ill health. His physician, Dr. John Buckler, whose letter I inclose, declares that confinement at the fort will be attended with fatal consequences. Doctor Smith, physician at the city infirmary, and Doctor Martin, of the Massachusetts Rifles, concur in the opinion of Doctor Buckler and represent Mr. Hinks as in the last stages of consumption.
>
> He has not been present in the city over a month having resided in the South on account of his health, and has not therefore participated in political affairs here until very recently. Upon inquiry among many prominent men I learn he is the least objectionable of any of the prisoners. His death in prison would make an unpleasant public impression. His release with proper declarations as to his future conduct would produce an agreeable impression. I would respectfully recommend that authority be given to release him whenever it can be done with safety to the public interests.[2]

Though the Civil War was the last "uncensored" American conflict, prisoners' mail was routinely searched, and their visitors closely monitored, as was the case at Fort Hamilton, in New York Harbor:

Twelve letters written by the prisoners received here yesterday from Fort McHenry. In my opinion some of them are of a very inflammatory nature, and if they should find their way into the press of Baltimore as it is evidently the intention of the writers they should it would be detrimental to the Government. Therefore I submit them to your inspection before forwarding them according to their directions. The writers you will see complain of the restrictions placed upon them and of accommodations which they receive. The restrictions are the same as those placed upon the prisoners confined here previous to their arrival and which in my judgment is the only means of securing the safety of the prisoners, my command being composed as you are aware entirely of recruits who might be influenced to a departure from their duty if the prisoners were allowed the free use of their money, private communications or interviews with their friends.[3]

The commander of Fort Hamilton explained that these prisoners were treated as well as his own men:

They are allowed all the liberty that the size, arrangement and situation of the post and the force under my command will admit. Their rooms are precisely the same as those occupied by the officers and privates. In consequence of the scarcity of apartments I am obliged to place twelve soldiers in each room, all of which are cleansed and well ventilated. The requisition made a week ago for blankets, bed-sacks and straw for the use of prisoners was filled to-day and they were supplied with the same. I this day (as directed by you in the presence of the prisoners) caused a requisition to be made for chairs, tables, wash basins and pitchers, plates and other articles necessary for their comfort. I have placed Mr. Alvey, Mr. Lyon and the three police commissioners in one room, they having made arrangements to provide themselves with meals. The other prisoners who draw rations are in another room. On taking their money from the prisoners I gave to each a receipt for the amount stating that I held it subject to their draft in such amounts as they may require for immediate use. On searching the prisoners who were first received here a revolver and a bowie knife were found upon the person of one of them.[4]

The U.S. House of Representatives, generally supportive of Lincoln's efforts to prosecute the war, in late July protested the detention of a class of political prisoners, naming the three members of the Baltimore Police Board and resolving

That the arrest and imprisonment of Charles Howard, William H. Gatchell and John W. Davis and others without warrant and process of law is flagrantly unconstitutional and illegal; and they should without delay be released, or their case remitted to the proper judicial tribunals to be lawfully heard and determined.[5]

General Dix ordered a group of Baltimoreans held in Fort McHenry to more permanent quarters in New York Harbor:

> You will receive on board the steamer Whitney the following persons, arrested by my predecessor in command of this department and charged with offenses against the Government and laws of the United States, viz: R. H. Alvey, John H. Kusick, John W. Davis, Dr. Edward Johnson, T. C. Fitzpatrick, William H. Gatchell, Charles M. Hagelin, Charles Howard, Samuel C. Lyon, James E. Humphrey. You will take care that all their wants so far as you have the means are supplied and you will also see that they are treated with proper kindness and courtesy. You will proceed without interruption or delay to Fort Lafayette in the harbor of New York and deliver them into the custody of the officer in charge of that fort. You will be held strictly responsible for their safety during the voyage as well as for the orderly conduct of your men.[6]

Charles Howard complained from Fort Lafayette that the government had reneged on its promise of better treatment:

> On Monday evening last we were placed on board the steamer Joseph Whitney with a detachment of soldiers, all information as to our place of destination being positively refused both to us and to the members of our families. Both General Dix and Major Morris, however, gave the most positive assurances that at the place to which we should be taken we would be made much more comfortable and the limits of our confinement would be less restricted than at Fort McHenry. Yesterday we were landed here and are kept in close custody. No provision whatever had been made here for us and last night we were shut up—eight persons—in a vaulted room or casemate about twenty-four by fourteen feet, having three small windows each about three feet by fourteen inches, and a close wooden door which was shut and locked upon us soon after 9 o'clock and remained so until morning. Some of the party by permission brought on our own bedsteads and bedding with which we had been compelled to supply ourselves at Fort McHenry, otherwise we should have been compelled to lie on the bare floor, the officers here stating to us that they had no supplies whatever and could not furnish us even with blankets of the most ordinary kind.[7]

Howard complained of censorship, denial of newspapers, and limited exercise and reminded Cameron that he and others were being held without trial or even charges:

> We were on our arrival here required to surrender all the money we had and all writing-papers and envelopes, our baggage being all searched for these and other articles that might be shown to be considered as contraband. It is unnecessary to give any further details to satisfy you that our condition as to physical comfort is no better than that of the worst felons in any common jail of the coun-

try. Having been arrested and already imprisoned for a month without a charge of any legal offense having been as yet preferred against me or those arrested at the same time with me it is useless to make any further protest to you against the continuance of our confinement. But we do insist as a matter of common right as well as in fulfillment of your own declarations to me that if the Government chooses to exercise its power by restraining us of our liberty it is bound in ordinary decency to make such provision for our comfort and health as gentlemen against whom if charges have been preferred they have not been made known (and all opportunity for an investigation has been denied) are recognized in every civilized community to be entitled to . . . I have written this letter on my bed sitting on the floor upon a carpet-bag, there being neither table, chairs, stool nor bench in the room.[8]

On August 8 Secretary Seward instructed General Scott and the U.S. attorney for the southern district of New York to ignore a writ of habeas corpus filed by the Baltimore Police Commissioners:[9]

In August, a guard reported a conversation he overheard to the commander of Fort Lafayette:

While in the room occupied by the police commissioners I heard John W. Davis, one of the commissioners, make use of the following language, viz: That Colonel Burke had outlawed himself toward him in not obeying the writ of habeas corpus; that he (Colonel Burke) was depriving him of his liberty, and so help him God if he ever got out of this place he would deprive him (Colonel Burke) of his life; that he would shoot him on sight and take the consequences. Some one told him that he was foolish; that Colonel Burke had nothing to do with it that he was only obeying the orders of General Scott. Mr. Davis said that Colonel Burke had no right to obey an order which was in violation of the laws of the land and he would hold him responsible for his confinement.[10]

In September, General Dix renewed his complaints about the prison facilities at Fort McHenry, which

has not sufficient space for the convenient accommodation of the number of men necessary to man its guns is crowded with prisoners. Beside our own criminals awaiting trial or under sentence we have eleven State prisoners. To this number six more will be added to-morrow. I do not think this a suitable place for them if we had ample room. It is too near the seat of war which may possibly be extended to us. It is also too near a great town in which there are multitudes who sympathize with them who are constantly applying for interviews and who must be admitted with the hazard of becoming the media of improper communications, or who go away with the feeling that they have been harshly treated because they have been denied access to their friends.

And worried about prison security:

> I certainly do not think them perfectly safe here considering the population by
> which they are surrounded and the opportunities for evading the vigilance of
> their guards.[11]

Three days later he suggested some prisoners be moved to Fort Delaware:

> I came to the city from Fort McHenry to-day to examine a quantity of articles,
> letters, &c., intended for the Confederate States, captured last evening by the
> police. Two parties of individuals were also taken with them. I have all these
> persons in custody; what shall be done with them I must again call your atten-
> tion to the crowded state of Fort McHenry. Every room is full and we had about
> fifty prisoners last night in tents on the parade ground with hardly room left for
> the guard to parade.[12]

After an escape Colonel Morris banned visitors from Fort McHenry:

> Major Alexander, formerly of the United States revenue service, but late an of-
> ficer in the Confederate army, and one of the political prisoners confined in Fort
> McHenry, made his escape from his cell at the Fort, and sometime between ten
> o'clock on Saturday night and yesterday morning, and succeeded in getting off,
> eluding the guards and outposts. It is thought his escape was effected by means
> of a disguise of some kind.[13]

Baltimore Attorney Thomas W. Hall, editor of the *Baltimore South*, was jailed at
Fort McHenry. Anticipating transfer to more permanent confinement in the North,
he asked his mother to send articles of clothing, books, and other necessities, including "tooth-powder, & bottle MacKenzie's Lustral for hair":

> This note, & my trunk when it comes, must both pass the inspection of the
> commandant; therefore, you will see the propriety of making no additions to the
> list, unless it be some article of necessary use which I have forgotten in the enu-
> meration. As it is not likely that I shall be permitted to see any of you before my
> departure or until my release, I bid you all *adieu* & *au revoir,* with a heart full of
> love, & hope that you will bear this temporary trial with as much tranquillity as
> I do, & rest in firm assurance of a speedy reunion. Kindest remembrance to all
> inquiring & sympathising friends.[14]

W. W. Glenn, arrested on September 14, commented on conditions there:

> Visited by Genl. Dix, whose Head Quarters were then at Fort, although he was
> in command of the Department, who informed that my wife would be permitted
> to visit me. I was transferred to a room on the ground floor. This evening politi-
> cal prisoners began to come in. They had been mostly seized upon the boats,

as they came to Baltimore, from the lower counties on their way to Frederick. They took their misfortunes differently. Some were despondent, one or two got drunk; most of them were thinking of the best way of getting free. Jim Maxwell had his fiddle & was very jolly. When the pinch came, it was he who showed the most pluck of this batch. As a general rule they were like the guests which were bidden to the marriage feast. One had his farm, another his merchandise & they got back to them as soon as possible. As they came in fifteen or twenty men were huddled together in the guard room. Half a dozen were crammed in with me. My room was about 12 x 14.[15]

On September 20, Thomas Hall asked his mother to send more items and urged she "dismiss all anxiety on my account; I am well, and but for the solicitude which I feel for you, and which your letters have not served to remove, I should be as contented as a prisoner can be." The following day he thanked her for the arrival of his "travelling bag" and asked for his spectacles:

When I wrote for eyeglasses, I mentioned (or intended to do so), that in my desk or bureau you would find some *broken pains,* which would give the right number for my eye. I find you have sent the broken ones, which, in their present state, are of no possible use. However, I have latterly accustomed myself in great measure to dispense with glasses altogether, and shall, probably, experience no great inconvenience from the want of them. Cards and books are our only resources in confinement, and as I care nothing for the former, I must repeat my request for a supply of the latter.[16]

Mayor George Brown spent some of his fourteen-month imprisonment in Fort Warren, where he described conditions to Emily Barton Brune, the wife of Frederick Brune, his law partner:

It is a strange feeling to be deprived of liberty. I have often wondered how prisoners felt, as I have seen them peering from grated windows. At first, I could hardly at times contain my indignation, but I am now calmly resigned to whatever may be in store for me. While I am in the house of bondage, and at all times, I am thankful for the prayers of those whom I love. I have read over the whole of the office of visitation of Prisoners, and see nothing in it which Every one who feels his sinfulness may not be glad to have said in his behalf.

Last evening Howard and I crawled out of the port hole and at on the edge with our feet over the moat, watching the beautiful sunset—the first since my incarceration.

There is a slight dampness about the casements, but the sea air is very wholesome and I am perfectly well. After a while, I think the very annoying restrictions which confine us within the walls, and practically exclude air and sunshine, will be taken off. The government can have no object, I suppose, except to prevent escape. Or rather it has another object is to prevent a free communication with the world, but this it will probably give up, for nothing can be gained by enforcing it. The sergeant who acts as deputy Provost-Marshal is very obliging, as indeed all the subordinates are who have come in contact with us. The business of playing jailer over prisoners of state is something new to the American mind and evidently not congenial to it.

I am surprised to find how rapidly day by day the time flies. Some of our Party are uncomfortably early risers, and this arouses the whole about 6 o clock. We breakfast at 8, dine at 2 take tea at 7 and retire when we please. As some are fond of late hours, the rest of those who are fond of sleep is somewhat interfered with. I read a good deal in a desultory way. I find much in Mosley's History which seems to shed light on passing events. When these sad days are over, we shall have much to talk & think of.[17]

In September, William Winder, perplexed by his arrest and confinement in Fort Lafayette, wrote to brother Charles:

On the day after my arrest, ignorant of your having been so too, I wrote you a letter. I have not since heard from you. My confinement is sadly injurious to my affairs, or I could be philosophic if I knew your family were not distressed by your confinement. I am cut off from my means, & fear to have recourse to such as were not seized lest everything might be taken. We have here over one hundred a letter from Washington of 16th stated you were to be sent here in a day or two, so I looked for you, until at length I have concluded that it was a mistake.

I am at work to try & find what it was which caused my arrest, as I am unable to act intelligently until I do. I much fear that your health will give way under your confinement. Cannot our friend [J] get you leave on parole to avert this. A publication of all letters & communications bearing upon natural matters, would be my complete vindication.[18]

In September Secretary Seward suggested General Dix consider releasing Brown:

No sooner is the conspiracy against the Government defeated than under a natural law of the human mind sympathy begins to rise in behalf of the agents of the crime held under duress. Among the prisoners recently arrested Mayor Brown is represented as having been harmless, unoffending and even loyal. Relying implicitly on your discernment and discretion I have to ask your opinion concerning the mayor and the reasonableness or unreasonableness of releasing him.[19]

On the same day, Dix wrote to Seward, referring to two testimonials on Brown's behalf and enclosing one of them, from George Shattuck, Brown's brother-in-law. With the disposition of political prisoners then the responsibility of the State Department (the War Department took charge of political arrests in February 1862), the stage seemed set for Brown's release:

Mayor George W. Brown of Baltimore, who labored mightily to prevent bloodshed in his city, suffered arrest and imprisonment for disloyalty— perhaps because of evidence that implicated him in destruction of railroad bridges in the spring 1861. MdHS.

He is a man of great amiability of character, behaved very well during the outbreak on the 19th of April and I think has been the dupe rather than the willing accomplice of such men as Wallis and Scott. I inclose letters from two of the most respectable gentlemen in Boston, both of whom you probably know. Doctor Shattuck is a man of great wealth and a warm supporter of the administration. I have also a letter from Mr. Sauerwein, of Baltimore, one of the most intelligent and stern of the Union men in the city, who suggests that the mayor should resign his office and take the oath of allegiance and on these conditions be discharged from custody.[20]

Seward replied:

If you think that George William Brown ought to be released upon his taking the oath of allegiance, resigning the office of mayor and residing in some one of the Northern cities for a time and if you think also that he would accede to these conditions you will please take such proceedings as you suppose necessary to have the propositions made by him to yourself. I shall not act in any of the cases without [your] advice.[21]

Brown was not released, but transferred to Fort Lafayette. His letter a month later to Emily Brune revealed his healthy state of mind:

> Our little community is constantly changing. Today two prisoners have been released, one Captain Hagelin of our city, a good man about whom I wrote the President. He promises to call at the office to see Frederick. Your long letter was very welcome and was read and reread by me with much pleasure. I am sitting on my trunk with portfolio on my knee while I write this, because the tables are otherwise occupied and our casemate is full of people. You would be amused to see our arrangements and various occupations. The marking ink which Clara's thoughtfulness supplied, has been in great requisition, and two days ago I marked a set of shirts for Gov Morehead. Frank Howard and Dr. Thomas are now tenants of our room No. 3, two vacancies having occurred which were filled by the vote of the remaining numbers. Our room is considered the most desirable, having a wood fire, a south exposure and *only* nine inmates.
>
> We are, on the whole, rather a cheerful community. There is much kindliness of feeling, the strong being willing to bear the infirmities of the weak, and much unanimity of sentiment about public affairs. Poor Haig has become deranged from distress and anxiety, but was an exception for very few give way to despondency. P.S. I had a bowl of nice calves foot jelly today from Mrs. Gelston.[22]

On September 30, George P. Kane wrote to Lincoln from Fort Lafayette with a litany of complaints, many to do with his health:

> On the 27th of June last I was taken from my bed at my dwelling in the city of Baltimore about 3 o'clock in the morning by an armed body of about 1,000 or 1,200 men and conveyed to Fort McHenry. The officers commanding the military referred to had no warrant for and as they informed me did not know the cause of my arrest. General Banks informed my counsel that I was not taken on any specific charge but merely detained as an act of military precaution, and also requested the commanding officer of Fort McHenry to make the same statement to me and that it was done by a special command of Your Excellency.
>
> Whilst at that post I contracted the fever resulting from the malaria incident to that locality at certain seasons with which I suffered for upwards of a month, and whilst still laboring under its effects was transferred to this place. On my arrival here notwithstanding my debilitated condition I was placed in a casemate on the ground floor paved with brick with just space enough for my bed between the gun by my side and the partition of the apartment in which have been incarcerated with me as many as between thirty and forty other prisoners at the same time thus rendering the atmosphere most offensive and pestiferous.
>
> Among other effects of the fever increased by my present confinement I am suffering with prostration of the bowels and required to repair to the only con-

venience for the purpose by the sea-side outside of the fort ten and twelve times in the twenty-four hours in all kinds of weather. I am locked in my prison room from 6 p.m. till 6 a.m. and only allowed to take with me one tumbler of water for use during that period. Whilst suffering great agony from the promptings of nature and effects of my debility I am frequently kept for a long time at the door of my cell waiting for permission to go to the water-closet owing to the utter indifference of some of my keepers to the ordinary demands of humanity. I am compelled to obtain at my own expense the mere substantial provisions which I require because the fare prescribed for the State prisoners is not fit for one in full health much less for a person in my present condition.[23]

On October 2, Thomas Hall reassured his mother about his prison life:

You ask the particulars of our condition. I do not know how far I should be permitted to disclose them; I am sure that if it were in my power to give you a full description, I should prefer to have you remain in ignorance, at least, until the period of any confinement is over. At the same time, I do not wish you to feel any unnecessary solicitude on my account; I am better able to bear the physical discomforts of our imprisonment than most of my companions, and have as much philosophy as any of them. I am well and hope to remain so.[24]

But provided more details to his father:

In spite of the frightful crowding to which we are subjected, exceeding anything ever witnessed in any well regulated barrack, prison, or even hospital in time of pestilence, the general health of the post continues to be remarkably good. My own never was better, and if constant care can avail for its preservation, I shall not suffer, *while the weather continues as at present*. I can not answer for the effects of rain and cold, in such quarters and with such accommodations. The present number of prisoners is about one hundred and seventeen—of whom a partial list is published in to-day's *New York Times*—fourteen were added on Saturday night, and while I write fresh arrivals are reported, and we are already packed like herrings in a barrel or the cargo of a slave-ship.[25]

By late November, George Brown was back in Fort Warren, where some prisoners rejected an oath of allegiance in exchange for release:

An unanswered letter always keeps my friends steadily in mind, but in your case no such reminder is ever necessary. Prison life is so monotonous that the record of one day very much resembles that of every other. Today however there was a little variety. We saw in the Boston papers of this morning a notice of release of various prisoners which I enclose. Soon afterwards the parties were sent for, but instead of an unconditional release, an oath of allegiance was presented.

Harrison Carter, [Erady] & Appleton at once refused to take it, but others were less stout.[26]

William H. Winder wrote from Fort Lafayette to his niece:

I was arrested on the 10th and on the 11th wrote Charles advising him of it, not knowing that he too had been arrested. I do not know whether he has received it or not. Of our accommodations here, he may judge by his own, as in all material respects I suppose they do not materially differ. We receive letters, after having undergone inspection, and the daily papers, & are allowed to obtain from outside many comforts. We have some one hundred confined here, many Baltimoreans & others acquaintances of bygone days

I learn with much satisfaction the considerate action of the Provost-Marshall, it tends to confirm my previous opinion of his soldierly qualities, & I doubt not he will do what he can to mitigate the hardships, his official action may cause.

I am however greatly distressed to learn the critical condition of Mollie's health, it affects me far more deeply than does my own confinement, how much so ever it injuriously affects my interest. I shall continue to feel solicitous about her until I learn her convalescence.[27]

In October, W. W. Glenn described his quarters at Fort McHenry:

By the first of this month I was, strange to say, tolerably comfortable in my prison quarters. I had received from home bedding and books, I was allowed provisions of liquors and my wife came to see me frequently. A few other friends were allowed to come from time to time. Other prisoners were detained at Fort McHenry only for a short time. They were allowed no comforts and as soon as a sufficient number had accumulated to warrant the expense, a steamboat was ordered down and they were shipped to some larger Fort. I never knew to what influences I owed my first detention.[28]

Glenn's description of Colonel Morris included reference to a prewar court-martial, on a charge of seducing a woman, whom Morris was later "compelled to marry":

His military views & his predictions as to the character and length of the War, showed decided capacity. On other matters he sometimes displayed unpardonable ignorance. At times he was a perfect brute; then again he would be kind and good natured. He often manifested a strong friendship & was willing to serve you, while at the same time his love of trickery so predominated that it was a real pleasure for him to catch a friend in a trap. He would call up prisoners and use every argument to induce them to forsake their opinions and take the oath of Allegiance and the moment it was done he would turn from them in contempt and speak of them most disparagingly.[29]

Glenn quickly discovered the colonel's weakness:

> I had some bottles of Seltzer Water in the room. "Colonel" said I "will you take plain or Seltzer Water with your brandy." "Seltzer" said he "What's that"? "Let me show you" said I and as I poured the water in the brandy and it sparkled up like champagne, he took it tossed it off, smacked his lips and evidently wished for more. From that day he was a constant visitor. He commenced by being fond of my liquor. He soon began to like my society.

And exploited it:

> I took care too from time to time to send him presents of Whiskey which proved very acceptable. Crittenden had sent father in from Kentucky in 1846 a barrel of Bourbon Whiskey. This Whiskey he sent as very fine. I had put it after five or six years in demijohns. It had not improved and as I had never liked Corn Whiskey, I had left it untouched, as not good enough for my friends. Crittenden was now a great card. I thought of the Whiskey, had some bottled & sent down labeled "Crittenden 1846". Morris used to call it the Crittenden Compromise. It had quite a reputation among these men, who knew no better. I kept him supplied with it. It was not the only time I used it advantageously.[30]

Richard Thomas, the "French Lady" who in May 1861 had hijacked a Chesapeake Bay steamer for the Confederacy, was in an adjacent cell:

> It was so small and so close. In it was Dick Thomas—alias Zarvona. He was under strict guard. His companion Col. Alexander had escaped some time before, he & Zarvona evidently having bribed the guard. Morris was of course furious. He considered it as a sort of personal disgrace to himself. Z. refused to give any parole & was very strictly guarded. There was a hole in the wall between his room & the guard room for a stove pipe. Two days after Henry J.'s arrival, Z. tossed a note through this. J.'s man got it & brought it to me. As we were under parole not to communicate with him here the correspondence stopped. I learned afterwards that Thomas soon after managed to obtain a key to the cell. He would doubtless have tried to escape had he not been transferred to Fort Lafayette, before he found a favorable opportunity.[31]

George Brown's release was conditioned on his resignation as mayor of Baltimore. On October 9, General Dix told Secretary Seward that Brown believed resignation tantamount to admitting disloyalty, and that city elections held that day would determine the next mayor. Dix quoted from a letter written by George Shattuck, Brown's brother-in-law helping broker his release:

> I would like his bounds to be the New England States because he has a sister in New Hampshire with whom another sister is now staying. Both these ladies are

strong for the Union. His second son is going to Saint Paul's school at Concord, N.H., and I should like him free to visit at those places. He can convince himself that throughout New England the sober, sensible, intelligent people are acting under a conviction that this war must be carried on vigorously and heartily; that the South gives us no choice. Can I have permission to see him again? I may be in New York early next week and his little daughter with me. Would she be allowed to go with me? I hope to get a favorable answer from Mr. Brown without seeing him a second time but the influence of his fellow prisoners about him may be adverse and prevail and I may wish to have another conversation with him.[32]

Two days later Seward replied:

If you approve Mr. Brown may be released on taking the oath and giving his parole not to do any act or hold any correspondence treasonable or injurious to the Union, and not to enter the State of Maryland or any insurrectionary State during the insurrection. These restraints to be removed only by direction of the Secretary of State.[33]

Frederick County delegate Thomas Claggett, who constantly petitioned for release from Fort Warren, described its conditions:

We have had religious services every Sunday since I have been in the forts except the first. At Lafayette an ex Lieutenant of the navy read the episcopal service and a sermon. Here we enjoy the services of a presbyterian preacher who was captured together with another big gun by Col. Geary at Harpers ferry. There are men here of almost all professions and classes in social life. We have an abundance of good society if intellectual and cultivated persons all of one sex can constitute good society, for altho in the land of the Pilgrim Fathers I have met with none of the pilgrim daughters.

Tell sister that I am much more comfortable here than she would suppose. I occupy a very good room finished nicely and intended for an officer of the Fort. Those who have money and think proper to use it can have almost any thing they may want. We have daily communication with Boston and get all important news as soon as we would at home. I heard of the arrest of Mr. Horsey and twenty others the day after it occurred. I did not receive nor hear until now any thing of the letter you enclosed to Gov. Hicks.

I do not in the least wonder that you were unable to find out why I became a state prisoner when I myself have no way of knowing. I can imagine no reason for it except my accidental connection with the Legislature and therefore have made no more in the matter, preferring to wait until after the election, when that reason for my detention will have ceased. Instead of my informing you of the charges against me, I have to ask you to try and find out what they are and what ought to be done.[34]

Dr. Thomas Maddox received a disappointing reply from the Episcopal bishop of Maryland, William R. Whittingham, whom he had asked to intervene on behalf of Claggett, his brother-in-law:

I am as ignorant as you of the causes or grounds of Mr. Claggett's arrest and detention. I am as little disposed as you can be to believe him capable of anything really deserving such treatment, or likely to have incurred it except under mistaken notions but too probably instilled by malicious misinformation.

But while I have no sort of knowledge of the causes or procurers of Mr. C's imprisonment, I am equally unacquainted with its authors or instruments. I have no personal acquaintance with either the present governor or his elected successor. With the latter I have never had any kind of communication, nor with the former. I know no member of the General Adminstration at Washington, and only know its chief organ in this State, General Dix, through his reputation in the public print; having only once in my life seen him, and then on horseback in the public street. I have never, on any occasion, asked a favour, of any Kind, for myself or for any one else, of any member of Government whether of the United States, or of this State.

Among the prisoners in Fort Warren are more than one for whom, besides Mr. Claggett, I have all the tender interests which spiritual relationship [?] adds to private friendship—more than one for whom I can say as of him, that I had ever held them to be all that characterized as Christian and a gentleman. To interfere in behalf of him and not of them would be to do violence to my own feelings towards them and afford them and their friends and relatives with whom I am in near and intimate relations, just cause for complaint. To interfere in behalf of all would be simply [?] impertinence on the part of one so utterly devoid of claims upon the attention of the authorities as I am.

I cannot but believe that the release of Mr. Claggett and others as little implicated in these unhappy troubles as I believe him to be, must follow speedily on the assemblage of the new Legislature of the State, now so soon to take place. Till then, I will not cease appealing in his behalf to a Higher Power; but I cannot, without a complete departure from the course presented to myself throughout my whole ministry become an applicant to the civil authorities in his behalf.[35]

By November, reports of Mayor Brown's actions in Baltimore on April 19 were being cited in support of his release:

I cannot but think it for the public welfare that every leniency should be shown him that is compatible with the safety of Baltimore. I can add my testimony to the inclosed that in private communications with Mr. Brown I was entirely satisfied of his good faith in regard to the President's expected passage through Baltimore; that he was at that time utterly opposed to the doctrine of secession and that his opinions regarding slavery were more liberal than that of any other prominent citizen of Baltimore of my acquaintance. I have the best authority for saying that on the 19th and 20th of April he said to the mob almost at the risk of his life that he was opposed to secession. I believe he is one of the men who ought to be on our side and if so would be of great value to us when the time comes for conciliation in Maryland. The circumstances of his arrest and first days of imprisonment were unfortunately very harsh and I cannot but think that it would be well for the Government to offer him a month's parole within the State of Massachusetts to attend to his private affairs, he first promising to have no communication of any sort verbal or written regarding Maryland politics. Such a course without committing the Government beyond thirty days would be entirely safe and would have a good effect in removing the remembrance of his too harsh treatment by subordinates at first.[36]

The chaplain of the Sixth Massachusetts Regiment stated in a testimonial that his men would not have survived the mob absent Brown's intervention:

To the officers and soldiers of the Sixth Massachusetts Regiment he is an object of especial interest. His manly and heroic conduct on the eventful 19th of April secured to him the esteem and praise of every one of us. I call testify to the admiration that every one in camp manifested in speaking of the events of that day. Those who were eye-witnesses of what he did were eloquent in their praises. I was at Camp Chase, Lowell, last Tuesday and took the liberty to introduce the subject to the field officers of the Twenty-sixth (formerly the Sixth) and I found that the same lively sense of indebtedness to Mayor Brown remained fresh as ever. I proposed that we should unite in an effort to procure some mitigation of the trouble under which he is laboring in the way of signing a petition for his relief.

I have often listened to the story as our men in camp related the doings of Mayor Brown as they fought their way through Baltimore. I have my doubts whether we should have gotten through at all without his aid; and if we had not God alone knows what would have been the present posture of our national affairs. My prayers and efforts shall never be wanting in behalf of a man who could do so bravely what he did on that memorable occasion.[37]

In October, Lincoln extended the suspension of the writ of habeas corpus north to Bangor, Maine. In December, the Republican House of Representatives protested this action and called on the president to release from military custody the Baltimore police commissioners so they might stand trial in civilian courts— by 108 to 26, resolving

That the Congress alone has the power under the Constitution of the United States to suspend the privilege of the writ of habeas corpus; that the exercise of that power by any other department of the Government is a usurpation and therefore dangerous to the liberties of the people; that it is the duty of the President to deliver Charles Howard, William H. Gatchell and John W. Davis to the custody of the marshal of the proper district if they are charged with any offense against the laws of the United States to the end that they may be indicted and enjoy the right of a speedy and public trial by an impartial jury of the State and district wherein the crime is alleged to have been committed.[38]

Thomas W. Hall told his mother on New Year's Day about Christmas in prison:

The day was spent far more pleasantly than I could have anticipated or imagined. Perhaps, it was because we had all indulged beforehand in such painful and gloomy anticipations of a Christmas spent in prison, that when the day actually arrived, we were agreeably disappointed to find that the sun did shine, that turkey & plum pudding retained their natural flavor and that eggnogg and apple-toddy brought in their train the usual increase of good humor & hilarity. Will our grieving sympathizing friends at home think their sympathy misplaced if we confess that on Christmas night, in Fort Warren, we could both laugh & sing, & even find places for a little innocent buffoonery? What jokes we cracked, what songs we sang, and the name of the obnoxious individual whose effigy we sentenced to an ignominious fate, after a solemn trial, verdict found & sentence rendered—these are secrets not to be communicated now or here.[39]

1862

When W. W. Glenn, still in Fort McHenry on New Year's Day, again refused to sign a parole, Colonel Morris threatened him:

"Now," said he, "Glenn, you are a good fellow and I like you very much. You have been here some time and we are friends. Take my advice, give a parole, go home, keep quiet and when this war is over we will meet again as friends & renew our intercourse with pleasure". I made no reply. "You need not think," he went on, "that you are going to Fort Warren where all your friends are and where Col Dimick the officer in command is a gentleman. You are going to Fort Lafayette, where you will be under a man who is known to be very severe, you will be put in a casement with half a dozen others, probably not fit associates for you, you will have no comforts and you will be treated like a dog."[40]

So Glenn prepared for transfer:

This morning I made my final toilet in my old quarters. I was only awaiting the arrival of the boat in which we were to embark. I had been shown the list of prisoners with the charges against them. Zarvona's name was at the head. Mine came second. There was no charge against me. I was styled W.W. Glenn, Editor Exchange. I was scarcely dressed when sister Anne came down in the carriage. Morris came in and told me I was ordered to report to Genl. Dix. At first, I did not wish to go. I told I was tired of talking. But he told me I had better go, as he thought I would be released.[41]

He pledged to return to Fort McHenry if not released and rode into the city to meet General Dix:

> Dix proposed a parole. I told him I knew no difference between that and an oath of Allegiance. At last he said "Very well! go home when I want you, I'll send for you". And I went.[42]

Early in January the U.S. marshal for Massachusetts reported that Brown was refusing to remain in Massachusetts as a condition of release—which would cost him another eleven months' imprisonment:

> I have the honor to report that George William Brown, of Baltimore, has this day surrendered himself to me pursuant to the terms of his parole. Not having any directions from the State Department in regard to his recommitment and this gale of wind making it very difficult if not impracticable to land at Fort Warren I have taken the liberty to retain him in custody and ask for instructions in the premises. He expresses no desire to have his parole extended but an earnest wish to be allowed to return to Baltimore and resume the performance of his official and private duties.[43]

Brown described a late January day in Fort Warren to George Shattuck:

> This has been a beautiful day. There was a parade of the fire companies, with the band of music, and an inspection by Col. Dimick. It seemed strange to be under the national flag, and to listen to Hail Columbia—not now however happy land—while I was held as a prisoner and regarded as an enemy.
>
> The military prisoners will depart on Monday, and the political prisoners are gradually being sent away, but I see no prospect of the liberation of my friends from Maryland or myself.
>
> The scales show that I weigh 132 lbs.—some fifteen more than my average, so that prison life has evidently not injured my health.[44]

William Winder described to brother Charles expectations of release and the granting of "paroles" that permitted prisoners to leave in exchange for promises to return:

> I wrote you last on or about Christmas; have you received that letter? I note by the papers that the typhoid is epidemic at Washington, colds taking that form. As you are constantly liable to cold during the winter, this statement has caused me much solicitude lest you may have become a subject of that dreaded disease.

I should be greatly relieved by learning of the good health of you & your family, & still further if I could know that other matters went well with you. The impression here is prevalent that the Maryland prisoners will soon be released, & as arrangements are in progress for the release of the prisoners of war, & of the officers of the Navy & Marines imprisoned on resignation, we shall soon be free, the Maryland men here alone numbering *some* thirty. Marshal Kane who had parole for 3 weeks, returned at its expiration, ordering to ask a renewal. Mayor Brown of Balto. was allowed to go to Boston on parole for 30 days, he declined to apply for a renewal or to allow application & is expected back to-day or to-morrow. Charles Pitts is in Balto. on a 30 days parole as is Mr. Brewer (all [readers] in the Md assembly) & yesterday Mr. Sangsten of Balto. an ex-member of the House, left on parole of 30 days. Mr. G. Harrison, H. Warfield, D. Thomas, T. Parkin Scott & some others will not even accept a parole.[45]

The following month Winder refused a conditional release:

Yesterday I was again offered a release, upon what Mr. Seward, in his letter directing my discharge, called a modified oath, or, as explained by him, the oath which did not require my support of the individual members of the Cabinet. He has, somehow, obtained only a partial view of my objection to any oath, as a condition of release; my position being simply this, that my discharge to be acceptable must send me forth cleansed of every ground which shall justify suspicion & its consequences. I had rather remain here until the end of the war than to return to my home, with a self imputed suspicion of myself, which would be the case, were I to accept release on conditions.[46]

In early 1862, Marylanders were being released from Fort Warren, though Thomas Hall did not mention conditional loyalty oaths in a letter to his mother. He wrote that he was alone in a room that until recently had housed eight—and that he "never had much fancy for letter-writing":

I know that many of my fellow prisoners, some of our Baltimore friends among the number, are able to indulge in daily outpourings upon paper, but I am as little able to make their ideas & practice a rule for my own conduct in this respect as in others. Had these same gentlemen written less and done more, six or twelve months ago, perhaps, things would be far otherwise than as they are. I will not be so uncharitable as to suggest a doubt as to the depth of feelings that lie so near the surface, or the sincerity of expressions that have grown into such daily & hackneyed use.[47]

A month later, however, Hall was thinking about conditional release:

Secy Stanton's order in reference to the release of state prisoners is still without practical points, and, perhaps, is destined to remain barren. Designed not improbably for the European market, its publication merely may have served all the purposes of the Govt and the prisoners will hear nothing more of it. My own acceptance of *any* conditions of release will depend entirely upon their character. Arrested & held, as Mr Stanton himself by implication admits, without authority of law & in violation of the constitution, I claim an unconditional release, and it is only in an extreme case that I should be willing to accept of any other. I should unhesitatingly reject any parole the terms & conditions of which resembled those by which some of my fellow-prisoners from Baltimore, how, I cannot say, regained their liberty—but exchanged the involuntary servitude of stone walls and bayonets for a servitude far more humiliating, because voluntary & self-imposed.[48]

In early April, he told his mother that more Marylanders had been released, and the "dozen or so of 'political prisoners'" remaining had either declined conditional release or been offered release—"in that last category, I find myself, and in that category I am likely to remain."[49]

Henry M. Warfield challenged the commander of Fort Warren over his imprisonment, complaining that no warrant or charges had been offered against him and that he was permitted no correspondence:

You ask me to accept a parole, to accept an amnesty from the President of the United States. For what? Is it to force me, without color of Law to acknowledge a partial criminality, when no charges have been preferred against me? When merely a Telegraphic Despatch, has arrested me and deprived me of my Liberty? The idea, is one, I cannot entertain, for a moment. I challenge a trial. I crave, to suffer for crimes, if I have been guilty of any. I ask for the Constitutional Rights, which you and the Secy. of War, have sworn to defend. Give me the means, by which, I may enjoy the right of the humblest citizen suspected of the highest crime known to the Law, and I will be satisfied.

It is proper for me, to state here, that at the time of my arrest, I was then a Member of the Legislature of Maryland, ready to perform my duties under the oath prescribed by the State, and faithfully.[50]

Thomas Claggett appealed for release to Secretary of War Stanton:

In consequence of the difficulties growing out of the election of the President of the United States and the subsequent action of some of the Southern States, a special meeting of the Legislature of Maryland to be held in April, 1861, was called by the governor and I attended as a member from my county.

The journal of the house will show my whole action there. I favored peace measures and I voted against a proposition for secession by the Legislature. I thought the Legislature had no authority to pass such an act. I have never to my knowledge done anything against the Constitution and laws of my country.

I was arrested in September last without any charge being made against me. I have been imprisoned ever since and I do not yet know what is charged against me. Under these circumstances I think I have a right to ask an unconditional release that I may return to my family and my farm in Frederick County. I confidently refer to the member of Congress from my district—Hon. Francis Thomas—for my character.[51]

Thomas Maddox continued his campaign to free his wife's brother. His plea to General Dix noted that Claggett—a Sunday school teacher and grandson of Maryland's first bishop who was "chaplain to our First Congress"—was no secessionist:

It is said that General Washington listened to the suggestions of his subalterns; that Dr. Rush inquired into the opinions of his nurses before forming opinions. I therefore hope you will excuse me for taxing your attention as to Thomas J. Claggett, an ex-member of the Legislature now a prisoner at Fort Warren.

How is a State prisoner to make his escape? The suspension of the habeas corpus deprives him of all legal remedy. He can have no hearing. Whether innocent or guilty he is a prisoner. We know not when he may have a hearing.[52]

B. Mills, another legislator in Fort Warren, asked Congressman Henry May to intercede with the secretary of war to secure a release or parole for Mills so he might visit his wife, who was severely ill:

He surely will not refuse me this when he remembers that I have been incarcerated over six months for no other offense than being by accident a member of the Maryland house of delegates. I would not ask this but I have been patiently waiting for more than a month from day to day for my discharge and yet it has not come. Others similarly situated, *i.e.*, members of the Legislature, have been discharged upon parole from time to time. Had I violated any law or done any act hostile to the administration there would be some excuse for my detention.

I beg of you to see Mr. Stanton without delay and urge upon him my release in order that I may return to my afflicted family, for a few days' delay may be productive of results I fear to think of. Your friends are all well here.[53]

Daniel Thomas, who avoided arrest, in March related the reaction of Baltimoreans to Confederate prisoners:

We have been put in a great state during the past week by the *Government* condescending to let us have some of their *prisoners* to make a fuss over. About 150 of them came to town on Tuesday & were safely lodged in the Town Jail. They at once became the exciting topic, and the Eagle of the Rebellion flapped its wings with joy. Such an ovation to the cause this town has not known since the

19th of April. Carriages lined the street in front of the Jail all day & every day. The people opened their purses, & showered down gold & precious gifts upon these distinguished martyrs to the cause. One rich lady supplied them all with blankets, another with shoes; a purse of $3350 was subscribed and all the Tailors in town were set at work making uniforms for them, and the ladies worked all day & half the night for three days & nights making them under garments.[54]

Thomas explained how people provided food for the prisoners—though the necessity for advance planning for the disposition of prisoners challenges his contention that their reception prompted an immediate transfer:

> Then in the matter of *victuals* they were stuffed and crammed to an extent unknown by them since the war, not only with substantials, but with ice cream & such like. The warden of the mail was very attentive in receiving & distributing what was sent for them—and said that they were supplied with more than enough for 500 men. Such was the mortifying outpouring of the hearts of the citizens towards them that the authorities at Washington in utter disgust would not let them stay here, but ordered them to be transferred to Fort Delaware; they were to have gone yesterday morning, but the crowd that collected to see them off was so great that the authorities fearing a demonstration postponed their departure, & sent them off quietly in the evening, when nobody expected it. But even then a large crowd was soon gathered and as they passed a deafening cheer was sent up for Jeff Davis & Beauregard, & one lady waved a Confederate flag over them as they passed her house.[55]

Lewis Holloway, one of those prisoners, expressed appreciation for the ministrations of city residents:

> I am sorry, that the iron bars of my prison home, prevent me from an intercourse with the ladies and citizens of Baltimore, which would be agreeable in one sense at least. I could express in person the deep gratitude I feel for the genuine kindness that has been extended to us in this, the first prison that has ever closed its bolts upon us.[56]

Holloway's letter is dated two weeks after Thomas reported, on March 13, that he had died:

> I send as an item of melancholy interest, copies of some letters written by poor Capt.n Holloway while he was in the jail here, and whose death at Fort Delaware you will have seen in the papers. Considering the disadvantageous circumstances under which they were written, they deserve a great deal of credit, and show a deep religious sentiment that is very gratifying in view of his subsequent sudden death. He was well when he left here and his death must have resulted from bad treatment and exposure.[57]

U.S. Senator Anthony Kennedy of Maryland, writing in March from the Chamber of the Senate, advised Thomas Maddox on the imprisonment of Thomas Claggett:

> I have endeavored to ascertain the cause of the arrest of Mr. Claggett and what charges have been preferred against him—and have recd for answer that his case will shortly be considered by Genl. Dix who has been charged to make investigations of all cases now under arrest. I have written Genl. Dix a statement of his character as you have given it to me, but I would recommend that you get up a paper endorsed by some citizens of Mr. Claggett's county in evidence of his loyalty, which would doubtless have great weight with Genl. Dix, who is disposed to act with moderation and regard for law.[58]

In April, W. W. Glenn recounted how several Baltimoreans, including Baltimore physician Richard Sprigg Steuart, kept a step ahead of the federal authorities:

> I was spending the evening out when a footstep approached my chair from behind and a hand was laid upon me. I turned and saw Dr. R.S. Steuart. He has been concealed for more than six months. His neighbors are so bitter against him that he dare not go home, and he committed himself so decidedly on the 19" April and is known to be so decided a Southerner, that it more than likely he would be thrown into a Fort. He goes about from place to place, sometimes staying in one county, sometimes in another and then passing a few days in the city. He never shows in the day time & is cautious who sees him at any time. He has several negroes in his confidence at different places.[59]

Mary Norris, wife of Baltimore attorney and Confederate Col. William Norris, was arrested for communicating with Richard Thomas, a.k.a. "Colonel Zarvona":

> Dr. Robinson was also concealed in this manner for a long time & had some narrow escapes. Mr. W.H. Norris was obliged to dodge about for a long time. It was very funny to see him as you approached his retreat, always on the *qui vive* as he was, warily watching every vehicle, horseman or foot passenger who came towards the house. He remained concealed in this way until he was allowed to come to town to see his wife. She had been seized in a brutal manner & carried off to the Old Capitol Prison. Her confinement there & rough usage had made her very ill. Having nothing really against her she was released. Norris soon went South. He has been in one or two battles, always volunteering where there is a fight & the last I heard of him he had a horse killed under him. She followed him. Both went underground.[60]

Thomas's mother pleaded with his captors for information about her son:

> I have written to Colonel Wood, also Lieutenant Wood, to know how my son, Colonel Zarvona, is situated. My letters have not been noticed by either Colonel

or Lieutenant Wood. Excuse a mother's anxiety in requesting you to inform me of the situation of my son; also the state of his health. Knowing the active mind that my son has I fear much the effect of solitary confinement on his mind. Direct Mrs. R. Thomas, care of St. George W. Teackle, corner of Courtland and Lexington streets, Baltimore.[61]

George Brown commented on the inevitability of war:

> I get on in the old way, and never suffer the time to hang heavily. Today Col. Dimick, Col. Hansen (Rebel) & myself walked up & down before our door engaged in pleasant talk.
>
> The more I think of the matter, the more do I grieve from the bottom of my soul over the dissolution of the ties political & fraternal which held this people together, and yet sometimes I think looking at the fierce antagonism that had grown up between North & South that the war was inevitable. The sections had got to the point where they must fight it out.[62]

The irrepressible "Zarvona" attempted an escape:

> Inclosed you will receive the report of an attempt to escape by a well-known state prisoner from Fort Lafayette. Not the slightest blame in my opinion can be imputed to my officer in command of that post. Unfortunately or fortunately one of the new soldiers instead of one of the old garrison was sent with him to the water closet by the sergeant of the guard. Had it been one of the latter he would have been shot at once. It was a stormy night, tide ebb and the wind blowing out of the harbor; a few minutes more and he must have been drowned, and it was not by any means a night suitable for lowering a boat.[63]

In May, Henry Warfield, in "the ninth month of my imprisonment in various fortifications of the government at Washington," in Fort Warren, demanded of Secretary Stanton an unconditional release:

> So disastrous has been my unwarrantable detention, that my household is about being broken up, and those most dear to me are suffering for the want of that support which my labor afforded. The highest ambition of my life, to maintain respectably those who of right claim my protection, has thus been crushed by the arbitrary proceedings and machinations of your parasites and my enemies, under the sanction of a government of which you are a prominent actor. I will not recount the indignities which I have been forced to submit to, nor will I fully describe to you the disgraceful proceedings of those who were empowered to enter my house at midnight, committing acts which you dare not sanction as having been required to secure me in the keeping of your agents, or the agents of your government. By the continuation of the oppression, under which I am now suffering, you have made yourself a party to the robbery of my house, and above

"Prison in Casemate No. 2, Fort Lafayette, New York Harbor." Many Maryland political prisoners were held in this federal prison. Harper's Weekly, *April 15, 1865.*

all, to the inhumanity which was experienced the night of my arrest by my wife, who was left alone in her home, after my being on my way to Fort McHenry, the privilege of having my own near relatives to be with her being denied.

After complaining about the search of his home and warehouse, the denial of hearing or counsel, and his treatment at Fortress Monroe, Warfield noted one improvement in his situation:

> Only since coming under the supervision of Col. Dimick has any regard to decency been realized by me or my fellow prisoners upon the part of the representatives of your government, and that I have attributed to his natural aversion to treat uncondemed citizens as convicts until so declared by the constituted authority, established for the purpose of passing judgment upon presentments duly made.

A week earlier Warfield had been summoned before General Dix's commission at Fort Warren:

> My interview was a short one, the commission evidently acting under orders from your department. My examination amounted to no examination; it was simply an offer of a parole and a tacit acknowledgment that no charges could be

substantiated against me. The acceptance of this parole would carry along with it an amnesty granted me by the President of the United States.

He demanded a trial:

> Before your commission, I asked to be transferred to my district for trial, if I am charged with crime, and was distinctly told by Judge Pierrepont, that it was not in its power to order this approach to justice. If my interview with the commission is considered an investigation, then all my anticipations of ever obtaining justice, whilst you have its administration, is at an end. I cannot close this without recording the fact that five of my fellow prisoners from my own State, were not even invited to appear before the tribunal created by you. On my own part, as I am confined without charge, I renew my claim to be discharged without conditions.[64]

A major in the Confederate army imprisoned in Fort Warren extolled the virtues of Baltimore's ladies, writing "God bless the ladies of Baltimore":

> I find myself the owner of a beautiful smoking cap, the ingenious workmanship of delicate hands. I congratulate myself; and give rein to fancy, that she may improvise for me an ideal of the fair donor. Who is she? Why am I found with a present, which not only blends the useful and the beautiful, but which has a peculiar value beyond and above these qualities. I am told upon good authority that it is the work of a young lady of Baltimore—a rebel young lady between whom and myself there is no bond of interest, no tie except that both are rebels—she loves Dixie and so do I.[65]

Randolph Jones Barton of the Thirty-third Virginia Regiment was captured in March at Kernstown. He passed through Baltimore en route to prison at Fort Delaware, where he received a letter from a Maryland cousin, Anne C. Thomas, the wife of Maryland Congressman John Hanson Thomas, who had also run afoul of the federal authorities:

> I tried very hard to visit you and your friends when you were staying in Baltimore but could not get permission. We sent you clothing and food however, which I hope made you at least comfortable.
>
> I have sent on a box containing some little comforts for you, your cousin, Mr. Barton, Mr. Burwell & Mr. Washington.
>
> I hope you will write me, if there is anything you or your friends desire. Have no feeling about the matter, for I have the deepest sympathy for all prisoners, and particularly those from my own State.
>
> My husband was a political prisoner for 5½ months which makes me wonderfully sympathetic to all who have lost their liberty. I am thankful you are under the charge of Capt. Gibson who is represented as being so kind and humane.

My own dear son is in the Army near Winchester and I am glad to know he is near your Father and Mother who will minister to him if he should be sick or wounded.

Will you remember me kindly to them when you write?

God bless you my dear young friend.[66]

In a June letter to his brother, William Winder speculated on reasons for his incarceration:

I do not think it advisable for you to see Mr. Stanton; it is evident, I think, beyond a peradventure, that I am detained here purely in revenge for my writings, which have made some one, at least, wince. The following state of facts would seem to justify this conclusion. My offence, as stated by the Commissioners, consisted of my correspondence & writings. I distinctly & unequivocally declared them to be in perfect harmony with the truest patriotism & loyalty to the Constitution & its Union.[67]

And kept a close eye on the status of political prisoners:

Not having heard from you since writing you several letters, I fear you are greatly worried by the perplexity of circumstances, public & private, & melted, sickened by the intense heat. How much I feel for you, especially on the hot days with your thermometer ranging 102 in the shade, while, amid all my troubles, am enjoying the cool, sweet sea breeze. On no one night yet, have I slept with less than two blankets. It is true, we have our windows & doors wide open, & our room is in the basement, with walls more than two feet deep or thick.

If a general exchange of prisoners should take place we should have probably only one or two in a room, & I suppose we may consider ourselves prisoners until the end of the war. The Bill which passed the house for liberation of the state prisoners seems to have failed in the Senate. Letters recd from Balto contain the improbable statement, that Gen Wool had said that all the State prisoners were to be exchanged.

A postscript noted that "the regulations in relation to the discussion of military & political subjects have lately been drawn tighter here, so as, in a great degree, to prevent any decided expression at variance with the administration."[68]

By August, most prisoners had departed Fort Warren:

The fort seems solitary now that the prisoners of war have gone. There are many noble & gallant fellows among them. The parting was quite affecting.

The thought of leaving the prisoners of the state behind, who had done so much for the general comfort was uppermost in their hearts, and tears rolled abundantly down many manly faces. When the tug full of officers went off from the wharf hats & handkerchiefs were waved in the air and a shout went up for Baltimore.[69]

Some of Charles Winder's letters from prison to his brother were returned, "being contrary to the regulations governing correspondence to refer to military or political matter. By order of Col. Dimick."[70]

By September, William Winder was reassured by the attitude of his captors and rumors that all Maryland prisoners would soon be freed. In a letter to his niece, he contrasted the congenial atmosphere at Fort Warren with the oppressiveness of Fort Lafayette:

> I am not sure I have given you an account of our Bastile. Fort Warren is on an Island in Massachusetts or Berlin Bay, about 9 miles from Boston by the channel, but about six only by an air line; the bay is picturesquely studded with Islands, & the main shore on each side to lakes cod & ann, studded with towns, rail roads connecting on either side; besides which several steamboats ply to several of the towns from Boston, passing & repassing the fort. On the north side of this Island & between it & another about 6 or 800 yards distant lies the main channel between Boston & the ocean—thus we have a near view of all vessels passing through this great channel. The Cunard line of steamers, all war vessels, & others of magnitude. In the wide expanse of the bay from the heights of the parapets, I have counted one hundred and twenty eight vessels in sight at one time. Within a few months we have had, during the day, the free run of the Island (some 40 acres), and at all times in a walk thee is some moving thing to be seen on the waters, and still more lately, we have been allowed to fish, & to trap for lobsters. We have from May to Nov. a steamer twice a day from Boston, with the papers. The friends & families of several of the prisoners have had permission to visit them. Mrs. Frank Howard, has been, for three months, to visit her husband, every day, if she likes. She did come for about a week, & may return again, indeed would have remained than come every day during the three months, but he would not allow her to be subjected to the inconveniences, necessarily attendant when this. Mayor Brown's family have visited him several times, & his son, has been spending a week with him in the fort. We have never suffered here from heat or cold. The Fort is a splendid structure, throughout, the work being beautifully & substantially done. There are three Companies stationed here of about 300 soldiers a Band discourses very sweet music, tho' guilty at times of playing 'John Brown.' A very civil state of feeling exists between the garrison & prisoners, who, however, have no communication, except on necessary business, or through the officers. The Commander of the Post manifests no disposition to impose restraints not required of him, & every willingness to have the confinement as little irksome as his instructions will allow, altogether a most marked contrast with the hated recollections of Fort Lafayette.[71]

Two weeks later, the staff of W. W. Glenn's paper, formerly known as *The South*, found themselves in Fort McHenry:

The News Sheet was seized today. Carpenter (the Editor), Neilson who had been chief compositor on the Exchange and Sultzer, the Clip, were thrown into Fort McHenry. General Morris with his usual cunning had tried to implicate me. He cross questioned these men closely to know if I was not in some way interested in and responsible for the conduct of the paper under its present name. He learned nothing.[72]

On September 24, 1862, two days after issuing the preliminary Emancipation Proclamation, Lincoln suspended habeas corpus throughout the nation for the duration of the war. Many Marylanders were released by the end of the year—attributed by Franklin Wilson to the Democratic protests, their good showing in the fall congressional elections, and disapproval of Lincoln's suppression of civil liberties:

The Administration has been severely rebuked by the voters in Indiana, Illinois and New York, which have given large majorities for the *Democrats*. Consequently the despotic practices have been modified. On Thanksgiving Day Nov. 27, all the Maryland prisoners in Fort Warren were *unconditionally* released, among them Mayor Brown, S.T. Wallis, and Marshal Kane. Others have been released from other Bastilles, and the order excluding opposition papers from the mails has been rescinded.[73]

Upon his release, an embittered George Kane blamed Secretary Seward for his imprisonment:

After an incarceration of seventeen months in four of the forts of the United States now converted by the Government into prisons which have no similitude but in the Bastile of France I avail myself of the first moment of my return to my native State to address a brief word to you.

In this imprisonment I am understood to have been the special victim of Mr. Secretary Seward, who in concert with his hired minions has omitted no occasion to heap upon me accusations which he knew to be false and therefore dared not bring to the ordeal of a public trial. To these charges the despotic censorship of the prisons in which I have been kept allowed me no reply; and I can only now promise that in due time and upon a proper occasion Mr. Seward shall hear from me in a way which will procure for him if he has not already acquired it the contempt of every honest man and woman in the land.[74]

Many were pleased to see George Brown upon his return to Baltimore shortly before Christmas 1862:

The prisoners have received the warmest reception, many have called to see me and visitors have not yet ceased. A great change has taken place I am told in the state of affairs here. There is a free expression of private opinion, and the press is gradually daring to speak out. Arbitrary arrests are no longer dreaded, tho' the removal of Gen Wood & the appointment of Gen Schenck is considered as somewhat threatening, for it is no doubt a concession to the radical & extreme element of the abolition party.

I am in danger of being more harmed by feasting than any thing else. I have had six invitations to dinner this week, and accepted four.[75]

1863

Kane's invective threatened the prospect of a treason trial, according to Attorney General Edward Bates, who promised the U.S. Attorney for Maryland, William Price, that "as far as I can I will shield you against all unjust assaults on account of the discharge of your official duties":

> Serious doubts are entertained here whether you could at this time safely go to trial in any treason case in Baltimore by reason of the supposed popular feeling and judicial bias. Of course you are far better informed than I can be in that matter, and I would be very glad to have your views upon it.[76]

Elizabeth Blair Lee described how Lincoln's trusted adviser—her father, Montgomery Blair—intervened to save the life of a relative, James S. Pleasants, whose conviction for treason in a court-martial had earned him a death sentence for "relieving the enemy with victuals, and knowingly harboring and protecting them." Lincoln commuted Pleasants' death sentence to prison for "duration of war":[77]

> Father had a brush with Mr. Stanton a few days ago about one of our Montgomery people who is a kinsman of John Key & to whom he gave shelter & food for a night & who he received as was proved with reluctance as he was always a Union man Stanton wanted to have him hung—the P. commuted that sentence to imprisonment & as his health is wretched & Father wanted his imprisonment shortened & so arranged as not injure his health—Father carried his point & to attain it the skirmish was sharp & long—Mr S. very bitter Mr. Bates sat mute—as all did all the Cabinet—but afterwards thanked Father for saving the life of his kinsman—[78]

Frustration characterized a June letter from Confederate soldier Samuel B. Rogers, imprisoned in Fort McHenry:

> They say they are going to hold us as hostages if so, we will be here some time. Bring my uniform as soon as it is finished, have it made tight in the waist. Oh! I wish they would exchange us. I dislike being a prisoner—to a person who has not slept in a house but very seldom in last two years, it is very disagreeable— slept all last winter in a fly.[79]

In October, Rev. Henry Slicer mourned the death of a young Baltimorean he claimed had died from the effects of imprisonment:

> I attended the funeral of Robt Henry Slicer Jackson of Monument St who died from disease brought on by imprisonment in Fort McHenry, from which place he was paroled, by the military authorities 2 days before his death—he was confined there in a stable, upon charges clandestinely made, but the nature of which, his friends were not allowed to know—He was 18 years of age, and an industrious and worthy youth—when will these arrests cease—& when will men recollect that there is "a judgment to come", where the poor, the weak, and the friendless will be righted, and where even Kings are sceptreless-Alas!—I had strange feelings as I stood over his coffin.[80]

1864

Some Baltimore women aided rebel prisoners, the subject of a letter Augusta Shoemaker, wife of Unionist Samuel Shoemaker, received in January from a prisoner in the "Officers Barracks" at Fort Delaware:

> If you deam me worthy please place me on your list of friends, for though I have not heard from you except in your kindness, since my confinement here, yet since the day I first met you I have desired to be known as your friend for though we may differ in some respects, yet we agree in the all important question, that is, should man prepare while on Earth for Heaven—if this be so, then let us be friends I thank the Lord for his kindness in puting it in your heart to do me a kindness I could so little expect at your hands, and for which I a under many obligations to you, by sending comfortable clothing, and interesting books—you alleviate in a great measure—the sufferings caused by confinement here.[81]

Optimism helped Baltimorean William Gordon cope with confinement in Fort McHenry as a spy:

> *My dear Mammy.* How are you this bright beautiful morning? Is it not beautiful weather? No time to enjoy in prison. But thank God, I still have the joy "the world knows not of." With the bright sunshine and spring air stealing in upon me. Could His Presence, and "my prison a palace seems," Dear Mother, how foolish it seems now. Our refining, our tears, our fears, and murmurs at God's recent chastisement. It was but the narrow gates leading to unknown sweets.—and four blind mortals.

He closed with reassuring words:

> I am well—both in mind and body. But very *anxious* to see *you.* Let us exercise patience—there are many nights in a life time, but every one is followed by a sunlit morning.[82]

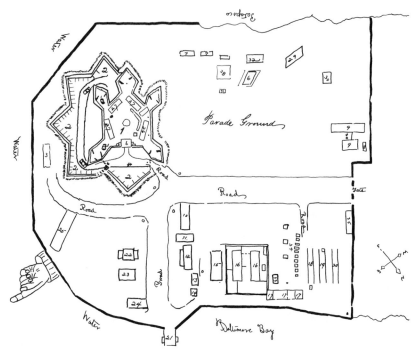

LEGEND
1 The Fort
2 " Water Battery[10]
3 " Armory
4 " Magazine
5 " Sally port
6 " Bomb Proof Magazine
7 " Sutler
8 " Carpenter Shop
9 " Hospital
10 The Quartermaster Dept
11 " Church
12 " General's House
13 " Bakery
14 " Stable (Gen'l)
15 " Stable
16 " Prisoners
17 " Cook houses
18 " Officers Barracks
19 " Company
20 The Company Barracks
21 " Pier where troops landed
22 Col Finch's Quarters
23 " Harris "
24 Wood Yard
25 Miscellaneous Barracks
26 Old Gen'l Office in the Fort
27 Barracks in the Fort
28 Hot Shot Furnaces
29 Hospital Tent
30 Spring
31 Scaffold
32 Store House
33 Tent
34 Tents (Soldiers)
35 Guard House
36 Reservoir
37 Stockade
38 Grave Yard

Robert Moore, a Union soldier posted to Fort McHenry, sent his mother a detailed map of the fort. The prison is at the lower center; the scaffold, where prisoners, usually spies, were executed, is in the center of the parade ground, at the top. MdHS. Redrawn by Betsy Mitchell from original art in MdHM, 54 (Sept. 1959), 299–300.

By March, candidates had announced for election to Maryland's April constitutional convention to consider emancipation. General Wallace conveyed his concern over the candidacy of the House Speaker to Governor Bradford:

> I am informed that Mr. E.G. Kilbourn of Anne Arundel County, was arrested by one of my predecessors, by order of the Secretary of War, and kept in confinement about one year; and that, though released, he refused to take the oath of allegiance to the Government of the United States, and has never taken it. Nor am I able to find that his hostility to that Government has been in any degree relaxed. His attitude at this time, from what I can gather, is that of an open sympathizer with the Rebellion.

I have no disposition to interfere with the elections in Maryland; but as Mr. K. is now a candidate for a seat in the Constitutional Convention, soon to meet at Annapolis, a proper regard for the honor of the General Government whose devoted servant I am, impels me to call your Excellencys attention to his political character and antecedents, and respectfully inquire if you have no power to prevent a result, to say the least, so incompatible with loyal interests as his election would doubtless prove.[83]

The governor told Wallace that he could do little about Kilbourne:

I never knew precisely the charges upon which this gentleman was arrested beyond his prominent connection with the famous Legislature of 1861, several members of which were arrested and imprisoned with him—whatever however were the precise charges against him, I entirely agree with you in thinking that his hostility to the Government is quite as determined to day as it ever was.— The fact that such a one should be now a candidate for the place he seeks, and may possibly be elected, is certainly to be deplored—but I am sorry to say, I possess no power to prevent his election or exclude him from the Convention if elected, other than by requiring him to take the oath which the Law providing for the Convention makes it my duty to administer to all its members.

They are required to swear that they "have never either directly or indirectly, by word, act or deed, given any aid, comfort or encouragement to those in rebellion against the Government of the United States"—and that this they "swear voluntarily without any mental reservation or qualification whatever"[84]

In November Samuel Shoemaker received a letter from the authorities at Fort Delaware:

I am desired by Capt Ahl to say that he encloses herewith a permit for clothing for Lieut Fitzpatrick, being all that he is allowed to receive as he is in rather a forlorn condition. Prisoners are not allowed to receive provisions from their friends. Capt Ahl desires to be remembered to Mrs. Shumaker, & is happy that he is able to serve your friend the Lieut.[85]

1865

Military authorities continued to threaten Marylanders, as Ella Thompson Carroll discovered in a February letter from Gen. Philip Sheridan:

Your communication of the 10th inst was duly received by me.

In reply permit me to express my willingness to release you from all the obligations embodied in your parole, excepting so much as relates to your not, directly or indirectly, by word or deed, aiding or abetting those in arms against the Federal Government.[86]

Samuel Cox, a farmer in Port Tobacco, Charles County, was swept up in the search for conspirators in Lincoln's assassination. He was held in Old Capitol Prison in Washington, where he confided his concerns to his wife:

Your most welcom letters of the 18th also that of the 16th have been received and gave me great comfort, to hear from you all, also I received one from Sammy to day dated yesterday stating that he would leave for home to day (also Mary) and I know my dear Wife it will give you as much pleasure to inform you, as it was for me to receive, permission just as your letter was received, to walk in the yard for exercise, which I have been deprived of until to day, having been confined to my room now for nearly four weeks. I there met several acquaintances, who are in my own predicament. I am glad to say I am as well as I could expect, my cough is not worse than it is sometimes at home. I have not heard a word from the authorities, but learned that all the witnesses supposed to be in my case, were released and have gone home. I hope my dear Wife it will not be a great while before I shall be released myself and will return to our dear old Home & loved ones, I feel exceedingly sorry to hear of the illness of Miss Matilou, I hope you will be able now that you have your horses, to go and see her and not let her suffer for any thing. I hope Sammy arrived home safe, Should you want any groceries & necessarys, you had better write to our merchants in Baltimore for them, unless you can wait until I can get home myself, but do not wait should you want *any thing*. Give my sincere love to Aunt [M] and all friends, continue my dear wife to unite with me in devout prayer to our Merciful Father to guide, sustain, and so direct all things, that we may soon be restored to each other.[87]

chapter nine

Rebels

1861

Years after the war a man recalled routes used to run Union blockades:

> Blockade Running of supplies down South was common. Some engaged in it from patriotism; some for the big profits made. The routes generally followed were by the Point of Rocks, then across the Potomac, or shipped down to the Eastern Shore, and they run across the Bay by night into the rivers and inlets of Eastern Virginia. Some high U.S. Officials in Baltimore were engaged secretly in the profits of Blockade Running.[1]

William Wilkins Davis wrote to sister Rebecca about the convergence of troops near his school in Hagerstown:

> We are beginning to be pretty lively up in this part of the world. An advanced guard of 1500 Virginians has encamped within four miles of us, at Williamsport, and we are daily expecting the advance guard of 10,000 Pennsylvanians at Hagerstown six miles on the other side of us. Just between the two fires we may have the pleasure of seeing a battle if not of participating in it.[2]

Somerville Sollers, a Baltimore deputy court clerk and brother of state delegate Augustus, joined the Confederate First Maryland Regiment in 1861. In an August letter to his brother from Fairfax Court House, Virginia, he expressed optimism about Confederate intentions toward Maryland, likely referring to comrades from neighboring Calvert County:

> I hope father does not now take such a gloomy view of affairs. We are in fine spirits, & look upon the recognition of the Confederacy & the redemption of Md. as a Sure thing. We are still encamped here expecting orders every day to March. We have nothing to complain off, but our rations, which are miserable, driving us very often to the Hotel to eat by which our funds are nearly all gone. This is evidently something wrong in the Commissary Department of our Reg. Our Colonel has promised to look into the matter & I hope this will be a change for the better.
>
> We received our uniforms a few days ago, grey pants & jackets & we look as gay as you please. Our's (Capt. Murray's Company) is the best I the Reg. numbering now 90 men—all gentlemen. Our Chaplain, Mr. Camerron, officiated last Sunday in the Episcopal Church of this village & preached a very good sermon. He has services to-day also. So you see, we have the privilege of hearing the word of God preached if we are "eleven dollar privates", as we call each other.
>
> Thursday night our Company were on Pickett duty, 7 miles from the camp, &

only 9 from Alexandria. The Yankees had two Regiments—only two miles ahead of us. The night before our pickets had been driven in, & we all were apprehensive of an attack. We laid by our arms, with scouts ahead, all night—not sleeping a wink. But we were not troubled, though we could distinctly hear their drums from our post. At daybreak we marched to the Camp accomplishing the distance in exactly 1½ hours. I tell you, we had a keen appetite for breakfast when arrived & the majority of us went into the village and made a terrific onsault upon the Hotel.

He concluded with a shot of bravado:

Meme, in conclusion let me tell you one thing—it is this, we will be in Maryland before the *leaves begin wither. This is true, & then look out.* Write soon, all of you. Give my love to all & tell everybody that the Calvert boys are well & hardy, though they sleep on the hard ground, with knapsacks for pillows & boots pantaloons all on. Good bye & may God bless & protect you all.[3]

Sollers was wounded in August. From Richmond's Robertson Hospital, he wrote his mother:

Since the commencement of the campaign, I am conscious that you suffered a great deal on my account—there has been so much fighting and you have not heard whether I am alive or dead. Thank God, I can inform you that although we have been either fighting or under fire. Since the 3d June, until last Friday 19th Aug on the Weldon Road I had passed through all unscathed, when I was wounded Slightly in the head. We were charging at the time & I was going full tilt, when the first thing I knew I was sprawling on the ground, with a stinging sensation about cranium. I soon found though, that only a piece of my scalp about the size of a Silver dollar had been carraid away. I got to the rear as quick as possible and am now here at this Hospital which is the best in Rich. It is conducted entirely by ladies of the best families, who are untireing in their kindness, & attention to our wants. I suppose I shall be all right again in 4 or 5 weeks.[4]

In August Robert Kirkwood, stationed in Williamsport, on the Chesapeake & Ohio Canal, described rebel activities just across the Potomac River in Virginia:

There was quite an excitement here yesterday evening and last night. The citizens came over from the Virginia side for protection some of them with their Famalies and some of them was run by the rebel cavalry we could see them plain from Williamsport across the river. News came over that they were going to come across into M.D. we was up all night in the rain along the Bank of the River, came in this morning wet to the hide some of the men got so tired of standing laid down when they waked found themselves laying in a puddle of watter some of us had not time to get our over coats they have threatened to burn Williamsport if

TO THE PEOPLE OF MARYLAND!

After sixteen months of oppression more galling than the Austrian tyranny, the Victorious Army of the South brings freedom to your doors. Its standard now waves from the Potomac to Mason and Dixon's Line. The men of Maryland, who during the last long months, have been crushed under the heel of this terrible despotism now have the opportunity for working out their own redemption for which they have so long waited and suffered and hoped.

The Government of the Confederate States is pledged by the unanimous vote of its Congress, by the distinct declaration of its President, the Soldier and Statesman Davis, never to cease this War until Maryland has the opportunity to decide for herself her own fate, untrammeled and free from Federal Bayonets.

The People of the South with unanimity unparalleled have given their hearts to our native State and hundreds of thousands of her sons have sworn with arms in their hands that you shall be free.

You must now do your part. We have the arms here for you.--I am authorized immediately to muster in for the War, Companies and Regiments. The Companies of one hundred men each.--The Regiments of ten Companies. Come all who wish to strike for their liberties and their homes.--Let each man provide himself with a stout pair of Shoes, a good Blanket and a Tin Cup---Jackson's men have no Baggage.

Officers are in Frederick to receive Recruits, and all Companies formed will be armed as soon as mustered in. RISE AT ONCE!

Remember the cells of Fort McHenry! Remember the dungeons of Fort Lafayette and Fort Warren; the insults to your wives and daughters, the arrests, the midnight searches of your houses!

Remember these your wrongs, and rise at once in arms and strike for Liberty and right.

BRADLEY T. JOHNSON,
Colonel C. S. A.

September 8, 1862.

Col. Bradley T. Johnson of Frederick exhorted Marylanders to join the Confederate army, just before Lee's first invasion of the state: "Remember the cells of Fort McHenry! Remember the dungeons of Fort Lafayette and Fort Warren; the insults to your wives and daughters, the arrests, the midnight searches of your houses!" MdHS.

they can but we have the citizens on our side it is a strong union Neighborhood and there is but few of over the river on the other side of the river but what is for the Union no one is alowed to go back that comes from the Virginia side we have the river strongly guarded and every man is searched that comes across and if a man can't give a good acount of himself we lock him in the guard house at once untill further hearing.[5]

In late summer, Confederate activity along the Potomac was disrupting two of Maryland's principal commercial arteries, the Chesapeake & Ohio Canal and the Baltimore & Ohio Railroad:

> Since the beginning of hostilities on the Potomac, little or no bituminous coal has been brought to this city, and the supply on hand is now well near exhausted. A large amount of it was used for steam purposes, both for boats and factories, but they have been obliged to resort to anthracite.[6]

The archbishop of Baltimore, Francis Patrick Kenrick, was obliged in December to defend the nuns at the convent in Emmitsburg from suspicion of spying:

> I have to state in reply, that Sisters of Charity were employed in the works of their institute at Richmond and Norfolk long before the formation of the S. Confederacy, and have extended their charitable services to the sick and wounded in the former place. In consequence of their dependence on the chief house of their institute at Emmitsburg, which supplies them with the peculiar dress of their order, and regulates the details of their domestic relations, they have occasionally passed to their home, and returned to the work of charity, but always openly, and without concealment, with the permission of the authorities, especially of General Scott, and they have not at any time lent themselves to any object of a political or treasonable character, or in the slightest degree departed from the objects of their calling.

He explained that one sister had been sent south to oversee the order's works, implying that the transit south by the larger group had ended:

> If any illicit correspondence has been carried on by any persons wearing the costume of Sisters of Charity, it has certainly not been by members of their Institute, or with means furnished by the Community of Emmitsburg. The Superiors of that Institution will cheerfully afford the Government any particulars in their power, and satisfy them that they have given no countenance or aid to any movement of an unlawful character.[7]

1862

Early in the year rebels troubled Maryland farmers along the numerous ferry crossings and fords on the Potomac River. One farmer

> had had a great deal of trouble with the Confederates, they only appraised his pair of mules, 215 dollars, and gave him a certificate for the amount, but he had not been able to get the money. They took corn, bacon and he had had much difficulty in saving his best horses & wagon, some one in the neighborhood has offered to buy them and Aaron Griffith thinks you had better sell, as you will be likely to lose them.[8]

From a Union camp at Kabletown, where men were "comfortably quartered, in a strong Stone Church," a captain wrote to the commander of the Potomac Home Brigade about his efforts to counter rebel activity:

> Notorious Captain Bailor may be in the area (8 miles from Castleman Ferry is Kabletown) The people here are very much freightened, and I am using every means in my power to protect, and if possible to allay their fears.[9]

Three days later the officer told of rebels prowling about his pickets at night, amid other complaints:

> This is not only annoying but very dangerous. Have the goodness to see that I receive the Countersign and Day signals regularly. This is indispensable for our safety. Our rations are consumed—I have sent my wagon to Bloomers Mills—I hope they will not fail to arrive, Co. F. have not rec'd any of their Camp Equippage—His wagon I believe has returned to Headquarters, pleas have it forwarded—
>
> I have about 30 Rounds of Cartridges per man which, if you will not be able to move forward to this place with the main body immediately I do not think sufficient—I am not alarmed yet the most intelligent people of this place insist that Col. Ashby with 800 Cavalry are but a few miles in my front—I do not regard it as true but a very lame endeavour to intimidate. They say his main body is at Berryville, his right resting upon the river at Castleman Ferry.
>
> If I did not misunderstand, our troops are in possession of Berryville, If so I am satisfied there are no enemies in our immediate neighbourhood on this side of the river.[10]

In March the Confederate army, worried about defending Richmond, began dismantling its huge commissary (containing more than 3.4 million pounds of supplies) at Manassas and retreating toward its capital. A Baltimore newspaper mocked this movement—though the rebels had the last laugh, for they were gone when General McClellan arrived at Manassas:

But is it possible now that "ye Secesh" of Baltimore, of Maryland, are thus incontinently to be left in the lurch? Can it be that the famous "army of deliverance" has forever turned its back on "downtrodden Maryland?" and have they who but lately were manufacturing "sympathy" by wholesale at Richmond, under the direction of ex-Governor Lowe, concluded to bottle up said "sympathy," and so transfer it to localities where it will be better appreciated?[11]

Baltimore & Ohio Railroad president John W. Garrett told Secretary Stanton that no military guards were posted west of Harpers Ferry, and with B&O workers in the vicinity worried about hostilities, General Banks

last night stated to our officers that he would endeavor to send some men but his forces are very short. Refuges at Winchester informed our men that Jackson expressed astonishment that the B&O Road could be opened soon, and a vicious determination to destroy it again at once. May I ask in view of the great importance attached by the enemy to its destruction as well as the great necessity to the interests of the country to maintain it, that you investigate whether a safe force has been left between Winchester and [Rummy] and whether the line from Harpers Ferry to Martinsburg should not at once be fully guarded.[12]

Throughout the Civil War, Maryland was a conduit for smuggled Confederate contraband and messages. W. W. Glenn delineated one method used by rebel sympathizers who operated on small schooners on the Chesapeake Bay:

These small bay craft at one time carried a great many men and a large amount of contraband. They loaded openly and went boldly over to Fort McHenry, to be searched if necessary. They were never detained until after some months the trick was found out. Important dispatches used to be sent this way. They wd. be put in a tin case, enveloped in lead. This was tied to a string and suffered to drop over the side of the vessel. In case of danger, the string was cut or broken at the last moment.[13]

Members of the clergy remained at the mercy of their congregations. An anonymous June letter from a pro-Southern member of St. Barnabas' Church in Baltimore criticized Bishop Whittingham's "frequent visits of late, (and participation in the services)" as "very offensive to many of the congregation of that Church":

We thus far have had the pure word of God preached to us, and have been permitted to offer up to his Throne the *primitive* prayers of his Church, free from *modern innovations* and from curses upon our Southern brethren, or rejoicings for feigned successes by Lincoln and his band of murderers and aides and abettors which are to be found in Church and State.

You have done as much in the Church & State as Lincoln has done in State to stir up strife and to array breathren & parents and children in hostility and to shed each others blood. *You* have created discord in our Church in Maryland by your unchristian and despotic course; it ought to make you shudder for the acts you have been guilty of.[14]

From Norfolk, the Rev. David J. Lee wrote Bishop Whittingham of his resignation from the "vestery" of St. Thomas' Church in Hancock, Washington County. Lee's letter refers to prisoner exchange and that "I may now consider myself free again":

> I hoped to the last, that I should be able to remain; but when, at the close of the year's services as Rector, I found the vestry would offer me no more than $300 for a second year. I was compelled to resign for want of a competent support. This meagre sum, I know is not the extent of their ability to raise; but being aware of the strong *secession proclivities* of several of the vestry, I readily accounted for their want of readings to support the gospels.[15]

In early September, Robert E. Lee made clear to Jefferson Davis his desire to establish good relations with Marylanders as he moved through the state in his first invasion of the North—movements that led to the battles of South Mountain and Antietam:

> I am taking measures to obtain all that this region will afford, but to be able to collect supplies to advantage in Maryland, I think it important to have the services of some one known to the people and acquainted with the resources of the country.
>
> I wish therefore that if ex-Governor [Enoch L.] Lowe can make it convenient, he would come to me at once, as I have already requested by telegram. As I contemplate entering a part of the State with which Governor Lowe is well acquainted, I think he could be of much service to me in many ways.[16]

On September 7, Lee again wrote to Davis, from headquarters "two miles from Fredericktown, Maryland," describing the reception his army was receiving and efforts to supply his men. Lee must have been bitterly disappointed at the likelihood of attracting Marylanders to his cause:

> I find there is plenty of provisions and forage in this country, and the community have received us with kindness. There may be some embarrassment in paying for necessaries for the army, as it is probable that many individuals will hesitate to receive Confederate currency. I shall in all cases endeavor to purchase what is wanted, and if unable to pay upon the spot, will give certificates of indebtedness of the Confederate States, for future adjustment.
>
> It is very desirable that the Chief Quartermaster and Commissary should be provided with funds, and some general arrangement made for liquidating the debts that may be incurred for the people of Maryland, in order that they may

The Confederate army crossing the Potomac into Maryland in September 1862, en route to the battles of South Mountain and Antietam. Harper's Weekly.

willingly furnish us with what is wanted. I shall endeavor to purchase horses, clothing, shoes, and medical stores for our present use, and you will see the facility that would arise from being provided the means of paying for them. I hope it may be convenient for ex-Governor Lowe, or some prominent citizen of Maryland to join me, with a view of expediting these and other arrangements necessary to the success of our army in this State. Notwithstanding individual expressions of kindness that have been given, and the general sympathy in the success of the Confederate States, situated as Maryland is, I do not anticipate any general uprising of the people in our behalf. Some additions to our ranks will no doubt be received, and I hope to procure subsistence for our troops.[17]

The following day Lee issued a proclamation to "The People of Maryland," stating the justification for rebelling against the federal government:

It is right that you should know the purpose that has brought the army under my command within the limits of your State, so far as that purpose concerns yourselves.

The people of the Confederate States have long watched with the deepest sympathy the wrongs and outrages that have been inflicted upon the citizens of a commonwealth allied to the States of the South by the strongest social, political and commercial ties.

They have seen with profound indignation their sister State deprived of every right and reduced to the condition of a conquered province.

Under the pretense of supporting the Constitution, but in violation of its most valuable provisions, your citizens have been arrested and imprisoned upon no charge and contrary to all forms of law; the faithful and manly protest against this outrage made by the venerable and illustrious Marylander, to whom in better days no citizen appealed for right in vain, was treated with scorn and contempt; the government of your chief city has been usurped by armed strangers; your legislature has been dissolved by the unlawful arrest of its members; freedom of the press and of speech has been suppressed; words have been declared offences by an arbitrary decree of the Federal Executive, and citizens ordered to be tried by a military commission for what they may dare to speak.[18]

As Lee pledged to help Marylanders cast off the yoke of oppression, the Hagerstown bank sent its reserves to New York, the town's post office moved to Chambersburg, Pennsylvania, and its citizens "skedadalled":[19]

Believing that the people of Maryland possessed a spirit too lofty to submit to such a government, the people of the South have long wished to aid you in throwing off this foreign yoke, to enable you again to enjoy the inalienable rights of freemen, and restore independence and sovereignty to your State.

In obedience to this wish, our army has come among you, and is prepared to assist you with the power of its arms in regaining the rights of which you have been despoiled.

This, citizens of Maryland, is our mission, so far as you are concerned.

No constraint upon your free will is intended, no intimidation will be allowed.

Within the limits of the army, at least, Marylanders shall once more enjoy their ancient freedom of thought and speech.

We know no enemies among you, and will protect all of every opinion.

It is for you to decide your destiny, freely and without constraint.

This army will respect your choice whatever it may be, and while the Southern people will rejoice to welcome you to your natural position among them, they will only welcome you when you come of your own free will.[20]

Franklin Wilson reacted to the initial movement of Lee's army:

Great excitement has been caused in this city by the well authenticated report that the Confed. have crossed into Maryland in heavy force at Point of Rocks & Nolan's ford. It is uncertain what their intentions are, some believing that they intend to invade Pennsylvania, and let them feel the horrors of war; others that they will come to Baltimore, and others that they intend to attack the railroad to Washington, and thus capture it by surrounding it. In any such event Baltimore will be a scene of confusion, anarchy, and perhaps a battle field. I have thought of taking my family away, but have about concluded to remain for the present, until the danger is more imminent.[21]

Another Baltimorean, not reassured by Lee, worried about renegade elements of the rebel army threatening Baltimore—though no evidence suggests that Confederates came close to the city during the Antietam campaign. The writer possibly referred to Governor Bradford's home on Charles Street, at the boundary of Baltimore City and Baltimore County:

For a few days it was a question whether or not five hundred rebels would not ride down the Falls Road & taken whence they pleased out of town. They did one night come as far down as Bradford who lives about three miles beyond me—as there were no force between them & me I thought best to get the "[?]" out of the way—provide an extra quantity of lead and be ready. Jimmy Littig was out there, and my boy Kelly, & we thought in a good thick-walled stone house we could account for some of the chivalry certainly. They made a haul of wheat & flour sugar loot & e & then ran away. Our secesh very much disappointed them. There was no rising. I don't think they gained as many recruits as they lost in deserters. They were miserably clad were very much given to scratching & were altogether uninviting.

And claimed to hear fighting just before Antietam:

we could distinctly hear the guns at the late fight but you have no idea how little effect wars alarms have upon us. We thought they might be 40 miles off and went to sleep as usual.[22]

Washington Hands enjoyed the reception from his fellow Marylanders:

On the 6th of Sept. the battery passed through Frederick city, and encamped on the suburbs. Many were the congratulations the brave fellows received from the citizens, and during the three days they remained, their wants were abundantly supplied.[23]

Joshua Hering described the appeal of the rebel army as it moved through western Maryland just before Antietam:

The first Confederate soldiers I saw during the war, was at Frederick in September 1862, just before the battle of Antietam. Lee's army had crossed the Potomac and entered Maryland, marching in the direction of Federick. The Farmers & Mechanics Bank of Westminster had some business with one of the banks in Frederick, which led the bank here to send Richard Manning, who was at the

This barricade on Saratoga Street in Baltimore could have been erected in 1862, 1863, or 1864—in response to the incursions of the Confederate army to the west. MdHS.

time a Director in the bank, to Frederick. I did know what the character of the business was, but as he was going in a buggy, he invited me to go with him. When we arrived in Frederick, a large part of the Confederate army had already passed through, but the town was full of soldiers, and the entire Corps of General D.H. Hill marched through after our arrival.

I was very much interested in seeing them. They were veterans and had seen hard service, with little pay and frequently short rations,—a splendid body of men, representing in almost every case, the very flower of southern manhood. Quite a number of Maryland men joined them at Frederick.[24]

Anne Schaeffer of Frederick recorded her impressions of the Confederate army moving into the city, followed two weeks later by the joyous reception given the federal troops who passed through in hot pursuit:

About the 4th of September came rumors of the Rebel army crossing the Potomac River, into Maryland. But we had heard similar reports before and gave little heed. At evening while sitting quietly in my parlor conversing with several friends we were startled by the cry of "Fire! Fire!' then we heard the fire bells ringing—the given signal of the approach of the enemy. No tongue or pen can describe our emotions. Seeing the street illuminated by a bright light, we learned the Union troops were burning the Hospital stores—making a grand bonfire in the street of all the bedding that could not be carried away, to prevent its falling into the hands of the Confederates, and the soldiers themselves were 'skedadling" as fast as their horses and their own legs could carry them, leaving the town defenceless. All sorts of reports were abroad and nobody knew what to do—what to expect. Fearing perhaps we would be obliged to fly during the night or forced from our houses by fire, I packed up a few necessary articles of clothing, shawls &c. in satchels—awaiting my Husband's coming home from his store. We confirmed the reports of the approach of the Rebels. Union men were flying, fearing arrest—Among others our neighbors on either side. Finally we learned the Confederates had encamped six miles south of Town and would not enter until the next day. Confident that his drug store would be ransacked my Husband had the most valuable articles brought home, where we hid them away, covered from view by ashes under an old fashioned outdoor bakeoven and not knowing what we might be called upon to endure the coming day, we lay down to rest after midnight and slept until 5 O'clock.[25]

From Havre de Grace, in Cecil County, Robert Spear wrote his wife about rumors that twenty thousand to forty thousand rebel soldiers were in the "upper part of Maryland" and that he had little to report,

except to say that Stone wall (or as some say) Stone fence Jackson had not made his appearance amongst us yet. Still there is a considerable excitement in this part of the country. Many people [?] looking for an invading army to make their appearance. But of this is but little if any danger.[26]

George Brown's son Arthur wrote to his father in Fort Warren that, thanks to the rebels, school was out, and that Baltimore was calm:

Stonewall Jackson has settled the question of the boys going to St. James in a most summary manner. The invasion of Md. puts that plan entirely out of the question for the present at all events. Until the purposes of the Confs. develop themselves, & we see whether the fortune of war will make their occupation of Md. permanent, we are completely at sea in regard to the future.

St. James can hardly reopen on the 24th inst, & just now it is impossible to say anything in regard to St Pauls. "We shall see what we shall see", is the very luminous & satisfactory reflection with which we have to console ourselves. I was yesterday (Sunday) in Balt. Of course there was a very great excitement, but it was rather deep than demonstrative. I never saw the town more quiet & orderly, a large number of special policemen being on hand in case of emergency—Strange as it may seem—we actually congratulate ourselves on having Gen. Wood to act as a check upon the folly & blind partisanship of our city & State authorities. So far there has been no breach of the public peace—The conciliatory course of the Confs. in Frederick & elsewhere has been most fortunate as affording to the dominant party here no cause for exasperation.[27]

After noting that the Confederates were behaving well, Brown speculated on their objectives:

> In regard to the movements of the Confs. you know quite as much as we do. Opinions differ as to whether they are bound for Penna or Washington, though present indications point to the former course. It seems to be generally thought by all that Baltimore is the prize whh. they hope to gain if successful, but that they would not risk an attack on the city at present, fearing that thro' the complications that would arise it might be injured or destroyed. In view of the *possibility* of our being placed in a state of seige, people are laying in stores of coal wood & the necessaries of life. The Calvert St. house is being furnished in these respects.
>
> In the midst of all this turmoil & uncertainty people possess their souls in a wonderful degree of peace & patience. The fact is, we have been kicked about so during the past twelve months that we have gotten quite used to it.[28]

Anne Schaeffer collected her valuables and planned to flee as the rebel troops marched into Frederick on September 6:

> Woke up—found all quiet. The fire in the street dying out leaving a horrible smell of burnt hair from the mattresses. What a dreadful waking up, to we knew not what! I went up street before breakfast to secure shoes for the children. Streets crowded with anxious faces. Returning home, I gathered together all the small valuable articles—silver spoons &c. and put them in large pockets, which I fastened to a belt around my waist under my skirts. I learned afterwards many ladies carried around a similar burden for a whole week. After breakfast my cook took leave—as the colored people are running away in all directions and was left alone with the children & white nurse. About 11 A.M. the Rebels came in by the southern pike, led by a former citizen of Frederick and were received with open arms by those who favored their cause, while the Union men hung their heads [n] sorrow and shame to see the 'Stars and Stripes' pulled down and trampled on. Our own small flags were all hidden out of sight. Soon the streets were swarming with ragged, filthy, worn out men—yet every one (to our astonishment) respectful and polite. Soon they were thronging the stores, offering their confederate notes, which not being regarded of much value in Maryland, about 4 P.M. most of the stores closed up. We were still in suspense, knowing, not what was intended by the enemy who now placed the City under martial

law—who can describe our feelings or paint the sad anxious faces? We feared to
go to bed, yet felt the necessity of rest.[29]

With rumors swirling about the approach of McClellan's army, residents of Frederick were afraid to leave home or attend church, and they were jolted by the explosion as the Confederates destroyed the railroad bridge over the Monocacy River, a few miles south of the city. Schaeffer nonetheless felt badly for the Southern soldiers:

> I ventured to the more public streets to day and could not help admiring the
> conduct of these poor men. Although in need of everything and our merchants
> refused to open their stores, they humbly acquiesced. I learned afterwards, they
> were simply obeying orders, for it is the policy of their officers, to do nothing to
> offend in Maryland, still hoping she may be induced to secede. Generals Lee,
> Stonewall Jackson, Stuart and Longstreet are all in Frederick—the men appear
> devoted to their officers, who seem to care kindly for them and cheerfully share
> their privations. The Southern sympathizers keep open house and our kind
> hearted Union citizens turn none away hungry who apply to them for food—so
> that they all declare, Frederick is the best place they have been quartered in
> for a long time. Their hatred of the "Yankees," as they call all Union men, is
> intense, though they admit they are heartily tired of this war. We can hear nothing of our troops approaching, although the slaves and contrabands, who wait
> at table, where the Rebel officers are dined and wined, listen attentively to all
> that is said and assure us "they *are* coming." Nobody pretends to work—everybody on the streets—standing in groups talking and eyeing the the quiet passing
> soldiers.[30]

Her apprehension grew on September 9, with one army moving and another poised
to replace it:

> Another night passed and we still spared from fire and bloodshed. The stores
> remain closed—Men still gloomy though getting a little accustomed to the state
> of affairs. Our supplies are all cut off—the bridge destroyed and R.R. track torn
> up—the mills taken possession of. Housekeepers are examining their stock of
> provisions. We succeeded to day in getting a bag of cornmeal, with a prospect
> of some flour. Many indications of the Federal army approaching and I dread
> a battle in our midst. We listen for every sound of gun or cannon, hoping they
> are coming. I learned to day with deep regret, that the brave scout, who brought
> us news of their approach, was arrested and yesterday shot at Camp Worman.
> Encouraging reports this evening of the Rebels leaving, but our streets are still
> crowded with the filthy, desperate looking, but polite strangers.[31]

The following day Lee's men began to leave:

> At 12 hrs. last night the Rebel army (the darkies were right) began moving and
> are passing through our streets out the Hagerstown pike as fast as they can travel.

Their destination (*They* say) Pennsylvania, but many think to endeavor to re-cross into Virginia at Williamsport. I have had some interesting conversations with several soldiers. One especially so homesick—he begged me for citizens clothing to facilitate his escape, which I supplied, he promising to inform me when safe and far away. (I never heard from him and suspect he was, like many other stragglers shot in crossing the mountains). This evening my husband got hold of a newspaper, which had been smugled into town—"The Philadephia Inquirer." It was almost worn out, having passed through so many hands. We read hurriedly for others were waiting their turn and felt much disheartened on reading the accounts therein given of a few panic stricken Rebels crossing into Maryland. They—the North—will not believe, with what a formidable force they may have to contend, until they see them at their doors.

"Poor most poor!" deprived of every comfort and yet an army of desperate men—well disciplined and well officered—in these respects vieing with, if not excelling our own army.[32]

On September 11, Schaeffer was "still in suspense"—"I tried to calm my nerves this afternoon by sewing"—as the rebels thronged the streets of Frederick, "wagons rumbling through the streets mingled with the lowing of the cattle they take with them. Almost afraid to go to bed."[33]

Late the following day the federal troops caught the rear of the Southern army at the town square:

About 4 P.M. my husband rushed into the house to tell me the Union troops were in sight—that from canon hill they could be seen fighting and driving the Rebels before them. I quickly donned my bonnet and going to a friends house ran up to the observatory, where with a glass we could plainly see our troops approaching, pursuing the Confederates along the Baltimore pike. Just outside of Town, the Union forces separated—a part coming through the fields and the Lutheran graveyard at the end of Church st. but the main body continuing on the pike up Patrick st. to the Square where the Confederates made a stand and charged on their pursuers, driving them back to the East end, where they turned and again the Rebels flew before them, compelling several unfortunates prisoners to keep up with their horse's. These however were taken at the west end of the Town. As the shots whistled through the streets, the citizens ran in every direction, seeking shelter. I started for home, but seeing the street deserted and hearing more shots, I returned to the observatory—we heard cheering and listening and watching, we beheld the stars and stripes borne aloft up Patrick St. Good Lord! Could I believe the sight of that dear flag would ever affect thus?—Unconsciously I screamed, shouted—jumped for joy. Again we flew down to welcome the small body of troops coming up Church st. Oh the frantic joy of that hour I shall never forget! And so with every body. Some shouted—some laughed—some cried. Cheers and hurrahs rent the air—People ran out of their houses—clasped each others hand—I went home to the children and found my little five year old daughter had somewhere found a hidden flag and was waving it—the first I know—on our street. The Union troops were pouring in—Every body at doors and windows cheering and waving flags and hankerchiefs—manyh on the side walks, engaged with buckets, dippers and cups giving the tired, heated soldiers, water as they passed.[34]

And then:

After awhile came Burnside himself—and now they cheered Many ran trying to grasp his hand, while he bowed again and again—Cheers rent the air—Surely was army never given a more uproarous welcome. At last we came home to super and this exciting day—another 12th of September ended in a quiet night, or at least we felt we could lie down to sleep in safety.[35]

As Confederate Gen. Daniel H. Hill questioned a local man about area roads, the day before the Battle of South Mountain:

Just then a shell came hurtling through the woods, and a little girl began crying. Having a little one at home of about the same age, I could not forbear stopping a moment to say a few soothing words to the frightened child, before hurrying off to the work of death.[36]

A Baltimore newspaper headline proclaimed "General Lee Reported Killed," and a reporter described the behavior of Frederick's ladies:

The loyal ladies of Frederick conducted themselves during the Rebel occupancy with marked firmness and propriety. They neither denied their devotion to the cause of their country, nor sought notoriety by parading it unnecessarily. At the proper time and in the proper way they let the invaders now that they were un-welcome visitors. When our army came, with McClellan at its head, they gave it such a welcome as ladies know how to give to a hero. They saluted him with kisses, (figuratively I mean—but they would have been actual ones had the Gen-eral come within reach,) showered flowers upon him, waved their flags over his head, and cheered him with their good wishes. Who doubts that "little Mac and his boys" fought better on Sunday for the hearty welcome that the loyal women of Frederick gave to him on Saturday?[37]

Some young ladies of Frederick accepted invitations from dashing Confederate Gen. Jeb Stuart to an impromptu ball, disrupted in full swing by the vicissitudes of war:

As the delightful strains of music floated through the vacant old house, and the dancing began, the strange accompaniments of war added zest to the occasion,

"General McClellan and His Army Passing through Federick City, MD, in Pursuit of the Confederates, September 12th, 1862. From a Sketch by Edwin Forbes." The Soldier in Our Civil War.

and our lovely partners declared that it was perfectly charming. But they were destined to have more of the war accompaniment than was intended by the managers, for just as everything had become well started and the enjoyment of the evening was at its height, there came shivering through the still night air the boom of artillery, followed by the angry rattle of musketry. The lily chased the rose from the cheek of beauty, and every pretty foot was rooted to the floor where music had left it. Then came hasty and tender partings from tearful partners, buckling on of sabers, mounting of impatient steeds, and clattering of hoofs as the gay cavaliers dashed off to the front.[38]

William Miller Owen, adjutant of the Washington Artillery of New Orleans, captured the mood of the Confederate troops as they passed through Frederick:

The army passed through in good order, and all in the merriest and jolliest mood possible, indulging occasionally in good-natured chaff, as was their wont. Any peculiarity of costume or surroundings of any person was sure to bring out some remark that would set whole regiments in a roar. On a small gallery stood a buxom young lady, with laughing black eyes, watching the scene before her; on her breast she had pinned a small flag, the "stars and stripes." This was observed, and some soldier sang out, "Look h'yar, miss, better take that flag down;

we're awful fond of charging breast-works!" This was carried down the line amid shouts of laughter. The little lady laughed herself, but stood by her colors.[39]

A Virginia private contrasted the reception in Hagerstown with that of Frederick during the Antietam campaign:

> The actions of the citizens of Hagerstown showed in vivid contrast to Frederick City, for not only were the men and women outspoken in their sympathy for the Southern cause, but they threw wide open their hospitable doors and filled their houses with the soldiers, feeding the hungry and clothing the naked as well as their limited means allowed.[40]

A Union soldier from Pennsylvania, having been on rebel soil for some time, was delighted at his reception in Frederick:

> Never was a more cordial welcome given to troops than was given to us. Bread, cakes, milk, water, fruit, and tobacco were freely given by the good people who crowded the doors and windows and lined the pavements, and flags and hand-kerchiefs were waved and flowers thrown as we passed. We felt then, for the first time during the war, we were fighting among friends.[41]

The poet John Greenleaf Whittier demonized the Confederacy. He made a legend of an old Frederick woman named Barbara Frietchie in his poem of the same name, in which she allegedly waved an American flag in the face of Stonewall Jackson as his men passed through the town:

> Up from the meadows rich with corn,
> Clear in the cool September morn,
>
> The clustered spires of Frederick stand
> Green-walled by the hills of Maryland
> Up rose old Barbara Frietchie then,
> Bowed with her fourscore years and ten;
>
> Bravest of all in Frederick town,
> She took up the flag the men hauled down;

Jackson's men then shot the flag from its pole, whereupon she waved it at Jackson from her window.

> She leaned far out on the window-sill,
> And shook it forth with a royal will.
>
> "Shoot, if you must, this old gray head,
> But spare your country's flag," she said.
> The nobler nature within him stirred
> To life at that woman's deed and word;

CAMP SONG

OF THE

MARYLAND LINE.

As Sung by the Baltimore Boys in Richmond.

Tune—"*Gay and Happy.*"

We're the boys, so gay and happy,
　Wheresoe'er we chance to be—
If at home or on camp duty,
　'Tis the same—we're always free.
　　So let the war guns roar as they will,
　　We'll be gay and happy still;
　　Gay and happy—gay and happy,
　　We'll be gay and happy still.

We've left our homes and those we cherish,
　In our good old Maryland;
Rather than wear chains we'll perish,
　Side by side and hand in hand.
　　So let the war guns, &c.

Old Virginia needs assistance,
　Northern hosts invade her soil;
We'll present a firm resistance,
　Courting danger, fire and toil.
　　So let the war guns, &c.

Then let drums and muskets rattle,
　Fearless as our sires of yore,
We'll not leave the field of battle
　Till we've ransomed Baltimore.
　　So let the war guns, &c.

"The Camp Song of the Maryland Line, as Sung by the Baltimore Boys in Richmond"—sung to the tune of "Gay and Happy"—noted the refusal of these Confederate troops from Maryland to "wear chains" and that "Old Virginia Needs Assistance." Rare Books and Manuscripts Department, Z. Smith Reynolds Library, Wake Forest University, Winston-Salem, North Carolina.

"Who touches a hair of yon gray head
Dies like a dog! March on!" he said.[42]

Eyewitness accounts suggest a different story. Anne Schaeffer, knowing the route of the troops through town did not pass the Fritchie house, doubted that Jackson's men even saw her:

> One little episode I must here record and give the true history of Barbary Frit-chie and her flag. A Confederate has recently said, she was bed ridden and prob-ably never saw a rebel soldier. This was untrue—I will relate here what one of her nieces told me, when Whittier's poem first appeared. Mrs Fritchie was very old—upwards of eighty years and looked much older. Before the door of her residence was a long low shaded porch and during the warm September days of that memorable week, the poor, worn out soldiers, would often seek rest there. She, leaning on her staff would sometimes come out among them and say "Get out you lazy, dirty Rebels" Without replying, they invariably made way for her.
>
> On the evening of Sept. 12th she sat at her open window waving a small flag to the advancing Federal troops, who were led by Gen. Reno. They halted in front of her door, just before crossing the town bridge. The soldiers seeing this very old lady cheered her and one and another begged her for the little flag. At length she gave it to one, who fastened it in the headgear of Gen. Reno's horse.
>
> Stonewall Jackson had led his men, just a few hours previous, up an alley coming out on Patrick street a little distance above Mrs. Fritchie's house and I doubt whether she ever saw him. This is I believe the true story[43]

In 1878, a nephew of Barbara Fritchie told a similar story to a Baltimore news-paper:

> Now in a word as to the waving of the Federal flag in the face of the rebels by Dame Barbara on the occasion of Stonewall Jackson's march through Frederick. Trust requires me to say that Stonewall Jackson with his troops did not pass Bar-bara Fritchie's residence at all but passed up what in this city is popularly called "The Mill alley," about three hundred yards above her residence, then passed due west toward Antietam, and thus out of the city.
>
> But another and still stronger fact with regard to this matter may be here presented, viz: The poem by Whittier represents our venerable relative (then 90 years of age) as nimbly ascending to her attic window and waving her small Federal flag defiantly in the face of Stonewall Jackson's troops. Now, what are the facts at this point? Dame Barbara was at the moment of the passing of that distinguished General and his forces through Frederick, bedridden and helpless and had lost the power of locomotion. She could at that period, only move as she was moved by the help of her attendants.
>
> These are the true and stern facts, proving that Whittier's poem upon the

subject is fiction, pure fiction and nothing else, without even the remotest resemblance to fact.[44]

Henry Kyd Douglas, of Jackson's staff, verified these accounts in his memoir:

As for Barbara Frietchie, we did not pass her house. There was such an old woman in Frederick, in her ninety-sixth year and bedridden. She never saw Stonewall Jackson and he never saw her. I was with him every minute while he was in the town, and nothing like the patriotic incident so graphically described by Mr. Whittier in his poem ever occurred.[45]

On September 13, Schaeffer awoke to frenetic activity, including the opening sounds of battle:

Awoke to find out streets crowded with Union soldiers. After breakfast I went to my sisters on one of the main streets. All bustle and excitement—McClellan expected—We heard a great noise and looking out, saw the Hero at the head of his staff approaching. Leaping down the steps we ran to the square and were among the first ladies to grasp his hand—Shouts and deafening cheers! people seemed beside themselves and forced him to stop—to receive their greetings—He sat as one confounded—the enthusiasm so unexpected—while ladies hung upon his horse's neck—patting his head stuck a flag in the gearing. At length he galloped away and when the streets cleared I hurried to the P-Office which had just opened to mail my letter.

All the morning we have heard the booming of cannon—for a battle is going on at the foot of the mountain—Again McClellan and Burnside passed through Town and now indeed came an army—Began passing at noon—continued marching as rapidly as possible until night. Oh what a different day from last Saturday! Still, most of the stores are closed and it is difficult to purchase anything—All articles of food are very high, but we hope for a change next week.[46]

Frederick residents heard the battle raging:

The Holy Sabbath and still the murderous work goes on. We have heard firing all day and know that many souls are appearing before their Maker, while many more are suffering excruciating bodily pain unseen and unpitied by human eye.[47]

Anne Schaeffer's entry of September 18 read simply, "Battle raging at Antietam."[48]

Washington Hands, sent to help liberate Harpers Ferry from Union occupation, arrived at Antietam:

The next instant the command "fire" was heard above the exultant cheers of the advancing columns, and twenty four pieces of artillery, double-shothed [?]

"Women and Children of Sharpsburg, MD. Taking Refuge in the Cellar of the Kretzer Mansion. During the Battle, Bursting of a Shell in the Window of the Cellar.—From a Sketch by F. H. Schell." The Soldier in Our Civil War.

with canister, belched forth their deadly contents into the very faces of the assailants. The scene that was presented as the smoke lifted beggars description. The ground was literally covered, nay, piled, with the slain and maimed of the enemy.[49]

Franklin Wilson described what he believed were one hundred fifty thousand Confederate soldiers crossing into Maryland toward Frederick, with detachments to other towns, and the distant "thunder of artillery" from Antietam:

On Friday Sept 5. the Confederates crossed into Maryland, in vast numbers, 150,000 it is said. On Saturday they occupied Frederick city, and sent detachments to Hagerstown, Westminster and even to Greencastle Pa. They supplied themselves with large quantities of shoes clothes and provisions, paying for them generally in Southern money, but partly in U.S. notes. They were under good discipline and did little or no damage to property. Some of them were close to this city and probably in its streets in disguise. Several were captured seven miles out on the Reis. Road. They are said as a body to be in a filthy, ragged, forlorn state, and those captured have certainly looked like paupers, many barefooted, and all ragged.

Pennsylvania was thoroughly frightened, and about 72,000 volunteers met at

Harrisburg & Chambersburg to repel the threatened invasion. Gen Lee (S.C.A.) issued an address to the people of Maryland offering the aid of the Southern army to help them throw off the despotic government under which they were groaning, but only a few hundred joined the standard of the "Stars and Bars." There was much excitement in Baltimore. Many sent away their goods and valuables, and a number went themselves. Dr. Lane and I were very much perplexed for a few days as to the proper course, but finally concluded to remain. The Union authorities here determined to destroy the city before it should be taken by the Confeds. I did not care to be in the neighborhood in such an event. However, the Confeds. did not come any nearer, they failed to make the expected raid into Penn.[50]

Young Maryland men tempted to enlist in the Confederate army had reasons to reconsider:

> Parties who arrived at Union bridge from Frederick state that a number of young men of Frederick had started out to join the Rebel army but that most of them seeing the forlorn condition of the men came to the conclusion that they could not stand such a service and prudently returned to their homes.[51]

From "Mondawmin," William H. Graham wrote to Thomas Winans, son of Ross Winans and a London resident, describing an aftermath to Antietam that sounded ominous for the Union and efforts of Marylanders to care for Confederate wounded. Graham explained that twelve thousand federals had been captured and paroled at Harpers Ferry before being sent to Annapolis:

> While smoking this evening I determined to write to you to find out what had become of you.

After discussing business matters, Graham moved to the war:

> The Confederates it is said have been obliged to leave many of their wounded in Maryland and Genl. Wool has given leave to parties here to nurse and attend to them. In a few hours some $5,000 was raised, some giving $500, some $200, some $100, etc., others gave groceries, others clothing, others went as nurses and four doctors went up and more are going. People who come from the battlefield say the papers do not give a true account of the conditions of things and the New York Herald says that the Flag of truce was first shown on the Union side.[52]

After the Confederate retreat from Antietam, civilians in western Maryland were not sure what they would find at home:

> The inhabitants in the vicinity of Frederick and Hagerstown are returning to their homes, and seem to be in great glee because the Rebels are driven across the river. No pillaging was allowed by the Rebels previous to the battle of South

Confederate troops outside Hagerstown in September 1862. A black man feeds an officer's horse, and the American flag flies in the town, in the distance. Harper's Weekly/*Pratt Lib.*

Mountain, but after that they cleared the country pretty thoroughly, particularly around Sharpsburg, almost every house in the town have been robbed, and goods which they could not use destroyed. Many houses were riddled by bullets and shells and several barns burned.[53]

Daniel Thomas saw hope for the South after Antietam, writing, "I am disposed to believe that McClellan has fallen very short of saving the country yet":

The past week has been the most eventful of the war. The greatest battle on record has been fought within 40 miles of us, and four days after it, all that the Government (which has not heretofore been mealy mouthed in telling of its successes) can make of the result is that the Federals *were not whipped.*[54]

Shortly after the battle the *American Sentinel* recounted the arrival in Westminster of 350 "chivalric Sons of the South," claiming to be the Fifth Regiment Virginia cavalry:

They entered town just after dark, as if ashamed to appear in open daylight, for a more dilapidated looking body of men we never again wish to see. The male sympathisers here was evidently disappointed, and was rather disposed to turn upon them the cold shoulder; but not so with some of the women—they indulged in the wildest demonstrations of joy, some so far exceeding propriety as to render themselves the objects of coarse jests by the soldiery.

After robbing the Post Office they proceeded to the Armory of the Carroll Guards where they wantonly destroyed the lamps and carried off a fine flag and drum, belonging to that Company. They next visited a number of stores, where they bought largely of hats, caps, clothing, boots, shoes and other articles necessary to present a more genteel appearance in the morning, paying for the larger portion in Confederate scrip, and other worthless Southern currency. Most of the Union men closed their places of business as soon as possible, and thereby saved their goods.[55]

After spending several days preparing food and caring for wounded prisoners, Anne Schaeffer expressed disbelief at how life had changed in a week:

Accompanied some ladies to the hospital at the Barracks. Time can never efface from memory, the scenes of suffering witnessed there. Oh this hellish war!—I could not help thinking how ridiculous our world must appear to superior intelligences—our incurring so much trouble, expense and suffering to maim and murder each other and after accomplishing this object, laying the poor creatures side by side—endeavoring to relieve their pain and save their lives. How terrible was the torture of some we saw—One especially who had just had one jaw removed—One just carried out to be buried—another was dying—far from home and friends.

Really I can scarcely believe I am living in Frederick—good old Frederick—Once so quiet orderly and clean Now all bustle and confusion—sidewalks crowded with soldiers, ladies and

A postscript to Schaeffer's diary—in handwriting suggesting it was written later—refers to "the glorious victory" at Antietam and hope for a "brighter future." Her final sentence suggests, for the first time, one of the personal impacts of the war: "and then the rupture with members of my family, for we were divided."[56]

1863

A young Marylander, in Richmond fighting for the Confederacy, wrote to Annie Woodward, a friend in his hometown of Cambridge, in Dorchester County:

Another year has passed, and I am still seperated from you and my friends at home; but I await with patience that happy day when we shall meet again as freemen.

God grant that the day may soon come when my *dear old sister* may be able to throw off her chains, and unite with her Southern Sisters, I know nine tenths of the people wish it, and if our noble army would get a foothold there, that there are thousands who cannot come here and leave their families, that would swell their ranks. Though there are many noble Marylanders in our Army, there are many young men, still remaining, who call themselves Southerners, that could very well leave home, and join their brothers in arms, but prefer to let others fight the battles and they share the spoils. I am sorry to say that though Cambridge has done, well, by sending many sons here, she is not without some of these of which I have been speaking who are afraid to face the iron hail in defence of their most sacred rights. When I left home to join our Army, there were some among that class of which I have been speaking who laughed at the idea of me, they called a little boy, going to fight. I noticed that they were afraid to come with me, and pass through the hardships and danger I have. How different are the beautiful and patriotic ladies in C[ambridge]. You have no idea how proud the boys from C[ambridge] are of them. We all still say that none in the world equal them in beauty and goodness.

The eighteen months that have passed since I last saw you seem as if they were as many years. I would give the world once more to enjoy your most agreeable society and listen to your sweet voice. I have always censured myself for not bidding you good bye when leaving home. I ask your pardon for this bad treatment. How often when having marched barefoot all day, and stop to rest for the night have I thought and dreamed of you and the pleasant days I have spent with you, in old C[ambridge].

These delightful recollections, would make me forget all my trials and sufferings. I pray that those happy days may soon return.[57]

Lieutenant Col. John A. Steiner of the Potomac Home Brigade recorded the capture of currency smugglers on the Patuxent River between St. Mary's and Calvert counties. The prisoners were sent to the Union prison at Point Lookout:

Lieu't Burk brough in last night 2 men taken near Spencers wharf Patuxent River. Viz L.E. Goldsmith & S. Kirtland. Goldsmith had letters & 2000$ in South paper. Lieu't Carroll brought in 8 men as follows.

After noting their names, Steiner noted that the men were

Captured in a coasting canoe, with about 9000$ Southern Bank paper & 180$ in Gold.[58]

Lee's second invasion of Maryland, in June, alarmed Baltimoreans. Volunteers, conscripted blacks, and disloyalists erected "barricades of carts, paving stones and earth." W.W. Glenn did not subscribe to the sense of danger:

The condition of things in Baltimore surpassed belief. The military authorities were frightened out of their lives and the most ridiculous defenses were erected. Negroes of every kind were impressed, so much so that the markets were entirely broken up for a day or two, absurd little forts were erected about in spots, around the city, many of which were commanded by hills close by, and about one half

"Rebel Prisoners Leaving Baltimore for Fortress Monroe." Confederate prisoners—soldiers or disloyal civilians—were feted as they left Baltimore for incarceration in Fortress Monroe in Virginia but under Union control. Pratt Lib.

of the city—the most populous part—was fortified with tobacco hogsheads and sugar hogsheads—the latter being empty & filled with dirt. The whole thing was ridiculous. These barricades were guarded by citizens, most of whom would have run away from a Confederate popgun.[59]

The Reverend Henry Slicer was no more impressed:

The Police are arresting the col'd men in the streets, and taking them to the station House, under the plea, that they want to set them to diging trenches for fortifications around the City, to keep out the Confederates—They have barricaded the streets on the outer portions of the City with Tobacco Hogsheads, Carts, Drays &c. Time will show the folly of all this—[60]

Archibald T. Kirkwood of the Seventh Maryland Volunteers in June described his friend's typhoid fever and camp life on Maryland Heights at Harpers Ferry, noting rebel movements presaging the Gettysburg campaign:

Went over today to see Henderson he is pretty bad with the Camp fever, I think some of his folks ought to come see him, they could get him home, Dr Robinson was over to see him today he would not have been out of his tent as soon as he was, if it had not have been Dr Robinson Lieut Quarrel is getting along fine he is not settling up yet it is reported that the Rebs are about to make another raid into Md about 15,000 strong it is a part of Lee's force and I would not doubt but what they will accomplish their act—it is reported they are in Martinsburg today if they are there they will be very apt to cross at or near Williamsport for we have got no force of any account there. I guess it is only to get something to eat and wear just like their other raids, Robert was up hear today he is well and hearty

We have got on the mountain again we are not in our old ground we are on the west side of the fort We are all stockading our tents we will have firstrate quarters water is pretty plenty the spring is stronger than it was last winter Well I have no news of importance to write I just fulfilling my promise to write every week to let you know how we are getting along

Give our best respects to all inquiring friends and relations but reserve a good share for yourself.[61]

Five days later poor Henderson was worse, as were some regiments of the Union army:

We expect pretty hot work here yet. You ought to have seen the troops coming in here yesterday broken regiments from the battle of Winchester the 5th Md has got 4 left all we have seen the 87 Pen. has got about 100 left Crosses Company has got 19 in it not a commissioned officer in that company they are either killed or taken prisoners James Thompson is one of the missing there was a big loss on both sides but from all accounts the rebs paid dear for their trip. I have not been to see Henderson since he moved over.

We have been in line of battle ever since Monday morning and not allowed to leave any distance from the line. I tell you it is not you were at home go and come when you please, Kenley's Brigade moved up on Md Heights yesterday, to support these batteries, he has got command of the heights we have got no mail for two days now.[62]

In late June, Frederick grappled with its second Confederate invasion in nine months:

Sunday dawned bright and clear. The citizens were greatly alarmed, for they knew not what excesses the raiders might commit. The churches, of which there are several fine ones in the city, were all open as usual, but rather slimly attended. The Rev. Dr. Zachariah, of the German Reformed, prayed for "the President of the United States, and all others in authority," while the rebels were racing and riding through the streets. At an early hour a party of about the same number as on the previous day came in town and commenced a search for horses. The stores were all closed, but the streets were alive with the citizens watching the doings of the raiders. Some of the citizens were very agreeable to them, and invited them to their houses to partake of refreshments.—Captain Davis, the leader of the gang, was feted and feasted, and was a gallant man among the ladies.[63]

Skirmishing occurred along much of the Potomac River, the border between Maryland and Virginia, throughout the war. Harper's Weekly.

On June 29, Archibald Kirkwood wrote again from Harpers Ferry:

> It is very disagreeable weather here this morning, we have no tents at all now, we have to build shelters out of our blankets. Joe was in our camp yesterday he was well Robert was here the other day he was well also, I guess you get as much war news as we do, I do not know any more than is in the paper
>
> I suppose the Rebs has a considerable to say now with you, about the rebels being in Md and Pa, if things are managed right I think this will the winding up job nearly, I am afraid if the rebels are not drove out of Md soon that we will not get home to the election.[64]

The diary of Margaret (Maggie) Mehring, a thirteen-year-old at a private school in New Windsor, described the evolution of the Gettysburg campaign, from June 19 through July 2:

> June 19: It is reported here that the Confederates are again at Frederick, but not much credit is given to the report as those reports usually come from Rebel sources. The birds have been singing merrily since early this morning.

June 22: It is reported on very good authority that the Rebels are in Frederick. They consist of part of Whites [Garibaldi] brigade. They have not molested any one as yet except to steal their horses a piece of art which they appear to be very near perfect in and one that I think is a pretty occupation for the much b[o]asted Southern Chivelry to be engaged in.

June 23: It is rumored here that the Rebels have left Frederick and that there is a force of fifty thousand at Getysburg if it is true I hope they will meet a warm reception from Pensylvania in the shape of balls for taking the trouble and liberty of calling on them without an invitation.

June 26: too thousand Rebels were in Tauneytown and would be in New Winsor before the following morning. I retired early expectin to see any quantity of Rebels the next morning or be called up at one o'clock to see them but was very arguably disappointed to wake and find all quiet and no Rebs about.

June 30: A little while after dark five thousand four hundred (union soldiers) passed through. They were dressed very nicely and rode handsome horses. It was a beautiful sight for the moon shown so brilliantly that one could almost imagine it was day and the horsemen riding six and eight abreast with their sords clatering while cheer after cheer rent the air. (*Maggie noted that "the girls" tried to remain awake to watch 25,000 infantry scheduled to pass through town at 4 AM.*)

July 1: The Union scouts brought in three captured Rebs—too of them held their heads down and look very sad but the third one was lively. They were mounted on farmers horses which they had stolen between here and Westminster. Our cavilry captured them and took their horses from them. They then march them out to the infantry camp. The infantry brigade was so long that when their advance guard entered Westminster their rear was just leaving [Jews]burg.

July 2: It was reported here to day that they had a fight at or near Tauneytown yesterday morning and that there was a General killed an his body conveyed through here early this morning on its way to Washington to be buried. Another report an most probably the correct one is that they had a fight at Hanover, Pennsylvania. Our General fell back twice an it was not until he was reinforced the third time that he drove the Rebels it was during the third attack that the commanding General was killed. It is said that the fight was in the streets of Hanover

July 2: It has been reported so frequently that the rebels are coming for the last few days that it has most ceased to cause an extra pulsation of the heart. This has been a beautiful day. Saturday will be the forth of July. I wonder if they will celebrate it in our army. It was that memorable day that our forefathers declared the little coliny of thirteen states free an independent It was hoped on last forth of July by the President, officers, an soldiers, of our army this forth would dawn upon them with the blessings of peace but unluckily for them an us the war appears but little nearer a close than then, I have known my lessons very well this week. Ikie Atlic said he saw four Soldiers ride up thrugh town yesterday an that one of them had something that looked like a ball in the side of his face. Mr Weaver asked him why he didn't have it taken out he replied that he had not time to stop. Ikie is certain that it was a ball for the blood was running down his face in a stream He must have been wounded by a Rebel. This is a beautiful day. We heard the cannons booming very distinctly last night and it is supposed that there is a battle going on between Littlestown an Gettysburg. The sun is shining so brightly an the air is so close tht they poor soldiers will suffer terribly for water. I must stop.[65]

Mary Louisa Kealhofer ("Lutie") was the daughter of a Southern sympathizer who was president of the Hagerstown Gas Light Company. The diary of this twenty-two-year old fiancée of a Confederate officer reflected the tenuous hold both sides had on Hagerstown during the Gettysburg campaign:

Feel rather better this evening but was really miserable all yesterday with my back. Things appear to be "In Statu Quo." Some persons who tried to get to Balt—returned today & report the R. Road torn up beyond Fred. These are stirring times—one hour we are under Jeff Davis—the next under Abraham & before the good Union people have time to congratulate themselves upon their release from Rebel rule in dashes a squad of these impudent Rebels & Jeff claims us again. So the world goes.[66]

Late in June four companies of the Second Maryland Regiment entrenched on Franklin Wilson's property—"They have depended on my pump for water, but have not disturbed me much, except by walking through the place at all hours":

For more than a week there has been a great excitement here and in Pennsylvania, on account of the advances of Lee's army, 125,000 strong into Md. and Pa. Last Saturday Gen. Schenck had our streets barricaded with tobacco hogsheads! and commenced erecting earth works around the city. In the evening as I went out to walk I saw them tearing down the fence of my cow-pasture, and without a word to me they went to work digging a huge rifle pit, 550 feet long, semi-circular in form, and faced inside with barrels. A large number of colored men were impressed and force to work all day Sunday June 21st. They made a great deal of noise, and our place became quite a thoroughfare.[67]

The same day Wilson, who probably lived northwest of Baltimore, recorded the ramifications of Lee's movements into Pennsylvania:

Trouble is predicted in this city, especially as the bitter feelings between the ultra Unionists and the Secessionists are almost on the point of bursting with a flame. In the even of an attack, the works near me would invite the balls and shells of the enemy, and my house would probably be destroyed. We have been kept remarkably calm during all this time, and trust that God will "deliver us from evil."[68]

A Baltimore paper described the depredations of that army on the Maryland side of the Potomac:

Notwithstanding General Ewell's orders commanding his troops to respect the property of all Marylanders, foraging parties are scouring the country in every direction, seizing all the horses and cattle they can lay hands on. Several thousand head of cattle and a large number of horses have been gobbled by the Rebels in Washington county alone. The neighboring counties are suffering in like manner. Most of the cattle have been driven across the river into Virginia, to feed that portion of Lee's army which still remains on the other side.[69]

Concerned about the vulnerability of Baltimore, Gen. Robert Schenck instructed Mayor John Lee Chapman to procure one thousand men to construct defenses, impressing them if necessary:

I am prepared, among other preparations for the defence of Baltimore against a possible attack of the rebels, to construct some lines of intrenchments at points commanding approaches to the city. You have apprised me that in this emergency the city authorities would furnish the required number of laborers, either by hiring, volunteering or otherwise. I desire to have immediately, to be put at the work by 4 o'c today, one thousand men, who, when ready, will report to Lieut. Meigs of Engineer Corps, on my staff, for the service. If you have any difficulty in furnishing the labor and find it necessary to obtain it, or any part of it, by some equitable system of impressments, give me notice to that effect at any time, and I will furnish you the military power to enforce such impressment.[70]

As three Confederate divisions marched north through western Maryland, quiet vigilance pervaded Baltimore on Sunday, June 29:

So, throughout the day the most stirring reports were received, but there was no panic visible, throngs of citizens visited the defences, the Loyal Leagues were at their armories, and quiet and order everywhere prevailed, the churches having their usual attendance.[71]

That night, though, the atmosphere changed:

At eleven o'clock last night our city was thrown into great excitement by the sounding of the signal by the fire bells agreed upon by General Schenck, to call the Union Leagues to arms for the defence of the barricades. The signal corps

"Invasion of Maryland—Citizens of Baltimore Barricading the Streets, Monday Evening, June 29.—From a Sketch by Our Special Artist, Edwin Forbes." Baltimoreans sprang to the barricades in late June 1863 as word spread of Lee's march into western Maryland. Pratt Lib.

stationed on the different roads had fired rockets announcing the approach of a Rebel cavalry force on the Reisterstown road. Through some parts of the city the cry "To Arms! To Arms!" was sounded, and men with muskets in their hands were seen running to and fro, and rapidly assembling at the points of rendezvous.

In a half hour several thousands were in arms and the headquarters of General Schenck was surrounded by bristling bayonets. All soon became quiet in the city, and considerable enthusiasm but no panic prevailed.

Up to the time we go to press, however, no enemy had appeared, and the alarm is presumed to have been occasioned by the near approach of a company of Rebel cavalry who were in the vicinity of the Pikesville Arsenal.

The number of our citizens at the barricades last night was estimated at from five to seven thousand. All the military in the city were also called out and were under arms all night.[72]

On June 29, with the rebel army moving through western Maryland, Schenck was fortifying the major roads into Baltimore:

A wagon to haul 50 Enfield Rifles, and horses to draw 5 mounted pieces of cannon from the Seminary of Rev. Mr. Van Bokelen at Catonsville, six miles out on the Frederick road are required immediately. The cannon are six pounders and the horses should have the gear for hitching onto them.

A guard will accompany the wagons.

Please report to me at what time you will have them ready at no. 8 Gay St.[73]

The following day, citing "the immediate presence of a rebel army within this department," he declared martial law "in the city and county of Baltimore, and in all the counties of the Western Shore of Maryland":

The response of the Union Leagues to the call to arms for the defense of the city on Monday night has elicited much praise from the military authorities. The various companies of Union Leagues remained on duty during Monday night. They were placed at the various street barricades and at some of the entrenchments around the city. The excitement all subsided after it was ascertained that no Confederates had approached nearer to this city than Pikesville, and, as we stated yesterday morning, where they remained but a short while, so that no conflict occurred during the night between the contending forces in the neighborhood of this city.[74]

Mindful of ransoms the Confederates were levying against towns in Maryland and Pennsylvania, the American beseeched Unionists to arm and protect the city. Two gunboats appeared at the end of Broadway and another at the bridge on the city's west side, "in admirable position to bear upon the city and its approaches":

The Union men of Baltimore are earnestly requested to assemble at their usual places of meeting in the different wards every evening this week for the purpose of forming independent military companies to aid the Government forces in defending our city.

It is anxiously desired that every Union man shall be under arms, and it would be a most gratifying result to have a Union Guard of at least ten thousand men fully armed.

The Rebel forces have levied a tax of $250,000 upon the people of York, such may be our fate, unless we promptly organize for defence. The time for action has arrived.

It is advised that all places of business be closed at 6 P.M.[75]

Until further orders all bars, coffee-houses, drinking saloons and other places of like resort shall be closed between the hours of 8 P.M. and 8 A.M. Any liquor dealer or keeper of a drinking saloon or other person selling intoxicating drinks who violates this order shall be put under arrest, his premises seized and his liquors confiscated for the benefit of the hospitals.[76]

Schenck ordered troops and "citizen soldiers" back to their encampments once the threat subsided.[77]

Union Mills lay on the route of both armies moving toward Gettysburg (Gen. George Meade, the newly appointed federal commander, planned to confront Lee in a line along Big Pipe Creek, just north of the Shriver homestead). On July 2, Eliza Shriver wrote to Henry Shriver about the arrival of soldiers of both armies and that "they are fighting in Gettysburg today, we can hear the firing distinctly the sound of the guns":

> Troops have been passing here from Monday night until this evening. They are all gone now, but a few stragglers. The Rebels came first, Monday night they came, between 11 & 12 and on Tuesday morning until 10 o'clock they were all gone, they were Stuart Cavalry. Their Generals had their Headquarters in our orchard. I tell you we were glad when they were gone, and then when our soldiers came, about 5—Thursday evening, you can imagine how glad we were to see them, The first came from Uniontown, (I think) and when we first saw them were coming over Wagers Hill. Kate and I ran down to Uncle [Jos?] to meet them, we told them we were so glad to see them, they were the staff officers finding a place for their General, we told them to bring him to our house, he was Gen Barns & had five staff officers, they all stayed here, and all slept out on the porch but the Gen, he slept up stairs, they were all real nice Gentlemen, all young fellows but the General. Kate and I tried our best to entertain them, I showed some of them your photograph.[78]

A Union army topographical engineer from Westminster wrote to his mother on July 2 about events at Gettysburg. His letter is notable on two counts—criticizing General Meade and intimating that it could fall afoul of military censors, even in the absence of systematic censorship during the Civil War:

> I have written you a line whenever I could do so and you must not be too anxious when you do not hear from Jim or myself, remember for the last two weeks we have both been working day and night and there has been no time for writing. I am down here now with the battalion guarding the wagon trains of the whole army about 4000 in number. I don't know whether that is engineering duty or not but suppose it is. I did not see Jim when I got to Taney Town yesterday but heard he was there and well. There is a battle going on at Gettysburg now (8 PM) and has been going on ever since 3 PM, but we get no news from there. They were fighting all day yesterday. I trust in God we may be successful for I think it will ruin the rebel army. I am sorry Meade had to take command just before such a battle and every thing scattered about as it was. I can't tell you any news for two reasons, in the first place *I don't know anything* and in the second this letter might be *gobbled up*. Now my dearest Mother you must not work yourself into a

nervous fever about Jim and myself but trust to an allwise Providence. I must say good night I must get a little sleep before going out to the pickets.[79]

He wrote again the next day, referring to the second day at Gettysburg, when the Union left flank repelled a furious Confederate attack on Little Roundtop:

I believe I told you there was a battle going on at Gettysburg it has also been going on this morning. We hear that Meade has beaten Lee in yesterday's fight very severely but there is no confirmation of the report yet. I have not seen any one from the front yet and can get no definite news. I have heard nothing from Jim yet but will write you just as soon as I do. I do not have time to write you any more today. I have a splitting headache for the first time in my life and I have got to go out in the hot sun. Give my best love to all the family. God bless you all.[80]

Frederick Shriver wrote to Henry Shriver on July 4 about a skirmish in Hanover, damage to Union Mills, and effects on residents:

We have suffered nothing except the damage that any large body of soldiers will make going through a neighborhood, I take it for granted you know we have had lots of soldiers here. I have returned from Hanover since Sis wrote to you. The people there were all safe, & in excellent spirits, though some of them had *very* narrow escapes. You must have learned from the papers of the cavalry fight there. The principal fighting was done in the town & there were men killed in every street in town. There was a Rebel battery about 800 yards from Winebrenners house which shot a shell into Winebrenners upstairs backporch door, which went through the old folks' room, from there to the girls, I think, from there to Dave & Peter's & from there down into the kitchen where the whole family were, & almost miraculously, none of them were hurt. You can tell Dave he will never sleep in his bed he left at home, again, it is shattered so it can never be used as a bed hereafter. The fight at Hanover was a complete surprise for all parties. At the time of the fight the streets were crowded with women & children who had to get out of the way as best they could & they embarrassed the Union forces not a little. The people had not time to get frightened—& they say the women could hardly be kept in the houses so anxious were they to see what was going on This does not apply to all for *some* were greatly scared—Mary W. tells me she peeped out of their door & saw two bodies of cavalry charge on each other right in front of their house She said as they came together they yelled & cursed each other awfully—

I forgot to say about them the shell that came into W.'s house did not explode. Uncle Henry also had a narrow escape from a shell It came down Balto Street from the woods way out towards Manchister, cut a large limb from one of the trees in front of his house, & then fell down, it did not explode either.[81]

Frederick provided an account of both armies passing through Union Mills on the same day:

> The rebels while here got into the Building & cut the best part out of a side of sole & greased their boots with the lard oil in the engine room, which with Charley, I believe was all the damage they done us. They did not get a great many horses in this immediate neighborhood, the people had run them all away. So much for the rebels, It is rather mixed up, I could not think of everything just as it happened—
>
> In the afternoon of the same day the rebels left, the advance of 1st division 5th Corps of the "Army of the Potomac" arrived on the Stone Bridge. They came from down the creek across by old Myers. They had glasses & were looking for the rebels. I went down as soon as I saw them & gave them all the information I could as to their whereabouts. They were soon joined by the neighbors who were overjoyed to see them. I don't think there *could* have been a more welcome sight to the neighborhood than the Union Army at that time—everybody had been perfectly disgusted with the rebels—Part of the division encamped on our & Uncle Wm's 1st old hills, the rest were around Sam Erbs & old [?]. On Thursday morn Gen. Sedgwick's whole corps passed they commenced at 2 o'clock & got by until 8 their near encamped on our & Uncle's meadows—Since the first appearance of the Union army there has been no scarcity of soldiers. This morning the road was lined with wounded soldiers returning from the Battle of Gettysburg. They were only slightly wounded ones. They don't seem to mind their wounds a bit though some must pain them a great deal—They all say the rebels are catching the d-l & I believe they are 800 rebel prisoners went by here yesterday & 2500 to-day.[82]

And offered advice about safeguarding the mills:

> Don't leave the mills for anything no matter whether rebels or union soldiers are as thick as grasshoppers. You can keep things safely much better by your presence than by locking up & leaving.[83]

Maryland cities and towns dealt as best they could with the passage of the rebel army. When V. A. Buckey, the "Mayor pro tem. of Cumberland" (acting in the absence of a federal commanding officer), surrendered his city to a rebel force, Confederate Col. G. W. Imboden acceded to the mayor's demand "that private persons and property, and the property of the state of Maryland, be respected":

> Our citizens then demanded of the rebel Colonel to know whether he intended to pay for private property taken from us by him for his use. He replied, that "he would either pay or receipt for it." He was also asked if he intended to allow his men to roam about unrestrained. He said, "assuredly not; and that any

John Singleton Mosby (standing, second left) terrorized Union troops assigned to fight Confederates in the Shenandoah Valley. Marylanders who served with him included two sons of Baltimore Police Marshal George P. Kane. MdHS.

violation of the terms of surrender, upon being made known to him, would be punished."

With this assurance, and having no means within reach to resist attack or defend the city, our citizens returned to the main street, and the rebel cavalry soon spread themselves over the town and were busy laying in supplies of muslin, calico, boots, shoes, etc., until about 11 o'clock a.m., when they departed by the same route the had entered.[84]

Baltimorean Charles Mayer, an engineer, described the losses sustained by Confederate Marylanders at Gettysburg and the appearance of Baltimore belle Hetty Cary in the Southern capital:

The Marylanders on the Rebel side suffered heavily in these last battles having asked for and been assigned the post of danger each day—They carried whatever they attacked, but paid for it with the lives of some of their best—among the dead are Col. Magruder (Mollie Hamilton's husband you know), one of the Lemons, Willie Murray & some others I don't remember. I supposed you know

[t]he young Miss Williamson is married—and that Hetty Cary is in Richmond engaged to the Rebel Genl Pegram.[85]

He made light of Baltimore's efforts at defense and extolled Lee's generalship:

Since the Rebels have been in Maryland & Penna, your native city has been in no enviable condition—the streets barricaded, martial law, long existing *in fact,* at last *proclaimed*—the citizens for the *third* time disarmed of everything like weapons or even parts thereof & the devil to pay generally. I wish you could see the barricades—they would give you cause for merriment for the balance of your days—The battles fought in front of Gettysburg for three days were very severe. But that [dam'd] Rebel Lee appears to have outgeneraled us again, for after inflicting terrible loss upon our troops, put down by the best informed at *1600 at least killed & wounded* (prisoners we know nothing of)—he quietly fell back taking his wounded, excepting nearly 500 too bad to be removed, with him, and quantities of horses & supplys.[86]

Walter G. Dunn, a New Jersey soldier lying wounded in the Jarvis U.S. General Hospital in Baltimore, described to his cousin Emma Randolph the behavior of loyal Baltimoreans in the face of invasion:

Yes, the loyalty of Baltimore has been rather dubious during this war but this last raid of Lees has much changed the tide of sentiment. When Baltimore was threatened, many who were thought to be disloyal, volunteered for its defence. A great many of its streets have been blockeadeded with large hogsheads filled with dirt and stone to prevent a rapid progress of cavalry. I like to sit in the front door of the hospital which opens into street and whistle at the secesh girls, as they promenade up and down the street, to tease them. A disloyal man has to be very carefull what he says now or down he goes. A few days ago while some prisoners were passing through on their way to Ft. McHenry, a citizen sung out three cheers for Jef. Davis, and the surgeon in charge of this hospital who was standing by knocked him down, a cavalryman saw him fall, run up and commenced cutting him over the head with his saber and would have killed him had not some one drug him out. Served him right; such a mans head should be severed from his body.[87]

On July 12 Frederick Shriver reported that:

The rebels did not get in the mill at all. Dave had locked it up & kept himself out of the way. Dozens of them rode their horses *up on t[he] steps* & tried to push open the door, but could not make it. They were in such a hurry when they went by here that they had not time to do anything of consequence, in the way of plundering—

Though fields were plundered:

> The oats on the field back of [Jas] Shuler's is entirely destroyed as is the fence between that & the clover field beyond. The Timothy this side of the grain field, fronting Shuler's is also destroyed. The grain was hardly disturbed both rebels & Union respected it. The second crop will hardly be good for anything. The whole *rebel horde* when they went up the Hanover road went through the creek at the bridges & on up through the meadow out at the red gate The meadow was all one mess after they had gone through—The raspberries as you seen were not disturbed by either party but the Cherry trees along the Hanover road present a woeful appearance. That is about the amt. of damage done us. We have got certificates from the Quartermaster putting our damages in all to about $100—which he told us then would be no difficulty in getting Uncle Wm lost a field of timothy & about 1000 rails by the Union forces for which he will never get anything. I tried to say a word from him to the quartermaster & almost got myself arrested in consequence—They though[t] I was one of his sons & were as saucy as could be but when they found out who I really was both Quartermaster & commissary were as good as pie—although we came out all night with the Union army, Charley & the other things the rebs took are a dead loss— Uncle Wm instead of losing by the rebs is in possession of a *first rate* horse which they left there & as he is not branded he cannot be taken from him. That horse will fully balance the losses he sustained by the Union troops so you will see he comes out without losing anything while we sustain a clear loss of about $200 in all.[88]

The Shrivers gave food to starving rebel troops:

> Father & Mother were down at Uncle's that night & got an introduction to Gen. Lee—When Gen. Barnes was at our house, Uncle was also up here talking to him—Uncle W. used his influence for us, but I believe the Confeds treated us just as they would have done, whether he had used it or not. I think the way we treated the rebels was of more use than all Uncle's influence. In fact we treated them entirely too well. I was for shutting up the house & not giving them anything at all but they all said they could not refuse giving to starving men, & and the rebs positively seemed to be so. They eat us out so clean that we had nothing for breakfast next morning.[89]

Rebecca D. Davis recorded a post-Gettysburg scene:

> Mr. Brown returned with us from church on Sunday last & remained till Monday. Gave me a sadly interesting account of his stop to the battle-field at Gettysburg. Many of the poor southerners only buried in a long trench a few inches 'neath the ground and parts of their bodies here & there exposed. Heart sickening scenes & sad that thus easily can men become hardened, few caring whether

or not the enemy be allowed even his narrow bed. Visited the hospital nearby &
found the wounded of both parties well cared for, at first their sufferings were
terrible, eighty almost lifeless Confeds were not found until five days after the
battle, there is little hope of their recovery. Through strategy sympathizers have
sent much to the poor prisoners.[90]

By 1863, Copperheads, also known as the Northern Peace Democrats, advocated
a negotiated peace with the Confederacy. Though they were not visible in Maryland, a September letter from Salisbury, in Wicomico County, implied a presence
nonetheless:

> I heard this evening that the Copperheads of the surrounding county are go-
> ing to organize a guerilla band to harass the Union population. I don't know
> whether the report is true, but if it is, I want you to enlist the best cavalry com-
> pany near you, and order it home to oppose them. It is doubtful though if your
> order would have any effect, isn't it? But seriously if there is such an organization
> being raised, men ought to be ordered here to protect the loyal people, for Cop-
> perheads are equal to anything evil.[91]

Six weeks after Gettysburg a Shriver visited the battlefield:

> I felt very bad in viewing the places of internment of the killed; the reflection
> could but force itself on my mind of the wickedness of a war which, brought
> together in deadly conflict relatives brothers and neighbors.—
>   About the rockey recesses of the Round Top can yet be found the remains
> of Rebel sharpshooters which have never been buried, laying, with their bones
> bleaching in the sun, where they had fallen.

And witnessed a grisly scene:

> a Boston Lady on the field, who with a stone smashed the teeth out of a rebel
> skull to take home as relics, and showing as plainly as manners could, that even
> to the bones of a Rebel she could not show the decency of good breeding. Re-
> ally I hardly know which I dislike the most a Rebel or a whining canting Yankee
> abolitionist.[92]

1864

Senator Lot M. Morrill of Maine related a story to John Nicolay, one of Lincoln's secretaries, about a Maryland woman seeking her son's release from a Union prison:

> I remember that at one time when I went into the room to President Lincoln,
> there were two women from Baltimore there who had come to try to obtain the
> release and parole of a prisoner of war who had been captured, and was then

confined at Point Lookout. One of them was the mother of the young rebel, and after detailing his alleged sufferings, wound up her sympathetic appeals with the usual *finale* of such interviews, a copious shower of tears. At this point the president, who had patiently listened to the recital, asked casually when and how the boy had gone into the confederate service? The mother with evident pride, quickly responded with the whole history; he had gone south early in the war, served in such and such campaigns, made such and such marches, and survived such and such battles.

"And now that he is taken prisoner, *it is the first time,* probably, that you have ever shed tears over what your boy has done?" asked the President with emphasis.

The question was so direct, and so completely described the true situation of affairs that the woman could frame no equivocation She sat dumb, and visibly convicted of her secession sympathies, by the very simple inquiry.

"Good morning Madam," said the President "I can do nothing for your boy today."[93]

In May, a friend in Gordonsville, Virginia, offered to help Gen. George H. Steuart find his son William, who was missing and most likely wounded on May 12 at the Mule Shoe at Spotsylvania Court House, during Grant's Overland Campaign:

> Permit me to introduce to you my friend Gen. G. H. Steuart of Md. He, attended by my servant, is in search of his son W.J. Steuart, Esq.—who was seriously wounded in the battle of Thursday last.[94]

After William Steuart was found with a hip wound and sent to Guinea Station, an Officer's hospital on 10th Street in Richmond, the friend wrote to his father:

> Your note to Major Boyle was duly rec'd and relieved us of a load of anxiety and the highest gratification that you had found William readily and that he was dong well. I trust he may soon be able to come with you to Hilton where you know he will be more quiet & have access to many country comforts not easily attained in the city at this time. Present to him my sympathy & sincere regards. Maj Boyle would not permit Baker to go in persuit of you, as it turned out to be unnecessary, and he returned with the waggons to the army.
>
> There was a battle yesterday and I am all anxiety conserning the safety of my dear boys. Baker brought off the guards two horses and Williams safely they are all with me. Mrs. N. will send you a Bucket of Butter by Express tomorrow.[95]

William Steuart died a few days later. A friend at the University of Virginia sent his father a note:

> You will not charge me, I trust, with intruding on the sacredness of your grief, if I cannot help giving expression to my deep, heartfelt sympathy with your great sorrow. You have sacrificed so much for the righteous cause already, that I know

Life became difficult for Gen. George H. Steuart after he fled Baltimore for the Confederate army. His home at Union Square was seized by the Union army, and his son died of battle wounds in May 1864. MdHS.

you will present this last and most precious offering also with the fortitude of your character and the submission of a Christian. Still, I know how valuable this son of yours had been to your interests, how dear to your heart, and I cannot tell you, with what deep and sincere grief I heard of your terrible loss.[96]

Mrs. H. S. Kettlewell, of 42 North Calvert Street in Baltimore, sought Bishop Whittingham's assistance in seeing her husband, who was in the Confederacy. She asked the Bishop to "use your interest which I should think would be the best I could have with Mr. Lincoln, whom I wish to deliver the letter to in person":

> I called twice at your residence this week, hoping to see you but you were engaged. The object of my visit was to beg you to write as powerfully as you could in my behalf to President Lincoln; begging him to allow myself and children to go south to join my husband as soon as it will be possible for us to get there and to be allowed to take whatever cloathing we have I have my British pass and have never at any time been disloyal to this government either in word or deed. My husband who is Southern in his feelings left me soon after the war broke out, and I have since been struggling hard to support my children by teaching.[97]

Mrs. Kettlewell wrote Whittingham three months later to report that she had decided to remain in Baltimore, "though hard be the conflict," and that she would accept a position as a governess if a home could be found for her children, wondering—"cannot they be admitted to the Church Home, through your powerful influence, where they would be under religious training and in a safe and respectful asylum."[98]

Confederate Gen. Jubal Early's plan to strike at Washington from Maryland soil would lead to the Battle of Monocacy, just below Frederick. General Lee wrote to Jefferson Davis about another objective of Early's foray into Maryland:

> Great benefit might be drawn from the release of our prisoners at Point Lookout if it can be accomplished. The number of men employed for this purpose would necessarily be small, as the whole would have to be transported secretly across the Potomac where it is very broad, the means of doing which must first be procured. I can devote to this purpose the whole of the Marylanders of this army, which would afford a sufficient number of men of excellent material and much experience, but I am at a loss where to find a proper leader. As he would command Maryland troops and operate upon Maryland soil it would be well that he should be a Marylander. Of those connected with this army I consider Col Bradley T. Johnson the most suitable. He is bold & intelligent, ardent & true, and yet I am unable to say whether he possesses all the requisite qualities. Everything in an expedition of the kind would depend upon the leader. I have understood that most of the garrison at Point Lookout was composed of negroes. I should suppose that the commander of such troops would be poor & feeble.

A stubborn resistance, therefore, may not reasonably be expected. By taking a company of the Maryland artillery, armed as infantry, the dismounted cavalry and their infantry organization, as many men would be supplied as transportation could be procured for. By throwing them suddenly on the beach with some concert of action among the prisoners, I think the guard might be overpowered, the prisoners liberated & organized, and marched immediately on the route to Washington.[99]

On June 24, W. W. Glenn, worried that Gen. Lew Wallace, now commanding the Maryland Department, might arrest him, fled Baltimore for New York, arriving in "Brattelboro" (presumably Vermont) on July 1. When Glenn learned that Early was moving into Maryland toward Washington—with cavalry strikes in Baltimore County that again alarmed Baltimore City—he criticized the government's overreaction. Glenn was overly optimistic, however, about Early's chances of taking Baltimore:

Cannot make out what is doing in Maryland. Am satisfied that the invading force is immensely overestimated. Tom Buckler & I went aboard restless with Travers & Louisa & Hatty to take an afternoon's sail & wait for further news. Went up to Oyster Bay & anchored.[100] Early seems to have abandoned his attempt on Baltimore. He could have captured it without firing a gun. The greatest panic prevailed last Saturday & Sunday after Wallace's defeat at the Monocacy (River, south of Frederick). The City Council or rather some of its members met and determined to surrender. The Military Authorities prepared to evacuate. Government stores were taken from warehouse & piled in vacant lots to be fired. Valuables from banks have been removed to steamers. Everyone was busy for two days packing. Police officers seized gentlemen in the street & put them to work.[101]

Mary Winebrenner told beau Henry Shriver of rebel cavalry movements:

My own dear Wirt, I wonder what you are doing and thinking of this morning. This morning before I was out of bed, John [Forney] from Gettysburg came with his horses saying the rebels were near Gettysburg. He said you hear everything—some say they are not across the river, others, the rebels will be in your midst in a few hours. Just now mother called me to see the numbers of horses, the farmers were taking away. Mamie's mother sent for her this morning, so she had to leave but she did not want to go at all. The stores are all closed and everything sent off. Cousin Jacob came from Waynesboro, on Monday, to Gettysburg with his horses and leathers and came to Hanover Tuesday. No one is doing anything. A little while ago, a Mr. Leuse with two horses came up short, saying there was three thousand rebel cavalry at Union Mills.

Two rare photographs of the Union army passing through Frederick in pursuit of the Confederates, either in September 1862 or July 1864. B'nai B'rith International, Washington, D.C.

Mary worried about his safety:

> Dear Wirt, you escaped the draft, did you not? Mother was reading yesterday who were drafted but no Shrivers were among the number, Oh I am so thankful and glad. If only the rebels don't come now, and destroy things for us. It was reported yesterday evening that there was a proclamation issued, for twelve thousand militia, to protect the capitol. I can't imagine where all these reports originate from. People are so excited every report they believe. They don't take time to considerate if it could be so.[102]

From July 5 to 9, Union soldier William H. James recorded descriptions of the Battle of Monocacy (Fanny was most likely his wife):

> July 5: Received a visit this afternoon from Lottie, Fanny and Freddie, obtained a leave of abscense and took supper with them at Mrs. Hanzsche's. Upon return to camp found the regiment packing up; orders having been received to that effect. Hard tack and forty rounds of ammunition issued to each man and pieces loaded. Marched down to the station about dark, and went aboard of cars, loaded the stores, and started up the road about eleven o'clock.
>
> July 6: About 8 o'clock this morning arrived at Monocacy Bridge, disembarked on the east side of the river, and marched on to a low piece of ground a short distance south of the railroad where we spent the day in the broiling sun.

July 7: This morning two or three companies of our regiment sent out on picket duty, rebels reported as being near. About one o'clock regiment ordered out, rebels reported coming. Alarm soon over, regiment ordered back, but kept in lines balance of the day. Late in the afternoon heard artillery firing very distinctly. By order of Col. Landstreet took a detail of four men to Genl. Wallace, found the Genl. on a high ridge overlooking the beautiful valley in which Frederick, is situated, viewing the artillery firing through a glass, which appeared to me to be five miles distant.

July 9: We were marched up the road at a very fast gait, too fast indeed for comfort, as the weather was intensely hot, though thanks to the high ridge and the trees on our right, we were protected from the scorching rays of the sun. After we had gone about a mile and a half up the river, we were marched across a field and down to what appeared to be an old mill-race, though it was much wider and was evidently a natural formation. Into this old race our company was posted in groups of from four to six, and were commanded to keep perfectly quiet and a sharp lookout for rebels, as the position our company occupied gave them complete command of a ford which it was thought the rebels would be likely to avail themselves of, in order to turn the right of our army which occupied the position around the railroad bridge and where it was determined to give the rebels battle.[103]

John W. Garrett of the B&O Railroad received a copy of a message from General Wallace, commanding Union forces at Monocacy, relating his efforts to impede the rebel advance east toward Washington and Baltimore:

> I have the honor to inform you that the following despatch has just been rec'd from Maj Genl Wallace at the Monocacy. "a battle now taking place at Frederick with fair chance to whip the enemy. I shall hold this bridge. Hurry up the veterans just arrived with all despatch, let them all come at once if possible. Inform Mr. Garrett of my purpose as to the bridge."[104]

William James described the Union retreat:

> I suppose that what tended most to make me believe that it was only a change of position, was the orderly manner in which the retreat was conducted. I always supposed that when an army was defeated in battle, and a retreat ensues, that there was great disorder, the men running off as fast as they could, but in this case it was not so.

> We had not gone many miles down the road before I commenced to lag behind, this was owing to my feet having become very sore from the loss of my stockings, the army shoes which I was wearing at the time being much larger than I had been accustomed to, in the abscence of any stockings chafed my feet a great deal.

The retreat continued on Saturday, July 9, through New Market, Maryland, where

> some of the citizens kindly set out buckets and pans of fresh water for our wearied men as we passed through which was very acceptable indeed.

Two days later, when his unit arrived in Baltimore, he briefly lost track of his regiment when he went home:

> Upon my arrival at home I shaved, took a bath and put on clean clothes and after a few hours rest was all most myself again.
>
> In the afternoon I ascertained that the regiment were encamped at Greenwood out Gay st. and joined them that evening, where I was gladly welcomed back by Capt. Courtney and my comrades who had feared that I had been gobbled up by the rebels.[105]

May Stevens—apparently sent to live with her aunt and uncle in West Chester, near Philadelphia, perhaps until any danger to Baltimore passed—wrote to her mother in Cambridge:

> Both Uncle and Aunt were afraid to let me go down to Baltimore today, thinking you would feel easier if I were here. I would not be at all afraid to be in Baltimore, but I don't like the ride down, I should have to go from here and all the

way alone—you know that road is used for transporting troops, and it would be unpleasant for me, besides, there might be some accident; I do indeed wish when I leave home, the Rebels would stay at home, they interfere with my plans every year.

I am anxious to get down to Baltimore and if I could only have gotten down before I should not mind being there. I have just been helping Aunt to make Maryland biscuits do you make them up stiff or work them soft—or the other way?

She urged her mother to be steadfast:

I want to be with you to help you put a bold face on for the sake of the *secesh*. I don't suppose there is any danger in Cambridge only it is disagreeable. I shall not go down to Baltimore until it gets quiet there.[106]

Another letter related the situation in Baltimore:

This has been quite an exciting day with us, and you folks also I presume, as it is likely you are well posted as to movements around you if the Rebs do not get down upon you it is likely our troops will, so you must look out for the live stock. Wallace made a brave fight yesterday, but was overpowered and his troops much cut up and scattered but they saved Hunter's train over two hundred wagons; they got to Ellicott's Mills last night and came down Pratt st. this afternoon. Report says the Rebs are at Popular Spring to day—I don't think they will attempt Balto. Washington is their aim. They have pressed some 2000 horses here and all the Negros and armed them and it is said they are pressing White men also, Johnny Palmer & most all the young men I know have Joined companies. I am in the *home guard,* for the present, but don't know how soon I may leave for the front. George Gilpin & some others started for Phila to day—the Rebs were getting most too near. I have some doubts as to whether this will go through—communications are very uncertain nowadays—the Rebs have plenty of fresh Horses now and their Cavalry will mostly likely look after the Bridge especially at Laurel. It is said a small squad were at Reisterstown this morning which is 18 miles from Balt. Our citizens are very cool—and the Sympathizers are the most alarmed at the approach of *their* friends would like very much to hear from you & hope we may tomorrow through one source or another.

It seems strange to see armed men (citizens) some mounted passing through the streets thousands of Cattle passed our house this morn between 4 & 5 o'clock. I told Harriet then the Rebs were coming—a sure sign. The Cattle were in a run, would not be surprised if there was a fight within 5 miles of you tomorrow and if I had a good horse I would go up—but Martial Law is in force here now & you have to have a pass to leave the City now.[107]

An officer on General Wallace's staff in Baltimore reported on efforts there to raise additional troops during Early's assault to the west:

I have the honor to report that matters are progressing favorably here. The Union Leagues are forming companies, and as fast as the companies are reported I send the captain a copy of the circular herewith inclosed, so as to prepare them for a call. They seem pleased with it. I think they will raise twelve or fifteen companies. They prefer battalion organizations, of four companies, to select their own field officers, and say there will be no great objection to your appointing the field officers. I have issued a special order to-night to arrest all officers in this city without authority. Copy of the special order is inclosed for your information. It is said there are a great many such officers in town.[108]

At 11:40 p.m. on July 9, Wallace reported a retreat:

I fought the enemy at Frederick Junction from 9 a. m. till 5 p. m., when they overwhelmed me with numbers. I am retreating with a foot-sore, battered, and half-demoralized column. Forces of the enemy at least 20,000. They do not seem to be pursuing. You will have to use every exertion to save Baltimore and Washington. Colonel Seward, son of the Secretary, is wounded, and is a prisoner. Brigadier-General Tyler is a prisoner. I think the troops of the Sixth Corps fought magnificently. I was totally overwhelmed by a force from the direction of Harper's Ferry arriving during the battle. Two fresh regiments of the Sixth Corps are covering my retreat. I shall try to get to Baltimore.[109]

May Stevens wrote to her mother again on July 12:

I beg you don't feel at all uneasy about me I am perfectly safe it is impossible for the Rebels to cross the Susquehanna and even if they could there is nothing to tempt them in W. Chester when Phila is so near. I was afraid you would be feel worried when you found the communication between Baltimore and Phila was cut but you must not it will all be fine soon and they will I hope be sent back if not captured.

She referred to the Confederate incursion at Monocacy and wrote that "I am thankful now that our home is on the Eastern Shore":

I suppose all those renegade Marylanders are with the troops ravaging their native state my dear State—it seems hard after all her troubles she should be subjected to *this*—think Cambridge will be visited as it was two years ago by *"the boys"*—Please write me if any of my friends were with Wallace in the battle.[110]

On July 16, Rebecca Davis began recording a series of impressions of the Monocacy campaign:

We heard many conflicting rumors of the Confederates. They had certainly crossed into Maryland, some said 7,000 strong, others 35,000 or more. Baltimore & Washington were expecting an attack & every effort made for the defense of the cities. Gen. Wallace had been defeated & obliged to withdraw to Balto. & no troops dared budge to encounter the *terrible rebels*. Secesh were jubilant, and Unions dreading they knew scarcely what.

Horses were hidden and

> hams were concealed in the garret, leaving a little musty bacon scattered through the meat-house, sugar & bag of coffee in wardrobe, wool in the cellar.

No Confederates were spotted on Sunday or Monday, but

> Tuesday morning I arose and as I glanced from the window spied several "grey-backs" dashing up the road. "They are coming, they are coming," was the cry, poor Ma, the picture of war proclaiming our ruin & shocked that we could smile. Such rapid toilettes as were completed, & I rushed foremost to find our portico crowed with hungry lambs (as such they came). Short cakes were soon ready, which with meat, milk and apples the poor fellows seemed heartily to enjoy. This troop of cavalry (2,000) were under Gen. Bradley Johnson, principally Mary-landers, among them found Messrs. Sam Lyons, Elder, Emory, Ned Bracco & in the rear guard Eddie Thompson & Harrie Dorsey, both handsome but the former is flourishing such long locks & so extensive a beard we scarcely recog-nized him.

Bradley Johnson's two thousand–strong cavalry detachment was in the area; most were Marylanders, of whom she knew a few. The following day fifty more men ar-rived, under Captain Burke of Harry Gilmor's cavalry unit, who:

> demanded feed for their horses & breakfast; but they were very gentlemanly & polite. The Captain made the men leave the fields, over which they were searching for horses, Pa having told him how severely he had suffered with his from their raid last summer & an infectious disease, indeed had none worth tak-ing. With them were four Federal prisoners captured on a train at Gunpowder bridge, which they had burned the previous day, & who were treated by them with every courtesy & deference, invited into breakfast &c.

Two prisoners were released:

> Two of them having been sick and promising they were returning home to resign were paroled here & as the Confeds left they shook hands, hoping they would reach home safely and regretting their trouble. The two Feds here paroled, were terribly scared & anxious to get into Federal lines, so Pa at the risk of losing his horse, sent them to Ellicotts Mills, one borrowed a linen coat & Yankee-like did not return it. Begged the driver to say they were rebels.

That afternoon the Davis family had a visit from Harry Gilmor, fresh from a cavalry raid around Baltimore:

Confederate army Capt. Harry Gilmor raised the Second Maryland cavalry battalion that operated behind Union lines. Imprisoned briefly in Fort McHenry early in the war, his destructive cavalry "ride around Baltimore" during the Monocacy campaign in July 1864 struck terror in the hearts of Baltimoreans. His rogue unit then played a prominent role in the burning of Chambersburg, Pennsylvania. Union forces captured him in February 1864.

Between 1 & 2 P.M. a cloud of dust announced another body approaching & soon Major Harry Gilmor and 100 men were upon us for dinner. At the sight of a plate of meat & bread they pitched en masse pell mell at me, grabbing in the best humor while I implored for more order, but they termed it too rare a sight not to have a little fun. Some of the officers begged us to give them some music and at Mr. Wilson's request Mary & I sang "Annie of the Vale." Almost forgot to be embarrassed, they were so free and easy, yet the idea of our tuning up our faint pipes for Major Gilmor & co. strikes me now as laughable in the extreme. The Major gave me a button from his coat, and we could bestow upon the importunate a no more lasting token than a rosebud.

A rebel friend appeared:

Thursday morning to my surprise up dashed Jimmie Williams with several Rebs. He had been taken prisoner by some Yankees in Confed uniform and deprived of horse, arms & his wife's photograph taken from his pockets & wantonly torn into pieces. Watching his opportunity after a day's detention he effected his escape, secured a horse & was anxious to overtake his command, desired me to write to Emily. These were the last of our visitors, a most independent set, in highest spirits, easy and affable in their manners and as one of the Federal officers here said to me he said "in every look, word & gesture from the highest to the lowest in rank, a determination that must carry success with it."

Davis described Early's retreat:

We have been virtually in Dixieland for several days, all communication cut with Baltimore and Washington, no mail and entirely at the mercy of the Rebels. Indeed we thought the city being so defenceless they might take Washington & bring the war upon us; but the immense force besieging the capital dwindled down to 500 men, only making a diversion while Gen. Early with all his booty safely recrossed the Potomac, to the great humiliation of the Federals.[111]

Benjamin Kirkwood avoided Monocacy but was in the defensive lines at Fort Sumner around Washington:

I am in very good health but still troubled a little yet with the Diarhoea but feell very well other ways. We left Camp Destribution last Monday and marched to the defence of the Capital where we have been ever since. There was about 1500 left there for the defence of Washington. We have not had no engagement yet with the rebs as the 6th Corps participated and kept us out of it I reckon there is quite an excitement in the neighborhood but I think the trouble is not over yet as the news is here that Lee is at Mannasses junction about a hundred thousand men with the intention of taking this place by storm.[112]

A letter in late July had what sounded like a reaction in Baltimore to the Monocacy campaign:

Grandma, and in fact all knew you would wonder how we succeeded in ridding ourselves of the Rebs who have recently visited us. Well *we* did nothing to get rid of them they left after having done what damage to property they could without entering our city—of course all damage was done to property—outside of its limits—we had no troops stationed here at all, a few came from the Potomac army and succeeded in holding them in check at 'Monococy' a little town west of our city; they (the 'rebs') could have entered had they seen fit, could not have stayed long but of course done immense damage to our inhabitence in different ways, They are now far enough off and I hope they will remain away for ever we care but little for their friendly visits; Mother has been troubled dreadfully by with a sore foot for some time back it does not seem to improve in the least, has opened in two or three places. I hope her trip to the country will improve it. I presume it is from overheating her blood, that started it.[113]

Early's forces had occupied Hagerstown and Frederick and, as retribution for David Hunter's destruction in the Shenandoah Valley, threatened to burn both towns if they failed to pay ransoms of $20,000 and $200,000, respectively. They paid. In August, a rebel force under Gen. John McCausland torched Chambersburg, Pennsylvania, when it failed to pay a $50,000 ransom. Rebecca Davis commented:

> We worshipped unmolested, feeling grateful that in these times of peril we were still privileged to repair to the House of God. The Confeds did not pay us a visit, but have carried fire & sword into Penna., having demanded a large sum of money from the citizens of Chambersburg, which they failed to pay, the town was fired by Gen. Early's order, and many poor creatures are now homeless and destitute. Much do I deplore this act by them & wish they could have refrained from following similar examples set them.[114]

A week later Davis mourned the death of "Ginny Griffin, a classmate from Mrs. Porter's school":

> Last Friday she ate many cucumbers, was taken that night with bilious dysentery, the extreme heat of the weather increased her disease, which baffled all remedies taken and so suddenly has snatched her from our midst.[115]

The Reverend Arthur C. Coxe, former rector of Grace Episcopal Church in Baltimore, wrote to the bishop from East Hampton, Long Island, expressing concern about St. James School in Hagerstown and its head, Rev. John Kerfoot, who with another school official had been captured by Confederates hoping to exchange them for a clergyman held in Virginia:

> What a strange turn in affairs! Dear St. James'—momentarily overcome by the rebels, & Kerfoot in Connecticut; no—in captivity! Can it be that Lincoln will suffer him to be carried into Rebel-dom? I think your influence will carry the day, in his favor. Poor, dear fellow! He has had his share of the war's troubles and alarms.[116]

Baltimorean William F. Gordon Jr., in confinement for seven months, appealed to Lincoln over his sentence as a Confederate spy, for which he has

> been sentenced to be shot to death with musketry on the 20th of this month. This sentence subject to your approval . . . as the Father, the lover of justice, and as the Head of a great nation—whose chief virtue should be "magnanimity to the fallen"—I appeal to you for Executive justice confidently hoping for your reversal of the sentence against me.[117]

In September, Daniel Thomas railed against Gen. William Sherman's seizure of Atlanta, a crippling blow to the Confederacy:

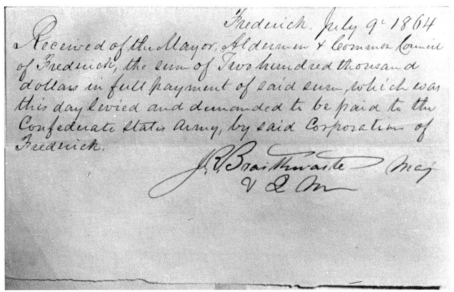

The Confederate army, seeking vengeance against Northern cities for the Union army's destruction in the Shenandoah Valley, vowed to put Hagerstown and Frederick to the torch unless they paid hefty ransoms. This receipt for $200,000 spared Frederick. Chambersburg, Pennsylvania, refused to pay and was burned. Courtesy of the Historical Society of Frederick County, Maryland.

Persons were very anxious to know whether the Bishop's most odious prayers giving thanks for the capture of Atlanta would be used to day in the churches, and many did not go to church for fear of hearing them. They were not used at my church, not at Emanuel. They are the *worst* he has prepared yet.[118]

From Port Tobacco Rev. Lemuel Wilmer wrote to Bishop Whittingham complaining of the busy contraband traffic through southern Maryland, where "the mails and stages instead of being in the hands of invalid soldiers still remain in the hands of those who thrive in contraband trade":

I go tomorrow, if Providence permits, to visit some troops lately arrived. For a considerable time the county has been left to riot in unfaithfulness. What infatuation! Could not fresh troops drill here, and at the same time crush out this immense contraband trade? But it is the Lord's day: other thoughts must have the ascendancy. Expecting to pass tomorrow by a wayside office, it is my intention to drop this—all offices are uncertain and will be, until there is an entire renovation. It is vain to think of palliatives, when every thing here is gangrened.[119]

William James's enlistment expired on September 23:

Our time of enlistment being out today we struck our tents early this morning, and left in a train of cars about ten o'clock this morning for Balto. where we arrived at three o'clock, having been absent just nine weeks.[120]

In October, Alban G. Thomas, a soldier in the reserve corps in Sandy Spring, was raised from his bed at midnight by a squad of rebels, who threatened to hang him if he did not surrender the key to his store:

> Before we knew it 11 Rebs had surrounded us and to surrender was the only alternative to being shot. They captured Uncle A's arms but I threw mine behind a goods Box and he only found a few chesnuts in my pockets which I *gave* the *sneak*.
>
> We were all so closely watched, that it was impossible to get off. Again the Key was demanded: they soon found out I was the clerk that had left the door so they pitched into me. Arthur had hid they key so I could not produce it but I could not satisfy them that I hadent it, so they took me up into my room and searched it but *nary key*. he took my fine boots and brought one down again to the Captain *"Bowie"* who seized a hold of my arm and ordered a man to take hold of the other side and sent a third to his horse and got a Rope & said he could get the Key, but [?] time he took me around in the back yard and threatened to *hang this,* but I told him *hanging* would not get it out of me, he then asked where he could get in & I told him there were some windows in the back side that were not very strong so with the aid of Uncle Gid's axe the end window on the N. side was opened then the door from the inside. We were all ordered in then and after getting lighted up (they had a candle) a confiscation of goods ensued. it is hardly worthwhile to say what kind of goods they took as they got a little of every thing and a goodeal of *somethings*.

The rebels stole items suggesting that a wedding was pending. Seventeen neighborhood men, including Thomas, formed a posse that ambushed the sleeping Confederates in Rockville, giving rise to the "Battle of Ricketts Ford":

> John fired a second time at the one on John Osburn's horse knocking him off and shoot the horses eye out, then Capt. Bowie took it up and shot at John several times and just as he was passing by Old Ent who was concealed behind a pine bush let him have a whole load of buck shot in the face & upper part of the head which knocked him sky high (the gun roared like a *cannon*).

Captain Bowie's body was put in a coffin and sent to his father in Prince George's County.[121]

The Reverend Alexander Falk, a Prussian native and professor at St. James College, also suffered at the hands of marauding rebels, noting that "during this war the college lost more than ½ of its students" and described the war's personal toll:

The incursions of the rebels also inflicted losses on me. Last year they took nearly all my linen, and—insignificant as the matter seems to be—the high prices of every thing and the diminution of my salary made me feel this loss severely. This year they robbed me of my watch, and I have not yet been able to replace it. I preached as a missionary for the last years alternately in Clearspring and Hancock. The small remuneration, I received for it, amounted to not much more, than to pay my expenses.[122]

The Confederate threat to Baltimore during the summer Monocacy campaign had prompted a July 11 Baltimore City Council resolution appropriating $100,000 for a "Defense Committee," which in October reported its expenses and requested reimbursement:

Cash paid expenses of the Citizen Guards	$2401.89
Cash paid for relief of families of members of the Guards	1165.
Cash paid expenses incident to the entrenchments in the streets	969.32
Cash paid expenses organizing the colored militia under Genl Wallace's order	4011.68
Cash paid for labor on the Barricades of 1863 under resolution Of 26th July	1598.17
Cash paid sundry expenses of the Committee, clerk hire, &c.	212.79
	$10,358.85[123]

In November, the provost marshal in Baltimore wrote from Relay House about rebel activity along the Potomac River:

Rumors coming down the Rail Road indicate that several bodies of Rebel Cavalry crossed the Potomac above Williamsport on yesterday or the day before: the report is that they crossed at Cherry Run and Hancock. I have heard nothing officially of these movements or of the skirmish said to have taken place yesterday in Loudon County opposite the Point of Rocks.[124]

The currents of life continued in Baltimore that autumn, when Dr. La Croix advertised his new book:

A Physiological View of Marriage—Consisting nearly 200 pages, and the fine Plates and Engravings of the Anatomy of the Human Organs in a state of Health and Disease, with a Treatise on Early Errors, its Deplorable Consequences upon the Mind and Body, with the Author's Plan of Treatment—the only rational and successful mode of cure, as shown by the reports of cases treated. A truthful adviser to the married, and those contemplating marriage, who entertain doubts of their physical condition, [?] free of postage to any address, on receipt of 75 cents, in stamps or postal currency, by addressing Dr. La Croix, No. 81 Maiden Lane, Albany, New York.

Marylanders were constantly told be vigilant about rebel spies. Here a Baltimore crowd gathered to watch the arrest of an alleged spy, at the corner of Orange Alley and North Street. Pratt Lib.

The author may be consulted upon any of the diseases upon which his book treats either personally or by mail, and medicine sent to any part of the world.[125]

1865

Daniel Thomas welcomed soldiers from the Confederate Army who were returning to Baltimore, which

> for the last few days has resumed a good deal of its old looks; so many of *our boys* have come back; you have no difficulty in distinguishing even those with whom you have no acquaintance, by their healthy sunburnt faces. I really cannot describe the emotions with which I greet the return of these splendid fellows, to many of whom I was so strongly attached, and who with all their old qualities retained come back so vastly ennobled by the trying events of their four years campaign. If all they went through would not make *men* of them their cases were indeed hopeless. Carvel Hall told me that when he was with Jackson in the valley he fought the enemy *seventeen consecutive days,* during which time he had seen

men (*gentlemen*) whose toe nails had dropped off from the incessant marching. Yet still they marched and fought. Though pleasant in one sense, yet in another it is very sad to see these poor fellows come back to begin life all over again, with the great blight of their failure weighing upon them. They bear it very well however, although it is very evident that beneath the surface there is a great sorrow rankling into their very hearts core.[126]

part three

Many Marylanders found some measure of redemption in October 1864 when, by a slim margin, voters embraced a new state constitution declaring freedom for more than eighty thousand slaves in their state. Though born at the ballot box six months before the end of the Civil War, the conditions that helped bring emancipation to Maryland had been gestating for decades.

Tobacco, that labor-intensive crop that thrived in the warm climate and rich soil of southern Maryland and the Eastern Shore, had long been the bedrock of Maryland slavery. However, years of overfertilization and lack of crop rotation had devastated soil and harvest. The response of Maryland planters, hiring free labor for seasonal crops such as wheat, grain, and cereals, had undermined slavery more insidiously than any outraged petition from abolitionists.[1]

Black Marylanders had much to do with winning their freedom. Beginning in 1861, slaves found sanctuary in two new places: federal army camps and, in the spring of 1862, the newly emancipated nation's capital. Starting in 1863 more than 8,700 black men from Maryland, free and slave, would join the United States Bureau of Colored Troops, to fight for cause and country alongside whites in the Union army.[2]

Since 1776, life had grown progressively worse for Maryland blacks. That year they could vote in House elections but by 1810 were disenfranchised by a Maryland legislature terrified of slave insurrection. Lawmakers managed to keep free blacks in a de facto bondage that could send them into slavery for such capricious reasons as being labeled runaways or being used to settle the debts of their former owners.[3]

Tobacco's decline during the first half of the nineteenth century meant fewer slaves. The free black population grew; slavery became concentrated in fewer areas and smaller numbers. "The most common slaveholding in Maryland in 1860 was one slave; half the slaveholders owned fewer than three slaves, three-fourths fewer than eight, and 90 percent fewer than fifteen slaves," wrote Barbara J. Fields. "A typical slaveholding in Maryland cannot have included both parties to a slave marriage, let alone all members of an immediate family." Owners mixed charity with frugality, freeing slaves or stipulating in newspaper advertisements and wills that they could not be sold outside of Maryland. But others unable to afford more than a few slaves tore families apart by selling husbands and wives, parents and children to different owners. Nonetheless, at the outbreak of the Civil War, many Marylanders who believed slavery constitutionally permissible by 1861 saw no profit in it. Others objected on moral grounds.[4]

Into this volatile mix marched the Union army. By mid-1861, slaveholders were confronting military authorities in Maryland over the flow of slaves, or "contraband," into military camps. Lincoln, wary of alienating Unionist Maryland slave-

Liberation

holders and their politician advocates, ordered commanders to repatriate escaped slaves. Compliance became a function of a commander's caprice, driven by the need for laborers or information about enemy activity, moral objections, or revulsion at the bad behavior of angry masters at camp gates. The president, having recognized the limited nature of tactics such as contraband policy, confiscation, and martial law to eliminate slavery in the border slave states, began pressing his strategy of gradual, compensated emancipation—though war would have to earn what politics could not.

Later in 1861 the Republican Congress began laying the foundation for blacks to join the Union army. In August came the First Confiscation Act, which permitted the seizure of property supporting the rebellion. In July 1862, the Second Confiscation Act and the Militia Act mandated freedom for slaves whose owners engaged in or assisted the rebellion and allowed black men to serve in the U.S. military and naval services. Many preferred the army to a life of actual or de facto slavery.[5]

In July 1863, the War Department authorized recruitment of black troops from Maryland for the new United States Colored Troops. (Gen. Robert Schenck, impressed by the efforts of four thousand free and enslaved blacks to fortify Baltimore against a possible rebel strike during Lee's Gettysburg campaign, had urged Lincoln to enlist black men in Maryland.) Col. William Birney, given charge of the effort, by month's end had raided Baltimore slave jails and liberated recruits for what would become six regiments for the cause. Birney, son of a black abolitionist, oversaw a vigorous recruitment campaign that infuriated Maryland slave owners and politicians. They complained that their slaves were enticed to enlist without the necessary permission of their masters and even kidnapped into the army by recruiting parties that plied the Patuxent River and other tributaries of the Chesapeake Bay.[6]

Lincoln and Maryland Unionists could not permit black recruitment to undermine the fealty of loyal slave owners. In the autumn of 1863, with the need for troops mounting as Grant pressed south amid growing losses, Lincoln declared that slaves of loyal masters were not to be recruited *"unless the necessity is urgent."* Following a brief recruitment suspension to clarify policies with state officials, in early October military authorities announced that Maryland slaves could enlist with the permission of their masters, who would receive federal compensation if deemed loyal. In November, Washington authorized the enlistment of all able-bodied black men; in March 1864, all black males, free or slave, became eligible to enlist. Maryland recruiting parties, now overseen by Col. Samuel Bowman, immediately raided slave jails and pens to free slaves sequestered by owners. In June, bounties were offered to black enlistees, and recruiters were ordered to accept all volunteers. For the black man, by summer the transition from slave to wage-earning military laborer to soldier was well under way.[7]

Congressional and state elections in the autumn of 1863 provided the political scaffolding for black freedom in Maryland. Two Unionist ideologies emerged: one conservative, the other unconditional, or radical. Both acknowledged the inevitability of emancipation, but their strategies differed. Radicals pursued the immediate, uncompensated brand, while conservatives sought compensation and to keep the election from becoming a referendum on black freedom. And they argued over the extent to which abolition could, or should, lead to equality.

The radicals trumped their rivals in November—their candidate for comptroller won 69 percent of the vote, and their men took four of five Congressional races and fifty-two of seventy-four seats in the General Assembly. Conservatives, citing military interference at the polls, cried foul. Egregious offenses were documented only in Somerset and Kent counties, where federal troops allegedly intimidated poll judges and suppressed votes of conservatives and Democrats by demanding loyalty oaths from those they accused of disloyalty. Some accusations were hurled by Unionist critics infuriated by the prohibition against Marylanders returning to vote from their new Confederate domiciles. Jean H. Baker argues that a more likely reason for the substantial decrease in 1863 voter turnout was the absence of many Marylanders who had either fled the state (south to the Confederacy, or north to more stable terrain) or joined the Union army (from which leave was required to vote)—a plausible alternative explanation to systemic, statewide vote suppression by the army.[8]

The new Maryland legislature scheduled an April 1864 referendum as a prelude to a September constitutional convention that would place the future of slavery before the voters in October. A hard-fought campaign, by the slimmest of margins, produced a new constitution to take effect the first day of November. Ninety-six convention delegates, who—after pausing to help erect fortifications around Annapolis against Jubal Early's strike toward Washington—approved the measure, which included a prohibition on the use of state funds as compensation for newly freed slaves. Emancipation had been won, if barely, by a relentless Unionist campaign and the votes of soldiers, who supported the new constitution by a ten-to-one margin.[9]

Some Maryland slaveholders refused to recognize this new era in Maryland. Within days they invoked Article 6 of the 1860 Maryland Code of Public General Laws, authorizing county Orphans' Courts to "summon before them the child of any free negro" and apprentice him or her to a white person if "it would be better for the habits and comfort of such child." White planters rounded up as many as three thousand black children—in some cases seizing them from their parents— and in wagons and carts hauled them before judges who quickly bound them out as apprentices in conditions that often differed little from slavery.[10]

On November 9, Gen. Lew Wallace issued General Orders 112, placing newly freed blacks under "special military protection" and creating a Freedmen's Bureau. Though unenforced by a Lincoln administration wary of prematurely alienating the

Maryland slave-owning constituency, Wallace's widely circulated order publicized the plight of these new citizens. Black parents—often mothers whose husbands were in the Union army—bombarded military and civilian officials with letters and affidavits detailing their futile battles with judges and masters in attempts to recover their children. Though the apprentice system was certainly used to the benefit of both parties, abuses would last well into 1868.[11]

White radicals, the Freedmen's Bureau, military authorities, and Maryland's new black citizens gradually coalesced into a force to remedy the misuse of apprenticeship laws. Though the state legislature in January 1865 failed to overturn them, the 1866 federal Civil Rights Act enabled Maryland agents of the Freedmen's Bureau to mount legal challenges in specific cases. In the autumn of 1867, the U.S. District Court in Baltimore ruled that Maryland's laws were unconstitutional, though almost another year would pass before most apprenticed black children were released.[12] The struggle for freedom in Maryland would continue well beyond 1868, with the old planter aristocracy arrayed against a coalition of radical Unionists, compassionate judges, federal military authorities, and the Freedmen's Bureau. Freedom, so long in coming, would for many remain elusive.

The Federal Writer's Project in the 1930s interviewed many former slaves, then well advanced in age. Though obtained long after the events described, these oral histories help convey the powerful story of American slavery. In 1936, Mary Ferguson recounted her sale in 1860 from Maryland's Eastern Shore to Georgia:

> In 1860 I wuz a happy chile. I had a good ma an a good paw; one older brother an one older suster, an a little bruther an a baby suster, too. One evening up rid my young Marstar on his hoss, an' up driv two strange white mens in a buggy. Dey hitch dere hosses an' cum in de house, which skeered me. 'Den one o' de strangers said, 'git yo clothers, Mary; we has bought you frum Mr. Shorter.' I c'mmenced cryin' an' beggin' Mr. Shorter to not let 'em take me away. But he say, 'yes, Mary, I has sole yer, an' yer must go wid em.' Den dese strange mens, whose names I ain't never knowed, tuk me an' put me in de buggy an' driv off wid me, me hollarin' at de top o' my voice an' callin' my Ma! Den dem speckulataws begin to sing loud—jes to drown out my hollerin'. Us passed de very fiel' whar paw an' all my fokes wuz wuckin', an' I calt out as loud as I could an', as long as I could see 'em, 'good-bye, Ma!' 'good-bye, Ma!' But she never heared me. Naw, suh, dem white mens wuz singin' so loud Ma could'n hear me! . . . I ain't never seed nor heared tell o' my Ma an' Pa, an' bruthers, an' susters from dat day to dis. My new owners took me to Baltymore, whar dey had herded tergether twoo two-hoss wagon loads o' Niggers. All o' us Niggers was den shipped on a boat to Savannah.[1]

Phillip Johnson was born in 1847 or 1848 in Montgomery County, between Edward's Ferry and Seneca. He was a slave owned by a physician named White, who, he said, "was good to his slaves." In 1937, at age 89, Johnson, living in Poolesville, recounted a Civil War episode involving Confederate raiders:

> I remember once during the war they came to town. It was Sunday morning an I was sittin in the gallery of the ole brick Methodist church. One of them came to de door and he pointed his pistol right at that preacher's head. The gallery had an outside stairs then. I ran to de door to go down de stairs but there was another un there pointing his gun and they say don't nobody leave dis building. The others they was a cleanin up all the hosses and wagons round the church. The one who was guarding de stairs, he kept a lookin to see if dey was done cleaning up de hosses, and when he wasn't watching I slip half way down de stairs, an when he turn his back I jump down and run. When he looks he jus laugh.[2]

In 1937, ex-slave Perry Ellis, "born on Kent Island, Md., about 86 years ago," lived at 1124 East Lexington Street in Baltimore. His father was a "freeman and my mother a slave," which made him a slave, owned by Thomas Tolson. Ellis described how blacks sabotaged slave patrols:

> The Eastern Shore of Maryland was the most productive slave territory and where farming was done on a large scale; and in that part of Maryland where there were many poor people and many of whom were employed as overseers, you naturally heard of patrollers and we had them and many of them. I have heard that patrollers were on Kent Island and the colored people would go out in the country on the roads, create a disturbance to attract the patrollers' attention. They would tie ropes and grape vines across the roads, so when the patrollers would come to the scene of the disturbance on horseback and at full tilt, they would be caught, throwing those who would come in contact with the rope or vine off the horse, sometimes badly injuring the riders. This would create hatred between the slaves, the free people, the patrollers and other white people.[3]

Richard Macks, born in 1844 as a slave in Charles County, described a town's hospitality:

> In Bryantown there were several stores, two or three taverns or inns which were well known in their days for their hospitality to their guests and arrangements to house slaves. There were two inns both of which had long sheds, strongly built with cells downstairs for men and a large room above for women. At night the slave traders would bring their charges to the inns, pay for their meals, which were served on a long table in the shed, then afterwards, they were locked up for the night.[4]

Macks recounted the fate of a young slave girl at the hands of a slave trader, explaining that "this attack was the result of being goodlooking, for, which many a poor girl in Charles County paid the price." Following emancipation she married and had three children, one of whom became a prominent Baltimore physician and another a schoolteacher:

> The slave traders would buy young and able farm men and well developed young girls with fine physiques to barter and sell. They would bring them to the taverns where there would be the buyers and traders, display them and offer them for sale. At one of these gatherings a colored girl, a mulatto of fine stature and good looks, was put on sale. She was of high spirits and determined disposition. At night she was taken by the trader to his room to satisfy his bestial nature. She could not be coerced or forced, so she was attacked by him. In the struggle she grabbed a knife and with it, she sterilized him and from the result of the injury he died the next day. she was charged with murder. Gen. Butler, hearing of it, sent troops to Charles County to protect her, they brought her to Baltimore, later she was taken to Washington where she was set free.[5]

Later in his interview Macks again spoke of the suffering of slave women:

> I have had many opportunities, a chance to watch white men and women in my
> long career, colored women have many hard battles to fight to protect themselves
> from assault by employers, white male servants or by white men, many times
> not being able to protect, in fear of losing their positions. Then on the other
> hand they were subjected to many impositions by the women of the household
> through woman's jealousy.[6]

Ex-slave Tom Randall was born in Oella, along the Patapsco River in Howard
County. His mother was owned by an Ellicott City tavern keeper named O'Brien;
she was a cook at the Howard House, "a gathering place of the farmers, lawyers
and business men of Howard and Frederick Counties and people of Baltimore who
had business in the courts of Howard County." Young Tom often accompanied his
mother to work. In his 1937 interview, Randall recounted the story of Joe Nick, a
slave owned by a Howard County farmer and lawyer named Rueben Rogers:

> When I was about eight or nine years old Joe ran away, everybody saying to join
> the Union Army. Joe Nick drove a pair of horses, hitched to a covered wagon,
> to Ellicott City. The horses were found, but no Nick. Rogers offered a reward
> of $100.00 for the return of Nick. This offer drew to Ellicott City a number of
> people who had bloodhounds that were trained to hunt Negroes—some com-
> ing from Anne Arundel, Baltimore, Howard and counties of southern Maryland,
> each owner priding his pack as being the best pack in the town. They all stopped
> at the Howard House, naturally drinking, treating their friends and each other,
> they all discussed among themselves the reward and their packs of hounds, each
> one saying that his pack was the best. This boasting was backed by cash. Some
> cash, plus the reward on their hounds. In the meantime Old Joe was thinking,
> not boasting, but was riding the rail.
>
> Old Joe left Ellicott City on a freight train, going west, which he hopped
> when it was stalled on the Baltimore and Ohio railroad a short distance from the
> railroad station at Ellicott City. Old Joe could not leave on the passenger trains,
> as no Negro would be allowed on the trains unless he had a pass signed by his
> master or a free Negro and had his papers.
>
> At dawn the hunters left the Howard House with the packs, accompanied by
> many friends and people who joined up for the sport of the chase. They went
> to Rogers' farm where the dogs were taken in packs to Nick's quarters so they
> could get the odor and scent of Nick. They had a twofold purpose, one to get
> the natural scent, the other was, if Old Nick had run away, he might come back
> at night to get some personal belongings, in that way the direction he had taken
> would be indicated by the scent and the hounds would soon track him down.
> The hounds were unleashed, each hunter going in a different direction without

result. Then they circled the farm, some going 5 miles beyond the farm without result. After they had hunted all day they returned to the Howard House where they regaled themselves in pleasures of the hotel for the evening.

In June of 1865 Old Nick returned to Ellicott City dressed in a uniform of blue, showing that he had joined the Federal Army. Mr. Rueben Rogers upon seeing him had him arrested, charging him with being a fugitive slave. He was confined in the jail there and held until the U.S. Marshal of Baltimore released him, arresting Rogers and bringing him to Baltimore City where he was reprimanded by the Federal Judge. This story is well known by the older people of Howard County and traditionally known by the younger generation of Ellicott City, and is called Old Nick: Roger's lemon.[7]

1861

The Union commanders at Poolesville issued General Orders No. 16 in response to concern that soldiers were causing trouble among slaves:

> The General commanding has with great concern learned that in several instances soldiers of this Corps have so far forgotten their duty as to excite and encourage insubordination among the colored servants in the neighbourhood of their camps, in direct violation of the laws of the United States, and of the State of Maryland in which they are serving.
>
> The immediate object of raising and supporting this army was the suppression of rebellion, and the putting down by military power of those ambitions and misguided people, who (unwilling to subject themselves to the constitution and laws of the country) preferred the carrying out of their own ideas of right and wrong, to living in peace and good order under the established Government. While, therefore, it should be the pride of every army to yield instant and complete obedience to the laws of the land, it is peculiarly the duty of every officer and enlisted man in this Army to give an example of subordination and perfect obedience to the laws; and to show to those in rebellion, that loyal national soldiers sink all private opinion in their devotion to law as it stands.[8]

Connecticut infantryman James Sawyer recounted in a letter to his family how Maryland slaves welcomed his regiment:

> We entered the state of Maryland at about 9 o'clock Sunday morning. You could see the difference between the free and slave states very soon. We could not see near as much cleared lands as we did in other states. The niggers were plenty enough and at the door of every log cabin near the railroad, they stood as thick as bees, shouting and waving their hats as we passed along . . . we came across a number of secesh houses as we went along. At all the loyal houses the inhabitants

were out cheering and waving their hats and handkerchiefs at us as we passed their houses while the rebels stood around their houses without giving a cheer or wave.

[Fort McHenry] is a very pleasant and healthy place and I am glad that we are stationed here. We have a good sea view and convenient places for bathing.[9]

W. & R. W. Duvall, near the Millersville "Postoffice" in Anne Arundel County, offered a $200 reward in May for the return of two escaped slaves:

Ran away from subscribers on Sunday, 5th May, two Negro Men, LLOYD and FRANK. Lloyd is very black, about 4 feet 6 inches high; pleasant when spoken to; had on a black coat and black hat. Frank is about 5 feet high, has thick lips, and very black; holds his head down when spoken to; his clothing is not known. The above reward will be paid, no matter where taken, provided they are both secured in jail, so that I get them again.[10]

In June, the commander of a Connecticut regiment informed his superiors of the status of slaves escaping into Union lines, a situation that would force slavery onto the administration's war agenda:

I have the honor to report to you that on the 10th inst, six men of color representing themselves to be fugitive slaves from Howard County in the State of Maryland appeared in the Camp of my Regiment and still remain upon my grounds. They also represent that their masters are secessionists in sentiment and opinion and members of secret military organizations hostile to the Government.[11]

Congressman Charles B. Calvert complained in July to the commander of the Department of Washington about slaves sequestered in Union army camps in Maryland and Virginia:

Since I saw you yesterday I have been called upon by a number of our Citizens relative to their Slaves being employed and concealed in the various camps in and around Washington. This has become a monstrous abuse of our rights and is rightfully causing a great deal of censure upon the Government for permitting it. I know from my personal intercourse with you on the Subject that it meets with our decided disapprobation and that of the Government because I have received assurances of the kind from the President and Secretary of War. These encampments not only employ these Slaves whilst Sojourning here but actually carry them off with them, as it is well known that many of the Regiments, now in Virginia, have large numbers of our Slaves concealed in their camps. The Regiment which left Washington last Sunday week on the cars, about Sunset for Baltimore, carried off Several & among them one of my own. As that Regiment passed through a portion of Pennsylvania I conclude those negroes, who accompanied it, were turned loose in the State, and are consequently a total loss to their owners unless the Government can be held responsible for their abduction. Under these circumstances I conceive I ask nothing unreasonable in behalf of our Citizens when I demand that the Government Shall order the immediate arrest of all Slaves now found in any Camps either in Maryland or Virginia and their confinement in Some place of Safety until their owners can reclaim them and that an order Shall be given to all Commanders and officers not to receive hereafter, on any pretense whatever, Such persons into their Camps or Stations. If Such orders were published in the papers of our State, and properly enforced afterwards, the public feeling, greatly exasperated at this time, would gradually subside and the enemies of the government would be disarmed of one of their most powerful weapons.[12]

In August, Gen. John A. Dix, commanding the Department of Pennsylvania at Fort McHenry, asked the secretary of war about the politically explosive matter of slaves finding refuge inside Union lines:

> Two negroes acknowledging that their master lives on the shore of the Chesapeake in Virginia below the mouth of the Potomac & is an active secessionist, were taken from a canoe at the mouth of the Severn, on their way, as they said, to Baltimore. I take it for granted they are fugitives. But I supposed that the matter should be treated precisely as it would be if we were in the occupation of Virginia. We would not meddle with the slaves even of secessionists.
>
> My letter to Col. Roberts takes the ground that we have nothing to do with slaves; that we are neither negro-stealers nor negro-catchers; and that we should send them away if they come to us. The matter is one of some delicacy.[13]

Two weeks later Dix, having received no reply from Cameron, told General McClellan that the Captain Nones, commander of the revenue cutter *Forward* at the mouth of the Severn River off Annapolis, had "captured three negro men going by in a canoe," and that he had ordered Nones to cease taking blacks into custody—"he now has five slaves on board his vessel doing nothing except consuming rations." Dix sought McClellan's guidance and elaborated on his view that accepting fugitive slaves would be harmful to the federal army, noting that "our cause is a holy one and should be kept free from all taint":

> Unless we abstain from the reception or the capture of fugitive slaves, I think we shall involve ourselves in the most serious difficulty. Their numbers will increase rapidly if it is understood that they are to be received and fed, especially as we advance into Virginia: and we shall not only be oppressed by a useless burden, but we shall expose ourselves to the imputation of intermeddling with a matter entirely foreign to the great questions of political right & duty involved in the

Nancy Davis, a slave of the Ridgely family of Baltimore County, refused freedom when slavery was abolished in Maryland in November 1864. Shown with Eliza Ridgely on her right, Davis was well regarded by the Ridgelys, the owners of Hampton Mansion, and is the only black buried in their family plot. Hampton National Historic Site, National Park Service.

civil strife, which [has] been brought upon us by disloyal and unscrupulous men.[14]

The Reverend Franklin Wilson believed that righteous abolitionists were exacerbating the crisis in Maryland:

> I consider the Northern agitators as intermeddlers with what was none of their business, and by their agitation only embittering the feelings of the South, breaking the bonds of our Union, and riveting the fetters of the slave more tightly.[15]

Though Wilson claimed to object to harsh treatment of slaves—who were prevented from learning to read and marrying and whose families were torn apart—he had a far higher regard for their Southern masters:

> As to my own views of this dreadful controversy, I can only say that I have always admired and loved our Union. I have believed it to be the best govt. on earth,

and the source of peace happiness and prosperity to our millions of citizens. I have dreaded and deprecated as a fatal calamity all tendencies to Disunion, and have always regarded the abolitionists of the North as fanatics, who in their zeal for the overthrow of a comparatively light evil would inflict the heaviest injuries upon the whole country, as well as upon the poor blacks they affected to befriend. I have looked upon Slavery as an evil, but as a despotic form of government, probably demanded by the character of the enslaved as a race, and as best removed by the gradual progress of the Gospel both among masters and slaves, rendering the one more humane and fraternal in his treatment of his servants, and the other more industrious, moral and intelligent, and thus better fitted for freedom. But I have no doubt that the Southerners as a whole are the truest friends of the blacks, and that the race in our South are far more elevated in every respect than anywhere else on earth.[16]

Archibald Kirkwood wrote to brother Robert from White Hall:

We received your kind letter dated 24th on yesterday we was all glad to hear from you, we are all well at present, and hope when these few lines reach you may find you enjoying the same great blessing, I am still going to stewardstown to school, the session is out the 27th of this month, I guess I will try and teach some this winter, Josiah Smith has got this school of ours, I can get the Narris Town school this winter, Robert I want to know what is rong with your watch, I have a notion of getting it fixed up if it dont cost to much, when you write again let me know will you.

William Robinson met with a severe loss last sunday, all of his negroes ran away, Jes is at Tom's yet, he will not go I guess Thomas Ayers, little Jake went too, Bill Robinson has got no house keeper, they went after them but did not get them, they took 3 of Bill's horses almost to the river they got them. Thomas Green and Uncle Hope went up among the Dutch on friday to trade Barny (horse) away he has got so he wont pull one bit, they went through Stewardstown flying, Giles has give out the notion of going to war, he went to York on last Tuesday to Join, but he give it out, he wife dont want him to go.[17]

In October Henry S. Briggs, commander of a Massachusetts regiment at Camp Brightwood near Washington, revealed the strong feelings of some Union officers about orders to "turn out from my camp any colored servant that may be claimed as a slave." Briggs had a colored servant with him whom he would not allow to be "claimed" as a slave and said he would choose the alternative of dismissal "from the service in which I have volunteered":

Whenever a claimant had made representation to me that his servant was in this camp and has come respectably accredited as a person entitled to confidence, or in company with a police officer, as in two cases in camp while I write, I have protected them in the search, and have assured them that no interference would be permitted in the exercise of any rights of ownership with which the local laws might have invested them. I have informed them as plainly that I shall neither give nor permit those in my command to give *aid* in the rendition of slaves beyond that required under due process of law. When such a requisition comes I shall then determine whether I will comply with the requirements of such a process or choose the penalty of a passive disobedience.[18]

Senior federal commanders, mindful of avoiding offense to Maryland slave owners whose slaves made their way into Union lines, instructed their officers to follow the administration's directive to relinquish slaves to masters who could prove "ownership." In October, Gen. John Dix clarified his policy to Col. A. Morse and ordered him to search for a slave belonging to S. R. Richardson:

You will please ascertain by the most searching inquiries among your Officers and men whether the colored boy belonging to Mr Richardson has been harbored within your lines since he was sent out by your order, and whether he is still within them.—

My order was not to allow fugitive slaves to come within the encampments at all.—The difficulty in this case arises from his having been allowed to enter yours. The owner now Seeks to hold you responsible for not giving him up when you knew he was a slave. I wish the matter put on such ground as to exonerate us from all responsibility, and it is for this reason that I direct the inquiries above Stated.—

Hereafter no fugitive slave should be allowed to come within your lines at all. But if he comes within them without your knowledge and the owner calls for him while he is actually in your possession or under your control he should be surrendered, on such call or demand. We may decline to receive them, and this is what I wished; but if we do receive them, we cannot decline to surrender.[19]

In November the lame-duck Governor Hicks wrote to Secretary Cameron on behalf of a slave-owning constituent regarding an incident at a Union camp near Annapolis:

I was called upon by a Mr. Tucker of this (Anne Arundel) County, who stated that he had a servant, that had left him, and taken refuge in the Encampment of the 25th Regt. from Mass, that he had repaired to the ground so occupied, and that Col. Upton, Commanding, at first refused, afterward, said to him go through and see if your man is here, He proceeded, but a short distance, when he *Tucker* was surrounded by quite a number, menaced him, and, applied opprobrious Epithets; such as Negro stealer, Negro catchers, and that the negro was better than he, the master was &c &c until he was obliged to leave the ground, without looking after his servant. Now whilst in this there is amusement, I must say there was much to provoke, and altho I care little for what becomes of the negroes, yet these things produce bad feeling and bad effect.

Hicks's letter demonstrated that even staunch Maryland Unionists wished to demarcate a line between preservation of Union and slavery:

> You are fully aware sir of the difficulty we have had in Md. things are working right now. let us have no stumbling blocks placed in our way—I care nothing for the Devilish Nigger difficulty, I desire to save the union, and will cooperate with the Administration in everything tending to that important result, that is proper. I know the difficulties surrounding us, and do not wish to mingle and mix up too much with the main design.
>
> I labored to have Md roll up a majority, that would smother secessionism. We have given them a heavy dose. I hope to strike them another blow by an early convocation of the Legislature of our state, and if we can but keep away outside Issues, and all things foreign from the, one, true great design of all Patriots, we shall save the union.[20]

General Dix's concern at the abduction of a young female slave by an Indiana regiment, guarding a railroad near Baltimore, was consistent with federal efforts to avoid antagonizing politically powerful Maryland slaveholders, many of whom were loyalists:

> The 20th Indiana Regiment, which was guarding the Northern Central R. Road, took with it when it left here, a yellow girl, a slave of Mr Jessup a strong Union man. She was dressed in boys clothes and was taken as is believed, for purposes of prostitution.
>
> If it be so I need not say how much such a transaction, if passed by unnoticed, is calculated to dishonor the Military service and the Government.[21]

An unsigned letter, likely from a Massachusetts soldier, described the arrest of two fugitive slaves (complying with orders issued by Gen. Charles Stone), at a Union camp at Poolesville. Massachusetts Gov. John Andrew sent the letter to the War Department, demanding that Secretary Cameron ensure "the protection of our men from such outrages in future and humanity itself from such infractions under color of military law and duty":

> On Sunday morning several negroes came into Camp as usual for the purpose of selling cakes, pies &c to the Soldiers.
>
> Although having eatables for sale, some of these negroes were themselves almost famished and were treated to a breakfast by the men of one of our German Companies. About the time of guard mounting the vigilant eyes of Lieut Macy espied the negroes as they were disposing of their wares through the Company streets, and, leaving the new guard to be mounted as it might, he beckoned two of the negroes to the Guard house when he ordered them into arrest and then

immediately *detailed a file of Soldiers under a sergeant with loaded muskets to escort them to their supposed owners and deliver them up.*

The procedure was therefore unknown to all save the officers who were parties to it and the parties who composed the escort had no knowledge that their prisoners were suspected fugitives.[22]

An official of the Freedmen's Bureau in the District of Columbia reported to a congressional committee in 1867 on "Outrages as shown by the records of this office," which included the 1861 actions of Samuel Cox, a Charles County planter who, in 1865, was imprisoned on suspicion of having aided the flight of John Wilkes Booth in April that year:

On the 28th of May 1866, Henry Seward made affadavit that in December 1861 while in Conversation with Mr. Samuel Cox living five (5) miles South of Port Tobacco, he (Cox) confessed that in August 1861 he had murdered one of his Slaves, Jack Scroggins by whipping him to death—

This statement is corroberrated by affadavits made by John Sims—and William Jackson—(at a different time) who testify that Scroggins was flogged to death for having escaped to the Federal lines, whence he was recaptured—and on the 12th of May 1866—Wm Hill, col$_d$ an employee at the Senate Post Office reports this case and states that in whipping Scroggins to death Cox was assisted by Frank Roly his overseer & 2 other men. all these parties are living now at the same place and have never been arrested.[23]

Late in 1861 the planter-dominated Maryland legislature addressed the matter of slaves fleeing toward the federal army—in the form of a resolution appointing a committee of three to exhort General McClellan to "solicit the adoption of some plan to prevent the admission of fugitive slaves within the lines of the army":

Whereas Maryland in her recent election has unmistakeably demonstrated through the ballot box her loyalty and devotion to the Union . . . and (whereas) it sometimes happens that through the actions of individuals among the troops, Negroes belonging to citizens of this State escape into the lines of the Federal Army thereby causing trouble and occasionally lost to their owners.[24]

A petition from citizens of Worcester County "praying for the passage of an act for the more certain and speedy apprehension of runaway slaves from the State of Maryland" was referred to the county delegation on December 13 and endorsed by the Maryland House of Delegates a week later, with one dissenting vote. Early in the new year the General Assembly would pass a law awarding to anyone apprehending an escaped slave $100 or half of the slave's market value.[25]

The Reverend Daniel Rideout of the African Methodist Episcopal Church in Hancock told Sarah Jervis, the mistress of Bowling Green (the Hood family farm at

Sykesville), of troop activity along the Potomac River in Washington County. Rideout, who was related to some of the Jervis slaves, evidently had a strong relationship with their mistress:

> In this part of the country there is a great number of union troops of soldiers come on from the north. This town is close to the northern river. Virginia persons can hulloo to each other across the river. And the soldiers is continuously crossing the river from the state of Maryland into Virginia. We hear nothing much here but the drumming of War, War, War, the rattling of the guns and sounds of the infantry, the hitting of the swords, shining of the bayonets, neighing of the horses. When will the time come that man will learn wars no more. Let us pray for the peace of God and for the Glorious United States of America.
>
> Dear Miss S. please give my love to all, both white and colored. I will come to you all as soon as I can. Hope all peace. May the God of Heaven bless you and yours.[26]

1862

A letter to his wife from John Boston, an escaped Virginia slave who found refuge in New York, was intercepted and sent to a committee of the Maryland House of Delegates, who demanded of General McClellan how Boston's owner, "a loyal citizen of Maryland," could recover his property (whether Boston's wife, Elizabeth, ever saw this letter is unknown):

> My Dear Wife it is with grate joy I take this time to let you know Whare I am i am now in Safety in the 14th Regiment of Brooklyn this Day i can Adress you thank god as a free man I had a little truble in giting away But as the lord led the Children of Isrel to the land of Canon So he led me to a land Whare fredom Will rain in spite Of earth and hell Dear you must make your Self content i am free from al the Slavers Lash and as you have chose the Wise plan Of Serving the lord i hope you Will pray Much and i will try by the help of god To Serv him With all my hart i am with a very nice man and have All that hart Can Wish But My Dear I Cant express my grate desire that i have to See you i trust the time Will come When We Shal meet again And if We dont met on earth We Will Meet in heven Whare Jesas ranes Dear Elizabeth tell Mrs Own[ees] That i. trust that She Will Continue Her kindness to you and that god Will Bless her on earth and Save Her In grate eternity My Acomplements To Mrs. Owens and her Children may They Prosper through life i never Shall forgit her kindness to me Dear Wife i must Close rest yourself Contented i am free I want you to rite To me Soon as you Can Without Delay Direct your letter to the 14th Reigment New york State malitia Uptons Hill Virginea In Care of Mr Cranford Comary Write my Dear Soon As you C Your Affectionate Husban Kiss Daniel For me[27]

One Annapolis man sought army help in recovering a slave:

> According to your instructions, I left with Capt Richmond a description of my
> Servant Man Wm Harris, who was coaxed away from this place on last Sunday
> evening, Either by one of the members of the 89th New York—or 9th New Jersey
> volunteers, for fear he may have lost it, I now give you a description, he is about
> 6 feet high, 23 years of age, dark complexion, with considerable impediment of
> speech, had on when he left, a striped cotton shirt, coat & pants of light drab
> country Cloth, coat very much worn, you will do me a grateful favour, if you
> will have him secured in the village prison at Annapolis as I hold him in Trust
> for other parties, and should fail to get him, may have to pay his full value, wich
> would be hard on me, especially at the present time.[28]

While another stressed his Unionist credentials as he did the same:

> A slave belonging to me, by the name of Samuel Offer, about 19 years old, stout,
> well made, with prominent mouth and short chin, dressed in new drab cloth,
> and new long boots, ranaway from me, and was taken with the "Burnside Expe-
> dition," by one of the Connecticut Regiments (the 8th or the 11th.)
>
> I send herewith letters substantiating my loyalty, which, I trust, will induce
> you to help me to reclaim my slave. Gen. Dix has kindly promised to intercede
> for me, and I trust his effort will be successful.
>
> A neighbor of mine, Wilson L. Wells, had a slave taken off in the same expedition.
> The negro is named Moses Hall, stammers badly, and bats his eyes while endeav-
> oring to speak. He is about 35 years old. Both these negroes were seen in soldier's
> clothes immediately previous to the embarkation of Gen. Burnside's troops.
>
> I will esteem it a great favor if you will aid me and Mr. Wells in the recovery of
> our property. We are both devoted Union men; and we deem it hard that Union
> soldiers should thus deprive us of our property.[29]

In February, the Maryland legislature unanimously passed a resolution expressing
dissatisfaction over the impending emancipation bill in the nation's capital:

> This General Assembly witnesses with great regret the efforts which are now
> making for the abolition of slavery in the District of Columbia. The agitation of
> the subject is calculated to disturb the relation of master and slave within this
> State; and the success of the agitators in this scheme would strike a serious blow
> at the interest of the people of Maryland and impress them with the belief that
> the Government of the United States have not a due regard for their rights, in-
> stitutions and feelings.[30]

A March affidavit from a Montgomery County slaveholder described difficulties
encountered when attempting to retrieve his slave from the camp of the Tenth Massachusetts Infantry Regiment, near the district line:

That six or seven weeks ago he went down and saw Col Briggs that Col Briggs told him to go into the camp and if he could find his Negroe to take him That he went there but was driven out and was not permitted to look for him That on 28th of Feby 1862 he went down again and spoke to Capt Ives about it that Capt Ives told him to go to the camp and take his Negroe and that no one would molest him that he did so and found him and attempted to take him out and that a large crowd got around him and knocked him about throwing small stones and dirt at him and otherwise ill treating him and finally driveing him out of the camp without allowing him to take his Negroe[31]

John Bayne, a delegate and slaveholder from Charles County, registered a similar complaint:

I learned by some of the soldiers my servants were in Camp and soon as my mission become general known a large crowd collected and followed me crying shoot him, bayonet him, kill him, pitch him out, the nigger Stealer the nigger driver at first their threats were accompanied with a few stones thrown at me which very soon became an allmost continued shower of stones a number of which struck me, but did me no serious damage. Seeing the officer who accompanied me too no notice of what was going on and fearing that some of the soldiers would put their threats of shooting me into execution I informed him that I would not proceed any farther, about this time Lieutenant Edmund Harrison came to my assistance and swore he would shoot the first man who threw a stone at me, the soldier hooted at him and continued throwing. I returned to Co Grahams quarters but was not permitted to see him again. I left the camp without getting my servants and have not been favored to get them yet.[32]

Gen. Joseph Hooker sought instructions on dealing with escaped slaves at Camp Baker, on the Maryland side of the Potomac:

Contrabands are arriving in such numbers at my camp from Virginia as to render it necessary for me to be advised of the disposition I shall make of them. Am I to understand Paragraph 8 General Orders 120.60 dated Head Quarters Army of the Potomac Febr. 21. 1862, as embracing this class of persons? To permit them to go at large in this secession district, would, I have no doubt result in many of them being returned to their rebel masters, and I hope that it will not be permitted. Please advise me.[33]

On March 10, Lincoln met with a group of border-state representatives to encourage them to accept his plan for gradual, compensated emancipation. Lincoln's visitors objected to the plan's constitutionality and worried about the consequences of a large population of freed slaves. Congressman J. W. Crisfield transcribed the interview (a portion of which follows):

Mr. Crisfield said he did not think the people of Maryland looked upon Slavery as a permanent Institution; and he did not know that they would be very reluctant to give it up if provision was made to meet the loss, and they could be rid of the race; but they did not like to be coerced into Emancipation, either by the direct action of the Government or by indirection, as through the Emancipation of Slaves in this District, or the Confiscation of Southern Property as now threatened; and he thought before they would consent to consider this proposition they would require to be informed on these points.

The President replied that "unless he was expelled by the act of God or the Confederate Armies, he should occupy that house for three years, and as long as he remained there, Maryland had nothing to fear, either for her Institutions or her interests, on the points referred to."

Mr. Crisfield immediately added: "Mr. President, if what you now say could be heard by the people of Maryland, they would consider your proposition with a much better feeling than I fear without it they will be inclined to."[34]

In April, Congress passed a joint resolution offering compensation for "the gradual Abolishment of Slavery":

Be it resolved by the Senate and House of Representatives of the United States of America in Congress assembled, That the United States ought to cooperate with any State which may adopt gradual abolishment of slavery, giving to such State pecuniary aid, to be used by such State in its discretion, to compensate for the inconveniences, public and private, produced by such change of system.[35]

On July 12, with Congress set to adjourn, Lincoln invited twenty-nine border-state representatives to the White House to press his emancipation plan. He told the border men: "I do not speak of emancipation at once, but of a decision at once to emancipate gradually."[36]

Two days later Lincoln proposed "the draft of a Bill to compensate any State which may abolish slavery within it's limits, the passage of which, substantially as presented, I respectfully, and earnestly recommend." That night the border-state representatives rebuffed him.[37]

On March 13, Congress passed an article of war prohibiting the services of Union soldiers in returning escaped slaves to their masters. A constituent wrote to Rep. Charles Calvert for help in the face of military interference with his "property":

As our representative in Congress I have thought you might be enabled to have abated a great grievance which we are suffering at the hands of the Federal Soldiery Stationed among us. Their camps with but few exceptions have been opened as receptacles for our slaves. Their emissaries are sent out among the

Slaves and all the young negroes are enticed to their camps where they are concealed from recovery by their owners. Within the last week large numbers have taken refuge in these camps. I have lost 3 boys and there is scarce a slave owner in my vicinity who has not lost one or more.

Burgess complained that Gen. Joseph Hooker must be able to enforce his orders to restore fugitive slaves to their owners, and that, with the army's impending move, he might lose his slaves for good:

I visited the camps on Saturday last when I met with no difficulty in obtaining an order authorizing me to search for and recapture my boys if they could be found but as soon as my purpose was known they were spirited away and concealed so of course I faild to [get] them though I have since learned they were certainly there. I learn the army is on the eve of crossing the river. General Hooker informed me that he had indirectly learned that an order had, or would be issued forbiding the negroes to be transported over the river with it I would therefore most respectfully suggest that if you could prevail upon the proper authorities to have such an order promulged before the army moves It might be the means of restoring to us our slaves now in these camps who otherwise will be lost to their owners.[38]

Calvert took up the issue with the War Department, enclosing his letter from Burgess:

One of our best Union men in Charles County in relation to a great abuse which is daily practised not only in Charles County but in most parts of Maryland and the District of Columbia. Genl Mansfield last Summer, under the direction of the President, issued an order that no negro Slaves Should be either permitted to enter the Camps or be transported with the Camps from place to place. I regret to Say this order has never been enforced and hence there are daily complaints against the Government for permitting this great abuse of the rights of our loyal people. therefore write at the request of Mr. Burgess and many other loyal citizens to know if this nuisance cannot be abated. Our people do not ask the army to arrest their Slaves but Simply that they will not entice them away and conceal them in their camps until Such times as they are ordered off and then taken them off with the troops.[39]

By the close of March, Maryland lawmakers had passed a number of measures designed to protect investments in slaves. That month, for example, sheriffs and constables were required to arrest nonresident free blacks entering Maryland; it became illegal to "sell, give or administer, to any Slave, any spirituous liquor or intoxicating drink," a misdemeanor meriting a $25 fine; and owners of slaves who escape via "railroad, steamboat, towboat or other vessel" became able to recover the slave's value from the owner of the railroad or vessel.[40]

Slave quarters near Harrisonville in Baltimore County. MdHS.

The abolition of slavery in the District of Columbia in April had immediate re-percussions in neighboring Maryland and Virginia. As owners tried to stop slaves from escaping to the nation's capital, some district masters risked their compensation by moving their slaves out of the capital into neighboring slave states. An 1864 affidavit from Grandison Briscoe, a Maryland native and freed slave "in the Service of the United States all the time & is now in Said Service in Virginia," recounted how in 1862 the owner of his wife and mother sought to keep possession of them:

That his wife & his mother were taken away from Washington in April (on the 7th day) 1862 & as fugitive Slaves & taken to Piscatawa to Broad Creek to their master's [farm] whose name is John Hunter & My mothers masters name was and is Robert Hunter—They were both taken to the barn & severely whipped Their clothes were raised & tied over their heads to keep their screams from disturbing the neighborhood & then were tied up & whipped very severely whipped and then taken to Upper Marlborough to jail My wife had a Child about nine months after my wife was imprisoned she had a Child but the inhuman master & mistress though the knew she was soon to be Confined or give birth to a Child made no arrangements provided no Clothing nor anything for the Child or mother I have sent them Clothing & other articles frequently until the first or near the first of January 1864 Since which the new jailor has refused to allow them to receive any thing from me[41]

A man in Rockville, Montgomery County, petitioned the U.S. Senate for $1,100 compensation for his slave Theodore (Tid), who he claimed joined the 102nd Pennsylvania Regiment, a Signal Corps:

> It is not improbable, that this claim may be disregarded, and even ridiculed, at the present time. But I have an abiding faith in the justice and loyalty of the people of the United States, and, upon a return of the "sober second thought," they will feel it to be a duty and a pleasure to pay all law abiding citizens for their negroes as well as other property destroyed, used, or carried away by the Government troops. One object of this petition is to notify the Government of my loss at the hands of its troops, and of my purpose now and hereafter to persist in my claim for compensation for my said property.
>
> A large number of slaves—perhaps several hundred—have been carried away by the Government troops from their owners in this County. Our slave population have been greatly demoralized by the Government troops, which has inflicted upon our people a heavy loss, hard to estimate. The effect upon our agricultural interests and upon the general welfare of the Community is exceedingly disastrous.[42]

In August 1861, Congress had passed the First Confiscation Act, permitting seizure of rebel property, including slaves, used in the insurrection. In July 1862, Congress passed the Treason Act (also known as the Second Confiscation Act), which freed slaves of anyone supporting the rebellion and mandated forfeiture of property owned by officers of the Confederate government—the act likely referred to in an April letter from Elizabeth Blair Lee:

> This emancipation act in the District which will undoubtedly soon become a law—has already passed the Senate—this reduced Nelly's household considerably—They now have a dowdy looking Irish cook & Luke takes care of the Stable—as they keep but one horse—I expect the planters in Prince George will emmigrate their slaves to the Cotton states & get good prices for them as so many there will be freed by Confiscation—Henry & Becky say that nearly all the owners of slaves have sent them into Virginia & Maryland from the District.[43]

Several weeks later Lee described the effects of emancipation in Washington on "Secesh" areas in Maryland. Though the Blair and Lee families might have evaded the new law (Elizabeth spent winters in Washington but summered at the Blair home in Silver Spring, Maryland, just outside the district boundary), Lee recounted her efforts to comply:

> Anniversary of the Baltimore Row & it is whispered the emancipation Bill in the District has renewed the rebellious spirit there & almost everywhere in the Secesh parts of Maryland Joe Cook was here this morning he is stationed near Balt & says things look very squally there—the Lovejoys were here today evidently to see the effect of the emancipation Act on us—They put direct questions on the subject when Father said his servants always knew they cold go when they wished—& they were of course now at liberty to do so—but all but one declined "the priviledge They looked amazed—said they had heard of such things but never saw them before—I have enquiring in the City & can get other servants if we need them I have an idea that Mary "*wants to see the* world too" & as I can get a better Cook for Mother I am inclined to suggest Marys departure as an experiment for awhile.[44]

The Unionist, pro-Lincoln posture of the *Baltimore American and Commercial Advertiser* accommodated no interference with the right of Marylanders to own slaves. Several days after Congress abolished slavery in the nation's capital, an editorial alluded to the dilemma Maryland posed for Lincoln—how to tighten the noose about slavery's neck without alienating the powerful slaveholding constituency in the border states:

> A visit of ex-Governor Hicks to Washington has been seized upon by the disloyal amongst us as the basis for a rumor that his business there was to urge the President to approve the bill for the abolition of slavery in the District of Columbia. We are so fully possessed of the facts in the case that we can assert with entire accuracy that Mr. Hicks' influence was used for a directly opposite purpose, and that he frankly represented to the President the considerations which he thought rendered the measure inexpedient and hurtful to the Union cause in the Border States.[45]

Elizabeth Blair Lee described broader consequences of the new District of Columbia emancipation law:

> I expected all of them would put out for the City & was rather surprised when Nannie Olivia & Henry told their purpose Nanny says she knows when she is well off but is evidently delighted that her children are free This Bill has liberated about one thousand blacks & has made about two thousand very miserable—by having them sent away in Maryland Kentucky & Virginia—All of Beckys sisters neices nephews have been liberated by the Miss Bell—who have always been emancipationists—the Lovejoys say the Presidents messages have

given the Republican party a policy—"Emancipation compensation & coloniza-
tion—satisfies all shades of Republicans."[46]

In May, Governor Bradford expressed concern over rumors of the government's
refusal to enforce the Fugitive Slave Law in Washington, D.C., thereby preventing
owners from recovering slaves who had fled there for sanctuary. He asked Attorney
General Bates to clarify federal policy:

> There are two classes of persons who are just now excited upon the subject of
> the late District law—the one made up of the politicians that have really no inter-
> est in the matter and are determined to agitate it simply for partisan effect, and
> the other of persons who are in pursuit of no object but their property and seek
> only to have the laws of the land honestly executed—It is hardly necessary for me
> to say that it is in behalf of the latter alone I deem it my duty to address you.

Bradford asked Bates:

> Will you therefore do me the favor to inform me whether it is true that the Gov-
> ernment has interposed and commanded, as reported, the Marshal of the Dis-
> trict to make no arrests in such cases; and if such is the case—and I sincerely
> trust it may not be—can it not be suspended until some such arrest in made
> and the question can be properly brought before a Judicial Tribunal—you will
> I think agree with me, that it is important this questin should be promptly de-
> cided, in order that if there is no such law now applicable to the District, our
> people should have the opportunity of bringing it before Congress before their
> adjournment.[47]

In his reply, Bates stated that he knew of no such refusal:

> I am honored with your letter of yesterday, informing me that large numbers of
> slaves owned in Maryland, are daily making their way into the District of Colum-
> bia, from the neighboring Counties of your state, which, you assure me is pro-
> ducing great anxiety and complaint in your community, and that such anxiety
> is greatly increased, within the last few days, by information received "that the
> Government has forbidden the Marshal of the District to execute any warrant
> for the arrest of these slaves, upon the ground, as it is suggested, that the fugitive
> slave law is not applicable to the District of Columbia."
>
> In these distempered times, I am not at all surprised to hear that Slaves in the
> border states are using all available means to escape into free territory; but the
> rumor you speak of, to the effect that the Government has ordered the Marshal
> of the District not to serve warrants in execution of the fugitive slave law, is to me,
> new, and unexpected.
>
> I know nothing of any such order, and do not believe any such exists. The Act
> of Congress of August 2d 1861, Chapter 37, charges this office with the general

superintendence & direction of the District Attorney and Marshal, as to the manner of discharging their respective duties. And hence, I suppose it very probably that, if such an order had been given, I would know it. I think none such was ever given. The rumor I suppose to be a mere fiction, started by some evil disposed person, to stir up bad feeling and to frighten the timid and credulous.[48]

A Harford County slave owner sought congressional redress when his slave fled to Washington:

Suffering the loss of my property by the recent act of Congress making the District of Columbia free soil and an outlet for all the slave property of Maryland— My slave George Giles having availed himself of the protection thus afforded to fugitives, and escaped from the service he was by law and justice bound to render, do hereby as my right and with all due respect petition your Honorable body either to return to service the said colored man George Giles, or pay to me the sum of One Thousand Dollars, the lowest estimated value of the services of said colored servant for the period He was bound to serve.[49]

In early spring, the Maryland General Assembly passed a barrage of resolutions defending the state's slaveholders, such as this one in March complaining about emancipation in the District of Columbia, in which the legislature

witnesses with great regret the efforts which are now making for the abolition of slavery in the District of Columbia. The agitation of the subject is calculated to disturb the relation of Master and slave within this state; and the success of the agitation in this scheme would strike a serious blow at the interest of the people of Maryland.[50]

In May, citizens of Maryland's "lower counties" asked Governor Bradford in a set of resolutions to establish "patroles" and intervene with federal officials to prevent slaves from escaping to Washington. Bradford's refusal cited the expense and dangers of arming a large force:

To suppress the evils to which these Resolutions point, by means of a force of the kind referred to, organized by the Executive, that force must not only be formidable in numbers, but,—as your Committee admitted—must be adequately armed, & there is every reason to fear that the employment of such a force of that character under the circumstances of excitement said to exist already in that portion of the State, would in all probability provoke serious collisions, and result in still more serious calamities—Your own Resolutions seem to contemplate some such results when they declare that "the people of said Counties are practically prevented from protecting themselves by lawful patroles because bodies of Federal soldiers occupy the termini of the roads leading into said District and threaten to prevent any interference with said escaping slaves—"

The governor noted that he had complained to Attorney General Bates and visited Lincoln, and he urged reliance on the Fugitive Slave Law for return of runaways:

> and though I saw the President for a few moments he was so engrossed by pressing engagements at the time, that it was manifestly no reason for such a conversation as I desired to have with him, and without mentioning the object of my visit I arranged for another interview with him to day. After leaving the President I met our Representative in Congress Mr. Crisfield, who informed me that he had on the day previous, been a witness to such an enforcement of the fugitive slave law by the marshal as fully assured him there would be no obstacle hereafter to its effectual execution. He had gone with a Gentleman from your County who had lost some slaves (attended by his Counsel—and the Marshal) to a House in the District where some of them were domiciled, had seen the owner point out his slaves, and the Marshal seize them, and was told afterwards by the owner himself that on proving his property before the Court, the slaves had been delivered to him by its order and he had sent them home. I am rejoiced to hear that this course has been adopted, and I am satisfied that the knowledge of such proceedings will do more to arrest the stampede of slaves than any remedy I could devise.[51]

Col. John Staunton, commanding federal forces in Annapolis, reported to General Dix on meetings of slave owners to discuss measures for preventing their slaves from absconding:

> I have investigated the report of meetings held at Owensville & other places in this vicinity and believe the object of Said meetings to be the prevention of negroes running away from their masters.
>
> On Thursday of this week I dispatched *Lieut. Tucker* of my command dressed in citizens clothes to a place called Annies Bridge one of the points designated for a meeting. At this place he met with a person named *Thomas Davison* who is represented as a Union Man and who informed *Lieut. Tucker* that some fifty persons had met there the evening previous to take into consideration the proper course to be pursued to prevent their negroes from escaping, avowing at the same time that no aid should be given to prevent the escape of negroes belonging to persons professing Union Sentiments.
>
> I will keep myself advised of any movements which may be prejudicial to the interests of the service and report accordingly.[52]

John Bayne, chairing a legislative committee studying preservation of slave owner property, intimated to Governor Bradford a correlation between the will of Marylanders to fight and their degree of assistance in preventing slave escapes:

> It occurs to me, Sir, that now since you have responded so patriotically in your Proclamation to the call of the President for more troops to suppress the rebel-

lion, [now] would be the opportune time for you as the Executive of the State to interpose for the restitution and protection of the slave property of the people of Maryland. I do not believe the people of this state or any of the border states will come to the rescue this time with half the alacrity and enthusiasm, that they would if they had some guaranty for their slave property. The people will not voluntarily embark in a cause which they believe will be suicidal to their interests. I know there are many cities of Maryland who are as loyal as Mr. Lincoln himself, and whose farms are uncultivated because their slaves are now fugitives and are under the protection of the Federal Army. There are at this time hundreds of slaves from Maryland now in the streets of Alexandria enjoying the most perfect immunity and defiantly confront their masters . . . the execution of the fugitive slave law has become a perfect nullity in Washington because all Maryland slaves have escaped to Alexandria and its vicinity where they receive military protection. Is it not possible for the people of this State to obtain some remedy?[53]

Bayne had met with Secretary of State Edwin Stanton during the winter of 1862 to discuss "the admission of fugitive slaves within the lines of the Federal Army." Late in July he complained that the problem had not abated:

The partial enforcement of the fugitive slave law in the District of Columbia, has had the effect of forcing all the fugitives from Maryland into Alexandria & its environs: where they receive military protection—The Provost Marshal there, has assumed the prerogative of deciding that no citizen of Maryland shall have the right to arrest any slave within the lines of his Department—This decision is tantamount to issuing an emancipation proclamation in the Counties of Maryland bordering on the Potomac River—Already hundreds and perhaps thousands of servants have absconded from Maryland & now are roaming about the streets of Alexandria & vicinity, & their legitimate claimants dare not interfere with them—

Bayne invoked the border-state slave owner strategy: proclaiming fervent Unionism that resonated with federal authorities, eager to mobilize blacks as wage-earning laborers and ensure Maryland's loyalty:

According to the very important order which has just emanated from the War Department—It is required, "that military and naval commanders shall employ persons of African descent for Military & Naval purposes, & that accurate accounts shall be kept to show from whom such persons shall have come, as a basis upon which proper compensation can be made in proper cases"—I believe sir, an order of similar import issued for the benefit of Maryland would be most acceptable to her loyal citizens—But to deprive Union men of their property without affording them any redress, as I have recently seen done in

Alexandria is a species of confiscation that I believe many of the extremists have never contemplated—

If the labor of slaves can be made to contribute in any way to the suppression of this iniquitous rebellion: it ought to be the policy of the Government to adopt it—And no patriotic citizen would hesitate to proffer it for that purpose—If in the prosecution of the war for the restoration of the Union the emancipation of slavery should become necessary, I would say let it go—But until then; justice to the loyal men in loyal states demands protection—

The Negro is naturally indolent & unless employed becomes demoralized & utterly worthless—[54]

One Maryland man blamed abolitionism for secession and war and saw the end of slavery as the only antidote for the conflict:

I am inclined to think there will soon one appear on the deck of our ship of State: The right kind of a commander who will get her on the course again & run her for awhile longer even if she must go down at last which now appears may be her fate—But we must hope for the best—as abolitionism may yet be destroyed & the country saved. But I see no hope for it in any other way. My disgust for that horid faction only increases as the awful fruits of their leanings are being manifested. Had it not been for them the bad men of the south could not possibly have succeeded in their state rights and state sovereignty doctrines. It now appears to many that the only way to put down the rebelion is to completely destroy slavery. If this is or can be done, will not the goose be killed which laid the golden eggs? Most certainly.[55]

A communication from an officer at Point Lookout described the contraband problem confronting military posts:

Contrabands are continually crossing over from the Eastern shore of va., and coming in from Md., all getting within our lines, by landing on the beech, until the number is greater than we know what to do with—

I have already handed over to the Post Q. Master, in addition to those who were her when I took command, more, than he can find employment for.

Now I would respectfully ask, what disposition am I to make of the surplus contraband? Have I the power to send them to Washington City or elsewhere?

Those already here claim that their masters are disloyal: but there may be some, whose masters are loyal, what shall I do with them?

We are in rather an exposed condition here—the great mass of the citizens in this county are disloyal, and are constantly crossing over into va.—Our condition, and the large amount of Hospital and other stores, might invite a raid upon us, with such numbers, that it would be out of my power to successfully resist them—My command is only 100 men, and they with only an average of 30 rounds of cartridges per man.[56]

A Frederick newspaper editorial in October presaged the Emancipation Proclamation, lending force to a nascent campaign for an end to Maryland slavery:

> The value and utility of slavery in Maryland have already been destroyed by the war . . . Emancipation would afford relief to thousands of slave holders and if accompanied with Federal compensation for the public and private inconvenience attendant upon a change of system . . . would promote the welfare and prosperity of the State. The time has past when we could delude ourselves with the hope that slavery would survive the ordeal of rebellion and come out of the fire unscathed. Every reflecting man now sees that its doom is written, let us, therefore, devise and pursue such prudent counsels as may prepare us for the impending social revolution and avert its calamities.[57]

A reaction to the proclamation was recorded in the Easton diary of Leonidas Dodson:

> In the Border States, it is feared the effect will be even more disastrous already in our community Secessionists chuckle over it as confirming all their accusations that the war is for abolition.[58]

A group of citizens of West River met with Governor Bradford in December to discuss the effects of the proclamation on Maryland. Bradford explained why he declined to issue a state proclamation:

> In the first place if the slaves at present believe that they are by law free on the first of January, it is doubtful whether any sudden change of that conviction produced by Executive action would not of itself incline them to make arrangements during a Holiday for a general stampede as the only alternative method of effecting their freedom.

And cited the perceptions that might arise from a Maryland version:

> Persons abroad would be very apt to deduce from it conclusions entirely unwarranted by the facts: It would for instance, in all probability be said that the slaves in Maryland were upon the eve of a revolt, which had rendered it necessary for the Governor to interfere and if possible prevent it by a proclamation—and the discussion or remarks which it would in all probability provoke, might be calculated in some parts of the state to stimulate similar movements among the slaves which there is now no reason to apprehend.[59]

1863

The Emancipation Proclamation greeted Americans at the New Year. Leonidas Dodson was not much impressed, noting that, as "slavery exists by virtue of state action," more forceful measures were necessary:

> There seems to be therefore as much good sense in the issue of this proclamation, as if the President had proclaimed that all the horses in the rebel domains should run into the gulf. The only vitality his edicts can have is by the march of his armies and if they march through the south, there will of necessity be no end of any windy proclamations to free the slaves. Invasion and occupation ends slavery.[60]

In January, G. Fred Maddox, the state's attorney for St. Mary's County, complained to Governor Bradford about another ruse employed by escaping slaves, in which he alleged military complicity:

> But the difficulty to which I now ask your attention and assistance arises from the fact of the location of a Military Hospital amongst us—which was established for that purpose, but has become the receptacle of runaway negroes—Not only are they taken within the Military lines but are protected by the Military in the hands of individuals belonging to the Hospital outside of these lines—I understand that the Col. Commanding states that until a runaway negro registers his name *he is free to leave if he choses*—If he does not chose to leave, his owner cannot force him—If his name is registered he in fact becomes the property of the General Government, because after such registering the Col. has no authority, and the party is referred to the Secretary of War.
>
> According to the law of Maryland a party who harbours a runaway negro is subject to an Indictment and if found guilty consigned to the Penitentiary.

Maddox expressed frustration at the Emancipation Proclamation's protection of slaves in areas such as Maryland, where it did not apply, and its failure to protect them in the South, where it did:

> A lady of the County living near Point Lookout has a runaway girl in the hands of one of the officers of the Point outside of the lines, but protected by the Military of the Post—the proper remedy would be a warrant directed to the Sheriff of the County to arrest this man, who holds this runaway—If the Sheriff is resisted, he can summon a posse from the whole County who can arrest him.
>
> The question is, will the Governor of Maryland protect the people of the County by the Militia of the state should the law be enforced by the Sheriff?
>
> I cannot understand the Government if by issuing the proclamation of the 1st of January the President intended to act in good faith to the people excluded by

said proclamation—We are excluded and worst served—worst served, because the proclamation bears upon its face protection to us, and comes into our midst in Peace and cheats us of our property—In the South where the proclamation is to take effect, the officers who are to carry it out, do not feel comfortable in going—[61]

An annoyed Bradford replied that extraordinary times required extreme measures:

But it must be equally obvious—though the tenor of your letter would seem to ignore the fact—that the circumstances now surrounding us are of a very extraordinary character, and such as much practically modify in many respects the usual course of judicial proceedings, whilst they would render utterly impracticable the particular Executive assistance you seem to contemplate—A single word explains this change of circumstances—We are in a state of War,—a war of such a character and extent as modern times have never witnessed, and which like all other wars carries in its train a fearful list of Calamities, surround us with Camps and Hospitals and fortifications, and compels the individual especially in the neighborhood of such posts—for the sake of great public exigencies—to submit frequently to exactions which at other times the laws of the land would promptly interfere to prevent.[62]

A January editorial from the *Talbot County Gazette*, pasted by Samuel Harrison into his journal, equated abolition and secession as fated to bring about the same end with regard to slavery:

The Gazette styles "Abolition" and "Secession" twin brothers—both laboring to the same end, the destruction of slavery—but characterizes the brother secession as most effective in his efforts, having accomplished in a few months, what the other had been laboring for during many years. It also accuses the secession party in the county of debauching the minds of the Negroes, and by constantly, persistently asserting that the object of the Government & its supporters here was the freeing of the Negroes, it has led them to expect confidently that their emancipation would be speedily declared. So up [until?] this date there seems to have been no party of emancipation in Talbot.[63]

The *Gazette* took note late of refusals by Union officers to relinquish slaves who escaped into their lines:

It is to be noted that about this time negroes in various parts of the state began to leave their masters, and take refuge within the army lines. In some cases they are delivered up, but the growing animosity against the institution of slavery, and the conviction that upon the support rendered by it the Rebellion was relying, caused many of the officers to refuse to surrender the slaves, and others to encourage their leaving their homes.[64]

In February, a group of twenty-six self-described Unionists petitioned Congress for compensated emancipation for Maryland slaveholders. The eventual split between those in favor and those opposed would weaken slavery:

> The undersigned Loyal Citizens of Maryland being sincerely anxious that Maryland shall cease to tolerate Slavery, and convinced that a grant of ten millions of dollars will suffice to compensate for the inconveniences, public and private, and to alleviate the shock to the industry of the State, incident to such a change, respectfully petition your Honorable Body for the passage of such an act, subject to such conditions as may be thought reasonable to exclude disloyal persons from taking any benefit under it.[65]

Gen. Henry H. Lockwood, commander at Point Lookout, in March ordered protections for slaves and other blacks within the prison's lines:

> That there shall be no interference with the slave population by the troops within his command except for certain specific purposes hereinafter named. Military Camps shall not be used as places of public resort or for idlers, and All those coming there, except on important business, or to give information, should be denied admittance, Such as have business will be conducted to the proper Officers of the Camp, Information will be sought for from all sources and rewards in money, with protection from danger from giving information may be promised to all, White and Black. Any one suffering from having given information will be protected, without or within the Camp, as may be necessary. Commanding Officers will generally be sustained in the protection afforded by them, but will be held responsible that there be just grounds for such protection. All cases of the kind, should be immediately reported to Head Quarters. All informants—where the information leads to a capture—will be remunerated, and with a view to this, their names should be taken, by the Officer to whom the information is given and reported. Negroes entering the Camps clandestinely, must be placed without the lines, but in no case *delivered*—either *directly* or *indirectly*—to their Masters.[66]

In June, the sheriff of Prince George's County sought guidance from Governor Bradford on dealing with "negroes running away from and through this County." The Sheriff was under pressure from citizens to call out a "Posse Comitatus," several of whose members had subsequently been arrested "by the authorities of Washington and imprisoned." Bradford's reply advised discretion in the performance of his duties:

> You are doubtless right in your suggestion that you have authority to arrest all fugitive slaves under the laws of our state, and if resisted in the discharge of that duty would have the right to summon to your assistance the Posse Comitatus.
>
> Whilst however it is your right to call such a power to your aid, the exercise of such a power at such a time as this is a proceeding of very doubtful expediency—

> With the war at our very doors and our state at this moment invaded, it would I think be manifestly imprudent to bring into operation in any County any such police power as might invite a Collision with the Military Authorities; and therefore whilst you might arrest all such fugitives that you quietly could; I think that the interest of the owner not less than the public peace, require that you abstain from surrounding yourself at present with any such County force.[67]

The same day Bradford wrote to Lincoln on behalf of Frank Stockett, a resident of Annapolis who had petitioned the president for assistance in retrieving his escaped slaves. Bradford told Lincoln that Stockett, who had been "Commissioner of Enrollment" in Anne Arundel County, "is one of our most esteemed Citizens, whose loyalty is unqualified in its character":

> The subject of his Complaint, as set forth in his Memorial, presents I think, just claims upon your interference—*Knowing* as his Petition alleges, that certain of his slaves are in, what is called the Contraband Camp in the District of Columbia, after arming himself with due process of law issued under the authority of the United States, he seeks merely to have such process served by the proper officer—Genl Martindale the Military Commander of the District, refuses to allow this service upon the ground "that said Negroes were under the Military protection of the United States Government"—In this view of his duty I would respectfully suggest that Genl. Martindale is clearly mistaken—[68]

Samuel Harrison commented on a meeting in Cambridge on August 24 that addressed a hitherto taboo subject in his part of the state:

> the question of emancipation was discussed freely—perhaps the first instance within 50 years upon the Eastern Shore, at least—if not in the state. H.H. Goldsborough one of the speakers, avowed himself an emancipationist, but desired the work of freeing the slaves should be of a gradual character, and that it should not be done in a "rough & unlawful manner.["] he said "when a man can prove his loyalty, he should be remunerated for his negro, just as he would be for his horse."

Noting that:

> H.H.G. became, in the end a warm advocate of immediate & unconditional emancipation.[69]

With congressional elections looming in October, Elizabeth Blair Lee commented on the Fourth Congressional District candidates: proslavery Unionist Charles B. Calvert and two favoring Maryland emancipation, Francis Thomas and John C. Holland:

> They hope to carry the emancipation M.C. in this District but I fear the Secesh will unite on Calvert who is proslavery Union Man—It is going to be a well contested election & if carried by Holland will soon emancipate slavery in this

State—for this District has some of the largest secesh counties in the State in it—Father puts much on their getting paid for their negroes & that is a point of much import—for they are fast losing them without any hope of recovery for loss in any shape Many that now stay hoping for emancipation & would leave if disappointed If I was a large owner of the property I would put them on wages now & be sure of my crops—Thomas goes for deportation & emancipation & made an admirable speech.[70]

Late in October four men from Upper Marlboro told Governor Bradford that they had complained personally to Lincoln about the tactics of black recruiting parties that conscripted their slaves. In their letter, the men said when in Washington they had seen Senator Reverdy Johnson, who "told us, there was mistake in the matter":

In behalf of our fellow-citizens of this County, we waited on the President yesterday, and complained to him; that a detachment of U.S. Troops had recently encamped here, collected a body of our negro-slaves, resisted and prevented the civil officers of the state from taking them, in execution of the laws of the state, and carried them off to the District of Columbia;

That detachments of armed negroes, among them our own slaves, are now occupying the landings on the Patuxent river, seizing and carrying off the slaves from the plantations, and greatly endangering the peace and safety of our defenceless families.

We submitted to the President the alarming and intolerable grievance of subjecting to Military authority, to be exercised over them by revolted slaves and armed negroes, a free white people entitled to the laws and liberties of the other people of the United States.

The President answered that the Governor of Maryland and the Secretary of War had come to an understanding in regard to the measures to be taken to recruit negro soldiers from the state of Maryland; that no complaint of these measures had reached him before ours; that he would order an enquiry into it; by a telegram to Genl. Schenck; and by sending an officer of the Adjutant Generals department immediately to the Patuxent; that *the soldiers must be had*; but, that he, in effecting it, had no desire to offend, insult, or needlessly injure our people; that our complaint of the employment of the colored troops in this matter seemed to him reasonable.[71]

In November, three black men were arrested and charged with helping slaves escape. In August 1865, almost a year following the abolition of slavery in Maryland, a slave wrote to an official of the Freedmen's Bureau in the District of Columbia requesting their release from prison and pardons:

I have the honor to state that in Nov. 1863, my husband, Jno. Jones, and Richard Coats, & Caleb Day—(Colored men) were arrested & tried at Port Tobacco,

Md, and sentenced to be confined in the Penitentiary at Baltimore, for the term of eleven years & eleven months, for assisting three colored women, & four children, to escape from slavery.

Richard Coats was the slave of Geo. Wm. Carpenter, of Harris Cove, (opposite Acquia Creek); Said Carpenter has several times, been confined in the "Old Capitol" for smuggling goods to the rebels.

Before turning my husband, Jno. Jones—& Richard Coats over to the authorities—Carpenter whipped them so severely with a stave—in which he had bored auger holes, that they suffered severely for over two months.—Caleb Day & my husband—Jno. Jones were free men.

I would earnestly, and respectfully request that you use your influence to procure for the parties named full pardon—& release from imprisonment.—Very Respectfully Your Obt. Servant,

    Her
    Dola Ann X Jones
      mark[72]

1864

Early in the new year a former Maryland slave at Camp Barker, a place of refuge for contraband slaves in Washington, testified about abusive treatment he and other slaves had suffered in Freedmen's Village, a facility thought to be in Virginia. The interviewer noted that this slave was ill with "catarrh of the bladder," and "there is every evidence of sincrity and reliability about this man & his testimony":

> I was a slave for a long time; my masters name was Lukie Pierce and we lived on Carrolls manor in Maryland. My master was a first rate man and if he was living to day I would be under him. I rather be under him by ten degrees than be with Nichols. My good old master never whipped any of his slaves, and he would never allow any of his overseers to abuse any of his slaves. He set us all free one year before the war began. My owners was better than many masters but I speak from my heart before the Lord when I say that the conduct of Mr Nichols was worse than the general treatment of slave owners.[73]

In March, Samuel Harrison summarized the arguments of the *Talbot County Gazette* and the emancipationists in noting that slave owners should not be compensated for any lost market value resulting from emancipation:

> The destruction of the value of slave property was owing to the war, & not to any state legislation; and therefore the owners have no more just claim upon the state than those persons who had lost property by the inroads of the enemy upon Maryland soil.[74]

One man expressed worry that disloyalists were organizing against the referendum on a convention to deliberate the merits of emancipation:

> I am sorry to hear that any Union men are being seduced by the Secession arguments that are so extensively circulated throughout the County & State. They ought to know that every vote cast against a Convention will be regarded by the Government as a vote in favor of the Southern rebellion. Slavery is, as we all know, is dead, and the sooner we get rid of it the better it will be for us all. We can soon accommodate ourselves to the change. But if the Convention Bill is beaten it will be considered as an evidence that our loyalty is conditional on the existence of slavery, which has caused so many difficulties & troubles. The secessionists are now opposed to a convention. The last time the question was before the people they were in favor of it. How is this? & why this consistency. The body of the vote against will be from secessionists who would rejoice to see the Southern rebellion succeed. Can any *good* Union man [?] in this with them. I hope not & I hope you will act energetically & get all the vote out. *The Rebels will have a ticket.* This I think you may rely upon. They profess they will not have, but this is a *mistake.* In secret they are working—& if we are not active we shall be defeated.[75]

Rebecca Davis recorded an April visit from Bishop Whipple, who preached at St. John's (the Davis church) and then ministered

> at night to a large number of colored servants at our house. During the service the Bishop requested them to sing some hymns with which they were familiar. This was done. The Bishop was much affected and said it recalled to his mind past years when he had preached to their brethren in South Carolina, & had united with them in singing the same hymn. After the sermon he called on the Rev. Mr. Enmegabowh to say something about the Indians. This he did in a feeling, dignified & impressive manner.

After further words about the Indians and "the pleasure he felt at being present at this christian meeting,"

> then followed the benediction by the Bishop, when the negroes, with one accord, sang spontaneously the Doxology. Mr. Enmegabowh ['a Chippewa divine'] said, with much emotion, I wish to shake hands with these Christian people, which was cordially responded to. The services throughout the day were unusually interesting, being participated in by not only different races of men, but different sects of Christians.[76]

In May, Laura Moody of Washington attempted to get her husband, George Moody, released from prison in Lower Marlborough. Moody and his companion, "Mr. Jones," had allegedly been engaged by Negro contrabands to take "some negro women to their husbands" when arrested, despite government authorization. Gen. E. B. Tyler reported on the case:

> On visiting Port Tobacco on Monday last, I learned that Moody, Jones and two negro men whose cases had been referred to me from the Secretary of War and Secretary of State, were as I had reported, confined in Charles County Jail having been transferred from Prince Georges. Being informed that they were not properly treated I called on the Sheriff and requested an interview with the prisoners; he very politely complied by showing me to a building to all appearances well secured with bars and bolts, at both doors, and windows. After unbolting two doors, I was shown into a medium sized room, where I found the four men heavily chained to the floor with fetters upon their feet, and was told the four were handcuffed together at night. I inquired of the Sheriff by what authority he held the prisoners, and he produced an order from a Prince George's County Magistrate, directed to the Sheriff of Prince George C. for the commitment of Jones in the Jail of his (Prince George) County, and said the others were charged with running off slaves; but exhibited no authority for holding them and I think he had none. At my suggestion the Irons were taken off.
>
> These men complained very bitterly of the treatment they had received in Prince George and Charles County Jails—and strongly disavowed any intention of committing an offence in what they did, believeing as they did, the pass of Provost Marshal Shutz of Washington all the authority they required. There is evidently a strong prejudice in the minds of a majority of the citizens of Prince George and Charles Counties against these parties and all who sympathize with the slave, and in the death struggle of their cherished institution they appear anxious to vend their spite upon any one that may fall in their power.[77]

In June, the commander of an Ohio regiment in Salisbury, in Wicomico County, sought guidance on the disposition of slaves recruited for the U.S. Colored Troops and subsequently rejected for service:

> I beg leave to refer a subject to the Brigr Genl commanding, that promises me no Small degree of Annoyance. Many Slaves have been recruited in this district, who upon examination, were rejected and sent home—the masters of these men wish to reclaim them. They come to me for protection, and refuse to go back to their masters. Under the Act of Congress and Gen Orders, what Shall I do with them—The master claims them under the laws of Maryland—And they claim they are fugitives. In one instance, and I learn there are many others, Masters have refused to feed and clothe their Slaves, and have beaten and illtreated them. They come and claim protection What shall be done. I do not fully understand to what extent I am to interfere in this matter. All those who conduct themselves in this manner are openly or covertly sympathizers with the Rebellion. I want

to do my whole duty in this Command, and Shall, if by possibility I can learn what it is.[78]

G. Frederick Maddox wrote to Governor Bradford about the case of Thomas Lynch, then in custody of the U.S. military on suspicion of murdering a slave. Maddox asked Bradford to facilitate Lynch's transfer to the civil courts—and indicated an intent to represent Lynch in the case:

> I concieve it to be my duty to represent to you the facts in a case which has occurred in this County—Dr. Thos. A. Lynch a respectable gentleman of the County, had a difficulty with one of his servants, and chastised, whether slightly or greviously I can not say—about ten days afterwards the woman went within the lines of Point Look-out and died the following day after her arrival—Dr. Lynch was immediately arrested by Col. Draper Commander of the Point—I proceeded immediately to the Point and requested that Dr. Lynch be handed over to the Civil Authorities—and in justice to Colonel Draper and the Provost Marshal Major H.G.B. Wymouth, I must say they were much inclined to listen to my request—but had already referred the case to Genl. Butler and were compelled to await his action in the matter—Since which time Genl. Butler has ordered a Commission to assemble to try Dr. Lynch for murder.
>
> I have also ascertained the reason that the order for the Commission has issued—that the testimony against Dr. Lynch is altogether negro and consequently will not be admitted as evidence in the Courts of the state of Maryland—[79]

An August letter to Lincoln from a Maryland slave in "Belair" may have been prompted by talk of emancipation:

> Mr president it is my Desire to be free, to go to see my people on the eastern shore. my mistress wont let me you will please let me know if we are free. and what i can do. I write to you for advice. please send me word this week. Or as soon as possible and oblidge.[80]

The *Baltimore American and Commercial Advertiser* recognized the difference between defeating the Confederacy and ending slavery, believed both objectives crucial, and that abolition would benefit slaveholders:

> The prevalent antagonism to it is so deeply seated that if the friends of the Union and the advocates of civil liberty fail to make Emancipation in Maryland a fixed fact in 1864, they will not rest until the blemish is wiped from her borders hereafter. The progress of the age demands it, and will be satisfied with nothing less. The people are convinced that Slavery is the cause of the Rebellion, and that if it is permitted to live after the Rebellion is suppressed, it will always be a spark on the brink of a powder magazine. All attempts on the part of the advocates of Slavery to arrest this growing conviction in the popular mind will prove futile.

It will increase and multiply, and become correspondingly imperative in its requirements. Lie the waves of ocean which cannot be at rest, its agitation will go on until the whole body politic is quickened and pervaded. Have not the more intelligent of our slaveholders the wit to perceive these facts? Have they not the good sense and discretion to give way quietly to the unerring and invincible decrees of fate, instead of rashly presuming to block the wheels of resistless progress? They surely know what their slave property has steadily depreciated until it has become valueless. Moreover, they are urged to acquiescence by their own interests. We have proved by statistical figures, by facts which cannot be controverted, by argument which cannot be refuted, that the abolishment of Slavery is largely conducive to their individual interests, while its beneficial influences upon the resources and prosperity of the State are beyond all calculation. We appeal to them as fellow citizens of our grand old Commonwealth, as men bound by common ties to memories we alike revere, and to associations which alike command the homage and the affection of our hearts, to ponder deeply upon these things. No sterner, no more solemn or more sacred obligation ever rested upon men to give up their idols, than is imposed upon the slaveholders of Maryland. The opportunity is given them to win the admiration and applause of the world, or to brave the reprobation of posterity.[81]

This newspaper was consistently Unionist and pro-Lincoln throughout the war and editorialized tirelessly for ratifying Maryland's new constitution banning slavery, exhorting supporters of freedom, especially soldiers, to vote. Its language sought to equate loyalty to the Union with opposition to slavery.

On the eve of the election, a "last grand rally for the new Constitution" was held in Baltimore's Monument Square. The October 10 gathering lasted until midnight and approved resolutions favoring the new constitution and the election of Lincoln and Andrew Johnson. Henry W. Hoffman, organizer of the meeting, read a letter from Lincoln "expressing his hearty approval of the new Constitution proposed by the Convention."[82] (In the middle of the affair, during which the Mayor spoke, a portion of the platform collapsed.):

As usual upon such occasions, a large platform (capable of seating one hundred and fifty persons) was erected below the eastern wall of the Court House, which was tastefully decorated by Mr. Louis Muller. Extending along the rail of the enclosure were United States flags, gracefully festooned, and immediately beneath were the names of Lincoln and Johnson, pained in large letters. Over the rostrum was the following inscription, in illuminated letters, extending across the entire front:

"A FREE UNION, A FREE CONSTITUTION, AND FREE LABOR"

In front on a line with the rostrum was a range of chandeliers, whose lights, supplied with shades, beautifully illuminated the Square. Whilst the Wards were marching into the Square the band of the 2d United States Regular Artillery, led by Professor Smith, and stationed at Fort McHenry, played several beautiful airs, which were received with applause by the crowd, which extended from Lexington street to a point south of Fayette. In the meantime, fireworks, consisting in part of rockets, blue-lights, revolving wheels, and Roman candles, were very liberally exploded and gave additional eclat and enthusiasm. Some of the Wards appeared in strong numbers, and in addition to the old style of transparence, displayed hundreds of Chinese lanterns.[83]

Marylanders received congratulations on their new "abolition" constitution from former fellow residents now in New York:

Allow us, who have gone from you to reside in New York and vicinity, to congratulate you upon the great event which has just marked a new era in the history of our beloved Maryland! Language fails to convey to you a full expression of the joy which we feel at the great victory which has been so peacefully achieved by you, through the ballot-box, over the worst of enemies to your prosperity. *Maryland* now stands for the "redeemed, regenerated, and disenthralled, by the genius of universal emancipation," from a material, social and political curse, which has long been seated upon her slumbering energies, and weighing them down like some hideous nightmare.[84]

Andrew Stafford, provost marshal of the First District of Maryland in Easton, advised his superiors the day after the new constitution took effect that military measures were necessary to prevent children of former slaves from being "apprenticed" to the "disloyal" (presumably ex-slaveholders):

Since the adoption of the New Constitution, in this state, there has been a very strong disposition on the part of the disloyal element here, to ignore that instrument, so far as it relates to Slavery and the Elective franchise. Many of the citizens are endeavoring to intimidate the colored, and compel them to bind their children to them, under the old apprenticeship law, and there is no means of preventing them from doing it, without their fears could be dispelled.—Many of them come to me, for advise, & I direct them to file their objections,—but many will be deterred from doing so by fear.—They are in a pitiable condition.

In some localities, the disloyal are determined to pollute the ballot box, by ignoring the law. Chas Key, a son of F.S. Key, says publicly, that he is disfranchised, but intends to vote. We need martial law here, if we expect peace—[85]

Gen. Henry H. Lockwood forwarded Stafford's letter to Gen. Lew Wallace, endorsing its contentions and urging that troops be dispatched to ensure that "disloyal slave-holders" did not hijack the new constitution by such methods:

I have no doubt of the truth of Capt Staffords statement and fear that unless some steps are taken to protect the colored people, of the lower counties the chief object of the new Constitution will be defeated and these people will still be slaves in truth though free in name. I respectfully recommend that a sufficient force be at once placed in these counties to protect the State & military authorities in their just and laudable effort to see that the organic law of the state is not rendered a nullity by chicanery and violence on the part of the disloyal slaveholders of Maryland. If the provisions of the new Constitution are not carried out and these rebels made to respect it it will be worse for the colored man than if it had never been adopted.[86]

Many Maryland slaves freed by the new constitution poured into Baltimore with no housing or job prospects. Gen. Lew Wallace, who took command of the Middle Department in March, years later described the scene in the city:

Directly that constitutional freedom in Maryland was proclaimed, the newly liberated, shaken off by many of their masters, and not knowing where to go or what else to do, toiled up in bewildered hundreds to Baltimore—men, women, and children. Their presence on the streets made itself observed, and became a subject of complaint. The police stations filled with them, and presently the mayor invited me to help him; they were starving, and he had no funds with which to care for them. The situation, really extraordinary, called for prompt action, and I buckled to it heroically.

After discovering that local asylums had no space for these refugees, Wallace seized the Maryland Club to house them, as part of "my Freedmen's Bureau":

The club-house happened to be eligibly situated, conveniently arranged, handsomely furnished—all by report, since I had never set foot in it—and though in style somewhat antiquated within and without, it also suited the new demand upon the city better than any other I could find. The kitchen with its great cooking-range seemed especially desirable. In short, I took possession of the house, and, putting it in charge of an officer of my own selection, before the week was out four or five hundred negro women and refuges, with their children, were in enjoyment of its luxurious shelter—women, be it observed—only women unable to go out and, like the men, seek employment.[87]

George B. Cole objected to extra measures for newly freed slaves. He also complained about "General Orders 112" that provided military protection for freed blacks and requisitioned the Maryland Club House—now called "Freedmen's Rest"—to house the "sick, helpless and needy."[88] (Military authorities considered a levy on rebel sympathizers to support this initiative should donations be insufficient.):

Union authorities had the Maryland Club under surveillance throughout the war. In the fall of 1864, Gen. Lew Wallace seized the club as a refuge for Maryland freedmen—knowing that "the hubbub it would raise would reach to Washington."

The *American* agreed:

> It is impossible to regard this order in any other light than as a premeditated outrage upon the feelings of all respectable citizens of this city and state. The new constitution has declared all slaves *free* . . . the existing laws and courts of the state are abundant to enforce its provisions. The Gen Gov has no authority nor need to put them "under military protection" . . . the Maryland Club House is entirely unfit. It is a large drinking house altered for Club purposes—being divided into a few suites of large apartments. It is in the center of the most admired and fashionable part of the city, very near the residence of Thomas Swann, the new Governor elect . . . and other prominent and conspicuous Union men of the city.[89]

A white Unionist and "district assistant assessor of internal revenue" in Prince George's County in December sought Wallace's opinion of what the writer characterized as emancipation's failure in Maryland:

> I take the liberty of asking a few Questions for the good of the Colored People it does appear from what they tell me that since they became free they are not cared for by their former masters and a number of them are women and children that

are suffering for food and raiment others say they are told that they will be sold into Bondage again the poor Creaturs do not know what to do they say they are whiped and abused very much the most of the young men has left and a number of them are in the army those women with their children cannot help them selfs they say they are afraid to look for a new home for fear while doing so their children will be thrown out this is their statement to me and I do not doubt it in the least, for, I know what a time we few Union men have hear for they do not hesitate to say that we robbed them of their property and such abuse as is hard to take you know our vote in the county was very small and we are few in number but we do not fear them for we think we have stood the hardist part of the storm and believe it is near to and end some information for their good would be thanfully received[90]

On November 10, Governor Bradford advised Wallace that General Orders 112 must not interfere with Maryland laws "relating to apprentices, whereby provision is made for binding out the minor children of free persons of Color, who have not the means or are unwilling themselves to take care of their offspring":

The general scope and object of your order as I understand it, is I think, if the order itself is discretely executed, calculated to be of much service in assisting a class generally very ignorant now for the first time thrown upon their own resources—I fear however that without some explanation it may mislead some of the Civil officers of the State in connection with their duties as prescribed in our Legislative Code—I do not refer to any thing connected with the *Slave* Code of the State; that of course is entirely abrogated in effect by the adoption of the new Constitution,—but there are other provisions of our Code having exclusive reference to the free Colored population of the State, now, more than ever requiring strict observance from the large and sudden increase made to that class of our population.

Bradford closed by suggesting that Wallace make clear that he had no intent to interfere with the power of Maryland's orphans courts to allow white masters to bind black children as involuntary apprentices.[91]

chapter eleven

Black Troops

1863

In February, four Charles County men wrote to Governor Bradford about the illegal recruitment of local slaves into the Union army.

> On the afternoon of Monday the 2nd Inst. he came up Port Tobacco creek in a steam-boat to Chappel Point, spent the night there, and left next morning with some fifteen or more slaves on board belonging to Citizens of this County—The exact number of slaves taken off we have up to this time been unable to learn, but we believe it will, when definitely known, be found to exceed rather than fall below, the figure above mentioned.
>
> The boat on her way up the creek, stopped opposite the farm of the Messrs. Ware and sent a boat ashore, which undoubtedly was done to notify their slaves of his being at Chapel Point, as six of them absconded that night, and were seen to leave next morning in the boat—Other Gentlemen living in that vicinity lost their property the same night, but not to the same extent as the Gentleman above named—These slaves far from being prevented, were openly invited and received aboard the boat—This can be proved by Citizens who were present and witnessed the proceedings.

The men complained further about the federal troops in the area:

> We would further call your Excellency's attention to the character of the troops now stationed in our County—It is such as tends very materially to demoralize the slave population in our midst, by enticing, harboring, and otherwise tampering with them; to say nothing of their continued depredations upon the stock and farms of the farmers of the neighborhood. There are now at Chapel Point three Companies belonging to "Scott's 900," two at least of which, we are credibly informed, were previously stationed at Poolesville Md. who became so exceedingly annoying and troublesome to the Citizens of that vicinity, that they petitioned the Secretary of War to remove them, which was done accordingly; shortly after this they were ordered to this County.[1]

Early in July Gen. Robert Schenck wrote to Lincoln about the eagerness of blacks to enlist in the Union army and the need to initiate recruitment immediately. Secretary Stanton informed Schenck two days later that Col. William Birney would oversee recruitment of the Second Maryland Regiment for the U.S. Bureau of Colored Troops:

> I have again and again in vain endeavored to get the attention of the authorities at Washington to the fact that at least one negro regiment might be raised here.

*On July 4, 1863, Gen. Robert
Schenck urged Lincoln to begin
recruiting black men for the
Union army immediately.
MdHS.*

I telegraphed you some days ago on the subject and venture once more respectfully to suggest that somebody be sent here or authorized to accept the services
of & organize these blacks who are now willing to be enrolled. I have had some
thousands of them at work on fortifications but will discharge the most of them
in a day or two. I had also upwards of two hundred (200) offering today from
Cambridge on the Eastern Shore but if not accepted and organized while this
spirit prevails among them it will be difficult to get them hereafter[2]

Birney began his work quickly. At the end of July, he reported on a raid he and his
men conducted on a slave jail in Baltimore City, for which "Special Order 202"
empowered him to enlist male slaves and "liberate all those confined there." His
report named ten male and ten female slaves and their masters, whom he noted as
disloyal. Birney was also ordered to free the slaves of "General Stewart, of the rebel

army," but did not do so—"they being confined in the Baltimore City Jail, and not in Camlin's Slave Pen":

> I have the honor to report that immediately on the receipt of Special Order No. 202, of this date, I proceeded to Camlin's Slave Pen in Pratt Street, accompanied by Lieut. Sykes and Sergeant Southworth. I considered any guard unnecessary.
>
> The part of the prison in which slaves are confined is a brick-paved yard about twenty five feet in width by forty in length, closed in on all sides. The front wall is a high brick one; the other sides are occupied by the cells or prisons two or three stories in height. The yard is not covered in. It is paved with brick. A few benches, a hydrant, numerous wash tubs and clothes lines covered with drying clothes were the only objects in it. In this place, I found 26 men 1 boy 29 women and 3 Infants. Sixteen of the men were shackled together, by couples, at the ancles with heavy irons and one had his legs chained together by ingeniously contrived locks connected by chains suspended to his waist. I sent for a black-smith and had the shackles and chains removed.[3]

One Baltimorean discussing the fallout from the Battle at Gettysburg mentioned a newly formed black unit in the city:

> While writing, a company of black soldiers have just passed. They were working at one of the forts near the City limits and have now organized as soldiers. I hear General Trimble has arrived here, a paroled prisoner, having lost his left foot but I hear he is doing well. Quite a number of Baltimoreans have been wounded, killed and taken prisoners.[4]

In July, Birney sought permission to enlist in the Fourth Infantry Regiment, U.S. Colored Troops, "now in process of formation in this city," twenty-four black men, "free from diseases and defects which would disqualify them from joining the army." Birney, having found these former slaves in the Baltimore City jail, courtesy of their masters, summarized the case of each, one being that of Peter Knox:

> The jail record shows nothing except that on the 1st June, 1862, he was commit-ted by Magistrate E.R. Sparks, as "a runaway slave." There is no statement of claim or ownership or hearing.
>
> Peter Knox states that he was the slave of a notorious secessionist, Captain John Fulton, of the rebel army, residing in Accomac Co., Va.; that on account of the open display of two secession flags by Captain Fulton, he, Knox, was de-clared free by General Lockwood, who gave him free papers, that he served for about seven months as waiter to an officer in the 150th N.Y.S.V.; that he lost his papers, was arrested here in Baltimore and thrown into jail where he has been lying ever since.[5]

Baltimore Judge Hugh L. Bond in August objected to the policy of recruiting only free black men into the Union army. The Unionist Bond believed the policy would lead to labor shortages that would inflate the value of slaves and thus support slavery. In arguing that all black men be recruitment candidates, Bond cited the Confiscation Act of July 1862, which authorized the president "to employ persons of African descent in any capacity to put down the rebellion":

> The objection which I have to this proceeding, in common with other non-slaveholders, is one which will strike your mind with great force. To take away from the State the hearty, strong & able free blacks who now do the manual labor on the farms of the seven comparitively free counties of the State, and in the City of Baltimore, will leave those sections of the State without labor, or else compel them, the most loyal sections of the State, to hire slave labor. This at once gives a new value to the institution which no loyal man desires should be permanent, and which it has been both hoped and conceded the war would destroy, and which, likewise, the Administration has taught us to believe it was its policy to rid us of for ever. I do not mean to assert that all slaveholders in this State are disloyal, but by far the greater portion of them are, and such as are hostile to the Government are by far the most bitter and active enemies in our midst. The course now pursued by Colonel Birney, under instructions as I understand it, viz: that of enlisting none but free persons, will double the value of slave property, as it is called, and actually indirectly put money in the hands of those hostile to the Government which is taken from the purses of the loyal non-holding people of the State.[6]

In August U.S. Colored Troops recruiting officer Col. John P. Creager was arrested and jailed in Frederick for allegedly recruiting slaves without the required permission of their masters. Creager, who did not try to make his bail of $1,000, summoned an attorney who "was a pro-slavery man & was opposed to taking negros into the army." From jail, Creager wrote to Colonel Birney about his misfortunes and requesting "a little money I have used all I had, and must have some," and noting "there are some, 8 Slaves in this Jail kept here by their masters who are all traitors":

> They charge me with having enticed Slaves to leave their masters. it is true I have recruited some, but did not know they were such at the time. the only thing I am sorry for is that I cannot go on with my recruiting. Col we can raise a Brigade in Md. I am sure of it if we can have a chance all, their [slaves] are running off and going to Washington or Baltimore. I have got the matter completely under way, they understand it, and if I had the chance I could send some 25 pr diem. on Sunday night 38 started from here, so one of the colord men told me yesteday, and there is 30 more who want to go to day these last are all free men, and I shall

HARPER'S WEEKLY.

A JOURNAL OF CIVILIZATION

Vol. VII.—No. 324.]   NEW YORK, SATURDAY, MARCH 14, 1863.   [SINGLE COPIES SIX CENTS.
[$3.00 PER YEAR IN ADVANCE.

Entered according to Act of Congress, in the Year 1863, by Harper & Brothers, in the Clerk's Office of the District Court for the Southern District of New York.

TEACHING THE NEGRO RECRUITS THE USE OF THE MINIE RIFLE.—[SEE PAGE 174.]

A March 1863 cover of Harper's Weekly *depicted training of blacks in the U.S. Bureau of Colored Troops. The legend reads "Teaching the Negro Recruits the Use of the Minie Rifle."* Harper's Weekly.

try to get transportation for them by sending the order to the agt and get him to fill a blank if he will do so. I can then send them forward to you. I will give you notice with each squad, but if I fail in this I do not know what couse to take.[7]

Several days later, in a letter to Secretary Stanton, the U.S. Colored Troops recruiting agent on the Eastern Shore stressed that slaveholders were the prime beneficiaries of the federal proscription against recruiting slaves and that non-slaveholding loyalists found the policy punitive. He urged the government to sanction slave enlistments:

> While I believe in the wisdom, and justness of intention on the part of the Government in all its efforts to put down the rebellion, you will allow me to call your attention to one thing which is very unjust, unfair, and which bears very hard on a large majority of the loyal men of Maryland, viz. the drafting and recruiting free colored men and leaving out the slaves.
>
> In this (Queen Anns) County, nearly all the slave holders are disloyal men and are doing all they can against the Government, while nearly all of the non-slaveholders are loyal and true men to the Government. By taking away the free colored men, you take away the labour from the very men who are doing their utmost to sustain the Government, and give every advantage to the men who oppose the Government. It ought not to be so. In nearly every case between master and slave, the slave is the only loyal man and anxious to fight for the country, but is prohibited from doing so. Can you not remove the barrier so that all the slaves who wish to, may join the army also? Under existing laws, the disloyal men of the county will be benefitted rather than hurt by the draft. If they happen to be drafted they will either pay the three hundred dollars, commutation money, or put in substitutes, and soon more than get their money back by the exorbitant prices they will demand for the hire of their slaves. But if you will allow the slaves to go, you strike a deeper blow against the rebellion than can be given in any other way.
>
> Sincerely hoping that you will give the matter due consideration, and speedily order the recruiting of slaves, I am, with great respect, your humble and obedient servant.[8]

An August transcription of a notice in Samuel Harrison's journal recorded the enthusiasm of black enlistees, and the disappointment of slaves denied:

> "*Colored Volunteers*"
> "The Spirit of volunteering among the colored population of the county, appears to be on the increase. On Monday morning last (August 17, 1863) there were some thirty five from Trappe District that took the steamer at [Clovas] Point, for Baltimore where all were accepted and mustered in except two, and they were rejected on account of physical disability. On Thursday morning (Aug

20) ten more left Easton in the steamer from Miles River Ferry. On the morning of their departure we learn that there were several slaves from the country made their appearance in town, and expressed a desire to play "sojer" but of course were denied the privilege."[9]

William Birney complained to the Bureau of Colored Troops about interference with his recruitment efforts. He cited the arrest of John Singer, "a free man of color," en route to enlist, on the basis of "a pretended writ" that Birney was "advised by counsel learned in the law, is not known to the law of Maryland":

> The scheme to obstruct and arrest the enlistment of U.S. Colored Troops in Maryland is prosecuted with activity by a few political schemers; while I have had every reason to believe that the great majority of loyal men in the state are ready to favor and promote the measure. The arrest of my agent, J.P. Creager, acted as was anticipated: it intimated the people of color, giving them the impression that the United States was powerless to protect them against their enemies in this state. That act alone caused me to lose between one and two hundred recruits who were ready to come to the rendezvous at Baltimore. It perplexed and disheartened the many respectable gentlemen who had, in different parts of the state, volunteered to aid me in gathering in the men willing to enlist. Nearly all of them have since been deterred by menaces from the further prosecution of the work; and the business of recruiting is going on but slowly. Encouraged by their success, the enemies of the enlistment of U.S. Colored Troops have within the last week resorted to the most inhuman outrages against the families of free men of color who have enlisted: the cornfields of these poor people have been thrown open, their cows have been driven away and some of the families have been mercilessly turned out of their homes. I shall immediately take measures to lay before you in an authentic shape the facts of some of these outrages designed to intimidate the men of color from enlisting.[10]

When William Bostick, the bailiff for Easton, and his son were arrested for impeding recruitment of black troops, Samuel Harrison spoke in their favor:

> These Bostics were people in an humble walk of life, as their avocation indicates. They were prompted to the course by their social & intellectual superiors.[11]

Ex-Gov. Thomas Hicks, now a U.S. Senator from Maryland, backed the use of black troops though he complained to Lincoln about blacks helping recruit slaves without the consent of masters, loyal and disloyal, and the consequences for farmers at harvest time:

> A deputation of good and respectable union men of Talbot County came over to see me to day, and are much troubled at the course things are taking, and say it will operate agst. us if persisted in. I say these were Union men because I know

them to be so, they represent that quite a number of slaves was taken from Miles River ferry in that county a few days since and their owners protesting agst. it.

Capt Lowndes had *his* negroes returned to him, whilst others were disregarded in their claims; and no one has faith in the loyalty of Lowndes.

Major Krauser was the officer, that took these slaves away as these gentlemen inform me. I do and have believed that we ought to use the col'd people, after the rebels commenced to use them agst. us. What I desire now is that if you can consistently do so you will stop the array of uniformed and arm'd Negroes here, let the recruiting go on as it is and all will be well.[12]

In September, Governor Bradford complained to Postmaster General Montgomery Blair that black recruiters were aggressively enlisting slaves. Bradford warned that the loyalty of Unionist slaveholders was being sorely tested by this activity, which he urged "either be expressly ordered or positively forbidden." He suggested that if "these practices are not speedily stopped we are given over in spite of all we can do, once more to the Democratic rule":

It sometimes really almost seems that there is a determination somewhere to get up if possible, something of a Civil War in Maryld. just as we are about to subdue it every where else. I went to Washington two weeks ago on this subject and regretted that you were absent. I had an earnest Conversation with the President and Mr Stanton, but I fear to little purpose, for though they both declared that the enlistment of slaves had not been determined on and no one had been authorized to enlist them, the practice not only continues but seems from what I see and hear to be every day increasing. They are being sent over from the Eastern Shore by scores and some of the best & most loyal men are among the sufferers.

I will not trouble you with many details, but refer only to the last Committee which waited on me yesterday.—They were four Gentlemen from St Michael's District in Talbot County, represented to me as of undoubted loyalty. The District itself, as perhaps you know, is notorious throughout the Shore for its early and inflexible loyalty. They said that a few days ago they went on board the Steamer when she was about to leave her landing, to see if their Slaves were not on board. They found a large number of slaves from the County huddled together in the Bow of the Boat armed with uplifted Clubs prepared to resist any close inspection. One of these gentlemen—and in his relation he was very calm & dispassionate—approached the officer having them in charge & told him that he had come merely to ascertain whether his Slave was among those on board—and respectfully asked to be allowed merely to see whether he was there told him at the same time that if he found him, he had no idea of demanding him, or interfering with the officer's possession of him or interfering in the slightest manner with his purpose. That he merely wanted to be able to identify his negro, that he might have some proof of his being taken by the Government in case it should think proper to pay for such—*And this request was denied.*—Now my dear Judge is it not almost a mockery to talk of paying loyal owners any thing, if the Contraband Camps are closed against them, and their negroes after being taken by the recruiting officers are at the very threshold of their own homes suffered to crouch together, conceal themselves from the possibility of identification, to club off their owners who make any such attempt, and then carried off before their face to—no one knows where?

I understand that the President & Secretary of War will say that such recruiting is unauthorized—Then why in God's name permit it?

In the same message, the governor sought Blair's help in keeping from Talbot County a black regiment from Baltimore:

These gentlemen whom I saw last evening said to me: "We have come to you Governor at this time not so much to get pay for our slaves—if the Government stands in need of them let it have them; but we have come earnestly to entreat that a *negro regiment* which they threaten to bring down from Baltimore and quarter in our neighbourhood may not be allowed to come. Our people are in a state of utter Consternation at the propect of such a thing.—Whilst we are willing that the Government shall take from us any thing it needs, for God's sake let it not suffer us to be pillaged by the Regiment of negroes."

I give you Judge the language as nearly as I can of one of the Committee—a plain straightforward, sensible loyal Farmer. I wish you could have heard him. And can not this poor boon at least be granted? Can not this Regiment be kept here where it is? or must it without the shadow of necessity be sent across the Bay only further to inflame, terrify and disgust our Citizens? Truly this would seem to be adding insult to injury.—Will you my dear Sir, see the President and if you can do nothing else, keep at least this negro Regiment at home.[13]

Bradford stated in a letter to Francis Thomas that Lincoln, recognizing Maryland's loyalty, would not sanction "this odious project" and complained about attempts

To force upon a people by means of military duress, the adoption of a particular policy, even in ordinary times and on far less sensitive subjects, would be a hazardous experiment with the temper of any community; but in times like the present, with our hearts intent on the preservation of the Union, and our united energies required to secure it, the seizure or seduction of all the slaves of the state capable of military service—whilst it would not probably, under any circumstances, add a single regiment to the ranks of the army—would awaken a sense of wrong, and a feeling of indignation and disgust, that, in their moral effect upon the loyal feeling of the state, would far outweigh all the advantage that fifty such Regiments could bring to the support of any cause.[14]

Troops of Company E of the Fourth Infantry Regiment, U.S. Colored Troops, organized in Baltimore in 1863 to serve for three years. They guarded Confederate prisoners at Point Lookout and saw action at Fort Fisher in North Carolina. MdSA.

Samuel Harrison described the scene aboard a steamer full of black recruits:

> I recollect to have witnessed the departure of the Champion with those recruits on board, as she left the wharf at Oxford, where she had stopped to take off others from the lower part of the County. It was a most impressive sight—the owners stood silent, and thoughtful upon the wharf & beach, while the steamer moved off, the colored people, waving their hats & good bye and the braking out into one of their jubilant himns, such as they sing in their meetings. They had no patriotic songs—but these hymns were converted into songs of deliverance from slavery.[15]

Leonidas Dodson was jubilant at the sight of black recruits and noted the opportunity that Maryland slave owners had missed:

> A bombshell has fallen in our midst! A week ago an officer was here recruiting *slaves,* on Tuesday morning (8) he started for the boat, with them (some 80 to

100) and for the first time in my life I saw slaves in the presence of their masters slaves no longer in a practical sense, any free to leave at pleasure. What wonderful changes result from a state of war.

This single instance served to illustrate more strikingly than any event that has yet transpired among us, how great the mistake of taking up arms to secure the permanency of slave Institutions. It served further to illustrate that instead of turning a deaf ear to the Presidents theory of compensated Emancipation, our delegates in Congress, should have foreseen the inevitable blow which the war had given slavery in Maryland.[16]

Capt. John Frazier, provost marshal on the Eastern Shore, told Secretary Stanton of robust slave enlistments in Talbot County and that "the disloyal utter no objection but seem to regard it as a matter of course." Frazier suggested a policy change that would both compensate loyal owners and count slaves toward the county's draft quota, ensuring that slave enlistment became universally embraced:

I have no hesitancy in saying that if the President would issue his proclamation—setting forth that it is the will of the Administration to accept all slaves who are willing to volunteer—there would be at once a universal acquiescence on all sides—particularly if it was known that loyal citizens would be compensated and the district receive a credit on the quota of troops required. Talbot has already furnished near 400 slaves and free persons of color since the enrollment of her citizens and will before the end of this week furnish probably two or three hundred more if the enlistment of slaves is continued as it should be. Poor men are rejoiced at the prospect of being exempt from draft. Loyal slave owners are glad of a last chance to receive some compensation for a property rendered worthless by the Rebellion and the cause of emancipation receives a constant accession of supporters. Nothing which has ever occurred has so strengthened the party favoring emancipation.

I trust therefore the Government will speedily develop its policy in this respect. The present doubt and uncertainty is the only source of trouble on the subject.[17]

A long letter to the president conveyed Governor Bradford's irritation with recruiting tactics in the state, which Bradford believed were permitted only in Maryland. He asked Lincoln to explain the authorization for this recruiting and reminded him, incorrectly, that the Emancipation Proclamation had freed slaves in Maryland:

Suffer me to make you acquainted with the course of proceeding usually adopted in these cases—as it has been reported to me—a steamer in Government employ provided with a recruiting officer and armed guard is sent into some of the many Rivers with which our state abounds, and this officer and guard immediately make known their presence and find means of communicating with the slaves on the neighboring farms; these slaves, usually under cover of the night are induced to quit their owners homes and to repair on board the boat—The officer in charge exercising his arbitrary discretion—by no means regulated by the question of the owners loyalty—in carrying off one man's slaves and allowing another's to return, and when his cargo of recruits is thus made up, he weighs anchor and delivers them at camps in a distant part of the state, sometimes before their owner is aware of their absence.

Bradford conceded that slaves could be recruited "when an imminent public necessity exists":

> If her property, whether in slaves or anything else, is really needed to put down the Rebellion, there is not a state in the Union that will yield it more cheerfully; but as your Excellency can well understand, she will not see her property of any kind wrested from her by armed force with no emergency Military necessity for it first proclaimed, with no adequate indemnity for it secured, with no similar process elsewhere instituted and not even an official order ever promulgated.[18]

On October 1, Secretary Stanton wrote to Lincoln about a meeting in which Bradford agreed to rules for recruiting black troops in Maryland. Stanton stated it a "military necessity" to enlist into the Union army as many troops as possible, "without regard to color, and whether they be freemen or slaves." Lincoln's response left a window slightly open, by prohibiting recruitment of slaves of loyal owners without owner consent "unless the necessity is urgent":

> The following propositions were understood to have received the assent of Governor Bradford:—First, that free persons of color in Maryland should be enlisted; second, that slaves should be enlisted by consent of their owners; third, that, if it were necessary for the purposes of the Government that slaves should be enlisted without regard to the consent of their owners, there would be no objection to a general regulation by which loyal owners of slaves could receive just compensation for the labor or service of such slaves, upon filing in the Department deeds of manumission—disloyal owners not being entitled to any such compensation.[19]

On October 21, Lincoln queried General Schenck about reports of disruption by black soldiers in southern Maryland:

> A delegation is here saying that our armed colored troops are at many, if not all, the landings on the Patuxent river, and by their presence, with arms in their hands, are frightening quiet people, and producing great confusion. Have they been sent there by any order? and if so, for what reason?[20]

MEN OF COLOR
TO ARMS! TO ARMS!
NOW OR NEVER

This is our golden moment! The Government of the United States calls for every Able-bodied Colored Man to enter the Army for the

Three Years' Service!

And join in Fighting the Battles of Liberty and the Union. A new era is open to us. For generations we have suffered under the horrors of slavery, outrage and wrong; our manhood has been denied, our citizenship blotted out, our souls seared and burned, our spirits cowed and crushed, and the hopes of the future of our race involved in doubt and darkness. But now our relations to the white race are changed. Now, therefore, is our most precious moment. Let us rush to arms!

FAIL NOW, & OUR RACE IS DOOMED

On this the soil of our birth. We must now awake, arise, or be forever fallen. If we value liberty, if we wish to be free in this land, if we love our country, if we love our families, our children, our home, we must strike now while the country calls; we must rise up in the dignity of our manhood, and show by our own right arms that we are worthy to be freemen. Our enemies have made the country believe that we are craven cowards, without soul, without manhood, without the spirit of soldiers. Shall we die with this stigma resting upon our graves? Shall we leave this inheritance of Shame to our Children? No! a thousand times NO! We WILL Rise! The alternative is upon us. Let us rather die freemen than live to be slaves. What is life without liberty? We say that we have manhood; now is the time to prove it. A nation or a people that cannot fight may be pitied, but cannot be respected. If we would be regarded men, if we would forever silence the tongue of Calumny, of Prejudice and Hate, let us Rise Now and Fly to Arms! We have seen what Valor and Heroism our Brothers displayed at Port Hudson and Milliken's Bend, though they are just from the galling, poisoning grasp of Slavery, they have startled the World by the most exalted heroism. If they have proved themselves heroes, cannot WE PROVE OURSELVES MEN?

ARE FREEMEN LESS BRAVE THAN SLAVES

More than a Million White Men have left Comfortable Homes and joined the Armies of the Union to save their Country. Cannot we leave ours, and swell the Hosts of the Union, to save our liberties, vindicate our manhood, and deserve well of our Country. MEN OF COLOR! the Englishman, the Irishman, the Frenchman, the German, the American, have been called to assert their claim to freedom and a manly character, by an appeal to the sword. The day that has seen an enslaved race in arms has, in all history, seen their last trial. We now see that our last opportunity has come. If we are not lower in the scale of humanity than Englishmen, Irishmen, White Americans and other Races, we can show it now. Men of Color, Brothers and Fathers, we appeal to you, by all your concern for yourselves and your liberties, by all your regard for God and humanity, by all your desire for Citizenship and Equality before the law, by all your love for the Country, to stop at no subterfuge, listen to nothing that shall deter you from rallying for the Army. Come Forward, and at once Enroll your Names for the Three Years' Service. Strike now, and you are henceforth and forever Freemen!

E. D. Bassett,	Rev. J. Underdue,	P. J. Armstrong,	Rev. J. C. Gibbs,	Elijah J. Davis,
William D. Forten,	John W. Price,	J. W. Simpson,	Daniel George,	John P. Burr,
Frederick Douglass,	Augustus Dorsey,	Rev. J. B. Trusty,	Robert M. Adger,	Robert Jones,
Wm. Whipper,	Rev. Stephen Smith,	S. Morgan Smith,	Heary M. Cropper,	O. V. Catto,
D. D. Turner,	N. W. Depee,	William E. Gipson,	Rev. J. B. Reeve,	Thos. J. Dorsey,
Jas. McCrummell,	Dr. J. H. Wilson,	Rev. J. Boulden,	Rev. J. A. Williams,	I. D. Cliff,
A. S. Cassey,	J. W. Cassey,	Rev. J. Asher,	Rev. A. L. Stanford,	Jacob C. White,
A. M. Green,	James Needham,	Rev. Elisha Weaver,	Thomas J. Bowers,	Morris Hall,
J. W. Page,	Ebenezer Black,	David B. Bowser,	J. C. White, Jr.,	J. P. Johnson,
L. R. Seymour,	James R. Gordon,	Heary Minton,	Rev. J. P. Campbell,	Franklin Turner,
Rev. William T. Catto,	Samuel Stewart,	Daniel Colley.	Rev. W. J. Alston,	Jesse E. Glasgow.

A Meeting in furtherance of the above named object will be held

And will be Addressed by

U. S. Steam-Power Book and Job Printing Establishment, Ledger Buildings, Third and Chestnut Streets, Philadelphia.

An 1863 recruiting broadside from Frederick Douglass summoned black men to join the Union army: "Join in Fighting the Battles of Liberty and the Union. A new era is open to us." The Gilder Lehrman Collection, courtesy of the Gilder Lehrman Institute.

Schenck's reply referred to the murder of Lt. Eben White by John H. Sothoron, former Maryland state senator and delegate and farmer on the Patuxent River, and his son:

> The delegation from St. Mary's County have grossly misrepresented matters. Col. Birney went by my orders to look for the site of a camp of instruction and rendezvous for Colored troops; see his report this day forwarded to the Adjutant General. He took with him a recruiting squad, who were stationed, each with an Officer, at Mill Stone, Spencer's, Saint Leonard's, Duke's, Forrest Grove, & Benedict Landings, on the Patuxent. They are under special instructions, good discipline and have harmed no one. The only order of violence has been that two secessionists, named Southoron, have killed Second Lieut. White at Benedict, but we hope to arrest the Murderers. The officer was a white man. The only danger of confusion must be from the Citizens, not the Soldiers, but Col. Birney himself visited all the landings, talked with the citizens, and the only apprehension they expressed was that their slaves might leave them. It is a neighborhood of rabid Secessionists. I beg that the President will not intervene and thus embolden them.[21]

The commander of St. Mary's District at Point Lookout sent a party to Leonardtown to suppress "contraband traded and all disloyal practices—arresting deserters and escaped prisoners and preserving the public peace." He also ordered an investigation into recruiting:

> It is reported that some persons are now engaged near the mouth of the Patuxent and above there in enlisting into the military service slaves and free persons of color without proper authority from the War department. You will enquire into the matter and if you find such to be the case you will cause them immediately to desist and to leave this military district forthwith if they are not residents therein.[22]

John Hay noted the problems created by forcible enlistments in Maryland, which, Hay wrote, Lincoln (the "Tycoon") suspected General Schenck tolerated, so "things in Maryland are badly mixed":

> Schenck is complicating the canvass with an embarrassing element, that of forcible negro enlistments. The President is in favor of the voluntary enlistment of negroes with the consent of their masters & on payment of the price. But Schenck's favorite way (or rather Birney's whom Schenck approves) is to take a file of soldiers into a neighborhood & carry off into the army all the able-bodied darkies they can find without asking master or slave to consent. Hence results like the case of White & Sothoron. "The fact is," the Tycoon observes, "Schenck is wider across the head in the region of the ears, & loves fight for its own sake, better than I do."[23]

A week later eight slaveholders from Upper Marlboro, on the western side of the Chesapeake Bay, complained to U.S. Senator Reverdy Johnson about illegal recruiting activities by black troops:

> The negro troops have *not* been withdrawn. The promise made to you last friday has not been kept. They are still harassing us, plundering us, abducting our negroes. So far from being withdrawn the field or their raid upon is much extended; now all way up the Patuxent. Yesterday a steamboat of them came up to Hill's landing, the head of navigation of the river, opposite this place. The negroes in the fields refusing their persuasions to go with them, they threaten them, that they will return to-morrow, thursday, and carry them off by force. We beg your prompt and urgent interposition. Judge Blair, we trust, will aid you.[24]

On November 8, Colonel Birney denied the slaveholders' allegations, defended the actions of his men, and accused the slaveholders of waging war on them:

> The authors of the within letter are reckless in their statements. I intend to recruit up the Patuxent but never have done so. Above Benedict, where my stockade camp is located, there never has been a recruiting station or party. The "steamboat of them" (negro troops) contained *three* colored soldiers placed on board to prevent slaveholders from burning the boat. There was one officer on board. The object of the trip was to observe the landings, with a view to future recruiting under order No. 329 and to give the regular pilot of the boat the advantage of the instruction of a Patuxent river pilot who accompanied him. There was no *"harassing," "plundering,"* or *"abducting,"* terms which I understand Senator Johnson's correspondents to apply to the Government recruiting of Colored Troops for the defence of the country.
>
> The threats to return next day and "carry them off by force" are the coinage of Messers Hodgkin and his associates. The officer & men on the boat fully understood they were *not* to return next day. The boat has never returned there nor has there since that date been a colored soldier or an officer of the U.S. Colored Troops up the Patuxent above Benedict for any purpose whatever.
>
> The Western Shore slave owners are more unscrupulous than the same class elsewhere. Two of them killed my Lieutenant, the unfortunate and noble-hearted White, others helped off the murderers, nearly all of them justified the murder; and now, we have strong grounds for suspecting that four of my soldiers, who have died suddenly—after an hour's convulsions—have been poisoned by the emissaries of these men.
>
> When there is sufficient loyalty and public virtue on the Western Shore to make it unpopular to run the blockade or to harbor rebel officers and spies, it will be time enough for its inhabitants to claim peculiar privileges from Government and to oppose the increase of the U.S. Army. At present, nearly all the loyal men here are among the class which I have been sent here to recruit.[25]

In November Reverend James W. Hoskins, rector of All Faith Episcopal Parish in St. Mary's County, sought Bishop Whittingham's influence in removing black troops from the Sotheron farm:

> You are aware of the tragedy which occurred lately on the farm of John H. Sotheron. Without saying anything about the circumstances of that occurrence, since it would not be profitable, I should ask why the family of innocent women & children should be persecuted and turned upon the world to starve and freeze, for what they are in no way responsible? The affair took place in the field, far away from the house where the family were. And yet they are beseiged in their dwelling by negro soldiers, who are eating up their substance, and soon what little they have in their storeroom will be consumed, when they must suffer and perhaps be turned out of doors to meet the approaching winter without provision, except such as they may find in the pity of those neighbors who feel for them, and are willing to share with them. I ask again why should they be thus punished? They are guilty of no rebellion against the Government. They have done nothing to merit such treatment.
>
> Let me beg you, Sir, to use your influence with the Powers that be, and have the negro soldiers removed from the Plains, and let the family enjoy what little is left, or at least let them remain until the winter has passed, unmolested. It seems to me that the seeking of vengeance upon innocent women and children cannot be approved by Him who takes cognizance of the affairs of men and metes out to them justice when and where due.[26]

Congressman John Creswell asked Judge Hugh Bond to clarify that Eastern Shore counties were receiving all due credit toward their quota for volunteers:

> After an interview with Col. Fry of the War Department to-day, I am very fearful that we shall have trouble in obtaining for the 1st District the proper credit for colored volunteers.
>
> If not appropriating too much of your valuable time, I would be greatly obliged to have you obtain from Col. Birney for me, as soon as possible a full return by counties of all enlistments of colored troops up to the day of this report. Please write to the Col. wherever he may be in relation thereto, and urge him to answer promptly.
>
> The authorities here have ordered a draft in my district without having made allowance for a single volunteer, white or black. This I think most unjust, and if carried out, will greatly damage us in the approaching contest for a convention, and emancipation. Indeed, unless we have the error corrected we shall be pretty obnoxious to the charge of indifference to the interests of the white laboring class, the influence and support of which is our great reliance in our battle against slavery.[27]

William H. Hunter,
chaplain of the Fourth
Regiment U.S. Colored Troops,
enlisted in October 1863.
Courtesy of Daniel C. Toomey.

At the end of September, Lincoln suspended black recruitment in Maryland pending agreement with state officials over policy specifics. In early October, General Orders No. 329 allowed slaves to enlist with their master's permission and provided compensation to loyal owners. On Christmas Day, the irrepressible John Creager sent from Monrovia, Frederick County, a status report to the Bureau of Colored Troops:

> Slaves are coming in tolerably fast. I shall be able to take from 80 to 90 recruits free and slave, Able bodied men to Baltimore or to our camp on the Patuxent on Tuesday next. I have already taken one one Squad down and am pushing ahead to the best of my ability, we still have trouble here with the Rebel and copperhead Factions, they are trying to have me removed, *"as you are aware"* they charge me with saying that I had power to go upon the farms and take the slaves, this is not the fact neither have I done any such thing, when they asked me if I had such authority I merely refered them to the 5th article of Gen orders no 329.

to these words, Enlistments may be made of slaves without requiring consent of their owners, and I merely added this seems to imply that they can be enlisted anywhere, but I have not recruited a man at any place but at my office.[28]

1864

Late in January William Birney, now a brigadier general, responded to a complaint from Charles Worthington, a Frederick County slave owner, that his slave had been coerced into enlisting:

> No slaves whatever have been mustered by me against their will; and no free persons. Every person prior to muster has full opportunity to say whether or not he will enter the service or not. I do not keep my recruits under guard.
>
> Slaveholders have frequently offered me their slaves, provided I would take them by force. I have uniformly declined having any thing to do with forcing them, although if the slaveholders had brought the men to me, I should have taken them, the orders recognising their right to enlist them.
>
> Nine owners out of ten will insist upon it that their slaves are much attached to them and would not leave them unless enticed or forced away. My conviction is that this is a delusion. I have yet to see a slave of this kind. If their families could be cared for or taken with them, the whole slave population of Maryland would make its exodus to Washington.[29]

A man near Upper Marlboro complained to Gen. Henry Halleck about an invasion of black recruiters and "that the recruiting of negroes should be by means of recruiting offices opened in public places only; and on due public notice":

> Yesterday a detachment of negro troops came to my landing on the river, my private property in which the public have no rights, took possession of one of my houses, are now quartered in it, have been roaming over my plantation, intruding into my barns, into my servants-quarters, and into my kitchen. a white man is sometimes with them, at the landing, who represents that he is their commanding officer, & that his name is Thorburn. He states that he has orders to send his negroes upon every plantation to persuade the farm-negroes to enlist; and afterwards to go himself upon the plantations.[30]

A recruiting officer sought permission in February to free black men who, upon trying to enlist, had been jailed:

> There are four or more Colored men who have been confined in Jail in this place, for several days, for no other crime than trying to get into the Service of the United States— Also that some twelve or more Colored men on their way to these Head Quarters as Recruiters for the U.S. Military Service, were last night taken up and lodged in Jail in order to prevent their enlistment.

I therefore beg to be authorized by you as Commander of the Post, to visit that Jail to release all such Recruits and to enlist all such who are willing to enlist, provided they are not Criminals except as above Stated.[31]

The commander of the St. Mary's district wrote to a county resident who had complained about black enlistments:

If you had given such advice I should have regarded it as very judicious and proper, but in point of fact you did no such thing. Those people who seem to think it a great wrong to have the negros exposed to the chances of battle would manifest a little more sincerity and be entitled to more respect if they would send their sons or go themselves to the field in defence of their government and country. But the time is close at hand when all these carpers and fault finders because the government chooses to employ colored soldiers will be regarded with the scorn and contempt that traitors are sure to receive. If you or any other loyal citizen is molested by unprincipled and disloyal men I will afford you such protection and adminster such punishment to them as will prevent a repetition of the outrage.[32]

On March 15, Gen. Henry Lockwood of the Middle Department of the Eighth Army Corps issued General Orders No. 11—which drew upon the Militia Act of July 17, 1862, and the Enrollment Act of March 3, 1863—directing recruitment of all Maryland blacks, free or slave:

Col. S.M. Bowman, Chief Mustering and Recruiting Officer for Colored Troops in Md., is authorized to enlist all such in the service of the United States; and for this purpose he is directed to send a recruiting officer, accompanied by a Surgeon, to jails, slave-pens, or other places of confinement, who shall be authorized to enlist all colored men found in these places, if passed by the Surgeon, upon their signifying their willingness so to enlist; provided, that none are held under criminal purposes.[33]

When Edward Belt, state's attorney of Prince George's County, wrote to Governor Bradford complaining about the behavior of black troops under the command of white officers, Bradford sent a copy of Belt's letter to Lincoln and demanded punishment of the perpetrators and cessation of such activities:

On the afternoon of the 8th inst. a large number of negro troops, from Birney's Camp at Benedict, arrived at this place, under the command of one Lt. Col. Perkins and other white officers and took possession of the Court House for quarters. The next morning a squad of the negroes was sent into the County Jail, of which they had previously demanded the keys, and set at liberty 21 of the prisoners—leaving only one person behind, a white man charged with Larceny—of those released, one was a white man brought here recently from Washington under a Requisition from your Excellency. *Eleven* were confined on various criminal charges, some being already under indictment and awaiting trial. The charges varied from Arson to Larceny, abducting slaves &c. one of the negroes released was actually under *conviction* of Arson—his sentence having been respited by the Court until April Term

As soon as our Sheriff reached the village, he hastened after the military who had started for Annapolis. The Lt. Col. had stated that his orders were only to takeout the *able bodied* negroes &c. and that the Jailer was responsible for the escape of the others, *yet all of them were released by a large armed squad,* and at the very point of the bayonet. Still the sheriff followed on to Queene Anne, hoping to have restored at least the women & boys &c.

But he met with no success, was roughly treated, and even threatened with personal violence.

The occurrence of so unprecedented an outrage within 18 miles of the National Capital, ought not probably to pass unnoticed. I had thought of communicating the facts to Mr Johnson of the Senate, and to our member in the House of Representatives—But upon reflection, I supposed I should best discharge myself of my duty in the premises by placing you in possession of the facts, and leaving the whole matter to your superior experience and discretion

Your Excellency will not fail to observe that the *practical working* of this affair is to invite the negroes to the perpetration of any crime and to offer practical protection and indemnity to them. It seems imposible that this man could have acted under orders.[34]

General E. B. Tyler, commanding the First Separate Brigade at Relay House, sent Lincoln a report describing trouble caused by the Purnell Cavalry, attached to the Nineteenth Infantry Regiment, U.S. Colored Troops, in Anne Arundel County:

On Thursday and Friday last the 19th U.S. Colored Regiment Commanded by Col Perkins passed through a portion of Anne Arundel Col. Md. which is in your command, and committed a great many depredations without any provocation, far as I can see and learn, at a placed called Taylorsville, or South River Ferry a Ware house containing grain and other things which had been deposited there for the purpose of being sent to Baltimore was entered and the troops were permitted to pour the grain out of the bags and use the bags to take away other things that were stolen by them. A young man whom I am well acquainted with was pushed off the wharf into the water by order of an officer because he asked the officer to prevent the negro troops from killing his chickens. After crossing the ferry they encamped on a poor widow woman's place who hardly has a support for herself, and took without Compensation, nearly all of her pigs; her tobacco was taken or destroyed, and her fodder fed to their horses. They also built fires in her barn. I have seen the depredations committed on the widow lady's

"Sergeant John H. Murphy, Sr., in Civil War Uniform, 1864." Murphy, the son of slaves, served in Company G of the Thirtieth Regiment, U.S. Colored Troops, which lost 225 officers and men fighting under generals Grant and Sherman. Of his experience he said, "I was in the wilderness with General Grant, and in North Carolina with General Sherman when he captured the Rebel army of General Joe Johnstone." Following the war, Murphy worked as a whitewasher, postal-service employee, porter, janitor, and Sunday school superintendent in Hagerstown before becoming president and publisher of the Baltimore Afro-American. *He died in 1922. MdSA.*

place, and am ready to *testify* to it. The Regiment is now stationed near Millersville, Md—and are still committing depredations. The men of the Command are allowed to insult gentlemen on the road without provocation. I feel it my duty as an officer of this Government, to report these facts, and am sure that immediate Stop will be put to these proceedings.

The Union men of the Co. are greatly insinced, and for their sakes, I hope the Government will not delay in making a thorough investigation into the matter.[35]

General Butler, now commanding the Department of Virginia and North Carolina, replied sarcastically to an Annapolis slaveholder who had complained about Union army recruiters forcibly removing his slaves:

No party, male or female, was taken away from your place against their will. Second, that negroes were enlisted in the United States services, and their families allowed to come with them.

For one, I could not consent to take the husband and father to fight for the United States and leave his wife and child in Slavery, and whenever the Government requires that of me, they will have to get some other gentleman to do that business. Besides, it would be manifestly unjust to you to take away the valuable servants, for the benefit of the United States, and to leave you to support their woman and children, and therefore I have ordered, in every case, where the wife and children choose to come with the husband and father, when he enlists, that they should be received, and taken care of, at the expense of the United States.

Long an abolitionist, Butler closed with a slow twist of the knife:

I can easily understand and sympathize with the trouble and discomfort the loss of servants occasions in a household, especially under such a system of labor as has been heretofore enforced in Maryland. But you, as a loyal man, will feel the necessity of submitting to that, as all of us have to submit to many discomforts, annoyances, grievances and troubles, because of this unhappy War.[36]

In March, Lt. Col. Joseph Perkins described to Col. Samuel M. Bowman (who in February 1864 had been assigned command of recruiting black troops in Maryland) a recruiting mission in Upper Marlboro, in which Perkins freed a number of imprisoned slaves:

The lower part of the Jail was in two rooms about ten feet square each, in the front room were about a dozen women with their children, all colored, who were confined there by orders of their so-called masters for safe keeping. I was informed by the Jailor (the only County Official I could see) that many of them had been there since the War broke out, and that their masters were some of them in the Rebel Army. The door of this room, when I entered the building was opened into the hall, but immediately on my entry, the Jailor, at my suggestion: closed and locked it.

At this time a guard was posted in the Court Yard, to prevent disturbance.

In the back room were eight able bodied men (Colored) all chained to one large staple in the centre of the room, by both legs, with Chains like ordinary cast chains, each manacle had been put on hot and rivetted down with a hammer and anvil. I was told that one of these men, belonged to the notorious murderer Colonel Southoron and had been there two years just because his master thought he would run away if he had a chance. The filth and stench was so utterly inhuman, that I had but little time to discriminate, although I was informed; and since then even in the communications referred to above; I have no reasons to think that any of them were confined for any greater offence than either trying to escape or assisting others to do so. I at once sent for a blacksmith, and told him to cut the chains off these men, saying I will not have any man enlisted into the Military Service of the United States with *irons* on

During the war, fifteen regiments encamped at Camp Belger, adjacent to Druid Hill Park. In 1863, it was renamed Camp Birney, after Maj. Gen. William Birney, who first oversaw recruiting in Maryland for the U.S. Colored Troops. Pratt Lib.

At this time the Mr Clark calling himself Provost Marshall, although without any insignia of rank, came to me and asked by what authority do you release these people? I answered, I do not recognise your authority to ask what my orders are, but I have released no one but the able bodied men, if any others have got out it has been through the neglect of the County Officer here. "Will you" said he "deliver up the women and children"? I answered "I have [not] released, neither do I take any woman or child under my protection, if you wish to, you can go and get them. My commission debars me from delivering them up to you, by act of Congress approved. But, as I shall put no obstacle in any ones way, so I shall not raise my hand to help, the men are enlisted and no one without a specific order can get them, the women take if you wish, no soldier shall interfere.[37]

In April, a Howard County mother described to her daughter the injurious effects of what appeared to be slave recruitment for the Union army from, and near, Bowling Green, the family farm:

Your father forgot to leave you some money. He did not receive a cent, and I sometimes fear he will never be paid. The rest of them are quite elevated with the idea of freedom. I do not know that we will own one by the first of May. I presume they will all be Emancipated. If so, I would like Compensation. There has been quite a Commotion in this neighborhood. Enlisting etc. They took 6 men from old Mr. Dickey Davis, Carroll's, and many others. Alice was up Easter. She said they had taken all of Rezin and Noah Worthington's that were able to go. They are nearly broken up. Labor is not to be had about here, and what the farmers are to do I do not know. My trust is in the Lord. I believe some way will be pointed out and provided for us.[38]

One free black man in "Annarunde County" gave an affidavit in April 1864 that "while sitting with my family at my home" on March 28 he was coerced into joining the Union army—reinforcing claims of Maryland slaveholders that blacks were being forcibly, and illegally, recruited:

I was asked by the officer my name & age and whether I wished to volunteer in the army and get the bounty of $400—or to be forced to go and get nothing—

I replied that my name was William Jackson and my age 36 years. That I did not wish to enter the army, and would not volunteer for any consideration of bounty, because of the del[icate] and uncertain state of my health, arising from the fact of my having been subject for the past ten years to constantly returning attacks of Epileptic fits. That I was totally unfit for military duty and could only expect to drag out a few months of a miserable existance, an incubus upon the United States Government If I was forced to enter its service

The officer declined to receive my statement, recorded my name at once upon his book as a recruit, and ordered me to follow him.

With difficulty and by solemnly pledging myself to report to him that evening at 4 oclock I obtained leave to remain at my home until the hour for reporting arrived. I immediately went to the two Physicians in my neighborhood Drs Waters & Hall one or the other of whom had been attending me for ten years or longer and obtained from each of them the certificates, (annexed herewith as part of this petition)—showing the fact of my having been subject to Epileptic attacks for many years, and of my being incompetant for military duty by reason of this painful and dangerous disease.

At the hour named viz 4 oclock P.M. March 28th I reported myself to Capt Read on board the Steamboat Cecil. as I had obligated myself to do. I stated my case and handed him my certificates. he said, I looked able to perform military duty and he would not take any certificate to the contrary.

I then begged leave to go back to my family and remain all night, pledging myself to report next day at 12 oclock. This permission was granted me. The next day at eleven oclock, I reported to the Captain and asked leave to go to Baltimore that morning and seek to obtain an exemption from the government surgeon before whom the recruits were examined. I pledged myself solemnly (and offered the Captain three or four hundred dollars security—from good Union men for the faithful discharge of my pledge) that I would report my self in Baltimore within ten days if I was not exempted in the mean time I obtained permission and came to Baltimore accordingly on the 29th day of March I was not allowed to go before the examening surgeon for two days but as soon as he would see me I reported to him and was pronounced fit for service and ordered on duty to the Camp near Baltimore where I have ever since and still am detained against my will.

And further that I have never at any time received or agreed to receive any money by way of bounty or compensation since I have been taken unwillingly from my home and detained in my present situation.

Your petitioner therefore upon the above recited facts prays that he may be discharge from performing service in the United States Army for which he is entirely unfit by reason of his delicate health and peculiar desease.[39]

Col. John Woolley, provost marshal in Baltimore, insisted that black troops receive the same respect as white troops:

While some of our Colored Troops were passing through Exeter Street this morning the ladies at the house No 80 indulged in hisses so loud that they were Easily heard across the street. They also brought a small dog to the window & endeavored to make him bark in order to show further their sentiments. I would like General to have the form of a bond which I can use in making such people feel that they cannot sneer & hiss at their Government or its troops without being brought to account for it. If consistent with your views please have Judge Marshal furnish me the form. The arrest of the parties at No 80 & placing them under bond of say 5,000 or 10,000 Dollars would no doubt prevent an immediate repetition of the "snakeish" offence.[40]

Under the headline "Riotous Colored Soldier," the *Sun* related the arrest of a black soldier:

On Saturday evening last a colored soldier named John H.W. Grey was arrested by policeman Stoddard, charged with riotous and disorderly conduct. It was alleged that Grey knocked several persons down on Union street, and declared that he would kill a white man before he left the city. He also, it was stated, resisted the policeman who arrested him. Captain Snavely, of the western district, sent the accused to the office of Col. Woolley, who ordered him locked up in the military prison to await trial.[41]

In April, Colonel Bowman believed that lack of pay parity for blacks and movement toward Maryland emancipation were impeding black recruitment efforts:

The prospect of recruiting Colored men in Maryland is not flattering: the bounty has ceased and free men will not enlist especially as the question of pay is not decided. Slaves won't enlist because they expect to be free by the action of the State Convention—

I have now only one boat and all the troops have been sent away. No recruits can be had unless I send detachments to particular localities and compel them to volunteer as I have done on many instances heretofore.[42]

Ten days later Bowman suggested recruiting cease in Maryland:

It is my opinion that Negro recruiting in Maryland is hurtful; negroes by force of circumstances and the costoms of the county have heretofore performed all the labor, and able bodied negroes between 20 & 45 have become exceedingly scarce, and whenever the U.S. gets a soldier, sombody's plow stands still; or sombody has lost a slave or servant of somekind.

They only way to prevent these outrages is to stop recruiting entirely[43]

In May, Thomas King Carroll, a citizen of Church Creek, in Dorchester County, complained to Governor Bradford that U.S. troops had forced all Negroes into their ranks:

On reaching home on Saturday last I learned that one of the more infamous outrages had been perpetrated upon the community the day before (Friday) that ever disgraced the annals of civilization. A press gang of negros dressed in U.S. uniforms and commanded by a white man whose name and rank I have been unable to learn, appeared in this neighborhood, having previously visited other sections of our county, and proceeded to *force* into their ranks every male negro they could find, free or slave, without regard to age or condition, threatening instant death to any who refused to go with them. The neighborhood was thoroughly searched, every farm visited and every negro they could find from the boy of 12 years to the man of 60, seized and carried off. In many instances the poor terrified wretches attempted to escape by flight, when the negroes would cock and point at them their guns threaten to shoot them dead if they did not stop. In no single instance, so far as I have been able to ascertain, was any one consulted as to whether he desired to go. *No one did go willingly.* Many of these thus taken were free negroes. I will cite one or two cases which may seem to illustrate the character of the whole proceeding.

Carroll provided specifics. His postscript identified one of the white officers as "Lieut. Foster," and "This man who said he was a captain gave his name as Booth":

One free negro man at least fifty years of age, was taken from the field of one of our farms, his plough and team left standing in the field, while he was not permitted to go home to obtain even necessary clothing. This man left five small motherless children with no human being to provide for them.

Another a free man over fifty years of age old and *lame* was taken, leaving behind him a perfectly helpless and now utterly destitute family to be provided for by public charity. Another a slave of nearly sixty years of age, almost *blind* and laboring under *consumption* was forced away. I could furnish many more but these are sufficient.[44]

Late in May Governor Bradford clarified to county commissioners in Maryland the policy that bounties were paid to all black volunteers—except slaves:

> The State designed these Bounties for the personal comfort and support of the volunteers and their families, and in case of their death leaving no family—or speaking more precisely in the words of the Bounty Act—leaving no wife or children, the unpaid bounty reverts to the State. To secure these results with the greatest possible certainty, and to prevent as far as practicable all abuses by which these ends my be defeated, I can suggest no better plan than to refuse altogether to recognize powers of attorney professing to be executed by colored volunteers, with perhaps the single exception of such as are executed in favor of the known wife or child of such volunteer and to whom you are thus able to make payment directly. Henceforth, therefore I advise you to observe this rule.[45]

Colonel Bowman complained that spring about the difficulties of recruiting for the U.S. Colored Troops:

> The position of Chief M.&R. officer Colored troops is difficult to fill, disagreeable and distateful. I occupy it much against my inclinations—The Secy. of War expects me to recruit every able negro I can get—I cant do it without hurting somebody. But in this case I encountered opposition where it was least expected. I was told by Citizens of Anne Arundel County there were slaves there fit for Military duty wholly useless to their masters. They proposed to put them in jail on some pretext so as to be seen by a recruiting officer. I sent Capt. Reed and squad there for the purpose stated. But the Jailor was adverse; he refused to allow Capt. Reed to take one who had been put there by the owner for the purpose and who had placed an order in Capt. Reeds hands authorizing him to take him, and it was not until after the owner remonstrated in person that he was able to get the negro.
>
> One other negro was put there for a like purpose. Two others were reported as being there for trivial offenses, and all those desired to enlist but the Jailor refused. An appeal was taken to Mr. McCullough the Sheriff, who also refused: He did not put it on the ground that the men were there charged with crime but on the ground that he should not "recognize military orders."
>
> Besides this it is currently reported and believed by Union men that the Sheriff is a strong rebel sympathiser, and that his hotel is a favorite resort for all such as drink toasts for the success of rebel arms.
>
> Whether all this or any of it is true or otherwise, it was the information upon

Among Confederate prisoners at Point Lookout was John Omenhausser, an Austrian-born Virginia soldier captured in 1864 and presumably the prisoner-artist who painted a series of watercolors depicting life in the camp, including interactions between captives and the African American troops who guarded them. One rebel conceded to the blacks a "soldierly manner," and a black sentry who recognized his master gave him $10, which the recipient described as "a curious inversion of old times." Here a guard stands over prisoners in punishment attire. "Ha! Ha! Ha!" he laughs. "I wonder if Barnum would not like to have them fellers in his Museum." Sketches from Prison.

which my action was based. If the facts stated are true a negro escort would be no outrage, but on the contrary might have a healthy influence.[46]

Henry Tydings, a slave owner at St. Margaret's in Anne Arundel County, described indignities suffered by his friends at the hands of recruiting parties that impressed slaves into military service without masters' consent:

> I was present when a band of some 8 or 10 negros and 1 white man came to a field where a negro man of Mr Thomas Pumphrey's was plowing; they surrounded the man, and compelled him, with presented bayonets, to accompany them; and I see them take him off.—I likewise heard Mr Pumphrey ask them if they tho't that was right? They replied, inquiring, "Do you not like it"? he remonstrated. They threatened him, *to serve him in the same way.* I saw one of the negros go to the fence, and on it level a gun, at Mr Pumphrey, while he was complaining.
>
> My own losses consist in the absence from work of my negros, concealing themselves, as did in like manner, nearly all the negros in this neighborhood, for several days, during all the time the Press Gang was in this neighborhood.—
>
> To Dr Wm Hammond, (an old practitioner) who asked of these men their

authority for seizing the negros, they replied by putting their hands on their swords, and saying "by this and by our muscle".—Dr Hammond has the words from their own mouths.

Numerous acts of a similar kind can be proved by other gentlemen, who have suffered losses.—

I also know that free negroes were carried off by them, to wit: Andrew Johnson & Horace Walker & others.—Some of them have escaped and got back.—

It is not necessary for me to repeat the fact that it is understood that *for money,* the slaves have been offered to be returned to some of the sufferers[47]

The commander of the Union prison camp at Point Lookout reported the escape of a prisoner who, after climbing a fence, was caught and returned by contrabands:

He declined, however, to explain the circumstances attending his escape, and as it occurred in the night, it is impossible to fix the responsibility upon any particular sentinel. The escape would seem to indicate some laxity of discipline in the regiment doing guard duty. The prisoner camp was guarded, on that night, by the 4th R.I. who have hitherto given no cause of complaint. I think the colored troops are the only guards from whom no prisoners have escaped, and they, as you are aware, are very prompt to use their pieces, perhaps too prompt.[48]

Mary Houser, a Maryland slaveholder, consented to her slave joining a black regiment:

Eligah [?] my colord man has been in the US service about nine months he is in the 4th Maryland US Rgt. We often get letters from him he likes the service. I am sorry for the necessity of employing Negro troops but it is so we were willing for him to go we miss him very much.[49]

In June, General Orders No. 47 outlined how the army would employ slaves unfit for combat:

The Secretary of War having ordered that all Slaves who are brought to the Recruiting Rendezvous, and found physically disqualified for Military Service, and who do not desire to return to their Masters, but seek Military protection, shall not be rejected, but enlisted and Mustered into U.S. Service, with a view to transfer to the Quarter-Master's Department; all Quarter-Masters in this Department are hereby directed to take charge of such persons when transfered to the Quarter-Master's Dept. and forward them to the Chief Quarter-Master of the Baltimore Depot.[50]

Colonel Bowman complained that the bounties due Maryland recruits had not been paid by the commissioners in the counties where they were enlisted, and that this failure to pay was causing much hardship and the black recruits to feel they had been deceived. Bowman explained that he had "advanced and disbursed" funds "for the benefit of the families of the men enlisted by me" and requested that unpaid recruits "be transferred to the City of Baltimore where their bounty will be paid immediately":

> Soon after relieving Genl Birney it became apparent that without extraordinary exertions, but few colored men could be enlisted in this State. I resolved to do all that could be done; I called a convention of negro preachers and prevailed upon them to open their churches for our use; I procured speakers to address them; sent out migratory recruiting parties into every neighborhood; published in all the papers; plastered huge posters on fences, walls, barn doors and wood piles, and set the black people crazy on the subject of enlisting, and the result was two fine regiments and eight hundred men besides for the Navy in about 40 days. A large proportion of these are free blacks whose enthusiasm and confidence were such that they left their families wholly unprovided for, having been assured by my officers and by myself that their bounty would be paid them as soon as mustered in or very soon thereafter. Hundreds of them could not have been induced to enlist except by this assurance The poor creatures believed that we were their friends and would not deceive them; they were proud of their uniforms; proud to become soldiers in the service of the U.S.—
>
> But it turned out they were ordered to the field before the bounty was paid. It will be remembered I plead earnestly to have them remain until after they were paid, but the answer was. "The exigencies of the public service require these regiments to be sent forward."—
>
> When the order came the men theretofore cheerful proud and enthusiastic became suddenly dissatisfied and dispirited. They felt, and had reason to feel they had been wronged and deceived.—
>
> The best thing to be done under the circumstances, that we could think of, was to have powers of attorney executed to collect their bounty for them, and disburse it according to the wishes of the men. Mr Hill the Secretary of State of Maryland undertook to collect for some of them; but both officers and men desired that I should do it and accordingly many of the powers were made out to me. At the same time the men gave directions for the payment over to their families by signing a printed form a copy of which is sent herewith.
>
> Under all the circumstances I could not well refuse to do all in my power to procure the bounty for the men who naturally looked to me for it. The business was not desirable by any means but my hope was to collect it at once, pay it over, and close the accounts.[51]

Samuel Harrison's October speculation about federal policy for black enlistment was consistent with Lincoln's approval of recruiting slaves even without the consent of masters. Harrison abided losing his male slaves to the army:

The enlistment of slaves continued to be the cause of much irritation to the slaveowners loyal and disloyal. Enlistments were not regularly conducted, but negroes suddenly, without warning left their homes, went off to Easton, or other places and thence were carried to Baltimore. The whole business was conducted as it were clandestinely, and without system, in the beginning.

My impression is this enlisting of slaves was at first without authority from the general Government, or the War Department; that it first began by receiving into the army the free negroes, and refugees, and at last culminated in the regular & systematic enlistment of any who should offer, without regard to their condition of freedom or servitude. Indeed they were finally enrolled & drafted as white men were previously. This enlistment of negro soldiers I opposed at the time, and I am not sure at this time, it was not a mistaken policy. But such was my devotion to the Union that I submitted with the best grace I could to the loss of my own slaves, all of the males of whom went into the army.[52]

In the summer of 1864, a U.S. Colored Troops' recruiting officer went to Middle River Neck in Baltimore County. He informed free blacks that enlistment would earn them "$300 bounty, $200 cash and $100 in monthly installments until the whole $300 is paid" and slaves "$100 Bounty and $40 worth of clothing, and your freedom, and be men, as other men, enjoying all the rights and privileges under the Government, that can be granted to you":

To all of which they answer, they are willing and would be glad to go, if their masters could not get them back. I assured them their masters could not take them back, if they were competent on examination to bear arms, and that their masters would be paid for them. They then offered the objection that they were to be made breastworks off, and to be put in the front, that the Government was deceiving them in the promise of bounty, wages, and freedom, and that they could be brought back again if they ran away. But as soon as we removed all these impressions, the men assented and said they would cheerfully, willingly go, in the presence of their rebel masters and mistresses. Some of their masters who were much attached to their slaves, were unwilling to believe that they had assented, until they questioned them in the presence of Lieut. Frick; and other witnesses whom we have. Some of them were told by their masters to make themselves either younger or older than the required age.[53]

John Q. A. Dennis, a former Maryland slave living in Boston, implied in a July letter to Secretary Stanton that he had been freed in November 1863 by enlisting in a regiment of the U.S. Colored Troops. He sought Stanton's aid in freeing his three children from slavery:

my Dear wife was taken from me Nov 19th 1859 and left me with three Children and I being a Slave At the time Could Not do Anny thing for the poor little

Children for my master it was took me Carry me some forty mile from them So I Could Not do for them and the man that they live with half feed them and half Cloth them & beat them like dogs & when I was admited to go to see them it use to brake my heart & Now I say agian I am Glad to have the honour to write to you to see if you Can Do Anny thing for me or for my poor little Children I was keap in Slavy untell last Novr 1863. then the Good lord sent the Cornel borne [*Birney?*] Down their in Marland in worsester Co So as I have been recently freed I have but letle to live on but I am Striveing Dear Sir but what I went too know of you Sir is is it possible for me to go & take my Children from those men that keep them in Savery if it is possible will you pleas give me a permit from your hand then I think they would let them go I Do Not know what better to Do but I am sure that you know what is best for me to Do

my two son I left with Mr Josep Ennese & my litle daughter I left with Mr Iven Spence in worsister Co [. . .] of Snow hill

Hon sir will you please excuse my Miserable writeing & answer me as soon as you can I want get the little Children out of Slavery, I being Criple would like to know of you also if I Cant be permited to rase a Shool Down there & on what turm I Could be admited to Do so No more At present Dear Hon Sir[54]

Colonel Bowman complained to Governor Bradford of invidious rumors about the bounties promised to black recruits. Bowman wrote, "I am satisfied if we could confer personally together in regard to the matters in controversy, we could settle the whole matter in two hours time":

I claim to have used all the care possible in enlisting in this State; to have prevented to the utmost extent of my power all colored men leaving the State to enlist elsewhere, to have preserved as near as possible the proper status of free and slave; to have credited to the different Counties the men belonging to them, and to have promised only such bounty as was provided by the laws of Maryland. This Bounty I promised should be paid before the men should go to the field, not anticipating their sudden removal, and when I found they were going disappointed and dispirited as they might well be, I consented as a matter of duty I owed to them, to collect their bounty for them, in case they were not paid in any other way. This is all I have attempted to do.

It is said I have threatened to credit all the slaves to Massachusetts or Pennsylvania. I beg you not to believe such nonsense. I have no power to do this and would not do it if I had. All I ask is that these men raised by me and promised bounty by me shall be paid the bounty provided by law.[55]

In August, an official of the U.S. Colored Troops in St. Mary's County sought guidance from Bradford in paying bounties to three black soldiers who had died before collecting them:

I was appointed a short time ago their Agent to pay the free colored Volunteers of this County their bounty. Having been informed by Col. Bowman that these troops were at the "front" of the "Army of the Potomac" I proceeded thither in search of them. After some time and difficulty I reached the Regiment that these troops were in; they were behind our breastworks in front of Petersburg, firing at the Enemy when I arrived. The Adjutant of the Regiment informed me that three of the number that I sought had been dead for some time, and the other three had been transferred to the Navy. From the Navy Department I learn that they are now in the Pacific Squadron.

Under these circumstances I ask for further instructions—In case one of the three who are dead left a free wife and children, another a slave wife and children, and the third, was a single man—how much I disburse this fund?[56]

The governor responded several days later:

In reply I would say that the unpaid Bounty due in the case of the one who died leaving a *free* wife, should be paid to her, and in the other two cases, the unpaid portion reverts to the State, and should be retained by the Commissioners for settlement with the State hereafter.[57]

In August, following an effort to organize militia companies in Baltimore amid the panic surrounding the Confederate strike on Washington during the Monocacy campaign, a group of black men demanded of Lincoln that black recruiters treat them as they did white troops:

Squads of colard soaldiers accompanied som times by white men come to our houses demand admitance under the authoritey of Col. Bowman. Surtches the house Curses our wives our sisters or mothers or if the man be found he is made to fall in and martch to the drilling room and thare give his name thare is one instance of a man being Shot at while trying to escape thare are others whare our white inemies go with thoas Soaldiers for the purpos of Maltreating us. Our ocupation sometime prohibits us from ariving home before those Squads do compel us to fall in the rank and march to the drilling room without supper all efforts of the people to come to gather in mass meting to protest aganst it has ben defeated by threts. The Congress of theas uninted States has made us a part of the National force then we hold that we ar subject to the same regulation of the National force We have responded to the call by enlistment We are allso subject to the draft the will of the Loyial Colard people of Baltimore citey is as a part of the National force to be treated no wors then the lawes Demand Governing the National force[58]

In September, an officer in a New York regiment at Fort McHenry asked that a black soldier in his command be transferred:

On the 17th ist I received 46 recruits from Depot N.Y.S. one of them is a negro, name, George Tankard Enlisted in town Platsburg, N. York State, by Capt Clendon. I have assigned him for the present to the Kitchen., it will be next to impossible to quarter him with the company or to drill him with them, and yet by his enlistment he is entitled to all the rights and subject to all the duties with other enlisted men, and must be reported the same,. I think under these circumstances it will be difficult to enforce Discipline in the company, I therefore most respectfully submit the case to Major Comdg 91st Regt. hoping some step may be taken to remedy the evil.[59]

An army official in Somerset County asked that action be taken about his discovery in the county jail:

I have the honor to report that numerous Complaints having been made to me conserning the treatment of certain colored persons confined in the jail of sumerset County in Princess Ann. I paid a visit to the jail to day. the jailor at first denied there was such persons confined there but upon my insisting upon being showed over the place I found confined the following persons one free born Colored man who is confined for the perpose of being forced into the Army. One colored man who has served six months in the army and has a discharge is confined in a cell and has been flogged untill the b[l]ood ran down on the floor by the same man who enlisted him when he first entered the service.[60]

1865

In February, a drummer in the Nineteenth Infantry Regiment, U.S. Colored Troops, sought a furlough:

I have the honor of writing you a few Lines To inform you that i Want to Apply for a furlough for i enlisted in December the 18th 1863 as a Drummer boy and now i am about 14 months from home and my mother has wrote for me several times for me to Come home I have ask for a furlough 3 different times now and they have put me off by saying that i was nothing but a boy and did not need one so i thought i would write to a higher authoritys and see what they would do for me I has respects for my folks at the Age of 14 as well as those of the age of 20 years i will now be 14 years of age the 25th of December 1865 i think that i have a right to my furlough at the end of 12 months any how a native of M.D. bred and born in St marys County.[61]

chapter twelve

Freedom?

In July 1862, the *Sun* reported on Lincoln's meeting with border-state congressmen to push his plan for compensated emancipation:

> A large number of the border slave State representatives had an interview yesterday with the President, at which they presented their views against current abolition legislation, and he appeared to take a stand in favor of his policy of emancipation, with compensation for slaves, and colonization of them. It was hinted about the capitol yesterday that the President's manner was curt and menacing, but I hear in an authoritative quarter that he was kind and courteous, he said to them, in effect, that the friction of war was wearing away or seriously damaging the slave interest in the border States, and that it was best for their people to at once inaugurate measures for emancipation, when the government has the will and the ability to pay, and when the former have slaves to dispose of.[1]

Even a clergyman such as Rev. Henry Slicer had limits on the extent of emancipation, noting in his diary that "the Crusade being now prosicuted for the black man, is likely to result in the ruin of the liberties of the white man."[2]

Governor Bradford's September letter to Francis Thomas revealed the evolution of his thinking about emancipation, which he now believed inevitable. He suggested revising Maryland's constitution through a convention, thinking that slaveowners would accept a legislative end to slavery:

> The Secessionists among us, still strangely clinging to the hope that the rebellion would succeed, the Southern Confederacy be established, and Maryland be made a part of it, have been, as a matter of course, opposed to every mode of emancipation, and determined to cling to Slavery as the great pillar of their new Republic. Bitterly, however, as they may hitherto have been bent on that purpose, the stubborn facts of their situation, the waning prospects of the rebellion, and the steady depreciation of slave property, are fast opening their eyes to the necessities of the case, and of providing by prudent legislation for such of it as is left.

The governor saw emancipation as a response to new dynamics of Maryland's economy:

> I am satisfied that the conviction has been slowly, but surely, maturing in the minds of our people for years past, that the future growth and prosperity of our state demanded a change in our system of labor, and the events of the last two years have only served to show the necessity of providing for that change with the least possible delay. When we speak of gradual emancipation it must not be supposed that the phrase is employed by way of postponement of the operation,

but it honestly expresses only what it truly means: that emancipation shall only be so gradual as to guard it against the evil consequences that must necessarily result to slave as well as master from too sudden a change in any system of labor that is of indigenous growth.[3]

Lieut. Col. John A. Steiner of Frederick County would disappoint future historians with his diary description of the consecration of the National Cemetery at Gettysburg:

> Morning cloudy & slight rain about 8½ o'clock left for Gettysburg arrived there about dusk. Stopped with Mr Thos Bevan
>> found there an immense crowd
>> very clear & pleasant[4]

> morning cloudy but pleasant after breakfast went over Battle ground with a number of friends. Then at the stand from where the dedicatory ceremonies of the National Cemetery were had. saw the President Mr Everett & many others of our distinguished Statesmen & was much gratified[5]

1864

In February, with emancipation stirring in Maryland, Frederick Douglass addressed a large Baltimore crowd—"one fourth were white ladies and gentlemen"—in the "spacious saloon of Temperance Temple, on North Gay Street." Following presentation of a sword to Col. Samuel Bowman, Douglass took the stage:

> And for fully two hours spoke on the topics which are of momentous interest to all thinking men of his color. His remarks were delivered in a very easy manner, every word being articulated with great clearness, and frequently the entire audience, in response to and in unison with his sentiments, loudly evinced their sympathy therewith. At other moments those present were convulsed with laughter as some droll expression escaped from his lips. He urged, with great force, the necessity of his colored brethren applying themselves diligently to the task of preparing themselves for the new position in which, by the new Constitution of Maryland, they were happily placed, contending that if they were true to themselves they would rise, socially, far above being merely hewers of wood and drawers of water.
>
> On this topic he enlarged with great impressiveness, telling his colored hearers that, unless they sought to be fully equal to their white brethren in all the branches of mechanical pursuits, they would always be an inferior race. Especially did he warn them against the evils resulting from extravagance, saying that $150 earned in the country was much better than $450 gained in the city, around the haunts of vice and luxury. In respect to education, he stated that he had the assurance of prominent men here, that Maryland should be really what the Con-

stitution professed to make it. In his concluding remarks he earnestly pleaded that if the negro was called on to take his share of the toils and dangers of warfare along with the white man, he should in time of peace also have the same privileges of the elective franchise, jury box, &c.

On the conclusion of his address three hearty cheers were given him by his colored brethren, on which he told them that they should commence aright by giving three cheers for the Union. These were given with a will. He then proposed three cheers for Abraham Lincoln, which not being given with the same heartiness as the others, he renewed the proposition, when the applause was tremendous.[6]

The following day the *Baltimore American and Commercial Advertiser* noted the readiness of the judiciary to deal with any conflicts between the apprenticeship laws and the proposed new constitution:

In the Orphans' Court of this city, yesterday, an order was passed stating that, as the provisions of the several sections of the Code of Public General Laws of Maryland in relation to negro apprentices were inconsistent with the new Constitution, the Court would decline to bind any negro apprentice until the General Assembly of the State shall have had an opportunity to provide for the binding of negro apprentices, as is required by the new Constitution.[7]

On the first Wednesday in April, Marylanders voted for an October constitutional convention whose delegates would deliberate a new constitution to go before voters in November. The key provision of a new constitution would be the abolition of slavery in the state. The *Baltimore American and Commercial Advertiser* welcomed the news:

The night of bondage is fading away in the dawning list of the morning star of Freedom. The oppression of which Pinkney and other sagacious statesmen complained is no longer to find an abiding place in Maryland. The bonds have been wrenched asunder, and the captives within her borders are to be set free. Henceforth we are to honor a barbarous custom by breach, instead of by observance. Truly, when error thus vanishes into its native night, and truth comes forth radiant with beauty, we can afford to indulge in mutual congratulations with those whose unwearied efforts have contributed to this grand result. The world will smile approvingly upon this act and bid us God speed. The nations will hail the coming day of Emancipation with rapturous shouts. The ages to come will look back upon the hour of our redemption with grateful memories. Maryland will awake to newness of life, and her half cultivated soil will blossom like the rose. Emigration will fill up her solitary places, and her growing commerce will unfurl its white sails upon every sea. Her citizens will arouse from their lethargy, and expand her bedwarfed agriculture and revive her waning trade. He who fails to see in all this just cause of congratulation is endowed with an obliquity of vision beyond our comprehension.[8]

By April, the U.S. government was seeking to reduce expenditures for government rations for former slaves. General Edward Hinks, the new commander of St. Mary's District, suggested to Butler, now commanding the Department of Virginia and North Carolina, that these ex-slaves be sent to cultivate farms whose owners had fled to the Confederacy. Hinks speculated on the suitability of several estates as "government farms":

> It would be advantageous, for the interest of Government, undoubtedly, to possess itself of some one of the many estates in St. Mary's Co. abandoned by rebel owners, upon which to employ the negroes that are accumulating at this Point, but I have hesitated to take any steps in that direction without positive instructions from the Maj. Genl. Comdg. the Department.
>
> The Thomas farm, on the Patuxent, can be made available for the purpose of employing some one hundred hands, but the mother of the three rebel Thomases resides in Baltimore, and has a life interest or right of dower in the estate.
>
> To the Forrest estate there seems to be no pretended loyal owner, but there are no buildings thereon.
>
> The Southern estate could be made available, but notwithstanding it is located within the limits of this District it is reported to be occupied by a portion of Gen. Birney's troops.
>
> There are other like estates within the County, but before attempting to possess, occupy and enjoy them I request specific directions from the Maj. Gen. Comdg. as to what course to pursue in relation to part owners, whose souls have been sold to the Southern Confederacy, but whose bodies are entitled to the protection of our laws, and in relation to claims of creditors of similar or more loyal characters.
>
> The season for farming operations will soon commence, and it is necessary that immediate action should be taken to secure the profitable employment of accumulating contrabands.[9]

Several weeks later Col. A. G. Draper, commander of the Thirty-sixth Regiment of the U.S. Colored Troops, began seizing rebel property in St. Mary's County. He sought approval to confiscate rebel property across the Potomac in Virginia:

> I have seized over 7,000 acres of land belonging to Rebels;—have turned over two of the farms to the Dept. for Negro Affairs to be worked by contraband labor.
>
> These farms are totally destitute of stock and tools, and I therefore respectfully ask permission to make expeditions with about 350 men to the Western shore of the Potomac for the purpose of seizing stock and tools belonging to Rebels, and of capturing any contraband goods of which I may get information.[10]

J. P. Kennedy expressed his outlook at the prospects for Maryland emancipation to the dean of St. Paul's in London:

> As one of the great events which have come up out of the defeat of the rebellion—you will be glad to know that this state (Maryland) is now in the very act of immediate and total abolition of slavery, through a convention elected especially for that Work. The war brings us, at least, this incalculable good.[11]

In June, Gen. Lew Wallace sent the War Department a subordinate's report about the attempts of Eastern Shore slaveholders to reclaim male slaves who, after escaping to join the Union army, had failed the army's medical examination. The solution was to engage them as laborers:

> Information having been received at the War Department that there are in Maryland, particularly at the military posts on the Eastern Shore a considerable number of Slaves, who after being brought to the recruiting rendezvous are found to be unfit for military service, who yet desire military protection, this Department has been advised that the Secretary of War has directed the acceptance into the United States service of all colored recruits presenting themselves;—those fitted for the active duties of a soldier to be retained as soldiers;—the remainder to be turned over to the Quarter Master's Department as laborers.[12]

W. W. Glenn, facing another arrest, left Maryland late in June for New England, despite the grave illness of his son, Billy. Upon hearing of the Confederate incursion into western Maryland in July he vowed to return—"this really looks like business & must hurry back to Maryland to take my part"—but when Early retreated after his abortive attack on Washington, Glenn remained out of the state until October, when:

> Lincoln hearing that I preferred him to McClellan sent me a card permitting me to return to Maryland & remain so long as I behaved myself. A great country truly—but I have no idea of Electioneering for him or any body else.[13]

Early in October national and local figures in Cockeysville gathered for a "Lincoln and Johnson Meeting," to support the president's reelection and the new Maryland constitution, coming to a vote on November 1. Guests included Postmaster General Montgomery Blair and Maryland Congressman Edwin H. Webster, who

> Delivered quite an eloquent and patriotic speech in support of Lincoln and Johnson and the adoption of the new Constitution; eulogizing the character of Abraham Lincoln, and setting forth the many advantages that would result from the adoption of the new Constitution; denouncing also McClellan and [Ohio Congressman George] Pendleton and the Peace Party generally. Mr. Webster was loudly applauded.[14]

A Baltimore newspaper reminded voters that the polls would be open for two days (October 12 and October 13) for the election that would determine the fate of slavery in Maryland—a moment "immeasurably more important than any event which has ever transpired in the history of Maryland":

> Do not forget that there are among us many who have given aid and comfort, countenance and support to the rebellion in some shape or other, who are so abandoned to the worship of false gods that they will not hesitate to carry deception to the extent of perjury in order to secure suffrage when they have voluntarily disfranchised themselves.
>
> Do not forget that Slavery, like every other monster of evil, dies hard, and that its extinction will require persistent and deadly blows.
>
> Do not forget that immediate and unconditional emancipation is the only policy that now accords with the spirit of Republican institutions, and is the only safe guarantee against future attempts at sedition, conspiracy and rebellion.
>
> Do not forget that the New Constitution will only be opposed by those in the slaveholding interest, and that though they constitute only a minority, they will make determined efforts to uphold the ebony idol.[15]

Baltimore's mayor and city council decreed that passage of the new constitution be marked by "firing a salute of five hundred guns." The *Baltimore American and Commercial Advertiser* likened the promise of ratification to Lincoln's 1863 Thanksgiving Proclamation:

> This is the birth-day of Maryland freedom. This day the shackles fall from the oppressed within our borders. The bonds are broken forever, and the captive is set free. This is a proud day for Maryland. It is the day of her regeneration. It is the dawn of a new regime and a healthier existence. The triumph of justice is consummated; the aims of sound economy are satisfied. Henceforth the first of November will be a blessed day in the calendar. It will be commemorated with thanksgiving and praise. The last Thursday of this month is selected, in accordance with the praise-worthy custom inaugurated by President Lincoln, as a day of National Thanksgiving. But Maryland will have another anniversary to celebrate hereafter in this autumnal month. And we venture to say that none will be more observant of its annual return, or more grateful for its memories, then those who have opposed the work whose fruition it represents. For they will become convinced of their error by the prosperity which will follow this day, and they will acknowledge that the prejudices of darkened reason faded away in the clearer light of reality.[16]

At the time of a 1937 interview by the Federal Writers' Project, "Parson" Rezin Williams, a former slave, was the "oldest living Negro Civil War veteran; now 116 years old." Born in 1822 at "Fairview," near Bowie in Prince George's County, he was a

Union army teamster whose father, he said, had worked for George Washington. Williams, who at Gettysburg helped evacuate wounded soldiers from the line of fire, recounted the reaction of slaves to the news of emancipation in Maryland:

> When the slaves were made free, some of the overseers tooted horns, callin the blacks from their toil in the fields. They were told they need no longer work for their masters unless they so desired. Most of the darkeys quit "den and dar" and made a quick departure to other parts, but some remained and to this day their descendents are still to be found working on the original plantations, but of course for pay.[17]

A Baltimorean complained to Maj. William Este, the newly appointed head of the Freedmen's Bureau, about men holding slaves the week after Maryland's new constitution freed them:

> You will please excuse me for troubling you but feeling much interest for my people, and being informed that you are to see that justice is to be done to them has prompted me to send this letter to you I have been informed that a Mr. Amos living on N. Charles st one door this side of Reed st has still several slaves which he still holds. I went there a few days ago and saw them there myself. Such has been his wife's System, that no one has ever been permitted ever to see them. Mr. Amos is a noted rebel sympathizer, and if his, and his friend—Dr. Doulan's houses Monument st were examined much rebel information would be obtained. praying that this communication may be strictly personal and that you will use all your influence in behalf of the oppressed.[18]

James Murray, the postmaster at New Town, Worcester County, related to General Wallace outrages against the black population:

> The Methodist Episcopal Church in New Town belonging to the Colored people was burned on the fourth Inst, about three oclock in the morning, I believe, and those I have talked with are of the same opinion, that It was set on fire by Secessionists or some one hired by them. The Colored peoples private property is threatend also to be destroyed. In the same District near Sandy Hill, Major Allen (a Colored Man) was Shot in the Back (by a white man in the vicinity) for no other purpose it is beleived than for entertaining a coloured Soldier at his house Union Mens lives have been threatened in a private manner, and some of them are really affraid that both their lives and property will be destroyed, and have besought me to enterpose for them. In Somerset County within twenty miles from New Town. the Colored peoples Church was burned, It is believed in like manner, about one month ago. I communicate to you these facts, and the State of Dread that hangs over the minds of union men in some parts of the District, hoping you will timely give us protection.[19]

Left: *In the eyes of rebel prisoners at Point Lookout, guards—many of them former slaves— made pointed reference to their new roles and responsibilities. A guard orders a prisoner away from the fence "or I make old Abe's Gun smoke at you. I can hardly hold de bolt back in der barrell. De bottom rail's on top now."* Right: *In this "Night-Scene," a guard inspires Confederate prayers for President Lincoln, the Union war effort, and the "Colored People."* Sketches from Prison.

The provost marshal in Easton, Capt. Andrew Stafford, characterized the use of Maryland's apprentice laws by slaveowners as a de facto continuation of slavery. Gen. Henry Lockwood sent Stafford's letter to General Wallace, suggesting that "immediate steps be taken to put a stop to these most outrageous and inhuman proceedings":

> There is a persistent determination of the disloyal people of this County, to totally disregard the laws of Maryland, in regard to Slavery. Immediately after the Governor issued his Proclamation, declaring the New Constitution adopted, a rush was made to the Orphan's Court of this County, for the purpose of having all children under twenty one years of age, bound to their former owners, under the apprentice law of the State. In many instances, boys of 12 and 14 years are taken from their parents, under the pretence that they (the parents) are incapable of supporting them, while the younger children are left to be maintained by the parents. This is done without obtaining the parent's consent, and in direct violation of the provisions of the Act of Assembly, and almost in every instance by

disloyal parties. Two of the members of the Orphan's Court being bitter enemies of the present organic law of the state, seem to be so prejudiced agains these poor creatures, that they do not regard their rights. The Court, as yet, has never taken any testimony relative to the capability of the parents to support their children, and where the parents are willing to bind them, they have been denied the choice of homes. In plain terms—the Rebels here are showing an evident determination to still hold this people in bondage, and call upon the Orphan's Court to give their proceeding the sanction of law.

My office is visited every day by numbers of these poor creatures, asking for redress, which I have not the power to give. They protest before the Court against binding their children to their former masters, who have dubtless treated them cruelly, and yet that same Court declares them vagrants, before they have enjoy liberty a single week.—in many instances before they have ever been permitted to leave their masters. The law in all instances requires the child or the parents' consent, but it is not done by Talbot County law. I am fearful there will be trouble here if measures are not taken to stop the proceeding. Loyalty is outraged, and justice has become a mockery.[20]

Thomas B. Davis, keeper of the Sandy Point Lighthouse off the western shore of the Chesapeake Bay, noting that he was "the only union man within ten miles of my Residence," described in graphic terms to Judge Hugh Lennox Bond the immediate postemancipation fate of some blacks in his area:

I Have bein Living or Rather Staying on the Bay Shore about Seven miles N. East from annapolis in the midts of a people Whose Hearts is Black in treason and a more fearless peopel for Boldly Expressing it Lives not outside of the Hosts that Bare Arms in upholding it

Since we the people have Proclaimed that Maryland Should Be free the Most Bitter Hatred has bein Manifested againest the poor Devils that Have Just Escaped from beneath there Lash there actions Since Tuesday Last Indicates to me that there is all Ready Orginized Bands Prowling apon Horse Back around the Country armed with Revolvers and Horse Whips threatning to Shoot every Negroe that gives Back the first word after they Lacerate his flesh with the Whip i Have bein told By Several Pearsons that a man By the name of Nick Phips on Last Wesnsday the first Sun That Rose apon the [wrech] in hes fredom after years of Bondage took in the Seller of Tom Boons the Post Master of St Margrets a negroe Woman stript her and with a Cow Hyde Lasarated her flesh until the Blood ozed from every cut and She with in a Month of giveing Burth to a child She appeared Before Court with the Blood Still Streaming from her To cover his guilt he ivents a Charge She is thrown in prson and he goes free the Same parties caught a Man By the name of Foster Eight Miles from annapolis hand cuffed him and Drove him before them and they on Horse With Such Rapidity that when he got to Severen Ferry he fell apon the Beach Exausted Covered with foam and this Man was Born free[21]

R. T. Turner, a Quaker in Kent County, described to his mother the post-emancipation conspiracy of slaveowners and judges against black Marylanders and asked for help from the Society of Friends "in providing places of refuge in the City until homes in the Country can be had—I have one family to look after now a mother and four children":

> Freedom is not established, notwithstanding our congratulations and celebrations and poetic effusions of rejoicing
>
> The slaveholders with Judge Chambers at their head are dragging the little children of Emancipated parents before proslavery magistrates and a proslavery Orphans Court, and are having them bound to their former masters without even a regard to the forms of Law. The Orphan's Court announces publicly that it will give the preference to former owners and the poor blacks have not the choice of a master, which is allowed them by this iniquitous law, nor do they stop to ascertain if the parent can support the children which is the very foundation and excuse for the Law. I wrote to Jno Graham to see eminent persons and write me what to do. But since then as I have investigated the subject. I see no hope from Courts Lawyers judges or juries,—for all with us in a general sense are oppressors.[22]

Typical of the chaos in emancipation's wake was a letter from a resident of West River, in Anne Arundel County, asking General Wallace to oversee the disposition of a black child:

> I have a man liveing with me that has A child at Geo. W. Hide's where it was a Slave its Mother being dead he wishes to obtain it and keep it under his care being apprehensive hat the said Hide will have the child bound to him The man Edward Wooden would respectfully ask the General commanding for an Order for the said Hide to give the child to him or to put it in his care and direct the Order to N.G. Glover West River A.A. County Md[23]

A statement given in Baltimore by a Maryland freedwoman noted that slaveowners were preventing many blacks from joining the military:

> My name is Harriet Anne Maria Banks & was the Slave of Dr. S.S. Hughes of Vienna Maryland I left Dr. Hughes & came to Baltimore. he treated me badly & this was my principal object in leaving they informed me that Abraham Lincoln Could not free me that he had no right to do so. there are Many coloured persons living in the Vicinity who desire to go into the Service of the United States but are prevented from So doing by their masters who disclaim the right of their being taken from them I wish the privilege granted me of returning to my former home & getting possession of bed & clothing left there by me.[24]

Another Maryland freedwoman described her post-emancipation ordeal:

> I was the slave of Wm Townsend of Talbot county & told Mr. Townsend of my having become free & desired my master to give my children & my bedclothes he told me that I was free but that my Children Should be bound to me [*him*]. he locked my Children up so that I could not find them I afterwards got my children by stealth & brought them to Baltimore. I desire to regain possession of my bed clothes & furniture.
>
> My Master pursued me to the Boat to get possession of my children but I hid them on the boat[25]

A Baltimorean told General Wallace about the fate of black children on the Eastern Shore:

> I have the honor to forward you a statement of facts, as to the binding of Negro Children in Dorchester County. I have seen them carried from different portions of the County in ox carts, waggons, and carriages to the County town (Cambridge) to be carried before the court to be bound out as apprentices, in some cases boys were bound out that would command wages at sixty dollars per year.[26]

A similar report arrived from the deputy provost marshal in Chestertown, in Kent County:

> The Orphans Court of this County have bound over one Hundred freed children without the consent of their parents. I do not think a greater injustice was ever committed.
>
> There is not a day but what there are from three to six poor women making complaints to me. If you wish the evidence I can send you a report of the proceedings and you will find there are but one or two cases but what are very unjust.[27]

At least one former Maryland slaveholder seemed intent on observing the distinction between slavery and apprenticeship:

> Mr. Hoopper was before the adoption of the new Constitution the owner of a negro woman & four children the oldest girl is over age. There is a boy a minor, him we do not want. The other two being girls are desirous of my retaining them. The mother is also anxious that we should have them bound to us. Major Este will please leave directions what I am to do. Until we know, presuming it not wrong, we will Keep them at home. We are in the dark, desirous to do right, but really not Knowing what to do—They had homes but the mother yesterday brought them home She, the mother is now with us under wages—The mother says she has been told she has entire control over them. We dont Know If it can

be done, we will have them bound to use. I will call Monday and get instructions—[28]

In November, Frederick Douglass's speech at the Bethel Church on Sharp Street in Baltimore described his feelings about emancipation in his home state. His sister, a freed Maryland slave, was with him; "a number of white persons were present, and the enthusiasm of the colored population was raised to the wildest pitch of excitement":

> What a wonderful change a few short years have wrought! I left Maryland a slave; I return to her a freeman! I left her a slave State; I return to find her clothed in her new garments of Liberty and Justice, a free State! My life has had two crises—the day on which I left Maryland, and the day on which I return. I expect to have a good old-fashioned visit, for I have not been there for a long time. I may meet my old master there, whom I have not seen for many years. I heard he was living only a short time ago, and he will be there, for he is on the right side. I made a convert of him years ago. He was a very good man, with a high sense of honor, and I have no malice to overcome in going back among those former slaveholders, for I used to think that we were all parts of one great social system, only we were at the bottom and they at the top. If the shackles were around our ankles, they were also on their necks. The Common Council and city authorities have promised to be present at the next meeting in Baltimore. I shall be glad to see them. I shall return to them with freedom in my hand, and point to her Free Constitution, and as the olive branch was a sign that the waters of the flood were retiring, so will the freedom which I shall find there be a sign that the billows of slavery are rolling back to leave the law blooming again in the purer air of liberty and justice.[29]

Late in November the judges of the Orphans Court of Anne Arundel County wrote to George W. Curry, the provost marshal at Annapolis, to explain their position regarding black children and the apprenticeship laws. The judges asked Curry if he felt they should suspend the binding of apprentices:

> We thot it due to simply state the course we are pursuing in reference to minor children particularly those under 14 years of age, & also to refer you to the Law under which we are called upon to act—the recent convention under which our new Constitution was framed in its deliberations deemed the existing Statutes, amply sufficient for any provision that might be required for negro children, leaving further Legislation, if necessary, to a future Legislature in the applications for binding apprentices we have quite a numerous class above the age of 14 soliciting the court to bind them to persons of their own selection. such selections, when known to the court to be a proper character, it has no hesitancy in granting—we would further state there is a very large number of *Orphan* chil-

dren whose ages ranging from infancy to 10 or 12 yrs require some immediate action in their behalf & when their previous owners are known to the court to be proper persons to care for & bring them up to habits of industry &c we invariably bind to them—we have also applications from former masters to have negro children that they have raised. bound to them but when it is satisfactorily shown to the court that the parents of such children are in a condition to provide for them in NO INSTANCE does the court interfere—we think it very probable our course has been misrepresented by some mothers. who think they can support themselves & family, their previous antecedents being enquired into by the court it is made too apparent their utter inability to properly provide & teach habits of industry &c in such cases the court regards it as an act of humanity when proper employers can be selected for them—[30]

Curry reminded the judges of General Order 112, which gave former slaves military protection pending action by the state legislature. Curry sent their letter to Adrian Root, commander of the U.S. Army post at Annapolis, requesting permission to invalidate all apprenticeships since the implementation of the new constitution:

I am fully convinced of the fact that since the adoption of the New Constitution by the State of Maryland that the Judges of the Orphans Court in and for the county of Anne Arundel. Md. have been binding out colored children to whoever might apply for them (but giving their former owners the prefference) against the express wish of their parents and in many cases said parents were entirely ignorant of the fact that their children were apprenticed untill they went to get them from their former owners.

It is to reach all of the above cases that I aim. and most respectfully ask for authority to annul indentures that have been made since the adoption of the New Constitution that are illegal as well as to stop further illegal proceedings of the court in this matter and it will be but an act of justice to a class of persons whose ignorance in regard to their rights is taken advantage of by men who in almost every case have always been known as sympathizers with (and to some extent) aiders of the rebels.[31]

General Lockwood informed a subordinate of his plan to permit Frederick Douglass to lecture in Harford County:

I have just been waited on by the Lieut. Comd's detachment at Havre-de-Grace who reports that the town authorities of the place are disposed to oppose the purpose of *Fred. Douglas* to deliver a lecture there some day this week, and asking for orders as a riot may ensue. Having myself heard this orator in this city, & believing his remarks eminently sensible & practical & calculated to do much good at this time, I have directed the Lieut. to oppose the intention of the town authorities, to support the lecturer in his purpose, and at all hazards to preserve the peace.[32]

In December, an officer at the headquarters of the Middle Department and Eighth Army Brigade in Baltimore informed General Lockwood that he was ordered by General Wallace to "protect loyal citizens," prevent misuse of the apprentice laws, and arrest two judges of the Somerset County Orphans Court (Jones and Bratton) and a Maryland senator-elect (Waters). Lockwood was to

> break up the practice now prevalent of apprenticing young negroes without the consent of their parents, to their former masters. If necessary, he will not hesitate to arrest all masters who refuse liberty to such apprentices, or withold them from their parents, and keep them in custody until they consent to such liberation. In case the parents of apprentices are not able to support them, and they desire it, he will send them to Baltimore, to the care of Lieut. Colonel *W. E. W. Ross* 31st U.S.C.T., in charge of Freedman's Bureau. He will endeavor to keep families to-gether as far as possible: but at the same time use his influence to discourage emigration for the present, and only send to Baltimore those who cannot find homes, occupation and labor where they now are—
>
> General *Lockwood* will arrest *Daniel Jones* and *Joseph Bratton,* of Somerset County, and *Levin D Waters* of Princess Anne, and send them as disaffected and dangerous men, by steamer to Fortress Monroe, to be sent across the lines, into Confederate jurisdiction—
>
> General *Lockwood* will resort to the most energetic and vigorous measures to quell the growing turbulence of secessionists in the counties along the Eastern Shore generally—[33]

James Murray complained to Wallace about the wide disregard of the general's November order placing freed slaves under military protection:

> To my great mortification I have found your Order to be contemtuously disregarded. The Citizens are laying hold, by violence, of Coloured peoples Children, carrying them to the Orphans Court and having them bound to themselves in Spite of all remonstrance upon the part of Parents, They are taking Boys and Girls as old as Sixteen years, Some of whom will hire out for Fifty and Sixty dollars a year, one case in particular, came under my own personal Knowledge, where the former owner laid hold of a boy Sixteen years old, The Mother refused to give up her Son, but was over powerd He threatend her with violence, The Mother came into the Post Office for Protection. The Man with a billet of wood came off his own premises crossed the Street and entered my door approached the Woman and Struck her on the Side of the head nearly Knocking her down, I spoke to him in an instant not to do that, when he desisted, They are

Judge Hugh Lennox Bond worked tirelessly to end abuse of apprentice laws invoked by former slaveholders as a way of re-enslaving black children. Baltimore American, November 16, 1892. MdHS.

JUDGE HUGH LENNOX BOND.

threatening Mothers with the severest punishment if they come on their premises, It is my opinion that the Orphans Court, The Register of Wills, and a certain Constable in this Community by the name of George Hargis is equally gilty with the Citizens in this matter The Mother who was Struck had her son hired out for ten dollars pr month at the time he was taken from her, The parents of Children thus taken, are comeing to me daily and almost hourly for direction, is there no redress for Such high handed viliany[34]

Nine days later Murray wrote again to Wallace, who ordered Lockwood to determine whether the blacks under Murray's care should be either supported locally or brought to Baltimore:

I am affraid I shall weary you, and yet I must write. Humanity compells me to do so. while Genl Lockwood was here adjusting the difficulties relative to the Coloured People, Some of the Slave Owners, after the Profitable Boys and Girls were taken away from them, turned off the old women, the Mothers with their helpless Children, and they of course had to be provided for. Genl. Lockwood applied to me, to provide Quarters, and Provision for all such cases as come to my knowledge. I have Secured Houses for two or Three Families and am providing them with provisions.[35]

Wallace sent Secretary Stanton a telegram he had received from Lockwood, expressing dismay at suspending his orders to protect the rights of freedmen on the Eastern Shore—noting in particular the binding of children who are then hired out to their own parents:

> On my return last evening I recd the following telegram from Gen Lockwood which explains itself: "Salisbury Md Dec 10 To Maj Gen Wallace. Just arrived here from below. Find a telegram from Lt Mulliken saying that orders have gone to me Cambridge countermanding my instructions so far as relates to the negroes. Presuming that this refers to the subject of the recent apprenticeship in these Counties, I beg leave to submit a few remarks, it is impossible to convey to you, by telegraph, any idea of the hundreds of abuses that have come to my knowledge of this system. I have knowledge of cases, where lads of sixteen (16) & eighteen (18) have been bound out and then hired to their father's who are prosperous farmers, for ten (10) and twelve (12) dollars a month. Both you and I are put in a false position, here, by stopping short now. I don't think any one (1) can visit these Counties as I have done, without seeing the importance of stopping this wholesale perversion, of what designed to be, a humane law.[36]

But having substantiated reports of coerced apprenticeship, Lockwood continued to act against the practice:

> I proceeded to the lower counties of the Eastern Shore and put forth a circular, of which I enclose copy, that I posted the same and in some cases executed it.—I found, that the binding-out had been very general and began as early as October last; masters having manumitted their slaves under 21 years of age for that purpose. I found, that the spirit of the apprentice law had been very generally disregarded, no attention being paid to whether parents could or could not support or to their wishes as to binding out. They were told, that they must select masters, willing or unwilling. In some cases the apprentices were at the time at hired service at good wages,—some 10—to 12$ per month. That many parents had rented small farms, expecting to have the labor of their childern,—that many poor tenants had made their arrangements to use this labor and are disappointed by the course pursued; That the apprenticing works advantageously only for the rich slave holder—generally *disloyal*—and disadvantageously for the poor white tenant and colored man. I could burden this report with cases, but deem it unnecessary, peticularly as I have not the names at hand. The feeling among

our friends in Somerset and Worcester seemed to be, that the law, executed in its proper spirit is a good one, but that, as these gross abuses have attended it, something should be done.[37]

The *Baltimore American and Commercial Advertiser* described Kent County's style of "voluntary consent":

> The little Ethiopians were carried by the dearborn and wagonload, for they were told they had to have their children bound out—"it was the law"—and thus, some of the most ignorant were opposed upon and willing consent obtained.[38]

John Diggs, a black military worker employed by the Commissary Department in Alexandria, Virginia, beseeched the Freedmen's Bureau for help in recovering his family:

> I have a wife and five children who lived with Somerset Parrin Prince Frederick Calvert Co. C.H. Md who, upon the issuing of the Emancipation Proclamation turned my wife and children out of doors, I rented a house from Henry Hutchins of the same County where my family resided untill last Thursday (15th inst), when Lum. Buckmarsh a Constable of the County went to the house my family occupied and by force carried them to the County Court, I was on my way to the house after my family had been taken away, when I was met by the said Buckmarsh who summoned me (verbally) to appear before the Court on Thursday, on being questioned by Nathaniel Dair P.M. in the Court House as to whether I was able to support my family and whether I intended going into the employ of the Government again? to which I answered yes, immediately upon answering, I was struck and cut at by the Constable L. Buckmarsh and pursued some distance from the building, I was afraid to make any further attempt to procure my family and returned to Washington. My family were sent to Jail, where I suppose they are now. I am able to support them, and would wish to have them under my charge, please have this done for me.[39]

Governor Bradford sent Diggs's letter to Joseph A. Wilson, the state's attorney for Calvert County. Wilson noted that no member of Diggs's family had been in jail and that Somerset Parran had been a member of the state convention that drafted the new constitution. On December 30, Parran denied that he had mistreated Diggs's wife and children:

> Instead of turning Eliza & her children out of doors she remained with her children in one of my negro quarters for about two weeks after she stopped working for me and during this time her family was fed by me.
>
> After she stopped work she went off in search of a place to live on & work during the year 1865. She returned in a few days and having informed me that she expected to rent a piece of land from Mr Henry Hutchins I offered no obstacle

or objection to her leaving my farm and several days afterwards when she wanted a conveyance to remove her effects to the land which she had rented I offered my cart for her use & the offer was accepted. Her husband John Diggs, who formerly belonged to a gentleman in Prince Georges Co, absconded I believe from his then owner and did not return to this neighbourhood until after Eliza & her children had left my farm not have I seen him since his return.

I have not had any of Elizas children bound to me, nor have I ever made any application to have them bound to me. I did not want them nor would I have them as bound apprentices to me. Although as a practising attorney I am often in Prince Frederick yet I have never heard of John Diggs children being in jail. Eliza left my premises of her own free will and I have not seen either her or any of her children since she left.[40]

On the last day of the year, Daniel Miller & Co., importers and jobbers of dry goods at 329 Baltimore Street, proclaimed its financial freedom:

We take great pleasure in announcing to you that we have to day assumed the payment of the entire, outstanding indebtedness of *Miller Cloud & Miller* & shall promptly pay *in full* all their obligations as they mature.

In making this announcement we must tender our heartfelt thanks to our creditors for the kindnesses they have shown us both in accepting our renewals so pleasantly & the kind sentiments they expressed for our success during the time we were struggling with difficulties that seemed almost insurmountable.

Previous to the breaking out of the war we were doing a large business with Virginia & other Southern States from which we were cut off almost instantly and we were suddenly left with a heavy debt hanging over us & the large bulk of our assets locked up in seceeded states.[41]

1865

On New Year's Day, a supporter of emancipation spoke in favor of educating Maryland's newly freed black citizens, noting that the weather was "very cold and the walking bad so I have concluded to stay home and amuse myself after reading Beechers sermon by writing a letter to you":

We are putting forth every effort to carry the provisions of our new Constitution to their logical consequences whatever they may be. First and foremost is the provision about education. On the Eastern Shore and indeed the Western Shore of the Bay that is resisted whether you mean to educate the blacks or whites. Strange is it not that you should I this day of grace have to write articles and use arguments which were worn out in England a hundred years ago, or that any one in this day should have to be convinced that ignorance is not bliss. In

"Arrival of the Freedmen and their Families at Baltimore, Maryland—an Every Day Scene," read the legend under this wood engraving from a September issue of Frank Leslie's Illustrated Newspaper. *MdHS.*

accordance with this letter of Introduction I received Wendell Phillips and his friend Stearns. We have a little fund out of which we give small entertainments at the club to such friends. I found Wendell Phillips one of the most agreeable men I ever met.

The writer recruited Wendell Phillips to speak and warned of the consequences of failing to provide education for these new Marylanders:

He agreed to come and make a speech for us, proceeds to be used in the establishment of free schools for the "darks." The only persons who made objection to his being introduced at the club were two Yankees, and when they did so a number of our Maryland members added their names to mine on the invitation book & swore the Yankees might resign if they did not like it. On Monday we have three free schools for the colored people open. We are determined this class of people should have an opportunity to get out of the slough. If they are to be kept in ignorance their viciousness will not make this a comfortable place to live in.[42]

John P. Kennedy praised the new constitution:

We have made a new era in Maryland which will become very significant in the future history of our republic. Our new constitution announces three dogmas of great value: 1. That the allegiance of the people of Maryland is due to the nation and not to the state. That all men have an indisputable right to the earnings of their own labor. & 3. That slavery is not only a moral but a political sin, entitled to no compensation for its destruction: and on that ground is forever abolished.[43]

The *Baltimore American and Commercial Advertiser* spoke out against forced apprenticeship:

These attempts to bind negro children in a manner indicative of utter recklessness of principle and of open defiance of the law cannot be too thoroughly exposed and help up to reprobation. We trust that our contemporaries in those counties will keep up a vigorous warfare upon such encroachments on the rights of a race which has been oppressed long enough, and for whose liberation from bondage the loyal people of the State have so earnestly contended. No reasonable citizen will oppose a system of binding which accords with the provisions of the law, and which will prove mutually advantageous to the parties concerned. But we strenuously object to the adoption of any plan whose transparent purpose is to renew in another shape what we have been striving to avoid. We object to refettering those who have been freed from the chains of Slavery by a process which is regardless of the spirit and intent of the New Constitution, and of the plainly expressed will of the people. We think, moreover, that every case of forced apprenticeship demands investigation at the hands of the County Courts. The loyal citizens of the State should insist upon a rigorous conformity to the Maryland Code, and upon acquiescence in the new organic law of the State. We hope that every case in which indentures have been illegally made will be reported to the proper authorities. Let the miscreants guilty of so improper a practice learn that they cannot escape surveillance and condemnation, and this form of injustice will soon cease.[44]

A surgeon with the Seventh Regiment of the U.S. Colored Troops asked General Wallace to intervene with the president of the Baltimore & Ohio Railroad about treatment of blacks aboard trains between Baltimore and Washington:

The company exacts of colored passengers the same fare it does for White, and then huddles them together in the front car with all sorts of persons, where smoking of pipes and segars continue all the time, and where they are subject to insults. In makes no difference how respectable a colored lady may be; how disagreable smoking may be to her; or how ill she might be, the Employees about the depot will not permit her to enter any other car, and should she by chance get into another and is found there, she is rudely thrust out.[45]

General Lockwood took up the case of Patrick Scott, a black man appointed to farm the estate of Col. J. Waring, a Southern sympathizer whose land was seized in 1863 by the military, consistent with federal policy toward disloyalists in southern Maryland. After Scott produced a bumper harvest in 1864, Waring returned and forced him from the land. William Burch, a white Unionist in Prince George's County, supported Scott's claim to a share of the crop:

> I fine that most every Bodey is agance the pore fellow it all groing out his being on Warrings place & I think that warring is the cose of it he wonts all that Partrick made thare he has taken from Partrick the kees of the corn houses & he is bringing up charges agance him about taking things of the place & selling them Mr Warring & his friends are seeking & finding out every thing thay can agance him & I dont know what will be the result I hav imployed him to work my place & I would like very much for the leading athoretys to deside what intrust Partrick has thare if aney I think that Govement aught to proteck him in it becose the govement put him thare to take care of the propety & toled him to make what he could to pay himself for the troble Now Mr Warring wonts to know what has becom of his poltrey & utentials & all of the little things left on the place those things was not put under Partrick charge but the farm & houses & Fenceing was & you know that partrick took care of what was put under his charge & toled him to pay himself of the place from what I can lern thay are trying to [reape] up all those charges agance him I beleave the fellow is truly honis & would state all of the facts in the case I wish you would asertane what he is entitel to he made a crop of corn last year at his on exspence & I think it would be a hard case if Govement will not alow him apart of what was rased as he rased it by his on laber & by hiering laber I wish you could so arange the mater so as partrick can get his writes & get the govement to cend thare wagones down & buy his share of corn & take it of & cend men with the wagons clothd with proper athorety to settel the bisness betwen Partrick & Mr Warring & ortherise those offercers to investergate the mater properly as Partrick is a black man & you very well know that a bleck man has no chance in this contrey & I think as Partrick has bin in the Govement imploy & imployed by them I think it is thare duty to protect him if he is entitel to aney thing he aught to have it & thay aught to see he gets it

Burch noted that his Unionist views and support of a black man in a dispute with a white man had caused him to be "now very unpoperlor withe the peopel":

> now if you can get the Govement to cend you down with other offercers to investegate the mater I would be glad as you are acquanted with maney of the facts in the case & farther if shuch a investigation was to be made doen in this contrey it mite alarm som of those hot headed Rebes & do som good it would be of benefit to the few that are loyal her & you know thare is few of them I am one & I hope I

will not be her long as sune as you & T.B. Burch can get me a place I shall leave I dont hardly leave my home unless I leave it for a distance I hav no friends her but my family & tharefor I cant fine aney consolatin aney whare elce it seames to me that every thing is glume & despare with me I think it worst now than ever it has bin & it will continue to grow worst I think

Now my Dear Friend if you will put yourself to som troble to help me out in getting away from her & also in getting Partricks rights I will ever be under obligations to you & I am shure Partrick will feale the same towards you[46]

As Lincoln began his second term in early March, W. W. Glenn complained about the shifting principles of fellow Marylanders:

In Maryland Men were decided pro slavery men & Southern, then became Union Men and now are almost abolitionists. Men, two years ago, who were willing to sacrifice everything for the Southern cause, or rather to stake everything on its success, now swear in Court that they never gave aid counsel or comfort to the South and that they will protect the Union and forever resist its dismemberment. All this is very Contemptible but amusing.[47]

Glenn captured the complexities of slavery's end, which, combined with military conscription, led to a severe labor shortage in Maryland that, he asserted, would drive prices higher:

Owing to the high prices of cereals & beef, produced by the scarcity arising from diminished production, the profits in farming have recently been very large. Men have received double and treble the incomes they ever received before and delighted with this change, which they forget is but temporary, discover that slaves are in incubus after all and that they are well rid of them; that is as Slaves. Of course the blacks are largely still employed as farm laborers. Now comes another phase. The new draft has created a great demand for men. The conviction that the Northern Armies are soon to crush the rebellion induces men to believe that the present campaign will be short and attended with little danger. Negroes are easily induced to offer themselves as substitutes or for bounty money. Quite a trade is being driven in human flesh and smart negroes are actually selling their more stupid brethren & pocketing more than half the money received. The withdrawal of a large number of hands from the fields is producing a scarcity of labor. Men who formerly received $9 or $10 per month & board, now receive $16 and before long will demand $20. The price of board too which was $8 is now at least $12 per month. This has again set the landholders to thinking and they are not certain now if the violent unsettling of an established system of labor is after all a good thing. Slavery was most profitable in the planting districts where women & children had but little out door work, but had to be fed & clothed.[48]

These six Union soldiers, from Company G. of the Ninth Maryland Infantry Regiment, spent four hundred days as prisoners in Andersonville. One of them, Henry Knipp of Baltimore, died in 1902. Baltimore Sun/Pratt Lib.

Even the most radical supporters of emancipation, such as Judge Hugh L. Bond, refused to put blacks on the same plane as whites:

> We do not encourage any benevolence toward them, which does not tend to make the colored man feel his duty and capacity to support himself. Whatever can educate his mind and equip his body for self-care is in the right direction. Everything else tends to lager houses, idleness, vice.[49]

Leonidas Dodson described the paroxysm of joy in Easton at news "that Richmond, the rebel Capital, for four dreary years the nest of traitors and the objective point of our war operations, has fallen":

> Easton has been in the wildest excitement all the evening, the Court House, and Church bells have rung, cannon jars the earth, bonfires blaze, and illuminations prevail. Even the disloyal seem to experience a kind of sympathy with the general jubilation. Further news of the pursuit of Lee's discomfited army will be looked for with intense interest.[50]

Jacob Engelbrecht recorded the scene in Frederick at 2 p.m. on Monday, April 10:

> Lee Rebel Army surrendered-yesterday about ock Lieut General Robert E. Lee of the Rebel Army Surrendered his whole army to Lieut General U.S. Grant of

the U. States army, it took place at Nottoway C.H. Va all the Bells of our city are now ringing & have been for Several hours the whole town is in Commotion.[51]

And in Baltimore:

It is impossible to describe the earnest and fervent enthusiasm evoked in Baltimore yesterday by the announcement of the capture of Richmond. The glorious news ran like wildfire through the city, and from all sections the masses came pouring by thousands on to Baltimore street. The people were wild. Congratulations were exchanged in a style which, in more quiet moments, would have savored of the ridiculous. An irrepressible enthusiasm animated our citizens, and again and again cheers broke out for the President, Gen. Grant, and the army. The meeting at night in front of the *American* office was a complete ovation when we consider the limited notice given and the brief time allowed for preparations. A dense mass packed the square from North to Calvert street, scarcely moving for hours, and listening with remarkable attention to the speakers. Altogether the day was such a one as rarely occurs twice in the experience of a lifetime.[52]

chapter thirteen

Murder

On April 14, 1865, Maj. Robert Anderson, the Union commander at Fort Sumter, was the guest of honor at the fort for a ceremony marking the defeat of the Confederacy—four years to the day of Sumter's surrender. Anderson, who disfavored the event's militaristic tone, was present under order of the secretary of war. In the crowd were William Lloyd Garrison, Rev. Henry Ward Beecher, and Lincoln secretary John Nicolay. At dinner that evening, Anderson offered a toast to the president, who had declined to attend:

> I beg you, now, that you will join me in drinking the health . . . of the man who, when elected President of the United States, was compelled to reach the seat of government without an escort, but a man who now could travel all over our country with millions of hands and hearts to sustain him. I give you the good, the great, the honest man, Abraham Lincoln.[1]

In Washington, the president and Mrs. Lincoln were at that moment setting off for an evening at Ford's Theatre.

Actors and patrons at Ford's were stunned to hear a pop and see a man jump from the president's box, race across the stage, and run out a side door. Attorney Seaton Munroe, walking on Pennsylvania Avenue, heard a man scream, "My God, the President is killed at Ford's Theatre." Munroe raced to the scene and made his way into the auditorium:

> I had never witnessed such a scene as was now presented. The seats, aisles, galleries, and stage were filled with shouting, frenzied men and women, many running aimlessly over one another; a chaos of disorder beyond control.[2]

John Wilkes Booth came under immediate suspicion and was thought to have escaped toward Baltimore, his hometown and a source of friends and benefactors. A reward was quickly announced:

> The major-general commanding this department is authorized to offer a reward of &10,000 for the apprehension of the assassin of the President of the United States and the Secretary of State. Please communicate this to the police and detectives of your department.[3]

On the next day, a Saturday, a Baltimore newspaper broke the news:

> We announce to our readers the most terrible, the saddest and the most sorrowful intelligence. Abraham Lincoln is dying. The President has been murdered. At the time when he had become most endeared to the nation, at the moment when the war was of the past, and he was bending the energies of his mind and the kindly feelings of a character more than usually forgiving toward the paci-

fication of the country, Mr. Lincoln has been basely, cowardly and traitorously assassinated.[4]

Mayor John Lee Chapman ordered closed "taverns and drinking houses," flags draped in mourning and bells tolled between 11 a.m. and noon. The military banned "assemblages of more than three persons" and ordered closed places of public amusement. The *Sun* described the scene on the morning of April 15:

> A crowd of persons assembled in front of Bendann's picture gallery, on Baltimore Street, and demanded of the person in charge of the establishment a likeness of J Wilkes Booth, the alleged assassin, but no such picture being there of course the demand could not be complied with, and the angry crowd left.

On the morning after Rev. Henry Slicer recorded his reaction:

> Learn'd through the Newspapers of this morning, that an attempt was made upon the life of President Lincoln, by an Assassin in Fords Theatre at Washington during the performance last night—a pistol ball entering his skull—he is said to have expired this morning about 7 AM—this is deeply to be regretted, as a great National Calamity, just when our national troubles seem'd upon the eve of adjustment—The life of the secy of State (Mr. Seward) was also attempted about the same hour in his bed—with his son & several persons in the room—[5]

The last line in Jacob Engelbrecht's diary entry, at "½ past 9 ock a.m.," captured the fury many felt about the episode:

> Mourn Columbia, mourn-by telegraph received this morning, we have melancholy information, that President Lincoln, and Secretary of State Wm H. Seward, were both assassinated last night (Good Friday night) at their residences in Washington City—the telegraph Says that Lincoln is dead & Seward was about dying—Remember God the avenger reigns—[6]

And on the following day, Easter Sunday:

> The fine weather, independent of the day being the religious anniversary of the resurrection of Christ, had the effect of filling all the churches of the city with full congregations. The death of President Lincoln was most feelingly alluded to by all the ministers, either in their sermons or prayer, and in many instances tears were shed by those present.[7]

All of which prompted sarcasm from W. W. Glenn:

> In Baltimore almost all the Southerners are frightened to death at the tragedy of last Friday night. They deplore pitifully the assassination of a man who has encouraged assassination for four years past and who has been the chief man to bring about the state of things which may render assassination frightfully common.

Last Saturday Mr W.J. Albert, one of the Vestry of Grace Church informed Mr Hobart, that if he did not remove all the flowers and floral decorations on Easter Sunday, that he would apply to the Military authorities and he forced Mr. H. to remove them. Such men as this compare Lincoln's entry into Richmond to Christ's entry into Jerusalem on Palm Sunday and his death to that of our Savior on Good Friday.[8]

A vitriolic anti-Lincoln editorial on April 6 by Joseph Shaw, editor of the *Western Maryland Democrat* in Westminster who had long been aggressively pro-Southern, seemed to presage the assassination:

Some people hope that Lincoln's life will be spared now, in order that the country may be saved the disgrace of an "incoherent" Vice-President. But is there not a slight chance of improvement in case that Providence should will it otherwise? Lincoln, it is true, is reported to be a sober man, but it is none the less true, that if he is always sober he is always wrong. So Johnson sober is Johnson wrong; but Johnson drunk might, perchance, be Johnson right.—As proof of this, in his "incoherent" speech in the Senate he talked about the "Constitution." He certainly never would have thought of talking of that document if he had been sober.—There is not a word about it in Lincoln's Inaugural! Not a word! It is evident, therefore, that a drunken Abolitionist is more likely to be right than a sober one.

This would be Shaw's last issue. Carroll County citizens shut the paper down on April 15; the following night a mob destroyed his presses. Accounts vary about what next transpired: Shaw was either hanged by the mob or, on April 24, shot and stabbed by four men at Zachariah's Hotel in Westminster.[9]

On April 21, Glenn recorded the scene as Lincoln's funeral cortege passed through Baltimore:

Lincoln's corpse passed through Balto. Procession passed up Eutaw St & down Baltimore. All business suspended. Streets densely lined with spectators. The Negro Masons joined in the procession. The negroes in town were all wild. It was utterly impossible to keep servants in the house or to get any work out of them. Draped flags were displayed from almost all the windows in the Main streets. Our people are like whipped hounds and now that such a display can only make them contemptible are eagerly manifesting their loyalty. On the 19", I draped one window sill, from 10 to 3 o'c—during the time prescribed by Military orders for mourning. All the family were much opposed to this, but I thought they were wrong. Today we are almost the only house without some symbol of mourning.[10]

As did Rev. Henry Slicer, a member of the procession:

I united with the clergymen of the City in the Civil & Military Procession, which recieved and accompanied the Remains of the late President, from the Camden st Depo, to the Rotunda of the Exchange building—by a route along Eutaw to Balt st—to Gay—to Chew—to Caroline, to Balt—to Gay—to Exchange Place, and through the Rotunda—the route was long and muddy, and the day damp & rainy—But I thought it due to the occasion that the Ministers of Religion should show that, respect—I fear'd the consequences to my health, but with the exception of some Rhumatic indications, I found no ill effects—[11]

Franklin Wilson expressed his sentiments about Lincoln and the man to succeed him:

It is a terrible calamity, especially at this stage of the war. Mr. Lincoln has been growing in public esteem, and breadth of view, in wisdom, calmness and true statesman-like feeling, and bid fair by his moderation and prudence to bring about a lasting peace and Union; but Andrew Johnson his successor is a violent, arbitrary man, Southern-born and bred, and one who has suffered much from the Secessionists, and who will be likely to revenge his wrongs in blood. Besides, he is a drunkard—disgraced the nation by being drunk when inaugurated Vice-President, and may plunge us into unspeakable difficulties. But God reigns, and may turn even this brutal dastardly murder into the means of ultimate good to the country and the world.[12]

On the morning after the shooting, George B. Cole referred to the simultaneous attempt on Secretary Seward's life:

A day of universal horror. At 7 this morning one of my domestics informed us that the report was abroad that the President had been assassinated last night at the theatre. The morning papers give the following account of the events—including an attempt on the life of Secy Seward at the same hour. (Seward was lying idle from an accident that fractured his arm and face some days since)

A silent gloom hangs over the whole city. It is raining from heavy clouds that have gathered since midnight. No business is done of course.

The present moment presents a more improbable future than any I have ever encountered. Congress is not in session and the conservatives rejoiced on the fact because nothing existed to turn the President from his cause of conciliation. He seemed determined to stand like a rock against the spirit of vindictiveness that the radicals and fanatics seemed governed by. Seward too was with the President the truest friend of the Southern people. What course will events now take? The Vice Pres' is known to be a man of bad and vindictive nature and a drunkard. Will the Cabinet and the army hold the reins of this Gov'? Several men of strong secession attachments have already expressed to me this morning their horror and apprehension of the effect this event will have upon the restoration of peace.[13]

On Easter Sunday, Cole attended services at St. Paul's, recording that "the City appears wholly draped in mourning," and that, "the views of this city so far as I can observe or hear are unanimous in a sentiment of horror at the great events—regardless of their politics."[14]

The same day the War Department sent terse instructions to the Provost Marshal in Baltimore regarding an alleged conspirator native to Baltimore, Mike O'Laughlin:

> Brigadier M. O'Lauglin here in the train which leaves Baltimore at 6 p. m. Have him in double irons, and use every precaution against escape, but as far as possible avoid everything which can lead to suspicion on the part of the people on the train and give rise to an attempt to lynch the prisoners. A carriage will be in waiting at the depot to convey him to the place of confinement.[15]

Two days later Walter Dunn, out of Jarvis Hospital, described the scene in Baltimore to his cousin Emma:

> Yes we have, indeed, had very bad news. In the midst of our rejoicings we were called upon to mourn the loss of our noble hearted President, by an All Wise Providence, who doeth all things for good, unto those who love him. Nearly every building is draped in mourning showing that all have lost a friend. The people are deeply affected with grief over the sad news of the murder, and the manner in which it was perpetrated. History does not record a more horrible crime. The news made me almost heart sick. I would not have been more shocked, had I received the news of the death of a near friend. I hope and pray that President Johnson will mete our death to all traitors as their portion. I would like to write more upon this subject but time will not permit.[16]

Martin J. Spaulding, archbishop of Baltimore, released a statement on behalf of the Catholic community:

> Fellow-Citizens—A deed of blood has been perpetrated which has caused every heart to shudder, and which calls for the execration of every citizen. On Good Friday, the hallowed anniversary of our Blessed Lord's Crucifixion, when all Christendom was bowed down in penitence and sorrow at His tomb, the President of these United States was foully assassinated, and a wicked attempt was made on the life of the Secretary of State. Words fail us for expressing detestation for a deed so atrocious—hitherto, happily, unparalleled in our history. Silence is, perhaps, the best and most appropriate expression for a sorrow so great for utterance.
>
> We are quite sure that we need not remind our Catholic Brethren in this Archdiocese of the duty—which we are confident they will willingly perform— of uniting with their fellow-citizens in whatever may be deemed most suitable for indicating their horror of the crime, and their feelings of sympathy for the be-

reaved. We also invite them to join together in humble and earnest supplication to God for the prosperity of our beloved but afflicted country; and we enjoin that the bells of all our churches be solemnly tolled on the occasion of the President's funeral.[17]

Gen. Lew Wallace warned the Baltimore clergy to keep politics out of their churches:

The conduct of certain clergymen in this city has, in some instances, been so positively offensive to loyal people, and, in others, of such doubtful propriety, to say nothing about taste, as to have become a cause of bad feeling with many well disposed citizens.

As you must be aware, the recent tragedy, so awful in circumstance, and nationally so calamitous, has, as it well might, inflame the sensibilities of men and women who esteem their loyalty only a little less sacred than their religion.

In this state of affairs, you will undoubtedly perceive the wisdom of avoiding, on your part, everything in the least calculated to offend the sensibilities mentioned. You will also perceive the propriety of requiring members of your congregation, male and female, who may be so unfortunate as to have been sympathizers with the rebellion, not to bring their politics into the church.

So profound is my reverence for your truly sacred profession, that, in the sincere hope of avoiding any necessity for interfering with the exercise of your office, I choose this method of respectfully warning you of the existing state of public feeling, and calling upon you, in the name of our common Saviour, to lend me your influence and energetic assistance, to be exerted in every lawful way, to soothe irritations and calm excitements. You know that what I thus request I have the power to enforce. You ought also to know that, to save the community from the dishonor and consequences of a public outbreak, it would be my duty to exercise all the power I possess, without regard to persons or congregations.[18]

While the police arrested anyone expressing solidarity with the Confederacy:

Policeman Woods yesterday arrested a man named Edward Hunt, charged with having hurrahed for Jeff. Davis. He was sent to Colonel Woolley for his action. Policeman Wright arrested Samuel Peacock, a watchman near the Belair market, for using disrespectful language of the late President and exulting over his death. He will be handed over to the care of Col. Woolley to-day.[19]

Leonidas Dodson described the reaction in Easton:

In our town this morning the bells of the churches at the hour of service tolled a solemn requiem, and sadness and gloom sat upon all faces, even upon the faces of those who never appreciated the personal or political worth of the illustrious patriot who has so untimely fallen.[20]

Samuel Harrison copied an editorial from the *Talbot County Gazette*:

The assassination of Mr Lincoln on Friday April 14, 1865, was announced in the Gazette of April 22, 1865. It says the spirit that prompted this deed is "just the spirit that has caused rebel sympathizers of this county to express, time after time, their desire for an opportunity to put a bullet in the heart of 'Abe Lincoln' while others who know more about drugs than bullets, (the women) appeared to entertain it as the chief desire of their hearts, to administer to him a pill. All these things have contributed to the formation of the dualish spirit that has grown to such dimensions.

"At the first announcement of the murder of Mr. Lincoln, rebel sympathizers were delighted with the opportunity of charging the murder upon radical Unionists, and at the first impulse appeared to be shown to rejoice, at least by some; but upon reflection, a large majority fell in with the side that was certain to be most popular. There were some however, mostly *women,* with more brass than brains, who could not suppress their great joy at the murder of the head of the nation."[21]

And noted the report in the *Gazette* that on Wednesday, April 19, "business was suspended in Easton, the houses draped in mourning, and services held in some of the churches."[22]

Archbishop Spaulding, mindful that several of the alleged conspirators were Catholic, ensured that the procession following Lincoln's body through the city included approximately one hundred fifty priests and seminarians. He also condemned the killing:

Words fail us for expressing detestation for a deed so atrocious, hitherto happily unparalleled in our history. Silence is, perhaps, the most appropriate expression for a sorrow too great for utterance.[23]

A Baltimore man described the mood in the city:

Everything here has been at a standstill since Saturday morning last, when the news of the horrible assassination of President Lincoln reached the city. There was much excitement on that day and for a while I feared violence would prevail, but everything quieted down and all were occupied in draping their residences and places of Businesses in the habiliments of woe. On Baltimore Street the sight was impressive and silent. Looking down the street, from every building flags of all sizes met your eye, at half mast and edged with deep black, whilst on the windows, signs, pillars &c.&c. which line the street, mournful black was lavishly displayed. At the same time the various bells of the City, including those of the different churches, were all dismally tolling, and nature herself seemed to mourn, for a drearier day rainy, cold and disagreeable could not well be imagined. Yesterday, the day of the funeral, was a holiday here;—business was suspended and all the churches had service, sermons being delivered and prayers offered with reference to the late calamity.

A great many of the Baltimoreans who went South and served in Lee's army, have returned since the late surrender, intending I suppose to settle down and take up again peaceful pursuits, as it is generally conceded that the war is about over.[24]

Robert Kirkwood, encamped at Manottaway Court House in Virginia, reacted with sorrow and anger:

The assassination of Abraham Lincoln has created much sadness the sad news reached us in the Height of our rejoicing over the bright prospects of peace but now each heart is filled with sorrow and burning with revenge, but those who are his Enemys will have greater reason to lament than we as they will be held accountable. they have received more kindness from his hand than they would have done from any other union man in the same position but they correspond with what they say about the niggers the more privaledge you grant them the more likely they are to cut your throat and sometimes I am inclined to think the Linch Law will have to be enforced before they can be made to know their place. but there is one consolasion he lived to see the back bone of the Rebelion chrushed and to visit the capital at Richmond when Jeff has failed to reach Washington as he boasted and had to leave in the night like A thief with A sheep on his back from amidst A People whom he has so sadly betrayed.[25]

On Thursday, June 1, a day of "National Humiliation and Mourning," Rev. James A. McCauley preached on the "Character and Services of Abraham Lincoln" at the Eutaw Methodist Episcopal Church—part of Baltimore's effort to expiate its grief. McCauley believed there no doubt that "his selection was one of God":

Minds of loftier mould could likely have been found; finer culture surely could. But it is doubtful if the nation had a single other mind, better qualified than his, to grapple with the great necessities of the Presidential office during his term. The world, I think, consents that he was a man remarkable for quick and clear perception; for cautious, acute, almost unerring, judgment; for a will in which pliancy and strength were combined, in a singular degree.

The reverend portrayed Lincoln as a savior:

Recently the land was lurid with the flames of war; the air was heavy with its woes. Now the noise of guns is hushed. The dust is lifting from the field. Columbia smiles from sea to sea. Grandly loom the great results: the Republic is safe; treason is dead, or dares no longer strike; one flag floats, and not a second will. These results, for which the nation has been toiling, as nation never toiled

The shot fired by John Wilkes Booth at Ford's Theatre on April 14, 1865, reverberates still. Harper's Weekly.

before, are facts accomplished now. And much of what they mean we already comprehend. We know that the questions, so troublous in the past, will no more disturb the nation's peace. State supremacy, that restless spirit which walked the land so long, and which no skill of Statesmen could compose, has been laid to sleep to wake no more. General Lee is rumored to have said, "the right of a State to secede was an open question till my failure settled it." It is settled now. No more will rivalries of rule disturb the nation's peace. No more the stars will leave the sun. In the Union every State will stay, each pursuing its allotted course, and dutifully doing its appointed work.

And closed with a prediction of Lincoln's place in memory:

Through all the ages yet to come, the generations of the American people will growingly revere and cherish him as the man, who, under God, preserved their imperiled institutions, and made them instrumental of the richer benefactions they increasingly dispense. Nor they alone. Throughout the world friends of liberty will keep fresh garlands on his brow, and consign the keeping of his fame to their best traditions. The appreciation of his character and deeds, as uttered in the tributes which have come across the sea, seems as warm and loving, if not so universal, in other lands, as in the land of which he lived and died. Like Washington, he is not ours exclusively: the world claims him.[26]

In June, John P. Kennedy described Lincoln's legacy:

> Abraham Lincoln lives forever in history as *the liberator of two continents.* He crushed out slavery from American and Africa. "The curse" is taken off the world and can find no lodgement on either side of the Atlantic. The extinction of slavery here makes it impossible any where.—Think of the grandeur of such a sudden and sublime exaltation as that—in the space of four years! The life of Lincoln seems like a heavenly [?]. This simple and shrewd and honest wood-man—thrown upon such a stage, with such a labor before him: the steady and almost inspired wisdom of his advance from each stage to the next, in the accomplishment of his task, and the final consummation of his appointed work, in the end of the war, by which he has saved the republic and which has secured the complete and perfect liberation of four millions of slaves—and then, the duty done, the departure from the scene of his labors.[27]

In December, P. M. Clark, a Washington man, wielding affidavits from the mayor of Washington and a colonel, laid claim for the reward offered by Baltimore for his role in the apprehension of the assassins:

> I have the honor to hereby notify you that I claim the award, offered by the authorities of Baltimore for the arrest of the assassins of the President and Secretary Seward, that may be applicable to the arrest of Payne and Mrs. Surratt.[28]

The disposition of Clark's claim is unknown.

Robert E. Lee's surrender at Appomattox brought a merciful end to what, for many Marylanders, had been four years of misery. Yet the emotions endure, long after that Friday in April 1865; indeed, the Civil War remains our most powerful national memory, defining who we are as Americans.

Contention over the merits of Northern and Southern war objectives persisted for decades among veterans' groups and in memoirs, lecture halls, funeral orations, cemetery statuary, textbooks, and battlefield markers. Postwar righteousness, having long ago reached the plane of moral certainty, is a staple of contemporary American culture. The impulse to remember the war and honor soldiers on both sides retains its power even in the early twenty-first century, when reenactors number in the thousands and scholars examine themes of reconciliation and race relations as they ponder the many dimensions of historical memory.[1] Cultural exposés such as *Confederates in the Attic: Dispatches from the Unfinished Civil War* and *The Civil War in Popular Culture: A Reusable Past* explore contemporary expressions of "memory" and demonstrate how deeply embedded the war remains in our national consciousness.

Much of the memory industry, especially in the immediate aftermath of the war, proceeded deliberately. In 1869, ex-Confederates founded the Southern Historical Society, with the stated purpose of arguing their perspective on the war—a campaign made all the more imperative by the fact that they had lost it. The Society portrayed those lost in battle as heroes fallen in the twin righteous causes of liberty and self-determination. Southerners since that time have worked diligently, perhaps at times unconsciously, to find mid-nineteenth-century concert of interest between rich and poor white Southerners, valiant common cause in wartime, and shared devotion to the Lost Cause.[2] This vision of internal white unity and postwar sectional reconciliation that served Southern political ends had no place for the complex legacy of slavery.

Former Maryland slave owners leapt immediately into the post-Appomattox fray. Having rejected Lincoln's 1862 offer of compensated emancipation, they fought to maintain the status quo before the ink dried on the November 1864 constitution banning slavery. Consorting with unscrupulous judges of county Orphans' Courts, their efforts to apprentice black children—too often successful—constituted a de facto extension of slavery in a state that had just banned it. Whites in southern Maryland and the Eastern Shore beat freedmen and terrorized black communities, torching their homes and schools. Passage of the Thirteenth, Fourteenth, and Fifteenth Amendments and the 1866 Civil Rights Act (the first such legislation in the history of the country) supplied the foundation for political change, though little of that would reach the South, including Maryland, before a century had passed.

Maryland's Southern partisans coped with their sense of loss by engaging in vigorous self-expression. Maryland civilians who had run afoul of Union authorities and endured prison published accounts that railed against the Northern tyrants. One of the best known, Frank Howard's *Fourteen Months in American Bastilles*, had appeared in the midst of the war. Published diaries by observers such as Southern Unionist William Wilkins Glenn regaled readers with tales of the heavy federal boot on Maryland; such highly personal accounts of the war years lent additional strength to the Southern view. Maryland's Union veterans published much less, perhaps believing "their record spoke for itself," in Robert J. Brugger's phrase;[3] their memoirs tended to take the form of letters, and few book-length works appeared. These men tended to go home to their families, farms, and businesses, where they collected pensions from the government for which they had sacrificed so much.

Postwar memoirs poured forth, some in response to a plea the Maryland Historical Society issued in the early twentieth century for personal accounts of the April 19, 1861, riot in Baltimore. Most of the published stories by and about Maryland soldiers, and all of the best known, featured the recollections of Confederates. They included Henry Kyd Douglas's *I Rode with Stonewall* (not published until 1940), whose self-absorbed tone led one reviewer to suggest the more apt title of "Stonewall Rode with Me"; McHenry Howard's *Recollections of a Maryland Confederate Soldier, 1861–1866* (1914); W. W. Goldsborough's *The Maryland Line in the Confederate Army, 1861–1865* (1900); and George Booth's *A Maryland Boy in Lee's Army: Personal Reminiscences of a Maryland Soldier in the War Between the States, 1861–1865* (1898). Former Confederate brigadier general Bradley T. Johnson, a Frederick native who spent most of his postwar life in Richmond, repeatedly returned to his home state to unveil monuments and establish organizations to commemorate the Southern fallen. Johnson characterized the Civil War as a continuation of the American Revolution; he labored mightily to place Maryland as the truest of Southern states, blaming the Confederate government for the failure of western Marylanders to join Lee's army during the invasions of 1862 and 1863.[4]

Shortly after the war, the federal government began to expand the National Cemetery system established in 1862 to manage the reburial of Union dead throughout the South. Plans included building a cemetery near Sharpsburg in Washington County. (Legislation passed in 1906 required federal maintenance of Confederate graves in cemeteries in the Northern states.) In Baltimore, in 1863, 139 Confederate prisoners of war captured at Gettysburg who died in Fort McHenry were buried in Loudon Park National Cemetery shortly after its establishment a year earlier. The Loudon Park Memorial Association began arranging burials of ex-Confederate soldiers and helping maintain their graves, which eventually numbered some six hundred (between Loudon Park National Cemetery, amid numerous monuments to both sides, and adjacent, preexisting civilian burial ground, also named Loudon Park). This association gave way in 1871 to the Society of the Army and

The graves of Union and Confederate dead in Maryland still draw visitors today. MdHS.

Navy of the Confederate States in the State of Maryland, whose first president was Pickett's Charge veteran Maj. Gen. Isaac R. Trimble. In September 1887, the group dispatched a delegation to Richmond for ceremonies dedicating the Lee statue on that city's Monument Avenue, where they participated in a spectacular parade. The society soon sprouted the Sons of Confederate Veterans, which by 1900 had three camps in Maryland. The state-funded Maryland Line Confederate Soldier's Home, on the grounds of the Pikesville Arsenal, operated from 1888 to 1932 and was the only facility of its kind in a former Union state.[5] The Maryland chapter of the Sons of Confederate Veterans survived until 1930. The last Maryland Confederate veteran, Eli Scott Dance, died in 1945, but the society reappeared in 1966 as a group devoted to commemorative activities; today it has approximately five hundred members.

Confederate women worked energetically on a variety of fronts throughout the South to honor the Lost Cause, painting it with a veneer of nostalgia. Women helped popularize Decoration Day, the precursor to Memorial Day, when graves of their noble fallen were festooned with flags and flowers by black citizens in a ritual first observed on May 1, 1865, in Charleston, South Carolina. These Southern women took seriously the work of erecting monuments, reburying the dead, and monitoring the "Lost Cause" content of history schoolbooks.

Maryland women played their part. In Baltimore, in 1867, the Ladies Southern Relief Society sponsored a fair that raised $162,000 for the benefit of charities in the ex-Confederate states and to aid indigent Southern veterans.[6] A year later, Baltimoreans had established chapter 8 of the United Daughters of the Confederacy, and by 1897, it had sufficiently established itself to host the fourth UDC convention.[7] As late as 1936, Maryland sustained thirteen UDC chapters —six in Baltimore and others in Annapolis, Ellicott City, Frederick, Hagerstown, Poolesville, Upper Marlboro, and Rockville, with more than eight hundred members statewide. The UDC staged elaborate annual conventions in Baltimore at the Alcazar Hotel, at Cathedral and Madison streets, or the Beaux-Arts Belvedere Hotel, at North Charles and Chase streets. In 1934, when the Baltimore chapter marked the birthdays of Lee and Andrew Jackson in the Blue Room at the Alcazar, Francis F. Beirne of the Baltimore *Evening Sun* offered the keynote address, and Dr. Henry Lee Smith wistfully read an original poem, "Victory." Attendees at the 1937 annual meeting at the Belvedere heard Stringfellow Barr, the president of St. John's College, proclaim that Confederate soldiers fought for "the right of independence and self-government."[8]

Proud if dispassionate Union veterans in Maryland, not to be outdone fraternally, gathered in posts of the Grand Army of the Republic (GAR), which organized in 1866 and by 1890 had more than four hundred thousand members (but being a group for men who had wielded arms for the United States, it would dissolve in 1956 following the death of the last Union veteran, in Minnesota). In 1885, Maryland members of the GAR invited Gen. George B. McClellan to give a Decoration Day oration at ceremonies honoring the Union dead at Antietam. In 1881, the Sons of Veterans of the United States of America formed as a group of descendants of veterans and, later, opened to all who subscribed to honoring the Union cause (in 1925, the name changed to Sons of Union Veterans of the Civil War). By 1892, Maryland, which shared in the explosive post-1880 growth of veterans' organizations, had almost 3,600 men enrolled in the Sons of Union Veterans and thirteen posts in Baltimore alone. In 2005, the Sons of Union Veterans had approximately one hundred members in posts in Baltimore, Frederick, and Fort Meade.[9]

War monuments, rare on the American landscape before the Civil War, began appearing soon after its end, reaching a zenith between 1903 and 1914, when most veterans were elderly. These monuments depicted veterans and women in a symbiotic embrace of honor. (World War I would bring a hybrid model, with women ministering to dying soldiers that paid tribute to both Union and Confederate.) Soldier monuments went up quickly after Appomattox, with the first, a Union sculpture, appearing in 1866. These monuments reflect the state's divided sentiments. In 1995, Susan Cooke Soderberg counted sixty-five monuments: twenty-nine Confederate, twenty-six Union, four honoring both sides, and six unassociated with either side. (The tallest—the prisoners-of-war monument at Point Lookout, erected in 1876 by the federal government—and the most expensive, the Lee-Jackson monument in Baltimore, both honor Confederates.) In 1886 on the field of Gettysburg, Maryland erected monuments to the First and Second Maryland Infantry (Confederate States of America)[10] and then, in 1888, honored Union veterans with markers for the three infantry regiments, single artillery battery, and one cavalry regiment that fought on that field.

After the Spanish-American War stoked patriotic fires throughout the nation, the Antietam Battlefield Commission of Maryland erected a splendid monument to the dead of both sides on that hallowed ground. Those who looked carefully could see reconciliation on the horizon. In Baltimore in 1909, at Charles and 29th Streets in Wyman Park, friends of the victorious side dedicated the Union Soldiers and Sailors Monument. Nine years later, a few blocks north, at Charles Street and University Parkway, Southern partisans unveiled a monument honoring Confederate women, a project of the Maryland Chapter of the UDC and beneficiary of a 1914 state appropriation of $12,000.

In the spring of 1865, with the prospect of peace finally at hand, an association of Baltimore black men purchased a building on Lexington Street. Called the Douglass Institute, for the renowned Maryland-born abolitionist and orator, it was dedicated to "the intellectual advancement of the colored portion of the community." On September 29 of that year, Frederick Douglass spoke of the importance of this new institution and the hope of black equality. The institute, he said to his racially mixed audience, "implies that the colored people of Baltimore not only have the higher qualities attributed to the white race. It implies an increased knowledge of the requirements of a high civilization, and a determination to comply with them. This Institute, in character and design, in some measure represents the abilities and possibilities of our race."[11] In the years following at black celebrations of Decoration Day and, particularly, Emancipation Day, speakers returned to the themes of hope, work, and progress that reflected a nascent black political activism.[12] Society would subsequently wrestle for decades with the incendiary challenges of portraying images of grateful slaves in freedom's pose—often with Lincoln—and black soldiers who had fought nobly alongside white men.[13]

Douglass returned to Baltimore in May 1870 for ceremonies marking ratification of the Fifteenth Amendment, which gave black citizens the right to vote (despite the failure of Maryland to ratify it). "The entire colored population seemed to have come forth upon the streets and entered into the spirit of the occasion," reported the *Sun*. A crowd of "from six to ten thousand persons had collected in the Square, representing every color, and shade of color, as well as every class and condition of men." After parades and processions culminated in Monument Square, letters from Massachusetts Senator and antislavery spokesman Charles Sumner and abolitionist and erstwhile Baltimore resident William Lloyd Garrison were read to the throng, which included "few white invited guests," the paper reported. Former Republican congressman John A. J. Creswell, then U.S. Postmaster General, was introduced as "the truest friend of the colored race," after which he, Judge Hugh Lennox Bond, and others spoke, and resolutions were passed thanking President Ulysses S. Grant. The crowd then grew quiet as Douglass, under clear sky and cool breeze, walked to the speaker's stand. He "had often appeared before the American people as a slave, and sometimes a fugitive slave, but always as an advocate for the slave," wrote the *Sun,* which paraphrased his remarks. Douglass noted that he had never fled from Maryland, but from slavery, and proclaimed that blacks now had two of three boxes—the cartridge box and the ballot box. Now, he said, they must achieve the jury box—a reference, surely, to the refusal of Southern states to recognize the provenance of the Fourteenth Amendment, which granted civil rights to black citizens. A public celebration of black achievement and new-found political legitimacy, the day ended with a ball at the Douglass Institute, where the *Sun* noted the paucity of white guests.[14]

Celebrations marking ratification were held in smaller Maryland cities as well. Jacob Engelbrecht's diary recorded how in early June a procession of "colored citizens" stretched a mile through the town of Frederick (his record of speakers is blank, as though he meant to write in the names later). Engelbrecht, a Frederick farmer, also noted that the graves of Union soldiers in Mt. Olivet Cemetery were honored on Decoration Day by citizens united in song—and that Confederate graves were similarly honored on June 4. The *American Sentinel* of Westminster delicately touched the racial issue, assuring readers that blacks did not seek equality with whites. It quoted remarks of Col. W. U. Saunders at "the recent celebration in this city" to the effect that the black population wished only for "an equal chance before the law, in the race for life."[15]

The race was, of course, far from being fairly run. At a time when war with Spain was encouraging national reconciliation, members of Baltimore's black GAR posts were making regular excursions to Gettysburg to commemorate the Emancipation Proclamation.[16] In 1913, when white organizers put together an ambitious fiftieth reunion of the battle, they pointedly excluded black veterans and studiously avoided mention of emancipation. The *Baltimore Afro-American Ledger* was moved to wonder whether Lincoln's phrase, as he dedicated the national cemetery there in 1863, "by the 'People'" really meant "only white people"—an observation made just as President Woodrow Wilson began segregating agencies of the federal government.[17]

The later twentieth century saw no less infatuation with Maryland's Civil War, and in the age of "separate but equal," such interest generally retained a Southern cast. The Maryland General Assembly set aside its real work long enough in 1939 to adopt James Ryder Randall's notoriously pro-Southern "Maryland, My Maryland" as the official state anthem. In May 1948, a crowd of three thousand turned out for the dedication of the double equestrian statue to Lee and Jackson on the northwest side of Wyman Park in Baltimore, a short distance from the classical architecture of the Baltimore Museum of Art. This major civic event, though marking no war-related anniversary, drew Mayor Thomas D'Alesandro Jr.; Noble C. Powell, the bishop of the Protestant Episcopal Diocese of Maryland, who gave the benediction; and Gov. William Preston Lane, the principal speaker. The music of the Army Field Forces Band leavened the oratory. Not many years later, with the centennial of the conflict approaching, Maryland's Civil War Centennial Commission, charged with establishing "a proper commemoration of the Centennial of the Battle of Antietam and other campaigns of the Civil War on Maryland soil," included in its activities a 1961 reenactment of the 1861 special legislative session that blunted secession and, in July 1964, a commemoration of the ransom Frederick paid Confederates to spare it the torch.[18] In the modern age, Marylanders of all stripes, led by reenactors, annually walk the route of the Pratt Street Riot of April 1861, and, in a moving tribute to the killed and wounded of both sides, each December volunteers light one candle in honor of each of the 23,110 men who fell on the Antietam Battlefield, on that bloodiest day in American history.

In 1994 a Maryland monument appeared on the Gettysburg battlefield, the first since the 1880s. Installed near Culp's Hill, where Maryland troops from each side clashed on the second and third days of struggle, the statue depicted two soldiers, one Union and the other Confederate, both seemingly wounded, each helping the other to safety.

This monument might have represented the final word on the war and Maryland's place in the North/South divide, but at the outset of many General Assembly sessions someone introduces a resolution calling for the demotion of "Maryland, My Maryland" as the state song. Its invidious lyrics include references to "Northern scum" and the "patriotic gore" of Southern sympathizers injured as they attacked the Sixth Massachusetts that fateful day in April 1861. Such resolutions are short-lived, and each year at the nationally televised Preakness Stakes in Baltimore, the U.S. Naval Academy glee club leads the crowd in singing less offensive stanzas.

For more than a century after the war, animus and segregation characterized Maryland's racial history, stoked by black activism—and corresponding white backlash—in the wake of landmark events such as *Brown v. Board of Education* and passage of the Civil Rights Act of 1965. Indeed, in Baltimore and several smaller Maryland cities, racial riots that exploded a hundred years after Appomattox remind us of the war's legacy, and that race and reunion remain entwined.

The myth that military force alone thwarted the will of Marylanders to secede is an essential story line in the romanticism of the Lost Cause. Sons and daughters of those who fought that war will sip mint juleps on soft summer evenings and argue over the viability of Maryland secession, and their debates will propel the story from each generation to the next. But military power did not drive the forces of Unionism that coalesced quickly to eradicate slavery, however imperfectly, before the end of the conflict. Enlightenment and redemption lie not in dogmatic rehash of oral traditions, but—if we listen closely—in the rich voices of Maryland's civil war.

In May 1870, Baltimoreans gathered in Monument Square to mark the passage of the Fifteenth Amendment to the U.S. Constitution. Maryland, however, would not ratify it until 1973. MdHS.

Abbreviations for Frequently Cited Sources

American
    Baltimore American and Commercial Advertiser
BCA
    Baltimore City Archives
Baker, *Politics of Continuity*
    Jean H. Baker, *The Politics of Continuity: Maryland Political Parties from
    1858 to 1870*, Baltimore, 1973
Ball Papers
    Thomas Sewall Ball Papers, 1863–1892, MS 1190, MdHS
Black Military Experience
    Ira Berlin, Joseph P. Reidy, and Leslie S. Rowland, *Freedom: A Documentary
    History of Emancipation, 1861–1867*, Series 2: *The Black Military Experience*, New
    York, 1982
Brown, *Nineteenth of April*
    George Brown, *Baltimore and the Nineteenth of April, 1861: A Study of the War*,
    Baltimore, 1887, reprinted Baltimore, 2001
Brown Papers
    George Wm. Brown Collection, 1862, MS 2398, MdHS
Brune Papers
    Brune-Randall Family Papers, 1782–1972, MS 2004, MdHS
E. Bonaparte Papers
    Elizabeth Patterson Bonaparte Papers, 1802–1879, MS 142, MdHS
J. Bonaparte Papers
    Jerome Napoleon Bonaparte Papers, 1805–1893, MS 144, MdHS
Bowie Papers
    Lucy Leigh Bowie Papers, 1759–1966, MS 1755, MdHS
Cohen Scrapbook
    Cohen Civil War Scrapbook, 1861–1865, MS 251.1, MdHS
Collected Works
    Roy P. Basler, *Collected Works of Abraham Lincoln*, New Brunswick, NJ, 1953
Creamer Scrapbook
    Creamer Civil War Scrapbook, 1871, MS 270, MdHS
A. B. Davis Papers
    Allen Bowie Davis Letters, 1855–1904, MS 1511, MdHS
Davis Diary
    Rebecca D. Davis Diary, July 19, 1863–September 17, 1864, MS 2111, MdHS
Destruction of Slavery
    Ira Berlin, Barbara J. Fields, Thavolia Glymph, Joseph P. Reidy, *Freedom:
    A Documentary History of Emancipation, 1861–1867*, Series 1, Vol. 1: *The
    Destruction of Slavery*, New York, 1985

Dodson Papers
    Papers of Leonidas Dodson, Series 1, UMdLib
Exec Ltr Bk
    Executive Letter Book, Maryland State Archives
Fuke, *Imperfect Equality*
    Richard Paul Fuke, *Imperfect Equality: African Americans and the Confines of White Racial Attitudes in Post-Emancipation Maryland*, New York, 1999
Furber Collection
    Lyman Van Buren Furber Collection, 1827–(1861–1862)–1879, MS 2442, MdHS
Glenn Diary
    Bayley Ellen Marks and Mark Norton Schatz, eds., *Between North and South: A Maryland Journalist Views the Civil War: The Narrative of William Wilkins Glenn, 1861–1869*, Rutherford, NJ, 1976
Graham Letters
    Graham-Winans Letters, 1862–1870, MS 2144, MS 2144–2147, MdHS
Graves Scrapbook
    Graves Civil War Scrapbook, 1860–1865, MS 405, MdHS
Hall Letters
    Thomas W. Hall Papers, 1861–1867, MS 2390, MdHS
Harris Papers
    J. Morrison Harris Papers, 1778–1898, MS 2739, MdHS
Harrison
    Harrison Collection (Political Annals), ca. 1790–1890, MS 432, MdHS
Hay Diary
    Tyler Dennett, *Lincoln and the Civil War in the Diaries and Letters of John Hay*, New York, 1939
Hering Recollections
    Hering Family Scrapbooks and Recollections ("Recollections of My Life"), 1774, 1833–1939, 1951, MS 1917, MdHS
Howard, "Crisis"
    Charles M. Howard, "Baltimore and the Crisis of 1861," *MdHM* XLI, no. 4, December, 1946
Kennedy Papers
    Papers of John Pendleton Kennedy, Peabody Institute, Baltimore
Kirkwood Papers
    Kirkwood Family Papers, 1857–1923, MS 2797, MdHS
Laas, *Wartime Washington*
    Virginia Laas, ed., *Wartime Washington: The Civil War Letters of Elizabeth Blair Lee*, Urbana, IL, 1991
Lee Papers
    Clifford Dowdey and Louis H. Manarin, eds., *The Wartime Papers of Robert E. Lee*, New York, 1961, reprinted New York, 1987

Marine Papers

Rev. Fletcher E. Marine Papers, 1829–1889, MS 1016.3, MdHS

MdHM

Maryland Historical Magazine

MdHS

H. Furlong Baldwin Library, Maryland Historical Society, Baltimore

MdSA

Maryland State Archives, Annapolis, MD

Mearns, *Lincoln Papers*

David C. Mearns, *The Lincoln Papers*, Vol. 2, Garden City, NY, 1948

NA

National Archives and Records Administration

Neely, *Fate of Liberty*

Mark Neely, *The Fate of Liberty: Abraham Lincoln and Civil Liberties*, New York, 1991

Noyes Letters

John G. Noyes Letters, 1861–1862, MS 2466, MdHS

OR

The War of the Rebellion: A Compilation of the Official Records of the Union and Confederate Armies, Washington, 1880–1901

Pratt Lib

Enoch Pratt Free Library, Baltimore

RG

Record Group

RG 94

Records of the Adjutant General's Office, NA

RG 107

Records of the Secretary of War, NA

RG 393

Records of United States Army Continental Command, 1821–1920, NA

Redwood Collection

Redwood Collection, 1828–1919, MS 676, MdHS (MS 1530 is a broader Redwood Coll.)

Schaeffer Diary

Ann R. L. Schaeffer: Records of the Past [Civil War], September 4–September 23, 1862, MS 1860, MdHS

Seward, *Reminiscences*

Frederick Seward, *Reminiscences of a War-Time Statesman and Diplomat*, New York, 1916

Shriver Papers

Shriver Family Papers, 1774–1957, MS 2085–2085.1, MdHS

Sketches from Prison

Sketches from Prison: A Confederate Artist's Record of Life at Point Lookout Prisoner-of-War 1865–1865, Maryland State Park Foundation, Inc., 1990.

Slicer Journal

Journal of Henry Slicer, Lovely Lane Museum and Archives, Baltimore

Spear Papers

Spear Papers, 1858–1866, MS 1428, MdHS

Spencer Letters I

Anna Bradford Agle and Sidney Hovey Wanzer, "Dearest Braddie: Love and War in Maryland, 1860–61," pt. 1, *MdHM* 88, no. 1 (Spring 1993)

Spencer Letters II

Anna Bradford Agle and Sidney Hovey Wanzer, "Dearest Braddie: Love and War in Maryland, 1860–61," pt. 2," *MdHM* 88, no. 3 (Fall 1993)

J. Steuart Papers

James E. Steuart Papers, 1785–1955, MS 758, MdHS

Sun

Baltimore Sun

Thomas Papers

The Papers of Daniel M. Thomas, 1674–1938, MS 1970.2, MdHS

UMdLib

Special Collections, University of Maryland Libraries

Wagandt, *Mighty Revolution*

Charles L. Wagandt, *The Mighty Revolution: Negro Emancipation in Maryland, 1862–1864*, Baltimore, 1964, reprinted Baltimore, 2005

Wartime Genesis

Ira Berlin, Steven F. Miller, Joseph P. Reidy, and Leslie S. Rowland, *Freedom: A Documentary History of Emancipation 1861–1867*, Series 1, Vol. 2: *The Wartime Genesis of Free Labor: The Upper South,* New York, *1993*

Wilson Papers

Wilson Papers, 1790–1952, MS 833, MdHS

Winder Papers

Winder Family Papers, 1817–1888, MS 2310, MdHS

Notes

INTRODUCTION

1. M. Ray Della, "An Analysis of Baltimore's Population in the 1850s," *MdHM* 68, no. 1 (1973): 20.

2. Charles B. Clark, "Politics in Maryland during the Civil War," *MdHM* 36, no. 3 (1941): 252, 254.

3. *Compendium of the Seventh Census,* Slave Population, Table 72 (Washington, D.C., 1854), 83. In 1850, Maryland had 90,368 slaves and 74,723 free blacks.

4. Augustus W. Bradford to Abraham Lincoln, March 6, 1862, *Exec Ltr Bk,* MdSA.

PART I: INDECISION

1. *Sun,* November 7 and December 3 (Beantown meeting), 1860. More remarkable was a peaceful Baltimore election, marred only by the accidental wounding (as recounted in the *Sun*) of a policeman by another member of the force, who had unholstered his revolver after being struck by a spittoon hurled from Bell headquarters.

2. *Sun,* December 4, 1860.

3. Daniel W. Crofts, *Reluctant Confederates: Upper South Unionists in the Secession Crisis* (Chapel Hill, NC, 1989), 90. South Carolina had chafed for years under the federal yoke, especially since the Nullification Crisis twenty years earlier, when the state had clashed with the federal government over import tariffs.

4. John G. Nicolay and John Hay, *Abraham Lincoln: A History* (New York, 1886), 4:93.

5. Constitutional reform in 1851 had rotated the governorship between Maryland's three principal geographic regions. At the time, the Maryland General Assembly met only in even-numbered years.

6. *Sun,* April 19, 1861.

7. Vivid accounts of the Pratt Street riot include Matthew Page Andrews, "Passage of the Sixth Massachusetts Regiment through Baltimore, April 19, 1861," *MdHM* 34, no. 1 (1919): 60–76; George Brown, *Baltimore and the Nineteenth of April, 1861: A Study of the War* (Baltimore, 2001); Charles Branch Clark, "Baltimore and the Attack on the Sixth Massachusetts Regiment, April 19, 1861," *MdHM,* 56, no. 1 (1961): 39–71; Frank Towers, "'Vociferous Army of Howling Wolves': Baltimore's Civil War Riot of April 19, 1861," *Maryland Historian* 23 (1992): 1–27; eyewitness reports at the Maryland Historical Society; and the April 20–22, 1861, issues of newspapers such as the *Sun* and the *American.*

8. Mark E. Neely, *The Fate of Liberty: Abraham Lincoln and Civil Liberties* (New York, 1991), 18. See chapter 1 for an overview of arrests in Maryland early in the war. Taney was not arrested.

CHAPTER 1. FALL 1860–1861 WINTER

1. *Centreville Advocate,* in *American,* November 14, 1860.

2. *Centreville Times,* in *American,* November 14, 1860.

3. *Baltimore Exchange,* November 7, 1860, in W. Bruce Catton, "The Baltimore Business Community and the Sectional Crisis, 1860–61" (M.A. thesis, University of Maryland, College Park, 1952), 53–54.

4. *Kent Conservator* in *American,* November 19, 1860.

5. Dodson Diary, October 26, 1860, UMdLib.

6. *Frederick Herald* in *American,* November 14, 1860.

7. *Catholic Mirror,* November 3 and December 1, 1860, in Thomas W. Spalding, *The Premier See: A History of the Archdiocese of Baltimore, 1789–1989* (Baltimore, 1989), 175.

8. Dodson Papers, November 7, 1860, UMdLib. Dodson noted that Stephen Douglas would have been elected had the Democrats nominated him in Charleston.

9. *Sun,* November 16, 1860.

10. *Sun,* December 5, 1860.

11. James Hicks in *Report of the Select Committee of Five,* January 30, 1861, No. 9, 34.

12. Frederick County meeting in *Sun,* December 20, 1860; other meetings in William J. Evitts, *A Matter of Allegiances: Maryland from 1850 to 1861* (Baltimore, 1974), 157.

13. Citizens of Anne Arundel County to Thomas H. Hicks, 1861, MS 1860, MdHS. (This version was given to the Maryland Historical Society in February 1954 by John M. Cates, who noted that Alexander Randall, the first signatory, was a strong Unionist.) William L. W. Seabrook, *Maryland's Great Part in Saving the Union* (Westminster, MD, 1913), 16, describes Randall, an ex-member of Congress, as a close confidante of Hicks and "one of the most consistent and ardent unionists in the state."

14. *Sun,* December 1, 1860.

15. Thomas H. Hicks to Thomas G. Pratt, Sprigg Harwood, J. S. Franklin, Llewellyn Boyle, and J. Pinkney, in *American,* November 29, 1860.

16. T. H. Hicks to W. L. Wilcox, January 24, 1861, MS 1860, MdHS. The *Sun* reported on November 24, 1860, that Minute Men were secretly organizing in Southern states to attack Lincoln's Wide-Awakes and block his inauguration.

17. "Parade of Minute Men" in Catton, "The Baltimore Business Community," 46; William Platt to Richard D. Fisher, May 25, 1909, MS 1860, MdHS.

18. George H. Steuart to editors of *The National Intelligencer,* November 19, 1860, J. Steuart Papers. The "other states" Steuart named were "New York, Ohio, Massachusetts and other Free States."

19. Dodson Diary, January 2, 1861, UMdLib.

20. E. B. Washburne to Abraham Lincoln, January 10, 1861, in David C. Mearns, ed., *The Lincoln Papers* (Garden City, NY, 1948): 2:398.

21. Woman to Lincoln, undated; W. G. Snethen to Lincoln, February 15, 1861, both in Abraham Lincoln Papers, Library of Congress, in Maury Klein, *Days of Defiance: Sumter, Secession, and the Coming of the Civil War* (New York, 1997), 269.

22. J[oseph] Medill to Abraham Lincoln, December 26, 1860, in Mearns, *Lincoln Papers,* 355–56.

23. Unsigned to Hicks in *American,* January 1, 1861.

24. George B. Cole to W. E. Cole, January 8, 1861, Redwood Collection. Cole published a photography manual for amateurs in 1858.

25. *Easton Gazette*, January 26, 1861, quoted in Harrison. Harrison served as superintendent of Talbot County Schools and wrote a history of the county.

26. Dodson Diary, February 6, 1861, UMdLib.

27. Lucius E. Chittenden, *Recollections of President Abraham Lincoln and His Administration* (New York, 1891), 37–39.

28. Norma Cuthbert, *Lincoln and the Baltimore Plot* (San Marino, CA, 1949), 4. The "Lady" was Mrs. Hattie H. Lawton. Cuthbert, who wrote the most comprehensive work on the Lincoln plot, examines four firsthand accounts: Pinkerton's original notes of his investigation (the *Record Book* of 1861); two letters he wrote to William Herndon, Lincoln's law partner, in 1866; and versions from each of two Lincoln advisers, Howard Judd and Ward H. Lamon. Cuthbert notes that the transcript of Pinkerton's notes includes only two reports from Webster, neither of which discusses either the military organization of Maryland secessionists or Governor Hicks (see Cuthbert, p. 126 n18). Pinkerton meant "Perryville," a small rail town on the Susquehanna River with a steamer landing.

29. Paul M. Angle, *Herndon's Life of Lincoln* (New York, 1961), 387.

30. Slicer Journal, February 14, 1861. Slicer, who in 1837 was appointed chaplain of Congress, voted for John Breckenridge in the 1860 presidential election.

31. George W. Walling, *Recollections of a New York Chief of Police* (Denver, 1887, reprinted Montclair, NJ, 1972), 68–69, 69–77 (men fleeing).

32. Allan Pinkerton, *Spy of the Rebellion* (Lincoln, NE, 1989), 59. Cuthbert, p. 138, notes that Pinkerton's manuscript misspells the name as "Farridina." Cypriano Ferrandina was listed in the Baltimore City Directory in 1860 as "hairdresser, Calvert (Street), under Barnum's Hotel, dw 250 e Baltimore (Street)."

33. Cuthbert, *Baltimore Plot,* 32–37, quote on 37 (italics Cuthbert's). Pinkerton's memoir differs somewhat; see pp. 63–66. I take the 1861 *Record Book* in Cuthbert, which presumably contains notes recorded during or shortly after the conversations took place, to be more reliable, though both works are likely infested with Pinkerton's grandiose claims. The *Baltimore City Directory of 1858–59* lists "Luckett & Young, produce com. merchts. 119 w Lombard (Street)." The 1860 directory lists "James H. Luckett, office 44 South (Street), dw Baltimore Co."

34. Pinkerton, *Spy,* 76–79.

35. Scott's note to Seward in Frederick W. Seward, *Reminiscences of a War-Time Statesman and Diplomat* (New York, 1916), 134–35. See pp. 134–39 for the complete account of Frederick Seward, who would serve his father as assistant secretary of state.

36. Allan Pinkerton to William Herndon, August 23, 1866, Herndon-Weik Collection, in David Herbert Donald, *Lincoln* (New York, 1995), 277 ("death in doing so"); Cuthbert, *Baltimore Plot*, 15.

37. George C. Latham to Jesse W. Weik, January 23, 1918, Herndon-Weik Collection, Library of Congress, in Cuthbert, *Baltimore Plot*, 132n31.

38. *Albany Atlas and Argus,* February 28 and March 5, 1861, in Robert Gray Gunderson: *Old Gentlemen's Convention: The Washington Peace Conference of 1861* (Madison, WI, 1961), 83.

39. Brown, *Nineteenth of April,* 11.

40. Ibid., 11–12.

41. William Louis Schley to Abraham Lincoln, February 23, 1861, Robert Todd Lincoln Papers, Library of Congress, in Cuthbert, *Baltimore Plot,* 149.

42. Chittenden, *Recollections,* 58–64.

43. Isaac N. Arnold, *The History of Abraham Lincoln and the Overthrow of Slavery* (Chicago, 1866, reprinted Freeport, NY, 1971), 171.

44. Thomas H. Hicks to John Contee, in *Sun,* December 21, 1860. (The reply to Contee was issued on December 6.)

45. Henry Winter Davis to Col. William Turnbull, December 25, 1860, Turnbull Collection, MS 1719, MdHS. Davis served in Congress in 1854–1860 and 1863–1864.

46. Thomas J. Hanson to John L. Manning, December 27, 1860, MS 1860, MdHS.

47. *Frederick Herald* in *Sun,* November 28, 1860.

48. *Sun,* November 13, 1860. Brown received 17,779 votes, to 9,675 votes for opponent Samuel Mindes.

49. Frank Moore, *The Rebellion Record: A Diary of American Events I,* Diary, 9, Documents, 17–18, in Bruce Catton, *The Coming Fury* (New York, 1961), 194.

50. *American,* January 7, 1861.

51. *Speeches and Addresses Delivered in the Congress of the United States, and on Several Public Occasions, by Henry Winter Davis of Maryland* (New York, 1867), January 2, 1861, 189–90.

52. *Philadelphia Inquirer,* November 20, 1860, in William Wright, *The Secession Movement in the Middle Atlantic States* (Cranbury, NJ, 1973), 26.

53. *New Orleans Picayune,* November 23, 1860, in Carl M. Frasure, "Union Sentiment in Maryland, 1859–1861," *MdHM* 24, no.1 (1929): 214.

54. *New York Tribune,* February 4, 1861, in ibid.

55. John Roberts to Magruder, Taylor & Roberts, December 23, December 28, and December 30, 1860, Magruder Papers, MS 553, MdHS.

56. A. R. Wright to G. W. Crawford, March 13, 1861, OR 4:1 (pt. 1), 152.

57. Bayly Ellen Marks and Mark Norton Schatz, eds., *Between North and South: A Maryland Journalist Views the Civil War: The Narrative of William Wilkins Glenn, 1861–1869* (Rutherford, NJ, 1976), entry "Jany 1861."

58. Gov. Thos. H. Hicks to the Right Rev. William Whittingham, January 11, 1861, MDA.

59. Daniel M. Thomas to Sister, February 10, 1861, Thomas Papers. Thomas was a vestryman of St. Luke's Protestant Episcopal Church in Baltimore and served on the Supreme Bench of Maryland.

60. Virginia Laas, *Wartime Washington: The Civil War Letters of Elizabeth Blair Lee* (Urbana, IL, 1991), 23 (entry of January 12, 1861).

61. John Fulton, *The "Southern Rights" and "Union" Parties Contrasted* (Baltimore,

1863), 16. In the winter's most serious attempt to patch the Union's cracks, Kentucky Sen. John Crittenden offered six constitutional amendments: no slavery above the old Missouri Compromise line of 36 30 (which would extend all the way to California), slavery sanctioned in current and future territories and safeguarded in the District of Columbia unless Maryland and Virginia agreed to end it, no congressional interference with slavery, and compensation for escaped slaves. The Senate rejected this compromise, in the early dawn of March 4, the day of Lincoln's inauguration; passage would have added the word "slavery" to the U.S. Constitution.

62. *State of the Union*, Speech of Hon. J. Morrison Harris of Maryland, U.S. House of Representatives, January 29, 1861, J. Morrison Harris Papers, MS 2739, MdHS.

63. *Richmond Enquirer*, December 25, 1860, in James Ford Rhodes, *History of the United States, 1850–1877* (New York, 1910), 3:300.

64. Thomas W. Gough in *St. Mary's Beacon*, March 7, 1861, in Edwin W. Beitzell, *Point Lookout Prison Camp for Confederates* (Leonardtown, MD, 1983), 5.

65. Benson J. Lossing, *Pictorial History of the Civil War I* (Philadelphia, 1866), 142.

66. Allan Nevins, *The Emergence of Lincoln: Prologue to Civil War, 1859–1861* (New York, 1959), 411; Lucius E. Chittenden, *A Report of the Debates and Proceedings in Secret Sessions of the Conference Convention, for Proposing Amendments to the Constitution of the United States*, held at Washington, D.C., 1861, 385–87.

67. John C. Robinson, "Baltimore in 1861," *Magazine of American History* 14 (September, 1885), 260.

68. Hester Anne (Wilkins) Davis to [Rebecca Davis], February 5, 1861, A. B. Davis Papers.

69. C. C. [Shriver] to F[rederick] A. Shriver, February 2, 1861, Shriver Papers.

70. Laas, *Wartime Washington*, 35 (entry of February 9, 1861).

71. Glenn Diary, 25 (entry of February 3, 1861).

72. Cuthbert, *Baltimore Plot*, 47. "A.F.C." was either Harry W. Davies or Joseph Howard. Pinkerton, who enjoyed the intrigue of numerous aliases, on p. 55 gives a short and colorful biography of Howard. Hillard testimony in *Report of the Select Committee of Five,* January 29, 1861, 144–55.

73. Cuthbert, *Baltimore Plot*, 48.

74. Edward Spencer to Anne Catherine Bradford Harrison, March 3, 1861, in Anna Bradford Agle and Sidney Hovey Wanzer, Spencers Letters I, 78. He refers to the Washington Peace Conference, which in February failed to reach a compromise that might have averted war.

75. L[uther] B[arnett] B[ruen] to [Augusta Forrer Bruen], March 3, 1861, Bruen Correspondence, MS 1891, MdHS. Bruen's correspondence in early spring 1861 suggests he was attempting to procure a high-level patronage job in the Post Office. In July 1861, he took command of Fort Hamilton.

76. Ibid., March 5, 1861.

77. Diary of John Pendleton Kennedy, March–April 1861, Kennedy Papers.

78. [William] Mentzel to Madame [Elizabeth Patterson] Bonaparte, March 6, 1861, E. Bonaparte Papers.

79. Edward Spencer to Anne Catherine Bradford Harrison, March 28, 1861, Spencer Letters I.

80. James Chesnut and Stephen D. Lee to Maj. Robert Anderson, April 11, 1861 (surrender demand and rejection), and April 12, 1861 (notice to open fire), both OR I: 1, 13–14.

81. Dodson Diary, April 12, 1861, UMdLib.

82. *Battles & Leaders of the Civil War* (New York, 1887), 1:76.

83. Abner Doubleday, *Reminiscences of Forts Sumter and Moultrie in 1860–'61* (New York, 1876, reprinted 1998), 152–53. Doubleday is frequently, and mistakenly, credited with inventing the game of baseball. See Harold Seymour, *Baseball, The Early Years* (New York, 1960), 1:5–12, for a discussion of this myth's origin and the authentic story of the game's beginning.

84. Glenn Diary, 27 (entry of April 13, 1861).

85. John Pendleton Kennedy, "The Great Drama: An Appeal to Maryland," in *Political and Official Papers by John P. Kennedy* (New York, 1872), 592, 598 (published originally as a pamphlet, May 9, 1861).

86. *Sun,* April 15, 1861.

87. *American,* April 15, 1861.

88. Allen Bowie Davis to William W. Davis, April 16, 1861, A. B. Davis Papers.

89. Baltimore correspondent "To Abem. Lincon Esqr," April 11, 1861, in Mearns, *Lincoln Papers,* 538.

90. Dodson Diary, April 19, 1861, UMdLib.

CHAPTER 2. APRIL 1861

1. Glenn Diary, 27 (entry of April 17, 1861). Severn Teackle Wallis was a respected Baltimore lawyer and a close friend of Glenn's; his Southern sentiments would land him in federal prison from September 1861 until 1862. Frank Howard, a grandson of Francis Scott Key, was Glenn's partner in the *Exchange* newspaper. In 1863, he published a memoir of his own prison experience, *Fourteen Months in American Bastiles.*

2. *Sun,* April 18, 1861.

3. Harrison, 5:114–15.

4. Ibid., April 18, 1861.

5. *Sun,* April 15, 1861.

6. George W. Brown to Abraham Lincoln, April 18, 1861, in Mearns, *Lincoln Papers,* 2:566–67. Brown dispatched three emissaries who delivered this letter to Lincoln.

7. J. J. Hooper to Capt. J. Lyle Clarke, Baltimore, April 18, 1861, OR I: 51, pt. 2 [5 108], 15. Benjamin was the Confederacy's attorney general from February 1861 to September 1862, then served as its secretary of war and secretary of state.

8. James Henderson to Abraham Lincoln, April 16, 1861, in Mearns, *Lincoln Papers,* 563.

9. Robert E. Lee to Anne Marshall, April 20, 1861, in Clifford Dowdey, ed., and Louis H. Manarin, assoc. ed., *The Wartime Papers of Robert E. Lee* (Boston, 1961, reprinted New York, 1987), 9–10.

10. Official report of Colonel Edward F. Jones, "Capitol, Washington, April 22, 1861," in Brown, *Nineteenth of April*, 43–44. The Philadelphia, Wilmington and Baltimore Railroad had opened the President Street Station in 1850.

11. Brown, *Nineteenth of April*, 46.

12. William Bowly Wilson, *Reminiscences of April 19, 1861,* June 13, 1910, MS 1860, MdHS.

13. Reminiscences of Henry C. Wagner, October 11, 1909, MS 1860, MdHS. (Gary survived and became postmaster general under President William McKinley.)

14. Augustus J. Albert, Account of Service in the Civil War (undated), 2, MS 1860, MdHS.

15. William Platt to Richard D. Fisher, May 25, 1909, MS 1860, MdHS.

16. Daniel M. Thomas to Sister, April 21, 1861, Thomas Papers. Evidence that Francis X. Ward survived his wounds is found in his April 19 account in a letter to Richard D. Fisher, November 8, 1909, MS 1860, MdHS. See also *American,* April 20, 1861. In October 1859, Ward resigned as secretary of the U.S. legation in Costa Rica and returned to Baltimore.

17. William N. Tuttle (for Bull & Tuttle, Proprietors) to George William Brown, April 19, 1861, RG 9 S2 Box 30, BCA.

18. Brown, *Nineteenth of April*, 48–49.

19. Ibid., 49. On p. 49 of the copy of Brown's memoir owned by the Baltimore County Public Library are handwritten notes apparently by an eyewitness to the day's events. Though incomplete, the notes refer to placing anchors on the tracks and state, "The fight was then furious. Paving stones on one side, muskets on the other."

20. Ibid., 50.

21. George W. Booth, *A Maryland Boy in Lee's Army: Personal Reminiscences of a Maryland Soldier in the War Between the States, 1861–1865* (Baltimore, 1898, reprinted Lincoln, NE, 2000, as *A Maryland Boy in Lee's Army*, 8–9). Booth's original manuscript, in which this quote appears on p. 8, is in the MdHS. Kane was Baltimore's chief of police.

22. Brown, *Nineteenth of April*, 50–51. In the middle of this passage, Brown interrupts his narrative to relate an exchange between himself and a Massachusetts officer and reflect on the role his own presence might have played.

23. Richard D. Fisher, April 19, 1908, in Ernest H. Wardwell, "Reminiscences of the March through Baltimore of the Sixth Massachusetts Infantry April 19, 1861 and the Riots Which Ensued," MS 1064, MdHS. Fisher added this comment at the end of a notebook in which Ernest Wardwell recorded his account of April 19.

24. L. A. Whitely to Simon Cameron, April 19, 1861, OR I: 2 [pt. 1], 580.

25. "Phil" to Mamie [S. Gardiner] [April] 19, 1861, Bowie Papers.

26. Mamie [S. Gardiner] to Phil, May 1, 1861, Bowie Papers.

27. J. E. Thomson and S. M. Felton to Simon Cameron and L. Thomas to S. M. Felton ("Governor Hicks has"), both April 19, 1861, OR I:1, 442.

28. Catherine N. Smith to Ellen, April 20, 1861, MS 1860, MdHS.

29. Slicer Journal, April 20, 1861.

30. Jabez David Pratt to John C. Pratt, April 20, 1861, MS 1860, MdHS. Quotations from this and subsequent letters between the Pratt brothers are from transcribed originals.

31. Daniel M. Thomas to "My Dear Sister," April 21, 1861, Thomas Papers. The Maryland Guards were established in the winter of 1859–1860. See McHenry Howard, *Recollections of a Maryland Confederate Soldier and Staff Officer under Johnston, Jackson and Lee* (Baltimore, 1914, reprinted 1975), 9–11.

32. *American,* April 22, 1861. One source refers to the destruction of a North Central Railroad bridge at Melvale by a Baltimore City Guard Battalion led by John G. Johannes. See Kevin Conley Ruffner, *Maryland's Blue and Gray: A Border State's Union and Confederate Junior Officer Corps* (Baton Rouge, LA, 1977), 56. In a colorful career in the federal Eighth Maryland Infantry, Johannes was convicted of striking an enlisted man with a stick, "nearly unhorsed but saved," and given a pension for eye disease caused by exploding ammunition near Harpers Ferry (Ruffner, *Maryland's Blue and Gray,* 381–82).

33. D. Wilmot to [General Scott], April 20, 1861, OR I:2, 582–83.

34. Tyler Dennett, *Lincoln and the Civil War in the Diaries and Letters of John Hay* (New York, 1939), 3–4 (entry of April 19, 1861).

35. Statement of I. R. Trimble (undated), MS 1860, MdHS (a letter from the donor states that Trimble wrote the statement in December 1864 from Fort Warren in Boston Harbor, where he was imprisoned following his capture as a Confederate general at Gettysburg). The statement in the *American* that "Truck Company No. 1 was summoned to the Mayor's office, and despatched with combustibles to the bridge at Canton, which was in flame before the arrival of the Philadelphia trains," seems to reinforce Trimble's claim. Hicks told Maryland legislators early in May that he "neither authorized or consented to the destruction of said bridges but left the whole matter in the hands of the mayor of the city of Baltimore, with the declaration that I was a lover of law and order" (see *Sun,* May 10, 1861).

36. Seabrook, *Maryland's Great Part,* 18–19.

37. *Sun,* May 15, 1861.

38. Orville H. Browning to Abraham Lincoln, April 22, 1861, in Mearns, *Lincoln Papers,* 582.

39. Thomas H. Hicks to Simon Cameron, April 20, 1861, *Exec Ltr Bk,* MdSA. Similar versions appear OR I:1, ix, 442, and Mearns, *Lincoln Papers,* 573.

40. *American,* April 20, 1861.

41. Ibid., April 22, 1861.

42. C. C. Shriver to [Frederick] A. [Shriver], April 20, 21, 1861, Shriver Papers.

43. Abraham Lincoln to Thomas H. Hicks and George W. Brown, April 20, 1861, in Roy P. Basler, *Collected Works of Abraham Lincoln* (New Brunswick, NJ, 1953), 4:341. After sending the letter, Lincoln telegraphed both men; Brown telegraphed that he was "coming immediately." (See also Abraham Lincoln to Thomas Hicks, April 20, 1861, OR I:2 [S# 2], IX.)

44. George W. Brown to Thomas H. Hicks, April 20, 1861, *Exec Ltr Bk,* MdSA (also OR I:1, 442).

45. Thomas H. Hicks to George W. Brown, April 20, 1861, *Exec Ltr Bk,* MdSA (also OR I:1, 442); George W. Brown to Abraham Lincoln, April 20, 1861, in Mearns, Lincoln Papers, 574.

46. Brown, *Nineteenth of April,* 74.

47. Ibid.

48. *American,* April 22, 1861; *Sun,* April 22, 1861; and Brown, *Nineteenth of April,* 74 (versions differ slightly).

49. *American,* April 22, 1861; *Sun,* April 22, 1861; and Brown, *Nineteenth of April,* 75 (versions differ slightly). The troops at Cockeysville, said to number three thousand, were commanded by Gen. George C. Wynkoop. See Festus Summers, *The Baltimore & Ohio in the Civil War* (New York, 1939, reprinted 1993), 56; Summers notes that the original Garrett telegram is in the Garrett Papers (see p. 237n36).

50. George Whitmarsh Diary, April 21, 1861, MS 896, MdHS.

51. C[harles]. C[offin]. Adams to [William R. Whittingham], April 23, 1861, MDA. Adams wrote again to Whittingham in August, asking him to endorse his son for a position as surgical assistant to Dr. Hammond, who was establishing a U.S. military hospital in Baltimore; see Charles C. Adams to [William R. Whittingham], August 24, 1861, MDA.

52. "Phil" to Mamie [S. Gardiner], [April] 21, 1861, Bowie Papers.

53. *Sun,* April 22, 1861.

54. *American,* April 22, 1861.

55. *Sun,* April 22, 1861.

56. *American,* April 22, 1861.

57. Brown, *Nineteenth of April,* 63 (Kennedy and Harris); Abraham Lincoln to Thomas H. Hicks and George W. Brown, April 20, 1861, in Basler, *Collected Works,* 4:340. The *Sun,* April 22, 1861, contains an account of the meeting between Lincoln and the Baltimore men. Other than Brown's comment that the latter two men were "sent to Washington" (Brown, *Nineteenth of April,* 63), I found no evidence of coordination between Hicks-Brown and Kennedy-Harris regarding their separate visits to the White House. Harris served Maryland's third district in Congress from 1855 to 1861, when he left office in March, just before this visit to Lincoln.

58. *Baltimore Evening Patriot,* April 19, 1861, in Summers, *The Baltimore and Ohio,* 54 (threatening crowd); *American,* April 22, 1861 (cars seized); *Report of Committees,* 37th Cong., 2nd sess., Vol. 2, 621n, in Summers, 237n (track damage).

59. "The Secretary" to John Garrett, Esq., Friday M, April 19, 1861, Garrett Papers, in Summers, *The Baltimore and Ohio,* 55.

60. Claim of stone-throwing in "Official Report of Colonel Edward F. Jones," April 22, 1861, MS 1860, MdHS; Jabez David Pratt to John C. Pratt, April 27, 1861, MS 1860, MdHS.

61. George Radcliffe, *Governor Thomas H. Hicks and the Civil War* (Baltimore, 1901),

70; Benjamin Butler, *Butler's Book* (Boston, 1892), 210. Butler was technically commanding various state militia companies in federal service; these companies would remain state organizations until their three-month enlistment periods expired.

62. Glenn Diary, 31 (entry of April 21, 1861).

63. Richard Sprigg Steuart, "The 19th of April, 1861" (Baltimore, undated), 3–4, courtesy of Arthur B. Steuart.

64. Daniel M. Thomas to "My Dear Sister," April 21, 1861, MS 1970.2, MdHS.

65. Thomas H. Hicks to Abraham Lincoln, April 22, 1861, *Exec Ltr Bk*, MdSA (also in Mearns, *Lincoln Papers*, 583, and OR I:2, IX, no. 4, 589).

66. Benjamin Butler to Winfield Scott, April 27, 1861, OR I:2 [S# 2], 9.

67. Kennedy in Cohen Scrapbooks ("spring, 1861").

68. Fulton, *"Southern Rights" and "Union" Parties*, 11–12

69. George Whitmarsh Diary, April 30, 1861, MS 896, MdHS.

70. *Sun*, April 23, 1861.

71. Charles Howard to Col. Isaac R. Trimble, April 21, 1861, Charles McHenry Howard, "Baltimore and the Crisis of 1861," *MdHM* 41, no. 4 (1946): 259.

72. Ibid., 261. In September 1862, Stonewall Jackson recommended Trimble be promoted to Major General for his battlefield success at Manassas Junction (see T. J. Jackson to Gen. S. Cooper, September 22, 1862, Trimble Papers, MS 1449.1, MdHS).

73. Hay Diary, 6 (entry of April 21, 1861).

74. Rev. Richard Fuller to Salmon P. Chase, S. P. Chase Papers, Vol. 44, MS Division, Library of Congress, in David Rankin Barbee, "Lincoln, Chase, and Rev. Dr. Richard Fuller," *MdHM* 46, no. 2 (1951): 109. An account of this meeting appears in the *Sun*, April 23, 1861. Barbee lists the eighteen signatories to the letter requesting the meeting with Lincoln—a group that included J. D. Pratt. Fuller, a South Carolina native, was at the time president of the Southern and Southwestern Baptist Convention.

75. *Sun*, April 23, 1861.

76. Emanuel Hertz, *Abraham Lincoln: A New Portrait* (New York, 1931), 2:830–31. Though Hertz gives the date of this reply as April 28, Basler, *Collected Works*, 4:341–42, includes the same passage and notes "although the source of Lincoln's remarks as printed by Hertz is probably a newspaper, the editors have been unable to locate it. Hertz dates the event April 28, 1861, but reports in the *Baltimore Daily Exchange* and *The South* of April 23, 1861, indicate conclusively that this reply was made on Monday, April 22. Reports in the Philadelphia and New York papers as well as the Baltimore papers give only fragments of Lincoln's remarks as printed by Hertz, and the editors have reproduced the Hertz text for want of a satisfactory contemporary source."

77. Hay Diary, 7 (entry of April 22, 1861).

78. John C. Pratt to Jabez David Pratt, April 27, 1861, MS 1860, MdHS.

79. Daniel M. Thomas to "My Dear Sister," April 21, 1861, Thomas Papers.

80. Jabez David Pratt to John C. Pratt, April 29, 1861, MS 1860, MdHS.

81. Ibid., May 1, 1861.

82. Charles Howard to Capt. [John C.] Robinson, April 20, 1861, John C. Robinson, "Baltimore in 1861," *Magazine of American History* 14, no. 3 (1885): 265. The Maryland Guard was commanded by Ben Huger, who had just resigned command of the Pikesville Armory.

83. Robinson, "Baltimore in 1861," 256.

84. Albert (undated), 3; MS 1860, MdHS. Albert, who would fight in the Confederate First Maryland Artillery, notes that the Maryland Guard was disbanded shortly thereafter.

85. Robinson, "Baltimore in 1861," 266–67. Robinson did not reveal any information about the letter.

86. Thomas H. Hicks to Benjamin Butler, April 21, 1861, *Exec Ltr Bk,* MdSA, Annapolis, MD (also OR I:2, IX, no. 4, 587).

87. Butler, *Butler's Book,* 194.

88. *American,* April 22, 1861.

89. Hester Anne [Wilkins] Davis to "My Dear Child," April 23, 1861, A. B. Davis Papers.

90. A. M. Hancock to Abraham Lincoln, April 28, 1861, Mearns, *Lincoln Papers,* 589. (Hancock wrote from Coleman's Eutaw House Hotel in Baltimore.)

91. Hay Diary, 9 (entry of April 22, 1861). Francis Elias Spinner was a member of Congress from New York (1855–1861) and treasurer of the United States (1861–1875).

92. Ibid., 9. Lane founded the "Frontier Guards," led the Free State movement in Kansas, and served as major general of the Kansas militia. A senator from 1861 to 1866, he supported Lincoln, emancipation, and arming slaves.

93. John C. Pratt to Jabez David Pratt, April 27, 1861, MS 1860, MdHS.

94. Robinson, "Baltimore in 1861," 267.

95. *American,* April 22, 1861 (A. H. Needham); death in *Sun,* April 29, 1861 (S. H. Needham).

96. Abraham Lincoln to Winfield Scott, April 25, 1861, Basler, *Collected Works,* 4:344. Lincoln incorrectly cited Annapolis, the state's capital, as the site for the Maryland legislature's special session, which Hicks had moved to Frederick.

97. Ibid.

98. Ibid.

99. *Sun,* April 26, 1861.

100. Original draft of proclamation of Mayor George W. Brown of Baltimore, April 29, 1861, MS 1860, MdHS.

101. *Sun,* April 29, 1861.

102. Whitmarsh Diary, April 30, 1861, MS 896, MdHS.

103. *Sun,* April 26, 1861.

104. William Chauvenet to George B. Cole, April 28, 1861, MS 676, MdHS.

105. Edward Spencer to Anne Catherine Bradford Harrison, April 28, 1861, Spencer I, 83.

106. Neely, *Fate of Liberty,* 7; Abraham Lincoln to Winfield Scott April 27, 1861, in

Basler, *Collected Works*, 4:347. Bracketed text is language given in another version of Lincoln's order, which had broader application in that it included established rail lines as well as the improvised water route from Perryville to Annapolis. Neely notes that "the order permitting suspension on any line was the one actually sent to Scott" because the secretary of state sent that one to Congress when it requested a copy of the order (Neely, *Fate of Liberty*, 8–9).

107. Seabrook, *Maryland's Great Part,* 18–19. Seabrook expressed his worries over the dangers of John B. Brooke, the president of the State Senate, seizing power and a rumor of an assassination plot against Hicks, involving a mysterious "Col. Harrison" (see pp. 21–22).

CHAPTER 3. MAY 1861

1. Thomas H. Hicks to John Letcher, May 1, 1861, *Exec Ltr Bk*, MdSA.

2. Isaac Mayo, pamphlet, May 1, 1861, MS 1860, MdHS. (Mayo died later that month. Emphases his.)

3. Franklin Buchanan in unnamed newspaper, May 4, 1861, Redwood Collection. Gideon Welles was Lincoln's secretary of the navy. At the time, Buchanan's home, The Rest, was near Easton.

4. Franklin Buchanan to George B. Cole, May 29, 1861, Redwood Collection.

5. Franklin Buchanan to Hon. J[ames] A. Pearce, June 26, 1861.

6. Edward Spencer to Anne Catherine Bradford Harrison, May 5, 1861, Spencer Letters I, 84.

7. [William] Di Mentzel to Madame [Elizabeth Patterson] Bonaparte, May 14, 1861, E. Bonaparte Papers.

8. *The Protestant*, May 25, 1861, Graves Scrapbook. William Graves maintained a scrapbook of newspaper clippings, primarily from Methodist sources, discussing the positions of religious denominations on secession and issues related to the war.

9. Thomas H. Hicks to Reverdy Johnson, May 1, 1861, *Exec Ltr Bk*, MdSA.

10. C. C. S[hriver] to [Frederick] A. [Shriver], May 4, 1861, Shriver Papers.

11. J. C. Delaney to Rev. John Hershey, May 3, 1861, Marine Papers.

12. Howard, "Crisis," 268–69.

13. I. R. Trimble, "General Order No. 18," May 6, 1861, MS 1860, MdHS. Mayor Brown agreed to allocate $3,200 to pay the volunteers, at Trimble's request. See Howard, "Crisis," 276–78.

14. Peter F. Shauck to family, May 10, 1861, MS 1860, MdHS. Shauck's home was "Morgan's Switch."

15. R. J. to "My Dear Cousin [Hester]," May 2, 1861, MS 1860, MdHS. The writer mischaracterizes Gen. Benjamin Butler, a Unionist, who did not join the Southern Democrats in bolting from the party's 1860 nominating convention in Charleston, South Carolina.

16. *Sun*, May 6, 1861.

17. "Van" to "Most Affectionate Sister," May 2, 1861, Furber Collection.

18. William Crane to "Brother Wilson," May 14, 1861, Wilson Papers. Wilson was a Baptist minister and founder of the Maryland Industrial School for Girls and the Baltimore YMCA. The *True Union* was published between 1849 and 1861 by the Maryland Baptist Union Association. The issue of April 26, 1855, included notes on revivals, temperance, sermons, and Christian life. The *Union List of Serials* indicates that publication ceased on December 26, 1861, and that it was published in Washington as well (probably at the end of its life). In 1855, its editorial office was at 146 Baltimore Street. Its title likely reflected religious doctrine rather than politics. (Russell L. Martin, American Antiquarian Society, Worcester, MA, personal communication, June 13, 2000, and June 14, 2000. The AAS has one issue, April 26, 1855; the American Baptist Historical Society, Chester, PA, may have more.)

19. Richard Sprigg Steuart, "The 19th of April, 1861," 1, courtesy of Arthur B. Steuart.

20. Brengle Home Guards Minute Book, May 7, 1861, MS 135, MdHS. The organization later became the Frederick Home Guard.

21. Creamer Scrapbook (p. 55), MS 270, MdHS. (Creamer was a hymnologist. His account of Maryland events during the Civil War consisted of a chronological set of newspaper accounts, serialized in a Baltimore newspaper in 1871 by Osmond Tiffany.)

22. G[eorge] H S[teuart] to George [H. Steuart], May 10, 1861, J. Steuart Papers. After Steuart joined the Confederate army in 1861, his estate near Union Square was confiscated and made into a Union garrison.

23. *Sun*, May 11 and May 13, 1861.

24. Lyman to "Dear Mother and Sister," May 10, 1861, Furber Collection.

25. West to "Friends All and Ed," MS 1860, MdHS. (A "spile," a wooden peg in a barrel, was also used to enable sap to flow from a tree.) Winans's arrest in *Baltimore Daily Exchange*, May 15, 1861.

26. Van to "Dear Mother and Sister," Relay House, May 17, 1861, Furber Collection.

27. Thomas H. Hicks to Benjamin Butler, May 10, 1861, *Exec Ltr Bk*, MdSA.

28. *Sun*, May 7, 1861.

29. "Civil War Scrapbook," undated newspaper [Spring 1861], MS 2602, MdHS. This scrapbook includes much pro-Southern material, most of it articles from newspapers.

30. C(atherine) N. S(mith) to Nelly, Baltimore, May 10, 1861, MS 1860, MdHS.

31. William Edes to Brother John Hershey, May 14, 1861, Marine Papers. (Hershey was a Methodist minister from Delaware who lived in Baltimore for many years.)

32. Allen B. Davis to Rebecca Davis, May 14, 1861, A. B. Davis Papers.

33. George N. Moale to "My Dear Uncle," May 15, 1861, MS 2489, MdHS.

34. John Milton Peck to Bishop [William R. Whittingham], May 14, 1861, MDA.

35. C(atherine) N. S(mith) to Nelly, May 10, 1861, MS 1860, MdHS.

36. [Frederick W. Brune] to Em[ily Barton Brune], May 6, 1861, Brune Papers. Emily Brune was in Fredericksburg, Virginia, at the time.

37. *The Protestant*, May 25, 1861, Graves Scrapbook.

38. Speech of John Pendleton Kennedy from the *Congressional Globe* (undated other than spring 1861), in Cohen Scrapbooks.

39. C. H. Bradford to George William Brown, May 14, 1861, RG 9 S2 Box 30, BCA. The incident was also reported in the *Sun,* May 8, 1861.

40. Daniel M. Thomas to Sister, May 8, 1861, Thomas Papers.

41. William [Edes?] to Brother John Hershey, May 14, 1861, Marine Papers.

42. Charles C. Grafton, *A Journey Godward* (Milwaukee, 1910), 35, in David Hein, *A Student's View of the College of St. James on the Eve of the Civil War: The Letters of W. Wilkins Davis* (Lewiston, NY, 1988), 33. William E. Wyatt was rector of Old St. Paul's Episcopal Church.

43. William Rollinson Whittingham to the clergy of the diocese of Maryland, May 15, 1861, Brand-Whittingham Correspondence Letterbook, 1861–1863, MS 122, MdHS. An edited replica appears in William Francis Brand, *Life of William Rollinson Whittingham: Fourth Bishop of Maryland* (New York, 1883), 2:18–19.

44. Edward Spencer to Anne Catherine Bradford Harrison, May 16, 1861, Spencer Letters I, 85.

45. Ibid.

46. *Sun*, May 18, 1861.

47. *Sun*, May 10 and May 18 (Locust Point), 1861. Troops were forbidden to visit the city without permission.

48. *American*, May 16, 1861.

49. *Sun*, May 18, 1861.

50. Robert Kirkwood to William Kirkwood, May 17, 1861, Kirkwood Papers.

51. William L. Winans to Thomas Winans, May 19, 1861, Winans Papers, MS 916, MdHS. See Wallace Shugg, "The Cigar Boat: Ross Winans's Maritime Wonder," *MdHM* 93, no. 4 (winter 1998): 428–42.

52. *Sun*, May 20, 1861.

53. Daniel M. Thomas to "My Dear Sister," May 22, 1861, Thomas Papers. Gen. George Cadwalader became commander of the Middle Department following Butler's departure.

54. Booth, *Personal Reminiscences*, 9. Booth departed for Harpers Ferry on May 18. The Army of Northern Virginia was so named in June 1862 by Gen. Robert E. Lee.

55. Walter F. Southgate to William [Southgate], May 28, 1861, MS 1860, MdHS.

56. Creamer Scrapbook, p. 55¾, MS 270, MdHS.

57. *The Protestant,* May 25, 1861, Graves Scrapbook.

58. Daniel M. Thomas to "My Dear Sister," May 27, 1861, Thomas Papers.

59. Allan Bowie Davis to Rebecca [Davis], May 14, 1861, A. B. Davis Papers.

60. W. W[ilkins] Davis to [Rebecca D. Davis], May 22, 1861, A. B. Davis Papers.

61. Hester Anne (Wilkins) Davis to Rebecca Davis, May 24, 1861, A. B. Davis Papers. Santo Domingo, now the Dominican Republic, was the scene of a brutal slave uprising in the 1790s, in which some saw parallels in John Brown's 1859 raid on Harpers Ferry.

62. Lotty Leigh Gardiner to [John] Leeds [Bowie], May 23, 1861, Bowie Papers.

63. "Inclosure No. 2," James Miltimore and William H. Abel, May 27, 1861, OR 2:1, 574–75.

64. Thomas Spicer to George Cadwalader, May 27, 1861, OR 2:1, 575.

65. Geo[rge] Cadwalader to Lt. Col. E. D. Townsend, May 27, 1861, OR 2:1 574.

66. Daniel M. Thomas to Sister, May 27, 1861, Thomas Papers.

67. William Chauvenet to George B. Cole, May 26, 1861, Redwood Collection.

68. Edward Spencer to Anne Catherine Bradford Harrison, May 24, 1861, Spencer Letters II, 338.

69. *The True Union,* May 30, 1861, Graves Scrapbook.

CHAPTER 4. SUMMER 1861

1. Glenn Diary, 33 (entry of June 2, 1861).

2. John P. Kennedy to Hon. R. M. Stewart, June 4, 1861, Kennedy Papers.

3. C. C. [Shriver] to [Frederick] A. [Shriver], June 6, 1861, Shriver Papers.

4. Ibid., June 21, 1861. This letter, with slight differences in transcription, appears in Frederic Shriver Klein, ed., *Just South of Gettysburg: Carroll County, Maryland, in the Civil War* (Westminster, MD, 1963), 18–19.

5. F[rederick] A. [Shriver] to "Lum" [C. C. Shriver], June 30, 1861, Shriver Papers. An abridged version appears in Klein, *Just South of Gettysburg,* 19–20.

6. Slicer Journal, June 30, 1861.

7. C. C. Shriver to F[rederick] A. Shriver, July 16, 1861, Shriver Papers.

8. Ibid., June 6, 1861.

9. Dodson Diary, June 12, 1861, UMdLib.

10. R. L. Merced to J. Morrison Harris, June 5, 1861, J. Morrison Harris Papers, MS 2739, MdHS.

11. Jacob Myers to George William Brown, June 15, 1861, RG 9 S2 Box 30, BCA.

12. Journal of the Senate, 251–54, Radcliffe, *Governor Thomas H. Hicks,* 99.

13. William Wilkins Davis to Rebecca D. Davis, June 12, 1861, in Hein, *A Student's View,* 125.

14. Edward Spencer to Anne Catherine Bradford Harrison, June 12, 1861, Spencer Letters II, 339.

15. Brengle Home Guards Minute Book, June 24, 1861, MS 135, MdHS.

16. Laas, *Wartime Washington,* 46–47 (entry of June 12, 1861). The Blair estate was in Silver Spring, where many of Lee's letters were written. Calvert served in Congress from 1861 to 1863 and became a voice for Maryland slave owners complaining that their slaves had "joined" the Union army.

17. Ibid., 47 (entry of June 14, 1861).

18. Senate Documents of 1861, Document D, in Radcliffe, 79 (document as shown).

19. Mrs. S. Kennard to Brother John Hershey, June 11, 1861, Marine Papers.

20. Wm. Mentzel to Elizabeth Patterson [Bonaparte], May 25, 1861, E. Bonaparte Papers.

21. Ibid., June 18, 1861.

22. R. K. Hawley to George William Brown, June 11, 1861, RG 9 S2 Box 30, BCA.

23. "Civil War Scrapbook," unnamed newspaper, June 15, 1861, MS 2602, MdHS. ("W.R.A." initials follow.)

24. Armstrong L. Berry to John Hershey, July 10, 1861, Marine Papers.

25. E. D. Townsend to Maj. Gen. N. P. Banks, June 25, 1861, OR 2:1 (pt. 1), 621.

26. Glenn Diary, 34–35 (entry of July 2, 1861). Thomas also called himself "Colonel Zarvona," later changing his name to Richard Thomas Zarvona. After his capture by federal troops, he was imprisoned until exchanged in 1863. See Virgil Carrington Jones, *The Civil War at Sea I* (New York, 1960), 135–42, and Gov. John Letcher, "Colonel Richard Thomas Zarvona," *Confederate Relief Bazaar Journal,* March 29, 1875.

27. Dodson Diary, June 12, 1861.

28. "Civil War Letter," July 2, 1861, MS 1860, MdHS.

29. Wm Augst White to [William R. Whittingham], July 9, 1861, MDA.

30. Rebecca Lloyd (Mrs. Edward) Shippen, 209 West Monument Street, January 30, 1908, MS 1860, MdHS. (The home of James Carroll was at 105 West Monument. Dulaney was the son of a noted Baltimore lawyer, Grafton Dulaney. Shippen wrote that her grandfather, Joseph Hopper Nicholson, set "The Star-Spangled Banner" to music.) She wrote two versions of the same letter, four years apart; they differ slightly.

31. James Glass to George William Brown, August 6, 1861, RG 9 S2 Box 30, BCA.

32. Benjamin Kirkwood to Robert Kirkwood, September 20 [1861], Kirkwood Papers. In 1864 Benjamin would have a leg amputated.

33. "(Signed) Simon Cameron," Brengle Home Guards Minute Book, July 19, 1861, MS 135, MdHS.

34. Edward Spencer to Anne Catherine Bradford Harrison [late July 1861], Spencer Letters II, 347.

35. Mary Jane Kirkwood to Robert Kirkwood, September 4, 1861, Kirkwood Papers.

36. Hannah [Kirkwood] to Robert Kirkwood, September 4, 1861, Kirkwood Papers.

37. Edward Spencer to Anne Catherine Bradford Harrison, July 20, 1861, Spencer Letters II, 344.

38. The *True Union*, July 18, 1861, Graves Scrapbook.

39. Richd. B. Carmichael to [James A. Pearce], July 23, 1861, James Alfred Pearce Papers 1843–1862, MS 1384, MdHS. Carmichael would be arrested in May 1862. In this letter, he refers to a letter he had just received from former President Franklin Pierce.

40. C. E. Brooke & Co. to George William Brown, August 28, 1861, RG 9 S2 Box 30, BCA. The folder contains an affidavit from Mohler attesting to the seizure of cannon.

41. *The True Union*, August 15, 1861, Graves Scrapbook.

42. Creamer Scrapbook, 57, MS 270, MdHS.

43. Laas, *Wartime Washington,* 53 (entry of June 28, 1861).

44. Both in Creamer Scrapbook, 69, MS 270, MdHS.

45. Glenn Diary, 36–37 (entry of September 13, 1861).

46. John A. Dix to M[ontgomery] Blair, August 31, 1861, OR 2:1, 590–91.

47. Fulton, *"Southern Rights" and "Union" Parties*, 22.

48. Diary of Anna Maria Tilghman, August 26, 1861, MS 1967, MdHS.

49. Henry N. Cox to "Mr. [George W.] Browne," July 27, 1861, RG 9 S2 Box 31, BCA.

50. Edward Spencer to Anne Catherine Bradford Harrison, August 6 [1861], 1861, Spencer Letters II, 349.

51. Ibid., 349.

52. Ibid., August 11, 1861, 353.

53. Ibid., August 17, 1861, 357.

54. Ibid., 358.

55. Ibid., editor's note, 358.

56. S. E. Horgewerff to [William R. Whittingham], September 23, 1861, MDA.

57. W[illiam] R. W[hittingham] to S.E. Horgewerff, September 24, 1861, MDA.

58. *American,* November 5, 1861.

59. Ibid.

60. Ibid.

61. *American,* November 6, 1861.

62. *American,* November 7, 1861.

63. L[eonard] J. [Mills] to [William R. Whittingham], November 18, 1861, MDA.

PART II. "OCCUPATION"

1. Neely, *Fate of Liberty,* 75. Neely's book is the most definitive analysis of the topic. He notes that "most modern estimates of the total number of civilians arrested by the federal military authority during the entire Civil War have put the number at over thirteen thousand" (p. 23). See chapter 1 (esp. pp. 23–31) and chapter 6 for discussion of sources and records used by historians to derive a reliable number, concluding "though we will never be able to ascertain exactly how many people were arrested, analysis of the available statistics can settle, once and for all, the larger questions about civil liberties under Lincoln" (p. 127).

2. Brig Genl Henry H. Lockwood to Colonel [Samuel B. Lawrence], July 19, 1864, filed as SW-4314, ser. 18, Letters Received, General Correspondence, Central Office, Records of the Office of the Chief of Engineers (RG 77), NA. The letter itemizes 500 laborers @ $1.50 per day, 20 foremen @ $2.00 per day, and four superintendents @ $3.00 per day, or $811 per day for an expenditure of $16,220 for the twenty-day project.

3. Union Club Record Books, MS 855, MdHS; undated newspaper clipping in Cohen Scrapbook. See also *American,* March 14, 1862. J. N. Bonaparte was elected chairman of the Union Club, whose board of managers included Johns Hopkins, Enoch Pratt, and John P. Kennedy. The club's last meeting was May 4, 1872.

CHAPTER 5. FEDERALS

1. Will[iam Hand Browne] to Josephine [Owings], Baltimore, January 8, 1861, MS 1860, MdHS.

2. C. C. [Shriver] to [Frederick] A. [Shriver], June 6, 1861, Shriver Family Papers, MS 2085, MdHS. Shriver may have meant a regiment—a thousand men at full strength—or erred on the number, as a company had one hundred men.

3. Van to "Dear Mother and Sister," June 15, 1861, Furber Collection. City delegates to the state legislature were being elected.

4. Van to "Friend Charley" (Charles S. Coburn of Lawrence, MA), June 16, 1861, Furber Collection.

5. Edward Spencer to Anne Catherine Bradford Harrison, July 4, 1861, Spencer Letters II, 341.

6. Daniel M. Thomas to Julia M. Thomas, July 8, 1861, Thomas Papers.

7. *Sun,* August 24, 1861.

8. Robert Kirkwood to Benjamin Kirkwood, August 24, 1861, Kirkwood Papers.

9. George W. Carpenter to Robert Spear, August 30, 1861, Spear Papers, MS 1428, MdHS.

10. Wilson Papers, September 10, 1861.

11. *Sun*, September 18, 1861. Military authorities in November 1864 would seize the club as a refuge for emancipated slaves. Dix served President James Buchanan as treasury secretary.

12. William Howard Russell, *My Diary North and South* (London, 1863), 2:280–81, in Robert J. Brugger, *The Maryland Club: A History of Food and Friendship in Baltimore, 1857–1997* (Baltimore, 1998), 20–21.

13. Ibid., 23.

14. *Sun,* September 18, 1861.

15. John A. Dix to Maj. Gen. G. B. McClellan, September 19, 1861, OR 1:5 (pt. 1), 604.

16. V[irginia] Warner to [Elizabeth Patterson] Bonaparte, September 23, 1861, E. Bonaparte Papers.

17. [John A. Dix] to Brig. Genl. Henry H. Lockwood, October 14, 1861, OR 1:5 (pt. 1), 620. These balloons were tethered.

18. Dodson Diary, October 23, 1861, UMdLib.

19. *Sun,* November 7, 1861.

20. "Reply to Delegation of Baltimore Citizens," November 15, 1861, in Basler, *Collected Works,* 5:24.

21. G. A. Farquhar to William H. Seward, December 9, 1861, OR 2:1 (pt. 1), 614–15.

22. John Donnell Smith to Ellen [Blair], January 13, 1862, MS 1860, MdHS.

23. H[arvey] Colburn to Edward [Colburn], January 16, 1862, MS 1860, MdHS. Edward Colburn previously had been assistant pastor at St. Luke's Episcopal Church in Baltimore.

24. John M. Buchanon to Horace Buchanon, January 19, 1862, The Buchanon Collection, MS 2053, MdHS.

25. Sister to Horace Buchanon, January [1862], The Buchanon Collection, MS 2053, MdHS.

26. "Charge and Specifications preferred against 2nd Lieut. 'George F. Young,'" January 29, 1862, MS 1860, MdHS. The charges were withdrawn when Young, who had been mustered in on June 28, 1861, resigned.

27. Louis James Wood[nare?] to Charles W. Dodge, February 8, 186[2], MS 1860, MdHS.

28. Glenn Diary, 53 (entry of February 18, 1862).

29. S[amuel] F. Streeter to Eudora [Jenks?], February 25, 1862, MS 1860, MdHS.

30. [Priscilla Bridges] to [Augusta Buck], February [1862], MS 1860, MdHS. The 1945 letter from the donor of this letter, Mary Delaplane Dongal, explains that Augusta Buck's father was Rev. James A. Buck and that "Jimmie D." was her father, Dr. James B. Delaplane.

31. J. V. Van Ingen to "William," April 1, 1862, MS 1860, MdHS.

32. B. Adelman Diary, May 12, 1862, MS 1860, MdHS. Adelman, who joined the Second Virginia Cavalry Regiment, kept this diary from May 2 to September 15, 1862.

33. B. Adelman Diary, May 26, 1862, MS 1860, MdHS.

34. Glenn Diary, 62–63 (entry of May 26, 1862).

35. United States Government to the Estate of Walter A. Haislip [1865], MS 1860, MdHS.

36. John Hay to [William R. Whittingham], September 3, 1862, MDA.

37. Schaeffer Diary, September 19, 1862.

38. Ibid., September 20, 1862.

39. Ibid., September 21, 1862.

40. Glenn Diary, 73 (entry of September 22, 1862).

41. William P. Preston to daughter, December 22, 1862, William Preston Papers, MS 711, MdHS.

42. "Speech of Gov. [Augustus Williamson] Bradford at the banquet given to welcome the advent of Gen. Schenck to the command of the Middle Military Department in Jany 1863 over which the Gen. Presided," January, 1863, MS 1860, MdHS (title noted in pencil, on the letterhead of Walter W. Preston, attorney at law, Bel Air, MD).

43. E. D. Townsend to Maj. Gen. John A. Dix, January 9, 1863, MS 1860, MdHS (this collection includes the pass and a list of Robinson's baggage).

44. Hering Recollections, 2:61.

45. Glenn Diary, 85 (entry February 1863).

46. Slicer Journal, February 24, 1863.

47. Ibid., March 1, 1863.

48. "Letters to Governor Bradford by a Marylander," Baltimore, April 1863, PAM S-2, 16–17, MdHS.

49. Glenn Diary, 82 (entry "April" [1863]).

50. Andrew Sterett Ridgely to Reverdy Johnson, May 30, 1863, MS 1840, Reverdy Johnson Collection, MdHS.

51. Robert Kirkwood to [William Kirkwood], June 8, 1863, Kirkwood Papers. The Copperheads were Northern Democrats who favored a negotiated peace with the Confederacy.

52. Hering Recollections, 2:90–91.

53. "Brother Lou" to "Girls," June 10 [1863], MS 1860, MdHS.

54. "Lou," the Quartermaster Lt. to "Girls," June 22, 1863, MS 1860, MdHS.

55. [Robert Kirkwood] to Mother, June 11, 1863, Kirkwood Papers.

56. Reverdy Johnson, May 30, 1863, MS 1840, Reverdy Johnson Collection, MdHS (draft written by a secretary).

57. *Sun,* June 29, 1863.

58. [Henry] W. [Shriver] to Mary (Winebrenner) and [Frederick] A. [Shriver], June 25, 1863, Shriver Papers. Shriver described this site as "Camp Disaster."

59. Diary of A. Steiner, June 28, 1863, MS 35.3, Historical Society of Frederick County.

60. Glenn Diary, 88–89 (entry of July 1, 1863). Glenn's escape to Canada is recounted on pp. 89–100.

61. George J. Cornwell to "Mother," July [5], 1863, Cornwell-Mead Letters, MS 2460, MdHS. Other letters in this collection suggest that this one was written just after Gettysburg, and as it is dated only "Tuesday," its actual date could be inferred as July 5.

62. *Sun,* July 3 and July 4, 1863.

63. F[rederick] A. Shriver to [Henry] W. [Shriver], July 9, 1863, Shriver Family Papers, MS 2085, MdHS. Sedgwick, called "Uncle John" by his devoted men, commanded several corps during the war and was killed by a sharpshooter at the Wilderness in May 1864.

64. Wilson Papers, July 7, 1863.

65. Mehring Diary, July 14, 1863, MS 1860, MdHS.

66. Wm. H. Chesebrough, General Order No. 42, July 11, 1863, MS 1860, MdHS.

67. Davis Diary, July 25, 1863.

68. Glenn Diary, 101 (entry of September 12, 1863).

69. A. W. Bradford to George Vickers, October 27, 1863, *Exec Ltr Bk,* MdSA. The radicals, also known as "Unconditional Unionists," favored immediate, uncompensated emancipation. Vickers, a Chestertown lawyer, was a general in the Maryland militia during the war. He later served in the state senate and as U.S. senator from Maryland.

70. A. W. Bradford to His Excellency President Lincoln, October 31, 1863, *Exec Ltr Bk,* MdSA.

71. A. Lincoln to Augustus W. Bradford, November 2, 1863, Basler, *Collected Works,* 6:556–57. A virtually identical letter of the same date appears *Exec Ltr Bk,* MdSA. (Lincoln referred to Isaac R. Trimble, whose name is spelled correctly in Bradford's correspondence.)

72. A. W. Bradford to His Excellency President Lincoln, November 3, 1863, *Exec Ltr Bk,* MdSA.

73. Fayette Thrall to Maggie Mullin, November 3, 1864, MS 1860, MdHS.

74. F[itz] J[ohn] Porter to Rev[erdy] Johnson, November 13, 1863, MS 1840, R. Johnson Papers, MdHS. Porter also commented that the Speaker of the House "(William) Etheridge can rule out the three members from Maryland—and also Slunck [?], Garfield & Blair."

75. S. W. Smith to J[erome] N. Bonaparte, November 28, 1863, J. Bonaparte Papers.

76. Henry M. Morgan to Mrs. Gehr, November 25, 1863, #299, Box M11, Historical Society of Carroll County (transcription). Morgan was a captain in Ames Battery.

77. Davis Diary, December 5, 1863. Davis also expressed chagrin at Gen. Braxton Bragg's failure to retake Chattanooga that autumn.

78. Ibid., December 17, 1863.

79. Message of the governor of Maryland to the General Assembly, January 7, 1864, *Journal of The Proceedings of the Senate of Maryland, January Session, 1864* (Annapolis, 1864), Document A, 33–35, MdSA.

80. Almon D. Jones to Carrie E. Jones and Ella, February 5, 1864, MS 1860, MdHS.

81. Jos. M. Cushing to J[erome] N. Bonaparte, February 5, [18]64, J. Bonaparte Papers. Bonaparte returned this letter with a note instructing McKim & Co. to pay the bill, in two installments.

82. M. M. W. to Mahlon [Hopkins Janney], March 5, 1864, Mahlon Hopkins Janney Collection, MS 1985, MdHS. (This letter contains a vivid description of other guests and costumes, including "bugle beads.")

83. Jacob V. Grove's Diary, March 5, 1864, MS 1860, MdHS.

84. William McKim to [Jerome N. Bonaparte], April 11, 1864, J. Bonaparte Papers.

85. John O. G. Allmand to "Friend," April 16, 1864, courtesy of Martha E. Marshall. Allmand lived at 75 North Charles Street.

86. *Sun,* April 19, 1864.

87. *American,* April 19, 1864. Governor Bradford's speech to the fair appears in this issue.

88. Thomas Sutton to "Uncle," April 18, 1864, Kirkwood Papers.

89. Glenn Diary, 127 (entries of April 27 and May 1, 1864). On June 4, Glenn would again be detained, briefly.

90. Ro[bert] Kirkwood to Father, May 2, 1864, Kirkwood Papers.

91. Baltimore Battery of Light Artillery Records, May 31, 1864, MS 176, MdHS. The unit was recruited in Baltimore in August 1862.

92. A. W. Bradford to Maj. Gen. Lew Wallace, June 5, 1864, *Exec Ltr Bk,* MdSA.

93. C. T. Simpers's Surgeon's Diary, July 13, 14, 18, 1864, MS 1860, MdHS. On July 19, Simpers wrote that his wife arrived and that his affliction was improving.

94. Minutes of Baltimore Union Club, Sunday, July 10, 1864, MS 1860, MdHS. Preston, an attorney, lived at "Pleasant Plains."

95. Robert R. Moore to Mother, July 14, 1864, MS 1860, MdHS.

96. *Sun,* October 4, 1864.

97. George Washington Kimball to Wife and Children, August 11, 1864, George Wash-

ington Kimball Papers, MS 2129, MdHS. Kimball was at Fort McHenry from August 10 to November 5, 1864, when he left for home.

98. George Washington Kimball to Wife and Children, August 21, 1864, George Washington Kimball Papers, MS 2129, MdHS. On August 29, he wrote that Lincoln commuted the death sentences but that "I had the machine all ready for them & was disappointed in not seeing how it worked."

99. Jacob V. Grove's Diary, October 10, 1864, MS 1860, MdHS.

100. Cole's Notes, November 9, 1864, Redwood Papers, MS 1530.1, MdHS.

101. Ibid., November 10, 1864.

102. E[udocia] Stansbury to May [Preston], December 5, 1864, MS 1860, MdHS. At the top of this letter is written, "Confeds on Prop. Darkies free."

103. Lew Wallace to Jerome N. Bonaparte, December 8, 1864, J. Bonaparte Papers. Lossing published a history of the Civil War in 1866.

CHAPTER 6. RECRUITS

1. Robert Kirkwood to William Kirkwood, May 17, 1861, Kirkwood Papers.

2. John A. Dix to M[ontgomery] Blair, August 31, 1861, OR 2:1 (pt. 1), 591.

3. William C. Hopkins to Robert Spear, August 14, 1861, Spear Papers, MS 142, MdHS.

4. Eliza S. Marsh to Charles Ridgely, October 11, 1861, Ridgely Family Papers, MS 1127, MdHS.

5. Thomas M. Cathcart to Brother John Hershey, October 21, 1862, Marine Papers.

6. "Objects of Benevolence," January 1, 1862, Shoemaker Papers 1824–1955, MS 1968, MdHS. Baltimorean Samuel Shoemaker was a Unionist with Southern business ties who rose to prominence in the Adams Express Co. He had a home, "Burnside," in Eccleston, now Brooklandville.

7. Washington Hands Civil War Notebook, MS 2468, 48, MdHS. Hands was a corporal in Company D.

8. Noyes Letters, February 7, 1862.

9. Lt. H. B. Boyd to John Lee Chapman, May 7, 1862, RG 9 S2 Box 31, BCA.

10. *Sun*, July 17 and 22, 1862, Cohen Scrapbook.

11. *American,* July 23, 1862, Cohen Scrapbook. Chapman, by virtue of being Baltimore City Council Chair, became mayor shortly after Brown's arrest.

12. Maryland Society Circular, 1862, MS 1860, MdHS (at a Richmond address, printed on circular).

13. John Donnell Smith to Ellen [Blair], January 13, 1862, MS 1860, 8–9, MdHS.

14. A. W. Bradford, July 4, 1862, MS 1860, MdHS.

15. Resignation of Jacob Eugene Duryee from Second Regiment Maryland Volunteers, 1862, MS 1860, MdHS.

16. Noyes Letters, July 7, 1862.

17. Lydia A. Thompson to Sarah Jervis, August 16, 1862, Letters and Papers of the

Hood-Jervis-Ridgley Families of Bowling Green Farm, Howard Co., MD, courtesy of Achsah Henderson.

18. Robert Wilson of Joseph to Father Hershey, October 25, 1862, Marine Papers.

19. *American,* July 24, 1862, in Cohen Scrapbook. (The council's first branch passed the appropriation unanimously.)

20. *American,* July 29, 1862, in Cohen Scrapbook.

21. Noyes Letters, July 20, 1862.

22. A. W. Bradford to E. M. Stanton, September 11, 1862, *Exec Ltr Bk,* MdSA.

23. Edwin M. Stanton to Governor Bradford, September 12, 1862, *Exec Ltr Bk,* MdSA.

24. A. W. Bradford to E. M. Stanton, September 27, 1862, *Exec Ltr Bk,* MdSA.

25. *Sun*, November 17, 1862, in "Draft List, Worcester and Somerset Counties," October 23, 1862, MS 1860, MdHS.

26. James Farnandis to [A. W.] Bradford, January 24, 1863, *Exec Ltr Bk,* MdSA.

27. A. W. Bradford to James Farnandis, February 5, 1863, *Exec Ltr Bk,* MdSA.

28. A. W. Bradford to S[amuel] H. Streeter Esq., March 13, 1863, *Exec Ltr Bk,* MdSA.

29. F[rederick] A. Shriver to [Henry] W. [Shriver], June 19, 1863, Shriver Papers.

30. Noyes Letters, July 26, 1862.

31. [R. H.] Ball to Corporal T[homas] Sewell Ball, September 8, 1863, Ball Papers. Ball, living in Pikesville in 1893, published the "Confederate War Map"; this collection contains letters to him from Lee's Secretary and Lee's nephew, Confederate Gen. Fitzhugh Lee, noting they had no knowledge of the map.

32. T. Sewell Ball to "Lou," August 16, 1863, Ball Papers.

33. "Lou" to Thomas S. Ball, September 10, 1863, Ball Papers (this portion of letter is dated September 11).

34. R. H. Ball to T. Sewell Ball, September 21, 1863, Ball Papers.

35. A. W. Bradford to Col. James C. Fry, October 10, 1863, *Exec Ltr Bk,* MdSA.

36. A. W. Bradford to Hon. E. M. Stanton, October 13, 1863, *Exec Ltr Bk,* MdSA.

37. A. W. Bradford to Captain Watkins, October 13, 1863, *Exec Ltr Bk,* MdSA.

38. Thomas Timmons and Levi Duncan to Major Henry B. Judd, November 23, 1863, vol. 100/204 8AC, p. 34, ser. 4900, Letters Received, Military Commander Wilmington, Del., RG 393, pt. 2 No. 316, NA.

39. J[ohn] Rose to [William R. Whittingham], November 28, 1863, MDA.

40. S. W. Smith to J[erome] N. Bonaparte, November 28, 1863, J. Bonaparte Papers.

41. James L. Baylies to J[erome] N. Bonaparte, December 1, 1863, J. Bonaparte Papers.

42. Ibid., December 8, 1863 (the second page of this two-page letter is glued so as to obscure a portion of the left margin).

43. B[onaparte], J[erome] N[apoleon] to J. L. Baylies, May 26, 1864, J. Bonaparte Papers.

44. Message of the governor of Maryland to the General Assembly, January 7, 1864, *Journal of the Proceedings of the Senate of Maryland, January Session, 1864* (Annapolis, 1864), Document A, 12.

45. James B. Fry to His Excellency A. W. Bradford, May 10, 1864, *Exec Ltr Bk,* MdSA.

46. Opinion of William Whiting, May 25, 1864, enclosed in James B. Fry to His Excellency A. W. Bradford, May 26, 1864, *Exec Ltr Bk,* MdSA.

47. J[ohn] W. Kerfoot to Hon. John P. Kennedy, May 31, 1864, Kennedy Papers. Kennedy contributed $50—see Kerfoot to Kennedy, June 4, 1864, Kennedy Papers.

48. Wm. R. Wilmer to Rt. Rev. William R. Whittingham, June 7, 1864, MDA. Wilmer was likely the son of Lemuel Wilmer.

49. Saml. B. Lawrence to Major-General Wallace, July 6, 1864, OR I: 37, pt. 2, 92.

50. Ibid.

51. Minutes of Baltimore Union Club, Sunday, July 10, 1864, MS 1860, MdHS. H. L. Bond was chosen chair and George A. Pope became secretary. Pope, George B. Cole, and J. B. Richardson received the three highest vote totals and thus became ranking officers. Men were quickly armed by Gen. Henry Lockwood, commander of the city's defenses; on July 11, ten men were sent to guard Adj. Gen J.S. Berry's house.

52. "Civil War Diary" of Horace Landon Shipley, 12–15, 53.304.6, Historical County of Carroll County. Shipley served in the Twelfth Maryland Volunteer Infantry Regiment. He was subsequently drafted for three years but avoided service beyond one hundred days by procuring a substitute in Baltimore for $675. He was discharged on November 16, 1864.

53. Davis Diary, September 3, 1864.

54. John E. Smith to [Gov. A. W. Bradford], October 21, 1862, MS 1860, MdHS. The document lists the five officers elected to lead the company.

55. Lt. Col. Gregory Barrett Jr. to Hon. H. L. Bond, December 15, 1864, Bond-McCullouch Papers, MS 1154, MdHS.

56. Walter [Shriver] to [Henry] W. [Shriver], July 26, 1864, Shriver Papers.

57. Hering Recollections, 2:63–64. Hering notes on p. 66 that "The substitutes who were put in for Mr Reifsnider and I were brought for Louisville, Kentucky." In this collection is an August 6, 1864, notice to Hering from James Smith, provost marshal of Maryland's Fourth District, informing him that he has been drafted, and a "certificate of non-liability" exempting him from the draft "by reason of having paid commutation."

58. Henry Michard Statement of Procure Substitute, Civil War Draft, North [1865], MS 1860, MdHS.

59. Geo L. Dolten & Co. [?]. Substitute [Civil War]—Agreement to Furnish One, January 3, 1865, MS 1860, MdHS (this organization may have found a market for procuring substitutes).

60. Certificate no. 370, for $900 (some handwritten changes), signed by Wm. Colton & Co., 24 Second Street, February 20, 1865, Shriver Papers. This file contains also a receipt for Frederick A. Shriver from Poland Jenkins & Co. for $900 for a substitute of Sub. District No. 51, Carroll County, Baltimore, dated February 27, 1865.

61. W[illia]m Colton & Company to A. K. Shriver, March 9, 1865, Shriver Papers.

CHAPTER 7. ARRESTS

1. Augustus J. Albert. Account of service in the Civil War, (undated), 3–4, MS 1860, MdHS.

2. Edward Spencer to Anne Catherine Bradford Harrison, May 16, 1861, Spencer Letters I, 86.

3. E. D. Townsend to George Cadwalader, May 16, 1861, OR 2:1, 572 (also OR 1:2, 639).

4. George Cadwalader to E. D. Townsend, May 16, 1861, OR 2:1, 572 (also OR1:2, 639–40).

5. Marriott Boswell to William H. Seward, June 27, 1861, OR 2:1, 622.

6. Nathaniel P. Banks to Mayor George W. Brown, June 13, 1861, and Banks to the People of the City of Baltimore, June 27, 1861, both OR—Banks to Brown 2:1, 624–25 (also OR 1:2, 585); Banks to People, 1:2, 140–41. The Department of Annapolis was at the time located at Fort McHenry.

7. Winfield Scott to Nathaniel Banks, June 24, 1861, OR 2:1, 621.

8. Robert Williams (assistant adjutant-general) to Edward Jones, July 1, 1861, OR 2:1, 622. Similar orders were sent the same day for the arrests of Gatchell, Davis, and Hinks.

9. Nathaniel Banks to Winfield Scott, July 1, 1861, OR 2:1, 623. Later in July Lincoln refused to comply with a House resolution for information about the detention of the Baltimore Police Commissioners, citing such information as "incompatible with the public interest"; see OR 2:1, 631.

10. Speech of John Pendleton Kennedy from the *Congressional Globe* ("Spring, 1861"), Cohen Scrapbook.

11. Simon Cameron to J. K. F. Mansfield, July 1, 1861, OR 2:1, 586.

12. Nathaniel Banks to Winfield Scott, July 1, 1861, OR 2:1, 623 (also OR 1:2, 139–40).

13. Ibid., 624.

14. Nathaniel Banks to E. D. Townsend, July 13, 1861, OR 2:1, 586. A July 17 reply to Banks informed him that nothing could be done, other than to send him "a regiment of three-years' men from Vermont" to help maintaORder and prevent escapes (see OR 2:1, 587).

15. Edward Spencer to Anne Catherine Bradford Harrison, July 14, 1861, Spencer Letters II, 343.

16. A. V. Colburn to Major General John A. Dix, August 20, 1861, OR 2:1 (pt. 1), 589. Dix commanded the Department of Pennsylvania from July 25 TO August 24, 1861.

17. *Sun*, August 24, 1861.

18. John A. Dix to Lieutenant General Scott, August 25, 1861, OR, 2:1 (pt. 1), 590.

19. Seward, *Reminiscences*, 175. See Neely, *Fate of Liberty*, 15–16.

20. Seward, *Reminscences*, 175–77.

21. Ibid., 177.

22. Ibid.

23. Ibid., 178.

24. John A. Dix to G. B. McClellan, September 4, 1861, OR 2:1, 591–92. See OR 2:1, 644, for Dix's letter to the Mayor.

25. Ibid., 592 (Marcy letter not found).

26. Simon Cameron to N. P. Banks, September 11, 1861, OR 1:5, 193.

27. Simon Cameron to John Dix, September 11, 1861, OR 2:1, 678. On September 13, Dix wrote to Gen. John Wool that a number of Maryland citizens and legislators were in custody (see OR 1:5, 194).

28. John A. Dix to E. D. Townsend, September 12, 1861, OR 2:1, 594–95. "Pegram" was likely John Pegram, a Confederate officer who surrendered to McClellan in July 1861 in western Virginia. Pegram, who became a general in 1862, married Hetty Cary of Baltimore in January 1865. He was killed less than a month later.

29. William H. Carpenter to Mrs. Edward Lucas, September 8, 1862, MS 1860, MdHS. Following his arrest Carpenter was imprisoned in Forts McHenry and Delaware.

30. Maj. Gen. N. P. Banks to Lieutenant Colonel Ruger, September 16, 1861, OR 2:1, 681.

31. R. Morris Copeland to Major-General Banks, September 18, 1861, OR 2:1, 682–83. See pp. 686–748 for the names of many of those arrested.

32. N. P. Banks to Governor [William] Seward, September 20, 1861, OR 1:5, 194–95.

33. "Statement Concerning Arrests in Maryland," September 15, 1861, Basler, *Collected Works,* 4:523. This statement also appeared in the *American* on September 21, 1861, according to Basler. Lincoln never provided an explanation.

34. Glenn Diary, 36–37 (entry of September 13, 1861).

35. Ibid., 37–38 (entry of September 14, 1861).

36. Ibid., 38 (entry of September 14, 1861). The glossary of persons and places describes James Lawrence McPhail as a "Baltimore hatter and politician" appointed Provost Marshal in July 1861 and who later served on the Baltimore City Council (p. 376).

37. W. G. Snethen to W. H. Seward, September 15, 1861, OR 2:1, 595.

38. Tho. H. Hicks to Maj. Gen. N. P. Banks, September 20, 1861, OR 2:1, 685.

39. Fort Warren Prisoners' Record, November 30, 1861, MS 1957, MdHS.

40. John E. Wool to Simon Cameron, September 15, 1861, OR 2:1, 596.

41. John A. Dix to Captain Bragg, September 20, 1861, OR 2:1, 597.

42. Samuel B. Rogers to Nathan Rogers, September 22, 1861, Butler-Rogers Collections, MS 1787, MdHS.

43. Citizens of Baltimore to Abraham Lincoln, September 21, 1861, Redwood Collection.

44. Diary of Anna Maria Tilghman, Monday, September 30, 1861, MS 1967, MdHS.

45. Harrison, 7 (October 1863): 107–8.

46. John A. Dix to Hon. William H. Seward, October 5, 1861, OR 2:1, 599.

47. L. C. Baker to "The Honorable Secretary of State," October 10, 1861, OR 2:1, 600.

48. C. E. Detmold to L. J. Brengle, Esq., October 11, 1861, OR 2:1, 601.

49. John B. Kerfoot to Hon. J. P. Kennedy, October 16, 1861, Kennedy Papers.

50. J. R. Giddings to Frederick W. Seward, October 22, 1861, OR 2:1, 603.

51. Glenn Diary, 40 (entry of September 17, 1861).

52. Ibid., 40–41 (entry of September 19, 1861).

53. John A. Dix to Hon. Simon Cameron and Hon. William H. Seward, October 23, 1861, OR 2:1, 603.

54. R. B. Marcy to Maj. Gen. N. P. Banks, October 29, 1861, OR 2:1, 608.

55. John A. Dix to Daniel Engel and William Ecker, November 1, 1861, OR 2:1, 609.

56. William Schley to Hon. William H. Seward, November 4, 1861, OR 2:1, 610.

57. Brig. Gen. O. O. Howard to Capt. H. W. Smith, November 9, 1861, OR 2:1, 612–13. Sollers was a delegate from Charles County.

58. John A. Dix to H. H. Lockwood, November 12, 1861, OR 2:1, 613. (Snow Hill is in Worcester County, on the Eastern Shore.)

59. *Gazette,* November 30, 1861, Harrison, 6:90.

60. Augustus R. Sollers to William H. Seward, n.d., "received December 9, 1861," OR 2:1, 615–16.

61. "Draft of a proclamation by the President of the United States found among the files of the State Department," OR 2:1, 617. This undated, unsigned draft is marked "File: January 1, 1862."

62. John M. Buchanon to Horace Buchanon, January 19, 1862, The Buchanon Collection, MS 2053, MdHS.

63. Isaac M. Fein, "Baltimore Jews during the Civil War," *American Jewish Historical Quarterly* 51, no. 2 (1961): 89.

64. Edward Bates to William Meade Addison, Esq., February 17, 1862, OR 2:1, 618.

65. Henry M. Warfield to Col. J[ustin] Dimick, February 22, 1862, MS 1860, MdHS. Warfield was imprisoned in Fortress Monroe briefly before being sent to Fort Lafayette.

66. Maj. Gen. John A. Dix to Police Commissioners, Baltimore City, March 17, 1862, OR 2:1, 619.

67. A. Chaplain to Honorable William Seward, March 20, 1862, OR 2:1 (pt. 1), 743.

68. Correspondence in *American,* July 1, 1862, in Cohen Scrapbook. Lincoln published his reply in Fulton's paper, attributing the editor's arrest to information Fulton obtained from Lincoln at a meeting at the White House regarding the Peninsula Campaign. Fulton was released after stating that publication of the information was unintentional.

69. Wilson Papers, July 26, 1862.

70. Ibid., July 10 and July 12, 1863. Pritchard was held at Gilmor House and sentenced to Fort Delaware, but following the intervention of "Dr. Lane," the family was sent south.

71. Glenn Diary, 68 (entry of August 2, 1862).

72. Ibid., 69 (entry of August 2, 1862). Glenn was promptly released.

73. E. Z. Chambers to Hon. J[ames] A. Pearce, May 28, 1862, James Alfred Pearce Papers 1843–1862, MS 1384, MdHS.

74. Glenn Diary, 72 (entry "Septr." [1862]). See Appendix C for further information about the Carmichael affair.

75. *American,* May 30, 1862.

76. Ibid., 80 (entry of November 28, 1862).

77. Daniel M. Thomas to Sister, March 15, 1863, Thomas Papers.

78. Daniel Thomas to Sister, March 22, 1863, Thomas Papers.

79. James S. Downs and J. Leeds Barroll to *Richmond Enquirer,* May 5, 1863, MS 1860, MdHS.

80. Dodson Papers, May 8, 1863, UMdLib. On May 14, Dodson noted that Robson was in fact sent south, to be treated as a spy if he returned—"a result not unlooked for by either political enemies or friends."

81. Slicer Journal, July 31, 1863.

82. Hering Recollections, 2:92.

83. Ibid., 2:93–95. Hering gives on p. 95 the text of the certificate "attesting to our renewed loyalty" and on p. 96 notes that his wife's brother, Dr. George H. Trumbo, refused the oath and was jailed in Westminster, then sent to Fort McHenry until spring 1864.

84. Thomas G. Pratt et al. to His Excellency Augustus Bradford, November 20, 1863, *Exec Ltr Bk,* MdSA.

85. A. W. Bradford to Thos G. Pratt, Jos. Nicholson, & Wm Tell Claude, Esqs., November 22, 1863, *Exec Ltr Bk,* MdSA.

86. Davis Diary, August 15, 1863.

87. Milton [?] to Mahlon H[opkins] [Janney], January 14, 1864, Mahlon Hopkins Janney Collection, MS 1985, MdHS.

88. *Sun,* April 7, 1864.

89. *Sun,* April 19, 1864.

90. Glenn Diary, 129, 131–32 (entries of June 4 and June 6, 1864). James M. Mason and John Slidell were sent in 1861 as Confederate emissaries to France. Their capture aboard the British mail steamer Trent by a Union warship generated much sympathy for the Confederacy in England. Secretary Seward averted a crisis by releasing the two men, who failed to procure French recognition of the Confederacy.

91. Edward A. Colburn to Father, December 5, 1864, MS 1860, MdHS.

92. Special Orders No. 47, February 23, 1865, MS 1860, MdHS.

93. William Wiegel to Charles Vocke, April 27, 1865, Vocke (Claas) Papers, MS 1453, MdHS. Vocke, a native German, was a naturalized American citizen.

CHAPTER 8. PRISON

1. Ch[arles] H. Winder to M[ary] H. Winder, undated (marked "corner 13 & avenue"), Winder Papers. William Winder was held for fourteen months in several Union prisons; many of William's letters to his brother survive. A list of prisoners "in the Building C on 13 St. and Penn ave Wash, DC," compiled by Charles H. Winder in October 1861, reveals his place of incarceration but not its duration; see Charles H. Winder, "List of Prisoners," Winder Papers.

2. Nathaniel Banks to Winfield Scott, July 3, 1861, OR 2:1, 627.

3. Chas. O. Wood to Bvt. Lt. Col. Martin Burke, August 1, 1861, OR 2:1 (no. 114), 633–34.

4. Chas. O. Wood to Bvt. Lt. Col. Martin Burke, August 1, 1861, OR 2:1 (no. 114), 634.

5. Resolution offered in House of Representatives, July 31, 1861, OR 2:1 (114), 633.

6. John A. Dix to Jacob B. Hardenbergh, July 29, 1861, OR 2:1, 631–32.

7. Charles Howard to Simon Cameron, August 1, 1861, OR 2:1 (no. 114), 634–35.

8. Ibid., 635. Howard wrote again to Cameron on August 7 and August 12, to Scott on August 8, and to Secretary of State Seward on August 19 about these matters.

9. William H. Seward to Winfield Scott, August 8, 1861; and William H. Seward to E. Delafield Smith, August 8, 1861, both OR 2:1 (no. 114), 638.

10. Chas. O. Wood to M. Burke, August 27, 1861, OR 2:1 (no. 114), 643.

11. Maj. Gen. John A. Dix to Maj. Gen. G. B. McClellan, September 5, 1861, OR 2:1 (no. 114), 592–93.

12. Maj. Gen. John A. Dix to Maj. Gen. G. McClellan, September 8, 1861, OR 2:1 (no. 114), 593.

13. *Sun,* September 9, 1861 (escape), and September 10, 1861 (visitors banned).

14. Thomas W. Hall Jr. to Mrs. Thomas W. Hall, September 13, 1861, Hall Letters. Hall's letter is addressed to his mother at "No 44 Monument St (near Calvert)." Two days later he wrote again, from Fortress Monroe. Hall was released in late 1862 and became a major in the Confederate army.

15. Glenn Diary, 38 (entry September 16, 1861).

16. Thomas W. Hall Jr. to Mrs. Thomas W. Hall, September 21, 1861, Hall Letters. On September 28 he wrote again, from Fort Warren in Boston Harbor.

17. George W. Brown to Emily [Barton] Brune, September 20, 1861, Brune Papers.

18. W[illiam] H. Winder to Chas. [Winder], September 27, 1861, Winder Papers.

19. William H. Seward to Major General John A. Dix, September 25, 1861, OR 2:1 (pt. 1), 645.

20. Maj. Gen. John A. Dix to Honorable William H. Seward, September 25, 1861, OR 2:1 (pt. 1), 645.

21. William H. Seward to Maj. Gen. John A. Dix, September 27, 1861, OR 2:1 (pt. 1), 647.

22. George W. Brown to Emily [Barton Brune], October 24, 1861, Brune Papers.

23. George P. Kane to His Excellency the President, September 30, 1861, OR 2:1, 648. On October 8, 1861, eighty Maryland prisoners, including Charles Howard, George P. Kane, George William Brown, William H. Gatchell, John W. Davis, and Henry M. Warfield signed a detailed letter of complaint to President Lincoln (see OR 2:1, 649–50).

24. Thomas W. Hall Jr. to Mrs. Thomas W. Hall, October 2, 1861, Hall Letters.

25. Thomas W. Hall Jr. to [Thomas W. Hall] October 7, 1861. By early November, Hall was in Fort Warren.

26. George William Brown to Emily Barton Brune, November 26, 1861, Brune Papers.

27. William H. Winder to Josephine S. Winder, October 4, 1861, Winder Papers. A notation on Charles H. Winder's October 1861 compilation of prisoners in a Washington, D.C., prison states that "his daughter Molly died Thursday 10th Oct 1861."

28. Glenn Diary, 40 (entry "October [1861]").

29. Ibid., 40–41 (entry "October [1861]"). Glenn noted that Morris was acquitted of the seduction charge.

30. Ibid., 41–42 (entry "October [1861]").

31. Ibid., 44 (entry "October [1861]").

32. Maj. Gen. John A. Dix to Honorable William H. Seward, October 9, 1861, OR 2:1 (pt. 1), 651. Brown's eventual resignation put John Lee Chapman, the presiding officer of the first branch of the city council, in the mayor's office.

33. William H. Seward to Major General John A. Dix, October 11, 1861, OR 2:1 (pt. 1), 652.

34. Thomas John Claggett to Dr. Thomas Maddox, November 12, 1861, MS 1860, MdHS. This letter also appears in William D. Hoyt, Jr., "Thomas John Claggett," *MdHM* 47, no. 2 (June 1952): 129–30.

35. W. R. Whittingham to Dr. T[homas] Maddox, November 22, 1861, MS 1860, MdHS. Claggett was ordered released on November 26, 1861; see OR 2:1 (pt. 1), 613–14.

36. I. M. Forbes to Seth Hawley, November 16, 1861, OR 2:1 (pt. 1), 657–58.

37. Charles Babbidge to George C. Shattuck, October 17, 1861, OR 2:1 (pt. 1), 658–59. See page 659 for other testimonials on Brown's behalf.

38. Resolution offered in the House of Representatives, December 10, 1861, OR 2:1 (pt. 1), 665.

39. Thos. W. Hall Jr. to Elizabeth Hall, January 1, 1862, Hall Letters.

40. Glenn Diary, 46–47 (entry of January 1, 1862).

41. Ibid., 47 (entry of January 1, 1862).

42. Ibid. Appendix B contains an order, dated December 2, 1861, from Dix to Morris discharging Glenn from custody.

43. John S. Keyes to Honorable William H. Seward, January 4, 1862, OR 2:1 (pt. 1), 664–65.

44. Geo. Wm. Brown to George [C. Shattuck], January 31, 1862, Brown Papers.

45. [William H. Winder] to Charles [Winder], January 1862 (no day), Winder Papers. Kane was granted three weeks' parole on November 28, 1861, to attend the death of his father-in-law.

46. W[illiam] H. Winder to Chas. [Winder], February 14, 1862, Winder Papers. Winder wrote on March 5 that conditional paroles had been eliminated. On March 24, he received a letter from Secretary of War Cameron saying that his arrest must have been directed by the State Department, for Cameron learned of Winder's arrest from the newspapers, but Winder claimed to have a letter from Cameron ordering his arrest.

47. Th[omas] W. Hall Jr. to Elizabeth Hall, January 20, 1862, Hall Letters.

48. Ibid., February 20, 1862.

49. Ibid., April 5, 1862.

50. Henry M. Warfield to Col. J[ustin] Dimick, February 22, 1862, MS 1860, MdHS.

51. Thos. J. Claggett to Honorable Edwin M. Stanton, February 25, 1862, OR 2:1 (pt. 1), 741.

52. Thomas Maddox to General [John] Dix, March 12, 1862, OR 2:1 (pt. 1), 741–42.

53. B. Mills to Honorable Henry May, March 20, 1862, OR 2:1 (pt. 1), 743. Mills was one of six released upon parole from Fort Warren on March 29; see OR 2:1, 744.

54. Daniel Thomas to Sister, March 30, 1862, Thomas Papers.

55. Ibid.

56. Lewis P. Holloway, C.S.A., to Mrs. C. McKenzie, March 27, 1862, Thomas Papers.

57. Daniel M. Thomas to Sister, March 13, 1862, Thomas Papers. (The inference is that "Holloway" is the same man in both letters. This letter resides in the Daniel Thomas collection.)

58. A[nthony] Kennedy to Dr. Thomas Maddox, March 30, 1862, MS 1860, MdHS.

59. Glenn Diary, 54–55 (entry "April 1862").

60. Ibid., 55–56 (entry "April 1862").

61. Mrs. R. Thomas to Colonel [Martin] Burke, April 3, 1862, OR 2:2 (pt. 1), 396.

62. Geo. Wm. Brown to George [C. Shattuck], April 11, 1862, Brown Papers.

63. Lt. Col. Martin Burke to Brig. Gen. L. Thomas, April 22, 1862, OR 2:2 (pt. 1), 396.

64. Henry M. Warfield to Edwin M. Stanton, May 13, 1862, MS 1860, MdHS.

65. H. B. Davidson (no recipient), May 22, 1862, Harwood Family Papers, MS 1022, MdHS.

66. Ann C. Thomas to Randolph Barton, June 10, 1862, in Margaretta Barton Colt, *Defend the Valley: A Shenandoah Family in the Civil War* (New York, 1994), 177. Augustus A. Gibson was then in command at Fort Delaware. Hanson was a delegate to one of the special sessions of the 1861 Maryland state legislature.

67. W[illiam] H. Winder to Charles [Winder], June 13, 1862, Winder Papers.

68. Ibid., July 18, 1862.

69. Geo. Wm. Brown to George [C. Shattuck], August 1, 1862, Brown Papers.

70. Edw[ard] R. Parry to C[harles]. H. Winder, August 24, 1862, Winder Papers.

71. W[illiam] H. Winder to Josie [Josephine S. Winder], September 7, 1862, Winder Papers. Winder noted that many prisoners had been released: "Since I first entered this, including those who came with me there have been some fifteen hundred, of whom only seventeen remain, three of these war prisoners, too sick to leave with the others on 31 July."

72. Glenn Diary, 70 (entry of August 14, 1862).

73. Wilson Papers, December 16, 1862. Democrats gained thirty-five seats in the Thirty-eighth Congress and captured Pennsylvania and Ohio, which had also gone Republican in 1860. Illinois Democrats made Lincoln's suppression of civil liberties a winning issue in the president's home state. See David Herbert Donald et al., *The Civil War*

and Reconstruction (New York, 2001), 413–14. For a view that historians have overestimated Democratic gains in the Fall 1862 elections, see James McPherson, *Battle Cry of Freedom: The Civil War Era* (New York, 1988), 561–62.

74. George P. Kane to "Fellow-Citizens of the State of Maryland," November 29, 1862, OR 2:1 (pt. 1), 666–67. Kane was elected mayor of Baltimore in 1878 but died in June the following year. He wrote this for a Baltimore newspaper.

75. Geo. Wm. Brown to George [C. Shattuck], January 31, 1862, Brown Papers.

76. Edward Bates to William Price, January 6, 1863, OR 2:1 (pt. 1), 667.

77. *Sun*, April 9, 1863. The court-martial occurred on March 25, 1863.

78. Laas, *Wartime Washington*, 259 (entry of April 17, 1863).

79. Samuel B. Rogers, "Civil War Data," June 25, 1863, Butler-Rogers Collections, MS 1787, MdHS. A July 27, 1864, folder in this collection contains a printed page noting that Samuel B. Rogers was killed in battle near Hagerstown, July 29, 1864; another page gives July 27 as the date of his death; and a third states that he was killed near Clear Spring. He may have been wounded on July 9 during the Battle of Monocacy. He was likely in Fort McHenry briefly.

80. Slicer Journal, October 8, 1863.

81. Lt. Jno. W. Fitzpatrick to Mrs. A[ugusta] C. E. Shoemaker, January 16, 1864, Shoemaker Papers 1824–1955, MdHS.

82. Wm F. Gordon Jr. to [Elizabeth Burdick Gordon], January 25, 1864, Burdick-Gordon Correspondence, MS 2585, MdHS. Gordon also asked for "oil" and "some good books."

83. Maj. Gen. Lew Wallace to Governor A. W. Bradford, March 24, 1864, *Exec Ltr Bk*, MdSA. Elbridge Gerry Kilbourn, an attorney from Howard County, was Speaker of the House of Delegates in 1861. He was arrested in September that year and imprisoned in Forts Lafayette and Warren; see OR 2:1 (pt. 1), 667.

84. A. W. Bradford to Maj. Gen. Lew Wallace, March 28, 1864, *Exec Ltr Bk*, MdSA. In a March 30 letter, Wallace asked Bradford to explain the power election judges would have to reject votes of the disloyal.

85. to S[amuel] M. Shumaker, November 13, 1864, Shoemaker Papers 1824–1955, MdHS.

86. Maj. Gen. Phil[ip] H. Sheridan to Ella Thompson Carroll, February 17, 1865, R. G. Harper Carroll Papers, 1863–1865, MdHS. Her husband, R. G. Harper, was in the Confederate Second Corps; his letters include vivid descriptions of troop movements and battles in 1863 and 1864.

87. Saml Cox to Mrs. W. A. Cox, May 21, 1865, courtesy of Lucy Neale Duke.

CHAPTER 9. REBELS

1. William Platt to Richard D. Fisher, May 25, 1909, MS 1860, MdHS.

2. William Wilkins Davis to Rebecca D. Davis, May 22, 1861, in Hein, *A Student's View*, 119–20.

3. Somerville Sollers to Brother "Meme" [Augustus Sollers], August 4, 1861, Sollers Papers, MS 1426, MdHS (emphases his).

4. Somerville Sollers to Mother, August 24, 1861, Sollers Papers, MS 1426, MdHS.

5. Robert Kirkwood to Dorcas Kirkwood, August 19, 1861, Kirkwood Papers.

6. *Sun,* August 26, 1861.

7. Francis Patrick Kenrick to Maj. Gen. [John] Dix, December 17, 1861, MS 1860, MdHS.

8. E.N.T. to James Wood Tyson, January 30, 1862, Tyson Papers, MS 1970, MdHS.

9. R. Ellsworth Cook to Col. [William P.] Maulsby, March 3, 1862, MS 35.1, Historical Society of Frederick County.

10. Ibid., March 6, 1862. (Maulsby, commander of the Potomac Home Brigade, was at Key's Ferry.) Turner Ashby commanded a Confederate cavalry brigade in the Shenandoah Valley and was killed in 1862.

11. *American*, March 12, 1862.

12. J. W. Garrett to ES, March 24, 1862, B&O Papers, Baltimore and Ohio Railroad Company Business Letters, 1854–1881, MS 1925, MdHS.

13. Glenn Diary, 56 (entry of March 28, 1862).

14. Anonymous to [William R. Whittingham], June 3, 1862, MDA.

15. David J. Lee to Wm R. Whittingham, June 18, 1862, MDA.

16. R. E. Lee to Jefferson Davis, September 4, 1862, Lee Papers, 294.

17. Ibid., September 7, 1862, 298.

18. R. E. Lee to The People of Maryland, September 8, 1862, Lee Papers, 299.

19. *Sun*, September 12, 1862.

20. R. E. Lee to The People of Maryland, September 8, 1862, Lee Papers, 299–300.

21. Wilson Papers, September 7, 1862.

22. Lew to Kate [Bond], September 16, 1862, Bond-McCullough Papers, MS 1159, MdHS. Confederate cavalry led by Bradley Johnson destroyed Bradford's home in July 1864.

23. Washington Hands Civil War Notebook, MS 2468, 88, MdHS. Hands's unit, moving to interdict Lee before Antietam, went through Boonsboro, Middletown, and Williamsport, then crossed the Potomac into Virginia and went to Louden's Heights, where they shelled Bolivar's Heights on the morning of September 15. Hands would fight at Antietam.

24. Hering Recollections, 2:41–42.

25. Schaeffer Diary, September 4, 1862.

26. Robert Spear to Sarah Spear, September 4, 1862, Spear Papers, MS 1428, MdHS. Robert Spear sent at least one letter to his wife in Boston and three to her in New Haven.

27. Arthur Geo. Brown to [George William Brown], September 8, 1862, Brown Papers, MS 2398, MdHS.

28. Ibid.

29. Schaeffer Diary, September 6, 1862.

30. Ibid., September 7 and 8, 1862.

31. Ibid., September 9, 1862.

32. Ibid., September 10, 1862.

33. Ibid., September 11, 1862.

34. Ibid., September 12, 1862.

35. Ibid.

36. *Battles & Leaders of the Civil War* (New York, 1887), 2:562.

37. *Sun*, September 16, 1862.

38. W. W. Blackford, *War Years with Jeb Stuart* (New York, 1945; reprinted Baton Rouge, LA, 1993), 141.

39. William Miller Owen, *In Camp and Battle with the Washington Artillery* (Boston, 1885, reprinted Baton Rouge, LA, 1999), 133.

40. Alexander Hunter, "A High Private's Account of the Battle of Sharpsburg," Southern Historical Society Papers, 10:511, in Kathleen Ernst, *Too Afraid to Cry: Maryland Citizens and the Antietam Campaign* (Mechanicsburg, PA, 1999), 83.

41. E. M. Woodward, *Our Campaigns* (Philadelphia, 1865), in Ernst, *Too Afraid to Cry*, 89.

42. John Greenleaf Whittier, "Barbara Frietchie," in *The Columbia Book of Civil War Poetry* (New York, 1994), 306–9.

43. Schaeffer Diary, September 12, 1862. She refers to Union Gen. Robert Reno, who was killed the following day in the Battle of South Mountain.

44. *American,* August 30, 1878.

45. Henry Kyd Douglas, *I Rode with Stonewall* (Chapel Hill, NC, 1940), 152.

46. Schaeffer Diary, September 13, 1862.

47. Ibid., September 14, 1862.

48. Ibid., September 18, 1862.

49. Washington Hands Civil War Notebook, p. 89, MS 2468, MdHS. Hands probably fought in the afternoon, at "Burnside's Bridge."

50. Wilson Papers, September 22, 1862.

51. *American,* September 22, 1862.

52. William H. Graham to Thomas Winans, Baltimore, September 23, 1862, Graham Letters, MS 2144 (typed script), MdHS.

53. *Sun,* September 22, 1862.

54. Daniel Thomas to Sister, September 22, 1862, Thomas Papers.

55. *American Sentinel*, September 26, 1862.

56. Schaeffer Diary, undated.

57. Correspondent to Miss Annie Woodward, January 1, 1863, courtesy of Martha E. Marshall.

58. Diary of [John] A. Steiner, April 8, 1863, MS 35.3, Historical Society of Frederick County.

59. Glenn Diary, 87–88 (entry "June" 1863). Charles Wagandt, *The Mighty Revolution: Negro Emancipation in Maryland, 1862–1864* (Baltimore, 1964, reprinted Baltimore, 2005), 103, describes Baltimore defenses.

60. Slicer Journal, June 21, 1863.

61. Archibald T. Kirkwood to Father, June 13, [1863], Kirkwood Papers.

62. Ibid., June 18 [1863].

63. *Sun*, June 26, 1863.

64. Archibald T. Kirkwood to Father, June 29 [1863], Kirkwood Papers.

65. Mehring Diary, June 19, June 22, June 23, June 26, June 30, July 1, and July 2, 1863, MS 1860, MdHS. Maggie lived in Bruceville, near Taneytown. The general of the July 2 entry may have been Union Maj. Gen. John Reynolds, the highly regarded Pennsylvanian killed at Gettysburg on July 1.

66. Fletcher Melvin Green, "Diary of Miss Lutie Kealhofer" [June 30, 1863], "A People at War: Hagerstown, Maryland, June 15–August 31, 1863," MdHM 40, no. 4 (December 1945): 257.

67. Wilson Papers, June 27, 1863.

68. Ibid.

69. *American*, June 27, 1863.

70. Robert Schenck to John L. Chapman, June 20, 1863, RG 9 S2 Box 33, BCA.

71. *American*, June 29, 1863.

72. *American*, June 30, 1863.

73. Major General Schenck to Captain Cumming, June 29, 1863, MS 1860, MdHS.

74. *Sun*, July 1, 1863.

75. *American*, July 1, 1863. Gen. Jubal Early's men levied ransoms against Hagerstown and Frederick, which escaped destruction by paying. Chambersburg, Pennsylvania, refused to pay and was burned.

76. Ibid.

77. *Sun*, July 1, 1863.

78. [Eliza Shriver] to [H. W. Shriver], July 2, 1863, Shriver Papers. "Stuart Cavalry" refers to Confederate Gen. Jeb Stuart.

79. [Charles Nisbet Turnbull] to [Jane Graham Ramsay Turnbull] [July] 2, 1863, Turnbull Collection, MS 1719, MdHS. Though the letter is dated "Junr 2nd/63," its content indicates the writer meant July 2, 1863. The Turnbull family lived in Baltimore.

80. [Charles Nisbet Turnbull] to [Jane Graham Ramsay Turnbull], July 3, 1863, Turnbull Collection, MS 1719, MdHS.

81. F. A. Shriver to [Henry] W. [Shriver], July 4, 1863, Shriver Papers. (This letter contains details on the battle at Hanover.)

82. Ibid.

83. H. Wirt Shriver to [Frederick] A. [Shriver], July 4, 1863, Shriver Papers.

84. *Sun*, July 2, 1863.

85. Charles F. Mayer to [Francis B. Mayer], July 13, 1863, Mayer Papers, MS 1574, MdHS. (Marylanders at Gettysburg: Union 1,953 wounded / 140 killed; Confederate 982 wounded / 228 killed.)

86. Ibid.

87. W[alter] G. Dunn to [Emma Randolph], July 10, 1863, in Judith A. Bailey and Robert I. Cottom, eds., *After Chancellorsville: Letters from the Heart* (Baltimore, 1998), 6. Dunn, in the Eleventh New Jersey Infantry Regiment, was wounded at Chancellorsville. Jarvis Hospital was on property in Union Square in West Baltimore confiscated from Gen. George H. Steuart, who had joined the Confederate army.

88. F[rederick] A. Shriver to [Henry] W. [Shriver], July 12, 1863, Shriver Papers.

89. Ibid.

90. Davis Diary, August 29, 1863.

91. Cousin Clara to Cousin [T] Sewall [Ball], September 21, 1863, Ball Papers.

92. Aug[ustus] Shriver to Andrew [Shriver], October 21, 1863, Shriver Papers.

93. "Conversation with Hon. Lot M. Morrill, Sec of Treasury," Nicolay Papers, Library of Congress, in Michael Burlingame, *An Oral History of Abraham Lincoln: John Nicolay's Interviews and Essays* (Carbondale, 1996), 55–56. Morrill was governor of Maine (1858–61), senator from Maine (1861–76), and treasury secretary (1876–77).

94. James Newman to Maj. Thomas Doswell, May 17, 1864, J. Steuart Papers. William Steuart had fought at Gettysburg.

95. James Newman to Gen. [George H. Steuart], May 19, 1864, J. Steuart Papers.

96. M. Schele de Vere to George H. Steuart, May 30, 1864, J. Steuart Papers.

97. H. S. Kettlewell to [William R. Whittingham], June 4, 1864, MDA.

98. Ibid., September 19, 1864.

99. Genl R. E. Lee to Jefferson Davis, June 26, 1864, Lee Papers, 807–8.

100. Glenn Diary, 137 (entry of July 13, 1864).

101. Ibid., 137–38 (entry of July 14, 1864).

102. Mary [Winebrenner] to [Henry] W. [Shriver], July 7, 1864, Shriver Papers.

103. William H. James Diary, July 9 [1864], MS 1860, MdHS. James, a member of the Lutheran Church, was married to Kate Francesca Harman, known as "Fannie."

104. Samuel B. Lawrence to J. W. Garrett, July 7, 1864, Baltimore & Ohio Railroad Company Papers, 1827–1864, MS 1192, MdHS.

105. William H. James Diary, July 9 and July 11 [1864], MS 1860, MdHS. James noted that the camp moved on July 16, from Greenwood to near Fort Worthington, a half mile east and on July 22 to Camden Station for the train to Relay House. His diary is a vivid personal account of the battle and aftermath.

106. E. May Stevens to [Sarah H. Stevens], July 9 [1864], MS 1860, MdHS.

107. R[ichard] P. T[homas?] to "Dear Bro," July 10, 1864, A. G. Thomas Letters, MS 2244, MdHS.

108. Saml. B. Lawrence to Maj. Gen. Wallace, July 6, 1864, OR 1:37, pt. 2, 92.

109. Maj. Gen. Lew Wallace to Major-General Halleck, July 9, 1864, OR 1:37, pt. 2, 145.

110. E. M[ay] S[tevens] to [Sarah H. Stevens], July 12 [1864], MS 1860, MdHS.

111. Davis Diary, July 16, 1864.

112. B[enjamin] F[ranklin] Kirkwood to Mother, July 16, 1864, Kirkwood Papers. Camp Destribution was near Alexandria, Virginia.

113. "Mollie" to "Judie," July 25, 1864, MS 1860, MdHS.

114. Davis Diary, August 6, 1864. History is unclear if the rebels actually demanded that much less of Hagerstown than Frederick or if a zero was omitted from the figure (intentionally or in error) by a disingenuous civic leader.

115. Ibid., August 13, 1864. Davis's last journal entry is September 24, 1864.

116. Rev. A. C. Coxe to Rt. Rev. William R. Whittingham, August 18, 1864, MDA. Coxe was elected bishop coadjutor of Western New York in 1864.

117. W[illia]m F. Gordon Jr. to President [Lincoln], no month, 1864, Burdick-Gordon Correspondence, MS 2585, MdHS. (This letter is in shreds and is difficult to read.)

118. Daniel Thomas to Sister, September 11, 1864, Thomas Papers.

119. L[emuel] Wilmer to [William R.] Whittingham, September 11, 1864, MDA.

120. William H. James Diary, September 23, [1864], MS 1860, MdHS. James was mustered out on October 4.

121. A. G. Thomas to "Brother," October 10, 1864, A. G. Thomas Letters, MS 2244, MdHS. On the reverse of this letter facsimile is a map of the scene, which occurred along Ricketts Creek, about 5.5 miles from Rockville. Thomas later became the president of the First National Bank of Sandy Spring.

122. Rev. Alexander Falk to Right Reverend Wm. R. Whittingham, October 8, 1864, MDA.

123. John Lee Chapman et al., to Baltimore City Council, October 24, 1864, RG 16, S1, Box 246, BCA. This folder includes a "recapitulation—Cost of Forts &c." itemizing costs of specific fortifications around the city that total $96,152.

124. John R. Kenly to Lt. Col. S. B. Lawrence, November 29, 1864, MS 1860, MdHS.

125. *American*, October 11, 1864.

126. Daniel Thomas to Sister, May 28, 1865, Thomas Papers.

III. LIBERATION

1. See Allan Kulikoff, *Tobacco and Slaves: The Development of Southern Cultures in the Chesapeake, 1680–1800* (Chapel Hill, NC, 1986), for an overview of the region's development as an agrarian slave society (esp. chap. 1); and on Maryland's transition from slavery to emancipation, Wagandt, *Mighty Revolution,* and the summary in Ira Berlin et al., eds., *Freedom: A Documentary History of Emancipation, 1861–1867*, Series 1, Vol. 2: *The Wartime Genesis of Free Labor: The Upper South* (New York, 1999), 481–99.

2. Maryland became the first border state and third slave state, after Arkansas and Louisiana, to ban slavery (the Arkansas ban was a partial one). Ira Berlin et al., eds., *Freedom: A Documentary History of Emancipation, 1861–1867*, Series 1, Vol. 1: *The Destruction of Slavery* (New York, 1985), argues that free and slave black cultures were inextricably linked and that in Maryland the Civil War exploited a "delicate balance of contradictory elements" that led to slavery's collapse; see 331–32.

3. Jeffrey Richardson Brackett, *The Negro in Maryland: A Study of the Institution of Slavery* (New York, 1969), 42–47.

4. Barbara J. Fields, *Slavery and Freedom on Middle Ground: Maryland during the Nineteenth Century* (New Haven, CT, 1985), 24; Robert J. Brugger, *Maryland: A Middle Temperament, 1634–1980* (Baltimore, 1988), 244–45. For details on the numerous legislative attempts to deny free black Marylanders the rights enjoyed by free whites, see James M. Wright, *The Free Negro in Maryland, 1634–1860* (New York, 1921, reprinted 1971), chapter 3. In 1850, Maryland had 74,723 free blacks, 90,368 slaves, and 417,942 whites. In 1860, the numbers were 83,942, 87,189, and 515,918, respectively. Only Delaware, a state with few slaves, had a higher percentage (91.6%) of freemen among its black population. See *Compendium of the Seventh Census of the United States* and *Compendium of the Eighth Census of the United States*.

5. The Second Confiscation Act was also known as the Treason Act. On the Confiscation and Militia Acts, see Donald et al., *The Civil War and Reconstruction*, 281–82, 329, 227; Russell F. Weigley, *A Great Civil War: A Military and Political History, 1861–1865* (Bloomington, IN, 2000), 86, 169; and McPherson, *Battle Cry of Freedom*, 500. See Jean H. Baker, *The Politics of Continuity: Maryland Political Parties from 1858 to 1870* (Baltimore, 1973), 102–10, for discussion of events related to the 1864 constitutional convention.

6. Between 1,500 and 1,800 black Marylanders would serve in the Union Navy; see Berlin et al., *Wartime Genesis*, 489, and Berlin et al., *Destruction of Slavery*, 339. See Wagandt, *Mighty Revolution*, chaps. 10 and 11, and Baker, *Politics of Continuity*, 82–102, for discussion of the political dynamics behind emancipation in Maryland.

7. Berlin et al., *Wartime Genesis*, 491. Those failing medical exams were dispatched to the quartermaster in Baltimore.

8. Baker, *Politics of Continuity*, 87–90; Wagandt, *Mighty Revolution*, 182–83. Baker discusses the claims of Democrats and Unionist critics and the roles of military men who in some cases were themselves candidates, states that the claims of military interference in the 1863 elections have been exaggerated, and explores the views of Unionist factions on emancipation.

9. Baker, *Politics of Continuity*, 109. See Wagandt, *Mighty Revolution*, chap. 16, for regional and county analyses of the vote and efforts of Democrats to overturn the results.

10. Maryland Code of Public General Laws (Annapolis, 1860), Article 6, Sec. 31, "Negro Apprentices." See Richard Paul Fuke, *Imperfect Equality: African Americans and the Confines of White Racial Attitudes in Post-Emancipation Maryland* (New York, 1999), chap. 4, for a discussion about abuse of the apprenticeship laws.

11. Fuke, *Imperfect Equality*, 72; Berlin et al., *Wartime Genesis*, 497–98. Three U.S. Colored Troops regiments in 1863 and 1864 had a total of 2,450 tidewater black men. Adjutant General, Rolls of Md. Troops, U.S. Colored Troops, 1863–1864, MdSA, in Fuke, *Imperfect Equality*, 72.

12. Fuke, *Imperfect Equality*, 80–83; Berlin et al., *Wartime Genesis*, 498.

CHAPTER 10. SLAVES

1. Mary Ferguson, interviewed in Columbus, Georgia, December 18, 1936, "American Slave," ser. 2, pt. 1, (Georgia), 12:326–31, in Ira Berlin, Marc Favreau, and Steven

F. Miller, eds., *Remembering Slavery: African Americans Talking about Their Personal Experiences of Slavery and Freedom* (New York, 1998), 153–54. Interviewer's text given *verbatim*.

2. "Maryland Narratives," in George P. Rawick, *The American Slave: A Composite Autobiography* (Westport, CT, 1941, reprinted 1972, 1975), Phillip Johnson interview, September 14, 1937, 41–43. This and other text from these slave interviews are given *verbatim* as recorded by the interviewers.

3. Ibid., Perry Ellis interview, 49–50.

4. Ibid., Richard Macks interview, 51.

5. Ibid., 53.

6. Ibid., 55.

7. Ibid., Tom Randall interview, 57–59.

8. Brig. Gen. Stone and Assistant Adjutant General C. Stewart, General Orders No. 16, September 23, 1861, in Berlin et al., *Destruction of Slavery*, 348–49. The camp was called "The Corps of Observation."

9. James Sawyer to Family, undated, Letters, Wyles Collection, University of California, Santa Barbara, in David Madden, ed., *Beyond the Battlefield: The Ordinary Life and Extraordinary Times of the Civil War Soldier* (New York, 2000), 46–47.

10. *Sun*, May 13, 1861.

11. Col. Alfred H. Terry to Capt. Theodore Talbot, June 12, 1861, in Berlin et al., *Destruction of Slavery*, 167. No response has been found.

12. Chas. B. Calvert to Gen. Mansfield, July 17, 1861, in Berlin et al., *Destruction of Slavery*, 169–71. Secretary of War Simon Cameron's response to a similar letter from Calvert in July noted the "importance of the subject" but "the pressure of business has prevented any definite action in the premises" (Simon Cameron to Hon. Charles B. Calvert, July 12, 1861, in Berlin et al., *Destruction of Slavery,* 347n). Background on Calvert, a founder of the U.S. Department of Agriculture, is at History Division, Maryland-National Capital Park and Planning Commission, Riverdale, Maryland.

13. OR 2:1, pt. 1, 763. Also see Maj. Gen. John A. Dix to Hon. S. Cameron, August 8, 1861, D-108, 1861, Letters Received, RG 107 (versions differ cosmetically).

14. Maj. Gen. John A. Dix to Maj. Gen. G. B. McClellan, August 21, 1861, ser. 2327, Letters Sent, vol. 27, 8AC, pp. 194–95, Department of Pennsylvania, RG 393, pt. 1.

15. Wilson Papers, September 10, 1861.

16. Ibid.

17. Archibald T. Kirkwood to Robert Kirkwood (brother), September 1, 1861, Kirkwood Papers.

18. Col. Henry S. Briggs to Brig. Gen. D. N. Couch, October 1, 1861, in Berlin et al., *Destruction of Slavery*, 349–50.

19. Maj. Gen. John A. Dix to Col. A. Morse, October 14, 1861, in Berlin et al., *Destruction of Slavery*, 350–51. Dix's order has not been found.

20. Tho. H. Hicks to Hon. S. Cameron, November 18, 1861, in Berlin et al., *Destruction of Slavery*, 351–53.

21. Maj. Gen. John A. Dix to Hon. S. Cameron, November 18, 1861, ser. 2327, Letters Sent, vol. 27, 8AC, p. 459, Dix's Division, Army of the Potomac, RG 393, pt. 1. Dix asked that Gen. John Wool investigate the incident.

22. Unsigned excerpt, November 28, 1861, in Berlin et al., *Destruction of Slavery,* 353–54. Emphasis in letter.

23. Excerpts from Bvt. Brig. Gen. [Charles H. Howard] to Hon. John P. C. Shanks, [20 Nov.] 1867, in Berlin et al., *Destruction of Slavery,* 347–48.

24. Joint Resolution 2, December 19, 1861, MdHR 50029-19, MdSA.

25. *Journal of the Proceedings of the House of Delegates, at a Special Session, December, 1861* (Annapolis, MD, 1861), 49, 107 (the dissenter was A. Chamberlain of Allegany County); *Laws of the State of Maryland* (Annapolis, MD, 1862), chap. 22, 22–23, MdSA.

26. Rev. D. Rideout to Miss Sarah [Jervis], December 30, 1861, Letters and Papers of the Hood-Jervis-Ridgley Families of Bowling Green Farm, Howard Co., MD, courtesy of Achsah Henderson.

27. John Boston to Elizabeth Boston, January 12, 1862, in Berlin et al., *Destruction of Slavery,* 357–58.

28. Thomas J. White to General [Ambrose E. Burnside], January 9, 1862, Letters Received, Burnside Papers, ser. 159, Generals' Papers & Books, RG 94.

29. Ezra Sheckell to Maj. Gen. Burnside, January 16, 1862, Letters Received, Burnside Papers, ser. 159, Generals' Papers & Books, RG 94.

30. Joint Resolution, February 17, 1862, *Journal of the Proceedings of the House of Delegates, at a Special Session, December, 1861* (Annapolis, MD, Thomas J. Wilson, 1861), 460. The resolution passed on February 18 (p. 475) and again, with slightly modified language, on February 27 (p. 615).

31. Affidavit of Richard Green, March 3, 1862, in Berlin et al., *Destruction of Slavery,* 177.

32. Jno. H. Bayne et al. to Hon. E. M. Stanton, March 10, 1862, in Berlin et al., *Destruction of Slavery,* 361–62.

33. Brig. Gen. Joseph Hooker to Brig. Gen. S. Williams, March 18, 1862, H-204 (1862), ser. 12, Letters Received, RG 94.

34. Charles Segal, *Conversations with Lincoln* (New York, 1961), 167.

35. *U.S. Statutes at Large, Treaties, and Proclamations of the United States of America* (Boston, 1863), 12:617.

36. "Appeal to Border State Representatives to Favor Compensated Emancipation," July 12, 1862, CW V, 317–19.

37. "To the Senate and House of Representatives," July 14, 1862, in Basler, *Collected Works,* 5:324–25. See discussion in Allen C. Guelzo, *Lincoln's Emancipation Proclamation* (New York, 2004), 107–9.

38. F. B. F. Burgess to Hon. Charles B. Calvert, March 27, 1862, in Berlin et al., *Destruction of Slavery,* 363–64.

39. Charles B. Calvert to Hon. E. M. Stanton, March 31, 1862, in Berlin et al., *Destruction of Slavery,* 363.

40. "Arrest Bill" passed March 4, 1862, as change to sec. 47 of art. 66 of the code, *Laws of the State of Maryland* (Annapolis, 1862), chap. 96, 102; "Liquor Bill" passed March 10, 1862, *Laws of the State of Maryland,* chaps. 238, 256; "Vessel Bill" passed March 4, 1862, *Laws of the State of Maryland,* Chaps. 128, 135, all in MdSA.

41. Affidavit of Grandison Briscoe, February 6, 1864, in Berlin et al., *Destruction of Slavery,* 365.

42. W. Veirs Bowie to the Hon. Senate of the United States, April 2, 1862, Thirty-seventh Congress, Records of the United States Senate (RG 46), NA.

43. Elizabeth Blair Lee to Samuel Phillips Lee, April 4 [1862], in Laas, *Wartime Washington,* 122.

44. Elizabeth Blair Lee to Samuel Phillips Lee, April 19, 1862, in Laas, ibid., 130. Owen Lovejoy was an Illinois congressman, abolitionist, and brother of journalist Elijah Lovejoy, who was murdered in Alton, Illinois, by a mob angry at his abolitionist sentiments.

45. *American,* April 18, 1862.

46. Elizabeth Blair Lee to Samuel Phillips Lee, April 19, 1862, Laas, *Wartime Washington,* 130–33.

47. A. W. Bradford to Edward Bates, May 9, 1862, *Exec Ltr Bk,* MdSA.

48. Edwd. Bates to Excellency A. W. Bradford, May 9, 1862, *Exec Ltr Bk,* MdSA; also in Berlin et al., *Destruction of Slavery,* 366.

49. Thos. Hope to the Honorable Senate and House of Representatives of the United States, May 15, 1862, 37A-H1.3, ser. 468, Petitions and Memorials Which Were Tabled, Thirtieth Congress, Records of the United States House of Representatives (RG 233), NA.

50. Joint Resolution 13, March 10, 1862, MdHR 50029-19, MdSA.

51. A. W. Bradford to William D. Bowie, May 19, 1862, *Exec Ltr Bk,* MdSA.

52. Col. John F. Staunton to Maj. Gen. John A. Dix, May 24, 1862, in Berlin et al., *Destruction of Slavery,* 366–67.

53. Jno. H. Bayne to A. W. Bradford, July 11, 1862, *Exec Ltr Bk,* MdSA.

54. Jno. H. Bayne to Hon. E. M. Stanton, July 25, 1862, in Berlin et al., *Destruction of Slavery,* 367–68.

55. Robert Spear to [Sarah Spear], September 4, 1862, Spear Papers, MS 1428, MdHS.

56. Capt. H. J. VanKirk to Capt. R. W. Dawson, September 8, 1862, P-47 (1862), ser. 5063, Letters Received, Dept. of Virginia & Seventh Army Corps, RG 393, pt. 1.

57. Otho Nesbitt Diary (Clear Spring, MD), in Ernst, *Too Afraid to Cry,* 226; *The Examiner* (Frederick), October 1, 1862, in T. J. C. Williams and Folger McKinsey, *History of Frederick County, Maryland* (Frederick, MD, 1910), 392, in Ernst, *Too Afraid To Cry,* 227.

58. Dodson Papers, October 3, 1862, UMdLib.

59. A. W. Bradford to A. C. Gibbs, December 17, 1862, *Exec Ltr Bk,* MdSA.

60. Dodson Papers, January 5, 1863, UMdLib.

61. G. Fred Maddox to A. W. Bradford, January 9, 1863, *Exec Ltr Bk,* MdSA.

62. A. W. Bradford to G. F. Maddox to, January 13, 1863, *Exec Ltr Bk,* MdSA.

63. *Talbot County Gazette,* January 17, 1863, Harrison, 7:70.

64. *Talbot County Gazette,* January 31, 1863.

65. Jno. T. Graham et al. to the Congress of the United States of America [February 1863], in Berlin et al., *Destruction of Slavery,* 369.

66. Brig. Gen. Henry H. Lockwood Circular, in Berlin et al., *Destruction of Slavery,* 371–72.

67. A. W. Bradford to Peter G. Grimes, Esq, June 23, 1863, *Exec Ltr Bk,* MdSA.

68. A. W. Bradford to President Lincoln, June 23, 1863, *Exec Ltr Bk,* MdSA.

69. Harrison [August 1863], 7:95.

70. Elizabeth Blair Lee to Samuel Phillips Lee, October 3, 1863, in Laas, *Wartime Washington,* 310.

71. Magruder, Lee, Sasser & Clagett to A. W. Bradford, October 22, 1863, *Exec Ltr Bk,* MdSA.

72. Dola Ann Jones to Col. Jno. Eaton Jr., August 16, 1865, in Berlin et al., *Destruction of Slavery,* 376–77. Berlin notes that Governor Bradford pardoned the three men in the fall of 1865 (see p. 377n).

73. Testimony of Lewis Johnson [Jan. ? 1864], in Berlin et al., *Wartime Genesis,* 296.

74. Harrison [March 1864], 8:14.

75. John E. Smith to [?], March 29, 1864, Shriver Papers.

76. Davis Diary, July 4, 1864.

77. Brig. Genl. E. B. Tyler to Lt. Col. S. B. Lawrence, June 15, 1864, in Berlin et al., *Destruction of Slavery,* 380–81. Berlin notes that Gen. Lew Wallace, upon learning that Governor Bradford would not order the release of the men, notified the governor that "I have no choice left me but to order Moody, Jones, and the negroes, brought to me, that I may forward them to Washington at once" (p. 381n).

78. Col. A. L. Brown to Captain, June 4, 1864, in Berlin et al., *Destruction of Slavery,* 382.

79. G. Fred. Maddox to His Excellency A. W. Bradford, June 5, 1864, *Exec Ltr Bk,* MdSA. Bradford petitioned Lincoln to bring about Lynch's release from military custody, claiming that, because no crime was alleged to have occurred on military property, Lynch should be remanded to civil authorities. See A. W. Bradford to His Excellency A. Lincoln, June 9, 1864, *Exec Ltr Bk,* MdSA.

80. Annie Davis to Mr. president, August 25, 1864, in Berlin et al., *Destruction of Slavery,* 384. No response to Annie Davis has been found in the records of the Bureau of Colored Troops or in other offices of the War Department.

81. *American,* October 10, 1864.

82. *Sun,* October 11, 1864.

83. *American,* October 11, 1864.

84. "Congratulatory Address" of J. E. Snodgrass et al. to People of Maryland, November 1, 1864, MS 1860, MdHS. Other signatories were M. Edward Stapleton, James Davis,

Eli Wells, Lambent S. Beck, Samuel B. Hayward, John A. Kennedy, Wm. B. Hayward, all former citizens of Maryland residing in New York. (Copy made for the American Historical Society.)

85. Andrew Stafford to General [Henry H. Lockwood], November 2, 1864, in Berlin et al., *Destruction of Slavery,* 390. For apprenticeship laws in the wake of emancipation in Maryland, see Fields, *Slavery and Freedom,* 139–42; and Fuke, *Imperfect Equality.*

86. Brig. Genl. Henry H. Lockwood to Major Gen. Wallace, November 4, 1864, in Berlin et al., *Destruction of Slavery,* 390.

87. Lew Wallace, *An Autobiography II* (New York, 1906), 689–91. Wallace claimed that his "Freedmen's Bureau" was established before that of the federal government's, under the command of Gen. Oliver Howard (691n).

88. "George Buchanan Cole's Notes on the Election of 1864," November 10 entry, Redwood Papers, MS 1530, MdHS. General Orders 112 was issued November 9, 1864; see next section.

89. *American,* November 10, 1864.

90. Kelita Suit to Genl. Wallace, December 26, 1864, in Berlin et al., *Destruction of Slavery,* 391.

91. A. W. Bradford to Maj. Genl. Lew Wallace, November 10, 1864, *Exec Ltr Bk,* MdSA.

CHAPTER 11. BLACK TROOPS

1. F. C. F. Burgess, James W. Neale, Geo. P. Jenkins, and Peregrine Davis to A. W. Bradford, February 4, 1863, *Exec Ltr Bk,* MdSA. Bradford replied that Colonel Swain, the recruiting officer, had denied the allegations and the matter had been referred to General Schenck.

2. Maj. Genl. Robt. C. Schenck to Abraham Lincoln, July 4, 1863, and Edwin M. Stanton to Major General Schenck, July 6, 1863, in Berlin et al., *Destruction of Slavery,* 197–98.

3. Colonel William Birney to Lt. Col. Wm. H. Chesebrough, July 27, 1863, in Ira Berlin, Joseph P. Reidy, and Leslie S. Rowland, eds., *Freedom: A Documentary History of Emancipation, 1861–1867,* Series 2, Vol. 1: *The Black Military Experience* (New York, 1982), 198–99. A footnote on pp. 199–200 explains that forty of the slaves had been imprisoned for more than a year and three for more than two years. Special Order 202 referred to "the slaves of Gen'l Stuart"—most likely Gen. George H. Steuart.

4. William H. Graham to Thomas Winans, July 9, 1863, Graham Letters, MS 2144, MdHS (typed transcript). General Isaac Trimble had lost a leg at Gettysburg.

5. Colonel William Birney to "Assistant Adj. General," July 13, 1863, in Berlin et al., *Destruction of Slavery,* 373. Birney noted that expenses at the jail were 30 cents per day, no doubt an attractive deal for owners worried about losing their slaves.

6. Hugh L. Bond to Hon. E. M. Stanton, August 15, 1863, in Berlin, *Black Military Experience,* 200. Bond enclosed a draft proclamation in which all black males ages 18 to 45 could enlist, with protections "against any person who may presume to impede their

patriotic purpose of offering their services to their country for the suppression of this rebellion." When Bond's proclamation appeared in Baltimore newspapers in September, Governor Bradford accused Bond of using slave enlistments to achieve emancipation (see Berlin et al., *Black Military Experience,* 203).

7. J. P. Creager to Col. Wm. Birnie, August 19, 1863, in Berlin, *Black Military Experience,* 204. The War Department declined to assist Creager with his legal difficulties, on grounds that he was a civilian—A. A. Gen. C. W. Foster to Col. Wm. Birney, September 9, 1863, Berlin, *Black Military Experience,* 205.

8. William T. Chambers to Hon. Edwin M. Stanton, August 22, 1863, in Berlin, *Black Military Experience,* 205–6.

9. *Gazette,* August 22, 1863, in Harrison, 7:94–95.

10. Col. William Birney to Capt. C. W. Foster, August 26, 1863, in Berlin, *Black Military Experience,* 206–7. Endorsement.

11. *Gazette,* September 5, 1863, in Harrison, 7:97.

12. Thomas H. Hicks to Abraham Lincoln, September 4, 1863, filed with A. W. Bradford to Hon. Edwin M. Stanton, October 8, 1863, M-101 (1863), Letters Received (Irregular), RG 107.

13. A. W. Bradford to Hon. M. Blair, September 11, 1863, in Berlin, *Black Military Experience,* 208–10.

14. A. W. Bradford to Francis Thomas, September 9, 1863, *Exec Ltr Bk,* MdSA.

15. Harrison, September 1863, 7:100–101. (A marginal note indicates that he was unsure what day he witnessed this episode.)

16. Dodson Papers, September 14, 1863, UMdLib. Dodson perceptively noted four days later that whites would likely welcome slave recruits as they would be counted toward the state's quota.

17. Capt. John Frazier Jr. to Honbl. E. M. Stanton, September 21, 1863, in Berlin, *Black Military Experience,* 210–11.

18. A. W. Bradford to Abraham Lincoln, September 28, 1863, *Exec Ltr Bk,* MdSA. Bradford cited Lincoln's preliminary Emancipation Proclamation.

19. Edwin M. Stanton to Mr. President, October 1, 1863, M-101 1863, in Berlin et al., *Black Military Experience,* 211–13.

20. A. Lincoln to Major General Schenck, October 21, 1863, ser. 390, "The Negro in the Military Service of the United States," p. 1687, Colored Troops Division, RG 94.

21. Maj. Gen. R. C. Schenck to A. Lincoln, October 21, 1863, Telegrams Collected by the Office of the Secretary of War (Bound), Records of the Office of the Secretary of War, RG 107. Lincoln replied the next day, asking Schenck to "Please come over here" to discuss using white men to recruit black troops; see A. Lincoln to Major General Schenck, October 22, 1863, "The Negro in the Military Service of the United States," ser. 390, Colored Troops Division, Records of the Adjutant General's Office, RG 94.

22. Brig. Gen. G. Marston to Lt. I. Mix, October 21, 1863, "The Negro in the Military Service of the United States," ser. 390, Colored Troops Division, Records of the Adjutant General's Office, RG 94.

23. Hay Diary, 105 (entry of October 22, 1863).

24. Thos. Clagett Jr., Thos. Hodgkin, Shelby Clark, R. H. Sasscer, C. C. Mapson, Wm. B. Hill, J. F. Lee, and Saml. H. Berry to Hon. Reverdy Johnson, October 28, 1863, in Berlin, *Black Military Experience,* 213–14.

25. Endorsement of William Birney, November 8, 1863, in Berlin, *Black Military Experience,* 214–15. Berlin notes that Lincoln had complained earlier in October about reports that armed black troops were disturbing the peace along the Patuxent River (Berlin, 215). Details of White's killing in J. W. Blassingame, "The Recruitment of Negro Troops in Maryland." *MdHM* 58, no. 1 (1963): 20–29.

26. J. W. Hoskins to [William R. Whittingham], November 19, 1863, MDA.

27. Jno A. J. Creswell to Judge Hugh L. Bond, December 5, 1863, enclosed in Hugh L. Bond to Hon. Edwin M. Stanton, December 8, 1863, B-62 (1863), Letters Received (Irregular), RG 107.

28. J. P. Creager to Col. C. W. Foster, December 25, 1863, C-416 (1863), ser. 360, Letters Received, Colored Troops Division, RG 94.

29. Endorsement by Brig. General Wm. Birney, January 28, 1864, on Chs. E. Worthington to Major C. W. Foster, January 15, 1864, in Berlin, *Black Military Experience,* 215–16.

30. Wm. B. Hill to Major Gen. Halleck, February 3, 1864, ser. 105, Letters Received by General Grant, Headquarters in the Field, Records of the Headquarters of the Army (RG 108), NA. In an endorsement, Colonel Birney notes that Lieutenant Thorburn was lent the house in question by the man leasing it and that "no outrages whatever were committed on the occupants of the 'solitary and unprotected' dwelling houses."

31. Lt. Charles R. Sykes to Colonel Carlos A. Waite, February 21, 1864, ser. 4882, Letters Received, Post of Annapolis, RG 393, pt. 2, no. 315.

32. [Brig. Gen. Gilman Marston] to W. E. Cole Esq., February 26, 1864, ser. 6843, Letters Sent, vol. 252/669 DW, District of St. Mary's, RG 393, pt. 2, no. 468.

33. General Orders No. 11, Middle Department, Eighth Army Corps, March 15, 1864, ser. 2352, General Orders (Printed), vol. 61, 8AC, Middle Dept. and Eighth Army Corps, RG 393, pt. 1.

34. Edward W. Belt to Governor Bradford, March 15, 1864, enclosed in A. W. Bradford to Abraham Lincoln, March 16, 1864, in Berlin, *Black Military Experience,* 216–17. An identical letter is in *Exec Ltr Book,* MdSA.

35. E. B. Tyler to Abraham Lincoln, March 20, 1864, enclosing Capt. Thomas H. Watkins to Brig. Genl. E. B. Tyler, President 297 (1864), Letters Received from the President, Executive Departments, and War Department Bureaus, RG 107. A notation by John Hay indicates that Lincoln referred the report to the secretary of war.

36. Maj. Genl. B[enjamin] F. B[utler] to Hon. John F. Dent, March 22, 1864, ser. 5046, Letters Sent, vol. 50, VaNc, pp. 218–19, Depts. of Virginia and North Carolina and Eighteenth Army Corps, RG 393, pt. 1.

37. Lt. Col. Joseph Perkins to Col. S. M. Bowman, March 28, 1864, in Berlin, *Black Military Experience,* 218–19.

38. Sarah M. H. Jervis to Sallie Ann Jervis, April 2, 1864, Letters & Papers of the Hood-Jervis-Ridgley Families of Bowling Green Farm, Howard Co., MD, courtesy of Achsah Henderson.

39. Affidavit of Wm. Jackson, April 13 1864, in Berlin, *Black Military Experience*, 220–21. Berlin notes on p. 221 that endorsements suggest that Lincoln ordered Jackson's discharge on May 21, 1864.

40. Lt. Col. John Woolley to Major Gen. Wallace, April 17, 1864, W-146 (1864), ser. 2380, Letters Received, Provost Marshal, Middle Dept. & Eighth Army Corps, RG 393, pt. 1. Attached affidavits from witnesses state that the women involved included the "daughters of Mr. Cole."

41. *Sun*, April 18, 1864.

42. Col. S. M. Bowman to Major C. W. Foster, April 29, 1864, endorsement on Col. S. M. Bowman to Major C. W. Foster, April 10, 1864, B-475 1864, Letters Received, ser. 360, Colored Troops Division, RG 94.

43. Col. S. M. Bowman to Lt. Col. Lawrence, May 11, 1864, in Berlin, *Black Military Experience,* 223.

44. Thos. King Carroll Jr. to Gov. A. W. Bradford, May 9, 1864, *Exec Ltr Bk,* MdSA. (On May 12 Bradford sent Carroll's letter to Lincoln, saying of Carroll that "no more truthful, highminded or loyal Gentleman can be found in the state.")

45. A. W. Bradford to the County Commissioners, May 27, 1864, *Exec Ltr Bk,* MdSA.

46. S. M. Bowman to Lt. Col. Lawrence, May 28, 1864, *Exec Ltr Bk,* MdSA.

47. Henry Tydings to Lt. Jno. S. Wharton, May 28, 1864, in Berlin, *Black Military Experience,* 221–22.

48. Col. A. G. Draper to Col. W. Hoffman, June 10 [1864], ser. 6844, Press Copies of Letters & Telegrams Sent, vol. 253 DW, pp. 254–55, District of St. Mary's, RG 393, pt. 2, no. 468.

49. Mary A. Houser to "Cousin Hattie," June, 1864, Burdick-Gordon Correspondence, MS 2585, MdHS.

50. General Orders No. 47, Head-Quarters Middle Department, Eighth Army Corps, June 22, 1864, vol. 61, 8AC, General Orders (Printed), ser. 2352, Middle Dept. and Eighth Army Corps, RG 393, pt. 1.

51. Col. S. M. Bowman to Major C. W. Foster, June 22, 1864, in Berlin, *Black Military Experience,* 225–26.

52. Harrison [October 1863], 112–13.

53. G. A. Hackett to Colonel Lawrence, July 6, 1864, H-162 (1864), ser. 2343, Letters Received, Middle Dept. and Eighth Army Corps, RG 393, pt. 1.

54. John Q. A. Dennis to Hon. Stan, July 26, 1864, in Berlin et al., *Destruction of Slavery,* 386. Berlin states that no response has been found.

55. S. M. Bowman to His Excellency A. W. Bradford, July 8, 1864, *Exec Ltr Bk,* MdSA.

56. Robert C. Combs to His Excellency A. W. Bradford, August 9, 1864, *Exec Ltr Bk,* MdSA.

57. A. W. Bradford to Robert C. Combs, August 15, 1864, *Exec Ltr Bk,* MdSA.

58. "Loyial Colard men of Baltimore Citey to His Exelencey The pesident of theas uninted States of america," August 20, 1864, in Berlin et al., *Wartime Genesis,* 508. The war department instructed Gen. Lew Wallace, who admitted some recruiting irregularities in this regard, to look into the situation; see p. 508n for related documents and background on the formation of local militia in Baltimore at this time.

59. Capt. Wm. Lee to Lieut. E. G. Shirly, September 20, 1864, L-264 (1864), ser. 360, Letters Received, Colored Troops Division, RG 94. Tankard was transferred.

60. Lieut. M. Karney to Lieut. James C. Mullikin, October 8, 1864, K-197 (1864), ser. 2343, Letters Received, Middle Dept. and Eighth Army Corps, RG 393, pt. 1.

61. Reason Brown to the secretary of war, February 21, 1865, B-126 (1865), ser. 360, Letters Received, Colored Troops Division, RG 94.

CHAPTER 12. FREEDOM?

1. *Sun,* July 14, 1862.

2. Slicer Journal, July 3, 1863.

3. A. W. Bradford to Francis Thomas, September 9, 1863, in *Exec Ltr Bk,* MdSA.

4. Diary of [John] A. Steiner, November 18, 1863, MS 35.3, Historical Society of Frederick County.

5. Ibid., November 19, 1863, MS 35.3, Historical Society of Frederick County.

6. *American,* February 23, 1864. Admission was twenty-five cents.

7. *American,* February 24, 1864.

8. *American,* April 8, 1864. For a discussion of the political environment surrounding the voting on the convention bill, the convention itself and ratification of its work, including the new constitution, see Wagandt, *Mighty Revolution,* chaps. 12–14.

9. Brig. Genl. Edwd. W. Hinks to Maj. R. S. Davis, April 15, 1864, in Berlin et al., *Wartime Genesis,* 502–3. Butler, who accepted the suggestion, appointed William G. Leonard, a Methodist minister, to supervise free blacks in St. Mary's County (see Berlin et al., *Wartime Genesis,* 491–94). Joseph Forrest owned two large farms on the Patuxent River in St. Mary's County; "Southern" was undoubtedly John H. Sothoron, who had murdered a white recruiting officer of black troops before fleeing south (see Fuke, *Imperfect Equality,* 31–35).

10. Col. A. G. Draper to Maj. R. S. Davis, May 6, 1864, in Berlin et al., *Wartime Genesis,* 503–4.

11. John P. Kennedy to [Very Revd. Henry Hart] Milman, May 4, 1864, Kennedy Papers.

12. Quarter Master Gen. M. C. Meigs to Major Gen. Lew Wallace, June 20, 1864, in Berlin et al., *Wartime Genesis,* 504–5. See also note and references to related documents on p. 505.

13. Glenn Diary, 137, 142 (entries of July 12 and September 21, 1864). On February 21, 1865, Glenn's diary noted that two cousins, Sewall Glenn and Elias Glenn, were imprisoned at Fort Delaware and Fort Lookout, respectively (p. 152).

14. *American,* October 3, 1864.

15. *American,* October 5, 1864.

16. *American,* November 1, 1864.

17. "Maryland Narratives," "Parson" Rezin Williams interview, September 27, 1937, 75–76.

18. Wm. A. Willyams to Major Wm. M. Este, November 11, 1864, in Berlin et al., *Wartime Genesis,* 517. Este had been aide-de-camp to the commander of the Middle Department and Eighth Army Corps.

19. James Murray to Major Genl. Wallace, November 14, 1864, filed with M-1932 (1864), ser. 12, Letters Received, RG 94.

20. Capt. Andrew Stafford to General H. H. Lockwood, November 4, 1864, in Berlin et al., *Wartime Genesis,* 510–11.

21. Thos. B. Davis to Hon. J. Lanox Bond, November 6, 1864, in Berlin et al., *Wartime Genesis,* 512–13. Bond, who had been a member of the Know-Nothing Party in the 1850s, became an ardent Unionist following the April 19, 1861, attack on the Massachusetts troops in Baltimore.

22. R. T. Turner to Mother, November 10, 1864, in Berlin et al., *Wartime Genesis,* 516.

23. N. G. Glover to General Lew Wallace, November 14, 1864, filed with M-1932 (1864), ser. 12, Letters Received, RG 94.

24. Statement of Harriet Anne Maria Banks, November 14, 1864, in Berlin et al., *Wartime Genesis,* 518–19.

25. Statement of Jane Kamper, November 14, 1864, in Berlin et al., *Wartime Genesis,* 519.

26. John E. Graham to Maj. Gen. Lew Wallace, November 15, 1864, filed with M-1932 (1864), ser. 12, Letters Received, RG 94. (See note in Berlin et al., *Wartime Genesis,* 525.)

27. Bartus Trew to Major Wm. M. Este, November 15, 1864, T-320, 1864, ser. 2343, Letters Received, Middle Dept. and Eighth Army Corps, RG 393, pt. 1.

28. Unsigned to [Major William M. Este], n.d. [received November 12, 1864], filed with M-1932 (1864), series 12, Letters Received, RG 94.

29. *American,* November 19, 1864. Douglass was reciting remarks he had given earlier, at Zion Church in Rochester (presumably New York).

30. Philip Pettebone, Chas S. Welch & J. W. Hunter to Geo. W. Curry, Esq., November 22, 1864, in Berlin et al., *Wartime Genesis,* 520–21.

31. Capt. Geo. W. Curry to Col. Adrian R. Root, November 23, 1864, in Berlin et al., *Wartime Genesis,* 520; Capt. Geo. W. Curry to the Honorable Judges of the Orphans Court for Anne Arundel Co. Md., November 18, 1864, in Berlin et al., *Wartime Genesis,* p. 521n. Additional correspondence between the parties on this matter is discussed in this note.

32. Brig. Gen. Henry H. Lockwood to Lt. Col. Lawrence, November 28, 1864, ser. 4915, Letters Sent, vol. 85/161 8AC, p. 100, Third Separate Brigade, Eighth Army Corps, RG 393, pt. 2, no. 319.

33. A. A. G. Saml. B. Lawrence to Brig. Gen. H. H. Lockwood, December 2, 1864, in Berlin et al., *Wartime Genesis,* 522–23. Lockwood arrested the three men, but Lincoln rescinded the order they be sent into the Confederacy and the secretary of war ordered Jones and Bratton released. Waters was tried by a military commission and, by late January 1865, took his seat in the Maryland Senate (Berlin et al., *Wartime Genesis,* 524).

34. James Murray to Major General Lew Wallace, December 5, 1864, in Berlin et al., *Wartime Genesis,* 524–25.

35. Ibid., December 14, 1864, 528–29. Endorsement of December 16, 1864, ordered Lockwood to ascertain where the people should be cared for; an endorsement of December 19, 1864, noted that eleven people were in Murray's care and that they would be sent to Baltimore.

36. Maj. Gen. Lew Wallace to E. M. Stanton, December 11, 1864, in Berlin et al., *Wartime Genesis,* 528.

37. Brig. Gen. Henry H. Lockwood to Lt. Col. S. B. Lawrence, December 15, 1864, in Berlin et al., *Wartime Genesis,* 532.

38. *American,* December 13, 1864, in Fuke, *Imperfect Equality,* 72.

39. John Diggs to Lt. Col. W. E. W. Ross, December 20, 1864, in Berlin et al., *Wartime Genesis,* 533. The bureau sent Diggs's letter to General Wallace, who referred it to Governor Bradford, inquiring about civil remedies available to the plaintiff.

40. C. S. Parran to His Excellency A. W. Bradford, December 30, 1864, in Berlin et al., *Wartime Genesis,* 534–35. On January 5, 1865, Bradford sent the states attorney's and Parran's letters to General Wallace, noting the discrepancies between the statement of those two and those of Diggs; see Berlin et al., *Wartime Genesis,* p. 535n.

41. Daniel Miller & Co. to Their Creditors, December 31, 1864, MS 1860, MdHS.

42. Lew to Kate [Bond], January 1, 1865, Bond-McCullough Papers, MS 1159, MdHS.

43. John P. Kennedy to E. Lynch Stanley, January 13, 1865, Kennedy Papers.

44. *American,* January 18, 1865.

45. Surgeon A. T. Augusta to Maj. Gen. L. Wallace, January 20, 1865, A-63 (1865), ser. 2343, Letters Received, Middle Dept. & Eighth Army Corps, RG 393, pt. 1.

46. Wm. N. Burch to Capt. Wm. H. Hogarth, January 24, 1865, in Berlin et al., *Wartime Genesis,* 537–39. William Hogarth was a white Unionist in Baltimore.

47. Glenn Diary, 167 (entry of March 8, 1865).

48. Ibid., 168 (entry of March 8, 1865).

49. American Missionary, 2nd ser., 9 (April 1, 1865), 80, in Fuke, *Imperfect Equality,* xx.

50. Dodson Papers, April 4, 1865, UMdLib.

51. William R. Quynn, ed., *The Diary of Jacob Engelbrecht 3,* April 10, 1865 (Frederick, MD, 1976).

52. *American,* April 4, 1865.

CHAPTER 13. MURDER

1. E. D. Townsend, *Anecdotes of the Civil War* (New York, 1884), in W. A. Swanberg, *First Blood: The Story of Fort Sumter* (New York, 1957), 339.

2. Seaton Munroe, "Recollections of Lincoln's Assassination," *North American Review* 162 (March 1898): 425, in Michael W. Kauffman, *American Brutus: John Wilkes Booth and the Lincoln Conspiracies* (New York, 2004), 17.

3. J. H. Taylor to Brigadier General Morris, April 15, 1865, OR 1:46, pt. 3, 777.

4. *American*, April 15, 1865.

5. Slicer Journal, April 15, 1865.

6. Quynn, *The Diary of Jacob Engelbrecht 3*, April 15, 1865.

7. *Sun*, April 17, 1865. The newspaper did not publish on Sunday and thus had no April 16 issue. The military ban on gatherings was in the *Sun*, April 15, 1865. The paper was able to include some information about the assassination in its Saturday issue.

8. Glenn Diary, 198 (entry of April 17, 1865). John H. Hobart was the rector of Grace Church.

9. Supplement to the *Democratic Advocate*, June 27, 1963 (facsimile of the *Western Maryland Democrat*, April 6, 1865, published for the Carroll County Observance of the Civil War). Accounts of Shaw's demise in Jesse Glass Jr., *The Complete Chronicles of Charles W. Webster* (The Fukuoka Jo Gakuin Literature and Research Journal, Fukuoka, Japan 2001, Historical Society of Carroll County), 61–62; and Klein, *Just South of Gettysburg*, 21–22.

10. Glenn Diary, 203 (entry of April 21, 1865).

11. Slicer Journal, April 21, 1865.

12. Wilson Papers, April 15, 1865.

13. George Buchanan Cole's Notes on the Election of 1864, April 15, 1865, Redwood Papers, MD 1530, MdHS.

14. Ibid., April 17, 1865.

15. C. A. Dana to J. L. Mcphaill, April 17, 1865, OR I:46 (3), 821.

16. W[alter G. Dunn] to Emma [Randolph], April 19, 1865, in Bailey and Cottom, *After Chancellorsville*, 209.

17. *American*, April 17, 1865.

18. *American*, April 21, 1865.

19. Ibid.

20. Dodson Papers, April 16, 1865, UMdLib.

21. Harrison [April 1865], 8:45–46.

22. Ibid., 46.

23. 39B-A-2, printed circular, in Thomas W. Spaulding, *The Premier See: A History of the Archdiocese of Baltimore, 1789–1989* (Baltimore, 1989), 181.

24. George William [Woodward?] to Lawrence, April 20, 1865, Woodward Collection, MS 1636, MdHS.

25. [Robert Kirkwood] to Brother, April 26, 1865, Kirkwood Papers, MdHS.

26. "Character and Services of Abraham Lincoln," by Rev. Jas. A. McCauley, June 1, 1865 (Baltimore, 1865), 10, 14–15, 16–17, MdHS.

27. John P. Kennedy to Prof. Goldwin Smith, June 8, 1865, Kennedy Papers.

28. P. M. Clark to Mayor of the City of Baltimore, December 19, 1865, BCA.

EPILOGUE

1. See, among others, Cynthia Mills and Pamela H. Simpson, eds., *Monuments to the Lost Cause: Women, Art and the Landscapes of Southern Memory* (Knoxville, TN, 2003), xv.

2. William A. Blair, *Cities of the Dead: Contesting the Memory of the Civil War in the South, 1865–1914* (Chapel Hill, NC, 2004), 173.

3. Robert J. Brugger, *Maryland: A Middle Temperament, 1632–1980* (Baltimore, 1988), 751.

4. See Thomas Will, "Bradley T. Johnson's Lost Cause: Maryland's Confederate Identity in the New South," *MdHM* 94, no. 1 (1999), 4–29, for a discussion of Johnson's efforts to create a Confederate image for postwar Maryland.

5. Ibid., 28n21. See C. Marion Dodson Collection, MS 236, MdHS, for documents related to the establishment of the Loudon Park monument to Union naval veterans, dedicated Thanksgiving Day (November 26) 1896.

6. Mills and Simpson, *Monuments to the Lost Cause*, 140.

7. David Blight, *Race and Reunion: The Civil War in American Memory* (Cambridge, MA, 2001), 273, 278.

8. "Early History of Maryland Division: United Daughters of the Confederacy," *The Southern Magazine Maryland Number,* vol. 1, no. 3, June 1934; *Sun*, January 18, 1934 (Lee-Jackson); *Sun*, October 28, 1937 (Barr). The 1897 Baltimore convention led to the formation of the UDC Maryland Division. By 1920, the national UDC had sixty-eight thousand members.

9. McClellan in *Sun* Supplement, June 1, 1885, in Kenly Papers, MS 507, MdHS; Susan Cooke Soderberg, *Lest We Forget: A Guide to Civil War Monuments in Maryland* (Shippensburg, PA, 1995), xxii; Kirk Savage, *Standing Soldiers, Kneeling Slaves: Race, War and Monument in 19th-Century America* (Princeton, NJ, 1997), 178 (growth 1880). A GAR National Encampment was held in Baltimore in 1882.

10. "Report of the State of Maryland Gettysburg Monument Commission to His Excellency E. E. Jackson, Governor of Maryland," Baltimore, William K. Boyle & Sons (Printer), 1891.

11. *American*, September 30, 1865.

12. Blair, *Cities of the Dead*, 167–68; Blight, *Race and Reunion,* 28.

13. Savage, *Standing Soldiers, Kneeling Slaves*, 18; see p. 180 for examples of soldier monuments that addressed emancipation.

14. *Sun*, May 20, 1870; *American*, May 20, 1870 (crowd size). Maryland did not ratify the Amendment until 1973. The *American* includes the text of Garrison's letter, Creswell's speech, and the resolutions, and in a lighter note describes the collapse of the speaker's platform, causing "an indiscriminate mingling of races on the paving stones below."

15. Diary of Jacob Engelbrecht, June 6, 1870, and May 30, 1870, MdHS; *American Sentinel*, June 2, 1870. W. U. Saunders was likely William U. Saunders, listed as "Q.M. Sergeant" and "Corporal" in Co. D, Seventh Regiment Infantry, U.S.C.T., in History and Roster of Maryland Volunteers, War of 1861–5, Vol. 2 (Baltimore, 1899), 159, 169.

16. Jim Weeks, *Gettysburg: Memory, Market and an American Shrine* (Princeton, NJ, 2003), 92–96. Black visitors often gathered in Round Top Park, an isolated part of the battlefield that opened in 1884.

17. *Baltimore Afro-American Ledger,* July 5, 1913, in Blight, *Race and Religion,* 390. Some made the case that black veterans had no place at a Gettysburg reunion, not having fought there.

18. Mill and Simpson, *Monuments to the Lost Cause,* 196; Soderberg, ix; "The Centennial Anniversary of the Civil War: A Report of the Functioning of The Maryland Civil War Centennial Commission, 1961–1965," Maryland Civil War Centennial Commission, Hagerstown, 1964. See Soderberg's Appendix B for a classification of monuments into three types: funereal, reconciliation, and commemorative; Appendix C for specific monument sites in Maryland and their dates of erection; and Appendix D for monument dates in chronological order. See "The Maryland Monument at Antietam," 18[98?], Benjamin Franklin Taylor Papers, MS 1863, MdHS (the Maryland General Assembly on April 7, 1898, created the commission and appropriated $12,500 for its work). The Lee-Jackson statue was underwritten by a $100,000 behest from Baltimore investment banker J. Henry Ferguson; sculptor Laura Gardin Fraser was chosen from the six who submitted designs.

Bibliographic Note

The literature on Maryland's Civil War is vast and rich. Letters, diaries, newspapers, and other personal papers abound in archives around the state, in the National Archives, and in the custody of individuals. *Maryland Voices of the Civil War* touches much, but certainly not all, of this trove.

Those interested in this period in Maryland history should consult at least the following ten secondary texts that offer interpretation of and context for various dimensions of the war. All are cited in this work and make expeditious use of primary sources to support their analyses. William J. Evitts, *A Matter of Allegiances: Maryland from 1850 to 1861* (Baltimore, Johns Hopkins University Press, 1974), analyzes elections and voting behavior to assess attitudes during the decade before the outbreak of the war in the spring of 1861. In *The Politics of Continuity: Maryland Political Parties from 1858 to 1870* (Baltimore, Johns Hopkins University Press, 1973), Jean H. Baker examines political parties, elections, and voting behavior to demonstrate that permanent political realignment in Maryland was well under way before the war. Evitts and Baker support the view that a Maryland secession was never very likely.

Charles B. Clark's *Politics in Maryland during the Civil War* (Chestertown, MD, 1952, n.p.) is a serialized and detailed narrative summary of the war in Maryland, concluding with efforts to thwart abuses of apprenticeship in the wake of emancipation. He gives particular attention to the results and ramifications of state and local elections during the Civil War. Clark's work, some of which has been published over the years in the *Maryland Historical Magazine,* is derived from his 1942 doctoral dissertation, now at the Wilson Library at the University of North Carolina–Chapel Hill.

Three volumes edited by Ira Berlin and colleagues in the series *Freedom: A Documentary History of Emancipation, 1861–1867,* published by Cambridge University Press—*The Destruction of Slavery* (1985), *The Black Military Experience* (1982), and *The Wartime Genesis of Free Labor: The Upper South* (1993)—present key documents from the National Archives related to the end of slavery in the United States. These volumes, which include incisive interpretative essays on each slave state, including Maryland, illuminate the particular circumstances of emancipation in the state. Barbara J. Fields, *Slavery and Freedom on the Middle Ground: Maryland during the Nineteenth Century* (New Haven, CT, Yale University Press, 1985), relates social history to economic and political dynamics introduced by the coexistence of two free populations, "one white and one black," as page xi of her introduction notes. In *Imperfect Equality: African Americans and the Confines of White Racial Attitudes in Post-Emancipation Maryland* (New York, Fordham University Press, 1999), Richard Paul Fuke examines the aftermath of emancipation and the early transition of Maryland from slave to free, as well as the new opportunities putatively available to black citizens. Charles L. Wagandt's *The Mighty Revolution: Negro Emancipation in Maryland, 1862–1864* (Baltimore, Johns Hopkins Press, 1964, reprinted Baltimore, Maryland Historical Society Press, 2005), is an early, comprehensive work that explores the political forces of the war era that coalesced to abolish slavery in Maryland before the end of the conflict.

No single secondary work is devoted to all military operations in Maryland, but Kevin C. Ruffner's *Maryland's Blue and Gray: A Border State's Union and Confederate Junior Officer Corps* (Baton Rouge, Louisiana State University Press, 1997) explores the backgrounds, careers, political attitudes, and experiences of 365 captains and lieutenants of both sides who served in the Virginia theater of operations: the Army of the Potomac's Maryland Brigade and the Maryland Line of the Army of Northern Virginia. Ruffner's 93-page glossary sheds further light on the lives of these junior officers.

Index

Page numbers with an *f* indicate figures.